Y0-AGK-057

Alternate Ways of Organizing the Contents of this Book

Process and Thought in Composition

SECOND EDITION

with Handbook

Frank J. D'Angelo

Arizona State University

Winthrop Publishers, Inc.

Cambridge, Massachusetts

Acknowledgments begin on page xv.

Library of Congress Cataloging in Publication Data

D'Angelo, Frank J.
    Process and thought in composition.

    Includes index.
    1. English language—Rhetoric.   2. English lan-
guage—Grammar—1950-   I. Title.
PE1408.D15   1980   808'.042   80-10239
ISBN 0-87626-645-6

Cover and interior design by Susan Marsh

© *1980, 1977 by Winthrop Publishers, Inc.*
17 Dunster Street, Cambridge, Massachusetts 02138

All rights reserved. No part of this book may be reproduced in any form or by any means without
permission in writing from the publisher. Printed in the United States of America.

10 9 8 7 6 5 4 3

Contents

Preface

The second edition of *Process and Thought in Composition* retains the original emphasis on writing as a thinking process, but it also includes the following features:

1. New material on aims, modes, and kinds of discourse, introduced in the opening chapter and reinforced throughout the book.
2. A completely rewritten chapter on invention (Chapter Two).
3. Two new chapters on persuasion as an aim (Chapters Eight and Nine), emphasizing logical thinking as it relates to writing essays, not merely to analyzing arguments.
4. Interesting new paradigms, based on the enthymeme, for writing arguments, with a step-by-step illustration of the process.
5. New material on paragraphing as a process, in relation to the writer's intention, audience, and kinds of discourse (Chapter Ten).
6. Expanded material on analysis, description (Chapter Four), and narration (Chapter Seven).
7. New professional and student models, exercises, and suggestions for student writing throughout the book.
8. A new handbook section—an *optional* feature—which serves as a reference guide and which offers chapters on grammar review, problems in grammar, punctuation, and mechanics.

The plan of the book is similar in many respects to that of the first edition. I have divided the main part of the text into three parts: invention, arrangement, and style. In each of these parts, I have tried to show how invention, arrangement, and style are organically related by providing connecting links wherever possible, especially in those chapters titled "Patterns of Thought."

The two chapters on "Persuasion as an Aim" may seem to depart from the original plan, but they do not. Rather they reinforce the new emphasis on aims introduced in the opening chapter and reinforced throughout. Because persuasion is such an important aim, I devote two chapters to it and to the writing of arguments. I continue the emphasis on aims in the new material on paragraphing which follows.

The chapter on the paragraph is almost twice the size as that of the original. It includes a discussion of paragraphing as a process, not just a discussion of the paragraph as a separate unit. There is also new material on beginning and ending paragraphs and on transitions.

I have tried to make the handbook material interesting and innovative. To what extent I have succeeded, I leave my readers to judge for themselves. In almost all instances, however, I handle most of the topics in a traditional way so that those teachers who want to take a more conventional approach to grammar or usage may do so.

In making these changes to the first edition, I have tried to write with my audience in mind. I am grateful for the constructive criticism I have gotten from my readers over the past few years. Whatever success I have had with the first edition, I owe to you, my readers.

*   *   *

I have been truly fortunate, in preparing both editions of this text, to have received the kind of helpful advice so necessary to making a book a critical success.

Richard Larson, Robert Gorrell, Gary Tate, and William Lutz were among those who helped with the first edition. Their influence is still a strong one in the second edition.

Many of those who helped with the second edition have used the first edition, and their criticisms have helped to make the second edition a better book. Among those who gave of their time and help are Erika Lindemann of the University of South Carolina, Constance F. Gefvert of Virginia Polytechnic Institute and State University, Tommy J. Boley of the University of Texas at El Paso, David E. Fear of Valencia Junior College, Kris Gutierrez of the University of Colorado, Melinda G. Kramer of Purdue University, Carolyn B. Matalene of the University of South Carolina, Roberta Pritchard of Texas Christian University, Richard Raspa of the University of Utah, and Woodruff Thompson of Brigham Young University.

In the preparation of both the first and second editions of this manuscript, I have received invaluable assistance from Terri Garchow, Robin Ruiz, and Robin Kendrick. They did an excellent job in typing and helping to edit the manuscript. I thank them for their patience and their unfailing good humor. Deborah Lay did a very fine job of helping me with various aspects of the text, as did Bob Johannsen and Rob Archer.

Herbert Nolan of Winthrop Publishers is one of the best editors

I have worked with, and I thank him for his patience, humor, and good sense.

Special thanks again go to Paul O'Connell of Winthrop Publishers, who first encouraged me to write this book several years ago and who is largely responsible for an improved second edition. His warmth, friendship, and sincerity go far beyond the bounds of a single textbook.

I would also like to thank the many students whose essays I have used. When the essays of professional writers seemed difficult for some students to emulate, their writing always seemed inviting, accessible, and interesting.

Finally, I would like to thank my daughters, Susan and Lori, and my sons, Frank, Marc, and Stephen for their patience and understanding, and my wife, Sylvia, for her love and support, and her unfailing sense of humor and great wit. "Holy, fair, and wise is she;/The heaven such grace did lend her."

F.J.D.
Tempe, Arizona

Acknowledgments

Aetna advertisement, from *Time* magazine, November 21, 1977. Reprinted by permission of Aetna Life & Casualty.

The Animal Kingdom, "Mollusks," August 1972; published by Bantam Books, by arrangement with Grosset & Dunlap, Inc., July 1971. Reprinted with permission of Grosset & Dunlap, Inc.

AP Newsfeatures, "7,000 Stolen Books Found in New York." Reprinted by permission of The Associated Press.

Arizona Republic. "Shoplifting Is A Crime," public service message from The Arizona Republic. Reprinted by permission.

Arrow Liquors advertisement, "Caramella by Arrow." Reprinted by permission of Arrow Liquors Company.

Isaac Asimov, "UFOs, Are They Visitors from Space—or Unreliable False Observations?" From TV GUIDE magazine, December 14, 1974. Reprinted with permission from TV GUIDE® Magazine. Copyright © 1974 by Triangle Publications, Inc., Radnor, Pennsylvania.

James Baldwin, "Go Tell It On the Mountain." From *Go Tell It On the Mountain* by James Baldwin. Copyright © The Dial Press, 1963. Reprinted by permission.

Ray Allen Billington, "The Frontier Disappears." In *The American Story* edited by Earl S. Miers. Copyright © 1956 by Broadcast Music, Inc. Reprinted by permission.

Ray Allen Billington and James B. Hedges, *Westward Expansion: A History of the American Frontier, 3rd edition.* Copyright © Macmillan Publishing, Inc., 1960. Reprinted by permission.

Ray Bradbury, "A Sound of Thunder." In *Golden Apples of the Sun* by Ray Bradbury. Copyright 1952 by Ray Bradbury. Reprinted by permission of Harold Matson Co., Inc.

Charles S. Brooks, "On the Difference Between Wit and Humor." From *On the Difference Between Wit and Humor* in Chimney Pot Papers (1919). Reprinted by permission of Yale University Press.

Bulova Watch advertisement, "Do You Have An Unfaithful Watch?" Reprinted by permission of the Bulova Watch Company, Inc.

Dinah Calhoon, "Rubbing Concepts." Reprinted by permission.

Willa Cather, "My Antonia." From *My Antonia* by Willa Cather. Copyright renewed 1954 by Edith Lewis. Reprinted by permission of Houghton Mifflin Co.

Stuart Chase, "Mexico: A Study of Two Americas." From *Mexico: A Study of Two Americas* by Stuart Chase in collaboration with Marian Tyler Chase. Copyright 1931, renewed 1959 by Stuart Chase. Reprinted by permission of Macmillan Publishing Co., Inc.

Chesebrough-Pond's advertisement, for "Ultra Vera" lotion. Reprinted by permission of Chesebrough-Pond's Inc.

Christian Children's Fund advertisement, from *Time* magazine, January 10, 1972. Reprinted by permission of the Christian Children's Fund.

Marchette Chute, "Shakespeare of London." From *Shakespeare of London* by Marchette Chute, copyright 1949 by E. P. Dutton & Co., Inc., and reprinted with their permission.

Coach Leatherware advertisement, from the *New Yorker*, November 8, 1976. Reprinted by permission of Coach Leatherware.

The New Columbia Encyclopedia, 1975. Entries for "pidgin" and "lingua franca." Reprinted by permission of Columbia University Press.

Joseph Conrad, "The Lagoon." From *Tales of Unrest* by Joseph Conrad. "The Secret Sharer." Excerpt from *The Secret Sharer* by Joseph Conrad. Copyright 1910 by Harper Bros. In the book *Twixt Land and Sea* by Joseph Conrad. Both reprinted by permission of Doubleday & Company, Inc.

Norman Cousins, "The Conquest of Pain." From the *Saturday Review*, March 17, 1979. Reprinted by permission of Norman Cousins.

Stephen Crane, *The Red Badge of Courage.* From the University of Virginia Edition of *The Works of Stephen Crane*. Reprinted by permission. "The Open Boat" in *The Open Boat and Other Tales*, Alfred A. Knopf, Inc., publisher. Also in *The Complete Short Stories & Sketches of Stephen Crane* edited by Thomas A. Gullason, Doubleday & Co., Inc., publisher.

Charles Dickens, *The Works of Charles Dickens*. From *Bleak House* in *The Works of Charles Dickens*, P. F. Collier & Son, publishers.

Gerald Durrell, *The Overloaded Ark*. Copyright 1953 by Gerald Durrell. Reprinted with permission from The Viking Press, Inc.

Empire Machinery advertisement, from *Time* magazine, July 3, 1978. Reprinted by permission of the Empire Machinery Company.

Leonard Engel, "The Sea." From Life Nature Library—*The Sea* by Leonard Engel and The Editors of Time-Life Books © 1961 Time Inc. Reprinted by permission.

Kenan T. Erim, "Aphrodisias: Awakened City of Ancient Art." From National Geographic Society magazine, June 1972. Reprinted by permission of the National Geographic Society.

Martin Esslin, *The Theater of the Absurd*, revised updated edition. Copyright © 1961, 1968, 1969 by Martin Esslin. Reprinted by permission of Doubleday & Co., Inc.

The Fantastiks, "Try to Remember." Copyright © 1960 by Tom Jones & Harvey Schmidt. Chappell & Co., Inc., owner of publication and allied rights throughout the world. International Copyright Secured. ALL RIGHTS RESERVED. Used by permission.

Ralph H. Faulkingham, "Where the Lifeboat Ethic Breaks Down." From "Where the Lifeboat Ethic Breaks Down" by Ralph H. Faulkingham, from *Human Nature*, October 1978. Copyright © 1978 by Human Nature, Inc. Used by permission of the publisher.

Ford Motor Company advertisement, from *Psychology Today*, October 1977. Reprinted by permission of Ford Motor Company.

E. M. Forester, "Aspects of the Novel." THE PLOT from *Aspects of the Novel* by E. M. Forster, copyright 1927 by Harcourt Brace Jovanovich, Inc., renewed 1955 by E. M. Forster. Reprinted by permission of the publishers.

W. Nelson Francis, "Revolution in Grammar," in The Quarterly Journal of Speech, Vol. XL no. 3 (October 1954). Reprinted by permission of the University of Wisconsin, Madison. *The English Language*, An Introduction by W. Nelson Francis. By permission of W. W. Norton & Company, Inc. Copyright © 1963, 1965 by W. W. Norton & Company, Inc. From "Usage and Variety in English."

Frontier Airlines advertisement, from Frontier Airlines inflight magazine, 1978. Reprinted by permission.

General Foods International Coffees advertisement. Reprinted by permission of General Foods Corporation. © General Foods Corporation 1976.

Edward T. Hall, "Let's Heat People Instead of Houses," from *Human Nature*, January 1979. Reprinted with permission of the author.

Robert Harr, essay on the composing process (untitled). Reprinted by permission.

Head & Shoulders shampoo advertisement. Reprinted by permission of Procter & Gamble Company.

Nancy Hechinger, "Discovering Human Nature." From "Discovering Human Nature" by Nancy Hechinger, from *Human Nature*, January 1979. Copyright © 1978 by Human Nature, Inc. Used by permission of the publisher.

Stephen W. Hitchcock, "Can We Save Our Salt Marshes?" From National Geographic Society magazine, June 1972. Reprinted by permission of the National Geographic Society.

Fred Hoyle, "When Time Began," in the *Saturday Evening Post*.

James Joyce, "The Dead." From *Dubliners* by James Joyce. Copyright © 1967 by the Estate of James Joyce. All rights reserved. Reprinted by permission of The Viking Press. Passage from *Ulysses*, by James Joyce. Copyright © 1914, 1918 by Margaret Caroline Anderson and renewed 1942, 1946 by Nora Joseph Joyce. Reprinted by permission of Random House, Inc.

Agnes Newton Keith, "Bare Feet in the Palace." From *Bare Feet in the Palace* by Agnes Newton Keith. Copyright © 1955 by Agnes Newton Keith by permission of Little, Brown and Company in association with the Atlantic Monthly Press.

Michael Kernan, story/article from the *Arizona Republic*, May 8, 1977. Reprinted by permission of *The Washington Post*.

Kitchenaid Disposal advertisement. Reprinted by permission of Hobart Corporation.

Joseph Wood Krutch, *The Desert Year* © 1951, 1952 by the author. From *The Desert Year*. Published by Explorer Books. Reprinted by permission of William Morrow & Company, New York.

R. D. Laing, *The Politics of Experience*. From *The Politics of Experience*. Copyright © 1967 by R. D. Laing. Reprinted by permission of Penguin Books Ltd.

Lindsay Olive advertisement, from *Sunset*, December 1978. Reprinted by permission of Lindsay International Inc.

James Livingston, "Two Women." Reprinted by permission.

(continued on page 618)

PROCESS AND THOUGHT IN COMPOSITION

The Writing Process

Preliminary Considerations

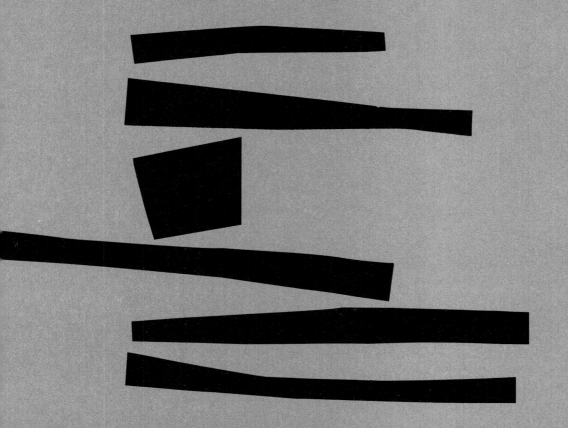

Chapter 1

Preliminary Considerations

The Importance of Writing

Despite the claims of some students of communications that there is little need for people to learn to write in an electronic age, there is still an insistent and persistent cry for effective writing.

We are all becoming weary of brainlessness in public language: of bureaucrats who cannot express themselves clearly in writing, of business people who cannot write letters that are accurate and concise, of writers of legal contracts who cannot explain coverage in everyday language, of politicians who deceive with language, of doctors and lawyers who use jargon to impress or befuddle, of friends and acquaintances who can't say what they mean.

Even in an electronic age, you can scarcely hope to succeed unless you can express yourself in writing with some degree of effectiveness. Television announcers work from a script. Movie and TV writers depend in large part upon writing. People in many occupations and walks of life write memos, reports, business letters, personal letters, letters of complaint, sympathy notes, invitations, letters of congratulation, articles, essays, theses, examinations, ads, brochures, manuals, catalogs, captions for posters and photographs—the list is endless. Writing is more pervasive and more important than you sometimes think.

But even if writing were not as important for many public uses as it was in the past, it would still be valuable in education because it facilitates thought. Writing can help you to think critically. It can enable you to perceive relationships, to deepen perception, to solve problems, to give order to experience. It can help you to clarify your thoughts. Often you discover what you really think and feel about people, ideas, issues, and events only in the actual process of writing.

Cultural psychologists have found that nonliterate people lag far behind literate people in a variety of cognitive skills. Their studies support the conclusion that literacy, especially writing, promotes intellectual development. More specifically, they have discovered that literacy transforms a person's mental processes by replacing practical, situation-bound thinking with abstract, theoretical thinking. Whatever may be the value of concrete, situation-bound thinking in nonliterate cultures, in a technological society a person who cannot think abstractly is at a disadvantage. To learn to write, then, is to learn to think in a certain way.

Invention, Arrangement, Style

Writing is a form of thinking, but it is thinking for a particular audience, and for a particular occasion. One of your more important tasks as a writer is to master the principles of writing and thinking that will help you to achieve your goals. The most important of these principles are those of invention, arrangement, and style.

Invention is the process of discovering ideas for speaking or writing. Although for many writers the process is intuitive, you can learn to guide the process deliberately by using formal procedures for analyzing and searching.

Arrangement is the process of discovering ordering principles so that you can organize your ideas in such a way as to make them understandable and believable to your readers.

Style is the process of making choices about sentence structure and diction while in the act of writing. You can also make these choices consciously and deliberately when you review what you have written.

To divide the writing process into invention, arrangement, and style is merely a convenience. Invention, arrangement, and style may occur or recur in all three stages. Try thinking, for example, about a movie that you have recently seen. If you begin to write down these thoughts, in the process of thinking about what you want to say, you cannot help but put your ideas into some kind of larger pattern and at the same time into sentences and words.

You may have heard various writers make exclusive claims for each of these processes: discovering ideas is the most important part of the writing process; the organization of ideas is all important; style is everything in a piece of writing. Writers can make these claims because there is a sense in which each claim is correct. Invention is everything because it includes arrangement and style. Arrangement is everything because it includes invention and style. Style is everything because it includes invention and arrangement. All are parts of a single, ongoing, mental process. (We shall take up these matters more fully in subsequent chapters.)

Finding a Subject

Why is it that some people who are such good conversationalists have so much trouble putting their thoughts into writing? To some people, writing a letter is a difficult task. Yet ask those same people to talk about a personal experience or give you an opinion about some social or political issue, and they can talk articulately for hours. Every time you make a telephone call, purchase something at the local supermarket, ask directions of a stranger, talk amiably with a neighbor, argue heatedly with a friend, you are putting thoughts together and expressing them in words. No matter how unconscious the process may be, you are engaging in oral composition.

Some people are never at a loss for something to *say*, yet when you ask them to *write* about a personal experience, or about current events, they vehemently declare that they have nothing worthwhile to write about. If someone were to record one of your conversations on a tape recorder, you might be surprised to learn that your conversation is filled with interesting ideas, bits and pieces of gossip, vivid descriptions of people and places, and vigorous opinions about social and political issues, all delivered in a lively and pleasing style.

All of us experience and observe the world around us. Yet students often feel unable to write about it. One of my students wrote: "I have an enormous amount of trouble picking a topic or thinking of something to write about. Once a topic is *finally* chosen, I grope and stumble for words like a blindman searching for a pen." Another wrote:

> Some people have a flair for writing—others don't. And unfortunately I am one of those people who doesn't have a talent

for writing. Picture a one-hundred-and-twenty pound man, anemic, pale, his skin hanging to his bones, trying to lift a weight of several hundred pounds, and you'll get some idea of the effort it takes me to write a good sentence. Words should come to my pen like rain, a gentle rain, steady, falling from a still blue sky, or better yet like a violent rain from a cloudburst, exploding, bursting out of the clouds and flooding the earth. But I'm lucky if I can force a drop out of a faucet, turned on as far as it will go, my fingers wrenching it 'til it can be forced no further, my fingers hurting and aching from trying.

Neither student realized how easily and beautifully each was using analogies to write eloquently about the difficulty of writing.

Personal Experiences

What to write about? Finding a general subject is easy enough. The possibilities for a given writer are almost unlimited, although some people have a wider variety of experiences to draw upon than others. The place to begin obviously is with your own *personal experiences*, your thoughts, feelings, and observations.

Every experience has within it the seeds for a potential flowering of significant ideas. No subject is intrinsically better than another. It all depends on the insights and the depth of perception you bring to the subject. Even much maligned subjects such as "What I did last summer" can be handled by some writers with sensitivity, skill, and wit.

College life offers some first-rate material for subject matter. One student who was taking a lecture class at the university wrote a paper based on a careful observation of his instructor. Another conveyed in very vivid language an experience she had while working in the university library. A third student gave a very humorous description of his last zoology lab.

Job experiences offer a source from which good writing can come. Almost all of you have a certain background of job experiences, whether these experiences be summer jobs, part-time jobs after school, or chores around the house. The familiar stuff of everyday experience can be made interesting for others to read about. Everyday experience, I'm sure, is a very common topic of conversation in your home and among your friends. The problem, however, is to find some point of view or some angle of vision with which to see your subject.

One student had a summer job working in a mortuary. He described his experience with concrete and vivid details, and with a curious detachment:

Someone Has To Do It

Working for a mortuary was a new experience for me. The job supplemented my summer earnings for tuition and also provided me with a free room. It was a good job—someone has to do it—and it helped me out considerably.

We kept the mortuary open in the evenings from 5:30 to 10:00 P.M., conducting people, relatives, and friends to the respective parlors where they would pay their last respects to their departed, dear ones.

In the evening and early mornings we answered death calls, coming in from hospitals, private residences, and old folks or convalescence homes. Then we would telephone a mortician, giving him the required information about the deceased.

The next step was the preparation of the one-man cot—two white sheets and pillow slips, locked beneath restraining belts, covered over by a silver-gray coverall. This we placed in the hearse, and then we drove to our destination, usually meeting the mortician or funeral director there.

We would wrap the last remains in sheets and head back to the mortuary where we would unload the corpse on a white porcelain table, all prepared for embalming.

The coolness of the milk-white flesh and the stench from uncontrolled sphincter muscles will long remain in my memory. Yet it was a good job—someone has to do it.

—Bob

There are subjects from daily experience all around you: joyful, painful, pleasurable, distressing, sad, delightful, fascinating, rapturous, heartfelt. Good writers will give their personal impressions of particular subjects, telling honestly how the experiences affected them. It would be impossible to attempt to catalog all the possible subjects from personal experience that you could write about. But here are a few that some students have found worth considering:

descriptions of people, places, and things; reflections about life; job experiences; death; illness; embarrassing experiences; sex; love; dating; marriage; war; alienation; civil disobedience; drugs; race relations; fears; hopes; dreams.

Vicarious Experiences

A second source of subjects for writing is *vicarious experiences* from books, records, movies, and television. Often you will find that you have enough knowledge about a particular subject from courses you are taking, from books you have read, or from movies and television programs you have seen, so that extensive research is not necessary. You need merely to recall this information or to find ways of getting at it to make it the basis of an interesting paper.

The following paper discusses a bit of the plot of a movie its author saw as a young child, but the emphasis is on the lasting impression it made.

Movie Impressions

I hope that if and when I become a parent, I have enough sense to keep a strict eye on the entertainment my children watch. I know from my own recollection what damage a movie viewed at an impressionable age can do.

I was *very* young when I saw this particular film, but even now, parts of it are as vivid to me as when I ran screaming out of the theater. If I had only been a little older, it likely would have had no effect on me at all, but at that time I was impressionable.

The plot went something like this. A young man and his bride lived in a swank high-rise apartment. Every night a strange woman with long, black hair and flowing gown would appear, holding a music box that played high-pitched, eerie music. She would go to the young couple's bedroom and the music would cause the young bride to walk in a deep trance. Out they would float to the balcony, about ten stories up. Here the music really got strange, enticing the girl to lean way over the railing, almost sure to lose her balance. Just then her husband would be heard calling for her, the odd enchantress would disappear, and the girl would be safe, but she would awaken, confused and frightened. The next thing I remember about the story was that somebody was murdered and the police were doing a thorough investigation of the apartment. In the bedroom, suspense began to build as that eerie music started playing softly. It was deathly quiet as the police reached the closet and began feeling the walls for clues. Nobody talked! Only that creepy music was heard, causing my tension to build. Then—B-O-O-M!!! With a horrible crash, a body fell out of the ceiling when the police hit a secret panel. With a chorus of screams ringing in my ears, I lit out of that theater as fast as my fat little legs would go, and bawled . . . and bawled some more.

I'm sure my parents never knew that for months I was scared to death to go to bed with the closet doors open. My heart always pounded a little harder when I went over to shut them. I think I realized there wasn't a music-box woman hiding there, waiting for a chance to lure me to my doom, or a body hidden in the ceiling, ready to come crashing down if I touched a certain panel, but my fear wasn't something I could rationalize. It was imprinted deep in my consciousness, just as is the habit I still have of faithfully closing our closet doors before retiring every single night.

—Linda

Magazines, Books, Reference Sources

Obviously, much of the writing you do in your college career or in other writing situations will not be this personal. Sometimes you will be called upon to give a relatively detached account of something you have read, to give an objective rendering of a subject about which you know little. A third source of subjects for your writing then is *magazines, books,* and *reference sources,* in the library, on the newsstand, or in your home, which you deliberately go to because you want to write about a subject with which you have little familiarity.

You can find general subjects in every conceivable place. Look at the table of contents in magazines such as *Time* or *Newsweek.* You will find such general headings as the following:

The Nation   Business
The World   Religion

People	Milestones
The Law	Books
Behavior	The Theater
The Press	Music and Dance
Education	Show Business and Television
Sports	The Environment
Science	Medicine
The Economy	The Sexes

Surely this listing will afford you with at least a beginning.

Another obvious place to look is in the dictionary. Just casually follow the alphabetical listings, stopping at topics that seem to hold some interest for you, jotting these down as they strike your fancy:

acting	clothes
advertising	comic strips
abstract (art)	dreams
Academy Award	music
babble	slang
bullfighting	words (new)

A third place is the alphabetically arranged subject index or table of contents of a textbook or essay anthology. I compiled the following list in about ten or fifteen minutes by looking in several books on my desk:

African art	humor
astrology	illiteracy
blind dates	movies
civil disobedience	nursery rhymes
collective bargaining	Olympic games
dance	prisoners of war
death	reading
devil worship	rock lyrics
drugs	rockets
ESP	solar energy
fashions	superstitions
feminism	television
flying saucers	theft

The card catalog in the library is another source of general subjects. The subject heading is what you want. Behind each heading you will find a stack of cards with titles related to the subject you have chosen:

Surrealism
Surrealism and Film
Surrealism and Its Affinities
Surrealism and Painting
Surrealism and the Literary Imagination
Surrealism and the Novel
Surrealist Art
The Surrealist Movement in England
The History of Surrealist Painting
Surrealist Poetry in France

Periodical indexes such as the *New York Times Index* and the *Reader's Guide to Periodical Literature* offer an even more promising beginning than some of the other sources. To begin with, you need merely to go through the alphabetical listing of, say, the *Reader's Guide* to come up with an interesting list of topics to write about:

abstract expressionism   basketball
acupuncture   cathedrals
American Indian languages   climate
apocalyptic thoughts   cosmic rays
ballet   dancing

Occasionally, one of these general topics will have numerous subdivisions, each of which might be a suitable subject in itself:

Moving picture critics and criticisms
Moving picture festivals
Moving picture industry
Moving picture plays
    criticisms, plots, etc.
        single works
            Alien
            Amityville Horror

Dracula
Gone with the Wind
Invasion of the Body Snatchers
Manhattan
Rocky II
Star Wars
Superman
Wedding, A
  production and direction
Moving pictures
  animated cartoons
  art films
  audiences
  bibliography
  comedy
  dance films
  documentaries
  moral aspects
  rating
  science films
  social aspects
  special effects
  study and teaching
  themes

In addition to the list of general topics, each entry makes specific references to titles of articles and their sources, for further reading:

DEATH
  See also
  Children and death
      Psychology
  Acceptance of the idea of mortality. Intellect 103:
    215–16 Ja '75
  Cold bright charms of immortality: study of death on
    television. M. J. Arlen. New Yorker 50:73–8 Ja 27 '75
  Nobility in our gramp's decision to die: F. Turgend. M.
    Jury. il pors Todays Health 53:18–23+ Ja '75

DEATH in literature
  Death. M. E. Stern. bibl Engl J 64:61–2 Ja '75
DEATH in Venice: opera. See Britten, B.
  —*Reader's Guide to Periodical Literature*, March 10, 1975

A final source is a good *encyclopedia*. If you know little about your general subject but you are interested in exploring it further, a useful first step would be to read the article to get an overview of it. The article itself would refer you to other books and articles. These in turn might have useful bibliographies you could pursue. Or you could look up the same subject in the *Reader's Guide to Periodical Literature* and read the articles related to it which are listed there.

Exercises

1. Write an essay in which you discuss which subjects would be most interesting to you if you had to write a personal experience paper.

2. Write an essay based on your personal experiences on *one* of the following general subjects: the death of someone near to you, an illness, a job experience, dating, love, marriage, an embarrassing experience, your fears and hopes, a dream (reverie, nightmare).

3. Draw up a list of subjects suggested by books you have recently read or by movies or TV shows you have seen.

4. Consult your dictionary or essay anthology. Compile a list of general subjects taken from these sources.

5. Consult the *Reader's Guide to Periodical Literature*. Go through the alphabetical listing and compile ten interesting topics to write about.

6. Consult a good encyclopedia. List ten topics from that source that interest you. Then read one or two articles in the encyclopedia to get an overview of your subject.

Limiting the Subject

Now that you have a general subject, do you just sit down and begin to write? Perhaps. If the subject is based on a personal experience, you might be able to do an interesting paper, exploring the subject as you go along, reducing it to manageable proportions. But more frequently, if the subject is a difficult one, or if it is a subject that needs focusing or demands a certain angle of vision, you need to be more methodical in how you go about handling it.

Sometimes in the very act of choosing a subject you can go a long way toward limiting it. For example, when looking for a general subject, instead of choosing a single-word subject from the table of contents or index of a book or magazine, choose the whole title or a portion of it. Although many of the topics are specific, others are general enough so that you can fill in your own content; or you may simply decide to handle the subject from your own point of view. The following are some typical subjects that are already partially limited:

> To drop out or not to drop out.
> This I remember.
> What _____'s second presidential term might be like.
> Why young people are giving up drugs.
> What are you scared of?
> What we must do about our junked-up landscape.
> How to put your trash to good use.
> What kind of person do you want to be?
> Women as sex objects in rock lyrics.

With just a little bit of thought, you could write about many of these topics. Further, the wording itself suggests a method of development. For example, the topic "To drop out or not to drop out" has the antithetical form of an argument. The title "This I remember" suggests a reminiscence. "What _____'s second presidential term might be like" is a hypothesis. The subject "Why young people are giving up drugs" can be developed by giving reasons. Other methods of development suggested by the remaining subjects are enumeration ("What are you scared of?"), problem/solution ("What we must do about our junked-up landscape"), process ("How to put your trash to good use''), and analysis (''What kind of person do you want to be?'' and ''Women as sex objects in rock lyrics'').

I have said that in the act of choosing a subject you can go a long way toward limiting it. Suppose, however, that you have selected or been assigned a very broad topic such as the urban crisis, prejudice, the generation gap, or clothes. Obviously, there is so much that can be said about each of these subjects that you would hardly know how to begin. Most general subjects need to be divided into manageable parts. This can be done in two ways.

The first way is by *free association*—by *listing under the general heading anything that comes to your mind* regarding the subject:

Movies

The Poseidon Adventure
Earthquake
disaster films
Airport
The Towering Inferno
stereotyped plots
action
suspense
emphasis on plot

Generation Gap

values
life-styles
clothes
politics
religious beliefs
education
attitude toward race
music

Clothes

fashion
skin
communication
class distinctions
Pucci

unisex
uniforms
best-dressed women
best-dressed men
movie stars
like packages

As you can see, the topics in the subcategories are still too broad for a 500-word essay, but at least they are much more manageable.

The second method is to consider the various aspects of the general subject by asking a few basic questions:

1. *What is it?*
2. *What are its parts?*
3. *How may it be classified?*
4. *In what respect is it like or unlike something else?*
5. *What are some examples?*
6. *How does it work?*
7. *What are its causes or effects?*

You could add many more questions to these basic few, but at this point you are not being asked to explore the subject thoroughly. Your main concern at this moment is to reduce your subject to manageable proportions. The following are just a few examples of theme topics on the subject of prejudice suggested by using this probe:

1. What is prejudice?
2. Are all people prejudiced?
3. Examples of stereotypes about races and nationalities.
4. Kinds of prejudice.
5. How children learn prejudice.
6. A comparison of the attitudes of the prejudiced person with those of the unprejudiced person.
7. Are people born prejudiced?
8. Is prejudice innate?
9. Does education reduce prejudice?
10. Language as a source of prejudice.
11. Causes of prejudice.
12. Effects of prejudice.

13. How prejudices are formed.
14. Epithets, pejorative terms, and prejudice.

Although it is not absolutely necessary that you limit every subject in this way, there are many advantages to limiting a subject. A limited subject is a more unified subject. It helps you to eliminate unnecessary material. It tells the reader more precisely what you intend to cover. And it makes clearer your whole approach to the subject. Naturally, in selecting and limiting your subject you should always be guided by your audience and your purpose.

Exercises

1. Limit one of the following general subjects by asking these questions of it: What is it like? What are its parts? How may it be classified? In what respect is it like or unlike something else? What are some examples? How does it work? What are its causes or effects?

   a. jogging   f. smog
   b. censorship   g. war crimes
   c. jazz   h. rock music
   d. magic   i. sports
   e. generation gap   j. feelings

2. Take one of the topics above and free-associate, putting down as much information about the subject as comes immediately to mind.

3. Take another topic from exercise 1 and use the journalist's questions (Who? What? When? Where? Why? How?) to explore it.

4. For this exercise, divide the class into groups of five or six. Then each group should list four or five specific essay subjects inherent in the following general subjects. Consider the audience appropriate for each subject and your purpose:

   a. music   d. bicycle racing
   b. values   e. theft
   c. fashions   f. noise

g. ethics   n. college education
h. childhood   o. taboos
i. shopping   p. prejudice
j. money   q. crime
k. superstitions   r. ecology
l. civil rights   s. TV
m. the cost of living   t. movies

5. What problems do you find with the following subjects for themes? Suggest ways to make each subject a suitable one:

a. nature   f. animals
b. proverbs   g. planets
c. Indians   h. machines
d. literature   i. sports
e. Arizona   j. studies

6. Examine the titles and headlines of articles in several current magazines and newspapers. Select a few general titles and then comment on how they can be narrowed in scope for purposes of composition.

The Writing Situation

As a writer, one of your tasks is to find something to say; but writing does not occur in a vacuum. It always occurs in some kind of context. In other words, a piece of writing comes into existence as the result of a response to a situation that often demands immediate attention. Let me illustrate this point with a particular example. You are away from home, attending a state university. The end of the semester is drawing near, and you discover that you are broke. You had enough money to last the entire semester, but recently you bought some record albums, a few books, and some clothing—things you could have done without, but they gave you satisfaction and pleasure. What to do? You decide to swallow your pride and to write to your parents, to a relative, or to a friend and ask for money. Your writing situation consists of the complex interrelations of persons, events, and objects which as a writer you must take into account in order to bring about a change in the situation.

A writing situation must take into account the **writer** (in this situation, the writer is you), the writer's **purpose** (the change you want to bring about in the reader), the **reader** or **audience** (your parents, relatives, or friends), and the **occasion** (the circumstances in which a particular event occurs, the time, the place, and the situation that demands immediate attention, the question that needs an answer, the problem that needs a solution, and so forth).

The Writer

Every writer puts something of himself or herself into a piece of writing. Even in so-called objective or impersonal writing, the writer appears as a certain kind of person. The writer takes on a certain role, and his or her writing takes on a corresponding tone. The doctor has a bedside manner, the lawyer has a business manner, the salesperson takes on a friendly tone, the judge sometimes appears stern. There is nothing negative about assuming a role or putting on a mask. When you are with your friends, you talk one way; when you are with your parents, you talk another way; at a job interview, you try to use your best speaking voice; when you tell a dialect joke, you assume another voice. The main idea of your essay may give the reader a hint about the role you are going to assume, but your whole text will reveal your attitude toward your subject.

Look at the following sentences and notice the difference in the writer's attitude toward the subject:

Crime in the streets is terrible; something must be done about it. Crime in the streets must end!

Crime in the streets is bad, but what can you expect when there is widespread unemployment?

Crime in the streets is no worse now than it ever was.

Crime in the streets is bad, but who cares? Live it up! Tomorrow we may all be dead from pollution or a nuclear war.

Obviously, a writer does not always write in an objective, dispassionate style. Sometimes he or she is angry, sometimes frustrated, sometimes hysterical. Other times the writer is reasonable or certain or skeptical or critical or joyful or ironic or dispassionate. Your attitude toward your subject is a part of your meaning, and discovering your attitude is an important step in the writing process.

Your attitude toward your subject, however, is not the only thing that you as a writer must keep in mind. Obviously, you ought to know your subject. And it is to be hoped that you will be interested in it. It is difficult to get your reader interested in your subject if you show no interest yourself. Finally, you need to consider whether your subject is appropriate to your readers. A good writer is knowledgeable, socially responsible, purposeful, and sensitive to the needs of his or her readers.

Exercises

1. Describe three writing situations in which you were involved as a writer. What was the occasion? What was the problem? Who was your reader? What was your purpose in writing?

2. Discuss in class some newspapers and magazines you read. What seem to be the predominant attitudes toward certain subjects in the editorials?

3. Write three sentences exemplifying in each one of the following attitudes: reasonable, angry, amused, frustrated, insensitive.

Audience

As a writer, you must not only choose an appropriate subject and determine your attitude toward that subject, but you must also determine your audience and your purpose. For example, if you were to write a paper for a classroom assignment, no matter how effectively you might construct a possible audience for your writing in your imagination, you know that one given is the instructor. He or she is the immediate audience for your writing. Another given is the other students in the class. Most writers for professional or popular journals have a pretty good idea of what the audiences are like, and their choices of subject matter, the main ideas of their essays, and their methods of developing their subjects usually reflect this knowledge.

Rather than simply assume your audience as given, however, you can determine the characteristics of your audience in a systematic way by asking certain basic questions:

What is the age of your readers?

What is their sex?

Where do they live?

What is their educational background?

What kinds of cultural interests do they have?

What are their social interests?

What do you know about their political beliefs?

What are their religious or philosophical beliefs?

What kinds of jobs do they hold? Are they professionals? White-collar workers? Blue-collar workers?

What kinds of leisure activities are they interested in? Movies? Sports? Reading? Jogging?

Is there anything not typical about this particular audience?

The result of asking these questions is that you will come up with a more complex picture of your audience.

In contrast to those who feel that writers should learn as much as possible about specific audiences and attempt to get views of their audiences that are as close as possible to reality are those who contend that writers *fictionalize* audiences, that is, they construct ideal audiences in their imaginations. According to Walter Ong, writers do not learn about their readers from daily life, but from other writers, who in turn have learned from still other writers the conventions of fictionalizing audiences. In fact, Ong argues, it might not be appropriate to talk about *audience* at all in relation to writing. Writers address *readers,* and readers do not form a collective audience in the same sense that an audience that goes to hear a speaker does. As the "readership" begins to read, it splits up into individual readers.

Ong has two things in mind when he says that the audience for writing is a fiction. First, in preparing to write, writers must assign some role to their imaginary audiences: concerned citizen, angry parent, intelligent layperson, belligerent redneck, alarmed voter, chagrined wife, disgusted consumer. Second, readers have to accept the role that writers have provided for them. When reading a work of fiction about some person in an exotic land, the reader must imaginatively project himself or herself into those surroundings. When reading an essay in a magazine about the dangers of pollution, he or she has to switch roles and become part of an audience that is concerned with pollution.

If we accept this point of view about the notion of audience, then it would seem that in the very act of formulating an idea or opinion we are choosing some roles for ourselves and assigning some roles to our audiences. For example, suppose you decide to write about religion and you use the thesis "My attitudes toward religion differ from those of my parents in a number of ways." The role you have chosen for yourself is that of a young adult who is struggling to come to grips with one of the most significant problems of the day. As a reader, I must accept the role of a concerned, older person who is honestly interested in your attitudes about religion and about the changing mores of the day. If you choose as a thesis "People tend to act out in life the things they see on television," then you are choosing the role of a concerned citizen who, because of recent newspaper accounts about adolescents acting out in real life the violence they watch on television, sees a cause-and-effect relationship between television shows and violence. As your reader, I must also assume the role of a concerned citizen.

Actually, these two views of how writers determine their audiences are complementary. Undoubtedly there are times when writers' audiences are so far removed in time and space that the writers must imagine their audiences. But there are other times when writers can with some assurance determine the actual characteristics of real audiences and can therefore proceed accordingly. Advertisers assuredly do more than imagine their audiences. They send out questionnaires, and as a result they can with amazing accuracy choose the appropriate audiences for their products.

Exercises

1. Using the questions enumerated in the section on audience, analyze an audience for whom you are planning to write.

2. You have been appointed fashion editor of a major magazine. As editor, your job is to write articles on some aspect of fashion or the clothing industry. Your boss has told you that your articles must go beyond a mere summary of what is in fashion. What subjects might you come up with if your readers were

   a. Women of limited income?   f. motorcycle riders?
   b. single men?   g. corporate executives?
   c. single women?   h. dry cleaners?
   d. weight watchers?   i. dog owners?
   e. travelers?

3. You have decided to write an essay on the influence of the blues on several rock groups. How will your strategies change for each of the following readers?

   a. a music professor
   b. a group of high-school students
   c. an all-black audience
   d. a group of rock fans
   e. a group of senior citizens

4. You have decided to write a letter to the editor of a local newspaper protesting the proposed building of a prison near your home. Your purpose is to encourage readers of the paper to join you in fighting the proposed building site. What arguments might you use to appeal to

   a. concerned parents?
   b. people who live near the site?

c. politicians?

d. students?

e. taxpayers?

5. Bring to class two letters to the editor in the local newspaper or in a magazine. Be prepared to discuss the following questions:

a. Who is the intended audience?

b. Is there more than one potential audience?

c. What is the purpose of each letter?

d. Is the purpose explicitly stated in a sentence or two, or is it implied?

Purpose and Aim

Every kind of writing has some purpose, but these purposes are so numerous that for the less experienced writer it would be helpful if they could be reduced to a few categories:

To inform or instruct   (car owner's manual)

To convince or persuade   (advertisement)

To entertain or please, by calling attention to language and form   (poem, joke)

To express strong feelings and emotions   (diary, love letter)

These categories, which are broad and general, I shall call the **aims** of writing to distinguish them from the numerous specific intentions that writers have. The writer's **intention** is the *response that he or she expects to get from the reader.* Over the years, writers have developed other terms to refer to these categories so that *writing that informs or instructs* is called **informative discourse.** *Writing that convinces or persuades* is called **persuasive discourse.** *Writing that entertains or pleases or has an aesthetic purpose* is called **literary discourse.** *Writing that expresses strong* *feelings and emotions* is called **expressive discourse.** Clearly, these aims overlap, and you could probably add some aims that are not included in the above list. But in most kinds of writing, one aim is dominant.

It ought to be obvious that as a writer you must first know your purpose before you can go about achieving it. Lawyers must develop strategies in relation to their aims if they expect to be successful in the courtroom. Contractors must know the purposes of the buildings that they are going to construct. If you formulate your purpose in terms of reader response, your writing will more likely be appropriate to your intended audience. The following scheme shows how the writer's purpose can be related to the desired response in the reader:

Writer's Purpose	*Reader's Response*
To inform or instruct	Understanding
To convince or persuade	Belief or action
To entertain or please	Aesthetic pleasure
To express strong feelings and emotions	Conduct or thought governed by emotion

Despite your good intentions, at times you might have difficulty keeping your dominant purpose in mind. One good strategy is to formulate a **purpose sentence.** This is a sentence that *explicitly sets forth your purpose in relation to your subject and to your audience.* Suppose, for example, you want to convince the director of freshman English that freshman English ought to be an elective. You might begin with an outline of the elements that will go into your purpose sentence:

Subject: Freshman English ought to be an elective.
Purpose: To persuade
Audience: The director of freshman English

Then you can easily combine the parts into a coherent whole:

Purpose Sentence: My purpose is to convince the director of freshman English that freshman English ought to be an elective.

The purpose sentence is not to be confused with your **thesis sentence**—one that *explicitly sets forth the main idea of your essay*, although it could be made into a thesis sentence:

Freshman English ought to be an elective.

The purpose sentence is designed to help you to keep your central idea in mind and to keep before you the response you expect to get from your reader. It can also be useful in helping you to plan your writing strategies.

Here are a few examples of purpose sentences related to the various aims:

My purpose is to get a friend who likes traditional art *to appreciate* a Jackson Pollock painting. (aesthetic aim)

My purpose is to get my parents *to understand* rock music. (informative aim)

My purpose is *to persuade* my uncle, who is a Democrat, to vote for a Republican governor. (persuasive aim)

My purpose is *to convince* my teacher to change the grade on my last essay. (persuasive aim)

My purpose is to help my sister *to understand* the basic sentence types of English grammar. (informative aim)

Notice that not all of these purpose sentences can easily be made into thesis sentences. Most are too formal and too general. Occasionally, you can take some of the wording of your purpose sentence and use it to compose a thesis sentence. ("You should vote for X for the following reasons.") But more often the purpose sentence serves mostly as a guide and as an attempt to make you self-conscious about the aims of writing in relation to your subject and to your reader.

Exercises

1. Using the following outline as a guide, fill in the content that might go into five purpose sentences:

   Subject: (fill in the subject)
   Purpose: (fill in the purpose)
   Audience: (fill in the audience)

2. Select a magazine advertisement and study it carefully. On a separate sheet of paper, answer the following questions:

   a. What is the purpose of the ad?
   b. Is there more than one purpose?
   c. Are some purposes immediate? Long-term? Hidden?
   d. In what way is the ad's purpose adapted to the audience?
   e. Who is the audience?
   f. Within the general readership of the magazine from which the ad was taken, how does the ad writer select out a more specific audience? By organizational strategies? By word choice? By the illustration?

3. Some writers would not agree that the writer's dominant purpose ought to be clearly indicated in a piece of writing. To some writers, writing is a process of discovering one's intention as one writes. Do you agree with this point of view? Are there certain kinds of writing, perhaps, that might lend themselves to one or another of these views.

4. What would you say would be the dominant aim of the following kinds of *discourse* (verbal expression in speech or writing)?

   a. a class lecture on black dialects
   b. a sermon
   c. an informal conversation with a friend
   d. a debate about nuclear power
   e. a patriotic speech on a national holiday
   f. an oral interpretation of a poem

Modes and Kinds of Discourse

After you have determined your subject, your purpose, and your audience, you must determine the manner of developing that subject and the kind of discourse. We will be looking at a variety of ways of developing ideas in subsequent chapters, but for the moment let's discuss briefly the general idea of modes.

A **mode** can refer both to *a way of getting ideas to write about* and to *the manner of developing those ideas.* These modes have labels that you are already familiar with, although you may have used different terms to refer to them. Perhaps you called them **techniques** or **processes.** As ways of developing paragraphs, they are sometimes referred to as **methods of development.** Some typical examples of these modes are the following: description, analysis, classification, definition, comparison, contrast, exemplification, narration, process, and cause and effect. Your choice of modes will necessarily be determined by your subject, your purpose, and your audience.

For example, imagine that you are a copywriter for an advertising firm and that your task is to write the copy for a food ad or a cosmetics ad. The subject matter seems to suggest that description would be the most appropriate mode. Suppose, on the other hand, that you are asked to write the copy for a stereo ad. Stereo buyers seem to like a listing of important features, so you would probably choose the mode of analysis, setting forth in much detail the outstanding features of the product. In much writing the modes are mixed. But in the beginning stages of learning to write, there is considerable value in isolating the modes and seeing them as simple.

The form or kind of discourse a writer chooses is usually the direct result of his or her purpose. For example, if your aim is to persuade, you might choose the form of a letter to the editor, a speech, a sermon, an ad, or a personal letter to convey your ideas. If your aim is to inform or instruct, you might write an expository essay, a book review, a movie review, a news article, a scientific essay, a literary critical essay, or an explanatory note. If your aim is to please or to entertain, you might tell a joke or write a poem, a limerick, a short story, a popular song, or a rock lyric. Finally, if your aim is self-expression, you might choose some form of personal or autobiographical writing, perhaps in a journal or diary.

At the beginning of the semester, you might find it useful to attach a cover sheet to your essays on which you list in outline form all of the elements that you must take into account in writing your essays. A typical outline for an assignment would look something like this:

General Subject: Automobiles
Purpose: To convince readers to buy a luxury car
Audience: Readers of *Esquire* magazine
Kind of Discourse: Magazine ad
Mode: Description

Exercises

1. Discuss in class: If you were writing advertising copy, what mode or modes might you choose to develop the following products?

   a. candy, gum, cookies, pastries
   b. drinks, staple foods, desserts
   c. perfumes, cosmetics, toilet articles
   d. men's suits, hats, stockings, dresses, shirts
   e. jewelry, silverware, watches
   f. moving pictures, novels, magazine subscriptions
   g. cars, tires, batteries, motor oil
   h. stereos, TV sets, radios, tape recorders

2. For what *readers* would you select any of the above-mentioned products?

3. It is often assumed in this age of mass media that writing is not as important as it used to be. Is this true? How could you verify this statement?

4. Interview the following people about the kinds of writing they do in their jobs: your mother or father; an uncle, aunt, cousin, brother, or sister; a friend; a celebrity. Then make a list and bring this list to class for discussion. Do not overlook even the seemingly most unimportant kinds of writing: a grocery list, a note, letters of various kinds, reports,

memos, invitations, and so forth. In compiling this information, use the familiar "who, what, when, where, why" questions of journalism. Who is doing the writing? What kind of writing is being done? For what purpose? When is it being done? Where?

Invention:

Probing the Subject

Chapter 2

Invention: Probing the Subject

Once you have decided upon a general subject and determined your attitude toward it, your purpose, and your audience, you are ready to explore your subject more fully.

To do this, you need a plan, a way to reach somehow into the recesses of your mind, to spin out of yourself, as a spider spins out a filament, a thread of thought that will develop into an orderly web. For invention is a thinking process. In its broadest sense, **invention** is *any mental activity that will bring to conscious awareness something previously unknown.* The process seems to have its origin deep within the human mind.

How Students Compose

Although many students are unsystematic in the way they go about getting ideas for writing and in the way they compose, the following student comments seem to indicate that there is a consistent pattern that some students follow in their prewriting and writing activities.

Maria

When I approach a writing project, I use very definite methods. I have not intentionally developed these methods. They have simply evolved over a period of years as habits which work well for me. They have proved to be consistently effective, and therefore I have retained them. They help me to achieve a certain balance and precision in my writing which I feel is essential to the validity of my work, and thus, if I were to discard even one of them, the quality of my writing would be diminished.

Invention

Before I begin the actual organization of my thoughts on paper, I usually research my subject for weeks, or even months, in advance. When I feel that I have done a sufficient amount of research and am satisfied that I know my subject well enough to begin writing,

Gestation Period

I then consciously try to stop thinking about the subject at all for several days, and instead occupy myself with very ordinary and usually rather quiet activities—long bicycle rides, evening walks, or perhaps some shopping I've been putting off. It is during this time that my thoughts begin to come together in my head, and when I feel

Readiness

that there is a flow, I begin to write. I cannot explain to the reader just exactly what this "flow" is. I don't understand it myself. I can only say that it is a sort of organic signal which tells me that I am ready—physically, emotionally, and spiritually—to begin putting thoughts into words.

When I finally sit down at the typewriter, it is always very late at night, for I have never been able to compose during the daylight hours. Usually I work for several nights like this, perhaps all through the night. But there is always a feeling of exhilaration the next morning—even if I have no sleep at all—because during those very quiet and private hours of the night before, I was able to reach out for a moment and touch . . . DELIGHT. And it is for that one moment that I write.

Conscious Composing

The most crucial period of the composition for me is the time I spend constructing my thesis or introductory paragraph. This may take hours to complete because it must convey to the reader, concisely and coherently, in just four or five sentences, the entire thought of the paper. Once this first paragraph is completed and I am satisfied with it, the rest of the words come relatively fast and almost seem to organize themselves. I always write in draft form. When this draft

Editing

is completed, I edit my work, usually making various changes and corrections in the text, then retype the paper in final form.

I don't know whether or not my methods of composition are very conventional. I suspect that they are not. But they are a very integral part of my writing and therefore an integral part of me.

Shirley

Often, when I sit down to do any kind of formal writing, I am reminded of Samuel Johnson's comment that anyone who writes except for money is a blockhead. I agree with Dr. Johnson's implication that writing is toil of the most arduous kind. Never, in my entire life, have I whipped out a paper. Hard work and mental anguish are always involved.

I have observed my husband's methodical composing process—note cards, outline, draft, final product—and tried to imitate it, hoping to lessen, if not the work, at least the anguish. For me, the result is guaranteed dullness. However, I do have a system for composing. Some processes are common to all my writing efforts.

Creative Tension

Indeter-minacy

As soon as an assignment is given or I decide to produce a piece of writing, the project is rarely off my mind until I complete it. While driving a car, I must consciously and repeatedly haul my attention back onto the road. If I clear a cluttered room, I will later have no notion of the disposition of its contents. Theses, arguments, quotations in scattered, shotgun patterns flash through my mind. Opening (never closing) sentences are born and inspected. By the time I begin serious work, I have developed a rough, tentative thesis and some supporting thoughts. If the paper requires research, I assemble my sources at this point, read, and make notes on sheets of lined paper.

Conscious Composing

If no research is involved, I sit down and start writing. I often start half-a-dozen times. Sometimes a great opening sentence emerges in the middle of the second page, and so I begin again. Some of the thoughts incubated over a sinkful of dirty dishes are now coaxed, prodded, or wrenched into being.

Revising While Composing

I do not write rough drafts. Such efforts have never rendered me a satisfactory product. I labor over each sentence as I write, revising until I accept it, before moving to the next. If I leave a line less than finished, the spark that lit it dies forever. So I write slowly, painstakingly, and sometimes painfully, head throbbing and stomach churning.

Endings are my particular torment. Rarely does one simply suggest itself as other parts of the project might. I write, reject, and rewrite until something works.

Creative Satisfaction

I have considered whether I would be relieved to know I would never agonize through another piece of writing. The answer is an unqualified no. A finished piece is exhilarating. I anticipate that feeling throughout the work; it is part of my sustenance. Perhaps I just suffer from the old "because-it-feels-so-good-when-I-stop" syndrome.

Dinah

When the movie houselights came on after my first viewing of *2001: A Space Odyssey,* it was an unwelcome intrusion; I was mentally and emotionally transcending earthly bounds. I had to go home to my typewriter to continue my transcendency.

Occasion

It is this kind of emotional lather, following a concrete experience, that often precedes my making an effort to compose something in writing. These concrete experiences can be as simple as listening to a frog chorus after a rain, or as complex as contemplating the process of regeneration presented in Shakespeare's *Tempest.*

Indeterminacy

Sometimes while integrating a particular experience I perceive a concept forming in my mind. I don't think of the concept in words, but become aware of it in a process I characterize, in my own thinking, as the "split-second movie." It's difficult to explain. I "see" the concept, but it is such a fleeting entity, I can't hold it. It is the after-image of the "split-second movie" that I refer to as the perceived concept.

Composing

The hardest work of composing now begins. I organize random ideas, but in the most rudimentary fashion. I don't worry about an introduction; I just start at the point most interesting to me, and write both ways. To generate material, I have imaginary conversations, starring myself and someone I'd like to impress. I dazzle this person with my profound insights, clever wording, and witty characterizations. The fun part is choosing only my best lines to build my written presentation.

Invention

Next, I read what I have written, to see what I think. While I don't always know in exactly what direction to write, I do know if what I have written fits the perceived concept I am working toward. In art, there is a process called "rubbing." A special kind of paper is placed over an impression of a design, picture, or sometimes tombstone and rubbed over with the flat edge of a piece of granite or colored wax. The process by which I discover words for my concept is similar. I place my typewriter "against" the mystery mass of the concept and type until a clear image emerges.

Composing and Revising

Gestation

Thus begins a tedious stretch of writing and revision—trial and error. I continue this process as long as I can stand it. Eventually, my ideas temporarily depleted, I leave the project for a period of time.

Unconscious Invention

A few hours or days later, I begin writing again. At this stage, new ideas make their appearance rapidly, not in an orderly way, but crowding each other. The disorder of their appearance can be overwhelming. When this happens, I'm temporarily about as pleased as the Sorcerer was with his Apprentice. Ideas stumble in end-over-end, march, interrupt, and sometimes make so much noise I can hardly write. I make an effort to classify at this point, but often settle for recording as quickly as possible—writing words, phrases, and incomplete sentences down randomly.

Composing

Arrangement and Revision

In the final process, I try to bring order. I sort, classify, fit, and revise for the finished work.

Kate

Because the process of writing has seldom been pleasant for me, I inevitably postpone composing a paper until the night before it's due (only, I add in defense, if it is fifty pages or less). When I finally sit down with a pen and paper, I continue to procrastinate by listening to the radio or splitting the ends of my hair. However, at this time I am also fretting over what I will say and how I will say it, as well as whether or not I will finish before the deadline.

Gestation Period

Creative Tension, Invention

Only after I am nervous and tense do I start to write. At first I only scribble ideas as they come to me, as though I am trying to empty my head. At this early stage, I have a tremendous amount of energy and have to fight to write down the barrage of words.

Gestation Period

After I have depleted my initial stock of ideas, though, I feel drained and usually have to procrastinate anywhere from fifteen minutes to three hours in order to feel sufficiently pressured to continue. However, I sense that while I am stalling, my subconscious is somehow still working on my paper.

Conscious Composing

The next stage of writing is more routine: I collect a thesis sentence from the ideas I previously wrote down and decide how to develop it. This is a systematic, logical process, and my energy level is much lower than before. After this, I write my first paragraph with care and deliberation before I allow myself more procrastinating, for if I don't start to write now, I never will.

Composing, Gestation

While actually composing the paper, I continue to alternate periods of wasting time with periods of writing. Wasting time appears to be as crucial as the actual writing, for besides allowing me an

Creative Tension — opportunity to rest and to clear my head, it increases my nervousness over not meeting the deadline. Consequently, my energy level is raised and my ability to concentrate increases. After I finally finish the paper (at three in the morning, to be precise), I hastily type it up (making numerous typographical errors), hand it in, go home, and sleep.

Robert

Invention — After long reflections on the question of how I compose, I have come to the conclusion that I am a masochist. When I am given a topic for composition, for example, that requires research, I do extensive research. For me there is no speculation, no attempt to reduce the topic to manageable proportions. I simply walk to the library and check out every source on that topic that I can carry out in my arms, and return home to begin reading. Since I haven't even begun to limit my topic, the only aspects that I specifically look for are those that strike my interest. If I get halfway through a book and decide that I'm becoming too bored, I merely close the pages and open another book.

Inchoateness — After two or three weeks of such haphazard research, I feel as if I have enough ideas floating around in my mind to begin the writing process. Of course, this is usually a day or two before the assignment is due, so that I have no choice but to attempt to make some sense of all I have read. Like my research techniques, my initial efforts at organization are completely unmethodical. With my lucky silver pen in hand, I open a notebook and begin to jot down ideas and facts which I have found particularly interesting or truthful, along with thoughts about the subject which were formed as I read.

Invention by Brainstorming —

Conscious Composing — Once I have finished compiling this personal set of notes, I sit and stare at them. This is the only logical part of my composition, for I seek out various relationships and pursue lines of thought suggested by my notes. This is the point at which I begin the actual physical act of writing. I try to expand upon a certain relationship or set of relationships, or develop a line of thought, often writing several pages and then discovering that I've reached a dead end.

Gestation Period — It's about this time that I close my notebook and flip on the radio or go outside for a walk. The theme is still prominent in my mind, but at least I don't have all of my aborted attempts to deal with it staring me in the face. Somehow, as corny as it may sound, I get an inspiration. A definite thesis statement will pop into my

Illumination   head, and suddenly the chaotic jumble of ideas begins to sort itself
Arrangement   out, each thought falling neatly into place. I hurry back to my notebook and begin to write, nonstop, the theme's organization logically suggested by my thesis and years of writing practice.

In the writing that I do which doesn't require research, my methods are much the same, without the weeks of extensive reading. Again, I jot down fragments of ideas and make several unsuccessful

Invention   starts until one of them seems to suggest a thesis and organization for the entire theme. It is a rare occasion that I know exactly what I want to say and how to say it from start to finish.

It has occurred to me as I have written this that I do have a method in my written composition, as unmethodical as it may seem. My processes are essentially the same for every composition I write, and they have always been successful.

I think it is clear from these student comments that *some* kind of systematic approach to writing is better than none at all. Those students who have a conscious awareness of what they are doing seem to have an easier time of putting their thoughts on paper. All of the students, however, use certain strategies that result in recognizable patterns.

The composing process begins with a kind of creative tension which, though it may be discomforting to the writer, seems necessary for the resolution of conflicts. In the beginning stage of invention, there is often a kind of indeterminacy, an inchoateness, a lack of clarity or precision. The process is dynamic. Ideas and images jostle one another. At this stage, there is also an order of sorts, a potentiality waiting to be realized, as the writer surrenders to an inner necessity. Sometimes even before he or she begins to write, the writer grasps the pattern to be developed in its full form. Sometimes the writer perceives a fragment of the whole, an image, a concept, but even at this stage, the part seems to contain the whole.

At some stage in the process, the writer must exert some conscious effort on the task at hand. In the prewriting stage, this might take the form of reading, taking notes, or thinking about the subject. In the writing stage, it consists of filling in details and making logical connections, giving to the writer's thought a determinate direction.

Often, this period of self-conscious activity is followed by a period in which the writer must while away the time or think about something else. Even in these moments of escape from the task at hand, the mind evidently continues to work, making connections, sorting out ideas. Some attention must also be paid to revision, either as one is writing or after the first draft is completed.

What also seems clear from these student comments is that seldom is the composing process strictly linear. A writer will gather ideas, think about these ideas, then procrastinate, gather more ideas, and begin to write, put the writing aside, try to think of other things, return to the writing with renewed vigor, write, revise while writing, reinvent, consciously follow a plan, unconsciously depart from that plan, make connections, revise again, and rewrite. Although the process is not strictly linear, it is useful to think of it as occurring in stages, even though these stages are idealized parts of what is really an organic and dynamic whole.

In my own writing, I follow a sequence of stages that can be described as prewriting, writing, and revision, even though there may be considerable overlapping in the stages. I gather ideas, consider my subject, my audience, and my purpose, and think hard about those ideas for weeks or months before I begin to write. The gestation period for me is at night, while I'm trying to go to sleep. Ideas jostle ideas as I make connections and perceive patterns. Sometimes the pattern for an entire essay will take shape in my head. When I begin to write, I continue to invent, but invention now means filling in details, giving examples, and so forth.

Exercises

1. How do you compose? Write a description of how you go about preparing for a writing assignment and how you actually do the inventing and writing.

2. Daydream! Deliberately put yourself into a situation that is pleasant and let your thoughts wander freely about the subject.

3. Imagine yourself in a strange new world. What do you see? What do you feel? What do you smell? What do you hear?

4. Think of a childhood memory, joyful or painful, happy or sad. Let the order of memory determine the process of invention.

5. Sit down in a room or outside under a tree. Write down freely what you see, hear, smell, touch, perceive.

Probing for Ideas

Although no two people would develop a general subject in exactly the same way, each of us to a certain extent must nevertheless, follow certain lines of development in our thinking because the mind is organized according to certain principles. It recognizes temporal, spatial, logical, and psychological principles and relationships in the universe.

Principles of composition such as analysis, classification, comparison and contrast, and cause and effect are *ways of thinking*. For example, not a day goes by that you don't analyze, classify, compare and contrast, or discover cause-and-effect relationships in the world around you. You see a tree and note the shape of its branches, the size of its trunk, or the color of its leaves. You classify it by naming it. You compare it to other trees. You observe it changing in time, notice that termites are causing it to decay or that it has been struck by lightning. When the tree is not in the immediate range of your vision, you substitute images or words to call it to mind, and these words or images facilitate your thinking about the tree. Every time you analyze, classify, exemplify, enumerate, compare, contrast, or discern cause-and-effect relationships, you are inventing ideas.

Compositional categories such as analysis, classification, and comparison and contrast, besides being principles of thought, are categories that suggest questions that can be used in exploring ideas for writing. These categories are sometimes called *topics*, a word that originally meant "places." (I have referred to them previously as *modes*.) The topics were literally conceived of as places in the mind or in books where ideas were stored, where one could go to get ideas. The term **topic** today is more frequently used to refer to the subject matter of a discussion or conversation. But I would like to use the term to refer to *categories that can be used to direct the search for ideas or the arrangement of these ideas into some orderly pattern.*

What I would like to propose is that in examining a subject to get ideas for writing, you use these topics or modes and the questions they suggest in a systematic way. To help you to do this, I have put these categories into a scheme to enable you to use them more efficiently:

Topics of Invention
A.
    Static
    1. Identification
    2. Analysis
      a. Partition
      b. Enumeration
    3. Description
    4. Classification
    5. Exemplification
    6. Definition
    7. Comparison and contrast
      a. Similarity
        (1) Literal
        (2) Figurative
      b. Difference
        (1) In kind
        (2) In degree

B. Progressive
    1. Narration
    2. Process
    3. Cause and effect

This visual scheme has two advantages. It shows you how the topics are related to one another, and it will enable you to remember them better for future use.

The static, logical topics are for the most part abstracted from time and space. Description, of course, is an exception, but what unites all of these topics is our ability to view them apart from their existence in time.

Obviously, many relationships exist among these categories. Probably all of the topics work together in the composing process, but for practical purposes you can separate them out. You can't classify without comparing or divide something into parts without noticing differences. All of these topics relate to dynamic processes in the human mind.

In order to use the topics to explore a subject, you need merely to move from one topic on the diagram to another, applying them to the subject at hand. You can start anywhere on the diagram that you like. Thus, you might begin by describing or defining your subject, dividing it into parts, classifying it, looking for significant examples, or comparing it to something else. Then you move on to the other topics, all the while obtaining a clearer idea of your subject as you apply each topic in turn. Once you have gone through the topics, you can repeat the procedure as often as you desire. The process is recursive. The result of applying these topics to a particular subject is that when you complete this procedure, you should have something to say, or at least you will be aware of the gaps in your knowledge and go on from there.

It may be that the topics may best be applied by putting them in the form of questions. The following are just a few of the many questions suggested by these topics:

Identification
Who or what is it?
Who or what is doing it or did it?
Who or what caused it to happen?
To whom did it happen?

Analysis
What are its pieces, parts, or sections?
How may they logically be divided?
What is the logical order?
What is the exact number?

Description
What are its constituent parts?
What are its features or physical characteristics?
How is it organized in space?

Classification
What are its common attributes?
What are its basic categories?

Exemplification
What are some representative instances, examples,
or illustrations?

Definition
What are its limits or boundaries?
What are its classes?
What are its common attributes?
What is its etymology?

Comparison
What is it like?
How is it similar to other things?
How does it differ from other things?

Narration
What happened?
What is happening?
What will happen?
When did it happen?
Where did it happen?

Process
How did it happen?
How does it work?
What are its stages or phases?
How do you make it or do it?

Cause and Effect
Why did it happen?
What are its causes?
What are its effects?
What is its purpose?
How is it related causally to something else?

Another plan is to put the topics in the form of statements and apply these directly to the topic you are exploring. The advantage of this procedure is that you will have fewer questions, statements, or topics to remember:

Identify the subject.
Describe it.
Divide it into parts.
Define it.
Classify it.
Give some examples.
Point out its similarities to or differences from something else.
Tell what happened, when it happened, and where.
Tell how it happened or how it is changing in time.
State its causes or effects.

In probing, clearly, you cannot apply all of the topics or questions to every subject. But merely by using some of them you will be able to get enough ideas to begin your writing.

To illustrate how the process of discovering ideas might work with an actual subject, let's take the general subject "automobiles" and explore it in a systematic way. I have chosen the subject of automobiles because it is one that is continually in our consciousness. (Perhaps you have recently bought a car or are about to buy a car, or someone in your family has bought a car, or a friend is about to buy one.) Automobiles are in our consciousness because of our concern with pollution, gasoline prices, traffic congestion, automobile accidents, and travel.

Identify the subject.

Cars of various makes and models. Chevrolets. Pontiacs. Cadillacs. Oldsmobiles. Buicks. Fords. Lincolns. Mercurys. Plymouths. Dodges. Chryslers. Hondas. Mazdas. Subarus. Toyotas. Volkswagens. Audis. Fiats. Datsuns. Subcompacts. Compacts. Large cars. Midsized cars. Luxury cars. Specialty cars. Gremlin. Opel. Skyhawk. Starfire. Sunbird. Chevette. Fiesta. Pinto. Arrow. Horizon. Rabbit. Malibu. Nova. Granada. Fairmont. Cutlass. Le Mans. Impala. Caprice. Cougar. Catalina.

Divide it into parts.

Noise-absorbing body mounts. Door and body seals. Vibration-dampening body mounts. Generous amounts of insulation. Acoustic-backed carpet and headliners. Smooth and quiet ride.

Wire wheel covers. Fiberglass-belted radial ply tires. White-wall radial tires. Surefooted grip in rain or snow. White-stripe glass-belted radials. Power windows. Side-window defoggers.

Electric clock. Courtesy lamp for ashtray. Reading lights on rear door. Two-tone paint treatment. Extensive corrosion-resisting treatment.

Power steering. Power brakes. Front disc brakes. Sport steering wheel. Custom leather-wrapped tilt steering wheel. Rack-and-pinion steering. Strong solid body. Tough frame. Body side molding. High-energy ignition system.

Four-cylinder engine. V-6 engine. V-8 engine. 98-cubic-inch engine. 134-cubic-inch. 231-cubic-inch. 260-cubic-inch. 305-cubic-inch. 1.6-litre engine. 1.7-litre. 2.2-litre. 3.8-litre. 4.3-litre. 5.0-litre. Four-cylinder, overhead cam engine.

Impressive space efficiency. Full-size room for six. Lots of room. Cramped. Too little elbow room. Fair comfort. Barely enough head room. Not enough leg room. More head room. More rear-seat leg room. Plenty of rear hip room. More usable trunk space. Twenty cubic feet of trunk space.

Five-speed manual transmission. Automatic transmission. Four-speed manual transmission. Crisp-shifting manual transmission.

Full carpeting. Color-keyed carpeting. Wall-to-wall carpeting. Cut-pile carpeting. Tufted seat backs. Notchback seats. Leather seating. Cloth fabrics. Vinyls. Vinyl upholstery. Reclining bucket seats. Corduroy bucket seats. Firm cushions.

Front-wheel drive. Four-wheel independent suspension. Electronic fuel injection. Battery that never needs refilling. Power sport mirrors. Instrument panel. AM/FM radio. Stereo. Cigarette lighter.

New fuel efficiency. High fuel economy. 21 mpg highway. 16 mpg city. 31, 32, 36, 40 mpg highway. 16, 20, 24, 25, 30 mpg city.

Describe the subject.

Great car. Beautiful. Ultimate in fashion and design. Remarkable design achievement. Elegant new luxury. Clean, functional lines. Clean and classic look. Luxurious comfort. Supple vinyls. Luxurious roominess. Comfortable. Elegant style. Handsomely detailed. Luxury and comfort. Color-keyed cut-pile carpeting. Elegantly tufted seat backs. Rich cloth fabrics. Sensationally smooth ride. Pleated and plush comfort.

Classify the subject.

General Motors (Chevrolet, Pontiac, Oldsmobile, Buick, Cadillac); *Ford* (Ford, Mercury, Lincoln); *Chrysler* (Plymouth, Dodge, Chrysler). *Chevrolet* (Monza, Chevette, Malibu, Nova, Impala, Caprice, Camaro, Monte Carlo); *Oldsmobile* (Starfire, Cutlass, Omega, Delta 88, 98, Toronado, Calais); *Buick* (Opel, Skyhawk, Century, Skylark, Le Sabre, Electra, Riviera, Regal); *Pontiac* (Sunbird, Le Mans, Phoenix, Catalina, Bonneville, Firebird, Grand Prix); *Cadillac* (Deville, Eldorado, Seville). *Ford* (Fiesta, Mustang II, Pinto, LTD, Thunderbird); *Mercury* (Bobcat, Monarch, Zephyr, Cougar, Marquis); *Lincoln* (Continental, Continental Mark IV, Versailles). *Plymouth* (Sapporo, Horizon, Omni, Arrow, Volare, Fury); *Dodge* (Colt, Diplomat, Monaco, Charger, Magnum XE); *Chrysler* (Le Baron, Newport, New Yorker, Cordoba).

Subcompact cars, compact cars, large cars, luxury cars, specialty cars.

Subcompact cars. AMC Gremlin, Buick Opel, Buick Skyhawk, Chevrolet Monza, Oldsmobile Starfire, Pontiac Sunbird, Chevrolet Chevette, Fiat 131, Ford Fiesta, Ford Pinto, Plymouth Arrow, Plymouth Horizon, Volkswagen Rabbit, Volkswagen Diesel, Datsun B210, Datsun F10, Dodge Challenger, Plymouth Sapporo, Dodge Colt, Dodge Omni, Honda Accord, Honda Civic, Mazda, Subaru, Toyota Corolla, Toyota Corona.

Compact cars. AMC Concord, Pacer, Audi Fox, Audi 5000, BMW 320, Buick Century, Buick Skylark, Chevrolet Malibu, Chevrolet Nova, Chrysler Le Baron, Dodge Diplomat, Datsun 810, Dodge Aspen, Plymouth Volare, Ford Granada, Ford Fairmont, Oldsmobile Cutlass, Oldsmobile Omega, Pontiac Le Mans, Pontiac Phoenix, Mercury Zephyr.

Large cars. Buick Le Sabre, Buick Electra, Chevrolet Impala, Chevrolet Caprice, Chrysler Newport, Chrysler New Yorker, Dodge Monaco, Plymouth Fury, Ford LTD, Mercury Marquis, Ford LTD II, Mercury Cougar, Oldsmobile Delta 88, Oldsmobile 98, Pontiac Catalina.

Luxury cars. Buick Riviera, Cadillac Deville, Cadillac Eldorado, Cadillac Seville, Lincoln Continental, Mark IV, Lincoln Versailles, Mercedes-Benz 2400, Mercedes-Benz 300D and 280SE, Oldsmobile Toronado.

Specialty cars. Buick Regal, Chevrolet Camaro, Pontiac Firebird, Chevrolet Monte Carlo, Chrysler Cordoba, Dodge Charger SE, Dodge Magnum, Ford Thunderbird, Oldsmobile Cutlass Supreme, Pontiac Grand Prix.

Define the subject.

A *subcompact* may be defined as a car that can accommodate four persons. It has a small four-cylinder engine. Although four-speed transmissions are common, some five-speeds are available. Automatic transmissions are also available in most models. Front-wheel drive is also becoming common in most subcompacts. Although a subcompact can usually accommodate four persons, the rear seat is often too cramped for adults.

A *compact* is a car about the size and weight of the Chevrolet Nova and some of the newly down-sized General Motors models such as the Buick Skylark and the Chevrolet Malibu. Most compacts are cars that have seating room for five or six persons. Most have automatic transmissions, but manual transmissions are also available in most models. Their engines range from the small four-cylinder to the large V-8.

Large cars are cars that tend to provide a quieter, more comfortable ride than do the domestic compact models. They are usually roomier inside. Large cars are often referred to as sedans. Included in this group defined as large cars are the old midsized models that haven't been down-sized yet and the new, so-called full-sized models.

According to automobile manufacturers, a *luxury car* is the best car that automakers can build. Luxury cars supposedly are cars with a truly superior ride, handling, and braking, but often they are no better than other good cars not defined as luxury cars. Unfortunately, the fuel economy of luxury cars is relatively low. The price of these cars is generally higher than that of other cars their size.

A *specialty car* has been defined by one automotive magazine as "basically a sedan showing off." Specialty cars have racy-looking coupe bodies in place of functional sedan bodies. The buyer of a specialty car gives up a little bit of practicality for style. Coupe lines result in a cramped seat. Some of the new, down-sized specialty cars offer fairly good gasoline mileage, but their overweight competitors have a relatively high fuel economy.

Consider the subject as a process.
Fuel-injected 89-cubic-inch four-cylinder engine starts and runs well. Not as peppy as last year. Standard four-speed manual transmission shifts crisply through forward gears. Downward push to engage reverse gear requires determined effort.

Ninety-eight-cubic-inch four-cylinder engine runs smoothly during warm-up. Starts fairly well from cold engine. Light acceleration in first and second gears produces annoying bucking and surging. Five-speed overdrive manual transmission shifts smoothly through first four gears. Fifth is often balky. Reverse requires firm downward push.

One-hundred-sixty-three-cubic-inch fuel-injected V-6 requires several seconds of cranking to start. Acceleration good. Car shudders during hard acceleration in first gear. Seats don't hold occupants well during hard cornering.

Engine runs smoothly and quietly. Automatic transmission stays in second gear for an annoyingly long time during gentle acceleration. Shift to third gear is abrupt during hard acceleration.

Two-hundred-cubic-inch V-6 stalls on cold start. Balky on partly warm starts. Once running, doesn't stall or hesitate. Stumbles and hesitates during warm-up driving. Runs reliably when fully warm.

Ride is somewhat stiff and always active. Motions fairly well controlled on average roads. Ride comfortable enough on expressways to prevent occupants from tiring on long trips. Ride deteriorates slightly when car carries its 725-pound capacity. Normal handling good. Accident-avoidance ability is very good.

Brakes are good. Regulating severity of stops somewhat difficult.

Ride is fair. Car jiggles constantly on almost all roads. Motions superficially cushioned on expressways and secondary roads. With recommended full load of 700 pounds, ride is a little worse. Normal handling good. Brakes shudder when hot.

Ride is good. Ride is firm, but well controlled on almost all types of road surface. Suspension soaks up most of harshness from broken pavement. Full 960-pound load actually improves the ride slightly. Normal handling is good. Brakes are good. Power brakes chatter and shake.

Ride is poor to fair. Car constantly snaps, jerks, and moves from side to side. Ride is tiring on expressways. Ride is painful on rough roads. Manual steering requires effort during parking in hard turns. Steering feels heavy. Sharp bumps provoke jolts. Rear suspension occasionally touches bottom when car is fully loaded. Rear end swings out on hard turns. Parallel ridges in the road diverts car from its straight course.

State some causes and effects.

Fuel tank is located under the floor and below the rear seat. Location protects it from crash damage. Fixed rearview mirror interferes with tall driver's view to the right front. Could cause accidents. Bumpers look sturdy. But one blow to the center of the front bumper and another to the center of the rear causes visible dents and bulges in both bumpers.

Seat belts are tight. Cause shoulder tension. Rear belts difficult to put on. Fuel tank safely positioned under the floor, below the rear seat. Well protected in a crash. Head restraint limits driver's view. Could cause accidents.

Head restraints prevent whiplash injury. Wipers leave upper corners of windshield unwiped. Sharp bumps cause suspension to bottom on the outer side. Effect is that the car skates outward from time to time. Fuel tank positioned on left side of car. Effect is that fuel tank is fairly vulnerable, more likely to be hit.

Front safety belts inconvenient and uncomfortable. Lap belt rides too high. Shoulder belt rubs against the neck. Head restraints provide whiplash protection for short persons only. Slight crash causes center of front and rear bumpers to bulge visibly.

Point out the subject's similarities to or differences from something else.

Car 1 has front-wheel drive. Car 2 does not. Car 1 has steel-belted radials. Car 2 has fiberglass-belted radials. Car 1 has rack-and-pinion steering. Car 2 does not. Car 1 takes regular gas. Car 2 takes unleaded.

Car A is a midengine car. Car B is not. Car A has 6 cylinders. Car B has 4. Car A has front-wheel disc brakes. Car B has front-wheel disc brakes. Both car A and car B have independent four-wheel suspension. Car A costs about $2000 less than car B.

Car X has a V-8 engine. Car Y has a V-8 engine. Car X has power windows. Car Y does not. Car X has side-window defoggers. Car Y does not. Car X has an electric clock. Car Y does not. Car X has a courtesy lamp for the ashtray. Car Y does not. Car X has reading lights on the rear door. Car Y does not. Car X has two-tone paint treatment. Car Y does not.

Car Y has extensive corrosion-resisting treatment. Car X does not. Car Y has a strong, solid body. So does car X. Car Y has a high-energy ignition system, but X does not. Car Y has a 260-cubic-inch V-8 engine. Car X has a 305-cubic-inch engine. Car Y has carpeting. Car X has color-keyed cut-pile carpeting. Car Y has 16 cubic feet of trunk space. Car X has 20 cubic feet of trunk space. Car Y has rich cloth fabrics. Car X has supple vinyls. Car Y has an AM/FM radio. Car X has a stereo/radio. Both cars have batteries that never need refilling. Car Y has no cigarette lighter, whereas car X does. Car Y gets 16 mpg in the city and 24 mpg on the highway. Car X gets 14 mpg in the city and 21 mpg on the highway.

Car 1 is a cat. A creature of fire and spirit. Car 2 is a classic piece of sculpture. Car 1 has catlike grace and surefootedness. Car 2 is sophisticated. The movement of car 1 is quick and agile. Car 2 is poetry in motion.

Now that we have compiled an undifferentiated body of material about the subject of automobiles, let's consider what we have done and where we go from here. We began systematically with some representative statements which the topics called to mind. We started with identification and ended with comparison. Actually, we could have begun at any point. You will notice that we didn't use all of the categories. The ones that we did use seemed to be the most appropriate for the subject. You will notice also that some categories generated a vast amount of material; others did not. This is to be expected. The amount of ideas generated by a particular topic will vary from subject to subject. Finally, you have probably observed that the ideas derived from exploring the subject are not too coherent. They seem to be more of a loose collection, a conglomeration, a catalog, a heap. This also is to be expected. When the ideas first come, you want to get them down on paper in any order, in sentences, in fragments, in catalog form, or whatever. Your primary purpose at this stage in the composing process is to "brainstorm" for ideas. The process is a little bit like that of free association, in which you jot down anything that comes to mind about a particular subject. It differs, however, in that the topics and the statements or questions they suggest give you a sense of direction often lacking in random associations.

Exercises

1. An important first step for many writers in inventing ideas is specifying the problem by putting the subject in the form of questions: What is pollution? What are the causes of pollution? Take one of the following general subjects and formulate as many questions about it as come freely to mind:

a. flying saucers	k. advertising
b. rock lyrics	l. prejudice
c. death	m. pollution
d. escapism	n. fashion
e. energy crisis	o. dance
f. blind dates	p. civil disobedience
g. TV	q. fantasy
h. the generation gap	r. materialism
i. boxing	s. acting
j. humor	t. religion

2. Now, in a more systematic way, take one of these same subjects and, using the probe outlined in this chapter, put the subject through the questions suggested by the topics of invention.

3. Putting the topics in the form of statements such as the following, probe one of the general subjects listed in question 2:

   a. Describe or define the subject.
   b. Divide it into parts.
   c. Classify it.
   d. Give some examples.
   e. Point out its similarities to or differences from something else.
   f. Tell what happened, when it happened, and where it happened.
   g. Tell how it happened or how it is changing in time.
   h. State its causes or effects.

4. Take a single topic, such as definition, division into parts, classification, exemplification, comparison, process, or cause and effect, and probe a general subject:

   a. nature   f. terrorism
   b. art   g. football
   c. slang   h. skyjacking
   d. music   i. fishing
   e. clothes   j. war

5. Take one of the following thesis statements and probe the main terms in the statement. Then write an essay, following the method of development suggested by the probe or the statement of the thesis:

   a. A liberal education is worthless in a recession.
   b. Love should (shouldn't) be the main reason for marrying someone.
   c. Suffering makes us better human beings.
   d. Love needs to be expressed in words.
   e. First impressions can be wrong.

From Subject to Thesis

Once you have put a general subject through a probe, your next step is to limit your subject. Some writers can do a good job of writing about a general subject. But for many, a general subject is often too broad to permit a significant handling of ideas. Therefore, instead of writing about the general subject of automobiles, you might instead want to limit the subject by adding qualifying words to it or formulating it as a title. For example:

How To Buy a Used Car.
Testing a New Car.
Why Buy a Specialty Car?
How To Save on a Car Loan.
Good Bets in Used Cars.

By narrowing your general subject to a more specific one, you have already gone a long way toward limiting it. But a subject is not a thesis. A **subject** is *the* **matter** *of a piece of writing, what it is about.* A **thesis,** however, is much more specific. It is *the* **working idea** *of a discourse, a theme, an assertion so clear-cut that the reader has no doubts whatsoever about what is to be discussed or proved.* "Daytime television" is a subject, but "Daytime television is of a very low quality" is a thesis. It is a proposition with a point of view. It makes readers nod their heads in agreement or disagreement. It has some kind of truth value. It can be the basis for a discussion.

A thesis underlies every kind of discourse. In poems or in stories, it is very seldom expressed explicitly, except in works inclined to teach or moralize too much, but with a little bit of effort it can be clearly expressed. For example, the theme of Nathaniel Hawthorne's short story "Young Goodman Brown" can be stated as "Evil exists in the hearts of all men." The theme of E. A. Robinson's poem "Richard Cory" may be expressed as "You can never judge a person's happiness from the outside." In literature, although the thesis may not be explicitly stated, there is a principle of unity, a concept, or a point of view that holds a story or the poem together. In an essay, the thesis usually appears in a clearly defined shape.

The thesis, then, is the main idea, the seed which contains in potentiality that which is necessary for the subsequent flowering of thought. If it were possible to summarize an essay in a single sentence, to reduce it to its most condensed form, then that form would be the thesis sentence. Formulating a thesis sentence is an important step in ordering your ideas.

Writers differ as to when they deduce their theses from the general subject. Should the thesis be formulated immediately after the determination of the general subject, or should it be formulated after the writer accumulates a body of ideas and explores them thoroughly? There is no simple answer to these questions. The thesis can either follow or precede the determination of the general subject or the exploration of ideas. Obviously, for many writers there is considerable overlapping in the process. In my own experience, more often than not I begin with a title or a controlling idea and then, by reading and note-taking or by some kind of mental probing of my subject, I gather sufficient material to get my writing under way. I have on occasion formulated my thesis in the process of writing, but even then, I usually have more than a general idea about what I am going to say. If you decide, however, to formulate your thesis before you explore your subject thoroughly, your thesis could give you a more definite direction in which to proceed in inventing ideas.

Naturally, in determining your thesis you will want to keep in mind your purpose and your audience. If your aim is to persuade, the wording of your thesis might be quite different than if your aim is to inform or instruct. Your purpose and your audience will also determine the kind of writing you choose. If you are a copywriter and your aim is to persuade, the kind of writing you choose to persuade your audience may be a magazine ad. If you're trying to convince a friend not to buy a certain kind of car, you might write him or her a letter.

So now you have a limited subject and you are ready to formulate your thesis. *State your thesis in a single declarative sentence.* Since the thesis is to be used primarily for your sake, state it in such a way that it clearly and precisely expresses your central idea. Then you can frequently return to it to get your bearings at every step of your writing. The thesis should be constantly in your mind as a point of reference. As the working idea of your writing, the thesis will also suggest the scope or limitations of your paper, and it can suggest ways of ordering your ideas.

The following are some typical examples of thesis sentences suggested by the subject of automobiles:

The automobile is the greatest single polluter of air.

Gas guzzlers not only waste fuel, they also waste money.

Few options are necessary for basic transportation, but some options do make sense.

In buying an automobile, there are two kinds of loans you should avoid: a consumer finance loan and a dealer's loan.

The new Plymouth Horizon gives you sporty features you'd pay extra for in many other cars.

Compare the features of the Chevrolet Citation with those of more expensive cars.

Down-sized spare tires can affect your car's performance.

Tax the gas guzzlers or ban them.

Buy yourself a Ford because it has the following outstanding features.

Here's how you can get a good deal on a new car.

You could easily have formulated thesis 1 ("The automobile is the greatest single polluter of air"). The wording of the thesis suggests that your plan of development would be to support the main idea with examples. This thesis could also be developed by cause and effect. Thesis 2 ("Gas guzzlers not only waste fuel, they also waste money") could be developed with examples. Thesis 3 ("Few options are necessary for basic transportation, but some options do make sense") can be developed by an enumeration of the options. Thesis 4 ("In buying an automobile, there are two kinds of loans you should avoid: a consumer finance loan and a dealer's loan") contains the kind of advice you might give to a friend. You could use a combination of enumeration and reasons to develop this thesis. Thesis 5 ("The new Plymouth Horizon gives you sporty features you'd pay extra for in many other cars") can be developed by an analysis of the car's features. The sixth thesis ("Compare the features of the Chevrolet Citation with those of more expensive cars") has the obvious structure of a comparison. Thesis 7 ("Down-sized spare tires can affect

your car's performance'') would be developed by causal analysis. Thesis 8 (''Tax the gas guzzlers or ban them'') could be the title of a
magazine article or the thesis of a persuasive essay. Thesis 9 (''Buy
yourself a Ford because it has the following outstanding features'')
could be developed into an analysis essay or an ad that sets forth
the features of the specific manufacturer's car. It is the only thesis
composed of two sentences. Finally, thesis 10 (''Here's how you can
get a good deal on a new car'') can be the basis of a process essay,
developed in terms of steps, or stages, or phases.

It is possible that after you have formulated your thesis, additional thinking or reading about your subject will force you to modify
your original conception or to recast your thesis completely in another
form. The invention of ideas is a process of thinking and rethinking
a subject or a thesis, for the process of thought rarely goes on un-
changed. The thesis, however, will give to your thought a particular
direction.

Exercises

1. Using the information about automobiles derived from the probe in this
   chapter, formulate five thesis sentences. First include in outline form
   the necessary information to include in each thesis sentence: subject,
   purpose, audience.

2. Using one of the thesis sentences from question one, write an essay to
   support the thesis.

3. Formulate a thesis sentence for each of the following general subjects:

   a. prejudice   f. daytime TV
   b. world hunger   g. nuclear energy
   c. dreams   h. freedom
   d. blind dates   i. identity
   e. fears   j. marriage

4. From your own reading and experience, construct five thesis sentences.

5. Discuss the methods of development suggested by each of the following thesis sentences. What kind of support would you use to develop each?

    a. My family background has influenced my life in a number of ways.
    b. "Exploitation" can have a number of meanings.
    c. Frustration is beneficial for three reasons.
    d. TV has a deep influence on our lives.
    e. Making a home movie is easy to do.

There are many other useful approaches to generating ideas for writing. This one is particularly interesting because of the close relationship of the topics to mental processes. It must be extremely discomforting to find yourself in a situation where you're called upon to write something for a specific purpose or for a particular occasion, and you have only a vague notion of how to begin to get ideas. The method discussed in this chapter is one useful way to discover ideas. Obviously, the process, at least in the beginning stages, is somewhat artificial. The goal is to make the process habitual so that instead of having to probe every subject in a formal way, you so discipline your mind that it will automatically explore ideas systematically, by analyzing, classifying, comparing, or contrasting.

Summary Exercises

1. Analyze a picture, a magazine ad, a newspaper article, or a short poem. Be conscious of your mental processes as you are analyzing and inventing. As you are analyzing, put the ideas from your probe on paper in the

same order in which they come to mind. Then analyze your paper to see if you've put the ideas into any intelligible order.

2. Analyze some short articles or essays. What is the plan of development? What mental processes must the writer have gone through in order to arrive at that pattern?

3. Now put the full discovery procedure into play. Choose a general subject. Consider your attitude toward it. Consider your audience. Using one of the formal methods suggested in this chapter, probe the subject, limit it, and formulate a thesis sentence. Write the sentence in such a way that it indicates your plan of development. Then write an essay supporting the thesis.

4. The topics enumerated in this chapter can be stated in other ways than as questions. Choose one of the following formulations of the topics to probe the subject:

   a. Classify the dates you have had.
   b. Give directions to someone about how to make something or how to get someplace.
   c. Explain a scientific process.
   d. Trace the cause-and-effect pattern of an accident you witnessed.
   e. Compare any two things point by point.
   f. Compare something by analogy; for example, "love is like a fire," "love is like a raging torrent," "hate is like poison." Extend the comparison as far as you are able.
   g. Tell a story about something that happened to you.
   h. Describe a painting or a movie you have seen.
   i. Define some modern slang term with which you are familiar that doesn't have a dictionary definition.
   j. Summarize a story you have read recently.

5. Discuss the suitability or lack of suitability of each of the following proverbs as thesis statements:

   a. Thirty days hath September.
   b. After a storm comes a calm.
   c. Do not wear out your welcome.
   d. Variety is the spice of life.

   e. There's no place like home.
   f. Speech is silver; silence is golden.

6. Quotations can make good thesis statements. Collect at least five quotations and bring them to class for consideration as theme assignments.

Arrangement:

The Whole Theme

Chapter 3

Arrangement: The Whole Theme

Thus far, you have been following a sequence of logical steps in the composing process that might be described as follows:

> *Find a general subject (if you have not already been given one).*
>
> *Limit the subject (unless you have been given a sufficiently narrow one).*
>
> *Consider your attitude toward the subject.*
>
> *Consider your audience and purpose.*
>
> *Consider the mode or modes you might use and the kind of writing.*
>
> *Probe for ideas.*
>
> *Formulate a thesis sentence.*

Beginning, Middle, End

What do you do now that you have probed your subject, collected your ideas, and formulated your thesis sentence? *Organize your ideas, giving them form.* As Thomas DeQuincy puts it, "The labor of composition begins when you have to put your separate threads of thought into the loom, to weave them into a continuous whole; to connect, to introduce them; to blow them out or expand them; to carry them to a close."

How is this done? By following a sequence of steps that can be outlined as follows:

In the beginning of your paper, perhaps in the first paragraph, indicate clearly what your general subject is, state your thesis, and indicate your plan of development.

In your middle paragraphs, take up the main ideas of your essay, allowing a paragraph or two for each main point.

In your final paragraph, conclude your essay, making sure that you leave your reader with a clear idea of what you have covered.

These three stages of development can be found in most kinds of writing. They are called simply the **beginning,** the **middle,** and the **end.**

The following student paper illustrates these stages nicely:

The Wasteful American

Beginning The economic slump is the biggest problem facing Americans today. Despite all the talk about deficit spending, oil prices, unemployment, and the impending depression, Americans continue to spend large sums of money on goods which are frivolous and damaging to the country.

Middle The economic boom in the fifties and sixties transformed Americans into the most wasteful people on earth. People in other parts of the world could live comfortably on our trash. Americans throw away disposable diapers, dishrags, and aprons. One company even developed disposable clothes. You wear them until they're dirty and then you throw them away. Americans also throw away paper plates, dishes, and cups and plastic knives, forks and spoons.

This tremendous waste also extends into other areas. While oil shortages increase, many Americans continue driving gas guzzling luxury cars. Younger Americans zoom around in their hot rods equipped with ridiculous devices which increase speed and power while diminishing gas mileage. While the price of paper products climbs, McDonald's continues to wrap a Big Mac in paper, put a cardboard strip around it, put it in a box, and then place it in a paper sack. While the prices for producing energy skyrockets, Americans continue to buy electric can openers, blankets, razors, knives, tooth brushes, and so forth. And while people starve all over the world, Americans buy tons of pet food to feed pets that range from aardvarks to zebras. I could go on and on with examples. Needless lights shine bright, tons of food go down garbage disposals, and litter covers the landscape. Yet for years little has been done. Wastefulness has become as American as apple pie.

End The recent recession has prompted some changes though. Car pools have been formed, speed limits have been reduced, and recycling centers have been established. One newspaper even reported that garbage cans are not as full as they used to be. However, much remains to be done. America can no longer afford to waste its resources as it has done for the past twenty-five years. Perhaps the current recession will awaken Americans to the realities of a world that is overcrowded and running out of natural resources and force them to change their extravagant life styles.

—Reed

Exercises

1. Analyze fully the student essay titled ''The Wasteful American.'' What is the thesis? What kind of details are used to support the thesis?

2. Poems have beginnings, middles, and ends too. Bring to class a poem that is organized in this way. Identify the three main parts and then discuss this three-part structure in terms of the ideas the poet is trying to convey.

Thesis and Support

In addition to organizing your ideas in three main parts, you want to break up the major divisions into a sequence of smaller steps that includes the statement of the **thesis** and the addition of **supporting details.**

The organizational plan of the following essay uses this method:

Beginning

Thesis

Despite the role that municipalities, industries, and agriculture play in polluting the environment, each of us is responsible in part for trash pollution. Rather than blame someone else for the mess we're in or expect the government to begin massive cleanup programs, *there are a number of things that we can do to reduce trash pollution.*

Middle

Supporting Details

The first thing we can do is to buy products in containers that disintegrate easily. Plastic containers and aluminum cans, for instance, are almost completely immune to biological decomposition. We should avoid, therefore, buying these. On the other hand, paper and cardboard products decompose fairly quickly. There is not much harm in purchasing these.

Supporting Details

The second thing we can do is refuse to buy throw-away items. We can refuse to purchase products that come in nonreturnable bottles. In planning for outings, we can forego styrofoam cups, plastic spoons and knives, and disposable plates. We can avoid using aluminum cans, plastic foil, and aluminum foil. On occasion, we can bring home unwrapped products, if the products are not perishable or if they won't soil easily, rather than have them wrapped in paper that will be discarded later.

Supporting Details

The third thing we can do is to recycle throw-away items. We can sell our old newspapers and magazines. We can give discarded clothing, furniture, and toys to charitable agencies for reuse. We can give our bottles and aluminum cans to agencies for recycling.

Supporting Details

The final thing we can do is to avoid littering. Instead of throwing plastic filter tips from cigarettes on the ground where they will not decompose, we should put them in the garbage. We should be careful not to discard gum wrappers, candy wrappers, and other trash on city streets and highways. We should carry litter bags in our cars and use them regularly.

End

Each year we throw away tons of cans, bottles, bottle caps, paper, aluminum cans, cigarette packages, milk cartons, and cellophane wrappers and discard countless rubber tires, old automobiles, newspapers, and magazines. To add to the problem, we are running out of burial space in our city dumps, marshes, and wastelands. There is a need for each of us to realize that we are all responsible for pollution.

Clincher Sentence

These are just a few of the many things we can do to reduce trash pollution, but we must do them now. Our goal is nothing less than a return to America the Beautiful.

The first paragraph introduces the essay. The second sentence of this paragraph states the thesis. The next four paragraphs add supporting details. The last paragraph concludes the essay.

Exercises

1. List some specific details that you might use to support one of the following statements:

   a. A casual encounter affected my life.
   b. People should be judged by what they do rather than by what they say.
   c. Anger can be beneficial.
   d. We need illusions to live by.
   e. A reasonable pride is justifiable.

2. Discuss the methods that you might use to develop one of the following sentences by thesis and support. Then choose one and write a thesis and support essay.

   a. There are two sides to every question.
   b. Opportunity seldom knocks twice.
   c. What's done cannot be undone.
   d. Absence makes the heart grow fonder.

Paradigms

Thinking of form in composition in such broad terms as beginning, middle, and end, or thesis and support can be useful to the beginning writer. But the approach to form in composition that I believe can be even more useful is one in which the writer conceives of form in terms of an underlying, abstract pattern. Quite obviously, in beginning a paper you cannot keep in mind all the specific details that go into making the finished paper. But you can envision a kind of core structure that bears the main burden of thought. Such a structure is called a paradigm.

A **paradigm** is *a kind of model or pattern that is abstract and general.* It is not to be confused with a traditional outline that is detailed and specific. Unlike a traditional outline, a paradigm is an **idealization,** a conception of a pattern in its absolute perfection. It represents the writer's **competence,** that is, *the writer's ability to use language.* But competence is always spilling over into performance so that it is possible to use these formalized patterns in your own writing. Because a traditional outline is so detailed, with its divisions and subdivisions, it can only be used for the specific piece of writing for which it is intended. A paradigm, however, represents a universal pattern that recurs from one essay to another. In other words, you can use the same paradigm and write completely different essays with it. A traditional outline is static. It represents a finished product. But a paradigm is dynamic. It represents *stages in thinking.*

The essay that we have just looked at is a good example of an essay that uses the paradigm as a principle of organization. The abstracted paradigm of that essay looks somewhat like this:

1. There are *a number of things* that we can do to reduce trash pollution.

2. *The first thing we can do* is to buy products in containers that disintegrate easily.

3. *The second thing we can do* is refuse to buy throw-away items.

4. *The third thing we can do* is to recycle throw-away items.

5. *The final thing we can do* is to avoid littering.

6. *These are just a few of the many things we can do* to reduce trash pollution.

Paradigmatic Structure

The value of paradigms is that they enable you to move your thinking in an orderly manner from the beginning of an essay to its conclusion.

For compositional purposes, you might best conceive of paradigms in relation to the topics of invention. You will recall that in the previous chapter we identified certain categories such as analysis, classification, comparison and contrast, and the like, and suggested that these categories symbolized corresponding thought processes, that is, that in the course of your everyday activities, you analyze, you classify, you compare, and you discover cause-and-effect relationships in the world around you. Further, these categories give rise to certain questions that enable you to explore a subject to get ideas for writing. Now I would like to make a related point: that the same categories that you use to probe a subject you can also use to arrange the details of that subject in an orderly pattern, that in fact the topics of invention are closely related to the patterns of arrangement. In other words, at the same time that you are probing a subject to get ideas, you are also arranging these ideas, putting them into some kind of intelligible form. Paradigms, at least the kind that we will be concerned with, represent *patterns of thought* that give your writing a sense of direction and provide you with a formal means of ordering your ideas.

What do these paradigms look like? The following are some typical examples of paradigms in their most abstract form:

Analysis Paradigm
Introduction (states the thesis)
Characteristic 1
Characteristic 2
Characteristic 3
Characteristics 4, 5, 6 . . .
Conclusion (restates the thesis, summarizes, and so forth)

Classification Paradigm
Introduction (states the thesis)
Type 1
Type 2

Type 3
Types 4, 5, 6 . . .
Conclusion (restates the thesis, summarizes, and so forth)

Exemplification Paradigm
Introduction (states the thesis)
Example 1
Example 2
Example 3
Examples 4, 5, 6 . . .
Conclusion (restates the thesis, summarizes, and so forth)

Cause-to-Effect Paradigm
Introduction (states the thesis)
Cause 1
Cause 2
Causes 3, 4, 5 . . .
Effect
Conclusion (restates the thesis, summarizes, and so forth)

Effect-to-Cause Paradigm
Introduction (states the thesis)
Effect 1
Effect 2
Effects 3, 4, 5 . . .
Cause
Conclusion (restates the thesis, summarizes, and so forth)

These patterns represent *stages in your thinking* as well as sections of an entire essay. You could, of course, write an essay consisting of five or six paragraphs if you were to follow each outline exactly, but it should be obvious that each of these paradigms can be shortened, lengthened, or modified to suit your own purposes. For example, in writing an analysis theme, you might decide to use several introductory paragraphs, rather than one. In addition, you might want to include qualifying or transitional paragraphs in key places in your essay. The result is that occasionally the abstract structure of your essay might look like this:

Analysis Paradigm
Paragraph 1 (introductory paragraph)
Paragraph 2 (a second introductory paragraph that includes the *thesis*)
Paragraph 3 (characteristic 1)
Paragraph 4 (qualification of paragraph 3)
Paragraph 5 (characteristic 2)
Paragraph 6 (qualification of paragraph 5)
Paragraph 7 (transitional paragraph)
Paragraph 8 (characteristic 3)
Paragraph 9 (conclusion)

In brief, what I am suggesting is that in composing an essay, in the process of discovering and arranging your ideas, you use paradigms to facilitate the movement of your thought. In subsequent chapters, I will be taking up the types of paradigms and discussing them at some length while relating them to the topics of invention and to underlying thought processes, but for the moment, let us consider in some detail specific ways of using paradigms to compose your own essays.

In the last chapter, we considered the general subject of automobiles. We probed it for ideas, using questions suggested by the categories of invention. Then we formulated some characteristic thesis sentences.

The thesis sentence not only gives direction to the composition as a whole, but it also suggests the kind of paradigm best suited to develop your ideas. Thus, if you select as your thesis "The new Plymouth Horizon gives you sporty features you'd pay extra for in many other cars," the word *features* suggests that you will develop your essay by means of analysis. If you select as an alternative thesis "Downsized spare tires can affect your car's performance," the word *affect* suggests a cause and effect pattern.

Composing an Essay

Let us take the process a step further and actually write an essay, using some of the ideas derived from the probe in the previous chapter. Naturally, in choosing a thesis you will want to keep in mind your subject, your audience, your purpose, the mode or modes of development, and the kind of writing. Not all of these elements, however, will be equally important in choosing your compositional strategies; at times, some will be relatively more important than others.

Consider now your choices. Your subject matter is given to you. You are going to write about automobiles. The kind of writing you choose will depend on the writing situation or on what the teacher tells you to choose. You can imagine yourself in any number of plausible situations in which you could write about cars. You could be writing an article in a popular magazine or a consumer magazine in which you give information about new cars to your readers. Or you might be writing a magazine ad in which you try to convince readers to buy a particular brand of automobile. Your writing could take the form of a letter to a friend in which you express satisfaction over the purchase of a new car. Each situation demands a different purpose: to inform, to persuade, or to express strong feelings.

What mode or modes might you use in developing your subject? If the car is a sporty car or a luxury car, you would probably decide to *describe* the sporty or luxurious interior. If it has safety features or gas-saving features you would probably choose the mode of *analysis.* If it has extra features or characteristics that its competitors do not have, you may decide to *compare* it to other cars.

What about considerations of audience? If your reader is a married couple with children, you might want to stress safety features or economy. If your reader is a mature man or woman with a large income, you might stress luxury. If your reader is a young college student, you might decide to emphasize sporty looks.

Suppose, after considering your subject, your audience, and your purpose, you choose as your thesis the statement "The Chevrolet Impala has the following outstanding features." This thesis suggests that you will be writing an analytic essay, perhaps supported by enumeration. If, however, you decide on the thesis "The new Thunderbird has sporty features you'd pay extra for in many other cars," your thesis would suggest either analysis or description. It would also suggest either an implicit comparison or an expressed comparison. Assuming that you decide to choose the first of these two theses, you can think of your overall compositional plan in terms of a kind of abstract pattern such as the following:

Introduction (states the thesis)
Feature 1

Feature 2
Feature 3
Feature 4
Conclusion (restates, summarizes, and so forth)

However, it is unlikely that you will confine yourself to discussing a single feature of the car in each paragraph. Instead, you would probably include a cluster of features or characteristics in each supporting paragraph. In that event, the paradigm would look like this:

Introduction (states the thesis)
Cluster of features
Cluster of features
Cluster of features
Cluster of features
Conclusion (restates, summarizes, and so forth)

Or you can employ a more detailed kind of paradigm in sentence form, as in the following scheme, keeping in mind that these patterns are not prior to but are the result of your thinking:

The Chevrolet Impala has the following outstanding features. . . .
The Impala has more space. . . .
The Impala has better fuel efficiency. . . .
The Impala has a number of luxury features. . . .
Chevrolet Impala is better than average. . . .

Then, using this sentence paradigm as the core structure of your thought, you write your essay.

You begin by putting your thesis sentence into your introductory paragraph. Then you put the supporting sentences of your paradigm into successive paragraphs. The resulting essay might end up looking something like this:

General Motors has done it again. They have come up with a new full-size car that is more efficient and more economical than full-sized cars used to be. This new car is the Chevrolet Impala. *It has the following outstanding features.*

The Impala has more space than the full-sized cars it has replaced. It has full-sized room for six passengers. It has plenty of head room, more rear-seat leg room, and plenty of hip room. It has more usable trunk space than ever before.

The Impala has better fuel efficiency. It has EPA mileage estimates of 21 miles per gallon on the highway and 16 miles per gallon in the city, and it gets this mileage with a 305-cubic-inch V-8 engine and an automatic transmission.

The Impala also has a number of luxury features. It has generous amounts of insulation and acoustic-backed carpet and headliners, for a smooth and quiet ride. It has wire wheel covers and whitewall radial tires. It has an electric clock, reading lights on the rear door, and a courtesy lamp for the ashtray.

Cars are shrinking. Almost all of the leading car manufacturers have down-sized their large cars. The best, however, among the large group of domestic models are the new General Motors cars. All get fairly good gas mileage and all give a fairly good performance. Of these cars, *the Chevrolet Impala is better than average.*

Suppose, however, that instead of using the essay form, you decide to write a magazine ad. Because of the mass audience your ad would have to appeal to and because of the contents of the magazine your ad would have to compete with, you would probably shorten your paragraphs and fragment your sentences to gain reader interest. The resultant copy might look like this:

The New Impala!
More Space Efficient, More Fuel Efficient,
More Luxurious Than Ever

General Motors has done it again!

They have come up with a new full-sized car that is more efficient. More economical.

The new Chevrolet Impala.

It has more space than older full-sized cars. Full-sized room for six passengers. Plenty of head room. And more usable trunk space than ever before.

It has better fuel efficiency. EPA mileage estimates of 21 mpg highway, 16 mpg city. With a 305-cu-inch V-8 engine and automatic transmission.

It also has generous amounts of insulation. Acoustic-backed carpet and headliners, for a smooth, quiet ride.

It has wire wheel covers and whitewall radial tires. An electric clock. Reading lights on the rear door, and a courtesy lamp for the ashtray.

Test drive a new Impala today! You won't go home without one.

In using paradigms to organize your writing, you need not follow the same kind of rigid order that was followed in the writing of the expository essay. The magazine ad above uses a paradigm. But the paradigm is less obvious than the one in the preceding essay, because the paragraphs and sentences have been broken down into smaller units and because some connecting links have been omitted. Ultimately, it is more important for you to understand *the principles that underlie these paradigms* than the paradigms themselves. Then, when you begin to write, you will automatically begin to think in terms of stages, or phases, or steps, or progressions of some kind.

Paradigms can be used with a great deal of flexibility as the following piece of professional writing illustrates:

The life of the ocean is divided into distinct realms. Each has its own group of creatures that feed upon each other and depend on each other in different ways.

There is, first of all, the tidal zone. Here land and sea meet. Then comes the realm of the shallow seas around the continents, which goes down to about 500 feet. It is in these two zones that the vast majority of all marine life occurs.

The deep ocean adds two regions, the zone of light and the zone of perpetual darkness. In the clear waters of the western Pacific, light could still be seen at a depth of 1,000 feet through the portholes of the *Trieste* on its seven-mile dive. But for practical purposes the zone of light ends at about 600 feet.

Below that level there is too little light to support the growth of the "grass" of the sea—the tiny single-celled green plants whose ability to form sugar and starch with the aid of sunlight makes them the base of the great food pyramid of the ocean.

—from *The Sea*, Life Nature Library

In this piece of writing, the paradigm is there, but it is not as formal or rigid as the paradigm in the previous essay. The opening sentence states the idea that the ocean is "divided into distinct realms." The next paragraph discusses two of these divisions. The third and fourth paragraphs discuss two more. But the divisions are not presented in lockstep fashion (e.g., the first, the second, the third). Numbers are used as signaling devices, but they are used flexibly. Synonyms are also used to help the reader follow the divisions.

You can easily pick out the key words that make up the paradigm, so that the resultant pattern looks like this:

1. The life of the ocean is *divided* into *distinct realms.*

2. There is, *first of all*, the *tidal zone.*

3. *Then* comes the *realm of the shallow seas.*

4. It is in *these two zones* that the vast majority of all marine life occurs.

5. The *deep ocean* adds *two regions*, the *zone of light* and the *zone of perpetual darkness.*

Notice that the key sentences that make up the paradigm are scattered in various places in the essay. The first sentence of the paradigm is the opening sentence of the essay. The second sentence of the paradigm is the first sentence of the second paragraph. The third sentence of the paradigm is also the third sentence of the second paragraph. The fourth sentence of the paradigm is the fourth sentence of the second paragraph. The fifth sentence of the paradigm is the first sentence of the third paragraph. It is obvious that the organization of this essay could have been quite different. For example, almost every sentence of the abstracted paradigm could have been used to start a new paragraph. But the writer decided to use this less formal pattern for his own particular purposes.

Exercises

1. Construct a paradigm in which you include a thesis sentence and supporting sentences in the form of steps, characteristics, types, details, or whatever.

2. Go back to chapter 2. There is more than enough material derived from the probe on automobiles for you to write several essays. Using this material, decide on the kind of essay you will write, your purpose, your audience, and your mode. Set this information up in outline form to be handed in on a separate sheet of paper, and then write your essay based on this information.
   The following is the format for the cover sheet:

   Subject:
   Aim or specific purpose:
   Audience:
   Kind of writing:
   Mode or modes:
   Thesis:

   Here is the same outline, with one possible handling of the material:

   Subject: automobiles
   Aim: persuasion
   Audience: college students
   Kind of writing: magazine article
   Mode: description

Form Consciousness

Although you impose order in the process of arranging your ideas in writing, you can also discover order in the writings of others. Research reveals that the best writers are those who can perceive form in their own writing and in the writing of others.

Following the processes of thought in the writing of others is analogous to recreating the processes of composition in your own mind.

In our discussion of the writing process up to this point, I have maintained that **formal principles of thinking are embodied in writing.** I have identified some of these principles as analysis, classification, comparison and contrast, and the like. They manifest themselves in the essay as principles of invention and patterns of arrangement. For example, comparison can be a means of probing a subject or of organizing an essay. If these principles are embodied in thinking as well as in writing, then you can get at them deductively, by moving through the stages of discovering ideas and arranging them in your writing, or inductively, by abstracting them from the writing of others and then using them in different subject matter. Thus, you can move from examining and describing principles and patterns of organization in the writing of others to using these principles and patterns in your own writing.

In order to get at these formal principles and patterns, I would like to suggest two methods of analysis. The first is *a type of structural analysis that follows the linear or chronological order of ideas from one sentence to another and from one paragraph to another.* I call this kind of analysis the **linear analysis** of a text. The second is *a type of analysis in which the paradigm is abstracted and placed in a formal scheme or pattern.* I call this kind of analysis the **paradigmatic analysis** of a text.

Exercises

1. Are you conscious of form in your own writing? In your sentences? In your paragraphs? In your essays? How do you organize your ideas in writing? Do you have a plan?

2. Look up the words *form, shape, structure, figure, outline, contour, configuration, profile, mold, design,* and *pattern* in your dictionary. Are there differences in the literal meanings? In suggested meanings?

3. What is meant by *form consciousness?*

4. Are you conscious of form in your own life? In your dancing? In your singing? In playing a game? In your speech? In thinking? Discuss.

Linear Analysis

To analyze the structure of an essay using linear methods, consider the essay as a kind of extended paragraph in which all the sentences are related to each other by coordination and subordination. Then, using a system of numbering and indenting the sentences to depict graphically the overall structure of the essay, go from sentence to sentence, considering the logical progression of ideas.

Begin with the opening sentence and label it number 1. Then go through each successive sentence carefully, searching for evidence of coordination and subordination. If the second sentence in the essay is like the first (is parallel in sentence structure or ideas), consider it as coordinate, label it number 1 also, and put it right under sentence 1. If the second sentence differs from the first (gives evidence of subordination of structure or ideas), give it the number 2 and indent it under sentence 1 as subordinate.

Do the same with the remaining sentences. As you consider each sentence in turn, indent it as subordinate or set it down as coordinate, and assign it an appropriate number. When you come to the last sentence in each paragraph, leave a space after this sentence and before the first sentence of the next paragraph, so that the paragraph divisions of the essay are obvious. Remember that even though you leave spaces between paragraphs, when you come to the first sentence of each paragraph, you disregard, for the moment, the part that these sentences play in their respective paragraphs and consider only their relationships to the last sentences of the previous paragraphs. Is the first sentence of the new paragraph subordinate to the last sentence of the previous paragraph? Then give it the next number and indent it. Is it coordinate to that sentence? Then give it the same number and set it down in parallel fashion.

The method of determining coordination and subordination between sentences in the essay is relatively simple. There are two kinds of subordination between sentences: grammatical subordination and meaning subordination. Some typical examples of grammatical subordination are the use of a pronoun in one sentence to refer to a noun or pronoun in a previous sentence; the use of transitional markers, such as *thus, therefore,* and *nevertheless,* to tie sentences together; the repetition of a word or a part of a word in a sentence to link it to a similar word in the previous sentence; and the use of a synonym to refer to an equivalent word in a previous sentence. Meaning relationships are much more difficult to determine, but in general, if a sentence gives an example, a fact, a detail, a reason, a qualification, or support of any kind, then consider it to be subordinate to a more general statement that precedes it.

Coordination, like subordination, can be based on grammatical structure or meaning. One of the clearest signs of grammatical coordination is parallel structure. Quite often, grammatical coordination will also contain meaning coordination. But if grammatical clues are not present or if they are difficult to discover, then look for groupings of examples, reasons, details, and consider sentences that contain these groupings as coordinate.

The following analysis of the introduction to Bertrand Russell's *Autobiography* is a good example of this kind of approach to form in composition:

What I Have Lived For

1

1. Three passions, simple but overwhelmingly strong, have governed my life: the longing for love, the search for knowledge, and unbearable pity for the suffering of mankind.

2. These passions, like great winds, have blown me hither and thither, in a wayward course, over a deep ocean of anguish, reaching to the very verge of despair.

2

3. I have sought love, first, because it brings ecstasy—ecstasy so great that I would often have sacrificed all the rest of life for a few hours of this joy.
3. I have sought it, next, because it relieves loneliness—that terrible loneliness in which one shivering consciousness looks over the rim of the world into the cold unfathomable lifeless abyss.
3. I have sought it, finally, because in the union of love I have seen, in a mystic miniature, the prefiguring vision of the heaven that saints and poets have imagined.
    4. This is what I sought, and though it might seem too good for human life, this is what—at last—I have found.

3

3. With equal passion I have sought knowledge.
    4. I have wished to understand the hearts of men.
    4. I have wished to know why the stars shine.
    4. And I have tried to apprehend the Pythagorean power by which number holds sway above the flux.
        5. A little of this, but not much, I have achieved.

4

3. Love and knowledge, so far as they were possible, led upward toward the heavens.
3. But always pity brought me back to earth.
    4. Echoes of cries of pain reverberate in my heart.
        5. Children in famine, victims tortured by oppressors, helpless old people, a hated burden to their sons, and the whole world of loneliness, poverty, and pain make a mockery of what human life should be.
            6. I long to alleviate the evil, but I cannot, and I too suffer.

5

1. This has been my life.
   2. I have found it worth living, and gladly would live it again if the chance were offered me.

This essay consists of five paragraphs. Paragraph 1 constitutes the beginning, paragraphs 2, 3, and 4 make up the body of the essay, and paragraph 5 constitutes the ending.

The first paragraph contains the *thesis* sentence:

Thesis   Three passions, simple but overwhelmingly strong, have governed my life:
the longing for love,
the search for knowledge, and
unbearable pity for the suffering of mankind.

(I have indented the sentence levels so that you can see the logical divisions more clearly.) The second sentence is subordinate to the first. It qualifies the statement in the first sentence. The phrase "these passions" in the sentence ties in with the phrase "three passions" in the first sentence.

In paragraph 2, the first sentence (beginning "I have sought love") picks up the first idea in the thesis sentence ("the longing for love") and comments on it. It is subordinate to the two previous sentences because it narrows down the general idea of love and begins to give reasons for Bertrand Russell's seeking it. The specific tie-in with sentence 1 is the repetition of the word *love,* and with sentence 2, the reference of the word *love* to the word *passions.*

The second sentence in this paragraph gives a second reason Russell has sought love. It also has a similar grammatical structure and thus is coordinate to the first sentence:

I have sought love, first, because . . .
I have sought it, next, because . . .

The third sentence in this paragraph gives a third reason for Russell's seeking love. It is parallel in structure to the two preceding sentences:

> I have sought love, first, because . . .
> I have sought it, next, because . . .
> I have sought it, finally, because . . .

The last sentence ("This is what I sought . . .") summarizes the ideas in the other three sentences. The word *this* refers back specifically to the words *love, it,* and *it* in sentences 3, 4, and 5, and more generally to the ideas about love in these sentences.

In paragraph 3, the first sentence is grammatically parallel to the first three sentences of paragraph 2. It is also parallel in meaning because it is an enumeration of one of the three passions Russell mentions in his thesis—love, knowledge, and pity:

> I have sought *love* . . .
> I have sought it . . .
> I have sought it . . .
>
> With equal passion
> I have sought *knowledge* . . .

The next three sentences are subordinate to the first sentence of paragraph 3 and coordinate to each other:

> I have wished to understand . . .
> I have wished to know . . .
> I have tried to apprehend . . .

Each sentence gives a specific example of the kind of knowledge sought:

> . . . to understand the hearts of men
> . . . to know why the stars shine
> . . . to apprehend the Pythagorean power by which number holds sway above the flux

The last sentence in this paragraph ("A little of this, but not much, I have achieved") summarizes the author's achievement of knowledge. The phrase "a little of this" ties this sentence to the three previous sentences.

In the fourth paragraph, the first two sentences are coordinate to each other:

> Love and knowledge, so far as they were possible, led upward toward the heavens.
> But always pity brought me back to earth.

The connecting word *but* points to the basis of the parallel ideas: love, knowledge, and pity. There is also a basic antithesis that links these two sentences together:

> Love and knowledge . . . *led upward toward the heavens.*
> But always pity brought me *back to earth.*

The third sentence is subordinate to the previous sentence. The whole sentence, "echoes of cries of pain reverberate in my heart," is a synonym for the word *pity*. It qualifies the idea in the preceding sentence and organizes the ideas in the last two sentences.

The next sentence ("Children in famine, victims tortured by oppressors, helpless old people . . .") gives specific examples of the "cries of pain" of the previous sentence and is subordinate to it.

The last sentence ("I long to alleviate the evil, but I cannot, and I too suffer") comments on the idea of evil and pain in the previous sentence and is subordinate to that sentence.

Finally, the first sentence of paragraph 5 ("This has been my life") summarizes the thought of the whole essay. It is parallel to sentence 1 at the beginning of the essay. These two sentences act as a kind of frame device for the entire essay:

> *Three passions* . . . have governed *my life.*
> *This* has been *my life.*

The last sentence of the essay ("I have found it worth living, and would gladly live it again if the chance were offered me") qualifies the ideas contained in the previous sentence and comments on them and on the ideas contained in the whole essay. The word *it* ties in to the word *life* in the previous sentence.

Exercises

1. Do a linear analysis of a magazine ad or a short news story, using the methods outlined in this chapter.

2. In class, do a linear analysis of one of the student essays in this chapter or of one of your own essays.

3. Select a short, well-organized article or essay from a magazine or from your own reader and do a linear analysis of it.

Paradigmatic Analysis

A linear analysis is a necessary first step in any kind of rhetorical analysis. It takes into account every sentence in the essay. The purpose of a linear analysis is to allow you to follow the logical progression of ideas in an essay to see what goes with what, to see how every sentence in an essay is related to every other sentence.

The purpose of a paradigmatic analysis is to allow you to abstract the underlying organizational pattern of the entire essay and to use this pattern to produce your own essays. The kinds of patterns we will be particularly interested in abstracting are those related to the topics of invention and the patterns of arrangement that were discussed earlier in this chapter: analysis, classification, comparison and contrast, and the like. These patterns represent *dynamic organizational processes*. In the act of composing, *our minds think along these lines*.

How do you get at these underlying patterns? Once you make your linear analysis, go back over the essay and read it carefully. Then proceed, sentence by sentence, through the essay, looking for instances of repetition (word, phrase, clause, or meaning repetition that relate to the pattern under consideration. For example, in classification themes, key words, and phrases, such as *types, parts, categories, classes, basic kinds of, fundamental kinds, divided into ___ classes,* and the like will recur with enough frequency that the pattern will be unmistakable.) Then abstract the sentences and phrases that relate to the pattern under consideration and put them into a paradigm. In the first stages, you might want to use as much of the original wording of the text as possible. But quite often, you may need to *regularize* the text for the sake of revealing the underlying pattern more clearly. You can do this by using a sentence paraphrase, recasting the sentences in simpler form. The paraphrase need not be exactly equivalent to the text, but it must be equivalent in meaning. The resultant pattern represents the principle by which your essay moves from beginning to end.

Many essays are so regular that it is fairly easy to detect the underlying pattern. The Bertrand Russell essay has a clear-cut organizational structure, so that the process of abstracting the pattern should be easy enough to do. In the first stage of your analysis, you should keep as close as possible to the original sentences of the text.

To begin our analysis, notice, first of all, that the opening sentence of the essay is the *thesis* sentence, the sentence that states the main idea. It is also the sentence that indicates the plan of development. The word *three* in the thesis suggests that a pattern of enumeration will follow. And the word *passions* coupled with the word *three* indicates a complementary pattern of classification. The first sentence is an *analytic thesis sentence.* It not only indicates that the writer is going to talk about three things, but it also enumerates what these three things are, then picks them up again in paragraphs 2, 3, and 4. A conventional thesis sentence would have this structure:

> Three passions . . . have governed my life.

But an analytic thesis sentence breaks the statement into parts and indicates the plan of development, like this:

> 1. Three passions . . . have governed my life:
>   the longing for love,

> the search for knowledge, and
> unbearable pity for the suffering of mankind.

This thesis gives us a clue, a hint of what is to follow.

The second sentence in this paragraph qualifies and expands the idea of passions in the first sentence. The explicit tie-in is the repetition of the word *passions:*

> These passions, like great winds, have blown me hither and thither, in a wayward course, over a deep ocean of anguish, reaching to the very verge of despair.

You will note that in paragraph 2, no one sentence advances the pattern. There is, for example, no topic sentence. Instead, the first three sentences advance the pattern by giving the reasons why the author sought love. So you provide a sentence that can serve as the top sentence of the paradigm and add to it those sentences or phrases that constitute its support. The result is the following pattern:

> I have sought love . . .
>> I have sought love, first, because it brings ecstasy. . . .
>> I have sought it, next, because it relieves loneliness. . . .
>> I have sought it, finally, because . . . I have seen . . . the prefiguring vision of the heaven that saints and poets have imagined. . . .

The first sentence of the next paragraph unmistakably advances the pattern. It enumerates the second of Bertrand Russell's passions, knowledge:

> With equal passion I have sought knowledge.

And the subsequent sentences in that paragraph form the support structure:

> With equal passion I have sought knowledge.
>> I have wished to understand the hearts of men.

> I have wished to know why the stars shine. . . . And
> I have tried to apprehend the Pythagorean power by which number
> holds sway above the flux.

The first sentence of the third paragraph repeats the words *love* and *knowledge* of the two previous paragraphs and continues the main idea. It is a transitional sentence. The second sentence of that paragraph advances the overall pattern by enumerating the third passion that has governed Bertrand Russell's life. So use this sentence and add to it the supporting details, but this time regularize the support pattern to make it parallel the structure of the support patterns of the previous paragraphs:

> But always pity brought me back to earth.
> [I have pitied] children in famine . . .
> [I have pitied] victims tortured by oppressors . . .
> [I have pitied] helpless old people, a hated burden to their sons . . .
> [I have pitied] the whole world of loneliness, poverty, and pain. . . .

Finally, the first sentence of the last paragraph completes the pattern, and coupled with the first sentence of the essay, it acts as a *frame device* for the entire paradigm:

> This has been my life.

If you put the various stages of the paradigm together, taking just a few more liberties with the phrasing, you get this overall pattern:

1. Three passions . . . have governed my life: the longing for love, the search for knowledge, and unbearable pity for the suffering of mankind.

2. I have sought love.
   I have sought love . . . because it brings ecstasy. . . .
   I have sought it . . . because it relieves loneliness. . . .

I have sought it . . . because [. . . it contains] a vision
of the heavens that saints and poets have imagined.

3. I have sought knowledge.
   I have wished to understand the hearts of men.
   I have wished to know why the stars shine.
   I have tried to apprehend the Pythagorean power by which
   number holds sway above the flux.

4. [I have sought pity.]
   [I have pitied] children in famine. . . .
   [I have pitied] victims tortured by oppressors. . . .
   [I have pitied] helpless old people. . . .
   [I have pitied] the whole world of loneliness, poverty, and
   pain.

5. This has been my life.

This pattern represents the organizational structure of the entire
essay. The first unit states the main idea. Russell is going to talk
about the three passions that have governed his life. The next unit
enumerates the first passion, *love,* then supports it with the reasons
why the author sought love. The next unit enumerates the second
passion, *knowledge,* and supports it with an explanation of the kinds
of knowledge Russell sought. The fourth unit names the last passion,
pity, and the supporting details tell whom it is the author pities.
The last unit concludes the pattern and returns to the beginning.

It is obvious that although the overall organizational pattern is
classification (what is being classified is kinds or types of passions)
reinforced by *enumeration,* the structure of the supporting paragraphs
could have differed. For example, paragraph 3 could just as easily
have been supported by reasons as by an explanation and enumeration
of the kinds of knowledge that Bertrand Russell sought. This leads
us to conclude that the main plan of the essay is carried by the
underlying patterns of classification and enumeration. This is the
pattern that represents the working idea of the essay and the principle
of forward motion. If you normalize the text again, reducing it to

its essential structure, you get a pattern that is more workable for compositional purposes:

> Three passions have governed my life.
> The first passion is the longing for love.
> The second passion is the search for knowledge.
> The third passion is the pity for the suffering of mankind.
> These are the passions that have governed my life.

For compositional purposes, you can abstract even more from the original pattern. You can then take the resultant pattern and put your own subject matter into it.

> Three passions have governed my life.
> The first passion is . . .
> The second passion is . . .
> The third passion is . . .
> These are the passions that have governed my life.

You can also vary the pattern by substitution:

> Three (four, five) things (passions, emotions, events) have governed my life.
> The first thing is . . .
> The second thing is . . .
> The third thing is . . .
> The fourth thing is . . .
> The last thing is . . .
> These are the things that have governed my life.

Or you can abstract even more, reducing the underlying pattern (or patterns) to a single abstract pattern:

> Introduction (states the thesis)
> Type 1 (or Characteristic 1)
> Type 2 (or Characteristic 2)
> Type 3 (or Characteristic 3)
> Type 4 (or Characteristic 4)

Types 5, 6, 7 . . . (or Characteristics 5, 6, 7 . . .)
Conclusion (restates the thesis, summarizes, and so forth).

Not every essay is as clearly organized as Russell's essay. Not every essay will have the paragraphs arranged in such a convenient order. Some essays may have several introductory paragraphs. The thesis, rather than being the first sentence of the essay, may be embedded in the second or third paragraph. In addition to containing the support paragraphs for the thesis, some essays may contain numerous transitional paragraphs or even paragraphs that digress from the main idea. Nevertheless, with enough practice and skill in analyzing, you should be able to abstract the underlying paradigm and make it generative in your own writing. In subsequent chapters, we will be looking at a large number of these patterns.

You should realize that the parts of the abstracted pattern do not necessarily bear a one-to-one relationship to corresponding paragraphs. The divisions represent "sections" of the essay. These sections could be paragraph divisions, or they could be larger thought units, as the following scheme indicates:

Paragraph 1 (Introduction)
Paragraph 2 (Statement of the Thesis)
Paragraph 3 (Characteristic 1)
Paragraph 4 (Qualification of Paragraph 3)
Paragraph 5 (Characteristic 2)
Paragraph 6 (Digression)
Paragraph 7 (Transitional Paragraph)
Paragraph 8 (Characteristic 3)
Paragraph 9 (Conclusion)

Exercises

1. Using the analysis of the Bertrand Russell essay as a model, select an essay from your reader or from a magazine and do a paradigmatic analysis.

2. Do a paradigmatic analysis of one of your own essays.

3. Using the paradigm from the Bertrand Russell essay, write an essay of your own in which you discuss passions or emotions or events that have governed your life. Try to follow the structure of Bertrand Russell's essay closely.

In subsequent chapters, I will be asking you to use paradigms of this sort in your own writing until you feel that you have such a firm grasp of compositional form that you can dispense with them. However, even more sophisticated writers use them in their writing. The idea is to *internalize the principles* upon which these patterns are based so that when you use them, they become intuitive rather than self-conscious. In this way, you will have acquired an invaluable resource to which you can return again and again.

Summary Exercises

1. Discuss some of the formal patterns that exist in nature, for example, the cycle of a storm, the change in seasons, the rhythmic movement of waves, the gradation of a sunrise, the ripening of crops, the beat of the heart, the rhythm of breathing.

2. Discuss some of the formal patterns that exist in art: plots, themes, motifs, refrains, climaxes, balance, hierarchies, rhythm, melody, movement, subordination, coordination, figure and ground, symmetry, genre.

3. Do dreams have a structure? Reveries? Daydreams? Trances? Hallucinations? Rituals? Incantations? Discuss.

4. Discuss the structure of a movie you have seen recently. Did it have a clearly laid-out plot? A thematic structure (for example, the themes of justice and honor in *The Godfather*)? A pattern of images? A central metaphor (life is a *Cabaret*)? A symbolic structure? A motif structure

(the hands in *The Pawnbroker, David and Lisa,* and *A Man and a Woman*)?

5. Did you know that there is a structure in the auditory memory? Try memorizing these telephone numbers: 9376532, 2357326, 5498514. Now memorize these: 9376-532, 235-7326, 54-985-14. Verbal structuring, as well as mathematical structuring, can help you to remember. It can also help you to reason.

6. Complete these opening phrases:

    a. Once upon a time _____.
    b. Long ago _____.
    c. There once was a _____.
    d. In the long and far-off times _____.
    e. It was an early spring morning when _____.

7. Consider the following quotations for possible thesis topics. What kind of pattern of development would you follow in writing about one of these statements?

    a. Character is higher than intellect.—Emerson

    b. A little learning is a dangerous thing.—Pope

    c. Sweet are the uses of adversity.—Shakespeare

    d. Reading maketh a full man, conference a ready man, writing an exact man.—Bacon

    e. Man is probably nearer the essential truth in his superstitions than in his science.—Thoreau

    f. Fear always springs from ignorance.—Thoreau

    g. Man is least himself when he talks in his own person. Give him a mask and he will tell the truth.—Oscar Wilde

    h. A man's worst difficulties begin when he is able to do as he likes.—T. H. Huxley

i. The course of true anything never does run smooth.—Samuel Butler

j. Understand that a man is worth just so much as the things are worth about which he busies himself.—Marcus Aurelius

Patterns of Thought:

Analysis and Description

Chapter 4

Patterns of Thought:
Analysis and Description

It would seem to be a valid statement that *for every process, there must be a corresponding system.* The topics of invention and the patterns of arrangement represent an unbroken line of development from process to system. Paradigms seem to mediate between the processes of discovering ideas and arranging these ideas into an orderly pattern. Thus, **paradigms** are on the one hand *patterns of thought* that give to your writing a determinate direction, and on the other hand *formal patterns* that help you to order your ideas.

To learn to compose, however, is not simply to memorize a set of paradigms. It is rather *to master the system of principles that will make it possible for you to understand and to produce discourse.* A paradigm is the result of paradigmatic thinking and should be considered as a means to an end, not an end in itself.

In the next few chapters, you will be looking at a number of these compositional principles, in their paradigmatic form as well as in their larger patterns in the composition as a whole. The following are some of the most important of these compositional principles:

Analysis/Description
Classification/Exemplification/Definition
Comparison/Contrast/Analogy
Narration/Process/Cause and Effect

Analysis

Most of your day-to-day analyses are informal and intuitive. As you walk along the street, you may notice a tree, look at one of its branches, and discern its size or the texture of the bark or the shape and color of the leaves. After you see a movie, you may talk about the plot, isolate an exciting moment, or discuss a suspenseful scene. Every day, in almost everything you do, you analyze, dissect, differentiate, and trace things to their sources. Analysis is not only an important principle in your everyday thinking, it is also an important compositional principle.

Analysis is *the process of dividing anything complex into simple elements or components.* It is also the exact determination of those elements. It is the systematic separation of a whole into parts, pieces, or sections. Ideally, in the act of analyzing, you trace things back to their underlying principles.

Anything taken as a whole can be analyzed: a landscape, a seascape, a configuration of buildings in a city square, a painting, a picture, a poem, an argument, a philosophical system, a movie, a day in your life, an idea of any sort. In a *physical analysis*, you separate an object in space and break it into its components. In a *conceptual analysis*, you divide an idea into other ideas.

Purpose, Audience, Kinds of Discourse

Analysis can be found in almost any kind of writing, and it can be a means of achieving any of the broader aims of discourse: to inform or instruct, to convince or persuade, to entertain or please, and to express strong feelings and emotions. Your intention in analyzing is especially important because it will become the informing principle that shapes your perception of the whole. Unless you keep your intention constantly in view, your analyses will become mere classroom exercises.

To avoid making your analyses sterile exercises, you might ask yourself a number of questions about the purpose of your analysis in relation to your subject, your audience, and the kind of writing best suited to your needs:

1. What *subject* am I going to analyze? A physical object? A political issue? An institution? A current event? An idea? A work of art?

2. What *specific problems* might I encounter in analyzing this particular subject?

3. What is my *purpose* in making the analysis?

4. For what *audience* is the analysis intended? What features of my analysis might I include for one kind of reader but exclude for another?

5. How will my reader use the *results* of my analysis?

6. What is the most appropriate *kind of writing* in which to put my analysis? A scientific essay? A report? A printed brochure? A news story? A magazine article? An advertisement?

Invention and Analysis

What is the thought process like? In the process of analyzing anything, you begin with a general impression of the whole, keeping in mind the response you want to get from your reader. Then you have to abstract some feature or features from the whole to support your general impression, and focus your attention upon them. Next you have to hold these features in your mind as the object of your immediate thought in order to remember them later. After this, you have to attend to other features, noticing the connection among them and their relationship to other parts of the whole. Then, in order to understand the object of your analysis, you have to pull all of these features together, to see them as a whole. Finally, you have to come to some kind of conclusion about your analysis. Your conclusion will depend in part on your purpose and may be a comment on your analysis or a summary of your main points. All of this is a part of what I mean by invention by analysis.

If you decide to generalize from your experience and put the results of the process of analysis into the form of questions for subsequent invention, you will get something like the following questions: What are its pieces, parts, or sections? How may they logically be divided? What is the logical order? What is the relationship of the parts to the whole? You can then ask these questions of any new subject that you want to analyze.

Let me illustrate the process by analyzing with you the following familiar poem by E. A. Robinson:

Richard Cory

Whenever Richard Cory went down town,
We people on the pavement looked at him:
He was a gentleman from sole to crown,
Clean favored, and imperially slim.

And he was always quietly arrayed,
And he was always human when he talked;
But still he fluttered pulses when he said,
"Good morning," and he glittered when he walked.

And he was rich—yes, richer than a king—
And admirably schooled in every grace:
In fine, we thought that he was everything
To make us wish that we were in his place.

So on we worked, and waited for the light,
And went without the meat, and cursed the bread,
And Richard Cory, one calm summer night,
Went home and put a bullet through his head.

After several close readings of this poem, you begin to notice that there is an interesting pattern of imagery in the poem relating to royalty and another relating to bearing or upbringing, and you begin to isolate and to examine words and phrases that seem to make up these patterns.

You notice that there are patterns of words related to royalty, and you associate certain meanings with these:

Word	Associated Meanings
Richard Cory	Richard Coeur de Lion
crown	king's crown
imperially	like an emperor
arrayed	dressed like a king
glittered	gold and kingship
grace	an attribute of a good king

Then you notice that there is an overlapping pattern of words related to bearing or upbringing:

Word	*Associated Meanings*
gentleman	polite, gracious, and considerate
clean favored	complete, free from alterations
quietly arrayed	not showy, impressively orderly
always human	kind and courteous
admirably schooled in every grace	effortless charm and refinement

With additional readings and close analysis, you notice other features of the poem. Each of the first three stanzas is divided between a description of Richard Cory and the reaction of the people to him. The last stanza describes the people's attitude toward life and Richard Cory's denunciation of it.

The specific lines relating to the people's increasing degree of reaction to Cory can be abstracted from the poem and presented in a systematic way as follows:

Stanza 1: We people . . . *looked* at him
Stanza 2: he *fluttered* pulses
Stanza 3: we thought that he was *everything*
Stanza 4: our reaction (implicit in the stanza) when he shot himself was to be horrified

You will notice in the process so far that you have followed most of the steps needed to make a competent analysis: a careful reading of the lines, a critical examination of the parts, the separation of the parts from the whole.

Your final step is to try to determine the nature of the whole. You can do this by trying to abstract from the elements and from the poem as a whole what you take to be its theme or main idea. The theme unifies the whole and helps to order the parts.

Several statements of the theme are possible:

You can never judge a person's happiness from the outside.
Things are not always what they seem to be.
All that glitters is not gold.
Appearances are deceiving.

Putting the parts together, you arrive at a conclusion about the *meaning* of the poem, which goes something like this. Richard Cory was a man whom people looked up to. He seemed to have many excellent qualities. He was regal in bearing, well dressed, polite, gracious, and considerate. He had effortless charm and refinement. Less fortunate people, who seemed not to have his attainments and certainly not his money, envied him and cursed their own status in life. Yet evidently something in Cory was lacking. Perhaps he was more superficial than people thought. Perhaps the *glitter* was just that, a kind of surface glamour with no real depth of feeling. There is a hint of this in the phrase "admirably schooled in every grace." The word *schooled* suggests that Cory's gracious and charming manner was not natural. The theme suggested by all these details, then, seems to be "that appearances are deceiving, that you cannot always judge people by their external appearance."

Exercises

1. Probe a subject using the questions related to the topic of analysis (What are its pieces, parts, or sections? How may they logically be divided? What is the logical order? What is the relationship of the parts to the whole?).

2. Analyze one of the following general topics in class and list the subdivisions revealed by analysis:

   a. a painting
   b. a picture
   c. a movie
   d. a television show
   e. a day in your life

   f. a sentence
   g. the layout of a supermarket
   h. a magazine ad
   i. an idea
   j. a poem

The Structure of Analysis

After you have made your analysis, your next step is to put your ideas into some kind of pattern. (Once you have mastered paradigmatic thinking, the process will be less artificial. *As you are analyzing, your ideas will naturally fall into an appropriate pattern.*) The paradigmatic structure of many analytic essays has a pattern somewhat like the following:

Analysis Pattern 1
Introduction (includes thesis)
Characteristic 1 (or part 1)
Characteristic 2 (or part 2)
Characteristic 3 (or part 3)
Characteristic 4 (or part 4)
Characteristic 5, 6, 7 (or part 5, 6, 7) . . .
Conclusion (summary, return to beginning)

The following pattern is less idealized, and probably more like the kinds of paradigms you will find in your everyday reading:

Analysis Pattern 2
Introduction (includes thesis)
Cluster of features
Cluster of features
Cluster of features
Cluster of features
Cluster of features
Conclusion (comment, summary, etc.)

If these paradigms seem too abstract to work with, you can supplement them with a checklist such as the following:

Checklist
1. *Identify the subject to be analyzed.*
2. *Give the basis or bases you will use to divide it into parts.*
3. *State your reasons for the divisions.*
4. *Point out the purpose these divisions might serve.*
5. *List the features, divisions, or subdivisions.*
6. *Discuss each feature as you go along or at appropriate points in your analysis.*
7. *Present these features to your reader in the best possible order, depending on your purpose.*

8. *Close with the final point, with a comment on the analysis,
or with a summary of the main points.*

Remember that the checklist is a reminder of the kinds of things
that might go into your essay, not an outline to be followed in the
exact order in which the items are presented.

Analysis patterns can be either inductive or deductive. If you
begin with the parts and then show how these are related to the
whole, you are proceeding inductively. If, in your writing, you begin
with the whole and then move to narrower elements, you are proceeding deductively, unless the process is one of inverse induction. But
whether you proceed inductively or deductively, you should keep
in mind the purpose of your analysis. The features you decide to
write about will depend on your purpose and your own interests.
You are not analyzing simply for the sake of analyzing, but for the
sake of some special point you want to make. In analyzing "Richard
Cory," for example, I picked out only those structural features of
the poem that seemed to reinforce the theme of appearance versus
reality.

The following professional essay is a good illustration of a well-
organized piece of writing that uses an analysis paradigm. I have
indented and numbered the sentence levels so that the pattern stands
out clearly:

The Frontier Disappears

1

Introduction 1. The United States of today is the product of a variety of forces:
its European origins, the continuing impact of ideas from abroad,
the constant mingling of peoples, and the changes wrought by
the Industrial Revolution.
2. Yet none of these forces was more significant than the frontier
in endowing the Americans with the traits that distinguish them
from other peoples of the world.
3. Down to the present time many of our basic attitudes toward
society and the world around us reflect that pioneer
background.

2

Thesis

4. What are the characteristics that are traceable to this unique feature of our inheritance?

3

Character-istic 1

5. We are a mobile people, constantly on the move, and but lightly bound to home or community.
    6. If you were to ask any group of Americans today how many live in the homes where they were born, only a handful would reply in the affirmative.
    6. If you asked that same question of a group of Englishmen or Frenchmen or Italians, an opposite answer would be given.
        7. Like our frontier ancestors, who shifted about so regularly that mobility became a habit, we are always ready for any change that promises to better our lives.

4

Character-istic 2

5. We are a wasteful people, unaccustomed to thrift or saving.
    6. The frontiersmen established that pattern, for nature's resources were so plentiful that no one could envisage their exhaustion.
        7. Within a few years of the first Virginia settlement, for example, pioneers burned down their houses when they were ready to move west; thus they were allowed to retrieve nails, and none gave thought to the priceless hardwoods that went up in smoke.
    6. As a people we still destroy much that others would save.
        7. I had this driven home to me when, during a year's residence in England, I received a letter from one of that nation's largest banks, enclosed in a second-hand envelope that had been readdressed to me.
            8. Such saving would be unthinkable in the United States, where even the most

insignificant bank would never address a
client save on elaborately engraved
stationery, usually with the names of all
twenty-eight vice presidents parading down
one side of the page.

5

*Character-
istic 3*

5. We are a practical, inventive people on whom the
weight of tradition rests but lightly.
6. In many lands of the world, people confronted with
an unpleasant situation will quietly adjust
themselves; in the United States, a man's first
impulse is to change things for the better.
7. This willingness to experiment came naturally
to the pioneers who had no precedents on which
to build.
8. It has remained a trait of the industrial
pioneers, whose ability to adapt and change
has laid the basis for America's supremacy
as a manufacturing nation.

6

*Character-
istic 4*

5. We are individualistic people, deeply resentful of any
intrusion into our affairs by government or society,
also a basic attitude among frontiersmen.
6. Aware that they were living in a land where
resources were so abundant that only their own
energies were necessary for success, they wanted
to be left alone above all else.
7. This trait persisted in American thought, even
though the passing of the frontier has forced
the government to adopt a more positive social
role.
8. Even today such activity is more resented in
the United States than elsewhere; and this
resentment also helps explain the almost
fanatical American hatred of political systems
such as facism or communism that are based
on the subjugation of the individual.

7

*Character-
istic 5*
5. We are a democratic people.
    6. Our pioneering forefathers originated neither the theory nor the practice of democracy; the western world was well on its way to political equalitarianism when the continent was settled.
    7. But conditions in frontier communities vastly stimulated the trend.
        8. There nature reduced men to equality by dimming the importance of wealth, or hereditary privilege.
        8. There poverty served as a great leveler.
        8. There the demand for self-rule was particularly strong, for frontiersmen knew that their problems were unique and must be solved locally.
        9. And so on the frontier the democratic tradition was strengthened, until it became a part of the American creed.
            10. The undying hatred of the United States for all forms of totalitarianism only mirrors the strength of this faith.

8

Conclusion
2. Thus has the frontier placed its stamp on America and its people.
    3. In the continuing rebirth of civilization during the three centuries required to settle the continent, nature modified the characteristics of its conquerors, even in the midst of their conquest.
    4. There emerged a new people, robust and strong, with an unwavering faith in the merits of the individual and an unswerving allegiance to the principles of democracy.
    5. The frontier is no more, but its heritage remains to give a strength as well as individuality to the civilization of the United States.
    —Ray Allen Billington, "The Frontier Disappears"

This essay has a very clear-cut pattern. Its structure can also be illustrated by the abstracted paradigm:

What are the characteristics that are traceable to this unique feature of our inheritance?

We are a mobile people, constantly on the move, and but lightly bound to home or community.

We are a wasteful people, unaccustomed to thrift or saving.

We are a practical, inventive people on whom the weight of tradition rests but lightly.

We are individualistic people, deeply resentful of any intrusion into our affairs by government or society, also a basic attitude among frontiersmen.

We are a democratic people.

Thus has the frontier placed its stamp on America and its people.

In an analysis essay, in addition to the characteristic paradigm, you come to expect words and phrases like the following:

characteristic	member	trait
feature	component	particular
aspect	constituent	division into parts
part	portion	subdivision
section	fraction	unit
sector	fragment	piece
segment	particle	detail
element	entity	ingredient

whole	analyze
totality	resolve
entirety	separate
collectiveness	dissect
unity	break up
embodiment	constitute
aggregate	compose
sum	embody
bulk	partition
mass	distinguish

These words and phrases provide meaningful clues that will enable your reader to follow the patterning of your ideas with less difficulty.

In your writing, it is more important for you to understand the principles of paradigmatic thinking and the principles of analysis than it is to follow these patterns exactly. At first, if you are having problems organizing your ideas, you might want to follow these patterns closely, until the kind of thinking that they represent becomes habitual. Later on, you will be able to use these patterns with a great deal of flexibility, as the following student paper illustrates:

A Diamond Is Forever

Rolling Stone magazine has never been a publication to concern itself with mushy, love-story-type themes. Most often, one finds articles on rock-and-roll music and the hazards of nuclear energy in the magazine. And yet, in the February 22, 1979, issue there is one full page of sentimental mush at its best (or worst). An advertisement for diamonds—specifically, what a diamond ring means to a young couple's budding romance—is nestled between an article on New Wave rock group Devo and a tongue-in-cheek ad suggesting a Valentine's Day gift of a Ted Nugent album. Has the diamond industry made a horrendous mistake? Probably. Not only is their ad laughably romantic and aimed at the wrong audience, but it is also poorly written.

A headline over the most prominent part of the diamond advertisement—a picture of a young couple enjoying a quiet moment together in a soda shop—starts the ad off in the wrong direction. It reads: "Our diamond means we now have the best of both worlds. Yours and mine." The phrase "yours and mine" takes up a separate line below the opening sentence and is centered between the tilted heads of the adoring couple in the picture. Now, *Rolling Stone* readers are *not* going to buy the premise of the opening sentence. A couple in love cannot miraculously attain a mixture of the best of their respective worlds simply by slipping a diamond ring onto a finger. What happens to the worst parts of their worlds when the ring goes on? Do his belching and her gum-cracking cease when the nineteen-hundred-dollar stone is purchased? *Rolling Stone* readers will, inevitably, ask these probing questions.

Next in line for rebuke is the centerpiece of the ad. The hairstyles and the clothing of the young couple in the picture seem to be right out of the late fifties or early sixties. The soft vignette of a young couple in an ice-cream parlor begs for criticism. A handsome male, not unlike Ryan O'Neal in appearance, leans over his dreamy-eyed, smiling gal to sip on an old-fashioned soda. The whipped topping of the soda appears about ready to topple onto the counter, and the moment is captured as if it were a candid snapshot. Sharing a soda with Sally went out with the Beach Boys. Injecting nostalgia into the ad is not going to sell diamond rings to readers of *Rolling Stone.*

The narrative form in which the ad is written continues below the ice-cream-parlor picture. The copy is written in the first person. The young woman, one would assume, does the narrating. "I still remember the day," she says, "you made this near-sighted musician see how exciting a game of football could be." She then goes on to reminisce about the time her boyfriend "sat through a concert without falling asleep." These recollections of times past are set apart in separate sentences so that the reader forms mental images of the events. Each mental image seems to pop into the frame occupied by the soda-fountain scene, so that the effect is like that of leafing through a photo album with the mind. This is a clever bit of psychology on the part of the advertisers, but it doesn't work for this audience. The reader that the diamond industry is reaching in *Rolling Stone* magazine is not one that is especially enthralled with football games and sitting through concerts. The type of concert implied in the ad is a classical concert. Just sitting through anything other than a rock concert would be almost unthinkable to most *Rolling Stone* readers.

A final point about the ad concerns the wording of the sentence "Being in love means we want to know what each other's all about." The wording here is awkward, if not grammatically incorrect. The phrase "each other's all about" in the sentence seems to be a shortening (decapitation might be a better word) of "each other's worlds are all about," but the omission of the two words leads the sentence, headed for sentimentality, into a brick wall of laughter and confusion. Because the reader must read the sentence again, this merely adds emphasis to the absurdity of the line.

The diamond industry would do better to include this kind of advertisement in a magazine whose readers are less apt to criticize and belittle established values. The ice-cream-parlor sweetness of this ad is laughable in almost any context, but buried within the pages of *Glamour* or *Seventeen* magazine, the absurdity would be less obvious.

—Ben

This is a well-written student essay. The student's purpose is to show how the magazine ad "A Diamond Is Forever" fails in relation to its intended audience. The features of the analysis are used as evidence to support his thesis. But these features are not presented without comment. The student writer sifts through the facts of the ad as he goes along, explaining and evaluating them and reaching conclusions about them.

In the professional essay entitled "The Frontier Disappears," the writer chooses to abstract the features of his analysis and present each one in a separate paragraph. In each paragraph, he expands on the particular characteristic by qualifying it, amplifying it, or commenting on it in some way.

In the student essay, the student writer, rather than devoting each supporting paragraph to a single characteristic of the ad, uses a cluster analysis as a way of presenting his ideas. In the first paragraph, he identifies his subject, provides the context for the reader's understanding of his discussion, and then states his thesis: "Not only is their ad laughably romantic and aimed at the wrong audience, but it is also poorly written." Then, in subsequent paragraphs, to support his thesis, he presents the results of his analysis in a cluster of features.

To achieve coherence, he organizes each cluster around a central idea. In paragraph 2, for example, he analyzes the headline and comments on its inadequacies. In paragraph 3, he criticizes the illustration. In paragraph 4, he discusses the narrative form of the copy. In the next paragraph, he isolates a particular phrase and comments on it. Finally, he concludes with a comment about "the ice-cream-parlor sweetness" of the ad and its inappropriateness in a magazine such as *Rolling Stone.* His concluding paragraph actually is a restatement of his thesis, a kind of return to the beginning. This is a suitable ending for his essay because he has been evaluating aspects of the ad in the supporting paragraphs.

These two essays are excellent examples of how the mode of analysis can be used in different kinds of writing, for different aims. The professional essay is a good example of historical exposition. The student paper is a good example of a critical essay, whose purpose may be to inform or persuade.

Here is one last example, an example of scientific writing, which uses the mode of analysis to inform or instruct:

The Anatomy of a Mollusk

Mollusks have a solid, unsegmented body which can be divided into four main parts unless greatly modified.

First is the head, bearing tentacles, eyes, and other sense organs. The mouth opens close to the anterior end and is often armed with teeth. The brain, or cerebral ganglia, is internal and is highly developed in the cephalopods.

The visceral sac is the next distinct part and it houses the gut, heart, and reproductive organs.

The foot is a muscular structure used for locomotion and burrowing and is developed into tentacles in the cephalopods.

The mantle is the fourth region of the body and is a fold of skin which develops from the posterior part and folds over, enveloping the visceral mass and separating it from the shell, thus forming a cavity between the shell and the rest of the body. The anus and excretory ducts open into the mantle cavity inside which the gills develop. The shell is secreted by the edge of the mantle and consists of an outer horny layer, with an internal pearly or nacreous layer of calcium carbonate.

—adapted from *The Animal Kingdom*

This is a good example of scientific analysis: The opening paragraph identifies the subject ("molusks") and sets up the division into "four main parts" ("head," "visceral sac," "foot," and "mantle"), then goes immediately into the analysis: The subsequent paragraphs each take up one of the divisions and extend the analysis initiated in the opening paragraph. The diction is Latinate and scientific ("anterior," "cerebral ganglia," "cephalopods," "visceral sac," "posterior," "nacreous," and "calcium carbonate") with some use of metaphorical language ("armed with teeth," "houses the gut, heart . . ."). Compared to the language of the student's critical essay which combines facts with evaluation, the language of this piece of writing is fairly objective.

Enumeration

Enumeration may be considered to be *a kind of informal analysis,* a subdivision of the topic of analysis. As a topic of invention, it answers such questions as What is the exact number? What is the logical order? How is it constituted? Like analysis, enumeration considers aspects or features of things as separate units. The mental process is concerned with *the sequential arrangement of successive things*: a group of objects, or events, or ideas, generally following each other in the order of time. Number can be thought of as a kind of abstract order, but when it is tied to time, it is related to narration, process, and cause and effect.

As a pattern of arrangement, enumeration presents ideas in numerical order so that there is a distinct separation of the elements of a group. Each part of the series reveals a definite pattern of advance. The numerical order reveals a recurrent causal or logical pattern. However, sometimes you may want to use an enumeration pattern in an essay to hold together parts of a subject that do not ordinarily lend themselves to a more logical form of organization. For example, if you are asked to give a speech, and you cannot think of a more logical way to present your ideas, at the very least you can announce to your audience that you are going to talk about three things or five things or some determinate number. This numbering will not only aid you in recalling the parts of your speech, but it will also give your audience a logical pattern to follow. There are times when you have some "things to say" about a subject, but the best you can do is to put them into some reasonable order. You could probably say more about the subject, but you limit yourself to a representative number, and this order at least serves your purpose.

Since enumeration is such a basic principle, it will often be found reinforcing other patterns such as partition, classification, process, and cause and effect. Whether you use it as a basic organizational pattern or in combination with other patterns, you will want to make clear to the reader your purpose and the basis of the enumeration. Usually your thesis will indicate your purpose and your plan of development.

Because we will be looking at a number of essays that use enumeration as a major or subordinate pattern of development, I will not present any special examples of the type at this time. But it is quite obvious that the paradigm will contain number words like *first, second,* and *next,* as the following scheme illustrates:

Enumeration Pattern
Introduction (includes thesis)

First (the first, one) . . .
Second (the second, two) . . .
Third (the third, three) . . .
Fourth (the next, four) . . .
Fifth, sixth, seventh (another, five) . . .
Finally (the final, six) . . .
Conclusion (summary, return to beginning)

Enumeration themes, like analysis themes, have a characteristic vocabulary. The following are a few representative words and phrases that can be found in enumeration themes:

number	string	list	to count
order	chain	item	to catalog
series	set	catalog	to number
succession	sequel	tally	to enumerate
progression	sequence	analysis	to itemize

Enumeration is probably the simplest kind of organizational pattern. Its simplicity, however, should not deceive you about its relative importance. In chemistry, in physics, in mathematics, number is of fundamental importance. In your everyday activities, numbering is so basic that you may sometimes forget its importance. You compute your grocery bills, number the pages of your letters, call the roll, catalog, count, list, tally, add, score, calculate, and itemize. Like time and space, number is an important principle in the universe.

Exercises

1. Write an analytic essay based on one of the following subjects. Be sure to consider your audience and your purpose for making the analysis. In this and in subsequent assignments, use a cover sheet, similar to the one suggested in chapter 3, that will include subject, purpose, audience, kind of writing, and mode.

   a. pop music
   b. a rock lyric

   c. a short poem
   d. a reproduction of a painting
   e. a life-style
   f. a political or social issue
   g. a magazine ad

2. Bring to class Xerox copies of a magazine ad. Distribute these to members of the class. Then analyze the headline, the picture, and the copy of the ad. Discuss these in relation to the purpose of the ad and the intended audience. Is the ad effective in achieving its purpose?

3. Analyze in class a movie or TV show the class has recently seen.

4. You are called upon to give a talk about the values college students hold. Write a speech in which you analyze these values and come to some kind of conclusion about them. (You can also use this topic for classroom discussion.)

5. Write a scientific analysis of a subject that interests you.

6. Select a newspaper article, a magazine article, or a short essay from your reader about a controversial issue (for example, nuclear power plants). Then do an analysis of the issues:

   a. Read the article carefully.
   b. Pick out all of the important *general statements.*
   c. Identify the *qualifying words: all, many, most, some, several, a few, always, sometimes, usually, never, seldom, occasionally.*
   d. Consider the *supporting evidence* for the general statements: examples, facts, statistics, details, descriptions.
   e. Look closely at the *connections* among ideas. Is the writer adding something new, qualifying, contrasting, or evaluating?
   f. Identify the *main idea.*
   g. Identify the writer's *conclusions.*

Description

Description is a mental process, a way of perceiving objects in space and time. It is really a mode of analysis. Like analysis, it is a process of dividing anything complex into simple elements. Like analysis, it deals with its subject as a whole and in its parts. And like analysis, it is more than an enumeration of the parts or qualities of an object. Unlike analysis, however, it deals with its subject more concretely. It relies heavily on sense impressions. Often, it depends for its effects on comparison and association. These are not absolute but relative distinctions, of course. As it pertains to composition, **description** is *a way of picturing images verbally in speech or writing and of arranging those images in some kind of logical or associational pattern.*

Embedded in the word *description* are two words: *scribere,* meaning "to write," and *de,* meaning "down" or "about." There is a hint in the etymology of the word *description* that something is being traced or drawn, that in describing you will follow the outline of an object visually and then write it down or "draw" it in words. The word *draw* is not an accidental association. Many writers have likened the process of describing to that of painting.

Purpose, Audience, Kinds of Discourse

Description can be found in almost any kind of writing, but it is frequently found in books of travel, history books, guidebooks, geography books, scientific articles, magazine ads, brochures for art galleries, books on architecture, magazine articles, descriptive poems, character sketches, novels, and short stories. Although it may be found in almost pure form, as in some magazine advertisements, description is usually mixed with the other modes.

Perhaps your most important prewriting consideration in describing a person, an object, or a scene is purpose, for your purpose will determine the nature of your description. For example, informative description will enable your reader accurately to identify the object you are describing. Persuasive description will enable you to appeal to the senses of your reader in such a way as to induce action. Evocative description will enable your reader to experience a mood or an emotion.

But to say that someone is describing something is immediately to give rise to the question To whom? The very act of describing implies an audience. Purpose and audience operate in the same fashion for description as they do for analysis.

Invention and Description

In getting ideas for writing a description, you might proceed exactly as a painter might. That is, whether you are looking at a landscape, a person, or an arrangement of fruit, you would tend to ask yourself certain questions that would make the process of invention easier. What does the object or objects look like, or feel like, or smell like? How would you group them logically or artistically? Would you follow the natural lines of the object or scene to be described? Is the object linear, angular, or circular? In describing an object or a scene, would you begin from left to right, from right to left, from bottom to top, or from top to bottom? Is the object or scene near or far away? If far away, would you depict it in the same way as if it were near? What is your point of view? What is the dominant impression of the object or scene? Does the scene evoke a mood or stir your feelings? How best can you convey sense impressions? Notice how easily questions like these come to mind when you are dealing with a particular pattern of thought. In answering these questions, you are inventing.

But you are a painter using words, not pigments. Instead of putting down your impressions on canvas, you will be putting them down on paper. But your task is very similar to that of the painter: to put into some kind of formal pattern the results of your mental perceptions. Like the painter, you will be concerned with form, position, color, light, sound, taste, touch, odor. Like the painter, you will be dealing with the particular and the concrete, with individuals of a class, not with generalized classes. You are not just interested in dogs, but in hounds, pups, whelps, curs, mutts, Saint Bernards, German shepherds, and collies. You are not just interested in birds, but in larks, starlings, robins, sparrows, canaries, finches, nightingales, and mockingbirds.

In the process of writing, you must select particular details and group them. At that time, other questions come to mind. Do you stress contours or outlines, definite lines, colors, or shapes? Do you stress masses and volumes of things? Do you see planes or successions of planes parallel to the picture plane? Do the forms recede—in and out, forward and backward? Are the forms confined in closed space, or are the representations of space infinite? Is there unity, balance, rhythm? Is the order intellectually formal or biomorphic, that is, developing in a natural way? Are the forms fantastic, never seen or imagined before, or seen perhaps only in dreams, myths, hallucinations?

At the moment, I am simply putting into words many of the things you do intuitively. Your mind is constantly questioning, inventing, probing, but I want you to make the process of invention and arrangement more self-conscious.

Exercises

1. Using questions such as those suggested (What is it? What are its constituent parts? How are the parts organized in space? What shape does the thing to be described have? What is its color, taste, feel, smell, sound?), examine a subject such as a landscape, a painting, a piece of fruit, a person's face, for a possible writing assignment.

2. Study a natural landscape, a cluster of buildings, a city scene, or a marketplace. Observe the choice of details, the arrangement of space, the landscaping.

3. Study some paintings, reproductions, or artistic photographs of a landscape, a still life, or a portrait. What is the central feature of the picture? How are the objects or figures grouped? What choices of details has the painter or photographer made? What kind of balance is there in the picture? What is the dominant impression? The point of view?

4. Compare a modern painting with a traditional painting. What is the difference in the handling of details, arrangement, point of view, and climax?

The Structure of Description

When you set out to describe a person, an object, or a scene, you have to decide at the outset your point of view, the choice of appropriate details, and the way you are going to arrange the details.

In description, *point of view* usually refers to physical location. But it may also refer to the mental angle from which you consider your subject. Occasionally, in describing, you may be able to *sense* your physical position in relation to the object. But it is usually better to determine your point of view in advance of your writing. In this way, your description will be more unified.

When moviemakers want to get several different views of a particular scene, they will move the camera from place to place. If they want to get a more general view of an object or scene, they will move the camera further away. If they want a more detailed view, they will move in close. Similarly, in describing, you may find it necessary to move from one point to another or from one scene to another.

Sometimes your point of view will determine your choice of details and the order of their arrangement. Sometimes the natural contours of the objects themselves will suggest a way of proceeding. But often you will have to impose some sort of order on your materials. The following selections illustrate a variety of patterns that you could follow:

Spatial Order: Depth

St. Mark's

And well may they fall back, for beyond those troops of ordered arches there rises a vision out of the earth, and all the great square seems to have opened from it in a kind of awe, that we may see it far away—a multitude of pillars and white domes, clustered into a long low pyramid of coloured light; a treasure-heap, it seems, partly of gold and partly of opal and mother-of-pearl, hollowed beneath into five great vaulted porches, ceiled with fair mosaic, and beset with sculpture of alabaster, clear as amber and delicate as ivory— sculpture fantastic and involved, of palm leaves and lilies, and grapes and pomegranates, and birds clinging and fluttering among the branches, all twined together into an endless network of buds and plumes; and, in the midst of it, the solemn forms of angels, sceptred, and robed to the feet, and leaning to each other across the gates, their figures indistinct among the gleaming of the golden ground through the leaves beside them, interrupted and dim, like the morning light as it faded back among the branches of Eden, when first its gates were angel-guarded long ago.

—John Ruskin, *The Stones of Venice*

Radiating Order: Moving Observer

A Tropical Landscape

On my right hand there were lines of fishing-stakes resembling a mysterious system of half-submerged bamboo fences, incomprehensible in its division of the domain of tropical fishes, and crazy of aspect as if abandoned forever by some nomad tribe of fishermen now gone to the other end of the ocean; for there was no sign of human habitation as far as the eye could reach. To the left a group of barren islets, suggesting ruins of stone walls, towers, and blockhouses, had its foundations set in a blue sea that itself looked solid, so still and stable did it lie below my feet; even the track of light from the westering sun shone smoothly, without that animated glitter which tells of an imperceptible ripple. And when I turned my head to take a parting glance at the tug which had just left us anchored outside the bar, I saw the straight line of the flat shore joined to the stable sea, edge to edge, with a perfect and unmarked closeness, in one levelled floor half-brown, half-blue under the enormous dome of the sky. Corresponding in their insignificance to the islets of the sea, two small clumps of trees, one on each side of the only fault in the impeccable joint, marked the mouth of the river Meinam we had just left on the preparatory stage of our homeward journey; and, far back on the inland level, a larger and loftier mass, the grove surrounding the great Paknam pagoda, was the only thing on which the eye could rest from the vain task of exploring the monotonous sweep of the horizon. Here and there gleams as of a few scattered pieces of silver marked the windings of the great river; and on the nearest of them, just within the bar, the tug steaming right into the land became lost to my sight, hull and funnel and masts, as though the impassive earth had swallowed her up without an effort, without a tremor. My eye followed the light cloud of her smoke, now here, now there, above the plain, according to the devious curves of the stream, but always fainter and farther away, till I lost it at last behind the mitor-shaped hill of the great pagoda. And then I was left alone with my ship, anchored at the head of the Gulf of Siam.

—Joseph Conrad, *The Secret Sharer*

Dominant Image: Repetition

Fog

Fog everywhere. Fog up the river, where it flows among green aits and meadows; fog down the river, where it rolls defiled among the tiers of shipping, and the waterside pollutions of a great (and dirty) city. Fog on the Essex marshes, fog on the Kentish heights. Fog creeping into the cabooses of collier-brigs; fog lying out on the yards, and hovering in the rigging of great ships; fog drooping on the gunwales of barges and small boats. Fog in the eyes and throats of ancient Greenwich pensioners, wheezing by the firesides of their wards; fog in the stem and bowl of the afternoon pipe of the wrathful skipper, down in his close cabin; fog cruelly pinching the toes and fingers of his shivering little 'prentice boy on deck. Chance people on the bridges peeping over the parapets into a nether sky of fog, with fog all round them, as if they were up in a balloon, and hanging in the misty clouds.

—Charles Dickens, *Bleak House*

Order of Memory: Fantasy

Night Town

The Mabbot street entrance of nighttown, before which stretches an uncobbled tramsiding set with skeleton tracks, red and green will-o'-the-wisps and danger signals. Rows of flimsy houses with gaping doors. Rare lamps with faint rainbow-fans. Round Rabaiotti's halted ice gondola stunted men and women squabble. They grab wafers which are wedged lumps of coal and copper snow. Sucking, they scatter slowly. Children. The swancomb of the gondola, highreared, forges on through the murk, white and blue under a lighthouse. Whistles call and answer.

—James Joyce, *Ulysses*

Order of Observations: Impressions

The Garden

I sat down in the middle of the garden, where snakes could scarcely approach unseen, and leaned my back against a warm yellow pumpkin. There were some ground-cherry bushes growing along the furrows, full of fruit. I turned back the papery sheaths that protected the berries and ate a few. All about me giant grasshoppers, twice as big as any I had ever seen, were doing acrobatic feats among the dried ground. There in the sheltered draw-bottom the wind did not blow very hard, but I could hear it singing its humming tune up on the level, and I could see the tall grasses wave. The earth was warm under me, and warm as I crumbled it through my fingers. Queer little red bugs came out and moved in slow squadrons around me. Their backs were polished vermilion, with black spots. I kept as still as I could. Nothing happened. I did not expect anything to happen. I was something that lay under the sun and felt it, like the pumpkins, and I did not want to be anything more. I was entirely happy. Perhaps we feel like that when we die and become part of something entire, whether it is sun and air, or goodness and knowledge. At any rate, this is happiness: to be dissolved into something complete and great. When it comes to one, it comes as naturally as sleep.

—Willa Cather, *My Antonia*

The first selection, by John Ruskin, displays an artistic grouping of details in space. The total effect is that of depth perception. In the Conrad selection, the observer first faces the sea and then turns completely around to face the shore. The effect is that of lines radiating from the observer to different parts of the picture. The Dickens selection uses a dominant image, the fog, as a way of organizing the description. The repetition of the word *fog* unifies the description and produces a dominant tone of dreariness. Quite obviously, not all descriptions are organized in space and time. The selection from *Ulysses* by James Joyce uses the order of memory, which is free from the confinements of space and time. It avoids logic. Memory, of course, is the voluntary calling to mind of past events. But this selection is further complicated by the fact that the mode of writing is a fantasy. The images therefore are bizarre, fanciful, hallucinatory, grotesque, whimsical, and unreal. In the absence of the objects of perception, the mind invents illusory images. Finally, the selection by Willa Cather uses no special order except that of reporting to the reader the random impressions received in the way in which they strike the observer.

The foregoing selections are specific examples of description, in all their concreteness.

The paradigmatic structure of description, however, may be illustrated as follows:

Paradigm 1: Vertical Order (bottom to top, top to bottom)
Paradigm 2: Horizontal Order (left to right, right to left)
Paradigm 3: Depth Order (inside, outside)
Paradigm 4: Circular Order (clockwise, counterclockwise)

A good example of horizontal order is this masterful description by James Joyce:

A fat brown goose lay at one end of the table and at the other end, on a bed of creased paper strewn with sprigs of parsley, lay a great ham, stripped of its outer skin and peppered over with crust crumbs, a neat paper frill round its shin and beside this was a round of spiced beef. Between these rival ends ran parallel lines of side-dishes: two little minsters of jelly, red and yellow, a shallow dish full of blocks of blancmange and red jam, a large green leaf-shaped dish with a stalk-shaped handle, on which lay bunches of purple raisins and peeled almonds, a companion dish on which lay a solid rectangle of Smyrna figs, a dish of custard topped with grated nutmeg, a small bowl of chocolates and sweets wrapped in gold and silver papers and a glass vase in which stood some tall celery stalks. In the centre of the table there stood, as sentries to a fruit-stand which upheld a pyramid of oranges and American apples, two squat old-fashioned decanters of cut glass, one containing port and the other dark sherry.

—James Joyce, ''The Dead''

Joyce uses a frame device to organize the details of this descrip-tion. The opening sentence presents an image of both ends of the table, with the goose at one end and the ham at the other. The rest of the description is organized from these points in space. Sen-tence 2 shows the progression of objects from the ends of the table to the center. Sentence 3 focuses on the objects in the middle of the table, laden with food. The reader can visualize the scene very vividly and grasp the relationships of the objects on the table to one another. Not only is there a spatial movement from the ends to the center, but there is also a movement from meat to drink.

Within this larger pattern, there are smaller patterns that help to make up the whole. The sentences are loose or cumulative sen-tences. (The main idea is stated first, followed by subordinate ideas.) Each sentence furthers the spatial description while at the same time giving the reader a catalog of the food in all its concreteness. Joyce puts the burden of the spatial patterning on the prepositional phrases:

> at one end of the table
> at the other end of the table
> on a bed of creased paper
> round its shin
> beside this
> between rival ends
> on which lay bunches of purple raisins
> on which lay a solid rectangle of Smyrna figs
> in which stood some tall celery stalks
> in the centre of the table

These phrases are phrases of location and direction.

The verb choices are primarily static verbs, the verb "to be" and verbs of rest *(lay, stood, was)*. These reinforce the spatial pattern and contribute to the effect the reader gets that he or she is looking at a static picture, a still life. The point of view is that of an observer who is close to the scene he is describing.

The word choice is specific and concrete. Joyce appeals to almost all the senses. He uses words and phrases pertaining to shape and size, color, texture, and taste:

Shape and Size

great	solid	blocks
little	round	leaf-shaped
full	shallow	stalk-shaped
large	fat	rectangle
small	bunches	pyramid
tall	squat	parallel

Color

brown	purple	peppered
red	gold	dark sherry
yellow	silver	chocolates
green	oranges	

Texture

creased	frill	glass
sprigs	peeled	cut
stripped	grated	
peppered over	crust	

Taste
Fat brown goose
peppered over with crust crumbs
a round of *spiced* beef
grated nutmeg
chocolates and *sweets*

Joyce also uses a number of figures of speech to lend concreteness to the description:

Figures of Speech
a large green *leaf-shaped* dish
a *stalk-shaped* handle
blocks of blancmange and red jam
a solid *rectangle* of Smyrna figs
two decanters of cut glass . . . as *sentries* to a fruit-stand
a *pyramid* of oranges and American apples

Strategies of Description

In this very small compass, Joyce manages to touch upon almost all the aspects of description:

    I. Methods of development
        A. Spatial (linear—left to right, right to left, bottom to top, top to bottom, clockwise, counterclockwise, and so forth)
        B. Repetition (same image repeated)
        C. Cataloging (accumulation of details and images)
   II. Point of view
        A. Near or far
        B. Above or below
        C. Direct line
        D. Oblique
        E. Inside or outside
  III. Imagery
        A. Literal
        B. Figurative
  IV. Sense Appeal
        A. Sight
            1. color (red, orange, lilac)
            2. form (spiral, star-shaped, tubular)
        B. Touch
            1. thermal (hot, cold, sunny)
            2. simple (soft, hard, featherlike)
            3. pressure (squeeze, whizz)
        C. Taste
            1. sweet   6. rough
            2. salty   7. smooth
            3. sour   8. soft
            4. bitter   9. crisp
            5. corrosive   10. cool and warm
        D. Sound
            1. high (shrill, piercing, screech)
            2. low (moan, groan)
        E. Smell
            1. pungent (sharp, stinging, caustic)
            2. tart (sharp)

3. sour (acid)
4. rancid (rank)
5. camphoraceous

6. musky
7. floral
8. peppermintlike

Most of you will have little trouble with visual images. But you will find, as this list shows, that there are few terms to describe touch or taste or sound or smell. So you may have to have recourse to comparisons, to figures of speech.

On the surface, it would appear that there is nothing easier to do than to describe. But to describe is to do more than simply follow the natural contours of an object in space. It is also to be discriminating in selecting details and in grouping objects.

Imitation

One good way to learn to describe is to imitate. The following student paper is based on the Joyce model:

A Thanksgiving Table

A fat brown turkey lay at one end of the table and at the other end, on a silver platter covered with waxen paper, strewn with sprigs of parsley and bits of onions, lay a great duck, stripped of its feathers and outer skin and drenched in pools of cranberry sauce, encircled by thick clusters of dressing and beside this was a platter of spiced rolls. Between these rival ends were concave lines of side-dishes: two tiny cuplets of jelly, purple and red, a large silver bowl filled with billowy mounds of white potatoes, a small pear-shaped dish with a stem-shaped handle on which lay clusters of pitted grapes and crushed walnuts, a companion dish on which lay a quivering rectangle of fruit-laden salad, a dish of chocolate pudding dotted with whipped cream, a small bowl full of almonds and peanuts and a glass vase in which stood freshly cut stalks of garden onions and green celery. In the center of the table there stood, like majestic pillars, two graceful, ornate containers of spun glass, one containing pink wine and the other bubbly champagne, flanking a fruit bowl, upholding a pyramid of oranges and apples, mixed with freshly picked cherries and grapes.

—Jim

If you feel too constrained doing a strict imitation, you might try a loose one like the following:

A Wedding Table

In the center of the long lace-covered table towered a white cake, six layers high and decorated with delicate, sugary, pink roses set against light green leaves. Silver dishes containing creamy mints molded into roses and tinted in pink and green lay to the right of the cake. On the other side of the mints were two deep silver bowls filled with a mixture of salted nuts. To the left of the wedding cake were the forks, their prongs gleaming, arranged in three perfectly even rows. Beside the forks were the napkins, snowy white with fine silver engraving, placed in a diamondlike pattern on the tablecloth. Steaming urns of black coffee stood at one end of the table together with glass cups, delicately etched in silvery swirls. A small pitcher of cream, thick and golden, and a bowl of sugar that was perfectly molded into cubes were close by. At the opposite end of the table sat a large cut-glass punch bowl containing a sweet ruby-red juice and bulky chunks of glittering ice. The tall and slender candles, flaming on each side of the cake, created a soft glow over the entire table.

—Donna

Exercises

1. Analyze one of the descriptions by Ruskin, Conrad, Dickens, Joyce, or Cather in class. Then, using one of these models, do an imitation, following the order of development indicated.

2. Using the Joyce selection as a model, describe a holiday table laden with food, using a frame device. Use specific concrete details and figures of speech.

3. Describe a person, a bowl of fruit, a floral arrangement, or some other grouping by the still-life method.

4. Using one of the four spatial patterns outlined in this chapter, describe one of the following:

a. a seascape   f. a junkyard
b. a desert scene   g. a supermarket
c. a spring morning   h. a street in the winter
d. a graveyard   i. a garden
e. an antique shop   j. a room

5. Describe a painting or an artistic photograph.

People, Places, and Things

Description is concerned mostly with people, places, and things. The student papers reprinted below give you a variety of models to follow, based on these topics.

You might wish to describe a roommate, a close friend, a parent, a child, a niece or nephew, a teacher, a landlord, a rock star, or a celebrity.

John

Of all my neighbors, the one that I find most interesting is John. He stands about six feet and one inch tall, lanky and thin, narrow in the hips and shoulders. He has one of those protruding Adam's apples that a person can get fascinated with as he watches it bob up and down. John's face is one of the most unique I've ever seen. His chin is square with a small cleft in the center. He's got a very thin mouth that is almost like a single pencil line, always turned up into a smile. Hanging over his top lip is a thick orange-brown mustache, extending from one corner of his mouth to the other, thick toward the middle and tapering at the ends. His long nose is thin and turns under a bit, off center, just above the mustache. His small hazel eyes are set deep into his head, forming two deep canyons on either side of his nose. His thick, black, horned-rimmed glasses make his eyes look even smaller, like two brown dots on flesh-colored paper. His eyebrows are thick and bushy, rising just above his glasses. His short hair is curly and wiry, like a poodle's, forming what looks like a cap upon his head. His whole structure is bowed and when he walks he takes long easy steps swinging his arms back and forth. All in all John looks like a curly-headed Ichabod Crane.

—Kris

Or you might want to describe a scene you know well.

An Afternoon in the Woods

As I sit here under this grotesque spreading oak which displays partial death in its upper limbs, my eyes squint from the raging brightness of the afternoon sun. Moving my eyes across a level plain, I see a descending cow path, twisting and turning until it abruptly comes to a granite ledge where the trail zigzags down a steep slope to a clear running spring. Loose sandstone and clay have been churned up by the cattle and deer which have quenched their thirst from the sweet water at the bottom of the slope. The cold water pours over a small ledge of red, orange-brown, and conglomerated rocks, resembling peanut brittle, making a plunging, gurgling rhythm like a public water fountain in Paris continuously flowing. Dark green moss grows along the banks, and a few ferns sprout between shales on the steep slope. The scoldings of the bluejays spread from treetop to treetop as they voice their disapproval of my visit, accompanied by the sounds of a sorrel-colored squirrel sitting on a low branch of a large oak tree on the other side of the stream, eating last year's nuts, while a mother pheasant and her ten young chicks ramble across the small level plain to a farmer's field that has not yet been plowed, hoping to find a few kernels of last year's corn. A rain crow demands another shower, but the sky promises no rain. A soft breeze gently rocks the tops of the aspens, maples, oaks, honey locusts, and weeping willows, whispering forest gossip to the trees in the next valley, and the sweet fragrance of blooming sweet clover drifts into the valley from a nearby field. No sounds of speeding cars on hot pavement or screaming jets enter this peaceful spot. Soon, shadows cross the green valley floor, darkening the once sunlit area, while unrecognizable forms of tree stumps appear as miniature men in the partial shadows.

—Mary

The Elegant Creation

On the table before me is a container, a simple, clear, transparent glass vessel, tall and slender, with the top edge flaring out. It curves inward toward the bottom, forming a short, thin neck, supported by a round base, just a little smaller than the circle formed by the top edge. This container, however, is merely the complement to the delicacy which lies within. A scoop of French vanilla ice cream is the first ingredient, slightly melting and cold, conforming to the roundness of the vessel's bottom. Another scoop, balanced on the first, is topped by spoonfuls of rich, thick, butterscotch syrup, dripping down the sides of the ice cream and oozing to the bottom in wavy, golden ribbons. Whipped cream, light and fragrant, is heaped on plentifully in soft puffs of wispy white clouds. Crunchy, toasty nuts rest temptingly on the delicate blanket of whipped whiteness. A perfectly formed, bright red maraschino cherry perches precariously on top of the creation, adding just the right touch of color and elegance. A small indentation in the cherry, where the cherry's stem had once been, is slightly visible, winking like the eye of a demon temptress, luring me on to enjoy the butterscotch sundae.

—Dorothy

These are just a few of the many subjects suggested by the topic of description.

Although description is generally conceived of as a static pattern of discourse, more often than not it is mixed with narration. It makes sense, nevertheless, in learning the characteristics of description to see description as being static.

Scientific Description

Description is sometimes divided into two kinds: scientific description and literary or artistic description.

Scientific description is sometimes called *technical* or *objective description. Objective description* attempts to *represent the object as accurately as possible.* It adheres strictly to a part-by-part analysis, exact measurement, and enumeration of details. It is factual, detached, and impersonal, uninfluenced by emotion or personal involvement. It is usually written in the third person singular, with the agent of the action omitted. There is seldom any hint that a person is involved in describing. The focus is on the subject standing apart, known in and of itself.

The following is a good example of scientific description:

The Emerald Tree Boa

The Emerald Tree Boa *(Boa canina)* is found in tropical South America. As its name suggests, it is arboreal and it has an extremely prehensile tail. It feeds mainly on birds and squirrels and also on iguana lizards. It possesses front teeth that are highly developed, probably proportionately larger than those of any other nonvenomous snake. Tree boas grow to about six feet.

When adult, emerald tree boas are a bright emerald green with creamy or white spots. These boas rest in a characteristically coiled position on the top of branches, with the front of the body above and inside the outer rings, looking a little like a bunch of green bananas. The color, posture, and the light spots break up the outline of the snake's body, leaving them almost impossible to detect at rest in the trees. Although the adults are this uniform and striking color, the young specimens are more variable and differ from their parents. They are yellowish, or even pink, with white markings edged with dark purple or green. As they become mature, the markings change to the adult pattern. In captivity, emerald tree boas are usually quiet and can be handled without attempting to bite.

—From *Snakes of the World.*

This selection has most of the characteristics of a good scientific description: specific details, comparisons, and precise diction. The writer combines a description of the behavior of the boas ("It feeds mainly on birds and squirrels and also on iguana lizards," "In captivity, emerald tree boas are usually quiet. . . .") with a concrete and specific description of its physical dimensions and characteristics. He describes the size of their teeth ("proportionately larger than those of any other nonvenomous snake"), by means of a literal comparison, and the size of their bodies ("about six feet"). He then describes the color, posture, and markings of the adults of the species ("a bright emerald green with creamy or white spots," "characteristically coiled position") and of the young specimens ("yellowish, or even pink, with white markings edged with dark purple or green"). In addition to color nouns and adjectives to describe the boas, the writer uses a metaphorical comparison ("looking a little like a bunch of green bananas") and a literal comparison (they are "more variable and differ from their parents"). Besides precise diction dealing with size, color, posture, and markings, the writer also uses formal and scientific diction for descriptive purposes ("arboreal," "prehensile tail," "*Boa canina*," "specimens"), yet the total description is not difficult to understand, written as it is for the general reader.

Literary Description

Literary description is *artistic description.* It is sometimes called **subjective** or **impressionistic description.** The *writer's aim* in this kind of description is not to give accurate, factual information, but to *create a mood, a feeling, or an impression by the use of imaginative language.* What is described is colored by the writer's subjective reactions to the object perceived. The style of literary description is characterized by colorful, suggestive, and vivid language and the artistic grouping of details. The selection from James Joyce's "The Dead" is a good example of literary description. Literary description is not confined to imaginative literature, however. Artistic description can be found in magazine ads where the aim is persuasion, in personal letters, in informal essays, and the like.

This selection from *The Red Badge of Courage,* by Stephen Crane, is an excellent example of literary description:

> The column that had butted stoutly at the obstacles in the roadway was barely out of the youth's sight before he saw dark waves of men come sweeping out of the woods and down through the fields. He knew at once that the steel fibers had been washed from their hearts. They were bursting from their coats and their equipments as from entanglements. They charged down upon him like terrified buffaloes.

Behind them blue smoke curled and clouded above the treetops, and through the thickets he could sometimes see a distant pink glare. The voices of the cannon were clamoring in interminable chorus.

The youth was horror stricken. He stared in agony and amazement. He forgot that he was engaged in combating the universe. He threw aside his mental pamphlets on the philosophy of the retreat and rules for the guidance of the damned.

The fight was lost. The dragons were coming with unvincible strides. The army, helpless in the matted thickets and blinded by the overhanging night, was going to be swallowed. War, the red animal, war, the blood-swollen god, would have bloated fill.

—Stephen Crane, *The Red Badge of Courage*

This passage describes a young soldier's panic and that of his fellow soldiers as they retreat in his direction. The action is seen from the young man's point of view. His horror is expressed by an extensive use of figurative language.

In the first paragraph, the retreating soldiers are viewed impressionistically by the youth as "dark waves of men . . . sweeping out of the woods and down through the fields." The wave metaphor is then replaced by a simile that describes the horror-stricken men as charging on the youth "like terrified buffaloes." The cannon's roar is personified as sounding like a chorus of human voices "in interminable chorus." In the last paragraph, the enemy soldiers are described as "dragons . . . coming with invincible strides." Finally, war itself is described as "the red animal" which would soon "have bloated fill." Crane's purpose in this passage is not to give a factual, objective picture of retreating soldiers, but to give us some insight into the young soldier's feelings. The description is dominated by a single mood—horror.

Exercises

1. Write a technical description of one of the following subjects. Aim for precision of diction, accuracy, and objectivity.

a. a stereo	f. a part of the body
b. a solar invention	g. a kitchen utensil
c. a new engine	h. a tool
d. a plant	i. a mechanism
e. a bird or an animal	j. a felt-tip pen

2. Cut a picture from a magazine. Describe the picture as accurately and as objectively as possible. Attach the picture to your description when you hand it in.

3. Describe a city scene, a marketplace, a landscape, or a similar subject from an objective point of view. Then write an impressionistic description of the same scene.

4. Describe some scene in fair weather. Then describe the same scene in fog, rain, or snow. Change the season, or time, or activity, or whatever.

5. Describe a strange or exotic landscape, perhaps on an unknown planet. Describe the plant life, the animal life, or the terrain.

6. One interesting kind of literary description is *expressionism.* Expressionism is the distortion of reality to communicate feelings and emotions. It is antirealistic, not being concerned with objective accuracy.

   Analyze the following excerpt from Poe's "The Fall of the House of Usher." How does the language of description contribute to the ominous atmosphere? Consider the impressionistic diction, the surrealistic images, the sound devices, and the narrator's comments.

> During the whole of a dull, dark, and soundless day in the autumn of the year, when the clouds hung oppressively low in the heavens, I had been passing alone, on horseback, through a singularly dreary track of country; and at length found myself, as the shades of the evening drew on, within view of the melancholy House of Usher. I know not how it was—but, with the first glimpse of the building, a sense of insufferable gloom pervaded my spirit. I say insufferable; for the feeling was unrelieved by any of that half pleasurable, because poetic, sentiment, with which the mind usually receives even the sternest natural images of the desolate or terrible. I looked upon the scene before me—upon the mere house, and the simple landscape features of the domain—upon the bleak walls—upon the vacant eye-like windows—upon a few rank sedges—and upon a few trunks of decayed trees—with an utter depression of soul which I can compare to no earthly sensation more properly than to the after dream of

the reveler upon opium—the bitter lapse into everyday life—the hideous dropping off of the veil. There was an iciness, a sinking, a sickening of the heart—an unredeemed dreariness of thought which no goading of the imagination could torture into aught of the sublime. What was it—I paused to think—what was it that so unnerved me in the contemplation of the House of Usher?

—Edgar Allan Poe, *The Fall of the House of Usher*

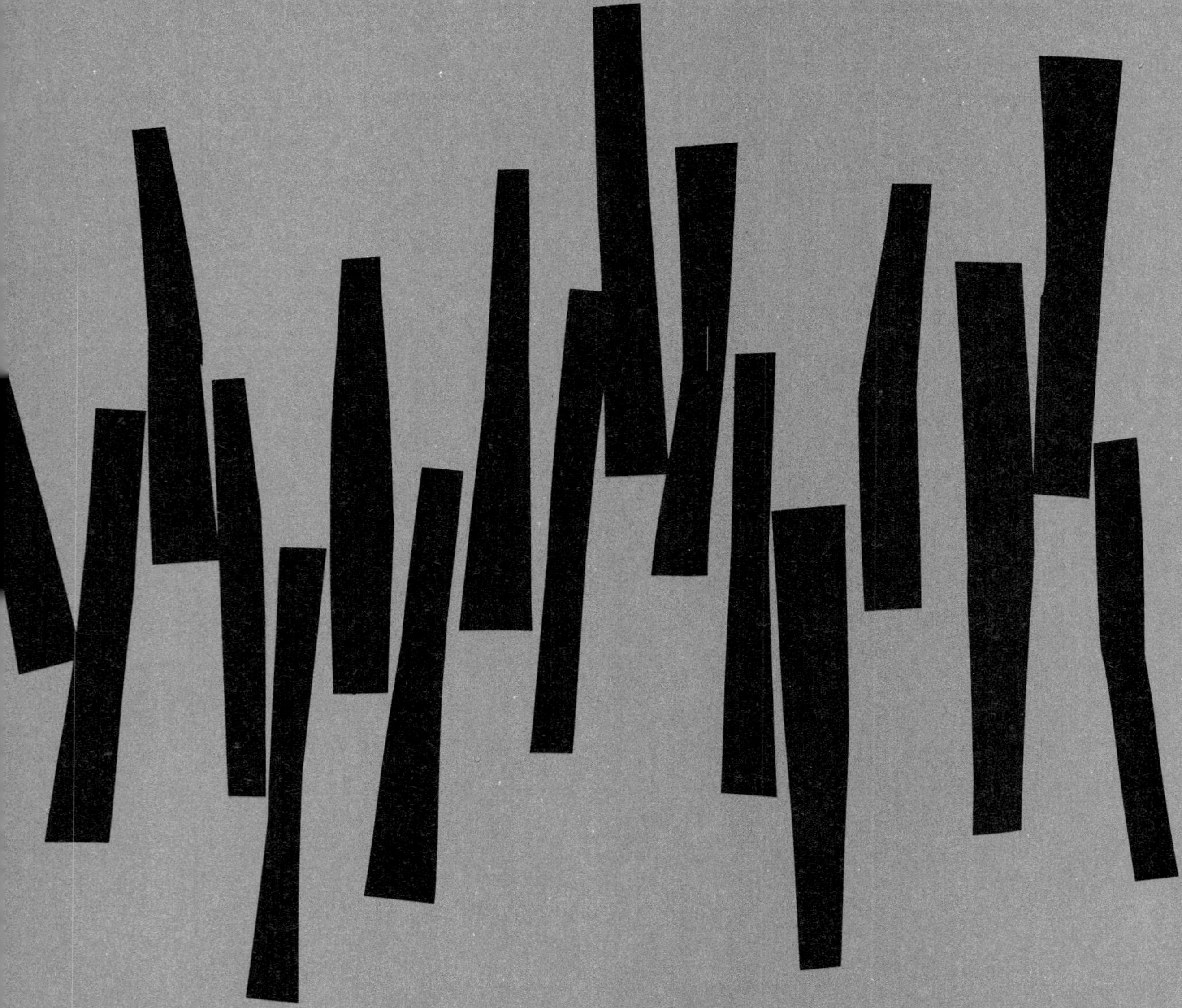

Patterns of Thought:

Classification, Exemplification, Definition

Chapter 5

Patterns of Thought:
Classification, Exemplification, Definition

Classification

Pick up the classified advertising section of your local newspaper and you will find broad categories such as the following: rentals, automotive, miscellaneous, livestock and produce, business and finance, business services, personals and services, educational, employment, and announcements. Then look at the subcategories of any of these broad categories and you will notice subdivisions such as these:

Automotive

Autos for Rent	Sports Cars
Autos for Sale	Trucks
Station Wagons	Autos
Convertibles	Imported Autos

Livestock and Produce

Dogs	Livestock
Cats	Poultry
Birds, Fish	Fruits
Pets	

Or go into a drugstore or a supermarket and look at the greeting cards. Some cards are classified according to official American holidays:

American Holidays

Christmas	Father's Day
New Year's	Independence Day

Valentine's Day   Thanksgiving
Easter   Halloween
Mother's Day

Others are classified under a miscellaneous category:

Miscellaneous
Formal   Birthday
Traditional   Death
Contemporary   Sickness
Humorous   Wedding
Floral   Anniversary
Cute   Sympathy

These are not very elegant ways of classifying things, but for special purposes it is sometimes convenient to group things together in a rough way, even though some of the categories may seem to be arbitrary. These examples illustrate that classifying is a familiar, everyday activity. Things may be classified; events may be classified; ideas may be classified.

Classifying is an important part of thinking. Yet the process as it develops in the child is a gradual one. In the first stage of concept formation, given an assortment of blocks or objects, a child will put them together at random, without any logical basis, because they appear together in time and space. But the objects have no intrinsic bonds according to the child's thinking. In the second phase of concept formation, the child puts objects together on the basis of bonds that actually exist between these objects. To be sure, the child's subjective impressions play some role in his or her thinking, but he or she no longer mistakes these impressions for connections between things. Instead, he or she groups objects on the basis of color, shape, or size. In the last phase of concept formation, the child is able to abstract and isolate elements and to view them apart from "the concrete experience in which they are embedded."

Is classification merely the process of giving a common name to things, or is it the discovery of universal properties that things have in common? Anthropological linguists have postulated a kind of linguistic and cultural relativity for classifying. The Hopi Indians, for example, have one class word that includes everything that flies except birds. Thus airplane pilots, airplanes, and insects all belong to the same class. The Eskimos have numerous names for snow: *wind-driven snow, snow on the ground, slushy snow, icy snow, hard-packed snow, falling snow.* Color classification varies in different cultures. The Shona, a tribe in Rhodesia, have three class names for colors. Other tribes have two. Botanists divide flower colors into blue (cyanic) and yellow (xanthic).

Purpose, Audience, Kind of Discourse

Classification is used constantly by people in hundreds of professions and occupations—by scientists, teachers, doctors, lawyers, historians, librarians, grocery clerks, and insurance agents. One of the simplest purposes to which classification can be put is the simple physical process of sorting. Consider the amount of sorting you do in your everyday life. You sort your clothes, your books, your record collection, stamps, coins, important papers of various kinds. In brief, one of your most important aims in classifying is to put experience in order.

Although classification can be found in many kinds of writing and used for a variety of purposes, one of the most important aims of classification is to inform or instruct. Therefore, you are more likely to find classification in expository than in persuasive or literary writing. Some typical examples of kinds of writing that use classification are articles and textbooks on botany, chemistry, biology, political science, anatomy, anthropology, psychology, and sociology, and library classification, scientific essays, magazine articles, museum catalogs, and classified ads.

Naturally, your audience will be an important factor in making your classification. If your audience has a specialized knowledge of your subject, your classification will tend to be formal or scientific. If your audience has little or no knowledge of your subject, your classification will probably be informal. In scientific classification, your focus will be on the subject itself, and your classification will tend to be exhaustive. But informal classification is more audience-centered. In informal classification, you may classify the same subject in any number of ways, depending on your purpose and on your reader's knowledge, interests, level of understanding, and so forth.

Invention and Classification

Classifying is a basic mental activity. It is *the process of grouping similar ideas or objects, the systematic arrangement of things into classes on the basis of shared characteristics.* As a topic of invention, it is related to definition (to define is to put the thing to be defined into a class); analysis (to classify is to divide into parts or categories); enumeration (to classify is to enumerate members of a class); and comparison (to classify is to group similar things). The topic of classification suggests questions that you can ask of any subject, such as How may an object or an idea be classified? What are its common attributes? What are its basic categories? What is the basis of the classification? What is the purpose of the classification?

Any group of individuals or objects possessing something in common can be classified. But you should not confuse classification with analysis. When you analyze, you begin with one object or idea and divide it into parts on the basis of differences. When you classify, you begin with many things and group them according to similarities. The term in an analysis is always singular: *a painting, a movie, the human body, an apple, a poem, a sentence, a house.* The term in a classification is always plural: *cars, jobs, popular songs, drugs, blind dates, clothing styles.*

When you classify, you should first determine the basis of classification, the common feature or quality that unites all the elements of the group. If, for example, you are classifying apples, you can classify them by color:

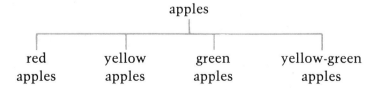

or you can classify them by taste:

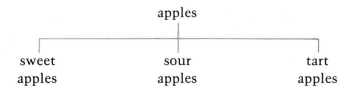

When you classify, always keep in mind the purpose of your classification. Your purpose should be clearly defined.

The principles of classification are similar in many respects to those of analysis:

> *There can be no classification unless the things to be classified are considered similar to each other in some respect.*

> *Only one principle of division may be applied at each level of classification.*

> *At each level, the classes must be mutually exclusive.*

> *In a scientific classification, the classes at each level must cover the whole field.*

To follow the principles of classification in your thinking is to participate in one of the most fundamental acts of the human mind.

Ludwig Wittgenstein gives some of the best practical advice about classifying for compositional purposes. Look at those events or proceedings, he says, that we call games: "I mean board-games, card-games, ball-games, Olympic games, and so on. What is common to them all?—Don't say: 'There *must* be something common or they would not be called *games*'—but *look and see* whether there is anything common to all."

Exercises

1. Probe one of the following subjects by using questions suggested by the topic of classification (How may it be classified? What are its common attributes? What are its basic categories? What is the basis of the classification? What is the purpose of the classification?).

   a. drugs
   b. drinks
   c. useful things
   d. cars
   e. school
   f. days
   g. movies
   h. voters
   i. tables
   j. crimes

2. Discuss in class the ways in which you are viewed (that is, classified) by different people.

3. Discuss national, racial, and other kinds of stereotypes as exemplified by the following:

   a. Athletes are dumb.
   b. Blacks have rhythm.
   c. Italians are amorous.
   d. Germans are stubborn.
   e. Irish are hot-tempered.
   f. Americans are materialistic people.

The Structure of Classification

The paradigmatic structure of classification essays has a pattern that may be depicted as follows:

> *Classification Pattern*
> Introduction (includes thesis and class words)
> Type 1 (or subclass 1)
> Type 2 (or subclass 2)
> Type 3 (or subclass 3)
> Type 4 (or subclass 4)
> Type 5, 6, 7 (or subclass 5, 6, 7)
> Conclusion (summary, return to beginning)

In addition to their basic paradigmatic structure, classification essays have a basic vocabulary that enables the reader to follow the logical progression of ideas:

kinds	categories	classify
sorts	sources	compile
types	orders	assemble
classes	clusters	string together
varieties	groups	collect

Put into the form of *suggestive statements*, the process of organizing classification essays may be described as follows:

Keep in mind your purpose before you begin to write.

In your thesis sentence, provide a clear statement of the basis of your classification.

In your introduction, supply a list of the types or classes into which you will group your subject.

In subsequent paragraphs, take up each type or class, defining or explaining each one and giving examples.

The essay that follows, taken from *Time* magazine of June 26, 1974, is a good example of an informative article that uses the steps outlined above.

Faces in the Crowd

Introduction   Who's playing at the local rock palace? One way to find out is to look at the marquee. Another, says California promoter Steve Wolf, is to watch the crowd strolling—or floating, in the case of heavy grass consumers—through the door. "Audiences resemble the groups they come to see," says Wolf. Those words are reckless understatements.

No one who has ever mixed with a San Francisco psychedelic-style concert crowd is likely to forget the experience. Going to see Boz Scaggs, Grace Slick, or Hot Tuna? Better take earmuffs and a flak jacket. Psychedelic rock crowds can be hostile collections of spacy Vietvets still suffering from post-Viet Nam syndrome, pimply feminists in granny glasses, and young high school dropouts. Bottles and firecrackers spin through the air. At a Grateful Dead concert, usually a four- or five-hour affair, the typical freak is a blend of drug hunger, male lonerism, and musical knowledgeability. He will attend somnolently to the music (probably after swilling a bottle of wine), sway ecstatically forward toward the performers. In contrast, the audience for balladeer James Taylor, or the country-rock group Poco, whose music has crisp pattern and infectious surfaces, has a well-scrubbed look and an enraptured response to the music.

Of course, when hallowed groups like the Rolling Stones, the Who, or Bob Dylan make one of their infrequent appearances, categor-

Thesis   ies crumble; everybody comes, just like the World Series. Still, it is possible to define five general types of audience on the basis of dress, manner, consumption, age, and music taste. The catetories:

Type 1   *Heavy Metal.* So named because of the massive banks of amplifiers, drums, and loudspeakers employed by Grand Funk, Led Zeppelin, Black Sabbath, and Blue Oyster Cult. The music is pure buzz—heavy, simplistic blues played at maximum volume and wallowed in mostly by young teen-agers, just experimenting with marijuana, the lingua franca of rock, and perhaps hard drugs too.

This audience can be trouble for concert-hall managers. Says Cleveland promoter Jules Belkin, ''They are up on the seats boogieing and running around the hall.'' Dress ranges from scruffy jeans to $200 velveteen jackets. The girls may come in couples to ogle, say, at topless Mark Farner of Grand Funk. Then there are the brassy groupies with their stevedore vocabularies who haughtily flaunt their backstage passes. The boys come in gangs and do what gangs do—fling lighted matches, fight the bouncers, sometimes toss empty wine bottles. Vomiting from too much beer or wine is a status symbol. If these kids do not have tickets, they break in. A heavy security force, sometimes including local police, is *de rigueur* at most rock concerts.

Type 2   *The Listeners.* Performing groups that attract this crowd include the Moody Blues, Yes, Weather Report, and The Eleventh House. The music is predominantly classical or jazz rock. The Listeners tend to be Heavy Metal graduates—youths ranging in age into the early 20's, who know and care about musicianship. Sedated by grass, Seconals, and Quaaludes, they tend to applaud rather than scream their approval.

Type 3   *Squeaky Cleans.* A description used by singer Bette Midler to characterize fans of the soft, often poetic songs of such bards as Cat Stevens, James Taylor, Joni Mitchell, Melanie. This is an orderly dating crowd in its late teens and early 20's who are interested in love songs. Girls generally outnumber the boys by 2 to 1. Melanie's ethereal fans tend to invade the stage, only to sit quietly at her feet, perhaps lighting candles. Mitchell's following emulates her. ''Since Joni started wearing gowns,'' says Wolf, ''the girls have started wearing dresses and makeup.''

Type 4   *Glitter Trippers.* Glitter stars do not seem so much to have created their fandom as to have been created by it. The fastest-growing audience in rock dotes on the finery of such brocade-, sequin-, mascara-, and rouge-wearing performers as Todd Rundgren, Suzi Quatro, Alice Cooper, and the New York Dolls. Occasionally a glitter singer like England's bisexual David Bowie is actually good. Mostly, though, admits the Dolls' David Johansen, "the whole glitter trip is just jive." A concert can also be simply an excuse for youngsters to come out for a reasonably harmless masquerade party. The kids go on parade to show off their white tuxedos and top hats, feather boas, and of course glitter, lavishly applied to face and body.

Type 5   *The Evening-Outers.* These are the young marrieds, who, says one New York promoter, "are dressed to the nines, and smoke where they're supposed to." As mellowed graduates of the 1960's rock revolution, they will naturally show up to hear the Stones or Dylan, but mostly they turn out for the Carpenters, or the Fifth Dimension. Promoters like the Evening-Outers because they spend money generously at the concession bars.

Conclusion   Begun by the Beatles a decade ago, the rock revolution succeeded beyond everyone's wildest dreams. Rock defined an emerging segment of America, financed a counterculture, and spawned a $2 billion industry. Its principal gift to those who were young in the 1960's was to provide a common means of expression—a common music, a common language, even a kind of cathartic theater in which a Janis Joplin assumed almost mythic dimensions as a tragic heroine and Dylan strolled the stage like an Orpheus. It is no secret that rock's classic era is gone forever, along with the social bonds that nurtured it. The current fragmentation of the rock audience certifies that. In fairness, it must be added that it also signifies a diversity of personal taste and music style unknown previously in American pop music. If rock can be described as being in a somewhat self-expressive romantic era, can its neoclassic period—or a pop Stravinsky—be far behind?

The first two paragraphs introduce the essay. Paragraph 3 states the thesis and helps to organize the classification pattern in the remainder of the essay ("It is possible to define five general types of audience on the basis of dress, manner, consumption, age, and music taste"). The next six paragraphs define the types of audiences (Heavy Metal, The Listeners, Squeaky Cleans, Glitter Trippers, and The Evening-Outers) and give specific examples of the types. And the final paragraph concludes the essay.

The following classification selection is less formal than the *Time* magazine essay, yet in many ways the classification scheme is more rigorous. In this passage, the author describes the Philippine market-place as it existed in 1953:

The Philippine Marketplace

1

1. Today, under the long skylit roofs of the market sheds, the long trestle tables are spread with miles of food.
   2. There is meat on the meat stalls now—carabao, pork, and beef in long, red, gluteal rivers—and entrails, organs, and tripe in slithering mounds.
   2. There are great mountains of cabbages, greens, beans, cucumbers, lettuce, white radishes, leeks, and squash, and of breadfruit, pineapple, mango, lansone, guava, blimbing, and durian in semiquarantine and smelling like cheese.
      3. One entire row of tables and stalls deals in nothing but blazing bananas, golden fingers clutched in clumps and clusters, yellow masses piled high, great green claws hanging down, and golden crowns swirling like blazing haloes as they hang on strings, and the air is alive with the gold of bananas and the smell of their ferment.

2

2. But more important than anything else, for it is the manna of the Philippines, there are fish in the fishmarket.
   3. I walk between hills of scales down aisles of opalescent sheen, and see fish with flattened gills shimmering and slithering, smelling of salt and sea and covered with slime; fish of every color, shape, and feel, soft, hard, red, yellow, black, blue, purple, jade, and green.
      4. Here are crustacea like round ribbon rosettes, like flowers just opening, like pools in surf-drenched rock; crab, crayfish, mussels, oysters, and clams.
      4. There are octopuses like wet black rubber tubing, and like dark purple bruises.
      4. There are fish like whales and fish like midgets, like balls and those like swords, fish wide and flat, tall and thin,

round and star-shaped, spiked and spindly, and fishes
not at all like fishes.

5. All these are fresh, but their like may be found
   shriveled, dried, salted, cured, and stinking high
   and loud, in all sizes, from minnow-size bait in
   countless hordes to huge cross-cuts of whale-like tunas
   and dried octopus hanging from strings overhead.
   —Agnes Newton Keith, *Bare Feet in the Palace*

The marketplace being described is a tropical market filled with
exotic sights and smells. The point of view is close up, with the
observer moving among the tables and stalls. Although the observer
is moving, the scene itself is static.

The initial sentence organizes the discourse: "Today, under the
long skylit roofs of the market sheds, the long trestle tables are spread
with miles of food." The general notion of the marketplace is introduced by the phrase "market sheds." Then you get a picture of the
trestle tables under the "roofs of the market sheds." Finally, you
are presented with the idea of a great quantity of food ("miles of
food") to be found in this marketplace. Subsequent sentences in
this paragraph and in the following paragraph add specific details
to the initial general statement and classify and describe the kinds
of food found in the marketplace.

The following scheme graphically depicts the relationships that
exist among the classes:

I. Food
   A. Meat
      1. carabao   3. beef
      2. pork
   B. Entrails
      1. organs   2. tripe
   C. (Vegetables)
      1. cabbages   5. lettuce
      2. greens   6. white radishes
      3. beans   7. leeks
      4. cucumbers 8. squash

D. (Fruit)
   1. breadfruit   5. guava
   2. pineapple   6. blimbing
   3. mango   7. durian
   4. lansone   8. bananas
E. Fish
   1. fish of every color, shape, and feel
   2. crustacea
   3. crab
   4. crayfish
F. (Mollusks)
   1. mussels
   2. oysters
   3. clams
   4. octopuses
G. Fish of various shapes and sizes
   1. minnow-size bait
   2. whale-like tunas

This graphic outline reveals the following things. First, there is a movement from explicit (food, meat, entrails) to implicit labeling (vegetables, fruit, mollusks). (I have put the implicit class concepts in parentheses in the above outline.) Second, the classification technique is that provided by the use of ordinary language, since this is not a strict scientific classification. (For example, were this a scientific classification, the fish would have been described as "vertebrate, cold-blooded craniate animals with permanent gills, belonging to the super-class Pisces in the phylum Cordata.") Finally, the classification becomes less formal and precise and almost disappears in the second paragraph, as the bountifulness of the fish seems to overwhelm an orderly perspective. The classification pattern, then, helps to organize the wealth of specific images relating to the copiousness and luxuriousness of the Philippine marketplace.

I think that the preceding examples and discussion make abundantly clear that classification is the normal way in which our minds perceive almost anything. But when you go to put the ideas received from your classifying into patterns for writing, perhaps it is best to follow some basic plan of organization, rather than to rely strictly on the order of your impressions.

Exercises

1. Write an essay in which you classify the audiences you have seen at a rock concert or at some other public affair.

2. Analyze a classification essay from your reader.

3. Write a classification essay based on one of the following topics:

   a. blind dates
   b. people
   c. clothing styles
   d. television shows
   e. popular songs
   f. kinds of art
   g. jobs
   h. people's voices
   i. vacations
   j. dreamers

4. Classify for a possible theme topic one of the following:

   a. your favorite movies
   b. the worst movies you have seen
   c. your favorite television programs
   d. your favorite songs
   e. the worst words you know
   f. the names of people you admire

5. Classify the students on your campus. Consider carefully the basis of classification (for instance, Catholic, Methodist, hippie, yippie, jock, cowboy, longhair, middle class, upper class, English, German, Armenian, freshman, sophomore, and so forth).

Exemplification

Exemplification is *the process of illustrating a general principle, statement, or law by citing specific examples.* It is the act of showing or illustrating by using examples.

Thinking by means of examples is one of the most important ways of making your ideas clear. Concrete ideas are almost always easier to understand than abstract ideas. How often in your own conversations have you paused after making a general statement and added, "for instance," "for example"? A significant and interesting example can lend much needed support and validity to your arguments.

Purpose, Audience, Kind of Discourse

Exemplification is generally found in those kinds of writing whose aim is to inform and persuade. Exemplification can be found in magazine articles; essays; critical reviews; legal writing, in which the example might serve as a precedent; scientific writing, in which examples serve as illustrations of laws or general principles; textbook writing, which uses the example to instruct; argumentative writing, where the example is used as proof; short narratives such as the fable and exemplum that point up a general truth; news articles; advertising, and manuals of various kinds.

By their very nature, examples seem to be audience-centered. If you supply your readers with appropriate examples to support a general statement in an expository essay or the proposition in an argument, you will be helping them to grasp your ideas in a way that a page of abstract exposition will not. But a mere enumeration of examples is not enough. You want to give your readers examples close to their own experiences, and insure their understanding of these examples by means of a short conclusion. In sum, examples can have both expository and persuasive force.

Invention and Exemplification

As a topic of invention, exemplification is closely related to classification (each example is a member of a group or class of persons or things); analysis (examples are parts of wholes); and definition (giving examples is one way of supporting definitions). Exemplification answers such questions as What are some representative instances, examples, or illustrations? What is the supporting evidence?

Exemplification almost always accompanies generalization. **Generalization** is *the process of forming general concepts on the basis of observing particular instances or examples.* When you generalize, you extract the common element from a number of particular experiences. The process is often intuitive, but it is easy enough to test the validity of a generalization by reviewing a sufficiently large number of examples in your mind.

A generalization must contain at least one general term:

All men are created equal.
Some politicians are dishonest.
Many citizens are fed up with white-collar crime.
Political writing is generally bad writing.
Most humor is basically sadistic.

In formulating generalizations, you might want to keep a few points in mind. *First, a generalization is an inductive conclusion. Be certain, therefore, that you can support your generalizations with a reasonable number of examples. Second, the general terms in a general statement may be unnecessarily broad. Qualify, when necessary, your general terms. Suppose, for example, you make a statement that "politicians are dishonest." Do you mean that "all politicians are dishonest," "most politicians are dishonest," "some politicians are dishonest," or "a few politicians are dishonest"? Finally, general statements may be statements of fact, statements of opinion, or statements of inference. Be sure that you are clear in your own mind about the differences and that you convey these differences to your reader:*

The price of gasoline is rising. (statement of fact)

It is unfortunate that the price of gasoline is rising. (statement of opinion)

The price of gasoline will go up after the first of the year. (inference)

Exercises

1. Formulate a general statement and be prepared to probe it in class and support it with specific examples.

2. Give some examples of a successful person, a happy person. What makes a person happy or successful?

3. Give in class some examples of movies that present an optimistic view of life, a pessimistic view of life. Then discuss.

The Structure of Exemplification

The process of organizing an exemplification essay is generally very simple. In its most abstract form, the paradigm looks like this:

Exemplification Pattern
Introduction (includes the generalization)
Example 1
Example 2
Example 3
Example 4
Example 5, 6, 7 . . .
Conclusion

Sometimes, instead of supporting your generalization by a series of examples in successive paragraphs, you might want to use a single extended example that you amplify over the course of several paragraphs. Or you may give several examples in the same paragraph.

Like classification themes, exemplification themes have a characteristic vocabulary:

example	typical	cite
instance	exemplary	quote
sample	to illustrate	as follows
case	commonplace	for one thing
specimen	as proof	generally
quotation	as a matter of course	on the whole

In writing an exemplification theme, you might want to keep these things in mind: *First, state your generalization in a single declarative sentence. If, however, your generalization needs qualification, add as many qualifying statements as you think necessary. Second, begin your first supporting paragraph with an expression such as "for example," "for instance," "one example," and so forth. Although this might seem a bit formal, it will force you to keep in mind the pattern you are following. Third, choose examples that are related to your experience. Fourth, arrange your ideas in order of importance.*

The following student paper uses a very simple exemplification pattern. The first paragraph states the thesis and qualifies it. The next four paragraphs give positive examples to support the thesis. The sixth paragraph gives a negative example. The next paragraph qualifies the idea in this one by analogy. And the final paragraph gives another negative example and concludes the essay.

Be a Touchable

Is American society full of untouchables? From my own experiences, I would say no. In fact, it never even occurred to me that some people might be repelled by a friendly pat on the shoulder. But after our discussion about this in class the other day, I did some visiting with several friends on the matter. My family and I seem to be somewhat in the minority.

For example, my family, while not being made up of the greatest cheek-kissers, has always been very generous with the hugs, hand squeezes, arm-in-arm walks, and comforting shoulder pats. All of this is spontaneous. Nobody has ever said to me, "Now, Linda, go kiss your Aunt Ada." It just so happened I thought enough of my Aunt Ada to *want* to kiss her now and then when she had been especially nice. When Dad introduces me to anyone, he always has that big protective arm right around my shoulders that tells me he is proud of me far better than his words could.

I wouldn't think of walking into Grandma's house without grabbing both of her hands in a tight squeeze and smiling into her eyes so that she can get a good look at her granddaughter.

My husband and I went bowling with my cousin and his wife the other night, and he often threw his arm around my shoulders or Virg's as we visited. I didn't think that was queer at all. In fact, I thought it was very sweet the way he has accepted Virg in the family.

How comforting it was to have my aunt's arm around me after my Grandpa's funeral! She knew how very close we were, and her words could never have been as warm and understanding as that arm was.

Several of the people I talked to about this had different thoughts. One lady I work with said she didn't like people "pawing" her. A girlfriend said she had no reservations about kissing her husband, but couldn't kiss her parents, although she wished she could.

My answer to that would be for heaven's sake TRY!!! Don't regret it later that you didn't. I was uneasy about going into a swimming pool for the first time, and even after that first step was taken, it was a long time before I felt comfortable in my role as a swimmer. Now I love to swim and I think what a loss it would have been if I had been afraid to try, then follow through. I think the analogy holds for life. If you *want* to be more affectionate with your loved ones, just try, and keep at it. Soon it may become so natural you will wonder what all the fuss was about.

Don't be like my cousin Jo, who loved her father dearly but just couldn't show it. When she was 18, she finally brought herself to kiss him, but it was too late; he was in his coffin, unable to feel the delightful sense of touch the living have to share, if we only will.

—Linda

The student paper reprinted below uses the same basic pattern, but is even simpler in form. The first paragraph states the thesis ("Professional athletes in a number of fields are making more money than ever before"). The next four paragraphs cite specific examples from different professional sports (golf, basketball, baseball, and football). And the final paragraph concludes the essay.

Playing for Pay

Recent years have been golden ones for professional athletes. Professional athletes in a number of fields are making more money than ever before.

For example, in golf there have been three professional golfers who topped the one-million-dollar mark in lifetime earnings.

In basketball, one player recently negotiated a contract providing him with an annual income of $200,000. And within the past year, several college All-Americans signed basketball contracts which made them millionaires overnight. Today the least amount that a pro basketball player can receive annually is in excess of $13,000.

Baseball's rosters contain a number of stars who receive $100,000 or more to play for a single season. Six-figure bonuses are commonplace.

The same is true in football. College stars sign contracts which guarantee them financial security before they have proven themselves on the field as professionals. Well-established players receive salaries comparable to the stars in the other sports.

All of the big names in the major sports profit handsomely from product endorsements, personal appearances, speaking engagements, and business opportunities made available to them. It all adds up to a highly lucrative business to those who possess the ability to participate.

—Bruce

Exercises

1. Write an exemplification essay on one of the following general subjects:

   a. local place-names
   b. peculiar personal names
   c. nicknames
   d. current fads

2. Formulate five general statements that can be supported by examples.

3. Support one of the following generalizations by means of examples:

   a. People are judged by their language.
   b. A person's early experiences with members of other races or nationalities determine his or her prejudice or lack of it.

c. People conform to what they think are the conventions of their own group.

4. Give examples of how slang may be effective in certain situations.

5. You have probably heard the expressions "The best things in life are free" and "The best things in life cost money." Write an essay in which you support one of these statements with examples from your experience. Begin your first supporting paragraph with a signaling device such as "for example" or "for instance."

6. Select one of the following proverbs and write a short paper in which you support the proverb with examples.

   a. Love is blind.
   b. Truth is stranger than fiction.
   c. Discontent is the first step in progress.
   d. We are all slaves of opinion.
   e. Everyone has his or her price.

Definition

Definition is closely related to classification. As such, it is *a way of thinking in classes.* But it is also *a way of thinking in differences.* Thus, definition is related to comparison and contrast. Definition and description are also closely related; definition is a kind of abstract description. Definition most resembles description when it restricts or sets boundaries to a thing, when it tries to tell exactly what a thing is. To **define,** then, is to *set bounds or limits to a thing, to state its essential nature.*

Purpose, Audience, Kind of Discourse

Definition has a number of purposes in your writing: to explain things to your readers, to make clear the key points in an argument, to make yourself understood in everyday affairs, to specify, particularize, itemize, individualize, and characterize.

Almost all expository or persuasive writing contains definitions. Definition often appears at the beginning of an expository or persuasive essay to explain unfamiliar terms or to make clear a specialized use of a word. It often combines with classification to limit class words. In analysis, it is used to characterize the parts that are separated from the whole.

Definition can be found in scientific essays, textbooks, dictionaries, books of reference, expository essays, magazine articles, encyclopedia articles, news stories, research reports, manuals, and government publications.

Invention and Definition

As a way of probing a subject, definition is closely related to both description and classification. It answers the questions What is it? What are its limits or boundaries? What is its genus? What are its species? When someone asks you what something is, if it is a concrete object, you will have a tendency to describe it; if it is an abstract entity, you will tend to define it. Of course, concrete objects can be both described and defined. Defining is such a natural mental process that it is difficult to keep a person from defining. But although the process is intuitive, not everyone defines effectively, and some conscious attention to the process can be helpful.

The idea that the process is a natural one is constantly being reinforced by the conversations I hear every day. Some time ago, I was watching the "Good Night, America" program on television. Geraldo Rivera was interviewing one of the leaders of the Hell's Angels. Rivera commented that when he tried to take some unauthorized pictures of the Hell's Angels, he was almost "thumped." *Thumping,* he explained, is "beating someone to within an inch of their lives." More recently, I was reading an interview between a local reviewer and a rock-music promoter. During the interview, the term *roadie* came up. "Roadies," the promoter was explaining, "are the male equivalent of groupies. They tag along with the band taking care of the equipment and doing odd jobs. They are attracted to the glamour surrounding the rock world. They only make $150 a week. They live on beer, chicks, and coke [cocaine]. Give them $150 a week and a motel room and they'll mutter, 'Hey, man, far out.'"

Although definition is a process that you use unconsciously almost every day of your life, in writing it has more formal uses. One use, quite obviously, is to clarify difficult or obscure terms in such a way that you will have no problem being understood.

Every discipline has its jargon. Linguists, for example, use terms such as *morpheme, phoneme, tagmeme, functional shift, clipping, blending,* and the like. Clearly, these terms need to be explained to a general audience. So if you are using a difficult or unfamiliar term in your writing, you should attempt to explain it before you go on to other ideas.

New terms also need to be defined. Within the past few years, you have absorbed, without any self-consciousness, hundreds of new words from newspapers, magazines, movies, and television, words such as *trashing, fragging, gig, grody, grunt, groupie, go-kart, granny glasses, mod, maxi, light show, jock, nerd, feelie, dove, hawk, dawk, Day-Glo, cop-out, acid trip, zizzi, zonked, tank tops, New Left, acid head, freak.* Granted that you know in general what these words mean; you want to be precise in your writing, and precision often means definition.

Sometimes you may want to define a word whose meaning is so broad that it needs to be restricted. *Free world* is one of those terms. In the so-called *free world,* there are dictatorships such as those in some Central and South American countries, whereas beyond the *Iron Curtain* there are countries such as Yugoslavia and Bulgaria that have shown remarkable independence. What do you mean by the word *free* in your definition?

A final use of definition is to make fine distinctions between terms. For example, some people often use the words *love* and *sex* as synonyms. Do they in fact mean the same thing? What is the difference between love and sex? Love and affection? Love and devotion? Love and infatuation?

How to Define
Logical Definitions

To define a word using **logical** or **formal definition,** *put the word to be defined into a class and then differentiate it from other members of the same class:*

Term	Class	Differentiation
To frag	is to kill or injure a superior officer	by using a fragmentation grenade.
Overkill	is the ability to destroy an enemy	several times over.
A granny dress	is a loose dress similar to those worn by grandmothers	which reaches from the neck to the ankles.
A freebie	is anything gotten	free of charge.
The mini	is a short dress	two to four inches above the knee.

In putting a definition into a single sentence, use the same part of speech for the term to be defined as for the class term. Define a noun with a noun, an infinitive with an infinitive, and so forth. Keep the class word restricted. The larger the class, the more distinguishing characteristics you will have to add in order to separate the word from other members of the class.

Sometimes definitions can be used for humorous or satirical purposes. The following graffiti use the definition form (sometimes without the verb *be*) for just these purposes:

Hit and run means never having to say you're sorry.
Love means saying I'm sorry every five minutes.
Happiness is a warm poppy.
Life is a hereditary disease.

Most of these definitions actually do not follow the strict logical form of the formal definition; they are rather closer to definition by synonym. Here are a few that define by **negation:**

Bacteria is not the back entrance to a cafeteria.
Free is not equal, is not free.
Graffiti is not the Italian defense minister.

And here are a few that define by apposition:

> Reincarnation: a split infinity
> Picnic: a meadow lark
> Oleo Acres: one of the cheaper spreads

Synonyms

To define a word using **synonyms,** simply *substitute for a word or phrase an equivalent word or phrase.* Although definition by synonym is not as exact as other methods of defining, it is a very common and useful method of defining words, because if you substitute a better-known or less difficult word for one that is difficult or obscure, your reader will at least have a partial understanding of your intended meaning:

> *Lewd* means lustful.
> A *gnu* is an African antelope.
> The word *cockamamie* means absurd or foolish.
> To *cop out* is to withdraw.
> *Grotty* means miserable.

Etymology

To define a word **etymologically,** *trace the origin and historical development of the word, including any changes in its form or meaning.* For example, suppose you use the word *lucid* in a conversation and somebody says, "What does the word *lucid* mean?" You might reply: "The word *lucid* comes from the Latin word *lux, lucis,* which means 'light.' If you shed light on something, you make it clear. Hence the word *lucid* means 'clear.' "

These are the three main methods of defining. Some writers add definition by examples, by comparison, by description, or by repetition, but these latter seem more properly to be aids to definition rather than ways of defining.

Dictionary Definitions

A **dictionary definition** is not a special method of defining. It includes, rather, most of the methods that we have been discussing:

logical or formal definitions, synonyms, and etymologies. Let us look
at a typical dictionary entry:

> **suburb** (sub'ərb) n. abbr. *sub.* **1.** a usually residential area or
> community outlying a city. **2.** *Plural.* The perimeter of country around
> a major city; environs. Used with *the.* [Middle English, from Old
> French *suburbe,* from Latin *suburbum: sub-,* near + *urbs,* city (see
> **urban**).]

The entry contains the word itself, the pronunciation of the word,
the part of speech, and either (or both) a formal definition or a definition by synonym, followed by the etymology of the word. In defining
a word, you need not be bound by the dictionary definition of the
word, but you will find it useful to take it into consideration.

Exercises

1. Write a one-sentence logical definition of five of the following words:

   a. Afro   e. macho
   b. charisma   f. superstar
   c. bummer   g. subcompact
   d. jock   h. honky

2. Define one of the following terms in a single paragraph by tracing its
   etymology:

   a. raccoon   f. bunk
   b. butcher   g. boycott
   c. colossal   h. Tabasco
   d. cockroach   i. zombie
   e. steward   j. dandelion

3. Coin a word and then define it in as many ways as you are able.

4. You are an advertiser with a new product. Invent a name for the product.
   Then define it and discuss it in a single paragraph. Think of some product
   names to get you started (*Tide* washes away dirt; *Duz* does everything).

5. Discuss in class the meaning of these terms:

   a. boredom
   b. morality
   c. responsibility
   d. good taste

   e. physical attractiveness
   f. progress
   g. individualism
   h. sportsmanship

6. Define one of the following, using the methods discussed in this chapter:

   a. the perfect woman (man)
   b. an ideal gift
   c. the perfect date
   d. soul music

   e. a good bargain
   f. soul food
   g. acid rock
   h. a great athlete

Patterns of Definition

How do you use definitions in your writing? Often at the beginning of an essay, you may need to explain key words necessary for understanding the meaning of what is to follow. Or you may want to explain a term that may be unfamiliar to the reader. In an argument, you would certainly want to make clear the terms of the argument. Definition is invaluable here.

Definition is seldom the length of an entire theme, although in some books or articles in which the author is trying to come to grips with the essence of a thing, it can be of essay length. More frequently, however, a definition goes on for a sentence or two or for the length of a paragraph. In the following selection from *The Theater of the Absurd*, Martin Esslin uses a variety of ways of defining:

> "Absurd" originally meant "out of harmony" in a musical context. Hence its dictionary definition: "out of harmony with reason or propriety: incongruous, unreasonable, illogical." In common usage in the English-speaking world, "absurd" may simply mean "ridiculous." But this is not the sense in which Camus uses the word, and in which it is used when we speak of the Theater of the Absurd. In an essay on Kafka, Ionesco defined his understanding of the term as follows: "Absurd is that which is devoid of purpose. . . .

Cut off from his religious, metaphysical, and transcendental roots, man is lost; all his actions become senseless, absurd, useless."

The first sentence defines by etymology. The word there that gives the reader a clue is the word *originally*. The second sentence is the "dictionary definition." It gives a string of synonyms. The third sentence defines by giving another synonym. The next sentence merely states, but does not define, Camus's stipulative use of the word. The last sentence is a logical definition, which is also stipulative; that is, Ionesco specifies the way he is going to use the term in an essay on Kafka.

In the next selection, E. M. Forster distinguishes between a story and a plot by first defining each term logically, then adding examples, and finally, toward the end, defining by function:

Let us define a plot. We have defined a story as a narrative of events arranged in their time-sequence. A plot is also a narrative of events, the emphasis falling on causality. "The king died and then the queen died" is a story. "The king died, and then the queen died of grief" is a plot. The time-sequence is preserved, but the sense of causality overshadows it. Or again: "The queen died, no one knew why, until it was discovered that it was through grief at the death of the king." This is a plot with a mystery in it, a form capable of high development. It suspends the time-sequence, it moves as far away from the story as its limitations will allow. Consider the death of the queen. If it is in a story we say, "and then?" If it is in a plot we ask, "why?" That is the fundamental difference between these two aspects of the novel. A plot cannot be told to a gaping audience of cave-men or to a tyrannical sultan or to their modern descendant the movie-public. They can only be kept wide awake by "and then—and then—." They can only supply curiosity. But a plot demands intelligence and memory also.

—E. M. Forster, *Aspects of the Novel*

The Structure of Extended Definition

How is a definition extended? One way is to begin with a logical definition, use it as a thesis sentence, and then expand the *class word* and the *attributes* in subsequent parts of the paper. The resulting paradigm would look somewhat like this:

Extended Definition
Introduction (includes logical definition)
Expansion of the genus
Expansion of the differentia
Conclusion (summary or restatement)

An alternative pattern might look something like the following:

Extended Definition
Introduction (includes sentence definition)
Supporting details
Supporting details
Supporting details
Supporting details
Conclusion (summary or restatement)

If you follow this paradigm, you would expand your thesis with examples, additional kinds of definitions such as synonyms or etymologies, comparisons, contrasts, analogies, explanations, quotations from authorities, and the like. The method of development is generally deductive, although an inductive order is possible.

The structure of the following professional essay by W. Nelson Francis is a good example of an extended definition that reveals the underlying paradigm very clearly. I have indented and numbered the levels so that the pattern stands out.

Three Meanings of Grammar

1

1. A curious paradox exists in regard to grammar.
    2. On the one hand it is felt to be the dullest and driest of academic subjects, fit only for those in whose veins the red blood of life has long since turned to ink.
    2. On the other, it is a subject upon which people who would scorn to be professional grammarians hold very dogmatic opinions, which they will defend with considerable emotion.

3. Much of this prejudice stems from the usual sources of prejudice—ignorance and confusion.

4. Even highly educated people seldom have a clear idea of what grammarians do, and there is an unfortunate confusion about the meaning of the term "grammar" itself.

2

5. Hence it would be well to begin with definitions.

6. What do people mean when they use the word "grammar"?

7. Actually, the word is used to refer to three different things, and much of the emotional thinking about matters grammatical arises from confusion about these three different meanings.

3

8. The first thing we mean by "grammar" is "the set of formal patterns in which the words of a language are arranged in order to convey larger meanings."

9. It is not necessary that we be able to discuss these patterns selfconsciously in order to be able to use them.

10. In fact, all speakers of a language above the age of five or six know how to use its complex form of organization with considerable skill; in this sense of the word—call it "Grammar 1"— they are thoroughly familiar with its grammar.

4

8. The second meaning of "grammar"—call it "Grammar 2"—is "the branch of linguistic science which is concerned with the description, analysis, and formularization of formal language patterns."

9. Just as gravity was in full operation before Newton's apple fell, so grammar in
the first sense was in full operation before
anyone formulated the first rule that began
the history of grammar as a study.

5

8. The third sense in which people use the word
"grammar" is "linguistic etiquette."
9. This we may call "Grammar 3."
    10. The word in this sense is often coupled
    with a derogatory adjective: we say
    that the expression "he ain't here" is
    "bad grammar."
    11. What we mean is that such an
    expression is bad linguistic
    manners in certain circles.
        12. From the point of view of
        "Grammar 1" it is faultless;
        it conforms just as completely
        to the structural patterns of
        English as does "he isn't
        here."
        13. The trouble with it is like
        the trouble with Prince
        Hal in Shakespeare's
        play—it is "bad," not in
        itself, but in the company
        it keeps.

6

7. As has already been suggested, much confusion
arises from mixing these meanings.
8. One hears a good deal of criticism of teachers
of English couched in such terms as "they
don't teach grammar any more."
9. Criticism of this sort is based on the
wholly unproved assumption that
teaching Grammar 2 will increase the

student's proficiency in Grammar 1 or improve his manners in Grammar 3.

10. Actually the form of Grammar 2 which is usually taught is a very inaccurate and misleading analysis of the facts of Grammar 1; and it is therefore of highly questionable value in improving a person's ability to handle the structural patterns of his language.

11. It is hardly reasonable to expect that teaching a person some inaccurate grammatical analysis will either improve the effectiveness of his assertions or teach him what expressions are acceptable to use in a given context.

7

7. These, then, are the three meanings of "grammar": Grammar 1, a form of behavior; Grammar 2, a field of study, or science; and Grammar 3, a branch of etiquette.
    —W. Nelson Francis, "Revolution in Grammar"

The thesis sentence is the second sentence of the second paragraph: "What do people mean when they use the word 'grammar'?" The word *grammar* is the key word which is to be defined. The next sentence indicates the plan of development ("The word is used to refer to three different things"). Then subsequent sentences and paragraphs enumerate a different meaning of the word *grammar* ("the first thing we mean . . . ," "the second meaning of 'grammar'. . . ," "the third sense in which people use the word 'grammar'. . .").

The abstracted underlying pattern has the following structure:

The word [*grammar*] is used to *refer* to *three different things*. . . .
The *first* [*meaning* of *grammar*] is "the set of formal patterns in

which the words of a language are arranged in order to convey larger meanings."

The *second meaning* of "grammar" . . . is "the branch of linguistic science which is concerned with the description, analysis, and formularization of formal language patterns."

The *third* [*meaning* of *grammar*] is "linguistic etiquette."

These, then, are the *three meanings* of "grammar": . . . a form of behavior, . . . a field of study, or science, and . . . a branch of etiquette.

In writing your own extended definitions, you may choose to follow a formal pattern very closely, as in the Nelson Francis essay, or you may want to use a less formal approach, as in the following student paper:

Environmentalist, Preservationist, Conservationist: What's the Difference?

The word *environmentalist* has been bandied about so much that a person can't be sure in a given instance whether the word is complimentary or pejorative, whether it applies to someone favoring an automobile noise-abatement program or someone wishing to close Yellowstone Park and convert it to a pristine wilderness. Once very modish, the word is now almost useless as a conveyor of precise meaning.

Until the 1960s, environmentalists were simply people who were concerned about the environment, about litter, polluted streams, and endangered wildlife. The word *environmentalist* was not a household word. But in the sixties, the term became identified with the youth protest movement and with causes as diverse as vegetarianism and antiwar demonstrations. Through the late sixties and into the seventies, the meaning of the word came to depend increasingly on the point of view of the user. Thus, land developers labeled Environmental Protection Agency officials as *progress-blocking environmentalists*. Concerned citizens who demanded that air- and water-polluting industries "clean up their act" proudly identified themselves as *concerned environmentalists*.

Probably the most serious consequence of the loose definition of the word has been the blurring of the distinction between *preservationist* and *conservationist*. Both are now indiscriminately referred to as *environmentalists*. A preservationist who advocates closing a wilderness area to all public use is termed an environmentalist, as is the conservationist who urges moderation that will permit public use of an area while preventing depletion of its natural resources. The term is more likely to be interpreted as the *radical preservationist*, with sometimes serious consequences.

If one can derive a moral from all of this, it might be as follows: There is a need for precision in the definition of words that one uses. Imprecise diction, whether deliberate or not, is potentially as dangerous as outright misrepresentation.

—Shirley

Exercises

1. Discuss in class the student essay entitled "Environmentalist, Preservationist, Conservationist." What methods of defining does this essay use? Is it effective in achieving its purpose?

2. Write an extended definition, in the manner of the Nelson Francis essay, of one of the following:

   a. curiosity
   b. jealousy
   c. culture
   d. leadership
   e. skepticism
   f. superstition
   g. patriotism
   h. a well-rounded person

3. Write an essay in which you try to explain to a friend the differences among a liberal, a conservative, a radical, a moderate. Include logical definitions and give specific examples.

4. Write an essay in which you discuss the differences in connotation (suggested meaning) between *naked* and *nude, drinker* and *drunkard, old man* and *geezer, drifter* and *hobo, original* and *eccentric*.

5. Discuss in class, by defining the differences, these terms:

   a. open-minded, bigoted
   b. love, affection, devotion, fondness, infatuation
   c. generousness, selfishness
   d. clever, stupid
   e. aggressive, timid
   f. free speech, license
   g. demonstration, riot

6. Select one of the following words or phrases to define, analyze, and illustrate in context. Consider the following points: (a) denotation (literal meaning) and connotation (suggested meaning) of the word, (b) any technical or limited uses of the word, (c) your own reaction to the use of the word and your reasons, (d) a critical evaluation of the meaning and effectiveness of the word in general communication.

   a. academic freedom   e. sophistication
   b. open mind   f. adult
   c. progress   g. individualism
   d. modern   h. culture

7. According to chronological age, you probably are one who can be described as a teenager, a youth, an adolescent, a juvenile, a young adult, a guy or a gal, a stud or a chick. Write a short theme analyzing your personal responses to these words as they apply to you. Do you like them or dislike them? Why? What does each connote? Are there any other words that you prefer as self-description?

8. Examine your attitude toward abstractions such as honor, virtue, love, loyalty, brotherhood, and truth. Cite specific experiences of the use of these words, avoidance of them, and so forth.

Patterns of Thought:

Comparison and Analogy

Chapter 6

Patterns of Thought:
Comparison and Analogy

Comparison

Comparison is such a familiar everyday activity that it may be difficult for you to think of it as an important mental process. Yet without the ability to perceive similarities, you could not classify, define, or generalize. And without the ability to perceive differences, you could not analyze, define, or describe.

Comparison is *the process of examining two or more things in order to establish their similarities or differences.* Both the word *comparison* and the word *contrast* conjure up all sorts of interesting images in the imagination, images that reflect their widespread use in everyday thinking. The word *comparison* calls to mind words and expressions such as *twin, double, counterpart, brother and sister,* and *look-alikes.* The word *contrast* calls forth words and expressions such as *mismatched, nonconformity, a shade of difference,* and *this, that, or the other.*

Although comparison and contrast are closely related, they can be regarded as different mental processes. In examining any two things, you can mentally explore their similarities without necessarily exploring their differences, or you can mentally investigate their differences without investigating their similarities. In actuality, any relationship between two or more things will involve some degree of similarity as well as some degree of difference.

Purpose, Audience, Kind of Discourse

Of the rhetorical modes, comparison may well be the most important. The word itself suggests choices from among alternatives. Seldom a day goes by that you don't have to make important choices. You have to choose between two careers, two or more products, two political candidates, two goals, two courses of action. In making your choices, you use comparisons for every aim (informative, persuasive, expressive, and aesthetic) and for any kind of audience.

Comparisons underlie everything we do. Scientists use comparisons in their experiments. Logicians use them to draw conclusions. Politicians use them to formulate policies. Judges use them to render decisions. Ministers and priests teach and admonish us with comparisons.

Comparisons can be found in any kind of writing: magazine articles, advertising, essays, news articles, letters, editorials, textbooks, scientific writing, reports, political speeches, pamphlets, instruction manuals, poems, fables, and parables.

Invention and Comparison

The topics of similarity and difference, with their subtopics of literal and figurative similarity, difference in kind, and difference in degree, are perhaps the most fundamental topics in the inventive process, giving rise to such questions as What is it like? How is it similar to other things? How does it differ from other things?

Literal similarity is based on perceiving likenesses between subjects that belong to the same class, as in these examples:

> This table is square. That table is square.
> Both trees have drooping branches.

Figurative similarity is based on perceiving likenesses between subjects that belong to different classes:

> The skin around his eyes is pulled tight, like the skin of an onion.
> We were as naked as stone.

Difference in kind is based upon perceiving differences in common *traits* or *aspects* of a thing:

> This flower has bright, colorful blossoms.
> That flower has pale, faded blossoms.
> Lincoln was largely self-educated: Ford was not.

Difference in degree is based upon perceiving the *extent* to which a thing is unlike something else:

> *Crest* toothpaste is better than other toothpastes.
> The influence of television is greater than that of newspapers.

In exploring a subject by using the topic of comparison, you would probably follow a sequence of steps that might be described as follows:

> *Choose subjects that are interesting enough to challenge your imagination.*
>
> *Try, if you decide to compare two commonplace subjects, to look at them from a fresh point of view.*
>
> *Consider your purpose and your angle of vision. What particular point of view, what particular insight can you give your readers to make them see what you see?*
>
> *Be certain that there are enough aspects of the things to be compared to make a valid and interesting comparison. An aspect is a characteristic or feature of the thing to be compared, considered from one point of view.*
>
> *Choose only the most significant aspects of a subject to compare.*

Exercises

1. For purposes of class discussion and as an exercise in invention, compare or contrast

   a. two styles of clothing
   b. two movies
   c. two television shows
   d. two songs
   e. two talk-show hosts
   f. two ideas
   g. two kinds of music
   h. two dances
   i. two magazines
   j. two sports

2. Discuss, as an exercise in invention, some of the cultural differences that exist between any two nationalities, racial groups, special interest groups, or subcultural groups in the United States.

3. Write five sentences in which you point out the similarities between two things. Write five sentences in which you point out differences. Make five of the comparisons literal and five figurative. Then discuss these sentences in class.

4. Bring to class magazine ads that use comparisons to make a point, and discuss the effectiveness or lack of effectiveness of the comparisons.

The Structure of Comparison

Once you have explored your subject, you have got to decide upon an organizational plan. In developing your overall plan, in your introduction indicate the purpose of your comparison (your purpose, of course, could be implicit in your paper), give your reader some idea of the things to be compared, and indicate your plan of development. Then, in subsequent paragraphs, take up the points of the comparison.

In developing specific patterns, there are a number of basic paradigms that you can follow:

The Half-and-Half Pattern
Introduction (includes thesis, sets up comparison)
Subject 1
   Characteristic 1
   Characteristic 2
   Characteristic 3
   Characteristic 4 . . .
Subject 2
   Characteristic 1
   Characteristic 2
   Characteristic 3
   Characteristic 4 . . .
Conclusion (summary, return to beginning)

The Characteristics Pattern
Introduction (includes thesis, sets up comparison)
Characteristic 1
    Subject 1
    Subject 2
Characteristic 2
    Subject 1
    Subject 2
Characteristic 3
    Subject 1
    Subject 2
Characteristic 4 . . .
    Subject 1
    Subject 2
Conclusion (summary, return to beginning)

The following student paper is a good example of the *half-and-half pattern*.

Myrtle and Peterbone

Thesis   In the days of my younger youth, the days of popsicle addicts and hula-hoop freaks, I had two great friends I divided my time with. Myrtle and Peterbone were both my friends, but that is the closest they ever came to having anything in common.

Subject 1   Myrtle was my childhood Doris Day. Her hair was so blonde that it would turn green from swimming in public pools, and the sunkissed freckles on her nose and knees was all the tan she ever got. Her nose was pug and turned up, and she always seemed to have her front teeth missing. She invariably wore that no-teeth smile together with a pink sunsuit to offset her aquamarine twinkling-star eyes.

Myrtle's parents were sort of hicks. They wore cowboy clothes and boots and someone was always cleaning catfish in the sink. Myrtle's mother must have been kind of quiet because all I remember of her are the swooshing and squeaking her levis and cowboy boots made as she did her Saturday housecleaning on Sunday morning. Myrtle's father is just as vague to me, but I think he wore flowered cowboy shirts and talked in kind of a twang whenever he wasn't engrossed in a beer can and the TV wrestling match. So while Myrtle's parents swooshed and squeaked and twanged, we would go off to see what new activities we could create for amusement.

The best thing Myrtle and I did together, aside from normal girlhood play, was tying strings onto locusts' wings and flying them around our heads like motordriven model airplanes. We never seemed to hurt them, as cruel as it may seem. We only did it in the summertime when the locusts drove everyone crazy with their noisy symphonies. The rest of the year we conjured up new species of paper dolls, tortuously hard games of jacks, or different schemes for not getting caught playing in the nearby irrigation ditch. When I would get tired of girlish pastimes, I would go over to Peterbone's.

Subject 2   Peterbone was Myrtle's opposite. He was a coffee-with-cream colored Catholic Mexican, with charcoal-black crewcut hair and the deepest ebony eyes I'd ever seen. No swimming pool could turn his near-bald head green, and if Peterbone ever had freckles, they were all run together into a tawny bronze. Peterbone had one front tooth missing, but no natural occurrence was responsible—it had been knocked out by a mean older brother. A white shirt and old jeans were what he wore the most, along with scuffed black shoes (untied) and two different kinds of socks.

Peterbone's parents were Mexican, but they nearly always spoke English, except when a family fight began. Then a tidal wave of Spanish words would crash into the air and I would, if present, stare dumbfounded as the deluge of Latin curses deafened my ears.

Choo-chee was Peterbone's mother. She wore red bandana scarves on her raven hair and yellow zoris on her size ten feet. She was very kind to her naughty boys and laughed with them lots of times when they got into trouble. She never kept a really neat house because she liked daytime soap operas, but her smiles and hot tortillas kept you from noticing. Peterbone's dad was a fireman. He didn't have much of an accent, but he wore white shirts too and liked boxing matches on Friday nights.

When Peterbone's parents were busy, we liked to stomp on caps in the driveway or sail boats down the ditch. That was only if Peter-bone was in a good mood. If he wasn't, he would hold back my arms and get his brother Bobby to sock me in the face or stomach. One day I retaliated and punched Peterbone right in the nose. It bled all down his white shirt and I played with Myrtle for a long time after; but Peterbone's mean streak was what I liked the most.

As a Kool-Aid wino, I had a childhood full of locusts and caps and two strange friends as different as jellybeans and brussel sprouts. Myrtle and Peterbone were as different as night and day. Or perchance they were more like two different novels, but both shelved under the title of friend in my faded rose scrapbook of people I know.

—Linda

This student paper is beautifully organized, interestingly written, and sensitively handled. The basic comparison between the two friends is set up in the opening paragraph ("Myrtle and Peterbone were both my friends, but that is the closest they ever came to having anything in common"). In the next three paragraphs, Myrtle, Myrtle's parents, and the activities of Linda and Myrtle are described. Then, in the following four paragraphs, Peterbone, Peterbone's parents, and the activities of Linda and Peterbone are described. Finally, the last paragraph returns to the beginning.

If you find the half-and-half pattern a bit restrictive, you might want to try the *characteristics pattern*, in the manner of this student essay:

My Old Ford and My New Maverick

Only a few short weeks ago, I guided my trusty Ford Galaxie over to the car lot where I exchanged it (and a large check) for a new Maverick. I had decided that the time had come when I'd have to break down and trade in the Ford before the Ford went ahead and broke down itself. Besides, it really wasn't safe anymore and my friends were afraid to ride in it. Although I have only had the new car for a short time, already I can see many significant differences between the two cars.

As far as size and comfort are concerned, the Ford has the Maverick pretty much beat to hell. The Ford's massive trunk could accommodate eight large suitcases, twenty full potato sacks, or three huddled bodies at a drive-in movie gate. It could sleep two comfortably, three less comfortably, or two couples quite cozily. In fact, it could carry at once the whole of my earthly possessions, including my ironing board and my coffee table.

The Maverick's trunk is smaller than the Ford's. Its ten cubic feet include all sorts of weird angles and a spare tire secured in a position so that it is always in the way. It will accommodate eight large handbags, twenty full popcorn sacks, or three huddled chihuahuas. It can sleep one uncomfortably, two very uncomfortably, or three contortionists quite nicely. As for overall load capacity, I'm lucky to be able to stuff in my clothes, let alone my furniture. In fact, the Maverick would be a great family car for crowded cities— it would discourage large families.

Economy is another story. The Maverick goes for 430 miles on a tank of gas, long enough to find a parking place even at ASU. It burns no oil and requires no coolant. Perhaps most important, it is very unlikely to fall apart, and if it does, it has a warranty.

With an equivalent amount of gas, the Ford would go about half as far as the Maverick or about long enough to find a gas station before running out again. In fact, it uses as much oil as the new car uses gas, and it needs coolant regularly because regularly it boils over anyway.

As far as extra features are concerned, the two cars are about even. This is, however, more the case of off-setting penalties than one of equal virtues. The Maverick has no air conditioner, but the Ford has no heater. The Ford has no gauge lights, but the Maverick has so few gauges that it doesn't really matter. The new car's plastic floor looks cheap compared to the Ford's thick carpet, but it isn't bothered by mud and spills like the carpet in the Ford was.

For better or worse, I'm stuck with the Maverick. Even if it doesn't prove to be better than the Ford, at least it's different.

—Phil

The first paragraph of this essay sets up the basic comparison between the old car and the new ("Although I have only had the new car for a short time, already I can see many significant differences between the two cars"). The next two paragraphs take up the first characteristic of the two cars, size and comfort. Paragraphs four and five take up the second characteristic, economy. Paragraph six takes up the idea of extra features. And paragraph seven concludes the essay.

Both the half-and-half pattern and the characteristics pattern are fairly easy to follow. The *point-by-point pattern* is a variation

of the characteristics pattern, in which the features of the subjects
to be compared are presented in single sentences, using words like
both, each, also, and *too.* The following article, which appeared in
the *New York Times,* after John F. Kennedy's picture replaced that
of Franklin on the half dollar, uses a combination of the half-and-
half pattern and the point by point pattern:

Kennedy and Franklin

Benjamin Franklin, symbol of American enlightenment in the Age
of Reason, now steps aside for John Fitzerald Kennedy, champion
of reason in the Age of the Atom. Franklin, whose profile has graced
the United States fifty-cent coin since 1948 is being replaced by the
image of the thirty-fifth President. That Kennedy should occupy a
place held by Franklin is appropriate, for there are many parallels
in the lives, outlooks, and interests of the two American figures.
Points of likeness range from the coincidental to the philosophical.

Both men were born in the Boston area: Franklin on Milk Street
in the city proper and Kennedy in suburban Brookline. Both lived
in England for a time, Franklin as an agent for the colonial
Pennsylvania Assembly and Kennedy as the son of the American
ambassador.

While in England, Franklin once considered establishing a
swimming school. He was an excellent swimmer who one day covered
the distance on the Thames from Chelsea to Blackfriars—about three
miles. Kennedy's swimming ability saved his life when, as a young
naval officer in World War II, he swam from his rammed PT boat
to the safety of a lonely southwest Pacific islet. The distance was
about three miles. At Harvard, he was a member of the swimming
team.

Before entering public life both men were active journalists—
Franklin was publisher of the *Pennsylvania Gazette* and, earlier, of
his brother's *New England Courant;* Kennedy was a reporter for the
International News Service in 1945. Both were authors of popular
works in the field of biography: Franklin with his *Autobiography*
and Kennedy with his Pulitzer-prize-winning *Profiles in Courage.*

Interests in culture and the intellectual life were common
characteristics. Kennedy held his alma mater, Harvard University,
in special esteem and served on its Board of Overseers. Franklin helped

found the Academy of Philadelphia, which grew into the University of Pennsylvania.

Both were intensely concerned with science (Franklin was a scientist in his own right) and keenly aware of its value to mankind. In 1783 Franklin watched the first hydrogen balloon's ascension from Paris' Champ de Mars. To a sceptic who questioned the worth of the experiment Franklin replied: "What good is a newborn baby?" In February 1962 Kennedy was personally on hand at Cape Canaveral to honor Astronaut John H. Glenn on his return to the spaceport from America's first manned orbital flight. Kennedy devoted time and much effort to promote the nation's technological development.

—From *The New York Times*, Jan. 5, 1964

In using comparison patterns, you need not restrict yourself to these patterns exactly as outlined. Paradigms can be used with a great deal of skill and flexibility, as the following student paper illustrates.

Two Women

The Phoenix Art Museum exhibits approximately fifteen sculptures on its grounds, all by twentieth-century artists, ranging from jagged iron abstractions to strictly representational bronze castings. The most commanding of these, at least in terms of sheer bulk, is Paolo Soleri's *Flying Woman.* One of the least commanding, or so it seems at first, is Francisco Zuniga's *Woman at Siesta.* Each is situated in the grassy mall area between the Phoenix Library and the museum, the Soleri rising from the lawn abruptly, the Zuniga sleeping peacefully beneath a Palo Verde.

Soleri's woman is constructed of welded plates of iron-ox, a sheet iron developed for commercial use, whose surface rusts evenly, creating a superficial shield against deeper rusting. The Zuniga is of cast bronze and has developed the light turquoise patina associated with that more traditional material. The rust-orange color of the Soleri heightens its distinctiveness from its grassy surroundings, while the greenish hue of the Zuniga causes it to blend even more unobtrusively with the grass and the blue-green leaves of the Palo Verde beneath which it rests.

The Soleri sculpture consists of two stacked cubes that rise to an overall height of fifteen feet. The lower, much smaller block has sides of five feet in length, with exactly centered circular openings in each of the vertical sides that are each three feet in diameter. The upper block duplicates this pattern on a larger scale: the sides are nine feet in length for the cube, with circular openings measuring almost seven feet in diameter. Through these circular openings the angular woman flies, parallel to the ground, one arm stretched in front of her, the other behind, in a sort of side-straddle swim stroke through the air and the cube. Her angular face is centered in the opening that faces the main entrance, her legs outstretched side by side behind her.

The Zuniga drapes over a folding chair, her head reclined against the topmost slat. From ground level to the top of her head measures four-and-one-half feet.

Each sculpture is an exaggeration. The Soleri is far too angular. The Zuniga is far too round. Soleri's woman owes more to geometry than to flesh-and-blood women; Zuniga's woman owes her rounded form to too many tortillas. The lines of the Zuniga woman are exaggerations taken from life—the high cheekbones and narrow nose are common features among native Mexican Indians. Soleri's woman seems, on the other hand, to be an exaggeration of an abstract idea. No woman I've ever heard of has eleven distinct planes in her left thigh. This is not an indictment. Artists are free to illustrate abstract ideas no less than to represent or exaggerate nature, certainly.

But this *is* an indictment. Soleri's woman, represented as flying, is actually supported beneath her rib cage by struts, which anchor her to the bottom inside of the upper cube. Her (angular) hair, as though duplicating the famous oversight of the *Boy Removing Thorn From Foot*, hangs straight down rather than streaming behind, as Newton's second law of motion insists that hair propelled through space at the speed necessary to keep such an enormous bulk aloft would do. Thus, the sculpture defies a law of craftsmanship—that the supporting elements be incorporated into the functional elements—and it also defies the laws of gravity and inertia we all must live with.

There is a worse flaw. The *Flying Woman* is one-dimensional. She was created to be seen from the front. Viewing her from any of the other three sides, one cannot discern exactly what the jumble of metal is—neither her function, her gender, nor her species is apparent, except from the front. Sculpture, by definition, presents a three-dimensional object.

By contrast, Zuniga's woman sleeps peacefully, not aspiring to much, perhaps—but still patiently complying with the laws of physics, the demands of careful craftsmanship, and the aims of sculpture. Approached from any angle, she is obviously a woman asleep, supported from the earth by a folding chair. Thus, her support is a functional part of the sculpture. She is three-dimensional, and she does not demand that the viewer temporarily discount physics.

The Soleri sculpture seems to me to represent a lofty idea that is attractive but not possible, or both attractive *and* possible—but in a form different from the expression. In either case, the sculpture fails. The Zuniga seems to take on a much smaller aim. This woman will never leap beyond the bounds of geometry. Instead, when she wakes, she is likely to eat again and perhaps call her children to her side. Except that she will not awaken. She is sleeping. We all sleep. We all at one time took for our domains of sleep the soft, inviting body of a mother. The Zuniga seems full of that invitation. It accomplishes what it seems to propose. It is a successful sculpture.

—Jim

In this paper, the student uses a comparison paradigm, but avoids the rigidity of a strict half-and-half pattern or point-by-point pattern. His purpose is aesthetic appreciation through evaluation and interpretation. His audience is the other members of the class, although one can imagine a similar kind of essay appearing in a newspaper or magazine. The kind of writing is a critical essay, and the mode is contrast. The comparison paradigms help the student to think through his subject and to illuminate the features of each piece of sculpture through contrast.

The opening paragraph provides the reader with the situation at the Phoenix Art Museum and sets up the comparison. The second paragraph uses a point-by-point comparison. It deals primarily with the materials from which the two pieces of sculpture are constructed. The next paragraph describes the physical appearance of the Soleri sculpture. Paragraph four describes the Zuniga sculpture. The juxtaposition of the two descriptive paragraphs provides the contrast. The next paragraph returns to a point-by-point comparison, on the sentence level, of the exaggerated details of each sculpture. Sometimes the comparisons are made by juxtaposing sentences ("The Soleri is far too angular. The Zuniga is far too round"). Sometimes the comparisons are made within the same sentence ("Soleri's woman owes more to geometry than to flesh-and-blood women; Zuniga's woman owes her rounded form to too many tortillas"). Paragraphs 6 and 7, which point to the ostensible flaws in Soleri's conception, contrasts with paragraph 8, which praises Zuniga's craftsmanship in relation to his aim. The last paragraph furthers the interpretation and concludes with an evaluation.

Exercises

1. Analyze the preceding student essay. Does it use any of the traditional linking devices to achieve coherence in the comparison? If not, how does the essay achieve coherence?

2. Rewrite the essay using a half-and-half pattern throughout. Rewrite the essay using a point-by-point pattern throughout.

3. Write an essay, using one of the patterns discussed in this chapter, in which you compare and contrast

   a. two paintings   f. two magazine ads
   b. two art objects   g. two sports figures
   c. two poems   h. two celebrities
   d. two people   i. two writers
   e. two cities   j. two political parties

4. Compare and contrast the same place at two different times of the day, at two different seasons of the year, or at two different periods of your life.

5. Compare adolescence with childhood or adolescence with adulthood.

6. Get Xerox copies of reproductions of the statues of David by Michelangelo, Donatello, and Verrocchio. Then write a comparison-and-contrast essay based on these artworks.

7. Compare Botticelli's *Venus and Mars* with Veronese's *Mars and Venus United by Love.*

8. Compare Henri Matisse's *The Red Studio* (painting) with W. D. Snodgrass's poem "Matisse: *The Red Studio.*"

9. Compare Vincent Van Gogh's picture *The Starry Night* with Anne Sexton's poem, "The Starry Night."

10. Compare the lyrics of two popular songs.

11. There are many other interesting comparisons that can be made of artworks in the same medium (two paintings, two sculptures) and artworks in different mediums (painting and poem, painting and sculpture, sculpture and poem). If you are acquainted with any of these, you can use them for class discussion or for a writing assignment. The pictures of magazine ads, especially those that are artistically done, may also be worth using.

Analogy

An **analogy** is *an extended comparison.* It is a kind of logical inference based on the premise that if two things resemble each other in some respects, they will probably be alike in other respects. If you wish to explain a concept and you find that your readers may not be familiar with your subject or that your subject is difficult and complex, you can compare it point by point with something similar, but more familiar and less complex. The etymology of the word, from the Latin word *analogia* and the Greek *analogos,* meaning "proportion" or "equality of ratios," supports this notion of a point-by-point comparison with something else. The Latin and Greek sources suggest equivalence, correspondence, and likeness of relations.

It is difficult to imagine thinking without analogies. The process of discovering ideas using analogies is very similar to that of discovering ideas using comparisons. You explore your subject by comparing it point by point with something similar. Thinking in analogies is so ubiquitous that it is hard to see how we could get along without such thinking.

The Structure of Analogy

The organizational patterns of analogy are very similar to those of comparison and contrast. The point-by-point comparison pattern seems to be especially suitable to expressing ideas analogically. In

organizing your ideas analogically, therefore, you might put them
in a pattern somewhat like the following:

Point-by-Point Analogy Pattern
Introduction (sets up the analogy)
Subject 1 is similar to subject 2 in this respect
Subject 1 is similar to subject 2 in this respect
Subject 1 is similar to subject 2 in this respect
Subject 1 is similar to subject 2 in this respect . . .
Conclusion (therefore, subject 1 is similar to subject 2 in some
respect known of one, but not known of the other)

In the following selection from *The Politics of Experience* by
R. D. Laing, the author uses a pattern of organization that might
be described as a point-by-point analogy pattern. In this passage, the
analogy of a plane formation is used to point out that schizophrenia
may be nothing more than a label that some people apply to others.

A revolution is currently going on in relation to sanity and
madness, both inside and outside psychiatry. The clinical point of
view is giving way before a point of view that is both existential
and social.

From an ideal vantage point on the ground, a formation of planes
may be observed in the air. One plane may be out of formation.
But the whole formation may be off course. The plane that is "out
of formation" may be abnormal, bad or "mad," from the point of
view of the formation. But the formation itself may be bad or mad
from the point of view of the ideal observer. The plane that is out
of formation may also be more or less off course than the formation
itself is.

The "out of formation" criterion is the clinical positivist
criterion.

The "off course" criterion is the ontological. One needs to make
two judgments along these different parameters. In particular, it is
of fundamental importance not to confuse the person who may be
"out of formation" by telling him he is "off course" if he is not. It
is of fundamental importance not to make the positivist mistake of
assuming that, because a group are "in formation," this means they
are necessarily "on course." This is the Gadarene swine fallacy. Nor
is it necessarily the case that the person who is "out of formation"

is more "on course" than the formation. There is no need to idealize someone just because he is labeled "out of formation." Nor is there any need to persuade the person who is "out of formation" that cure consists in getting back into formation. The person who is "out of formation" is often full of hatred toward the formation and of fears about being the odd man out.

If the formation is itself off course, then the man who is really to get "on course" must leave the formation. But it is possible to do so, if one desires, without screeches and screams, and without terrorizing the already terrified formation that one has to leave.

Laing's main point is that many people are labeled schizophrenic because they are "out of formation" with society. But being "out of formation," he contends, is not necessarily the same thing as being "off course." Quite often, it is society and society's values that are "off course." "The perfectly adjusted bomber pilot may be a greater threat to species survival than the hospitalized schizophrenic deluded that the Bomb is inside him," argues Laing.

The points of the comparison may be illustrated as follows:

society = formation of planes
people = planes
"abnormal" person = "out of formation" plane
"normal" person = "in formation" plane
"abnormal" person = "off course" plane
"normal" person = "on course" plane

To many writers, an analogy is nothing more than an extended metaphor in which the comparison is put in terms of relationships. The following scientific analogy illustrates this process.

Observations indicate that the different clusters of galaxies are constantly moving apart from each other. To illustrate by a homely analogy, think of a raisin cake baking in an oven. Suppose the cake swells uniformly as it cooks, but the raisins themselves remain of the same size. Let each raisin represent a cluster of galaxies, and imagine yourself inside one of them. As the cake swells, you will observe that all the other raisins move away from you. Moreover, the farther away the raisin, the faster it will seem to move. When the cake has swollen to twice its initial dimensions, the distance between all the raisins will have doubled itself—two raisins that were a foot apart will have moved two feet apart. Since the entire action takes place within the same time interval, obviously the more distant raisins must move apart faster than those close at hand. So it happens with clusters of galaxies.

The analogy brings out another important point. No matter which raisin you happen to be inside, the others will always move away from you. Hence the fact that we observe all the other clusters of galaxies to be moving away from us *does not mean that we are situated at the center of the universe.* Indeed, it seems certain that the universe has no center. A cake may be said to have a center only because it has a boundary. We must imagine the cake to extend outward without any boundary, an infinite cake, so to speak, which means that however much cake we care to consider there is always more.

—Fred Hoyle, ''When Time Began,'' *The Saturday Evening Post*

In this selection, the analogy is pretty straightforward. Hoyle wants to explain to the general reader a scientific concept: ''that the different clusters of galaxies are constantly moving apart from each other.'' The basic metaphor he uses is that of a raisin cake baking in an oven. The cake is the universe, constantly expanding. Each raisin represents a cluster of galaxies. The raisin is one of the clusters of galaxies, and the observer is inside.

Not every analogy is a scientific analogy or an explanation of a complex subject. The following magazine ad uses an analogy as a way of selling a product.

Judgment From the Bench

Those who sit in judgment of a piano come from many branches of musical achievement. But they all look for the same signs of truth to emerge.

Responsiveness, for instance, is always called upon—especially when a new concerto is being tried.

Clarity must come forth—as in the case of enunciating vs. blurring the inner voices of Bach's fugues. Reliability, above all, will figure hard in the outcome of every rock concert.

To all these points, Yamaha pianos plead guilty as charged.

Judge one at your nearest Yamaha dealer. But whatever you do—

don't sentence yourself to life without a piano. In fact, we'd rather you buy another piano than no piano at all.

—ad for *Yamaha* piano

Exercises

1. Analyze the Yamaha ad in class. Set up a kind of outline or equation showing the points of the comparison. Does the analogy break down at any point? Is the ad effective? This ad was taken from *The New Yorker*, October 7, 1972. Discuss the ad in relation to its intended audience.

2. Write an essay, using one of the following analogies:

   a. Thinking is like exploring.
   b. Courting is like playing a game.
   c. Life is a river (stream, tributary, eternal sea).
   d. Life is a journey (hourglass, book, plant).
   e. My moods are like the seasons.
   f. _____ is like falling leaves (a dying fire, a shooting star).

3. Select one of the following as the basis of an analogy and then write an essay using the analogy to illustrate an idea:

   a. a merry-go-round   d. a clock
   b. a bridge   e. a puzzle
   c. a broken mirror   f. a wasp's nest

4. Use one of the following proverbs as the basis of an analogy paper:

   a. Time is like an arrow.
   b. Words are like bees: they have honey and a sting.
   c. Marriage is a lottery.
   d. Lost credit is like a broken mirror.
   e. Courage is fire; bullying is smoke.

5. Write a scientific analogy to explain an idea.

6. Write a persuasive essay in the manner of the Yamaha ad, using an extended analogy.

Patterns of Thought:

Narration, Process, Cause and Effect

Chapter 7

Patterns of Thought:
Narration, Process, Cause and Effect

Narration

Seldom a day goes by without friends or acquaintances coming up to you and telling you a joke, an interesting story, an incident that happened to them, or the plot of some movie or television show they have just seen. What happens to people in their work and in their leisure time constitutes the very pulse of life. Much of your conversation as well as much of your writing consists of narration.

Narration, as a pattern of thought, consists of *the act of following a sequence of actions or events in time.* It is *a recounting of the facts or particulars of some incident or experience.*

Purpose, Audience, Kind of Discourse

Narration can be used to achieve any aim: to inform or instruct, to convince or persuade, to entertain or please, or to express strong feelings and emotions. Narration as a process in and of itself does none of these, except perhaps in an indirect manner. It all depends on the uses to which you put your narration. Tell a story in one context, and it will be entertaining. Tell the same story in another context, and it may be instructive or persuasive.

Narration can be found in numerous kinds of writing: the narration of personal experiences, biographies, autobiographies, journals, diaries, memoirs, reminiscences, logs, records, genealogies, newspaper stories, magazine ads, short stories, novels, ballads, folk songs, movie scripts, travel accounts, chronicles, histories, anecdotes, obituaries, and sermons.

Many of these forms have their own distinctive puposes, although the same narrative techniques and the same forms can be put to many different uses. Literary narratives such as the novel or short story usually have an aesthetic aim. Narration in sermons or magazine ads has a persuasive aim. Biography usually has an expository aim, which is to set forth a part or the whole of a person's life to explain his or her character, influence on others, or accomplishments. The aim of autobiography is similar to that of biography. Some obvious differences, of course, are that biography is an account of a person's life written by someone else, whereas autobiography is written by oneself. Biography is written in the third person; autobiography is written in the first person. Biography has a different aim from that of autobiography. Historical narratives, like biographies, have informative and instructive aims. In such writing, the author seeks to explain general trends, customs, worship, warfare, commerce, governments, and agriculture. Or the writer may seek to illuminate the characters of men and women, their wisdom or foolishness, intelligence or passions.

Whereas the autobiography puts its emphasis on introspection, journals and diaries, because they are so brief, are usually less introspective. They do, however, often give us personal impressions and fresh insights into experience. What they lack as connected narratives, they gain in vividness and immediacy. They are less structured than biographies and autobiographies and more anecdotal, containing brief observations, direct impressions of life, bits and pieces of information, personal reactions, and intimate thoughts.

Invention and Narration

As a method of invention, narration answers such questions as What happened? What is happening? What will happen? When did it happen? Where did it happen?

Because of its concern with time, narration is related to process and cause and effect:

Narration	*What* happened?
Process	*How* did it happen?
Cause and effect	*Why* did it happen?

In narration, however, the emphasis is on the *what* (although, for example, the elements in a plot are related by cause and effect). In process, the emphasis is on the *how*. And in cause and effect, the emphasis is on the *why*. To recount the particulars of an occurrence in time and space is to invent.

It is interesting to note that time is usually conceived of in terms of space. Events are conceived in relation to one another:

$$event_1 \quad event_2 \quad event_3 \quad event_4$$

Yet your awareness of time comes not from space, but from some inner sense of the passage of events. Number is sometimes associated with time, and this helps to give you some notion of what is meant by a "time sense." An important synonym for *narrate* is *recount.* But an equally strong synonym, *relate,* brings you back to the spatial relation. Whether you think of time as sequence or relation, your feeling for time helps you to penetrate deeply into the nature of reality.

I have said that narration is a recounting of particulars in a temporal sequence. The word *recounting* suggests a self-contained series: "This happened, and then this happened, and then this happened." The word *particulars* assumes that narration will be concerned with the individual and the concrete. The basis of narration, the *what,* is concerned with the simplest kind of progression in time, contiguity. Particulars are related to each other because they occur in time. But in a plot or in a scientific process, they are also causally related.

In any event, to narrate is to invent. In the process of invention, you must come up with a succession of details, and shape and proportion each part. You must also keep in mind the end to be achieved. Each part must prepare for what is to follow.

Narration is a dynamic mode, for experience is dynamic and changing. The squirrel you looked at in the yard yesterday is no longer there. The tree you trimmed last summer has long since shed its leaves. You yourself are now probably taller, bigger, wider, or thinner than you were last year. When you go home for the Christmas holidays after a semester at school, you notice that everything seems strange or different. Your little brother or sister has grown an inch taller. Your father has another wrinkle. Your room seems different than you had imagined it, perhaps because your mother has moved the furniture around.

How do you express these changes in narration? By verbs, by prepositions, by adverbs. "It started snowing on Saturday night," wrote one student, "the wind whipping about the house, moaning low and then shrieking high and shrill like a banshee, whirling gusts of snow around, blotting out the black of the night sky." Another wrote: "The raindrops fell against my window, tapping rhythmically against the glass, then spattering in all directions from the middle, slithering lazily down the smooth surface, and finally dripping from the corners of the sill."

In narratives, you normally think of the verb as carrying the burden of the action. Action verbs are much more vivid than passive verbs: *glide, slide, ramble, stroll, amble, plod, tramp, strut, stride, toddle, spurt, sprint, scamper, dash, crawl, loiter, waddle, slouch, hobble, limp, jostle, clash, crash, smack, whack, jab.* Prepositions and adverbs help to convey action: *now, then, afterwards, later, since, therefore, after, from that time on, hereafter, today, tomorrow, eventually, while, early, slow, fast, till, by, in, at, from, to.* Narration, like the other modes, has a characteristic vocabulary that gives the reader a sense of the passage of time:

now	first	previously
then	second	every day
before	third	a long time ago
after	once	one of these days
earlier	former	last year
later	latter	up to this time
soon	prior to	on that occasion

Exercises

1. Using the questions suggested by the topics of invention, probe a narrative subject.

2. As a classroom exercise, relate to other members of the class some simple experience that actually happened to you.

3. Tell the plot of a movie or television show that has a strong narrative interest.

4. Reinvent! Take a plot from an old story and bring it up to date with a new setting and new characters.

The Structure of Narration

Because narration follows the laws of chronological succession, in writing your own narratives, you can follow a kind of abstract paradigm that might be depicted thus:

> *Narration Pattern*
> Introduction (time, place, persons, beginning of action)
> Event 1 . . .
> Event 2 . . .
> Event 3 . . .
> Events 4, 5, 6 (or incidents 4, 5, 6)
> Climax (point of intensity of action)
> Conclusion

Translated into more specific terms, the pattern might look like this, with, of course, considerable overlapping in the stages:

> Introduction
> Initial incident
> Rising action
> Suspense (foreshadowing, withholding information, surprise, and so forth)
> Turning point
> Falling action
> Climax
> Conclusion

The *introduction* sets the time and place of the action, introduces the characters, and shows their relationship to one another. The *initial incident* is the foundation of the plot. It brings the inciting force into action and moves the story forward. The *rising action* consists of a connected series of incidents or episodes which increase suspense. *Suspense* is that moment in the action that stirs excitement in the reader. It is an emotional appeal, making the reader fearful, or angry, or happy. *Foreshadowing* is a hint of something to come. *Withholding information* is one way of achieving suspense. Another way is to *surprise* the reader, to mislead deliberately. The *turning point* is that part of the narrative at which the conflicting forces of the story meet. The *falling action* is an intense series of events in which the writer begins "to tie the knot." The *climax* is the result of all of the elements of the story. It is the *resolution,* the point of highest intensity, and the place where the conflict rages fiercely. The *conclusion* is the logical ending of the story. It should be clear and satisfying and make sense. Not all of these elements of course will appear in a given narrative.

The *action* of a story may be *physical* or *mental.* Since a story involves people in action, there is usually some kind of *conflict* involved in the action. The main character is tested in some way and emerges victorious or defeated. Some familiar conflicts at the heart of most stories are the individual versus nature, the individual versus society, the individual versus God, the individual versus the supernatural, the individual versus other men or women, the individual versus himself or herself. When the conflict is internal or between an individual and another man or woman, the basis of the conflict is usually good or evil, virtues or vices: honesty/greed, hope/despair, courage/cowardice, generosity/selfishness, duty/lack of responsibility, forgiveness/revenge, chastity/lust, patience/impatience, compassion/lack of compassion, and so forth.

In many narratives, *character development* is more important than plot. The characters are the "actors in a story." Characterization can be developed by *personal action,* by *speech,* by *introspection,* by what *other people* tell us about a character, by the *author,* and by the *interests, tastes, possessions,* and *surroundings* of a character.

The *theme* of a story is its main point. It is an idea the writer wants to impress on his or her readers. It usually is expressed by means of character and incident.

In telling a story, a writer may use the *first person* or the *third person.* The first person is limited in that all of the events are seen through the eyes of one person. The third person allows the writer to portray the events from many angles.

Not all of the narratives that you write will have an extensive depiction of character or long, involved plots. Perhaps most will be merely a recounting of a series of events, as in personal narratives, reminiscences, and news stories. Autobiography and biography may or may not have plots. Journals, diaries, memoirs, and letters are usually too brief and too unconnected to allow for an extended treatment of plot.

The following narrative, taken from Willa Cather's *My Antonia*, is an excellent example of a literary narrative with an aesthetic aim. It follows very closely the pattern of a well-plotted narrative.

The Men Who Fed the Bride to the Wolves

When Pavel and Peter were young men, living at home in Russia, they were asked to be groomsmen for a friend who was to marry the belle of another village. It was in the dead of winter and the groom's party went over to the wedding in sledges. Peter and Pavel drove in the groom's sledge, and six sledges followed with all his relatives and friends.

After the ceremony at the church, the party went to a dinner given by the parents of the bride. The dinner lasted all afternoon; then it became a supper and continued far into the night. There was much dancing and drinking. At midnight the parents of the bride said goodbye to her and blessed her. The groom took her in his arms and carried her out to his sledge and tucked her under the blankets. He sprang in beside, and Pavel and Peter (our Pavel and Peter!) took the front seat. Pavel drove. The party set out with singing and the jingle of sleigh-bells, the groom's sledge going first. All the drivers were more or less the worse for merry-making, and the groom was absorbed in his bride.

The wolves were bad that winter, and everyone knew it, yet when they heard the first wolf-cry, the drivers were not much alarmed. They had too much good food and drink inside them. The first howls were taken up and echoed and with quickening repetitions. The wolves were coming together. There was no moon, but the starlight was clear on the snow. A black drove came up over the hill behind the wedding party. The wolves ran like streaks of shadow; they looked no bigger than dogs, but there were hundreds of them.

Something happened to the hindmost sledge; the driver lost

control—he was probably very drunk—the horses left the road, the sledge was caught in a clump of trees, and overturned. The occupants rolled out over the snow, and the fleetest of the wolves sprang upon them. The shrieks that followed made everybody sober. The drivers stood up and lashed their horses. The groom had the best team and his sledge was lightest—all the others carried from six to a dozen people.

Another driver lost control. The screams of the horses were more terrible to hear than the cries of the men and women. Nothing seemed to check the wolves. It was hard to tell what was happening in the rear; the people who were falling behind shrieked as piteously as those who were already lost. The little bride hid her face on the groom's shoulder and sobbed. Pavel sat still and watched his horses. The road was clear and white, the the groom's three blacks went like the wind. It was only necessary to be calm and to guide them carefully.

At length, as they breasted a long hill, Peter rose cautiously and looked back. "There are only three sledges left," he whispered.

"And the wolves?" Pavel asked.

"Enough! Enough for all of us."

Pavel reached the brow of the hill, but only two sledges followed him down the other side. In that moment on the hilltop they saw the whirling black group on the snow. Presently the groom screamed. He saw his father's sledge overturned, with his mother and sisters. He sprang up as if he meant to jump, but the girl shrieked and held him back. It was even then too late. The black ground-shadows were already crowding over the heap in the road, and one horse ran out across the fields, his harness hanging to him, wolves at his heels. But the groom's movement had given Pavel an idea.

They were within a few miles of their village now. The only sledge left out of the six was not very far behind them, and Pavel's middle horse was failing. Beside a frozen pond something happened to the other sledge; Peter saw it plainly. Three big wolves got abreast of the horses, and the horses went crazy. They tried to jump over each other, got tangled up in the harness, and overturned the sledge.

When the shrieking behind them died away, Pavel realized that he was alone upon the familiar road. "They still come?" he asked Peter.

"Yes."

"How many?"

"Twenty, thirty—enough."

Now his middle horse was being almost dragged by the other two. Pavel gave Peter the reins and stepped carefully into the back of the sledge. He called to the groom that they must lighten—and pointed to the bride. The young man cursed him and held her tighter. Pavel tried to drag her away. In the struggle, the groom rose. Pavel knocked him over the side of the sledge and threw the girl after him. He said he never remembered exactly how he did it, or what happened afterward. Peter, crouching in the front seat, saw nothing. The first thing either of them noticed was a new sound that broke into the clear air, louder than they had ever heard it before—the bell of the monastery of their own village, ringing for early prayers.

Pavel and Peter drove into the village alone, and they have been alone ever since. They were run out of their village. Pavel's own mother would not look at him. They went away to strange towns, but when people learned where they came from, they were always asked if they knew the two men who had fed the bride to the wolves. Wherever they went, the story followed them. . . .

The first two paragraphs set the scene in time and place (a wedding in a small village in Russia in the middle of winter); introduce the characters (two brothers, Peter and Pavel, the bride and groom, the wedding guests); and set forth the initial incident (the wedding party, after much dancing and drinking, setting out at midnight for the groom's village). Subsequent paragraphs then take up each incident in turn.

The narrative progression might be depicted as follows:

The wedding party sets out in sledges at midnight for the groom's village.

The wolves come together to attack the sledges.

The hindmost sledge is lost.

Another driver loses control.

The sledge of the groom's father overturns.

The horses panic, and the second-to-last sledge overturns.

Pavel knocks the groom over the side to lighten the sledge, then throws the bride after him.

Finally, Pavel and Peter drive into the village alone, with the "bell of the monastery of their own village, ringing for early prayers."

Of the sixteen paragraphs in this selection, the shortest are those with dialogue. Most of these consist of a single phrase or sentence. The longest paragraph is paragraph 15, the second-to-last paragraph, which contains the largest number of words (135) and the largest number of sentences (10). The length seems natural when you consider that this is the most action-packed and suspenseful part of the narrative, that climactic moment when Pavel throws the bride and groom to the wolves.

Most of the sentences are short, or give the appearance of being short due to extensive use of coordination. Most of the short sentences come in the chase scenes, to convey rapid action and increase the excitement and tension. The longest sentences come at the beginning of the story (to set the scene in time and place), at the beginning of the chase scene, at the end of the chase scene (with Pavel and Peter riding into the village), and at the end of the narrative.

The sense of passing of time and the action is conveyed by prepositional phrases:

after the ceremony
at midnight
over the hill
behind the wedding party
over the snow
at length
down the other side
in that moment
across the fields
at his heels
behind them
beside the frozen pond

abreast of the horses
over each other
into the village

adverbs and adverbial nouns:

over	too late
all afternoon	out
then	far
far	now
in	away
beside	alone
presently	ever since

and verbs:

sprang	breasted
drove	reached
set out	followed
were coming together	screamed
came up	overturned
ran	shrieked
left	ran
overturned	was failing
rolled out	got tangled up
sprang	overturned
stood up	must lighten
lashed	knocked
lost control	threw
were falling behind	drove
shrieked	run out
sobbed	went away
went	

In just sixteen paragraphs, Willa Cather is able to convey a wide range of human emotions: merriment, fear, tension, unspeakable horror, anger, and sadness. All the structural elements work together to produce a masterful narrative.

The following student paper has most of the characteristics of a good narrative.

To Surf

I had been out all day. I had been too exhilarated by the huge, rolling waves, the taste of saltwater, the sting of coral cuts to notice hunger or fatigue.

For the first time in my life, I had body-surfed. I was excited with my new knowledge. Wanting to show the natives of the islands I could take any wave they could, I swam farther and farther out, looking for a bigger wave, a higher crest.

I would swim out to where the waves rose the highest, wait for just the right one to come swelling across the sea, time my start to the exact moment, and ride the wave until it was nothing but a ripple. Then I would repeat the process.

Often on my way back out I would come head on with a surfer. But I had been taught just when to go under the board and how long to stay under. The boards didn't scare me unless I became aware that the rider was scared. These were the ones who tried to go around you or ditch the board. You couldn't be sure when you were under a "green rider" that he wouldn't bounce the board right over your skull. But this too was a part of the game. This was one of the reasons I had traveled so far from home.

I didn't even mind the coral cuts. They hurt like everything when you suddenly find yourself thrown right into a bed of the sharp, cutting animals. If you had time to think, you could tell by the flow of water where these piles of deadly skeletons lay. But if an unexpected wave caught you and carried you into it, you knew you had to get out of the coral and get out of it fast. Because if another sudden wave were to come beating down on you, you would be crushed further into the sea's torture chamber. Even this I hadn't minded earlier.

But now I was beginning to tire. I felt a hollow, heavy sensation in my stomach. I had had nothing to eat since breakfast and it was late in the afternoon. Most of the swimmers were already going home. Boats were coming in. The waves were growing smaller and smaller until now there were hardly any. My girlfriend Cindy had been lying on the beach for well over an hour. Although I could not see her,

I imagined her resting, asleep in the last rays of the day's sun. I envied her as my muscles began to ache. My eyes burned from the salt. My skin was dry and would have been red from the sun except for the white, sticky layer of salt covering it. My swimsuit was full of sand and my legs and feet hurt from the tiny cuts. I started swimming back to shore. I had not realized I was so far out. In my attempt to catch the last dying waves I had swum far out past the breakwater. The water, fortunately, was not over my head and I thanked God for small favors. As my arms tired of swimming I decided to float in. It was then, with absolute terror, that I discovered that the tide was going out and going fast. That explained why the waves had diminished. The tide was reversing! The native swimmers had known this and had long since swum in. There were only a few stragglers left, inexperienced, dumb tourists like myself who had gone out looking for that last wave, that last thrill. In panic I started swimming madly. This lasted only a few minutes though. Reality told me to save my strength. If I could only get within calling distance of Cindy, I could yell to her. I stood up and walked now. It seemed with each step I took the water pulled me back three. The water was just below my shoulders now. I tried to think of anything but what was happening to me. This failed. All I could think of was calling out to Cindy. I must have been making progress. The water was at my waist.

I could now make out the people on the beach. I scanned each girl, looking for Cindy's familiar suit. My eye caught the flash of bright purple suit on dark-tanned skin. That was no mistake. That was Cindy. I was overjoyed. Then I realized she was with three guys. Probably servicemen on R and R. I was mad. REALLY MAD. Here I was nearly drowned, at the very brink of death, and she was lining up a date. With my anger I gained new strength. I walked the rest of the way in. The tide, although low, was getting stronger now, but in my fury, so was I. At last I had made it. I walked up onto the beach and picked up my beach mat. As I headed for the hotel Cindy called out to me. "How was your swim?" she asked. "Great," I bellowed back. With that, my remaining strength drained. My knees shook as I walked the half-block back to the hotel. In the elevator I thought I would collapse. I finally reached the fourteenth floor and practically crawled to the door. The door was locked! Cindy had the key. I sank to the floor. Covered with salt and sand, my skin burned, my hair tangled, I didn't want to go to the main lobby to get the other key. Besides I wasn't sure I could take another elevator ride. So I sat in front of my door.

—Vada

This story, with its irony, is very suggestive of the Stephen Crane short story "The Open Boat" in which four shipwrecked men in an open boat are distraught when they realize that some bathers they see on the beach are not even remotely aware of their plight. In the student's surfing story, the additional irony of being locked out of her room adds just the right final touch to the conclusion.

Not all narratives need to be this well plotted. Some instead may have a thematic unity, such as this student narrative based on a reminiscence:

Try to Remember . . .

Try to remember the kind of September
When life was slow
And oh so mellow
Try to remember the kind of September
When grass was green and grain was yellow
Try to remember the kind of September
When you were a tender and callow fellow
Try to remember, and if you remember,
Then follow . . .

That's such a lovely, lovely song. I have the entire album from the *Fantasticks*, but I always hover over the record player, catching the needle before it goes to the next song, and play "Try to Remember" over and over. Someday, that band will be worn out, and all the others will be like new.

I probably never would have even thought of it today, except that I received a call from grandfather's friend, who lives in Lincoln. My grandparents live in Iowa, and these people had gone to visit them, and get some apples from the orchard. My grandfather had

"Try to Remember" copyright © 1960 by Tom Jones and Harvey Schmidt. Chappell Co., Inc. owner of publication & allied rights. *All rights reserved.* International Copyright Secured. Used by permission.

asked them to drop off some apples for me, and so they did. A brown grocery bag full of red delicious, jonathans, and even a banana apple, and one yellow delicious. I looked at those apples and remembered. . . .

When I was a child, "tender and callow," we would go to my grandfather's and pick those apples ourselves. Mom would dress my sister and me, and my brother, who was too young to reach most of the branches then, in sturdy shoes, and jackets, and long jeans, to protect our little legs from the poison ivy that usually was already dead by then, anyway. But it was a ritual. We'd load my grandparents up in the car, and head for the orchards.

My grandfather had planted those trees by himself, when he was young. And my grandmother would herd the cows through the fields nearby. Now, my grandfather was nearly ninety, and he had been crippled for years. He could barely get into the car, let alone walk through his own orchard. And my grandmother was not too much better. She would get out of the car, and take quick little steps in her old-ladies' shoes, the weeds catching on her brown cotton stockings. Her back was kind of hunched now, and she had to breathe hard if she reached up too far over her head. But we, who were young, would run through those orchards, through the prickly thistles, through the tall grass, now yellow and dried, through the tangled vines of orange bittersweet, over the road with countless ruts left from the last rainstorm when the tractor came through in the mud. We would run from tree to tree, taking only the biggest and best apples, and comparing each other's baskets full to one another. Occasionally, we would stop, polish a particularly choice red apple, and bite into it, the juice dribbling down our chins, mixing with the brown dust already on it. Then we would toss the cores into the woods, as far as we could throw them, and listen for them to drop in a crackling pile of fallen leaves. It was usually very cold when we went to the orchards, or at least it always seemed so, and most often we would be picking apples while the sun set in a lovely pink, yellow, and blue autumn sky. The air was fresh and clean. And we ran and ran until our freedom was ended not by our choice, but by fatigue, and the falling darkness.

I slowly took each apple out of the brown grocery sack they had sent, and very nearly polished them with my tears along with a pink terry-cloth towel. I put them in an old metal pot that I had in the room, and they are sitting there gleaming at me now. They're picked now, but they grew in freedom all summer, on trees, in the calm country. Funny they should find their way into a stuffy, cramped college dorm room. Sometimes, I wonder that about me too.

—Laura

Here the emphasis is not on a rigid plot structure, but on the order of memory.

Sometimes, in writing a story, you may wish to make your theme explicit. The following student narrative follows an inductive pattern (from particular to general), with the narrative as a kind of extended example for the concluding generalization in the last paragraph.

The Promise That Grew

Some years ago, I was caught in a sudden, blinding snowstorm near Indiana, Pennsylvania. My car stalled at the edge of town. I floundered into town and into the nearest store. The proprietor phoned for help to get my car out of the snowdrift.

In a short time, a tall blond man showed up with a team of horses and pulled me out of the drift into town. I asked him how much I owed him for his trouble. He refused any pay, saying, "I will charge thee nothing but the promise that thee will help the next man thee finds in trouble." I thanked him and made the promise.

After he left, the storekeeper explained that my Good Samaritan was a Mennonite who considered it wrong to charge anyone for a service made necessary by an act of God.

Four years later, a friend and I were driving over flooded land south of St. Louis, Missouri. We crossed through water a foot deep without any trouble, but through my rearview mirror, I could see that the small car behind us stalled. I waded back while my companion reversed the car so I could hook up onto his bumper with tire chains.

We pulled the man out and waited until he got his engine started. Then he offered to pay me. I told him of my experience in Indiana, Pennsylvania, then repeated the Mennonite's words: "I will charge thee nothing but the promise that thee will help the next man thee finds in trouble." He promised, and we parted.

About one year later, my family and I were camping about one hundred miles from Aurora, Missouri, and we pitched our tents near the James River. We'd been told that it never flooded at that time of year, but the river evidently misread the calendar, for I awakened in the middle of the night with a very cold back from water deep enough to cover the canvas cot. We loaded our soggy equipment into our car, but we were unable to drive it to higher ground. I waded back to an inn some distance from our camping spot and asked the innkeeper if he could get help to pull us out.

In a short time, a farmer showed up with a tractor and a long rope and pulled us to safe ground. When I offered to pay him, he told me of a man who had helped him get his tractor out of the mud and then said: "I will charge thee nothing but the promise that thee will help the next man that thee finds in trouble." The quotation was identical to that of the man in Pennsylvania, although I know of no Mennonites or Quakers in that section of Missouri.

How far one man's act of kindness had traveled!

—Fred

In writing your own narratives, it is not necessary to develop long, involved plots. Unless you intend to become a novelist, most of your narratives will be of the kind found in the narration of personal experiences, anecdotes, autobiography, letters to friends, journals, diaries, and newspaper stories. Your stories may indeed have a built-in plot, but your main purpose will be to tell a compelling and interesting narrative based on personal experiences. Then the kind of concreteness that you can get only from firsthand experiences may carry into your more abstract writing.

Exercises

1. Analyze in class the student narratives titled "To Surf" and "The Promise That Grew," using the outline of traditional narrative techniques discussed earlier (introduction, setting, characters, initial incident, rising action, and so on).

2. Write a brief *autobiographical sketch* of your childhood or adolescence.

3. Write a *brief narrative* on one of the following general subjects:

   a. a job experience
   b. a date
   c. falling in love
   d. a college experience
   e. an accident

   f. a dream
   g. a racial incident
   h. a humorous experience
   i. a death or illness
   j. a natural disaster

4. Write a *newspaper account* of a fire or some other incident.

5. Write a *character sketch* in the form of an obituary notice.

6. Someone interested in employing a friend of yours has asked you to give a frank summary of his character. Imagine the exact situation and write the letter.

7. Write a *biographical sketch* of someone you know well.

8. Recount some episode in the *history* of your county, parish, city, or state. Emphasize the people involved.

9. In the manner of the student narrative "To Surf," give a first-person account of one of the following: a narrow escape, a brave act, an embarrassing experience, a journey, a practical joke.

10. Write a short paper, based on a *reminiscence,* in the manner of the student paper "Try to Remember."

11. Expand one of the following into a full-length narrative:

    a. For one day, you will express all of your feelings about people truthfully, no matter whom you may hurt.

    b. You go to a party, only to discover that six people have on the same outfit as you do.

    c. You have been drinking, and you hit an old man or woman at a crossing while you are driving.

    d. You arrive at the air terminal just as your plane is departing.

    e. You are eating in a fancy restaurant, and when it is time to pay the bill, you discover that you have left your wallet at home.

12. The TV show *Roots* has reawakened our interest in genealogy, history, biography, and autobiography. Trace your genealogy or that of someone in your family. Write down all you know about your family, beginning with yourself, your parents, your grandparents, your great-grandparents. Include dates of births, marriages, and deaths, places of residences, and so forth. Interview your uncles, aunts, or grandparents. Check family records: old photo albums, letters, newspaper clippings, notes, diaries, journals, and other such sources of information.

Process

A **process** is *a series of actions, changes, functions, steps, or operations that bring about a particular end or result.* Like narration, process suggests ongoing movement and continuous action. The emphasis in a process theme, however, is on the *how,* rather than the *what.* These are relative rather than absolute differences, of course, since like narration, a process can be concerned with the *what,* and like cause and effect, it can be concerned with the *why.*

When you think of a process, you generally tend to think of slow, gradual changes and of a series of interlocking steps whereby an end is achieved. Some synonyms for the verb form of the word *process* are *change, alter, vary, modify, transform, convert,* and *transmute.* The word *change* is perhaps the most important synonym, suggesting as it does a transition from one state to another. A change alters the quality of a thing and modifies its form or appearance. Like the other topics and patterns with which you will be concerned, this one carries a train of rich images and expressions: *mutation, transformation, transfiguration, metamorphosis, transubstantiation, transmigration,* and *a kaleidoscope of colors.*

Purpose, Audience, Kind of Discourse

Process as a mode of developing a subject can be found in any kind of discourse that emphasizes a system of operations or steps in the production of something or a series of actions, changes, or phases that bring about an end or result. Although the primary aim of process exposition is to inform or instruct, it can also be used to persuade, as in certain magazine advertisements which outline the steps in the making of a product to convince the reader of the product's excellence.

Since process is by definition a sequence of actions, changes, or operations that brings about some desired end or result, then as a writer you can best appeal to your audience by logically presenting the connected series of actions that lead to the desired end.

Process can be most profitably employed in the following kinds of writing: scientific essays, instruction manuals, booklets, research reports, cookbooks, directions for doing something, natural history, biology, chemistry, explanations of a mechanism, explanations of a social process or a historical process, explanations of a natural process, explanations of a creative process, advertising, and argumentation.

Invention and Process

As a topic of invention, process answers basic questions such as How did it happen? How does it work? How do you make it or do it? What are the stages, phases, steps, or operations? To recount a series of changes, a sequence of steps, a particular method of doing something, an explanation of a scientific process, the steps in an argument, a course of action, a series of operations, a procedure, a function, or the alteration in the position, size, quantity, and quality of something is to invent.

Your awareness of process comes from a sense of some kind of change. You notice that the hands on your watch have changed position. You observe that the plants in your garden are changing in size and quantity. You change the quality of the water in your shower from hot to cold. You watch people, animals, and plants around you come into existence, mature, grow old, and die. You observe that the sky grows dark, it begins to rain, leaves fall from the trees, autumn comes, then winter, then spring, then summer. You notice the yellows in a sunset shade into the oranges, the oranges into the reds, and the reds into blues, purples, and greens. Life ebbs and flows, moves, pulsates, palpitates, throbs all around you.

Process analysis is a special form of exposition in which you present a step-by-step description of how some process takes place:

a natural process, a scientific process, a mechanical process, a historical process, a social process, a creative process. Process exposition is concerned with *how* topics: how flowers changed the world, how the universe was formed, how the American Revolution began, how LSD was discovered, how liquor is made, how to operate a car, how the heart works, how to eat crabs, how to bake a cake.

Because process is a kind of dynamic exposition, its characteristic vocabulary tends to emphasize change:

phase	state	inconstancy
occurrence	condition	inversion
step	conversion	permutation
change	displacement	modulation
alteration	transformation	qualification
mutation	fluctuation	metamorphosis

Some process terms are very similar to those of narration: *now, then, next, afterwards, later, thereafter, from, to.* Others are similar to those of enumeration: *first, second, third, one, another, a third.* The verb tenses in a process may be present (if you are giving directions) or past (if you are explaining something that has already taken place). The voice may be active or passive (generally used in scientific descriptions). The person may be first (in an informal account), second (in giving directions), or third (in an objective description of a process).

Exercises

1. Using the questions suggested by the topics of invention, probe a process subject.

2. In class, for purposes of invention, analyze a natural process, a scientific process, a mechanical process, a historical process, a political process, a social process, or a creative process.

3. Explain in class how one of the following works:

    a. an eggbeater
    b. a bicycle
    c. a razor
    d. a rifle
    e. an engine

4. Play the game of "Charades" in class. Choose sides and take turns acting out a process.

5. Explain to someone in class how to

    a. swim   f. sell something
    b. box   g. put down someone
    c. skate   h. make coffee
    d. lie   i. play a musical instrument
    e. tell jokes   j. clean a rug

The Structure of Process

The rhetorical structure of a process may be conveyed by a very simple paradigm:

Process Pattern
Introduction (thesis)
Step 1 (phase 1) . . .
Step 2 (phase 2) . . .
Step 3 (phase 3) . . .
Step 4 (phase 4) . . .
Step 5, 6, 7 (phase 5, 6, 7) . . .
Conclusion (summary and so forth)

In writing process themes, you want to divide your subject into stages, phases, or operations. If the process you want to explain involves giving directions or making something, your introduction will usually contain a description of the material and the tools or implements or materials to be used. If it does not involve directions, as in the explanation of a natural process, your introduction may contain an explanation of the principles involved, but the primary emphasis will be on the chronological order, on the *what, how,* and *when* of the process.

The following student description of the process of making candleholders is an excellent example of the directions-for-doing-something theme. It follows the process paradigm fairly closely, but without using the enumeration pattern throughout.

The Process in Making Candleholders

If you are stuck for a gift but short of time and money, beautiful, stained-glass candleholders, which sell in candle shops for five dollars each, are relatively easy and inexpensive to make. These candleholders take about ten hours to complete, but the process is fun and easy.

Before beginning, you must have the needed materials. These consist of a wide-mouthed drinking glass about five inches high, an old windshield, glass stain, tile grout, glue, and black acrylic paint. With these materials you can make up to fifteen candleholders (if you have that many glasses).

The first step is breaking and staining the windshield. To break the windshield, wrap it in an old blanket and hit it several times with a hammer. The glass will shatter, but not separate. After this is done, break off small pieces of various shapes and sizes, and stain them any color. The stain will dry almost immediately.

While the pieces are drying, cover the drinking glass with a thin coat of glue. This will give the shattered, stained pieces of glass something to hold on to.

When the pieces have dried, attach them to the drinking glass. This is done by gluing each piece separately to the drinking glass, as close to each other as possible. It is important to remember that the stained side of the pieces must be glued toward the inside of the glass. If this is not done, the stain will wash or peel off the candleholder.

Once the drinking glass is completely covered with the brightly colored pieces, it is time to grout the candleholder. To do this, fill the spaces between the stained glass with grout, forming a smooth, rounded edge around the mouth of the glass, and then cover the bottom of the glass with a smooth layer of grout. Allow the grout to dry the amount of time specified by the instructions on the package of grout.

With a damp rag, remove any grout which covers the stained glass after the grout has dried. After removing the excess grout, smooth out the grout with a piece of sandpaper.

Now it is time to paint. Carefully paint the grout with black acrylic paint. Do not be concerned if the paint covers parts of the glass since acrylic is a water-base paint and washes off easily. After the paint dries, use a damp cloth to remove any paint on the glass.

If you follow these directions carefully, you can finish a candleholder in a matter of a few hours. Candleholders cost approximately one dollar apiece, and they are very beautiful to own or to give as gifts.

—Ina

Because process themes are relatively easy to write, you may be turned off by a straightforward account. Instead, you might want to try your hand at a humorous approach to writing a process theme, in the manner of the following student essay:

Lobe-Botomy

The first thing you need for a do-it-yourself-pierce-your-ears kit is a sadistic friend. Then you need lots of ice, a sharp sewing needle, and a good bottle of booze.

Obtaining the sadistic friend was no problem for me. In fact, Linda had been "needling" me all semester to let her do the job. She had had her lobes gored since high school "and it looked so easy anybody could do it," she said, eager eyes fastened on my little lobes. My ears are tiny anyway and my earlobes are attached like a button-down shirt. This gave Linda momentary doubts because she remembered something about a nerve in the upper lobe that, if punctured, would paralyze that side of the body. This gave me more than momentary doubts, but she assured me that the story was just a rumor. Besides, the surgical tray and anesthesia were all ready.

It was the night before my last final exam, first semester, freshman year. The next morning I was to take my seventh test. Since I had been gorging my head with knowledge for two solid weeks, I was so out of it I didn't even require the friendly Southern Comfort winking at me from the table.

The lobe-botomy operation took place at Linda's apartment, which was abundantly stocked with ice cubes. There I sat limply in a cushiony old chair watching detachedly the frantic activity around me. First, Linda banged the ice tray against the sink, trying to chip a few hunks from the frozen mass in which she had forgotten to place the cube divider. Then, with a caldron of boiling water popping on the stove (you'd think I was having a baby), she scrounged through a drawer full of thread, paper clips, bottle openers, wire, plastic bags, thumbtacks, ashtrays, and Elmer's glue for a big-enough knitting needle.

While Linda sterilized the needle, only slightly smaller than a whaling harpoon, I held a two-pound ice chunk in a washcloth to my right earlobe. After about fifteen minutes it was deadened enough so that I couldn't feel a pinch. Meanwhile much of the ice had trickled down my sleeve. After fifteen more minutes both patient and doctor were ready. I closed my eyes as Linda walked over to me, smiling, her hands behind her back. A few seconds later she plucked my ear away from my head and I felt the needle's searing jab. In the first place she had forgotten to let it cool, and secondly it hurt like hell. I yelped and at the same instant heard cartilage crushing inside my head. "My God! She missed," was my first thought, confirmed by blood trickling down my neck. But no, Linda had been only slightly off target due to my sudden jerk. But my scream and the blood had scared her, along with the difficulty she had getting the needle through my lobe. "I should have had a thimble," she berated herself. "Why not a hammer," I said tearfully.

That made her mad. "Ungrateful," she muttered. "You can just go around with a hole in one of your ears like a goddam pirate," she sniffed. I apologized and soothed and convinced Linda to take up the knife again because, no matter how much it hurt, I wasn't going to go around unbalanced. So this time I held the ice to my ear a whole hour and didn't feel the penetration nearly as much as before. But the blood—and especially the sound of popping cartilage—I'll never forget.

That was three and a half years ago. Since then my sadistic friend has kept her ears clean and abandoned the ear-bobbing business. And I've developed an allergy to gold and can't wear my much-suffered-for earrings.

—Carol

The pattern in this essay is less formal than that of the preceding student essay, but the puns, the concrete description, and the wit make this a delightful model to emulate.

Descriptions of processes in the natural sciences are very easy to come by. Although this example is taken from a book, it is not unlike the more popular kinds of scientific writing you might find in magazines. Its aim is to explain and inform:

How Snakes Shed Their Skins

When a snake has grown a new epidermis and is about to shed its skin, it secretes a thin layer of fluid between the old and new skin (which are no longer touching), giving the snake a clouded milky appearance. This can be seen especially at the eyes, for the milky fluid covers the pupils and makes the snake almost, if not completely, blind. This condition may last for as much as a week; during this period, snakes normally remain in hiding.

A day or two after the cloudiness has cleared, the snake will shed its skin. This is accomplished by opening and stretching the mouth and rubbing it on surrounding objects until the old skin at the edges of the lips begins to split. Rubbing continually, the snake starts to wriggle out of its skin. This is usually sloughed off in one piece from head to tail, turned inside out in the process by the emerging snake. Sometimes the skin will break up, however, and come off in pieces, as during the shedding of lizards.

The sloughed-off skin is a perfect cast of the snake. The large belly scales, the pattern of scales on the back, the eye spectacle and even casts of facial pits can all be seen. It is completely devoid of color as the pigment cells remain in the dermis, which is never shed. The shed skin is transparent with a white tinge. After it has been detached from the snake for a while, it usually becomes brittle. The sloughed-off skin is not especially attractive, but the newly emerged snake is seen at its best. Most species show their best bright colors in the days immediately following molting; as the upper skin gets older, the colors do not show through as well.

—From *Snakes of the World*

If you are asked to write a description of a scientific process, you may want to use the third person rather than the second, and make the tone more impersonal and objective.

Industrial Alcohol

Industrial alcohol is produced by a process known as fermentation. Fermentation is the process of producing alcohol and carbon dioxide from simple sugars such as glucose (a colorless, yellowish syrupy mixture) and fructose (a very sweet sugar that occurs in fruit and honey). The chemical change that occurs is brought about by the catalytic action of ferments (or enzymes).

The chief ingredient for the production of industrial alcohol is molasses, either cane-sugar molasses or beet-sugar molasses.

In the process of making industrial alcohol, the molasses is first diluted with water. It is then made slightly acid to promote the growth of yeast and to retard the growth of bacteria. Afterwards it is heated to 70 degrees Fahrenheit and to it is added a yeast culture. The yeast secretes an enzyme known as invertase which converts the sucrose in the molasses to glucose and fructose. The concentration of the alcohol can then be increased by distillation.

In addition to using cane-sugar or beet-sugar to produce alcohol, manufacturers use corn, potatoes, various kinds of grain, and other substances containing starch. When starch-containing substances are used, the starch is converted to sugar in the preliminary stages.

Although descriptions of scientific, mechanical, or natural processes tend to be impersonal and objective, you can make them less impersonal, if you wish, by basing them on personal experiences. The following student theme describes the process of canning pineapple with great accuracy, without sacrificing the personal element.

How to Can Pineapple

Two summers ago, our family flew to Hawaii. When we arrived at the hotel, the Royal Hawaiian proved how it had acquired its "royal" reputation. At five o'clock the evening of our arrival, a handsome, dark-skinned Hawaiian boy knocked on our door and presented us with a large, boat-shaped pineapple shell. It was filled with bright, juicy chunks of pineapple. This welcome became a daily ritual which we all looked forward to. The Dole Pineapple Cannery was on our list of places to visit. It proved educational as well as lots of fun!

The pineapple is a sweet, yellow fruit, especially thirst-quenching when eaten in the warm, humid climate of the Hawaiian Islands. It is grown on large plantations. The luscious fruit is produced in slices, chunks, tidbits, spears, and crushed form. How is this done? The process may be described as follows:

After the ripe pineapples arrive at the cannery in specially designed bins or trucks, and are unloaded mechanically for their long, rapid trip through the cannery, they are washed and sorted according to size. Then they enter the "ginaca" machine which removes the shell, cuts off both ends of the fruit, punches out the core, and leaves each fruit a golden cylinder. It even scrapes the shell, leaving the husk nearly dry, ready to be made into bran.

Next, the trimming tables receive the pineapple cylinders at the rate of fifty to one hundred a minute. Here women in white caps, aprons, and rubber gloves pick up each cylinder and trim away any eyes, bits of shells, or overripe portions left on the fruit.

The trimmer then puts the clean cylinder on a moving, stainless-steel conveyor which takes it through a cold-water spray to the slicer where guarded knives cut it into uniform slices. Then other white-capped workers select perfectly matched slices and place them in cans according to grades.

After the cans are filled with slices, chunks, or whatever size fruit is being processed, they move on to syrupers and through vacuum seamers where covers are attached and sealed. Still moving fast and steadily, they come to cookers where they are sterilized and heated at 200 degrees Fahrenheit, for five to fifteen minutes, depending upon the size of the can and the kind of product.

The fruit, of course, is now very hot, so without pausing a second the cans move through water coolers. The cans of crushed fruit go through a cold-water spray device aptly called a "hula cooler" which shakes as it sprays, getting the contents cool in the center as well as on the outside.

The cans are then placed in cases, and the cases are stored in warehouses, where they leave the state as a finished product under many competitive brand names.

I'll always remember my first taste of fresh Hawaiian pineapple. I can still see the rows and rows of pineapples growing in the fields. I can hear the roar of the giant machines in the plant and the workers efficiently handling the fruit. I know now why Hawaii supplies 80% of the world's pineapple.

—Jackie

Like narration and the other temporal modes, process exposition is not simply the recounting of a sequence of actions or events. To be effective, a process theme must involve the idea of purpose. Here is a sequence of events, but what holds them together? A random sequence of events will make neither an interesting narrative nor a successful process theme. But if you keep in mind the question "What is it for?" you will be well on your way to writing a successful process theme.

Exercises

1. Analyze in class the scientific essay "How Snakes Shed Their Skins." Outline the steps in the process. Discuss the language. Is it formal or informal? Does it use scientific diction or popular diction? Pick out the figures of speech. How are they used to support the writer's purpose?

2. Discuss in class a process that you have observed in a factory or in some other place.

3. Write an analysis of a natural process such as the cycle of the seasons; the beat of a heart; the composition of an essay, a painting, or a piece of music, a thought process; a learning process.

4. Write a scientific essay in the manner of "How Snakes Shed Their Skins."

5. Write on one of the following topics:

   a. How _____ was formed.
   b. How to play a certain game.
   c. How to cook a certain dish.
   d. How to make a particular drink.
   e. How to perform a particular operation.
   f. How _____ was discovered.
   g. How to control a crowd at a rock concert.
   h. How _____ works.

6. Write a humorous process theme in the manner of "Lobe-Botomy."

7. Write on one of the following:

  a. How to produce _____. e. How to sell _____.
  b. How to extract _____. f. How to eat _____.
  c. How to make _____. g. How to build _____.
  d. How to prepare _____. h. How to plan _____.

Cause and Effect

Why does the wind blow? What causes it to rain? Why does the sun shine? Where does the rainbow come from? Why is the sky blue? Where do babies come from? How did the elephant get his trunk?

Almost all these questions a child would be likely to ask, but the questions should not be dismissed lightly for this reason. Scientists such as Sir James Jeans have written articles explaining why the sky is blue. Doctors have prepared manuals for parents and children explaining where babies come from. And Rudyard Kipling wrote a beautiful tale of causation in which he gave a fanciful explanation of how the elephant got his trunk. All these questions and their answers are related to the rhetorical process that we call cause and effect.

A **cause** is *a force or influence that produces an effect.* It is *an agency or operation responsible for bringing about an action, event, condition, or result.* The word calls to mind other words and expressions such as *origin, source, first principle, author, producer, agent, instrument, ground of being, prime mover, foundation, support, influence, font, genesis, rationale, intention,* and *the straw that broke the camel's back.*

An **effect** is *anything that has been caused.* It is the *result* of a force or an action. Another meaning of the word **effect** is *something worked out, accomplished, or produced.* The word *effect* calls to mind such related words and expressions as *consequence, result, derivation, end, outcome, denouement, development, production, performance, offshoot, creation, handiwork, outgrowth, harvest, emanation,* and *issue.*

Cause and effect are correlative terms. The one always implies the other. If a tire on your car blows out and your car hits a lightpole, there is a correlation between the blowout and the accident. We say that one *causes* the other.

Cause-and-effect relationships are embedded in our language:

> February brings the rain
> Thaws the frozen lake again.
> March winds and April showers
> Bring forth May flowers.
> If in October you do marry,
> Love will come, but riches tarry.
> When December snows fall fast,
> Marry, and true love will last.

But in dealing with cause-and-effect relationships, you want to go beyond language, since language encodes relationships that are already operating in the universe.

What is it that you do when you discern cause-and-effect relationships? You notice that a particular cause or combination of causes is followed by a particular effect, or that a combination of effects follows from a particular cause or causes. A man lights a match near a leaking gas pipe. The man is subsequently killed by a gas explosion. The coroner concludes that the man's carelessness is the cause of his death. Actually, the juxtaposition of the flame and the gas caused the accident.

Another man is driving down the highway in the middle of the winter. It has been snowing, and the road is now covered with ice. The car hits a slick spot in the road, and the man swerves the car in such a way that the car skids and runs off the road, causing the car to overturn. Who or what caused the accident? Philosophers and scientists would say that any causal explanation should take into account not only the *immediate cause* of an effect, but also the *necessary conditions*. The immediate cause was the poor handling of the car by the driver. The necessary conditions were that it had snowed, the snow had turned to ice, and the ice had made the road slippery.

According to scientists, no effect is ever the product of a single cause. A cause is the sum total of all the conditions that help to bring about an effect. It is the combination that constitutes causality. Thus, in strict scientific terms, it would be inaccurate to say that "B is the cause of A" or "A is followed by B." It would be more accurate to state that events A, B, C, D, E in combination caused an event: X. But in everyday matters, it is usually sufficient to pick out one or two of the most conspicuous events and maintain that these produced a particular result. In such cases, you accept the necessary conditions as given.

A familiar old nursery rhyme illustrates this chain of causality beautifully:

> For want of a nail the shoe was lost,
> For want of a shoe the horse was lost,
> For want of a horse the rider was lost,
> For want of a rider the battle was lost,
> For want of a battle the kingdom was lost,
> And all for the want of a horseshoe nail.

It is customary to compare causal events to the links in a chain. But causal events are not merely links in an observable chain. They are part of complex conceptual patterns. Causes *are* connected to effects, but this is because you tie them together through experience and reflection. Consider an accident in which one car goes through a red light and plows into another. According to the police, the driver of the first car caused the accident by negligence. The driver claims that his brakes did not hold, yet he just had new brake shoes put on the car. The automobile mechanic blames the failure on faulty construction by the maker of the brake shoes. The brake-shoe manufacturer blames the foreman, who in turn blames the workman, who in turn blames faulty equipment. When you discern cause-and-effect relationships, then, you bring to your understanding of causality certain assumptions and presuppositions. Otherwise you would not be able to explain anything. For compositional purposes, however, you would not be expected to take into account the total cause, including all the necessary conditions of an event. You are expected to be as careful as possible in your causal analyses.

Purpose, Audience, Kind of Discourse

Cause-and-effect thinking can be found in any kind of writing, for any purpose. Ordinarily, you associate cause-and-effect thinking with scientific writing. But it can be found in everyday reasoning, formal arguments, reports, magazine articles, textbooks, historical explanations, scientific explanations, news articles, proposals, manuals, accident reports, political analyses, TV commentaries, and magazine ads.

Cause and effect can be used for any of the writer's purposes: to justify or condemn some action; to prove or disprove an idea, belief, or assertion; to explain; to give an account of something; to produce a feeling; to investigate; to draw conclusions.

Insofar as your readers are logical beings, they will be looking for reasons in your writing, especially when you want to inform them or ask them to accept or reject a course of action.

Invention and Cause and Effect

As a topic of invention, cause and effect answers such fundamental questions as Why did it happen? What are its causes? What are its effects? What is its purpose? How is it related causally to something else? In inventing, you follow a sequence of events in time, notice the transference of a force or condition from one thing to another, and attempt to explain these relationships.

Cause and effect is related to narration and to process because all three are concerned with chronological progression. But in cause and effect, you are more interested in the *why* than in the *what* or the *how.*

Cause-and-effect exposition is a special form of exposition that presents a step-by-step description of *associated* sequences of events. Something more than just contiguity is involved in the process. Even though frequently all that you observe is two or more events following each other in time, you reason from your knowledge of other kinds of causal connections that there is some kind of bond holding these events together, and you imagine what this connection might be. Experience teaches you that certain events are always followed by other events, and you ascribe to the sequence the idea of cause and effect.

The average person understands how to use the word *cause*. Ask her or him what a cause is, and the reply will probably be, "Something that makes something else happen." Cause-and-effect themes have a commonsense vocabulary to convey logical relationships that even the average person will have no trouble with:

cause	in	as a result of
effect	by	for this reason
bring about	of	therefore
produce	so	consequently
give reasons for	thus	accordingly
accomplish	since	on account of
originate	due to	owing to
follow from	because	by the agency of
make possible	if	by means of
result from	then	in effect

In addition to characteristic words and phrases, sentences that convey action imply cause-and-effect relationships:

The intruder was killed by a bullet.
Robert smashed the window with a rock.
The wind lifted the edge of the roof and sent it crashing to the ground.
Amy kicked George in the leg.
The leaves changed from a dark green to a bright orange.

In your sentences, you usually attribute some cause to an agent, an instrument, or some agency.

Exercises

1. Probe a cause-and-effect subject by using the questions in this chapter suggested by the topics of invention.

2. Write five thesis sentences for a causal analysis.

3. Discuss in class the cause of an accident which you witnessed or in which you were involved. Discuss the effects of the same accident.

4. Discuss in class your most embarrassing (happiest, saddest, maddest) moment. What caused this embarrassment? What were the effects?

5. Discuss the effects of

   a. watching television late on a school night
   b. no breakfast before school
   c. no meal before heavy drinking
   d. staying outdoors on a freezing night

6. Discuss the causes of a solar eclipse, a rainbow, a flood, bird migration.

The Structure of Cause and Effect

Causal essays tend to fall into two basic types: those in which you proceed from cause to effect and those in which you move from effect to cause.

Cause-and-effect sequences fall into relatively simple paradigms:

Cause-to-Effect Pattern
Introduction (includes thesis)
Cause 1 . . .
Cause 2 . . .
Cause 3 . . .
Cause 4, 5, 6 . . .

Effect . . .
Conclusion (summary and so forth)

Introduction (includes thesis)
Cause . . .
Effect 1 . . .
Effect 2 . . .
Effect 3 . . .
Effect 4, 5, 6 . . .
Conclusion (summary and so forth)

Keep in mind that the numbers of the paradigms refer to sections of the paper and not necessarily to paragraph divisions.

Effect-to-Cause Pattern
Introduction (includes thesis)
Effect 1 . . .
Effect 2 . . .
Effect 3 . . .
Effect 4, 5, 6 . . .
Cause . . .
Conclusion (summary and so forth)

Introduction (includes thesis)
Effect . . .
Cause 1 . . .
Cause 2 . . .
Cause 3 . . .
Cause 4, 5, 6 . . .
Conclusion (summary and so forth)

In composing cause-and-effect essays, you divide an event into the number of *necessary* conditions involved in the event. Naturally, the particular elements you abstract from an event will be determined by your purpose and your interest. If, for example, an adolescent dies from an overdose of drugs, the doctor may rule that the OD was the cause of death. The police, on the other hand, may blame the drug pusher. And parents will search their hearts to see if there was something in their own behavior to contribute to the cause of death. In ascribing a certain cause to an effect, be aware that your purpose determines the way you interpret the effect.

The following cause-and-effect essay, based on an Associated Press news story, is a good example of an essay that moves from cause to effect.

Liquor Prices Could Go Down

Introduction   A few years ago, the United States sold millions of bushels of corn and wheat to the Soviet Union. At that time, some critics advocated that Americans should drink less in order to make more grain available for food. That idea went over like a lead balloon with the liquor industry. They argued that only a small amount of grain, comparatively speaking, goes into the production of hard liquor. Eliminating booze production, they maintained, would make very little difference in the food supply. Now, a few years later, prospects for a record grain production are so good that these critics have been silenced, and liquor consumers may look forward to some relief from the higher prices.

Cause   The Agriculture Department estimates the 1975 corn crop will yield a record 6.05 billion bushels. Farmers are delighted at what they expect to be a record harvest. Already over 177 million bushels of corn have been sold to the Soviet Union, and the Agriculture Department expects corn exports to exceed 1 billion bushels.

Effect 1   One effect of this projected record harvest is expected to be lower prices for whiskey drinkers and drinkers of other kinds of alcoholic spirits, although one industry liquor spokesman maintains that a record grain crop would have a negligible effect on whiskey prices. It would, however, keep prices from going up.

Effect 2   Another effect of a bumper corn crop would be that the cost of livestock grain would go down, thus resulting in lower prices for milk, meat, and poultry.

Conclusion   Whiskey imbibers are being warned, however, not to cheer too soon. Some critics are complaining that the recent grain deal with Russia could send prices skyrocketing again.

This news story is based on a very simple cause-and-effect pattern. The opening paragraph provides the introduction, giving the reader some background concerning fluctuating prices for grain and liquor. The second paragraph states the cause for a possible reduction in liquor and food prices. Paragraphs 3 and 4 give the effects of a bumper grain harvest: lower liquor prices and lower food prices. And the last paragraph concludes with a warning.

Many news stories contain cause-and-effect patterns embedded in the narrative. Headlines such as "Driver is killed as auto overturns and hits an embankment," "Yastrzemski drives in two runs to beat the Detroit Tigers," and "Gunman takes $2 million in gems from London safe-deposit center" are based on cause-and-effect relationships. Many books and magazines present cause-and-effect articles about the dangers of taking heroin, speed, alcohol, or some other drug.

The student paper that follows uses a cause-to-effect pattern of development.

Why Preventative Detention Is Wrong

I recently read that President Nixon and Attorney General John Mitchell had sent a piece of legislation to Congress, modeled after their infamous "D.C. Crime Bill," which would permit the federal government to hold suspects in jail for up to sixty days pending trial. The plan is to prevent crime by incarcerating presumably dangerous criminals, rather than allowing them freedom on bail. In actuality, this measure would thwart justice, not crime, if enacted, through the perversion of our Constitution and some of our most basic legal principles which have long been the hallmark of our system of jurisprudence.

The most flagrant effect which would result from adopting the President's bill would be a major deterioration of the presumption of innocence which has guided criminal proceedings ever since the Star Chamber Court was abolished in the 17th century. Imagine locking a man behind bars for a period of two months *before he has even had a trial!* Whatever happened to the Constitution which guarantees the right to a speedy trial? Or what about the Eighth Amendment which assures the suspect of his right to reasonable bail?

This matter of bail is one long entrenched in our constitutional history. And without exception, the Supreme Court has held time and time again that the only purpose for bail is to assure the appearance of a defendant at trial. In a case where the suspect owns a home in the community, has a job, and appears to be a sound risk in terms of showing up for trial, then a low bail, or none at all, is called for. Where the suspect is likely to run, then a high bail is required. But there is *no* provision in the Constitution for *pre-trial* punishment. We have traditionally believed that it is wiser to see if the accused is *guilty* before inflicting a sentence.

President Nixon would have us believe that with the present backlog of criminal cases on the docket it is dangerous to permit certain people to roam the streets after they have been accused. The obvious answer to this argument is to hire more judges, more court personnel, more prosecuting attorneys in order to speed up the trial progress. It is not at all uncommon for a case to be delayed for several years due to the volume of cases. In comparison, sixty days may not be very long, but for something which has not yet been proven in court, it can well be sixty days too many. We must speed up the process, not file the cases away behind iron bars. The old adage "Justice delayed is justice denied" is all the more critical if someone is rotting in jail.

—Barry

The student paper reprinted below moves in the other direction, from effect to cause.

No one familiar with the four televised Kennedy-Nixon debates during the presidential race in 1960 can deny the effect of television on American politics. The charisma of a candidate has become as important a factor as his political program, thanks to the mass exposure he gets through the medium of television. Nixon, for example, could not compete with John F. Kennedy's charm, dry wit, and warm smile, as they debated on nationwide television in the autumn of Kennedy's presidential victory. Viewers responded to the style of the young Democrat—of the estimated 120,000 Americans who had seen at least one of the four debates, an opinion poll showed that seventy-five percent of those whose vote had been swayed by the television confrontation were influenced in favor of the charismatic senator from Massachusetts. Television had truly come into its own as a major factor in American politics as it exposed the public not only to the political facts but also to the political personalities in a way no other medium could.

Politics is not the only area of American life in which television has had a significant effect. Family life, too, has changed as a result of television. Conversation is a virtually nonexistent form of meaningful communication in many American households, for the family gathers only to eat and to cluster in front of the twenty-six-inch, full-color screen in what is called the living room. Often, even meals are eaten in front of a TV program that is too good to miss, and the evening dinner, traditionally a family gathering accompanied by a discussion of the day's events, is turned into an exercise in futility, as forks grope for nutritious food while eyes remain glued to the screen. Family games, outings, songfests, and reading are abandoned in favor of prime-time fare. Sometimes the only verbal communication two family members will have in a day is an argument over which TV program will reign on the evening's agenda, although the popularity of a second or even third television set is wiping out even this meager contact.

Social customs have also been affected by television. TV dates are common, eliminating the need for any involved verbal contact between those who date, and guests in a household are frequently invited to join the host in viewing a particular show, rather than in socializing by pleasant talk or by some more active form of entertainment such as a game. Indeed, much socializing has been eliminated by television, for it is much easier to sit at home and be amused than to force yourself to get up, make yourself attractive, and go out and amuse others.

Television has affected many varied and seemingly separate areas of American life, from politics to the dinner hour, from education to the crime rate. In 1938, E. B. White wrote, "I believe TV is going to be the test of our modern world. . . . We shall stand or fall by TV—of that I am quite sure." The boob tube, the living room babysitter, the electronic pacifier, whatever you call it, this 20th-century invention has affected the lives of virtually every modern American. It is now up to the American public to realize the significance of these effects and to channel them into more positive currents in American life.

—Sandra

Exercises

1. Select a brief cause-and-effect essay or magazine or newspaper article and do both a linear and a paradigmatic analysis of the essay.

2. Analyze the picture of a magazine ad for cause-and-effect relationships.

3. Write on one of the following:

   a. the causes of inflation
   b. the effects of inflation
   c. the effects of smoking
   d. the effects of taking some drug or hard liquor
   e. the causes of _____
   f. the effects of _____

4. Describe in detail the effects of your first smoke (drink, kiss, lie, or the like).

5. Write an essay on one of the following topics:

   a. likely effects of early marriages
   b. short-term effects of the energy crisis
   c. effects of movie censorship
   d. causes of your attitude toward sex (God, religion, politics, education, or other controversial subject)
   e. moral standards

6. You are a mad scientist. Describe the effects of a diabolical experiment on one of your enemies.

7. Discuss the effects of air (noise, visual) pollution in a place you know well.

8. Discuss the effects that certain television programs (or movies) might have on children.

Persuasion as an Aim:

Induction and Deduction

Chapter 8

*Persuasion as an Aim:
Induction and Deduction*

In the preceding chapters, you have been asked to use a variety of modes of invention and organization in your writing and to consider a variety of aims: informative, persuasive, aesthetic, and expressive. Because persuasion is such an important aim, in this chapter and in the next I want to focus on the kinds of thinking and compositional techniques appropriate to this aim.

Actually, all of the compositional strategies you have learned so far can be used in the service of persuasion. Modes of invention and organization such as analysis, description, exemplification, narration, comparison, analogy, and cause and effect can be used for any of the writer's aims, for any audience, and for any kind of discourse. Traditionally, however, the kinds of logical thinking that go into the making of arguments have been given the names *induction* and *deduction.*

Every day you encounter numerous situations that depend upon persuasion. Advertisers try to get you to buy their products. Politicians solicit your vote. Priests and ministers try to lead you on the path to salvation. Newspaper editorial writers attempt to convince you to vote for or against nuclear power plants. Your friends and neighbors argue with you about anything and everything—religion, politics, nuclear energy, the oil crisis. . . . And you argue back—sometimes convincingly, sometimes ineffectively, usually un-selfconsciously. In your writing, however, a selfconscious attention to the process can be helpful.

Public issues must necessarily be resolved by influencing the beliefs and actions of other people. Skill in argumentation and persuasion can be a means to help you get things done and to combat the evils of doublespeak and propaganda. You might think that all you have to do to get your point across is to be forceful and sincere, but to be persuasive, your arguments have to be presented effectively.

Argumentation is *the giving of reasons to support the truth or falsity of a proposition.* A **proposition** is *a statement upon which an argument is based or from which a conclusion is drawn.* It is a sentence phrased in such a way that it can be the basis of a discussion. It is the thesis of an argument. Think, for a moment, of what such a statement might contain: an opinion, an authoritative decision, a judgment, a sentiment, a conviction, an attitude, a belief, a criticism, an impression.

To write an argument, then, you begin with a proposition. Next you add other sentences to it, and other sentences to these sentences, and you depict the relationships among these sentences in such a way as to lead your readers to accept your conclusions and perhaps to act on them. Your proposition, in other words, must be supported by reasoning and evidence. Otherwise, it stands as an unsupported generalization. **Reasoning** is *thinking in a connected, logical manner by induction or deduction.* It is the drawing of conclusions from observations, facts, or hypotheses. **Evidence** is *the material used to prove your point—facts, ideas, statistics, examples, testimony, and so forth.*

Reasoning by Induction

When you reason inductively, you begin with particular bits and pieces of evidence and then draw a conclusion from this evidence. **Induction** is *reasoning from the particular to the general.* It is coming to a conclusion about all members of a class from examining only a few members of the class. Because the evidence is incomplete and the facts limited, you must "leap" from these facts to a general conclusion.

Induction tells you what to expect. If you reach into a basket of tomatoes and pick out six or seven that are rotten, you might conclude that the rest of the tomatoes are rotten, too. You might be right or you might be wrong. Your conclusion would be *probable,* but the only way you could be certain would be to examine every tomato.

Many of our conclusions are based on an *inductive leap.* We believe that aspirin cures headaches because we've taken aspirin in the past, and indeed aspirin did cure our headaches. Therefore, it is reasonable to believe that aspirin will cure our headaches in the future.

In its logical form, an inductive reasoning process looks like this:

Aspirin cured my headache a year ago.
Aspirin cured my headache six months ago.
Aspirin cured my headache last month.
Aspirin cured my headache two weeks ago.
Therefore, aspirin cures headaches.

Reasoning by Deduction

When you reason deductively, you begin with a general statement as a premise, apply it to a particular instance, and then draw a conclusion from it. **Deduction** is *reasoning from the general to the specific.* It proceeds through steps that comprise what is called a syllogism. A **syllogism** consists of three sentences or propositions. The first two sentences are called premises. The last sentence is called the conclusion. In its traditional form, the syllogism looks like this:

All women enjoy dancing.
Joan is a woman.
Therefore, Joan enjoys dancing.

The conclusion is valid because the reasoning is sound. But it may not necessarily be true. If the premises (sentences 1 and 2) are true, then the conclusion (sentence 3) is true. But a moment's thought will reveal that the major premise ("all women enjoy dancing") is not necessarily true. Therefore, the conclusion may be false.

Inductive reasoning generally takes the form of examples, testimony, analogy, and cause and effect. Deductive reasoning often takes the form of the syllogism and the enthymeme (the sentence form of the syllogism). However, even though you reason to a conclusion inductively, in your writing you can state your conclusion first and then supply reasons for supporting it.

Because of the close relationship that exists between induction and deduction, in this chapter we shall be moving back and forth between the two kinds of thinking. But we will also be looking at a wider range of categories than is ordinarily dealt with in discussions of argumentation. Besides the usual methods of reasoning by induction (examples, testimony, analogy, cause and effect), we will be examining categories such as analysis, description, narration, and comparison, usually associated with expository or literary writing. In the next chapter, we will be dealing almost exclusively with deduction as it relates to the syllogism and the enthymeme.

Arguing by Analysis

In chapter 4, you learned that **analysis** is *the process of dividing anything complex into simple parts.* Besides being a thought process, analysis is also a method of getting ideas as well as a way of organizing those ideas. Although analysis can be used for any of the writer's aims and in any kind of writing, most of the analyses you have looked at thus far have been examples of informative writing. Yet analysis is also an important mode of developing arguments.

In writing an argument, giving features or characteristics or details amplifies the central idea. In using analysis for persuasive purposes, you divide a whole into its component parts. But in writing expository essays, you proceed in much the same manner. Wherein lies the difference? The most obvious difference is in the writer's intention. In persuasive writing, your purpose is to secure conviction or action. In expository writing, your purpose is to inform or instruct. In expository writing, all you have to do to achieve your purpose is to convince your readers of the soundness of your thinking. But in persuasive writing, you must also provide your readers with motives and reasons for believing your assertions. If you want your readers to do something, you've got to ask them to do it: to get out and vote, to fill in a questionnaire, to buy a particular product, to travel to a mountain resort, to fly to Hawaii.

How is this done? Not only by logical reasoning and evidence, but also by *direct command*, by *invitation*, and by *suggestion*. The most effective arguments extend the call for action throughout the text, embedded in the reasoning process, but many persuasive essays get action by calling for it near the end of the discourse. Here are some examples:

The Command
See and drive this great new car today.
Vote for _____.
Ban nuclear energy!
Impeach_____.

And in a more humorous vein:

Repeal inhibition.
Fight air pollution—inhale.
Be alert—the world needs more lerts.
Get high on helium; it's a gas.

The Invitation
We invite you to join us at the Holiday Inn.
We hope you'll make your next cake with Swans Down
Cake Mix.
Please try our coffee today.

The Suggestion
Why not give minorities job preferences?
Your girl will be impressed if you say it with flowers.
You will look so much better if you buy an Arrow shirt.

The direct command makes an urgent appeal to the reader. It uses exhortation to get action. The invitation employs polite and courteous language. It sometimes resembles a social invitation. The suggestion uses implication and inference. Like the invitation, it is courteous, but in addition it makes use of coaxing, flattery, and pleading.

In arguing by analysis, you can use both inductive and deductive thinking. In an inductive analysis, you proceed from the parts to the whole. In a deductive analysis, you go from broader to narrower elements.

The paradigmatic structure of analytic arguments is very similar to that of expository essays, except that the thesis is a proposition to be argued:

Analysis Pattern 1
Introduction (includes proposition to be argued)
Feature 1 (or detail 1)
Feature 2 (or detail 2)
Feature 3 (or detail 3)
Feature 4 (or detail 4)
Feature 5, 6, 7 (or detail 5, 6, 7) . . .
Conclusion (includes call for action)

Analysis Pattern 2
Introduction (includes proposition to be argued)
Cluster of features (as evidence)
Cluster of features
Cluster of features
Cluster of features
Conclusion (includes call for action)

An inductive pattern is also possible. Here is an example of an inductive pattern in a slightly less abstract form:

Analysis Pattern 3
This political candidate has this qualification.
This political candidate has this qualification.
This political candidate has this qualification.
This political candidate has this qualification.
This political candidate has outstanding qualifications.
Vote for him/her.

The following is a good example of a persuasive essay that uses inductive reasoning toward a conclusion:

> If you've never driven a car with front-wheel drive before, you're in for a new and rewarding experience. GM's new Chevrolet Citation, Pontiac Phoenix, Oldsmobile Omega, and Buick Skylark are front-wheel-drive cars that will be GM's frontrunners for the '80s.
>
> They all have *transverse-mounted engines*. Because the engine sits sideways, overall length is reduced, yet each car has plenty of room for passengers and luggage. A 4-cylinder engine is standard, but a V-6 is also available.

Each car has a *MacPherson Strut front suspension* that helps create a roomier passenger compartment.

Each has *rack-and-pinion steering* for quick, easy response.

All have *front disc brakes* with a new low-drag design with audible wear indicators.

All have *radial tires* in a new design, with a special rubber compound to lower rolling resistance even more than conventional radials.

Each has a maintenance-free *Delco Freedom battery* that never needs water.

Each has maintenance-free *wheel bearing assemblies,* completely sealed, preset for precise clearance, and lubed for life.

These are just some of the *outstanding standard features* that you get on these exciting new front-wheel-drive cars. Drive one at your GM dealers today and draw your own conclusions.

—adapted from a General Motors ad

This essay uses an inductive chain of reasoning very much like that exemplified in analysis pattern 3. Each paragraph highlights a feature of the new GM front-wheel-drive cars. As the evidence mounts, paragraph by paragraph, the reader is led into *(induced)* the generalization in the final paragraph. The essay concludes with a call to action.

Advertisers make extensive use of the mode of analysis to convince their readers of the relative superiority of their products. In an inductive arrangement, the ad opens with attributes of the product, with features, facts, or other proof, and then shows how these selling points are beneficial to the reader. This inductive sequence gains conviction because it piles up facts about a product, explains its qualities, and then leads the reader to conclude that the product has benefits from which he or she can profit.

Arguing by Description

Description is *a mode of analysis,* and like analysis it can be found in any kind of writing, to achieve any of the writer's aims. In literary writing, where there may be long stretches of description, it tends to follow a spatial pattern. Often, however, it is subordinate to the mode of narration. But in persuasive writing, descriptive elements and details are arranged largely in the order of observation.

A good example of descriptive reasoning for persuasive purposes can be found in magazine advertising. As in magazine ads that use a kind of abstract analysis of features to win conviction, magazine ads that use concrete sensory details present descriptive material in the form of product attributes or benefits. Advertisers present this material in such a way as to differentiate their brand from competitive brands and to convince their readers that the quality of their merchandise is consistent with the price.

In advertising, descriptive copy is often called human-interest copy because it appeals primarily to the senses and the emotions, and the reader's response to it is instinctive. Consequently, persuasive writing that uses description relies heavily on suggestion rather than deliberation. If all of our actions were based on deliberate choices, there would be little place in persuasive writing for description. But human beings are not always logical. They are also moved by instincts and feelings of hunger, anger, fear, and desire.

Writers who use description for persuasive purposes often give conflicting advice about the kinds of techniques best suited to win conviction from their readers. According to some writers, vague, general words such as *beautiful, magnificent,* and *luxurious* have little human-interest value. They claim that the best descriptions individualize the person or object to be described. Therefore, the writer should fill his or her writing with concrete and vivid sensations of sight, smell, taste, and touch. Other writers claim that description need not always be concrete and specific to be good. Sometimes certain objects are difficult to describe precisely. Other times, it seems better to give the observer's reactions to the perceived object than to give a precise description of the object. Whatever may be true in other kinds of writing, in persuasive writing a combination of suggestive and concrete description can be effective.

Here is an example of a magazine ad that uses a combination of concrete and suggestive description to achieve its purpose:

Caramel-Vanilla: A Golden Merger of Two of Nature's Richest Flavors

We've blended the taste of luscious vanilla with creamy caramel and now have a deliciously mellow cordial with a rich flavor that's more than equal to its parts. Sip it straight, blend it half-and-half with fresh cold milk, or be creative and experiment. It's delicious fun.

And its name, Caramella, is as soft and mellow as its taste. Look for the distinctive white bottle from Arrow.

The headline serves the function of a thesis sentence: "Caramel-Vanilla [is] a golden merger of two of nature's richest flavors." This sentence organizes the descriptive details that follow by repeating the idea of the blending of ingredients in successive sentences. The word *caramel-vanilla* in the headline, which is a compound, introduces this idea, and then the idea is repeated in the words *merger, two, blended, Caramella, more than equal to its parts,* and *blend.*

Within this framework, the ad uses a combination of concrete and suggestive details to convince the reader to buy the product. The concrete details appeal directly to the senses: *mellow* ("soft, sweet, juicy, full-flavored"), *creamy* ("rich in cream"), *caramella* ("caramel and vanilla"). The suggestive details direct the reader to feel a certain way about the product: *delicious* ("pleasing, enjoyable"), *luscious* ("pleasant"), *rich* ("excessive proportion of pleasing ingredients"), *distinctive.* There is also an effective use of sound devices to reinforce the idea that Caramella is a pleasant experience: *creamy caramel,* de*liciously mellow, Caramella,* soft and *mellow.* There is no direct call for action at the end of the ad. Instead, the act of description, with its appeal to the reader's sensations and feelings, makes an effective selling appeal.

Although magazine advertising may seem to be a specialized kind of persuasive writing, politicians, businessmen and -women, and religious organizations have borrowed techniques from copywriters to sell ideas, goods, and services. You can learn much from ad writers about how to use description for persuasive purposes.

Exercises

1. Bring to class a magazine ad that uses the mode of analysis to secure conviction (for example, car ads, stereo ads, ads for soap, and so on). Discuss the chain of reasoning. Is it inductive or deductive? Is the argument convincing?

2. Bring to class for discussion a food ad, a perfume ad, a cosmetic ad, a clothing ad, or a jewelry ad that uses description for persuasive purposes. What is the method of organization: inductive? deductive? What is the order of impressions? What is the diction like? Is the selling appeal explicit or implicit?

3. Describe your home in such a way that you make it appealing for someone who wants to swap homes for a summer vacation. The form of writing can be a letter or an ad.

4. You work for Japan Air Lines. Write an ad to get people to take a trip to the Orient.

5. Write an ad describing a Las Vegas holiday for two.

6. Describe the benefits of a pleasure cruise to South America or Europe.

7. Using the mode of description, write a persuasive essay to get your reader to do one of the following: see an exhibit; visit a special place; reevaluate a song, a painting, or another work of art; visit a place of historical interest; avoid a certain place.

Arguing From Example

Reasoning by example is *the typical inductive form of reasoning.* When using this method of developing ideas in persuasive writing, you cite a series of particular examples, all of which display a certain relationship to one another, and then draw a general conclusion from them.

The following ad for Coach Leatherware uses this process effectively. The illustration is simple. It consists of four pictures of leather bags or purses, arranged in a rectangular shape, two pictures at the top and two at the bottom. The text reads as follows:

Example 1: This is a Coach bag. You can get it at Goldwater's.
Example 2: This is a Coach bag. You can get it at Bonwit Teller.
Example 3: This is a Coach bag. You can get it at Dayton's Oval Room.

Example 4:   This is a Coach bag. You can get it at Garfinckel's.
Conclusion: Coach bags are sold in the nicest stores.

Here is an ad for Aetna Life and Casualty that uses a similar chain of reasoning:

> A truck without brake lights is hit from behind. For "psychic damages" to the driver, because his pride was hurt when his wife had to work, *a jury awards $480,000 above and beyond his medical bills and wage losses.*
>
> A 67-year old factory worker loses an arm on the job. His lawyer argues that he should receive wages for all the remaining years of his life expectancy. He had been earning about $10,000 a year. The jury awards him a sum equal to almost $89,000 a year.
>
> Then there's the one . . . but *you* can probably provide the next example. Most of us know hair-raising stories of windfall awards won in court. Justified claims should be compensated, of course. Aetna's point is that it is time to look hard at what windfall awards are costing.
>
> What can we do? Several things:
>
> We can stop assessing "liability" where there really *was* no fault—and express our sympathy for victims through other means.
>
> We can ask juries to take into account a victim's *own* responsibility for his losses. And we can urge that awards realistically reflect the actual loss suffered—that they be a fair *compensation,* but not a reward.
>
> Insurers, lawyers, judges—each of us shares some blame for this mess. But it is you, the public, who can best begin to clean it up. Don't underestimate your own influence. Use it, as we are trying to use ours.
>
> Aetna wants insurance to be affordable.

Although reasoning by example is generally inductive, for purposes of writing persuasive essays you can present your conclusion in the beginning of your essay and then follow it up with representative examples to support your conclusions.

This ad for Texaco uses a single extended example to make its point:

> Texaco is working to get more than oil out of the ground.
> Texaco doesn't just look for new sources of oil, it also looks for new ways to conserve the oil we already have.

For example, Texaco has developed a way to produce one of the raw materials for making chemical fertilizer. This method, which is a coal gasification process, uses coal instead of natural gas or petroleum liquids.

Recently, Texaco's coal gasification process was selected by the Tennessee Valley Authority for use in its National Fertilizer Development Center in Alabama.

In the future, this process may be widely used and America will be able to save some of the natural gas and petroleum liquids which it so desperately needs.

This coal gasification process is just one example of how Texaco puts its resources to work for you.

In reasoning by example, try to avoid common weaknesses by keeping in mind the following advice:

1. *Cite a reasonable number of examples.*   In arguments using examples, there is a danger of generalizing from too few examples. It is difficult, however, to determine how many examples are necessary to lend force to an argument. Sometimes a single long example can be effective.
2. *Cite typical examples.*   If you select examples that are unusual or exceptional, you might draw misleading conclusions from them. Your examples should be representative.
3. *Account for negative examples.*   In generalizing from examples, you might come across negative examples that do not support your conclusion. Nevertheless, you must account for these negative instances, perhaps by showing that they are not significant or that they are exceptions.

Hasty Generalization

A **hasty generalization** is *one that is based on insufficient evidence.* The problem arises when the writer tries to extend his or her conclusion beyond the examples on which it is based. All arguments of this kind leap from the known to the unknown. But the difficulty lies in justifying this leap with too few examples, with the lack of typical examples, or with the failure to account for negative examples. Is it true, for instance, that "Americans are the most waste-ful people on earth"?

Sweeping Generalization

A **sweeping generalization** is *one that needs to be qualified* by words and phrases such as *some, a few, many, most, usually,* and *sometimes.* Advertisers use sweeping generalizations extensively to make claims of exclusivity (note my use of the sweeping word *extensively*), as in the following examples:

> No other product lets you bake so many things so quickly.
> Nothing performs like a Saab.
> Did you know that no leading oil tastes lighter than Mazola 100% corn oil?

In your own writing, you will be more effective if your generalizations are less sweeping:

> All politicians are dishonest. (sweeping)
> *Most* politicians are dishonest. (still too sweeping)
> *Many* politicians are dishonest. (less sweeping)
> *A few* politicians are dishonest. (you're on safer ground)

Exercises

1. Analyze the Aetna ad. Besides the inductive use of examples, the ad uses other methods of development. What are they? Are they effective?

2. Write an inductive argument supported by examples.

3. Evaluate these generalizations:

   a. Children who read are not dropouts.

b. The best American-made movies are the ones the major studios have absolutely no part in making.

c. All Democrats are liberal.

d. Most Republicans are conservative.

e. Nothing can be perfectly safe. Should we ban automobiles, cigarettes, and bathtubs? The biggest danger of nuclear power is that we won't have enough.

f. Most women are conceited.

g. You mean you wear contact lenses, too? You're the fourth person with blue eyes I've met recently who wears contact lenses. Blue-eyed people must have weak eyes.

h. Dan had his wallet stolen downtown. Carol lost her purse. If I go downtown, I'll be robbed.

i. I asked everyone in class if he or she smoked grass. Not one said yes. Marijuana is not used in this school.

j. This morning I got a flat tire. An hour later I got a speeding ticket. On the way home I got into an accident. Today sure was a lousy day.

Critical Review

The **critical review** makes widespread use of all of the kinds of reasoning we have discussed thus far, in the form of features, characteristics, particulars, and examples. The writer studies a movie, a TV show, a book, a record album, a painting, or a piece of sculpture and comes to a conclusion about it. In the review, the writer cites particular passages from a book in the form of examples, or the descriptive features of a movie or a painting, and uses them as evidence for the conclusion.

The chain of reasoning in the critical review can be inductive or deductive. If you begin with particular features that account for your conclusion, then the pattern is inductive. If, however, you begin with a judgment about the work and then support your judgment with evidence, then the pattern is deductive. The details of the analysis constitute the body of the review.

Here is one pattern that you might find useful in writing a critical review:

1. In the opening paragraph, *identify the work you are reviewing* (title, genre, name of artist, singer, director, writer, and so on). For example: *"Youth Terror: The View from Behind the Gun* is a disturbing TV documentary on teenage crime"; *"The Stories of John Cheever,* published by Knopf, is a collection of sixty-one short stories dating from 1947."

2. In the same paragraph, in a sentence or two, *give an overall evaluation of the work.* (*"Last Embrace* is a film in which a stylish director and a superb cast . . . do their best to triumph over a script that lacks witty writing and genuinely suspenseful substance.")

3. If necessary, in the first or second paragraph, *give your reader any background information necessary for understanding your review.*

4. *Give a brief summary of the contents of the work you are reviewing,* as objectively and as accurately as you can.

5. *Cite evidence, in the form of details, to support your earlier judgment* of the work. Point out specific strengths and weaknesses.

6. *End* your review *by restating your earlier evaluation, by making a recommendation* to your reader, or *by coming to a significant conclusion* about the work.

The review that follows uses most of the steps outlined above:

Norma Rae is a warm-hearted story about the realities of working and living in a small Southern town in America. This film was directed by Martin Ritt. The screenplay was written by Irving Ravetch and Harriet Frank.

Norma Rae is an account of a young Southern woman (played by Sally Field) who has little education and a routine job at a local cotton mill. She has two children and no husband. Her life changes when an educated union organizer (Ron Leibman) comes to the mill from New York to unionize the workers. He breaks through her suspicions and convinces her to help him organize a union in a union-busting mill. She gets into trouble at the mill, and when it appears that her children might hear about her sexual past, she confides in them and in her new husband (Beau Bridges), who feels she is neglecting him and the children because of union work.

The strengths of this movie are considerable. Sally Field plays a tough, vulnerable, and high-spirited woman with a somewhat questionable sexual past. Yet she has a moral spirit that is awakened by Reuben's friendship and their attempt to organize the workers. Ron Leibman, as Reuben, is a New York intellectual who wins out over small-town suspicion and prejudice. He reveals himself in his dealings with Norma Rae and the mill workers to be sensitive, witty and human.

As the story of a woman who copes with adversity and who realizes her moral potential, the film is a success. Its weaknesses are the result of a plot that is somewhat stereotyped and didactic (Norma Rae causing the machines in the mill to stop, company goons to the attack, the mill workers rallying round, the triumph of justice) and a story that takes too long to get going. The moviegoer is not quite sure if the main interest is to be in the possible romantic attraction between Norma Rae and Reuben (left undeveloped) or in the ordinary lives of the mill workers.

If the story is weak, the acting of Sally Field and Ron Leibman, and the characters they portray, make this a movie worth seeing. We need more movies that depict the everyday trials and tribulations of real people.

Exercises

1. Although the above review follows a logical plan of development, at times it makes generalizations about the movie without sufficient support. For class discussion, isolate all of the general assertions and then determine if there is enough evidence to support these assertions.

2. For discussion, bring to class a review of a movie you have recently seen. Do you like the review? Do you agree with the conclusions? Does the reviewer offer evidence for the evaluation?

3. Compare two reviews of the same movie, record album, play, TV show, or novel.

4. Write a review of a movie, a TV show, a book, a painting, a record album, a new building that has distinctive architectural features, a play, or a poem.

5. Reviews can be about a variety of subjects. Bring to class, for discussion, several of the following: a book review, a movie review, an art review, a TV review, a music review, a dance review, a theater review, a cuisine review, or a travel review.

Arguing by Narration

In **arguing by narration,** *you present your narrative in such a way that it serves as an inductive example to support your conclusion.* Narration as a mode of developing ideas has great human-interest appeal for readers. The narrative mode is intensely dramatic and dynamic. Because it is filled with action, it leads naturally to inducing action in others.

In using this mode of persuasion, you try to get your readers to identify with the characters in the narrative or with the situation being dramatized. This attempt to get your readers to identify with the characters or the situation is an important part of the persuasive appeal.

Narratives in argumentation can be of various kinds: factual narratives, fictional narratives, monologues, or dialogues. **Factual narratives** are *based on actual events,* and even when some liberty is taken with the names and places, the situation must be recognized as one that could take place in everyday life. **Fictional narratives** are *invented stories whose content is largely produced by the imagination.* However, a part of the content may be based on fact.

The following ad is a good example of a fictional narrative. The illustration depicts a man looking wistfully through a store window at a Steinway piano:

The Man Who Thought He Couldn't Own a Steinway

To him it had always been "the only piano."

Yet a little voice in the back of his head kept whispering, "You can't afford it."

Then one day he sharpened a pencil, quieted the voice in the back of his head, and did some serious figuring.

To his surprise, he discovered that the Steinway was not too much more expensive than the piano he'd been considering. Which didn't have the tone of a Steinway. Or the Steinway touch. It didn't have Steinway's Hexagrip Wrestplank. Or Steinway's Diaphramatic Soundboard. Or any of the exclusive features that makes a Steinway feel and sound like a Steinway.

"I'm being penny-wise but pound-foolish," he cried. So he bought the Steinway he's always wanted, which he and his wife and family are all enjoying.

He has only one regret. "I should have done it years ago," he says.

For more information, please write to John H. Steinway, 109 West 57th Street, New York 10019.

Monologues are *narratives in which the talk is by a single person.* The advantage of using a monologue instead of a fully developed story is that it allows a single character to act as a spokesperson for the writer. It is important in this kind of writing that the speaker talk with a believable voice.

The following ad for Timberland boots uses monologue copy very effectively. The illustration depicts an old man from the country sitting in the cab of his truck, with his feet extended from the cab. Naturally, he has on Timberland boots.

> "It was two of those fellers from the city come up the road in a big green car, asked me if I wanted some new boots. I didn't. Already had boots, had 'em for seven years. But they talked and we drank some, and then we looked at the boots some, and I tried 'em on. Now, I have to say, they did seem to have my size. So I walked 'em about for maybe a week, and once I went over and stood in Orville Wade's creek, just to see if they were waterproof, which they were. When those boys came back from the city, this is what I said. One, I said thank you for the fine boots, which are warm and dry as a hen's bottom. Two, I'd like a pair of 13 wides for Cousin Luther, double wide on the left foot where the tractor run it over."

> TIMBERLAND.   A whole line of fine leather boots that cost plenty, and should.

Dialogues are *narratives that have at least two speakers.* In writing dialogues, use dialogue tags such as "said he" and "she said" sparingly to avoid monotony.

The dialogue reprinted below, taken from a Whirlpool ad, moves inductively from the telephone conversation to the conclusion and selling appeal at the end of the ad:

How One Family Got Their Laundry Done Over the Phone (Based on an Actual Call)

(telephone rings)

Cool-Line Consultant: Whirlpool Cool-Line. May I help you?

Man: I certainly hope so. I rush home from work, gobble down dinner, pack the kids in the wagon, and head out to pick up our new Whirlpool washer. Then back home, hook it all up, and . . . nothing.

Consultant: Nothing?

Man: Absolutely zotz. Our four-year-old can make the door open and close, but that's all. So now, the store's closed, my wife's really steamed, and I'm not too thrilled myself. Now what are you gonna do about it?

Consultant: Our Cool-Line service is here to help get things working for you. Let's run through a quick checklist. First—now, don't get mad—did you plug it in?

Man: We're not that dense.

Consultant: Both water lines hooked up and the water turned on?

Man: Of course.

Consultant: And you set the dial to regular wash and pulled out the control knob?

Man: Look, the washer really doesn't work! Might take the repairman a whole day to fix it.

Consultant: Might take just a few minutes. You see, Whirlpool appliances are designed to make servicing as quick and easy as possible. But before you call for service, let me ask you one more question.

Man: Shoot.

Consultant: Why did you buy a new washer? What was wrong with the old one?

Man: It was really on the fritz. Blowing fuses and stuff. The service guy said it was hopeless.

Consultant: Is there any chance that old washer blew a fuse one last time without your knowing it? Will you check?

Man: Oh my aching. . . . hang on. *(minutes later)* This is embarrassing. All we needed was a new fuse. I'm sorry I hassled you.

Consultant: Sorry you had trouble. Glad we could help.

Man: Hey, thanks again.

This is the kind of two-way communication we've been having on our Whirlpool Cool-Line service for the past eleven years. It's just one example of the continuing concern we have for our customers who purchase Whirlpool appliances.

If you ever have a question or problem with your Whirlpool appliance, call our toll-free 24-hour Cool-Line service at 800–253–1301.

Appeal to Pity

The **appeal to pity** is *an emotional appeal,* often using the mode of narration combined with description, *in which the writer attempts to persuade his or her readers to accept a conclusion on the basis* *of pity or sympathy.* A good example of the appeal to pity is the ever-recurring situation in which a student asks a teacher to change a grade, saying that he or she will flunk out of school or lose a scholarship unless a higher grade is given.

An appeal to pity is not necessarily a logical fallacy. A relevant appeal is one that addresses an issue which *by its nature* arouses sympathy. If, for example, a charitable organization makes a plea for money in order to aid needy children and shows a picture of a starving, wretched child, this strategy is bound to evoke an emotional response in the reader. The child's wretched condition *is* the issue. Therefore, the emotional appeal is appropriate. If, however, the appeal to pity fails to touch on the issue, as in the case of the student who receives low grades because of poor performance, then the appeal is irrelevant.

Here is an appeal designed to get sponsors for needy children in India, Brazil, Taiwan (Formosa), Mexico, and the Philippines, which appeared in *Time* magazine several years ago:

She Needs Your Love

Little Mie-Wen in Formosa already knows many things . . . the gnawing of hunger . . . the shivering of fear . . . the misery of being unwanted.

But she has never known love. Her mother died when she was born. Her father was poor—and didn't want a girl child. So Mie-Wen has spent her baby years without the affection and security every child craves.

Your love can give Mie-Wen, and children just as needy, the privileges you would wish for your own child.

Through Christian Children's Fund you can sponsor one of these youngsters. We use the word *sponsor* to symbolize the bond of love that exists between you and the child.

The cost? Only $12 a month. Your love is demonstrated in a practical way because your money helps with nourishing meals . . . medical care . . . warm clothing . . . education . . . understanding housemothers. . . .

Little Mie-Wen and children like her need your love—won't you help? Today?

Exercises

1. The Steinway piano ad appeared in *Harper's* in 1977. Discuss the relation to the intended audience. Is there a conflict in the story? Who are the characters? What is the diction like? How does the persuasive appeal work?

2. Does the voice of the speaker in the Timberland ad seem believable? Examine the ad closely. What is the language like? Pick out dialect features, words and phrases, or other stylistic devices that characterize the speaker. Is the ad convincing?

3. How would you characterize the customer in the Whirlpool ad? What is his language like? Does the language of the consultant seem as if it were part of the conversation of the actual telephone call? Is this ad persuasive?

4. Bring to class examples of writing that use narration for persuasive purposes. Try to find examples of each type: factual narratives, fictional narratives, monologues, and dialogues. Then discuss how the narrative mode is used in the service of persuasion.

5. Write an argument, using the mode of narration.

6. Write an essay in which you use an appeal to pity as the basis of your argument.

Arguing From Authority

When you argue from **authority,** you include in your argument *statements from an expert in some particular field.* A mere assertion, such as "Everybody knows that . . . ," is not enough. You should name the authority, quote his or her exact words, or paraphrase them.

The statement of the authority may take the form of a letter of recommendation, a quotation, a testimonial, an opinion poll, a best-seller list, a critical statement about a book or a movie, or the testimony of a witness at a trial. The logical structure of an argument by authority consists simply of repeating the words of the expert. A more sophisticated form of argument by authority is that in which the statement of the expert becomes the premise of a deductive form of reasoning.

You must often rely on the opinions of others because you don't have firsthand evidence yourself, or because such evidence is difficult to obtain. You also draw on these opinions because the experts who offer them have special training and experience in a particular field and are thus more qualified to make judgments in that field than is the average person.

Authorities can be of various kinds. There is the *prestige authority*, whose fame is known to the audience. He or she may or may not be an expert. There is the *expert authority*, who has special knowledge and experience. There is the *nonexpert authority*, who has had no special training or experience. There is the *lay authority*, the common man or woman who constitutes the majority of people, whose opinion is solicited *because it is typical.*

The **testimonial** is *an effective form of arguing from authority in which a real person gives a sincere statement about a product or service.* The people are real in the sense that they are not fictitious, but they may be professional models rather than actual users of the product.

Here is a testimonial, in the form of a monologue, of a Head and Shoulders shampoo ad. The speaker is a young woman, seated in a chair, with a magazine opened before her and a bottle of Head and Shoulders dandruff shampoo prominently displayed in the foreground. The ad appeared in *Mademoiselle* magazine in March 1977. The text reads as follows:

> I never tried a dandruff shampoo. I just sort of ignored my occasional itches and flakes. After all, my hair had bounce and shine and was very delicate. And since I washed my hair an awful lot, I really wanted a mild shampoo.
>
> Then my best friend (who has gorgeous hair, by the way) told me about Head & Shoulders. She said I'd love the fresh smell, the thick, rich lather. And it would leave even my baby fine hair soft and shiny, while controlling dandruff at the same time. She told me Head & Shoulders was the only shampoo she used.
>
> I sure am glad I listened to her. Head & Shoulders is everything she said it was. You can see for yourself how wonderfully shiny

my hair is. And not a worry about those itches and flakes. Now I wouldn't trust my hair to any shampoo but Head & Shoulders.

It is difficult to determine the age of the young woman in the illustration. She could either be a high school student, perhaps a senior, or a college student. Not only is she young looking, but also she uses characteristic phrases such as *sort of, awful lot,* and *sure am glad* that a teenager might use.

It is also difficult to tell if the young woman in the ad is an actual user of the product or if she is a model. She is not identified by name, nor are her words included in quotations. Perhaps we would be justified in accepting this testimonial as a fictional narrative.

Many testimonials use *celebrities* to endorse products. People like to look at pictures of celebrities in magazine ads and to read about them. The extent to which testimonials from celebrities are effective is in direct proportion to the extent to which the reader believes the endorser actually has knowledge of the product he or she is credited with using.

The following testimonial by Carol Lawrence for General Foods International Coffees is a good example of the type.

Carol Lawrence Presents Orange Cappuccino

"I love Italy. I love oranges. I love coffee. I suppose that's why I love everything about Orange Cappuccino.

"Of all the countries I've visited, I've always had a special affection for Italy, land of good food, good art, and lots of my good relatives.

"So it wasn't surprising how much I enjoyed Orange Cappuccino. This flavor from General Foods International Coffees, inspired by Italian Cappuccino, is a delightful treat.

"It has a creamy brown color and a delicate aroma. Yet it's a wonderfully full-bodied coffee with an extra note of flavor: the enticing taste and bouquet of lively orange.

"Orange Cappuccino has such a satisfying flavor I drink it the way the Italians drink their own Cappuccino—in a relaxed and unhurried way. As you know, Rome wasn't built in a day."

Argument from authority frequently takes the form of *massed evidence* or *group authority*. **Massed evidence** is *a large collection of facts or quotations of the same kind, with little explanation or comment.* Massed evidence is used in magazine advertisements, on book jackets, and in movie ads. One ad for Woody Allen's film *Manhattan* consisted entirely of quotations such as these:

> *"Manhattan* is inspired! One of Allen's most brilliant movies!"— Gene Shalit *(Today)*, NBC–TV
>
> *"Manhattan* deserves a stream of bravos! I can't urge you strongly enough to see *Manhattan.*"—Rona Barrett, ABC–TV
>
> "A masterpiece! A perfect blend of style, substance, humor, and humanity!"—Richard Schickel, *Time*

Recently, while I was flying to Colorado on Frontier Airlines, I happened to run across these massed quotations in a Frontier Airlines magazine:

Frontier. For the Long Stretch

"You allow an amount of legroom that I thought had disappeared years ago."—B. W. McPherson, Huntsville

"I especially enjoyed the roominess offered in your seating arrangement."—J. W. Moeller, Wichita

"Thanks, Frontier, for your legroom, good food, and friendly service— don't change it."—C. Schuld, Ft. Collins

"We wish to compliment you on the roominess of the aircraft."— Mr. & Mrs. R. O. Zincke, St. Louis

"Frontier is definitely far superior to other airlines. Thank you for being you."—K. Bolles, Denver

FRONTIER AIRLINES: First-class comfort at coach prices.

Although there is a sense in which testimonials prove nothing, they have great psychological appeal. First, they present the point of view of the user of a product or service. Second, people tend to believe a statement if it comes from an authority. Third, people want to associate themselves with others whom they like or admire.

Fallacious Appeals to Authority

In the writing of arguments, the fallacious appeal to authority can take several forms: citing an authority in one field (for instance, Reggie Jackson in baseball) when deciding a question in a completely different field (automobiles); citing an all-inclusive or vague authority ("Experts agree," "Everyone knows"); citing authorities that may be outdated (such as quoting from an old science book); citing authorities that are biased; citing authorities who may have been paid for their testimony.

Here are some questions that you might ask to determine if the appeal to authority is valid:

1. *Is the argument you are preparing really a matter for authority?*

2. *Is the authority an expert on this subject (rather than on some other subject)?*

3. *Is the authority prestigious? What positions does he or she hold? What kind of training and degrees does he or she have? Publications, awards, or grants?*

4. *Is the authority reliable?*

5. *Is the authority prejudiced? Is he or she influenced by self-interest? Does he or she represent a special interest group?*

Exercises

1. Over the past few years, cigarette advertisers have switched from the green-world archetype, where the Salem smoker takes his girl, to testimonials. Bring to class a group of ads for Vantage, Salem, or Winston cigarettes, and discuss the effectiveness or lack of effectiveness of the testimonials. Does the endorsement come from real people? How can you tell? Is the voice authentic? Compare the language of the various ads. Is the language similar?

2. Bring to class for discussion ads that use celebrities to sell a product.

3. In celebrity ads, there ought to be some kind of association between the celebrity and the product. Consider the following: Elizabeth Ashley for Je Suis skin fragrance, Redd Foxx for Teachers Scotch, Reggie Jackson and Wilt Chamberlain for Volkswagen, Farrah Fawcett-Majors for Wella Balsam shampoo, Catherine Deneuve for Chanel, Yul Brynner for Lauder's Scotch, Lola Falana for Hanes pantyhose, Florence Henderson for Wesson oil. If possible, bring to class the original ads. Are the ads convincing? Is the voice of the celebrity authentic? Is there a proper association between celebrity and product? Is any of the celebrities an authority for the product?

4. Bring to class some examples of massed evidence or group authority for discussion.

5. Bring to class examples of best-seller lists, best popular albums, and so forth. Discuss their use as arguments from authority.

6. Proverbs, maxims, and wise sayings are a form of argument from authority. Discuss their uses to win arguments in everyday life. For example, did your parents ever use them on you? Have you ever heard politicians use them?

7. A friend is applying for a job and has given your name as a reference. Write a complimentary letter of recommendation for that friend. Now imagine that the friend has personal habits that would make you hesitate in writing a letter. Write the letter anyway, but qualify it in such a way as to point out the friend's shortcomings, but without jeopardizing the friend's chance for a job.

8. Write an argument, using some form of authority to support your argument. It can be in the form of an essay, a letter to the editor, or a magazine ad.

Arguing by Comparison

In **reasoning by comparison,** *you state a resemblance between two things and then draw a conclusion from that resemblance.* When you argue by comparison, you present two units of thought to your reader and then point out how one is different from, or superior to, or more desirable than, the other:

Spanish Olives: How To Tell the Original From the Reproduction

The olive on the left is a true-blue Spanish green olive. The olive on the right just looks like one.

The olive on the left was grown in Spain, where the dry climate and mineral-rich soil help an olive ripen to its tangiest best. There's no telling where the olive on the right was grown.

The olive on the left was treated with meticulous care. By people who learned long ago that a bruised olive hurts business. As for the olive on the right, you really can't be sure how it was treated.

How do you tell them apart? Simple. Just read the label.

The olive on the left comes in a jar with the Spanish Olive Man symbol on it. The olive on the right doesn't.

So now you can be sure of the green olive you're getting, before you lay down your hard-earned green for it.

This ad for Spanish olives was taken from *McCall's* magazine, October 1977. Because there are so many ads in magazines, a successful ad has to grab the reader's attention immediately and then attempt to gain conviction. The illustration is the means of getting attention in this ad. It consists of a picture of two green olives, juxtaposed against a background of dark blue shading into royal blue and then gray.

The writer of this ad uses a simple point-by-point comparison pattern. Never mind that this paradigm has been used repeatedly. It is effective *because* it is conventional. The very shape of the comparison pattern has persuasive force. I am convinced that when the reader finishes this ad, he or she is persuaded of the relative superiority of one product over the other on the basis of the reasoning process alone, for if you look carefully at the evidence within the process, you come away with the impression that there are very few facts on which to base a buying decision. Isolated from their context, the "facts" look like this:

The Olive on the Left	*The Olive on the Right*
true-blue Spanish green olive grown in Spain	looks like one
	no telling where the olive on the right was grown
treated with meticulous care	can't be sure how it was treated
comes in a jar with the Spanish Olive Man symbol on it	doesn't [come in a jar with the Spanish Olive Man symbol on it]

In using comparison as a mode in developing arguments, many writers find it natural to consider *both sides of a question.* Is the subject under discussion good or bad, desirable or undesirable? Use the **pro-and-con method of comparison** to present a balanced view of a subject. The process allows you to move from a narrow or one-sided view of a subject to a larger perspective. You begin by stating one side of the question, then contrast this view with a counterstatement, moving back and forth until you come to a conclusion.

You can see the process at work in the following article by Isaac Asimov, taken from the *TV Guide* of December 14, 1974:

UFOs: Are They Visitors From Space—or Unreliable False Observations?

When most people think about flying saucers or, as they are more austerely called, "unidentified flying objects" (UFOs), they think of them as spaceships coming from outside Earth, and manned by intelligent beings.

Is there any chance of this? Do the "little green men" really exist? There are arguments pro and con.

Pro.   There is, according to the best astronomical thinking today, a strong chance that life is very common in the universe. Our own galaxy, containing over a hundred billion stars, is only one of perhaps a hundred billion galaxies.

Current theories about how stars are formed make it seem likely that planets are formed also, so that every star may have planets about it. Surely some of those planets would be like Earth in chemistry and temperature.

Current theories about how life got its start make it seem that any planet with something like Earth's chemistry and temperature would be sure to develop life. One reasonable estimate advanced by an astronomer was that there might be as many as 640,000,000 planets in our galaxy alone that are Earth-like and that bear life.

But on how many of these planets is there intelligent life? We can't say, but suppose that only one of a million life-bearing planets develops intelligent life forms and that only one out of 10 of these develops a technological civilization more advanced than our own. There might still be as many as 100 different advanced civilizations in our galaxy, and perhaps a hundred more in every other galaxy. Why shouldn't some of them have reached us?

Con.   Assuming there are 100 advanced civilizations in our own galaxy and that they are evenly spread throughout the galaxy, the nearest one would be about 10,000 light-years away. Even assuming coverage of that distance at the fastest speed we know of—the speed of light—the trip would take at least 10,000 years. Why should anyone make such long journeys just to poke around curiously?

Pro.   It is wrong to try to estimate the abilities of a far-advanced civilization, or their motives either. For one thing, the situation may not be average. The nearest advanced civilization may just happen to be only 100 light-years away, rather than 10,000.

Furthermore, because we know of no practical way of traveling faster than light doesn't mean an advanced civilization may not know of one. To an advanced civilization, a distance of 100 light-years or even 10,000 light-years may be very little. They may be delighted to explore over long distances just for the sake of exploring.

Con.   But even if that were the case, it would make no sense to send so many spaceships so often (judging by the many UFO reports). Surely we are not that interesting. And if we are interesting, why not land and greet us? Or communicate without landing? They can't be afraid of us, since if they are so far advanced beyond us, they can surely defend themselves against any puny threats we can offer.

On the other hand, if they went to be merely observers, and not interfere with the development of our civilization in any way, they could surely so handle their observations that we would not be continually aware of them.

Pro.   Again, we can't try to guess what the motives of these explorers might be. What might seem logical to us might not seem so logical to them. They may not care if we see them, and they also may not care to say hello. Besides, there are many reports of people who have seen the ships and have even been aboard. Surely some of these reports must have something to them.

Con.   Eyewitness reports of actual spaceships and actual extraterrestrials are, in themselves, totally unreliable. There have been innumerable eyewitness reports of almost everything that most rational people do not care to accept—of ghosts, angels, levitation, zombies, werewolves, and so on.

What we really want, in this case, is something material; some object or artifact that is clearly not of human manufacture or Earthly origin. These people who claim to have seen or entered a spaceship never end up with any button, rag, or other object that would substantiate their story.

Pro.   But how else can you account for all the UFO reports? Even after you exclude the mistaken, the gags and hoaxes—there remain many sightings that can't be explained by scientists within the present limits of knowledge. Aren't we forced to suppose these sightings are extraterrestrial spaceships?

Con.   No, because we don't know that the extraterrestrial spaceship is the only remaining explanation. If we can't think of any other, that may simply be a defect in our imagination. If any answer is unknown, then it is simply unknown. An Unidentified Flying Object is just that—unidentified.

The most serious and levelheaded investigator of UFOs I know is J. Allen Hynek, a logical astronomer who is convinced that some UFO reports are worth serious investigation. He doesn't think they represent extraterrestrial spaceships, but he does suggest that they represent phenomena that lie outside the present structure of science, and that understanding them will help us expand our knowledge and build a greatly enlarged structure of science.

The trouble is that whatever the UFO phenomenon is, it comes and goes unexpectedly. There is no way of examining it systematically. It appears suddenly and accidentally, is partially seen, and then is more or less inaccurately reported. We remain dependent on occasional anecdotal accounts.

Dr. Hynek, after a quarter of a century of devoted and honest research, so far ends with nothing. He not only has no solution, but he has no real idea of any possible solution. He has only his belief that when the solution comes, it will be important.

He may be right, but there are at least equal grounds for believing that the solution may never come, or that when it comes, it will be unimportant.

The organizational pattern of this article is very pronounced. Asimov sets up his thesis in the second paragraph ("Do the 'little green men' really exist?"), and then uses the last sentence in that paragraph to organize the essay ("There are arguments pro and con"). Then, in subsequent paragraphs, he takes up one point at a time, explores it thoroughly, and then considers a contrasting point of view. The resultant pattern is pro/con, pro/con, pro/con, pro/con, followed by a conclusion. The following scheme reveals the basic paradigm:

Introduction (includes thesis)
Pro (for)
Con (against)
Pro (for)
Con (against)
Pro (for)
Con (against)
Pro (for)
Con (against)
Conclusion

In this article, Asimov dispassionately analyzes the question as to whether life exists on other planets. He presents evidence and logical reasoning, refuting each argument point by point, but he does this within the framework of a comparison paradigm. He tries to convince his audience intellectually, by conviction, rather than by emotional appeal, and each step in the process is clearly formulated. Conviction is the logical part of argument that avoids the shaky emotional basis of some persuasive arguments.

Faulty Comparison

In reasoning by comparison, try to avoid the following errors in reasoning. These are most commonly found in advertising writing, but the principles are applicable to any kind of writing that uses the mode of comparison.

Avoid the **floating comparison.** This is *a comparison in which one half of the comparison is missing, so that the comparison seems to be floating in the air.* One tire company claims to have a new tire that lasts "20 percent longer." 20 percent longer than what? Last year's tire? A competitor's tire? A food manufacturer advertises an all-vegetable shortening that "is lighter, creamier, and more digestible." Lighter, creamier, and more digestible than what? Than it was before? Than all other brands? Than any brand of all-vegetable shortening? Than any brand that sells for the same price? What is missing, of course, is reference to the other product. The comparison is made to things that don't even exist.

Avoid **excessive use of superlatives.** When every medicine ad promises the "fastest" relief, every soap powder gives the "whitest" wash, every toothpaste the "fewest" cavities, every cigarette the "mildest" smoke, then you've got to believe that these claims are idle boasts. The test is whether or not a superlative claim is *factually* true. Can the claim be verified by objective standards? Quite often, the language is not clear enough or believable enough to be meaningful.

Superlative claims can also be made by using such words as *the, only,* and *exclusive.* This strategy is often used when it is difficult to determine significant differences between products. It's *"the* car of the decade," one advertisement reads. "It's the *only* tire made with. . . ." reads another.

Arguing by Analogy

An **analogy** is an *extended comparison.* It is *a process of reasoning based on similarity.* When you reason by analogy, you go from one particular case to another, basing your conclusion on similarities between two sets of circumstances. In arguing by analogy, you argue that if two things resemble one another in certain respects, they also resemble one another in other respects.

Analogies are often confused with metaphors. Both are based on similarity, but an analogy *argues from those similarities.*

An analogy may be literal or figurative. A **literal analogy** is *based on the same class of objects.* A **figurative analogy** is *based on different classes of objects.* Thus, if you compare a Buick with a Ford, that's a literal analogy. If you compare a Ford with a mustang, that's a figurative analogy.

Here is an example of a figurative analogy that appeared in *The New Yorker* on October 7, 1972:

Do You Have an Unfaithful Watch?

At first you tell yourself, "What's a few minutes off?"

But when you catch your watch cheating on you time and time again, when you're forced to turn to the wrist of some stranger . . .

That's when you wish you had an Accutron watch. Accutron by Bulova. The true-blue tuning-fork watch.

Its tuning-fork movement is guaranteed to keep it faithful to within a minute a month.

It can't be led astray, like others can, by an unbalanced balance wheel.

And it's so loyal that even if you deserted it for months, it would do nothing but lie there and count the seconds until you returned.

Testing the Analogy

Test all arguments from analogy to determine if the reasoning is valid. Determine what the main issues are. Figure out precisely what is being compared. Determine if the similarities and differences are relevant. Extend the analogy. Attack half of the comparison. Attack the whole analogy.

Faulty Analogy

It has become a cliché to state that analogies never prove anything. Yet they do have persuasive force. An analogy is faulty if the points being compared *are not alike in all essential respects;* if there are *negative instances;* and if there is a *single comparison* on which to support the conclusion, rather than an extended series of comparisons.

Exercises

1. Evaluate the following comparisons and analogies:

    a. Try Handle With Care on *your* summer washables. You'll say it really does more.

    b. Smooth some Balm Barr [cocoa butter] on your skin and see why it's better.

    c. Nothing performs like a Saab.

    d. Reach toothbrush. Designed like a dental instrument.

    e. Rise is thicker than the leading foam.

    f. The Three Mile Island "event" will do for nuclear power what the Hindenburg did for zeppelins.

    g. After the Three Mile Island accident, I intend to vote against any politicians who say "Maybe" to nuclear power, regardless of their opinions on all other matters. What good is a chicken in every pot if the broth is radioactive?

    h. Strengthening the CIA is a step in the right direction. If we're so intent on being the world's babysitter, we need to know what the kids are doing.

    i. Wake up to an ocean-fresh shave. Old Spice makes every shave smooth sailing.

    j. Unless we are careful, the computer may soon warp our thinking abilities as a nation, just as the automobile has withered our walking ability.

2. Analyze and evaluate the Accutron watch ad.

3. Bring to class for discussion an ad that uses comparison or analogy for persuasive purposes.

4. Write a comparison paper, using one of the following, in which you argue the superiority of one over the other:

    a. two songs   f. two cars
    b. two political candidates   g. two sports commentators
    c. two similar movies   h. two magazines
    d. two talk-show hosts   i. two products
    e. two paintings   j. two TV shows

5. Discuss in class how the analogies in the following proverbs might be extended for a persuasive essay:

    a. Anger is a stone cast at a wasp's nest.
    b. Courage is fire; bullying is smoke.
    c. Confidence is a plant of slow growth.
    d. Lost credit is like a broken mirror.
    e. Gratitude is a heavy burden.

6. Write an argument, using a pro-and-con format, on one of the following topics:

    a. abolition of capital punishment
    b. motion-picture censorship
    c. federal control of the oil industry
    d. state or federal ownership of all utilities
    e. strict wage and price controls on gasoline
    f. nuclear power plants
    g. keeping or doing away with the 55 mph speed limit

7. You marry young. Your spouse is critically injured shortly after in an automobile accident. On his or her deathbed, your spouse asks you to promise not to remarry. Less than a year later, you fall in love again. Give arguments (reasons) for and against having to honor your promise.

Arguing From Cause and Effect

When you reason from **cause to effect** or from **effect to cause,** you note that certain actions produce certain effects and that certain effects are produced by certain causes. If, in writing an argument,

you start off with causes and move to effects, you advance ideas
deductively. The following public-service message that appeared in
a local newspaper uses this method of development.

Shoplifting Is a Crime

Cause   Shoplifting a 20¢ candy bar or a $1 lipstick doesn't sound like a
serious crime. But if the shoplifter is caught, it will add up to more
than $1.20. Storeowners are no longer giving a "second chance"—
not even for a candy bar, and *an arrest for shoplifting can follow
you the rest of your life.*

Effects   Convicted shoplifters are denied admission into many colleges
and are barred from holding government or bonded jobs. Professions
that require special licensing, like law or insurance, are closed to
them. They can't even get a mortgage, loan, or credit card. What
can be even more tragic than the jail sentence or fine is the teenager
delivered in a police car to his home or the business executive earning
$25,000 a year who has to explain to his family why he shoplifted
a couple of ties.

No matter how little the item costs, shoplifting is stealing.

If you first describe certain effects, results, or consequences in
writing an argument, and then move to the causes or agents that
produced them, you advance ideas inductively. This ad by Caterpillar
Tractor Company, which appeared in *Time* magazine on July 3, 1978,
proceeds from effect to cause:

The Arizona Floods Cost Less Than the Copper Depression!

The March 1978 floods, dangerous and overwhelming as they were,
caused a statewide property loss of 24 million dollars. But there is
a copper industry depression in Arizona that caused far greater losses.

Effects   One effect of the copper industry depression is the loss of more
than 46 million dollars in wages last year alone. Another is that
Arizona businesses lost more than 39 million dollars in copper industry purchases. A third is that state and local governments lost more
than 9 million dollars in taxes. A fourth effect is that one out of
every four Arizona copper workers is unemployed. And there is no
end in sight.

Causes   There are two main causes of the depression. The first is that foreign copper is cheaper than Arizona copper because of lower wages and lower environmental standards. American industry is buying copper from Chile, Peru, and other nations. An environmental tariff is one solution. A second cause is our own governmental policy. America should maintain a copper stockpile for defense purposes. It is not doing so. Yet its purchases would help.

Here's something you can do. Our statistics for Arizona's copper depression are verified. They are likely new to you. We suggest you send them to your state legislator. They may be new to him, too.

Faulty Causal Reasoning

Faulty causal reasoning, sometimes called by its Latin name, *post hoc, ergo propter hoc* ("after this, therefore because of this"), consists in *assuming that because one event comes before another in time, the first event is the cause of the other.* It is true that causes come before effects, but it does not follow that because one occurrence precedes another, there is necessarily a causal relation between them.

This form of reasoning is sometimes found in political arguments. It goes something like this: "After the Carter Administration came into power, the country suffered an energy shortage. Therefore, the policies of the Carter Administration are responsible for the energy crisis."

Superstitions are based on faulty causal reasoning. "Pretty soon," said Huckleberry Finn, "a spider went crawling up my shoulder, and I flipped it off and it lit in the candle; and before I could budge, it was all shriveled up. I didn't need anybody to tell me that that was an awful bad sign and would fetch me some bad luck, so I was scared and 'most shook the clothes off of me."

Exercises

1. Evaluate these causal arguments:

    a. Smoking causes cancer. Don't smoke.

    b. You take away gasoline and you destroy the family.

    c. Antiscience and anti-intellectual activity is much more widespread than even a few years ago. There are ten times as many American college students enrolled in astrology courses as in astrophysics courses.

    d. If thousands of Catholics are turning to Pentecostalism, it is because they miss the ecstasy and mysticism of the old Mass.

    e. Last Saturday there were more people in line for confession than I have seen in years. Your story must have scared the hell out of them.

    f. We figure if we can make driving safe for these people, we'll be making driving safe for everybody.

    g. Like anyone who has been in party politics for a long time, our senator is tainted with ideological impurity.

    h. Your hair is a mess, and your face is as red as a beet. You must have gotten drunk last night.

    i. Listerine antienzyme toothpaste offers you continuous protection against tooth decay.

    j. Those students who type their themes get better grades than those who do not.

2. Bring to class several magazine ads that use cause-and-effect arguments for persuasive purposes, and discuss their effectiveness.

3. Write an essay, using cause-and-effect reasoning, in which you argue that television shows which depict physical violence cause violence in everyday life.

4. Imagine that because of an Arab boycott of oil in the Middle East or because of a dwindling supply of gasoline, Congress has voted to limit drastically the private ownership or use of cars to conserve energy. Write an argument in which you discuss the effects of such a policy.

5. Write an essay in which you argue against teenage marriages, citing harmful effects of early marriages.

6. Write a letter to your campus newspaper, in which you argue that doing away with final examinations will have beneficial (or negative) effects.

7. Write a persuasive essay, using a topic of your own choice, in which you argue from cause to effect or from effect to cause.

Persuasion as an Aim:

The Syllogism and the Enthymeme

Chapter 9

Persuasion as an Aim:
The Syllogism and the Enthymeme

If a superstitious friend comes up to you and says, "I shall be unlucky today, because today is Friday the thirteenth," you might be amused at his sur···stitious beliefs, but you can't fault his logic. He has been engaged in a process called deductive thinking. The superstition is, of course, arrived at inductively. But the superstitious friend is applying that superstition to a particular case, and so is reasoning deductively. **Deductive thinking** is *the process of reasoning from a general statement to a logical conclusion.* The syllogism is one form that deductive thinking takes.

The Categorical Syllogism

The **syllogism** is a *mode of thinking in which you reason from two statements, or propositions, called premises, to a third statement, or proposition, called the conclusion.* A **premise** is *a statement that serves as the basis of an argument.* An argument, in the form of a syllogism, looks like this:

> All people are basically honest.
> Joan is a person.
> Therefore, Joan is basically honest.

The first sentence is called the **major premise.** In an argument, the major premise is usually drawn from experience or assumed to be self-evident. The second sentence is called the **minor premise.** The minor premise states a new idea. It is a particular instance of the previously stated general idea. It needs to be supported with evi-

dence. The third sentence is the **conclusion.** The conclusion follows logically from the two premises.

There are four kinds of statements that enter into a syllogism:

1. A *universal affirmative* statement (All people are basically
   honest. Everyone watches television.)

2. A *universal negative* statement (No person is basically honest. Not everyone watches television.)

3. A *particular affirmative* statement (Some people are basically
   honest. Some people watch television.)

4. A *particular negative* statement (Some people are not basically honest. Some people do not watch television.)

You can recognize a universal statement because it contains words
such as *all, every, everyone,* and *everybody.* A particular statement
will have words such as *some, many,* and *a few* in it. A negative
statement uses words such as *no, not, not any, never, nothing,* and
the like. An affirmative statement is one in which the predicate asserts
that something is true of the subject

The simplest form of a statement that goes into a syllogism is
the **categorical proposition.** (The *categorical syllogism* is so
called because its major premise is a categorical proposition.) It consists of a subject, a copula (a form of the verb *to be*), and a predicate
term. It has the following form:

Subject Term	*Copula*	*Predicate Term*
All women	are	beautiful.
No woman	is	beautiful.

Logicians use variations of this form, with the verb *to be,* because
it is easy to spot the terms. The wording of the proposition below
is found more in speech and writing. But because it contains no linking
verb, it is harder to pick out the terms:

All Europeans appreciate jazz.

If you rewrite the sentence, however, to include a form of the verb *to be*, the terms are easier to pick out:

> All Europeans   are   people who appreciate jazz.

In addition to having three sentences, a syllogism contains three terms: a major term, a middle term, and a minor term. In the following syllogism, the **major term** is the predicate term in the major premise and in the conclusion *(appreciate jazz)*. The **middle term** is the common term in each of the premises *(all Europeans, European)*. The **minor term** *(Marcello)* appears in the minor premise, and it is the subject term of the conclusion:

> All Europeans appreciate jazz.
> Marcello is a European.
> Therefore, Marcello appreciates jazz.

A syllogism is **valid** if the relationship among the terms is logical and if it follows certain set rules. In the above syllogism, there is a common term in each of the first two sentences *(all Europeans, European)* which allows us to connect the ideas in each sentence:

> All Europeans appreciate jazz.
> Marcello is a European.

This term drops out in the conclusion, and the remaining terms combine to form a sentence:

> Marcello appreciates jazz.

If the major premise had read *"Most* Europeans appreciate jazz," you would have had to qualify your conclusion with a word such as *probably:*

> Most Europeans appreciate jazz.
> Marcello is a European.
> Therefore, Marcello *probably* appreciates jazz.

Here is another valid syllogism, with a negative major premise:

No Europeans appreciate jazz.
Marcello is a European.
Therefore, Marcello does not appreciate jazz.

Rules for a Valid Syllogism

1. You can have only *three terms* in a valid syllogism. The following syllogism is not valid because it contains four terms:

   All women are *independent creatures.*
   No girls are *servile.*
   Therefore, no girls are independent creatures.

   Because there are four terms *(all women, independent creatures, no girls, servile)*, there are no logical links to allow the writer to go from one sentence to another.

2. You must be sure to distribute the middle term at least once. A middle term is distributed if it refers to all or most of the individuals in a class *(all, every, most, no, not any)*. A middle term is undistributed if it refers to particular individuals in a class *(some, a few, many)*. The following syllogism is not valid because the middle term *(some women, woman)* is not distributed at least once. What is true of some women is not necessarily true of Joan:

   Some women are vain creatures.
   Joan is a *woman.*
   Therefore, Joan is a vain creature.

3. You cannot extend a term in the conclusion if it has not already been extended in the premise:

   All men are vain creatures.
   Some Arizonans are men.
   Therefore, *most Arizonans* are vain creatures.

   In the above syllogism, the term *most Arizonans* in the conclusion is an extension of the term *some Arizonans* in the minor premise. Therefore, the syllogism is not valid.

4. You cannot draw a conclusion from two particular premises. The following syllogism is not valid because the major and minor premises are particular statements:

   Some women are vain.
   Some Arizonans are women.
   Therefore, some Arizonans are vain.

5. You cannot draw a conclusion from two negative premises. The syllogism that follows is not valid because the conclusion follows from two negative premises:

   No men are vain.
   No Arizonans are men.
   Therefore, no Arizonans are vain.

6. Finally, if one of your premises is negative, then your conclusion must be negative. The syllogism below is not valid because the major premise is negative, but the conclusion is affirmative:

   All women are *not* vain.
   Joan is a woman.
   Therefore, Joan is vain.

A syllogism is **valid,** then, if the form is such that you can logically deduce a conclusion from the premises. A syllogism is **true** if certain facts and evidence make the statements true.

In deducing conclusions, sometimes you can go immediately from one proposition to another, without a middle term. Common sense should help you in doing this. For example, what's true of the universal must be true of the particular. If it is true that all people are basically honest, then it must be true that some people are basically honest. If it is true that no people are basically honest, then it must be true that some people are not basically honest.

Similarly, contradictory statements cannot both be true. If it is true that all people are basically honest, then the contradictory statement, some people are not basically honest, must be false. If it is true that no people are basically honest, then the contradictory statement, some people are basically honest, must be false.

Contrary statements cannot both be true. If it is true that all men are basically good, then it can't be true that no men are basically good. If it is true that some men are basically good, no deduction can be made about the statement that some men are not basically good.

The Hypothetical Syllogism

The **hypothetical syllogism** has a conditional proposition (a sentence containing an *if* clause) as its major premise. This premise expresses a hypothetical (*uncertain* or *conjectural*) relationship of causation or resemblance:

> If the rain continues, the bridge will be lost.

In a conditional proposition, the *if* clause is called the **antecedent.** The second clause (the clause to which the "condition" is applied) is called the **consequent.**

The hypothetical syllogism, like the categorical syllogism, consists of three propositions: the major premise containing the *if* clause, the minor premise, and the conclusion:

> If the rain continues, the bridge will be lost.
> The rain will continue.
> Therefore, the bridge will be lost.

Rules for the Hypothetical Syllogism

1. If you affirm the truth of the antecedent (the *if* clause) with the minor premise, then the consequent (stated in the main clause) necessarily follows, and your conclusion is valid:

> If you inject heroin, you will die.
> You inject heroin.
> Therefore, you will die.

2. If you affirm the truth of the consequent, it does not necessarily follow that the antecedent is true, and your conclusion is invalid:

If you inject heroin, you will die.
You will die.
Therefore, you inject heroin.

3. If you deny the consequent, you may draw a valid conclusion. But be certain to make both the minor premise and the conclusion negative statements:

If you inject heroin, you will die.
You will not die.
Therefore, you do not inject heroin.

4. If you deny the antecedent, then your conclusion is not valid:

If you inject heroin, you will die.
You do not inject heroin.
Therefore, you will not die.

The Disjunctive Syllogism

The **disjunctive syllogism** has a disjunctive proposition (one that gives alternatives, such as *either . . . or . . .*) as its major premise. A disjunctive statement is one that sets forth alternative possibilities:

Either you are mortal, or you are immortal.

Like both the categorical syllogism and the hypothetical syllogism, the disjunctive syllogism contains three sentences: the major premise (which has the words *either, or*), the minor premise, and the conclusion:

Either you are mortal, or you are immortal.
You are not immortal.
Therefore, you are mortal.

In speech and in writing, the conclusion of a disjunctive syllogism is sometimes omitted:

Either you are coming, or you are not.
You are not coming?

Rules for the Disjunctive Syllogism

1. When formulating a disjunctive proposition, be careful to set up alternatives that are mutually exclusive and therefore contradictory. In the following example, the alternatives are not mutually exclusive:

   Either she is a singer or a dancer.
   She is not a singer.
   Therefore, she must be a dancer.

   Actually, she could be both a singer and a dancer, or she could be a musician or an actress. But if you recast the major premise to read

   Either she is a singer, or she is not a singer,

   then the alternatives are mutually exclusive.

2. Be sure to include all of the possibilities in a disjunctive syllogism. Failure to do so destroys its validity, as in the following example:

   Either excessive heat or excessive moisture killed her roses.
   Excessive heat did not kill her roses.
   Therefore, it must have been excessive moisture.

   All that is needed to destroy this conclusion is to show that other causes, such as insects, heavy winds, frost, or hail, might have been responsible for killing the roses.

Exercises

1. Analyze the following syllogisms and comment on their validity or lack of validity:

   a. Those who succeed in life work hard.
      Everyone is anxious to succeed in life.
      Everyone works hard.

b. All X is Y.
   Some Y is Z.
   Therefore, some Z is X.

c. No fish are mammals.
   No fish are birds.
   No birds are mammals.

d. Some soldiers get killed in battle.
   Some civilians get killed in battle.
   Some civilians are soldiers.

e. Some X is Y.
   All Y is Z.
   Some Z is X.

f. All lawyers are articulate people.
   Some doctors are not articulate people.
   Lawyers are not doctors.

g. Because some people are honest,
   and honest people want to avoid jail,
   some people want to avoid jail.

h. No sensible people are smokers.
   Some Americans are sensible people.
   Some Americans are smokers.

i. All left-wing liberals are radicals.
   All radicals are communist.
   Therefore, all left-wing liberals are communist.

j. Switzerland loves freedom.
   I love freedom.
   Therefore, I am Switzerland.

k. All Martians are green.
   Jeffrey is not green.
   Therefore, Jeffrey is not a Martian.

l. No Chinese are North Americans.
   All Americans are North Americans.
   All Americans are Chinese.

m. All drunken drivers are potentially dangerous.
No thinking person is a drunken driver.
No thinking person is potentially dangerous.

n. All price-fixing is immoral.
Some immoral actions are illegal.
Some price-fixing is illegal.

o. Since only lunatics want to go to the moon,
this man cannot be a lunatic,
because he wants to stay here on Earth.

p. If it rains, I will get wet.
It rains,
Therefore, I will get wet.

q. Unless you stop, I will get mad.
You will not stop.
Therefore, I will get mad.

r. Either Hitler is dead or he is hiding in Argentina.
He is not hiding in Argentina.
Therefore, he must be dead.

s. Either his shoes are Italian-made or they are British-made.
They are Italian-made.
Therefore, they are not British-made.

t. Obviously, whales have warm blood.
They are mammals.

The Enthymeme

The **enthymeme** is *a shortened form of the syllogism in which one of the premises or the conclusion is missing.* It is the form usually encountered in speech or writing.

Here is an enthymeme in which the major premise is missing:

The price of meat will go up
because of the poor corn crop.

The conclusion is stated in the main clause: "The price of meat will go up." The minor premise is stated in the *because* clause: "because of the poor corn crop." The major premise, which is missing, can easily be supplied:

> The price of meat will go up whenever the corn crop is poor.
> The corn crop is poor.
> Therefore, the price of meat will go up.

Here is an enthymeme in which the conclusion is missing:

> Either Chris Evert or Virginia Wade will win the match.
> Chris Evert's chances were lost when she sprained her ankle.

The conclusion of this enthymeme, like the major premise of the previous enthymeme, can easily be supplied:

> Therefore, Virginia Wade will win the match.

In writing, enthymemes take various forms. They may take the form of a complex sentence with a *because* or *since* clause; a compound sentence joined by words such as *therefore, consequently, so,* and *for* ("The corn crop is poor; therefore, the price of meat will go up"); or two sentences placed together ("The corn crop is poor. The price of meat will go up.").

Enthymemes, like the syllogisms they replace, can be categorical, hypothetical, or disjunctive. A good example of a hypothetical enthymeme in a recent ad for Kent cigarettes depicts two cigarette packages with the following text:

> Come for the filter.
> You'll stay for the taste.

If you reword the sentences slightly, you get this conditional enthymeme:

> If you come for the filter,
> you'll stay for the taste.

Presumably, the reader will affirm the antecedent and be led to accept the inevitable conclusion.

A recent ad for Texaco oil company uses a similar strategy. The illustration pictures an oil rig in the Gulf of Mexico with this caption:

> If we don't go into deep water,
> we'll all be in hot water.

Besides the argument embedded in the enthymeme, there is a larger argument implicit in the entire ad: Drilling in deep water costs money. We are in hot water because we're dependent on imported oil. We will be less dependent on imported oil if we explore more offshore sites. But leasing costs and expenses are higher for offshore wells than they are on land. Nevertheless, Texaco is continuing to drill deeper wells, literally getting into deep water. Of course, the ad doesn't say that the costs will be passed on to the consumer, but the argument is clearly designed to placate customers who are concerned over the increasing cost of gasoline and the high profits of the oil companies.

The disjunctive enthymeme, like the hypothetical enthymeme, can be found in many magazine ads, where it is used very effectively. Whatever one may think about the validity of the enthymeme in the following ad for True cigarettes, there is no doubt about its effectiveness. The picture depicts a man sitting on a log with his bare feet in the sand, holding a True cigarette. The text reads as follows:

> After kicking around everything I'd heard about smoking,
> I decided to either quit or smoke True.
> I smoke True.

It's pretty obvious that the alternatives are not mutually exclusive. Yet the smoker seems to be given only two choices: quitting or smoking True. If he decides to smoke (what he has heard, of course, is that smoking is dangerous to his health), then he could smoke any kind of cigarette, not just True. But the alternatives are set up in such a way that if he decides to smoke, he must smoke True. The complete argument, reconstructed, goes something like this: "I've considered seriously everything I've heard about the dangers of smoking, but I enjoy smoking, so I've decided to continue. True cigarettes have the lowest tar and nicotine content. That's why I smoke True."

To test the validity of an enthymeme, simply rewrite it, putting it into the form of a syllogism. Then follow the same procedures you would follow to determine if a syllogism is valid.

One of the most important errors to guard against in using enthymemes is *hasty generalization in the major premise.* Ordinarily, in a syllogism, the major premise is there to be examined and evaluated. But in an enthymeme, the major premise must be assumed by the reader or listener.

The following is an example of a statement attributed to the Republican senator from California, S. I. Hayakawa, in the early summer of 1979, when long lines began to form at the gas pumps and some Congressmen began to cry for decontrol of gas prices:

"Let gas go to $1.50, even $2.00 per gallon.
A lot of the poor don't need gas because they are not working."

Needless to say, Senator Hayakawa's remarks were greeted with public indignation. What is missing from this statement is the major premise:

Major Premise:
Minor Premise: They are not working.
Conclusion: A lot of the poor don't need gas.

Reconstructed, the chain of reasoning goes something like this: "Anyone who is not working does not need gas. The poor are not working. Therefore, the poor don't need gas." The argument is valid, but not true because the assumed premise is faulty. The poor may need gas so they can obtain jobs. And, of course, all of us need gas for reasons other than to go to work: to go to the grocery, to visit friends, to run errands, perhaps to make an emergency trip to the hospital, and so on.

Exercises

1. Supply the missing proposition in each of the following enthymemes. Then determine if each is valid or not.

a. If you're Spanish or Italian, you may as well resign yourself to being emotional.

b. When we were in New Orleans, we went to the French Quarter. All of the architecture there is excellent.

c. Most of Fellini's pictures are offbeat, so *Amarcord* is probably offbeat too.

d. Smith must be crooked; all of those politicians are.

e. These new clothes are really expensive, so I refuse to buy at Frederick's Department Store, because all their clothes are expensive.

f. If you read about it in the local paper, don't believe it.

g. There is no sense in paying high prices for coffee, since it is well known that coffee has no nutritional value.

h. Because they are gas guzzlers, most large cars are not very economical.

2. Convert the following categorical syllogisms into enthymemes:

a. All criminals ought to be prosecuted.
   Price fixers are criminals.
   Therefore, price fixers ought to be prosecuted.

b. All nutritional foods are healthy.
   Sugar is not a nutritional food.
   Sugar is not healthy.

c. All excellent movies are works of art.
   No Westerns are works of art.
   No Westerns are excellent movies.

d. Most hard drugs are habit-forming.
   Heroin is a hard drug.
   Heroin is habit-forming.

e. No man wants to be untruthful.
   Michael is a man.
   Michael wants to be truthful.

3. Bring to class magazine ads that use enthymemes, hypothetical syllogisms, or disjunctive syllogisms to sell a product or make a point. Then analyze the arguments in class.

Planning an Argument

You seldom state arguments in complete syllogisms, although recently I have come across an ad for Snowdrift shortening that uses the deductive sequence of a syllogism to make its selling point:

What Every Good Cook Knows

Just a little difference in ingredients makes a big difference in cooking results. Snowdrift is just a little lighter than ordinary shortening— and that can make the big difference in giving your family lighter, more digestible foods.

The major premise offers benefits that have a general appeal to the reader. ("Just a little difference in ingredients makes a big difference in cooking results"). The minor premise—the proof part—gives supporting details in the form of product attributes ("Snowdrift is just a little lighter than ordinary shortening"). The proof part is flexible. You can use it to enumerate several product attributes or, as in this ad, one or two. The conclusion applies directly to the reader ("and that can make the big difference in giving your family lighter, more digestible foods").

The advantage of the deductive sequence is that it enables the writer to analyze the proposition carefully and to pick out the facts that will be most effective with the reader. The deductive order gives the major premise or assertion first and then backs it up with evidence, explanations, and logical reasoning.

Most arguments, however, are based on the enthymeme rather than the syllogism. *The logical structure of an argument consists of a series of enthymemes that exhibit the framework of the chain of reasoning and the evidence upon which the argument is based.*

To write an argument based on the enthymeme, begin with the conclusion of the syllogism as your thesis. Then add the minor premise to it in the form of a *because* clause. The minor premise is the proof part of your argument. You must support it with the kinds of evidence considered in the previous chapter: facts, personal opinions, attributes, descriptive details, examples, statistics, testimony and other evidence from authority, narrative examples, comparisons, analogies, causes, and effects.

The following example, adapted from a public declaration by musicians and celebrities such as John Denver, Art Garfunkel, Mia Farrow, Israel Horovitz, John Simon, Stevie Wonder, and Howard Johnson, who oppose nuclear power plants, is a good example of a thesis in the form of an enthymeme:

> Nuclear power should be banned
> because it represents a grave threat to life on this planet.

In this thesis statement, the *main clause* states the conclusion of the enthymeme ("Nuclear power should be banned") and the *because* clause states the minor premise. Put into the form of an incomplete syllogism, the statement reads:

Major Premise:
Minor Premise: Nuclear power represents a grave threat to life on this planet.
Conclusion: Nuclear power should be banned.

Taking the process one step further, you can easily supply a major premise so that the syllogism is complete:

Major Premise: Any form of power that represents a grave threat to life on this planet should be banned.
Minor Premise: Nuclear power represents a grave threat to life on this planet.
Conclusion: Therefore, nuclear power should be banned.

Why not write an argument in the form of a syllogism, you might ask at this point? Well, you could write an argument in this way if you so desired. But in many arguments, you don't need to state the major premise, because the major premise usually contains assumptions that you already share with your reader. It is the common ground from which your argument starts. You don't need to prove the statement that "any form of power that represents a grave threat to life on this planet should be banned." Common sense and the law of self-preservation will tell you that none of us wants to endanger our lives. More important than explicitly stating the major premise in this argument is setting forth the conclusion that you want your readers to accept. And they will more readily accept your conclusion if your reasoning is sound and your evidence is substantial.

Stating your thesis in enthymeme form will spell out for your reader your specific intention. Second, it will help you as a writer to keep your intention clearly in mind. Third, it will help you to organize the sections of your essay more effectively.

You can expand the enthymeme which constitutes your thesis statement in a number of ways. One way is to state your proposition and its proof (the conclusion and the minor premise in the form of a *because* clause) and then add to your main reason *subordinate reasons* in the form of additional *because* clauses or phrases. These subordinate ideas will be the proof of the main idea, and each subordinate idea must be supported with evidence (facts, examples, testimony of witnesses, opinions of authorities, and so forth). The resulting paradigm for the proposition on nuclear power would look something like this:

Thesis:	Nuclear power should be banned
Main Reason:	because it represents a grave threat to life on this planet,
Sub. Reason:	because of the unresolved question of nuclear-waste storage,
Sub. Reason:	because of the failure of the emergency core-cooling system in tests,
Sub. Reason:	because of the danger of theft or accident during the transportation of nuclear materials, and
Sub. Reason:	because of the continuing rise in incidence of cancer, leukemia, and genetic disease, which are known to be radiation-related.

This paradigm is in the shape of a single sentence, but for purposes of writing an argument, the thesis and the main reason could go together to form your thesis statement ("Nuclear power should be banned because it represents a grave threat to life on this planet"). Then each subordinate reason could be put into sentence form, each sentence marking a division of your essay. Naturally, each of the subordinate propositions has to be supported by evidence of some kind. So the thesis and the main reason (the enthymeme) constitute the proposition to be proved, and the supporting reasons constitute the proof of your argument. A more idealized version of the paradigm would look like this:

> Introduction (includes thesis and main reason)
> Reason 1 (plus supporting evidence)
> Reason 2 (plus supporting evidence)
> Reason 3 (plus supporting evidence)
> Reason 4 (plus supporting evidence)
> Reason 5, 6, 7 . . . (plus supporting evidence)
> Conclusion (application of above to reader)

Another way to expand an enthymeme for organizational purposes is to state your thesis in a single sentence. Then, instead of adding to it a single main reason, which has to be supported by subordinate reasons, you add a series of parallel reasons—all of which, presumably, are main reasons to support your assertion.

Here is an example of a thesis statement, taken from a recent article in *Esquire* magazine about an attempt to abolish the fraternity system at Dartmouth College. Incensed by what he believed to be immoral and uncivilized behavior on the part of some fraternity brothers, English professor James Epperson made a stirring speech to the Dartmouth faculty on November 6, 1978, in which he urged the college's board of trustees to ban fraternities from the campus. The outline of his argument goes something like this:

> Fraternities should be abolished
>> because they are racist,
>> because they encourage destructive behavior,
>> because they are anti-intellectual,
>> because they encourage drunkenness, and
>> because they are sexist.

What looks like a single enthymeme here is really a series of connected enthymemes, with the independent clause ("Fraternities should be abolished") serving as the conclusion of each enthymeme and each *because* clause serving as a minor premise:

Minor Premise: Fraternities are racist.
Conclusion: Therefore, they should be abolished.

Minor Premise: Fraternities encourage destructive behavior.
Conclusion: Therefore, they should be abolished.

Minor Premise: Fraternities are anti-intellectual.
Conclusion: Therefore, they should be abolished.

Minor Premise: Fraternities encourage drunkenness.
Conclusion: Therefore, they should be abolished.

Minor Premise: Fraternities are sexist.
Conclusion: Therefore, they should be abolished.

If you put these enthymemes into an outline, you get the following paradigm:

Thesis: Fraternities should be abolished.
Reason: They are racist.
Reason: They encourage destructive behavior.
Reason: They are anti-intellectual.
Reason: They encourage drunkenness.
Reason: They are sexist.

In its more abstract form, the paradigm would look like this:

Introduction (includes the thesis or proposition to be proved)
Reason 1 (plus supporting evidence)
Reason 2 (plus supporting evidence)
Reason 3 (plus supporting evidence)
Reason 4 (plus supporting evidence)
Reason 5 (plus supporting evidence)
Conclusion (application of above to reader)

The paradigm can then be used as the basis of the essay:

Fraternities should be abolished because they are racist, they encourage destructive behavior, they are anti-intellectual, they encourage drunkenness, and they are sexist.

Fraternities are racist. They do not encourage blacks and other minorities to join.

Fraternities encourage destructive behavior. Their members are uncivilized. Theft and vandalism are frequent among their members.

Fraternities are anti-intellectual. Their members go to college to have a good time and to make social connections rather than to enrich their minds. Those who do study are scorned.

Fraternities encourage drunkenness. Heavy drinking is the norm. Then, when fraternity brothers get drunk, their drunkenness is used to justify vandalism and other forms of offensive behavior.

Finally, fraternities are sexist. Almost all of them exclude women from being members. But even worse, they are actively and aggressively sexist. Women who walk along Fraternity Row at night must put up with obscene proposals. At fraternity parties, some women are scorned, ridiculed, and physically intimidated. Fraternity brothers who "make out" are frequently required to give detailed descriptions of what went on.

For these reasons, fraternities should be abolished.

This is not a complete argument, to be sure. The argument needs a more suitable introduction and a conclusion, and each of the reasons in the respective paragraphs needs more supporting details as proof of the argument. But the model does show how the enthymeme can be used to construct effective arguments.

In the beginning stages of learning to write deductive arguments, you might want to follow these paradigms closely. Ultimately, however, what is more important is that you make the process of deductive thinking habitual, so that in your written arguments, the paradigms will be a direct result of your thought processes.

I said earlier that arguments are seldom stated in complete syllogisms because the major premise usually contains assumptions that you share with your reader, and therefore they need not be stated explicitly. But what if your reader does not share the assumptions in your major premise? They you might want to use the syllogism rather than the enthymeme to present your argument. In that case, you would want to present supporting evidence for both your major and your minor premise.

The following syllogism is one formulation of a very traditional argument for the existence of God:

> Major Premise: Anything that displays design, order, and harmony must have some intelligence directing it.
>
> Minor Premise: The world displays design, order, and harmony.
> Conclusion: Therefore, the world is the work of an intelligent being in the universe.

It can be embedded in the larger patterning of an essay to produce the following argument:

The Argument From Design

The idea that the universe exhibits an orderly design and that this design is proof of a purposeful intelligence in the universe is exemplified by the psalmist who sang, "The heavens declare the glory of God, and the firmament showeth his handywork." Yet modern men and women, in an atmosphere of technical accomplishments and what might be called the new hedonism, often have doubts about the existence of God. To many modern thinkers, the existence of God has become the central religious problem of the twentieth century. In view of modern people's skepticism, is there any evidence that God exists? To many thinkers, proofs of God's existence have always been available, and many of these proofs are just as relevant today as they were in years gone by. One of the most popular of these proofs is the argument from design. The argument goes like this.

Anything that displays design, order, and harmony must have some intelligence directing it. Can there be a design without a designer? If you were asked to give an account of anything man-made, such as a car, a building, or a machine, you could not give a complete account if you omitted the maker. Similarly, if you were to try to give an account of the workings of the universe, of its organic regularities and its orderly structures and processes, you would have to conclude that the principle of order is an intelligence operating and directing it for some purpose toward some intelligible goal.

Order itself must have a cause. A work of art does not produce itself, but is the result of the intentions of an artist. Language is a formal creation in which a writer imposes form on his or her materials. A pool player striking a ball can be said to be operating with a purpose. Everything has a purpose. Why are there doors and windows at regular intervals in the walls of a house? Why are the streets of cities laid out in orderly designs? Why is the produce in supermarkets arranged in such an orderly fashion? What is the probability of an orderly structure in the universe coming into existence by chance? An intelligent order in the universe is the work of an intelligent being.

Everywhere, *the world displays design, order, and harmony.* The planets revolve around the sun in the same plane. The simplest molecules contain several thousand atoms, all intricately organized. The universe is an intricate and orderly balance of rhythms, forces, and processes. Numbers, scales, times, crystal forms, symbolic forms, sentences, and languages of all kinds reveal order and complexity. Order is a necessary condition for anything in the universe to function: the human body, plants, machines, athletic teams. Recurrent features in the world repeat themselves over and over again: the patterns of leaves, the colors in sunsets, the symmetry of plants and flowers, the shapes of birds, the odor of roses, the rhythm of waves.

When things in the universe show orderly progression, design, and harmony, they cannot be said to do so of their own nature. It follows, therefore, that this order is a matter either of chance or of design. But as you have seen from numerous examples, whatever comes about in this world is not the result of accident. *Therefore, the world is the work of an intelligent being in the universe.*

Let us assume, now, that your readers do share the assumptions in your major premise. In that case, you turn your syllogism into an enthymeme:

The world must be the work of an intelligent being in the universe because it displays design, order, and harmony.

Then you use the enthymeme as the thesis in your argument and add the supporting evidence. But this time, let us consider possible objections to the argument and include them near the end of the essay:

> The idea that the universe exhibits an orderly design and that this design is proof of a purposeful intelligence in the universe is exemplified by the psalmist who sang, "The heavens declare the glory of God, and the firmament showeth his handywork." Yet modern man, in an atmosphere of technical accomplishments and what might be called the new hedonism, often has doubts about the existence of God. In view of modern people's skepticism, is there any evidence that God exists? To many thinkers, proofs of God's existence have always been available, and many of these proofs are just as relevant today as they were in years gone by. One of the most popular of these proofs is the argument from design, which states that *the world must be the work of an intelligent being in the universe because it displays design, order, and harmony.*
>
> Everywhere, *the world displays signs of design, order, and harmony.* The planets revolve around the sun in the same plane. The simplest molecules contain several thousand atoms, all intricately organized. The universe is an intricate and orderly balance of rhythms, forces, and processes. Numbers, scales, times, crystal forms, groups, symbolic forms, sentences, and languages of all kinds reveal order and complexity. Order is a necessary condition for anything in the universe to function: the human body, plants, machines, athletic teams. There are recurrent features in the world which repeat themselves over and over again: the patterns of leaves, the colors in sunsets, the symmetry of plants and flowers, the shapes of birds, the odor of roses, the rhythm of waves.
>
> But some skeptics have serious objections about the argument from design. If the universe exhibits order and harmony, they say, it also exhibits an absence of order and harmony. Does not evil exist in the world? Are there not natural disasters and calamities such as floods, storms, tornadoes, cyclones, and earthquakes? The answer to these questions is that for order and harmony to exist in the universe, it is not necessary for it to be detectable in all parts of the universe. Besides, in order for us to experience disorder, we must first have had to experience some kind of order. If you were to go into a dormitory in which there were a hundred beds and see one unmade bed, would you necessarily conclude that the one unmade bed proves

that disorder is characteristic of that dormitory? What is disorder, anyway? According to some scientists, disorder is the clash of uncoordinated orders, not the absence of order.

When things in the universe, then, show signs of orderly progression, design, and harmony, they cannot be said to do so of their own nature. It follows, therefore, that this order is a matter either of chance or of design, or the product of a designer who had a particular purpose in mind. But as we have seen from numerous examples and analogies, and as you know from personal experience, whatever comes about in this world is not the result of accident. *Therefore, God must be the designer of the universe.*

Exercises

1. Discuss the essay on fraternities. From your experience, give supporting evidence for the thesis "fraternities should be abolished." Then take the opposite point of view, that fraternities should *not* be abolished, and give supporting evidence for your opinion.

2. Bring to class magazine ads that use deductive arguments to sell goods and services. Then discuss the arguments, including the thesis and support.

3. Bring to class a letter to the editor that uses deductive reasoning.

4. Complete the following theses by adding at least three reasons in the form of *because* clauses. Then, for class discussion, choose one or two and consider the evidence you might use to support each reason:

   a. Cheating is wrong.
   b. All wars are immoral.
   c. English is the most valuable subject in the curriculum.
   d. Personality is more important to success than brains.
   e. Gambling should (should not) be legalized.
   f. _____ is a lousy movie.

5. Assume you believe that smokers have a right to smoke in public places:

    a. Write a dialogue that might take place as you try to convince a non-smoking friend of your position.

    b. Write an ad a cigarette manufacturer might use to convince the general public that smoking should be allowed in restaurants.

    c. Write a letter to your parents (who won't let you smoke in their house) which persuades them to let you smoke when you go out with them in public.

6. Write an essay on one of the following. (These topics can also be used for class discussion.) In your essay, add to the thesis at least three reasons in the form of *because* clauses, or include one main reason and several subordinate reasons:

    a. There should (should not) be complete and open honesty between prospective marriage partners before marriage. (In other words, you must tell your fiancé all that you did before marriage.)

    b. Final examinations should (should not) be abolished.

    c. Killing animals for sport should (should not) be prohibited by law.

    d. Shows that depict violence should be banned from television.

    e. Smoking in public places should be prohibited.

    f. Minorities should be given job preferences.

    g. Price controls should (should not) be lifted on gasoline.

    h. Nuclear power plants should be banned.

    i. Peaceful demonstrations should be allowed on college campuses.

    j. The pass-fail system should be allowed for all undergraduate courses.

    k. Lobbying should be prohibited.

l. Congress should pass an emergency gasoline rationing plan.

m. The selling of handguns should be prohibited.

n. A college education should be free.

o. Capital punishment should be abolished (restored).

p. The jury system should be abolished.

q. The president of the United States should be elected by direct popular vote.

r. Women should serve in the armed forces.

s. Universities should provide day-care centers for the children of married students.

t. Colleges should teach only salable skills.

7. To write an argument based on either a hypothetical syllogism or a disjunctive syllogism, you substitute a hypothetical proposition or a disjunctive proposition for a categorical proposition. The following propositions or syllogisms can be used for discussion or for a writing assignment:

a. If a law lacks support, it can't be enforced. The 55 mph speed limit lacks public support. Therefore, it can't be enforced.

b. Nuclear power is either a good way of solving our energy problems or a lousy way.

c. Either price controls will be imposed or there will be a recession.

d. If human beings were basically good, then laws would not be necessary.

e. If telling a certain kind of lie is not always wrong, then telling a lie can sometimes be ethically better than telling the truth.

Errors in Reasoning

A **fallacy** is *an idea or opinion based on faulty logic.* It is an error in reasoning that may be deliberate or due to ignorance. The following fallacies are intended as a checklist to make you alert to possible errors in reasoning in your own arguments and in those of others. Ironically, as strategies of persuasion, they can be very effective. But as logical arguments, they are fallacious.

Begging the Question

This is a fallacy in which you assume the truth of the premise that you are supposed to prove in your argument. If you state, for example, "Everybody knows that minorities commit most of the crimes in large cities," and then argue from that premise, you would be guilty of **begging the question.** Another form that begging the question takes is **arguing in a circle,** that is, assuming the truth of a premise, drawing a conclusion from this premise, and then using the conclusion to prove your initial premise. For example, if a salesperson says to you, "You should buy the new Chevrolet Impala because it's the best car on the market," and you ask why, and he or she answers, "Because it's made by Chevrolet," that's arguing in a circle. Still another form that begging the question takes is the use of prejudicial words in the proposition—for example, "Who wouldn't oppose this *idiotic* piece of legislation?"

Argumentum Ad Hominem

If in an argument you attack or insult the person you are arguing against rather than deal with the issues, then you are guilty of **argumentum ad hominem** (arguing against the person). Opponents of John F. Kennedy, for example, argued that he was unfit for the presidency because he was a Catholic who would owe allegiance to the Pope. Opponents of Nelson Rockefeller criticized him because he had been divorced—as if his being divorced had anything to do with his qualifications for office. Other politicians have been accused of being socialistic or ultraconservative or too radical, the intent being to discredit the person rather than to address the argument.

Name-Calling

This fallacy is similar in some respects to that of the argumentum ad hominem. In arguing, you give bad names to a person, an issue, or an event, rather than examine the issues. Down through the years, people have been called heretics, fascists, communists, demagogues, and troublemakers by adversaries who appeal to hate and fear rather than to logical reasoning. Thus, if someone doesn't agree with an action taken by some group, they can avoid dealing with the action by calling it "communist-inspired," "radical," "left-wing," or "right-wing."

Argumentum Ad Populum

Like the previous two fallacies, this is an emotional appeal in which you turn away from the real argument and appeal to the irrational fears and prejudices of your audience. You can do this by praising your audience extravagantly, praising the American way of life, resorting to appeals of God, country, home, and motherhood. In other words, you associate something good or bad with your argument. Writers who habitually include in their arguments stock appeals for or against "our free enterprise system," "bureaucracy and red tape," "government interference," and "big business" are guilty of appealing to the crowd.

Shifting Ground

This fallacy consists of ignoring the question by shifting from one question or proposition to another when you are cornered. This fallacy is also called **confusing the issue** and the **Red Herring.** You argue beside the point you are trying to prove. In other words, if you can't answer a question or meet your opponent's arguments straight on, you simply ignore the question and raise another one. Pat Brown, the former governor of California, was once asked, "Governor, what's your opinion of the rising crime rate in California?" He answered: "Rising crime is not the decisive factor. It is the increasing efficiency of crime reporting with the more accurate use of computer technology." Here is how his son, Jerry Brown, answered the same question: "Why don't you ask an intelligent question? You sound like you're giving me the Rorschach test, asking me what I think of the crime rate."

The Bandwagon

This is a technique used to get people to follow the crowd. Any time you call for an action or an opinion because it is popular, because "everybody's doing it," you are using the **bandwagon technique** of arguing. Because people are imitative, they like to do what everybody else does and to believe what other people believe. So this appeal has human-interest value. Advertisers use this appeal when they make claims about the popularity of an advertised product, based on the large number of people who buy the product or who remain faithful to a name brand: "Everybody loves delicious Wrigley's Spearmint Gum"; "Today, more people ask for Coke than for any other soft drink."

Slanting

This is a technique in which you phrase a statement in such a way that you encourage your reader to take a favorable or unfavorable view of a subject. You can do this by selecting certain facts and details of your subject that are favorable and omitting others that are unfavorable. Or you can distort the facts in such a way as to suggest things that are not completely true. **Slanting** can be achieved by using words connotatively, by ordering words in a certain way, by italicizing or underlining words you want to emphasize, by punctuating, and by using emotional or charged language. A humorous example of slanting is this conjugation of an irregular verb, attributed to Bertrand Russell: "I am firm; you are obstinate; he is pigheaded."

Either-Or Fallacy

This is a logical fallacy in which you oversimplify an issue by narrowing your reader's options to just two alternatives. The linguistic form of the **either-or** statement forces your reader to think in terms of black or white. If the options are genuine, there is no problem. But sometimes there may be an unnoticed third possibility hidden by the false dilemma. Thus, if someone argues that lifting price controls on gasoline will produce either more oil at cheaper prices or less oil at higher prices, what may go unnoticed is the possibility of producing the same amount of oil at higher or lower prices. The reader can escape the "horns of a dilemma" by going between them—that is, by not being caught by the one or the other, but considering all of the alternatives.

The Complex Question

This is an error in reasoning in which you ask a question in such a way that it assumes an answer to another question, which has not even been asked. The fallacy is committed when a single answer is demanded of the question. "Why" or "how" questions are frequently of this type. Thus, the question "How long are we going to tolerate interference with our national interests by these large international corporations?" assumes that there has been such interference. The question "Why is it that girls are less interested in science than are boys?" contains the answer to the hidden question "Is it a fact that girls are less interested in science than boys?"

Hypothesis Contrary to Fact

If you begin an argument with a hypothesis that is not true or that is speculative and then draw conclusions from it, this is an error in reasoning called **hypothesis contrary to fact.** It takes the form: "What would the consequences have been *if* such and such had been true?" For example: "If the Shah of Iran were still ruler of that country, gasoline prices would be much lower in this country." There is, of course, evidence to show that the Shah encouraged higher prices when he was the ruler of that country. Another example that keeps making the rounds is the statement "If Columbus hadn't discovered America, we wouldn't be living here today."

Argument From Ignorance

This fallacy is committed if you argue that a statement must be true because it has not been proven false, or that it must be false because it has not been proven true. In other words, if you try to justify a belief when there is no evidence for it, you are guilty of **arguing from ignorance.** For example: "There must be life on other planets, because no one can prove that there isn't." Or, "Psychic phenomena must exist, because eyewitnesses have given us reports of them for years, and nobody has ever disproved these reports."

Exercises

1. Identify the errors in reasoning in the following:

   a. Ever since we put men on the moon, we've been having unusual weather.

b. When I get married, either I will run the house or my husband will.

c. I cooked it. That's why it's good.

d. I'd never vote for Carter. I don't like his Southern accent.

e. The ranting of *Time* and the pseudo-Americans over the CIA disclosures would be comical were it not so childish and tragic. What the United States needs is a stronger CIA, and let the chips fall where they may.

f. You accuse me of going over the 55 mph speed limit, but everybody speeds on the highway.

g. Everyone has a new car but me. Why can't I get a new car? After all, I'll be going to college next year.

h. The West would have been won ten years sooner if the pioneers didn't have to stop and ride back forty times a day to pick up their hats.

i. My teacher is a hard grader. Three of my friends got "F's" on the midterm exam.

j. You are either a Republican or a Democrat.

k. The energy crisis could ultimately destroy our economy and bring down the world economy along with it. Such a collapse would precipitate world conflict and probably atomic war. We cannot escape the danger of the atom. But I would rather risk a mishap from a nuclear power plant once every twenty or thirty years than face one nuclear holocaust.

l. Everybody watches the NBC evening news. You ought to watch it, too.

m. The first chapter was so boring I concluded that it must be a lousy book.

2. Bring to class magazine ads that commit the fallacies cited in this and the previous chapter.

3. Bring to class for discussion examples of fallacies taken from letters to the editor in magazines such as *Time* or *Newsweek,* in your local newspaper, or in the campus newspaper.

4. Discuss the arguments and the errors in reasoning in the following letter to the editor:

Dear Editor:

The letter of Mrs. _____ is outstanding in that she links evolution with the proposed sex education in schools supported by tax money.

We are in this fight against great odds and powers, "against spiritual wickedness in high places" (Ephesians, chapter 6, especially verse 12).

With this thought in mind, we should make every effort to withdraw our children from such influence and place them in a Christian school where only dedicated teachers are employed.

If we do not believe the account of Creation and the Flood, then we call God a liar. If we make God a liar, then we cannot believe any part of His word. This is the position of the supporters of evolution.

God, the essense of life, is life itself, the source of life, plant and animal. This the evolutionist denies, and yet he goes to the swamp and steals from God's creation the smallest form of life, a microorganism, the physicochemical basis of living matter that forms the essential part of plant and animal life.

The microscopic bit of life the evolutionist stole from God and placed into a never-never time resembling eternity, namely, billions upon billions of never-never years before time or matter were created. The amoeba is that bit of protoplasm that the evolutionist has made to be his god, his idol, for he has claimed for it the power to evolve itself in billions of never-never years into great animals such as lived before the Deluge.

There is no halfway point between evolution and the Creation, as some would have us believe. As Mrs. _____ says, "It is either evolution or God." The promoters of evolution despise and violate the moral law which contains the law of chastity. This law forbids the practice of the marriage act outside of marriage.

Adultery, fornication, rape, and what have you already have such a hold on our moral life, as a nation, that we do not need sex instruction by licentious teachers to foster a further drop in morality. Go-go girls, miniskirts, Bikini suits: what next?

Remember, Rome and other great nations of the past have gone into oblivion by a similar route.

Paragraphs and Paragraphing

Chapter 10

Paragraphs and Paragraphing

The Paragraph as Part of A Longer Unit

There are several ways of looking at paragraphs. One way is to see the paragraph as a division of a longer piece of writing. Another is to think of the paragraph as a group of logically related sentences, composed of unified parts, based on a single idea. A third way is to view the paragraph as a kind of extended sentence.

Writers paragraph for a variety of reasons—for instance, to change tone, to shift rhythm, or to emphasize a point. One of the most important reasons for paragraphing, however, is for logical considerations. Understanding the logical basis of paragraphing is of primary importance in developing in the writer a sense of form consciousness.

Some writers claim that they are always conscious of paragraphing and of the logical basis of their paragraphing *when they write.* Others assert that they often go back *after they have completed their writing* and then make their paragraph indentations. These are not opposing points of view, in my opinion, but complementary ones. Writers who claim that they go back and paragraph after they have completed their writing usually end up paragraphing similarly to the way in which writers who use the opposite method do. Both kinds of writers know in general the end they want to achieve. Both have an intuitive grasp of the overall structure of their essays. But some writers are more self-conscious about the logical basis of their paragraphing *as they are writing.* Others are less so. Nevertheless, the latter necessarily have to group their ideas into thought units as they are writing, *whether they paragraph them as such or not.* I am not saying that writers cannot go back and paragraph their essays for reasons that have little to do with the logical progression of ideas.

What I am saying is that the logical basis for dividing essays into paragraphs is there, if writers want to avail themselves of it. It is there because composition is an organic development that begins with an intuitive grasp of the whole. The writer knows in general the end he or she wants to achieve. **Paragraphing** is *the process of differentiating the parts within the whole to achieve the writer's purpose.*

The truth of this idea is easy to illustrate. Give an experienced writer a completed piece of writing, one that has been written without traditional paragraph divisions, and he or she can invariably divide that piece of writing into thought units that make sense. Although some writers may disagree slightly as to where some of the paragraph divisions should be, the extent to which they will agree is amazing.

To illustrate this point, let's look at two kinds of writing: the kind of writing that is **overdifferentiated,** in which there seem to be too many paragraph divisions and in which the basis of the paragraph divisions seems to be almost arbitrary, or at least nonlogical; and the kind of writing that is **underdifferentiated,** in which there are few or no paragraph divisions.

Overdifferentiated writing occurs in magazine ads and in newspaper writing, where considerations such as the educational level of the mass audience, the neat, orderly appearance that shorter paragraphs present, the readability of such paragraphs, and the balance achieved by making the paragraphs the same average length are of paramount importance. Underdifferentiated writing occurs in encyclopedia articles, to give just one obvious example.

Overdifferentiated Paragraphing

Let us look at a few examples of overdifferentiated writing, the first an ad for Kitchen Aid disposers:

> OTHER DISPOSERS CAN'T COMPARE
> TO KITCHEN AID.
>
> Kitchen Aid disposers have a cast
> iron drain chamber to fight corrosion.
> Other disposers don't.

Kitchen Aid has a push-button Wham
Jam Breaker to break up stubborn jams.

Other disposers don't.

Kitchen Aid has a powerful motor.
Stronger start-up power than any other,
to handle tough stuff like steak bones
and corn husks.

Which some disposers can't.

In fact, when you make a point-by-
point comparison, it turns out there
really isn't much comparison.

And, perhaps, that's why so many
people choose a new Kitchen Aid
stainless steel disposer when it comes
time to replace their worn-out disposers.

This ad appeared in the October 1978 issue of *Better Homes and Gardens.* The paragraphs are written in typical advertising-copy fashion. The copy is broken up into eight short paragraphs. Each contains a single sentence or a fragment punctuated as a sentence, with the exception of paragraph 5, which contains both a sentence and a fragment. Paragraph 1 has eleven words; paragraph 2, three words; paragraph 3, thirteen words; paragraph 4, three words; paragraph 5, twenty-two words; paragraph 6, four words; paragraph 7, eighteen words; paragraph 8, twenty-four words. The average paragraph length is twelve words.

The typical short paragraph in advertising copy is composed of three or four sentences. The paragraphing in this ad is even more extreme. If breaking up a block of printed matter into smaller units makes it easier to read and more inviting to the eye, then it follows that the more you break up the copy, the better it will be.

In the typical short paragraph in an ad, there is little opportunity for extensive internal development. Yet most advertising copy has a logical progression of ideas, found in the various sections of the text. The section in advertising copy is often the equivalent of the paragraph in a longer essay. Naturally, the arrangement of logical units into paragraphs and sections will differ from advertisement to advertisement.

Are advertisers being perverse in writing such short paragraphs? Indeed not. They know a great deal about the psychology of their audiences. Ads with long paragraphs (as in some stereo ads) look like *hard reading* before readers even know what's in them. Short paragraphs look like *easy reading*. They are easy on the eyes. They are simple to follow. They aid emphasis. They get attention and hold it. This is especially important in magazines, where the ad has to compete with stories, feature articles, editorials, and reviews to make its selling point.

Yet despite the copywriter's grouping of the sentences into eight paragraphs, the logical basis for grouping these sentences into new paragraph units is there. A reorganization of the sentences based on logical considerations gives us four paragraphs that look like this:

OTHER DISPOSERS CAN'T COMPARE TO KITCHEN AID

Kitchen Aid disposers have a cast iron drain chamber to fight corrosion. Other disposers don't.

Kitchen Aid has a push-button Wham Jam Breaker to break up stubborn jams. Other disposers don't.

Kitchen Aid has a powerful motor, stronger start-up power than any other, to handle tough stuff like steak bones and corn husks, which some disposers can't.

In fact, when you make a point-by-point comparison, it turns out there really isn't much comparison. And perhaps that's why so many people choose a new Kitchen Aid stainless steel disposer when it comes time to replace their worn out disposers.

This rewritten version uses a point-by-point comparison paradigm. In the first two paragraphs, the first sentence in each lists a feature of Kitchen Aid disposers. The second sentence negates these features in the competitor's product. In the third paragraph, consisting of a single sentence, the first part of the sentence comments on Kitchen Aid's powerful motor and on what it is capable of doing.

The second part denies this capability in the competitor's product. The last paragraph makes the point that there really isn't much of a comparison between Kitchen Aid and other products and concludes with an implicit appeal to the reader to buy Kitchen Aid disposers.

Here is a second example of overdifferentiated paragraphing, this time a slightly more elaborated piece of writing, from a newspaper article:

7,000 Stolen Books Found in NY (Associated Press)

NEW YORK—A middle-aged man with eclectic reading taste and sticky fingers brought public library officials to their knees Monday as they sorted through 7,000 volumes valued at $100,000 that were stashed in his apartment.

Inspectors from the New York and Queens public libraries picked their way delicately through wall-to-wall books stacked in the back bedroom of the Queens apartment abandoned three months ago by Caio A. D'Aurelio.

"It looks like they've all been stolen," said Cecil Greenidge, a Queens library inspector. Some of the books were stamped with library logos as distant as Florida State University in Tallahassee, but most were from libraries here.

"Now we can't be sure this guy stole these books. But somebody sure did," Greenidge said. Authorities at first thought the books had been checked out and never returned.

D'Aurelio rented the apartment for 10 years, said Armando Arias, the building superintendent. He stopped living in the apartment about two years ago, and he stopped paying his monthly $200 rent three months ago. No one has seen him since.

Arias and city marshals entered the apartment a week ago and found a riot of books—on the bed, the floor, even packed into the kitchen cabinets. They included books on Cicero, architecture and design, chemistry and archeology, flowers, Greek and Russian, and a guide to the rhythm method of birth control.

Some were dated as having been taken as long ago as 1952.

D'Aurelio was described by neighbors as an average-looking man in his 50's, with receding red hair and quiet demeanor. Arias said he once worked for the city as an architect, and apparently kept the Queens apartment as a place to work and study.

The street-level, one-bedroom apartment also had a litter of papers and magazines. Arias, once a military librarian in Ft. Polk, La., said he spent four days stacking most of the volumes in the bedroom because it would be easier for library officials to remove them through windows.

Arias said he used a shovel to plow through the strewn books and knee-high yellowed newspapers and magazines—some 11 years old—but it was two days before he could see the apartment's parquet floor.

At 10 cents a day, D'Aurelio's overdue charge in New York City for all 7,000 volumes would amount to $700 daily. Any book overdue since 1952 would have an accumulated fine of about $912. If all had been due back then, the bill would total more than $6.3 million.

Like the paragraph structure of the Kitchen Aid ad, the paragraph structure of this news story is not completely logical. This does not mean that it is less effective, however. As I have previously pointed out, there are many reasons a writer would want to vary his or her paragraph structure: ease of reading, balance, emphasis, and the psychology of the audience being just a few. Like the paragraphs of the Kitchen Aid ad, the paragraphs in this news story contain few sentences. There is a total of eleven paragraphs in this article, ranging in length from one to three sentences.

Although the paragraph structuring is not strictly logical, the overall plan is logical. In typical journalistic fashion, the opening paragraph answers the questions who (public library officials), what (found 7,000 stolen or borrowed books), when (Monday), where (in the apartment of a middle-aged man with eclectic reading taste).

If you regroup the sentences from the original paragraphs and place them together in new paragraphs based on similar ideas, you get the following logical divisions:

7,000 Stolen Books Found in NY (Associated Press)

1

NEW YORK—A middle-aged man with eclectic reading taste and sticky fingers brought public library officials to their knees Monday as they sorted through 7,000 volumes valued at $100,000 that were stashed in his apartment.

2

Inspectors from the New York and Queens public libraries picked their way delicately through wall-to-wall books stacked in the back bedroom of the Queens apartment abandoned three months ago by Caio A. D'Aurelio. "It looks like they've all been stolen," said Cecil Greenidge, a Queens library inspector. Some of the books were stamped with library logos as distant as Florida State University in Tallahassee, but most were from libraries here. "Now we can't be sure this guy stole these books. But somebody sure did," Greenidge said. Authorities at first thought the books had been checked out and never returned.

3

D'Aurelio rented the apartment for 10 years, said Armando Arias, the building superintendent. He stopped living in the apartment about two years ago, and he stopped paying his monthly $200 rent three months ago. No one has seen him since.

4

Arias and city marshals entered the apartment a week ago and found a riot of books—on the bed, the floor, even packed into the kitchen cabinets. They included books on Cicero, architecture and design, chemistry and archeology, flowers, Greek and Russian, and a guide to the rhythm method of birth control. Some were dated as having been taken as long ago as 1952.

5

D'Aurelio was described by neighbors as an average-looking man in his 50's, with receding red hair and quiet demeanor. Arias said he once worked for the city as an architect, and apparently kept the Queens apartment as a place to work and study.

6

The street-level, one-bedroom apartment also had a litter of papers and magazines. Arias, once a military librarian in Ft. Polk, La., said he spent four days stacking most of the volumes in the bedroom because it would be easier for library officials to remove them through windows. Arias said he used a shovel to plow through the strewn books and knee-high yellowed newspapers and magazines—some 11 years old—but it was two days before he could see the apartment's parquet floor.

7

At 10 cents a day, D'Aurelio's overdue charge in New York City for all 7,000 volumes would amount to $700 daily. Any book overdue since 1952 would have an accumulated fine of about $912. If all had been due back then, the bill would total more than $6.3 million.

Paragraph 2 depicts inspectors from the New York and Queens public libraries picking their way through wall-to-wall books in D'Aurelio's bedroom in Queens and records their comments. Paragraph 3 discusses the length of time D'Aurelio stayed in the apartment and when he left. Paragraph 4 gives a catalog of D'Aurelio's eclectic reading tastes. Paragraph 5 describes D'Aurelio. Paragraph 6 emphasizes the litter of books, papers, and magazines. Paragraph 7 gives an account of the overdue charges.

Underdifferentiated Paragraphing

If overdifferentiated writing can be described as the kind of writing in which the writer, for whatever reasons, makes a large number of paragraph divisions, then underdifferentiated writing is the type in which the writer makes few, if any, paragraph divisions. Nevertheless, there are units of thought within this kind of writing that can be separated into paragraphs.

A typical example of this kind of writing is the following article, taken from *The Columbia Encyclopedia:*

Lingua Franca

[A lingua franca is] an auxiliary language, generally of a hybrid and partially developed nature, that is employed over an extensive area by people speaking different and mutually unintelligible tongues in order to communicate with one another. Such a language frequently is used primarily for commercial purposes. Examples are the several varieties of the hybrid pidgin English; Swahili, a native language of East Africa; Chinook jargon, a lingua franca formerly used in the American Northwest that was a mixture of Chinook, other American Indian languages, English, and French; and a variety of Malay (called *bazaar Malay*), which served as a compromise language in the area of British Malaya, the Dutch East Indies, and neighboring regions. The original lingua franca was a tongue actually called Lingua Franca (or sabir) that was employed for commerce in the Mediterranean area during the Middle Ages. Now extinct, it had Italian as its base with an admixture of words from Spanish, French, Greek, and Arabic. The designation "Lingua Franca" [Language of the Franks] came about because the Arabs in the medieval period used to refer to Western Europeans in general as "Franks." Occasionally the term *lingua franca* is applied to a fully established formal language; thus formerly it was said that French was the lingua franca of diplomacy.

The structure of this article is very much like that of many encyclopedia articles. The entire article consists of a single unit the size of a long paragraph. The opening statement is not a complete sentence, but it could be made into a complete sentence by the addition of a main verb. Despite the lack of paragraph divisions, however, this article has a logical progression of ideas that could be paragraphed like this:

Lingua Franca

1

[A *lingua franca* is] an auxiliary language, generally of a hybrid and partially developed nature, that is employed over an extensive area by people speaking different and mutually unintelligible tongues in order to communicate with one another. Such a language frequently is used primarily for commercial purposes.

2

Examples are the several varieties of the hybrid pidgin English; Swahili, a native language of East Africa; Chinook jargon, a lingua franca formerly used in the American Northwest that was a mixture of Chinook, other American Indian languages, English, and French;

and a variety of Malay (called *bazaar Malay*), which served as a compromise language in the area of British Malaya, the Dutch East Indies, and neighboring regions.

3

The original lingua franca was a tongue actually called Lingua Franca (or sabir) that was employed for commerce in the Mediterranean area during the Middle Ages. Now extinct, it had Italian as its base with an admixture of words from Spanish, French, Greek, and Arabic. The designation "Lingua Franca" [Language of the Franks] came about because the Arabs in the medieval period used to refer to Western Europeans in general as "Franks."

4

Occasionally the term *lingua franca* is applied to a fully established formal language; thus formerly it was said that French was the lingua franca of diplomacy.

The logical basis for grouping these sentences into paragraphs is as follows. Paragraph 1 defines a *lingua franca*. Paragraph 2 gives examples of an auxiliary language. Paragraph 3 gives the origin of the word and traces the original language that was used as a *lingua franca*. Finally, paragraph 4 discusses another application of the term.

What, then, can you conclude about paragraphing from the study of overdifferentiated writing and underdifferentiated writing? That the structure of sentences, paragraphs, and sections of the whole essay interact. That paragraphing is the process of differentiating the parts within the whole, whether that differentiation comes as you are writing or after you have completed your first draft. And that paragraphing can be based on a number of considerations, depending on the writer's intention, although the logical basis of paragraphing may be the most important one.

Exercises

1. Rewrite the following news story, regrouping the sentences into new thought divisions:

Chair Commands High Spot in Human History

Michael Kernan
Washington Post

Is civilization possible without the chair?

Think about it. Plenty of animals make their own beds, but did you ever see even the sharpest rat sit in a chair?

The chair is no mere piece of furniture; it's a concept. It says something about human power. Long before the kings of Scotland were crowned on the Stone of Scone, the idea of a throne must have existed.

After all, if you could afford to sit down in the presence of strangers, that is, enemies, and not stand ready for combat, it must mean you didn't fear them very much. Where do you think the word chairman came from?

In our homes, this curiously ambiguous emblem of authority and relaxation is almost a member of the family.

My grandfather, an old soldier from the Gold Rush days, took up wood-carving in his last years and made a marvelous mahogany armchair with claws and scrolls.

It was always my father's chair in the dining room, and mine in my turn. My father also had his special armchair, by the fire in the library, deep, profoundly comfortable, with a high back and generous arms: it was a chair to take a nap in. Sometimes I would sit in this chair to read his paper, but never when he was around.

Something made me get up and offer it to him when he came in the room. Not that he was in the least threatening, or that I was in the least polite. It was something about the chair.

We still have that chair, all but reupholstered to death, and are about to retire it, but people still shy away from sitting in it unless I insist.

Even today, in an executive office, the chair has mojo. Try asking the boss for a raise when you're sitting in a chair lower than the one across the desk.

My mother also had her special chair: elegant, dowell-backed and efficient. It was the chair she sat in to write checks. If she wanted to relax, she would lie on the sofa.

Another one, a fine old wing chair, used to be stationed by a window in the living room overlooking the lawn and the valley beyond. It was in a nook, so you could sit perfectly still in it and someone looking for you to do a chore would walk right past.

I decided to make it my official reading chair. But it was too formal, too sternly straight-backed, so I never warmed to it. We still have that one too, in the attic, too valuable to throw away, not valuable enough to sell. It's as unaccommodating as ever.

Another disaster is the loveseat, which is good for nothing except arm wrestling.

You can tell a lot about a family by its chairs: whether it's socially ambitious, puritanical, lazy or whatever. Some living rooms contain all those springy-bottomed, stiff-backed antique chairs. You can't feel really welcome in such a place, and you wonder if even the people who live there do.

Doubtless those chairs were Louis XVI, Chippendale or some such. Which brings up the question: Why didn't the master chaircrafters make comfortable chairs? Was there some social prestige attached to sitting up straight? Is this the origin of "Don't slouch"?

The more you think about chairs, the stranger they get. The electric chair: Why? Wouldn't it be much more practical to put the poor soul on a stretcher? Even in the gas chamber, the executee sits on a chair. Maybe it is a vestige of the homage paid to the sacrificial victim from times primeval.

2. Rewrite the following encyclopedia article, dividing it into paragraphs that "make sense":

[A *pidgin* is] a LINGUA FRANCA that is not the mother tongue of anyone using it and that has a simplified grammar and a restricted, often polyglot vocabulary. Pidgins that have developed from English and other tongues have been employed in different regions since the 17th century. An example is the variety of pidgin English that resulted from contacts between English traders and the Chinese in Chinese ports. In fact, the word *pidgin* supposedly is a Chinese (Cantonese) corruption of the English word *business.* Another well-known form of pidgin English is the Beach-la-Mar (or *Beche-de-Mer*) of the South Seas. The different kinds of pidgin English have preserved the basic grammatical features of English, at the same time incorporating a number of non-English syntactical characteristics. The great majority of words in pidgin English are of English origin, but there are also Malay, Chinese, and Portuguese elements. As a result of bringing to the Caribbean area large numbers of Negro slaves from West Africa who spoke different languages, other pidgins evolved in that region that were based on English, Portuguese, French, and Spanish.

The Paragraph as a Group of Logically Related Sentences

The paragraph as a group of logically related sentences represents, for the most part, the traditional approach to composition. In this view, the paragraph is a collection of sentences on a single subject. It expresses a single thought, and it contains no idea that does not advance the main topic. The thought of such a paragraph can usually be expressed in a single, concise statement called the **topic sentence,** which is ordinarily stated at the beginning of the paragraph. The **topic sentence** is *the sentence that expresses the main idea of the paragraph.* In this position, all the subsequent ideas in the paragraph are developed from it:

1. Apart from teaching him Latin, *Stratford Grammar School* taught *Shakespeare* nothing at all.
2. *It* did not teach *him* mathematics or any of the natural sciences.
2. *It* did not teach *him* history, unless a few pieces of information about ancient events strayed in through Latin quotations.
2. *It* did not teach *him* geography, for the first (and most inadequate) textbook on geography did not appear until the end of the century, and maps and atlases were rare even in university circles.
2. *It* did not teach *him* modern languages, for when a second language was taught at grammar school it was invariably Greek.
   —Marchette Chute, *Shakespeare of London.*

In this paragraph, the first sentence is the topic sentence and each of the next four sentences adds a supporting detail. The paragraph is unified because it deals with a single topic, the things that Stratford Grammar School did not teach Shakespeare.

In the traditional view of the paragraph, the relationship of every sentence to every other sentence and to the main idea is made clear and orderly through logical development and proper transitions:

1. Applied to language, the adjective *good* can have *two meanings:* (1) "effective, adequate for the purpose to which it is put" and (2) "acceptable, conforming to approved usage."

  2. The *first* of *these* is truly a value judgment of the language itself.
    3. In this *sense* the language of Shakespeare, for example, is "good English" because it serves as a highly effective vehicle for his material.
    3. On the other hand, the language of a poorer writer, which does not meet adequately the demands put upon it, might be called "bad English."
  2. The *second meaning* of *good* is not really a judgment of the language itself but a social appraisal of the persons who use it.
    3. An expression like *I ain't got no time for youse* may be most effective in the situation in which it is used, and hence "good English" in the first *sense*.
    4. But most people, including those who naturally speak this way, will call it "bad English" because grammatical features like *ain't, youse,* and the double negative construction belong to a variety of English commonly used by people with little education and low social and economic status.

         —W. N. Francis, *The English Language*

  This paragraph has the form of an extended definition. The opening sentence is the topic sentence. It introduces the term to be defined, *good language.* It also indicates the plan of development. The adjective *good,* the writer states, can have two meanings when it is applied to language: "effective" and "adequate for the purpose," or "acceptable" and "conforming to approved usage." Then he goes on to comment on the two meanings. He does this by dividing the remaining sentences into two groups. Sentence two and the two subordinate sentences related to it extend one part of the meaning of the term (the first meaning of *good,* followed by two examples). The language of Shakespeare is *good* because Shakespeare uses it effectively. The language of a poorer writer is bad, not because it is intrinsically bad, but because the poor writer does not use it effectively. Sentence five and its qualifying sentences take up the second meaning of the term, "a social appraisal of the persons who use it." Most people will label an expression *bad,* regardless of its effectiveness, if it has grammatical features that people of little education and low economic status use, the writer contends in the last two sentences.

In addition to the logical order of ideas, this paragraph uses a number of other methods to achieve unity and coherence:

Parallelism
the first of these is
the second meaning . . . is
in this sense
on the other hand
the language of Shakespeare
the language of a poorer writer

Repetition
the adjective *good*	highly effective
good English	most effective
the second meaning of *good*	language
bad English	the language of Shakespeare
good English in the first sense	the language of a poorer writer
bad English	the language itself
effective	

Synonyms
meanings
these
sense
meaning
sense

Transitional Expressions
in this sense
on the other hand
and hence
but

Exercises

1. Compose five topic sentences to be used in developing paragraphs.

2. Develop a paragraph from one of the following topic sentences:

   a. Education reduces prejudice.
   b. All people are motivated by self-interest.
   c. People should always be honest with each other.
   d. I was startled by what I saw when I entered the room.
   e. There are at least two good arguments to be made against pornography.
   f. Aside from its interest, _____ is an informative book (or television show, movie, and so forth).

Modes of Developing Paragraphs

Because writing is a unified process, the same principles which apply at the essay level also apply at the paragraph level. You have learned in earlier chapters that a **mode** is *a way or manner of developing ideas.* At times, I have used the term to refer both to the process of invention and to that of arrangement. But a mode is also a way of developing paragraphs.

Categories such as analysis, classification, comparison and contrast, and cause and effect, besides referring to mental processes and processes of invention and arrangement, also represent methods of developing paragraphs. They appear in paragraphs because our minds think along those lines.

Although it is true that in much writing the modes are mixed, it is useful in the beginning stages of learning to write for you to see them as simple. Just as in invention, the modes rarely appear in pure form (for instance, when you classify, you must also compare), in paragraphs, the modes are often mixed.

The following are typical examples of the modes as they appear in paragraphs. (You might want to go back and review the discussion of modes in the first chapter and in the chapters titled "Arrangement" and "Patterns of Thought.")

Analysis

Organize *analysis paragraphs* by dividing a complex subject into its component parts. In the following paragraph by Bertrand Russell, the topic sentence introduces the term *patriotism* (in the first sentence), and the following sentences break this term into its elements:

> Patriotism is a very complex feeling, built up out of primitive instincts and highly intellectual convictions. There is love of home and family and friends, making us peculiarly anxious to preserve our own country from invasion. There is the mild instinctive liking for compatriots as against foreigners. There is pride, which is bound up with the success of the community to which we feel that we belong. There is a belief, suggested by pride but reinforced by history, that one's own nation represents a great tradition and stands for ideals that are important to the human race. But besides all these, there is another element, at once nobler and more open to attack, an element of worship, of willing sacrifice, of joyful merging of the individual life in the life of the nation. This religious element in patriotism is essential to the strength of the State, since it enlists the best that is in most men on the side of national sacrifice.
>
> —Bertrand Russell, *Why Men Fight*

Description

Descriptive paragraphs consist basically of sentences representing objects arranged in space. In its simplest form, the principle of organization is based on the way you perceive objects in space—left to right, right to left, bottom to top, top to bottom, and so forth. In writing descriptive paragraphs, you can make the scene easier to follow if you use a particular principle of spatial arrangement:

> As you enter the forest, your eyes used to the glare of the sun, it seems dark and shadowy, and as cool as a butter dish. The light is filtered through a million leaves, and so has a curious green aquarium-like quality which makes everything seem unreal. The centuries of dead leaves that have fluttered to the ground have provided a rich layer of mold, soft as any carpet, and giving off a pleasant earthy smell. On every side are the huge trees with their

great curling buttress roots, their thick smooth trunks towering hundreds of feet above, their head foliage and branches merging indistinguishably into the endless green roof of the forest. Between these the floor of the forest is covered with the young trees, thin tender growths just shaken free of the cradle of leaf mold, long thin stalks with a handful of pale green leaves on top. They stand in the everlasting shade of their parents, ready for the great effort of shooting up to the life-giving sun. In between their thin trunks, rambling across the floor of the forest, one can see faint paths twisting and turning. These are the roads of the bush and are followed by all its inhabitants.

—Gerald Durrell, *The Overloaded Ark*

Classification

Classification deals with systems of classes. Begin classification paragraphs with a general statement and support this statement by an enumeration and explanation of the types or subtypes:

Meteorites are of three general classes: irons—composed 98 percent or more of nickel-iron; stony irons—composed roughly half and half of nickel-iron and of a kind of rock known as olivine; and, finally, stones. The stones are further subdivided, depending on whether they contain tiny bodies (or chondrules) of the minerals olivine and pyroxene. The stones that possess them—more than 90 percent of all known meteoritic stones—are called chondrites. The few stones that lack these minerals are known as achondrites. All these categories offer useful clues to those who try to reconstruct the history of the earth, for not only are meteorites fellow members of the solar system, but radioactive dating indicates that they are as old as the earth itself. .

—Time-Life Books, *The Earth*

Exemplification

Exemplification paragraphs use supporting examples to illustrate a generalization. Begin exemplification paragraphs with a general statement and then support this statement by specific examples:

Almost no feature of the interior design of our current cars provides safeguards against injury in the event of collision. Doors that fly open on impact, inadequately secured seats, the sharp-edged rearview mirror, pointed knobs on instrument panels and doors, flying glass, the overhead structure—all illustrate the lethal potential of poor design. A sudden deceleration turns a collapsed steering wheel or a sharp-edged dashboard into a bone-and-chest-crushing agent. Penetration of the shatterproof windshield can chisel one's head into fractions. A flying seat cushion can cause a fatal injury. The apparently harmless glove-compartment door has been known to unlatch under impact and guillotine a child. Roof-supporting structure has deteriorated to a point where it provides scarcely more protection to the occupants, in common roll-over accidents, than an open convertible.

> —Ralph Nader,
> "The Safe Car You Can't Buy,"
> *The Nation* (April 11, 1957).

Definition

Definition paragraphs tell what a thing is. They also explain what words or phrases mean. One way of developing paragraphs of definition is to lead off with a general statement or with a logical definition. Then expand the general statement by other methods of defining:

"Desert" is an unfortunate word all around and most of its usual associations are inaccurate as well as unfavorable. In the first place the word doesn't even mean "dry," but simply uninhabited or deserted—like Robinson Crusoe's island. In that sense, the expanse about me is far from being a desert, for it is teeming with live things very glad indeed to be right there. Even in its secondary meaning, "desert" suggests to most people the rolling sand dunes of the Sahara. Something like that one may find in Death Valley; perhaps in parts of the Mojave; and especially, with an added weirdness, in the hundreds of square miles of New Mexico's White Sands, where the great dunes of glistening gypsum drift like the snowbanks one can hardly believe they are not. Most of my Lower Sonoran Desert, however, is not at all like that. The sandy soil is firm and hard-packed; it supports life, less crowded than in wetter regions but pleasantly flourishing. Nature does not frown here. She smiles invitingly.

—Joseph Wood Krutch, *The Desert Year*

Comparison and Contrast

Comparison and contrast paragraphs deal with similarities and differences. One way of organizing such paragraphs is as follows. In the first half of the paragraph, deal with one subject or aspect of a subject, and in the second half, take up the second subject or aspect of the subject to be compared:

> The way of the desert and the way of the jungle represent the two opposite methods of reaching stability at two extremes of density. In the jungle there is plenty of everything life needs except more space, and it is not for the want of anything else that individuals die or that races have any limit set to their proliferation. Everything is on top of everything else; there is no cranny which is not both occupied and disputed. At every moment, war to the death rages fiercely. The place left vacant by any creature that dies is seized almost instantly by another, and life seems to suffer from nothing except too favorable an environment. In the desert, on the other hand, it is the environment itself which serves as the limiting factor. To some extent the struggle of creature against creature is mitigated, though it is of course not abolished even in the vegetable kingdom. For the plant which in the one place would be strangled to death by its neighbor dies a thirsty seedling in the desert because that same neighbor has drawn the scant moisture from the spot of earth out of which it was attempting to spring.
>
> —Joseph Wood Krutch, *The Desert Year*

Narration

In *narrative paragraphs*, the emphasis is usually on the action, on the connected series of events that take place in chronological order. Of course, description is often included in narrative paragraphs in order to present the action in the most vivid terms. Organize narrative paragraphs chronologically. Since narrative paragraphs seldom use topic sentences, begin with a sentence that gets the action started. Then add sentences to advance the action:

> Slowly the minutes ticked away toward the zero hour. Officers, their watches synchronized, waited with guns in the air, ready to fire the shots that signaled the opening. At last the revolvers barked, and along the line pandemonium broke loose. Men whipped up their horses, wagons careened wildly forward, horses freed from overturned vehicles galloped madly about—all was hurrah and excitement. The Santa Fe trains, streaming slowly forward at a regulated pace which would not give their passengers an undue advantage, disgorged riders along the route as men leaped from roofs or platforms and rushed about in search of a claim. Noise and confusion reigned as the shouts of successful "Boomers," the crash of hammers on stakes, the clatter of wagons, the crash of overturned vehicles, and the curses of disappointed homeseekers mingled to create a bedlam unique in the annals of the nation.
>
> —Ray Allen Billington, *Westward Expansion*

Process

Organize *process paragraphs* chronologically, as you would narrative paragraphs. Place the emphasis, however, on *the steps* involved in the process:

> The process of précis writing is fivefold: (1) The student reads slowly the entire selection he intends to summarize, concentrating his attention on getting at the author's central idea. (2) He then rereads the selection, picking out the essential points or subdivisions; and, if the selection is long, jotting down the points made in successive paragraphs. (3) Either with or without reference to these notes, he next constructs sentences expressing the different points concisely but accurately, and groups these sentences into paragraphs representing sections or larger divisions of the whole. (4) He reads the selection a third time, comparing it with the summary he has prepared, and making sure that nothing important has been omitted,

nothing unimportant included, and nothing at all unclearly expressed. (5) He finally revises and recopies or rewrites his summary. The précis which results from this process will generally be from one-quarter to one-third the length of the original.

—Harry Robbins and Roscoe Parker, *Advanced Exposition*

Cause and Effect

Compose *cause and effect paragraphs* by moving from cause to effect or from effect to cause. The assumption is that an event takes place in time *because* an initial event caused it to occur or because it is part of a causal chain:

The intellectual life of the nineteenth century was more complex than that of any previous age. This was due to several causes. First: The area concerned was larger than ever before; America and Russia made important contributions, and Europe became more aware than formerly of Indian philosophies, both ancient and modern. Second: Science, which had been a chief source of novelty since the seventeenth century, made new conquests, especially in geology, biology, and organic chemistry. Third: Machine production profoundly altered the social structure, and gave men a new conception of their powers in relation to the physical environment. Fourth: A profound revolt, both philosophical and political, against traditional systems in thought, in politics, and in economics, gave rise to attacks upon many beliefs and institutions that had hitherto been regarded as unassailable. This revolt had two very different forms, one romantic, the other rationalistic. (I am using these words in a liberal sense.) The romantic revolt passes from Byron, Schopenhauer, and Nietzsche to Mussolini and Hitler; the rationalistic revolt begins with the French philosophers of the Revolution, passes on, somewhat softened, to the philosophical radicals in England, then acquires a deeper form in Marx and issues in Soviet Russia.

—Bertrand Russell, *A History of Western Philosophy*

Exercises

1. Analyze the foregoing paragraphs. Usually the topic sentence is the first sentence of the paragraph. Is this true in these paragraphs? What are the specific sentences in each paragraph that relate to the respective modes of development?

2. Write an analysis paragraph, listing the characteristics, features, aspects, or parts revealed by your analysis, based on one of the following topics:

   a. a song lyric
   b. the human body
   c. a day in your life
   d. a landscape
   e. an album cover
   f. a part of your room
   g. some object or possession
   h. a poster
   i. a picture or painting
   j. a magazine ad

3. In a single paragraph, describe a person, an object, or a scene.

4. Write a classification paragraph based on one of the topics listed below:

   a. popular songs
   b. clothing styles
   c. graffiti
   d. people
   e. blind dates

5. Write a paragraph giving examples of:

   a. things that disturb you
   b. prejudiced people
   c. current fads
   d. doublespeak in language
   e. ads that use subliminal appeals

6. In a single paragraph, write an extended definition of one of the following terms: *trashing, grodie, hippie, groupie, myth, romance, love, beauty, truth, success, pacification.*

   Coin a word and then write a paragraph defining it.

7. In a well-written paragraph, compare or contrast:

   a. two songs (rock lyrics)
   b. two people
   c. two dances
   d. two ads
   e. two of anything

8. Write a one paragraph narrative on one of the following subjects: an embarrassing moment, a frightening experience, a college experience.

9. In a single paragraph, describe a process:

   a. how to cook something
   b. how to play a certain game
   c. how to eat a certain dish
   d. how to produce (sell, prepare, build, plan, solve, and so forth)

10. Write a cause and effect paragraph based on one of the following topics:

   a. the effect of inflation on my life
   b. the effects of taking some drug (or of drinking a certain liquor)
   c. the cause of an accident in which you or a friend was involved
   d. the effects of a love affair
   e. the cause of some natural occurrence

The Paragraph as an Extended Sentence

Another way of looking at paragraph structure is to think of a paragraph as an extended sentence. This approach to paragraph construction is based on the work of Francis Christensen, who sees a close relationship between a particular type of sentence that he calls the **cumulative sentence** and the paragraph. According to Christensen, the cumulative sentence begins with a sentence base. This base contains the main subject, the main verb, and any bound or restrictive modifiers:

   1. The boys ate warily,

To the base is added an accumulation (hence the designation *cumulative*) of details, in the form of free or sentence modifiers:

   1. The boys ate warily.
     2. trying not to be seen or heard,
       3. the cornbread sticking,
       3. the buttermilk gurgling,
         4. as it went down their gullets.

—Katherine Anne Porter

The base clause is often stated in general terms. The modifiers add specific details to the base so that there is a deductive movement from the general (level 1) to the particular (levels 2, 3, and 4). The sentence levels are numbered and indented to show the grammatical and logical progression of ideas.

If sentences tend to have a base, to which details in the form of modifiers are added, then paragraphs, according to Christensen, have a similar movement. The paragraph, in this view, is a kind of extended sentence. The top sentence of the paragraph is similar to the base clause of the cumulative sentence. The supporting sentences in the paragraph are similar to the sentence modifiers. The successive sentences in the paragraph are related to each other by coordination and subordination.

If it is possible to consider the paragraph as having the same kind of structure as the cumulative sentence, then clearly some sentences can be rewritten as paragraphs. Below is a rewritten version of the Katherine Anne Porter sentence (cited above) as a paragraph:

1. The boys ate warily.
  2. They were trying not to be seen or heard.
    3. The cornbread was sticking.
    3. The buttermilk was gurgling.
      4. It went down their gullets.

Implicit in Christensen's approach to paragraph construction is the idea than an inductive study of the paragraph can be useful in learning to write paragraphs, that analyzing paragraphs will enable the writer to see what goes with what. Since all writers must necessarily use the same basic compositional principles, one can learn a great deal about these principles by studying the writing of others.

Analyzing Paragraphs

For the purpose of analyzing paragraphs, therefore, Christensen has suggested a sequence of steps that may be described as follows. First, assume that the first sentence of the paragraph is the top or topic sentence of the sequence, not the traditional topic sentence, but the sentence that gets the paragraph going. Give it the number 1. Then examine the subsequent sentences carefully, searching for similarities and differences. If the second sentence in the paragraph is like the first (is parallel in structure or ideas), set it down as coordinate and assign it the same number. If the second sentence differs from the first (gives evidence of subordination of structure or ideas), indent it as subordinate and give it the number 2. Do the same with the remaining sentences.

The following paragraph has been analyzed using the method indicated above. (Key transitional words and phrases are italicized to supplement the indentation and numbering of sentence levels):

1. The intellectual life of the nineteenth century was more complex than that of any previous age.
   2. *This* was due to several *causes*.
      3. *First:* The area concerned was larger than ever before; America and Russia made important contributions, and Europe became more aware than formerly of Indian philosophies, both ancient and modern.
      3. *Second:* Science, which had been a chief source of novelty since the seventeenth century, made new conquests, especially in geology, biology, and organic chemistry.
      3. *Third:* Machine production profoundly altered the social structure, and gave men a new conception of their powers in relation to the physical environment.
      3. *Fourth:* A profound *revolt*, both philosophical and political, against traditional systems in thought, in many beliefs and institutions that had hitherto been regarded as unassailable.
         4. This *revolt* had two very different forms, one *romantic,* the other *rationalistic.*
            5. (I am using these *words* in a liberal sense.)
            5. The *romantic revolt* passes from Byron, Schopenhauer, and Nietzsche to Mussolini and Hitler; the *rationalistic revolt* begins with the French philosophers of the Revolution, passes on, somewhat softened, to the philosophical radicals in England, then acquires a deeper form in Marx and issues in Soviet Russia.
            —Bertrand Russell, *A History of Western Philosophy*

This paragraph has a structure similar to that of the cumulative sentence. The first sentence is the top sentence or base. It also happens to be the topic sentence, the sentence that contains the main idea of the paragraph (the idea that "the intellectual life of the nineteenth century was more complex than that of any other age"). I have given it the number 1. The second sentence (level 2) is subordinate to the first, the word *this* referring to the idea of the complexity of intellectual life. Further, this sentence acts as the organizing sentence for the ideas in the subsequent sentence. (The word *causes* in the sentence "this was due to several causes" leads us to expect an enumeration of causes.) The next four sentences, labeled 3, enumerate specific causes of the complexity of intellectual life. The repetition of the cardinal numbers ("First," "Second," "Third," "Fourth") makes the logical progression of ideas and the tie-in with the word *causes* explicit. The next sentence (level 4) expands the idea in the previous sentence about the philosophical and political revolt, and the next two sentences (level 5) comment on the two forms of this revolt.

Let us look at another paragraph, this time doing a more extensive analysis:

1. It is impossible for Mexicans to produce the humblest thing without *form and design.*
2. A donkey wears a load of palm leaves *arranged* on either flank in great *green* sunbursts
2. Merchants hang candles by their wicks to make *patterns* in both *line* and *colour.*
2. Market coconuts show *white* new *moon strips* above the dark, fibrous *mass.*
2. Serapes are thrown with just the right *line* over the shoulders of ragged peons, muffling them to the eyes.
2. Merchants in the market will *compose* their tomatoes, oranges, red seeds and even peanuts into *little geometric piles.*
2. *Bundles* of husks will be *tied in a manner suitable for suspension in an artist's studio.*
3. To the traveler from the north, used to the treatment of the cold, dead produce as cold, dead produce, this is a matter of perpetual wonder and delight.

—Stuart Chase, *Mexico*

This paragraph follows a rigid, logical order. The first sentence is the topic sentence. Sentences two, three, four, five, and six are coordinate to each other but subordinate to sentence one. Each gives a specific example of the general idea contained in the topic sentence. Sentence seven is immediately subordinate to sentence six, but the word *this* in sentence seven could also refer to all the previous coordinate sentences.

The logical movement of this paragraph is from the general to the particular. The rhetorical pattern is exemplification. The first sentence states the main idea, the inductive generalization, that Mexicans produce even the humblest things with form and design. The next six sentences give specific examples of humble things with form and design. The load of palm leaves on a donkey are arranged in the shape of great green sunbursts. Candles are hung by their wicks in symmetrical patterns. Market coconuts are cut to show white moon strips. Ragged peons throw serapes over their shoulders with just the right lines. Merchants arrange their produce in geometrical piles. And husks are tied in bundles in such a way that an artist could have arranged them. The last sentence ties all these ideas together and concludes that this attention to form and .design in the simplest, everyday objects is a matter of wonder and delight to the traveler from the north.

The logical structure is also developed by the use of synonyms and related ideas that tie together the ideas of form, design, and color. The key lexical patterns can be schematized as follows:

Form and Design
palm leaves . . . *arranged* . . . . in great green *sunbursts*
candles [hung] . . . to make *patterns* in both *line* and *colour*
coconuts [with] . . . white new *moon strips*
serapes . . . thrown with just the right *line*
merchants . . . *compose* their tomatoes, oranges, red seeds and even peanuts into little *geometric piles*
bundles of husks . . . *tied in a manner suitable for suspension in an artist's studio*

Color
palm leaves . . . in great *green* sunbursts
coconuts show *white* new moon strips
dark, fibrous mass
tomatoes, *oranges*, *red* seeds

The value of this kind of analysis is that it not only graphically depicts the sentences in a paragraph in relation to each other, but it also enables you to understand the meaning relationships that obtain in paragraphs. You can subsequently use this kind of analysis to check your own paragraph structure, or you could go on to write your own paragraphs, using the same basic principles.

Composing Paragraphs

For the purposes of writing your own paragraphs, you could follow a sequence of steps very much like those listed below:

> *Begin with a base sentence.*
> *Add a supporting sentence.*
> *Add a second supporting sentence.*
> *Add a third supporting sentence.*
> *Conclude with a final supporting sentence.*

Or you could use some variation on the basic pattern:

> *Write a base sentence.*
> *Qualify that base.*
> *Add a specific detail.*
> *Add another detail.*
> *Qualify that detail.*

Visually, the two basic movements of thought in such paragraphs can be depicted as follows:

The Two-Level Paragraph

1. _____
   2. _____
   2. _____
   2. _____
   2. _____

The Multi-Level Paragraph

1. _____
  2. _____
    3. _____
    3. _____
      4. _____

In the two-level paragraph, all the sentences in the paragraph follow from and "depend" upon the base sentence. In a multi-level paragraph, the sentences follow from and "depend" upon each other.

Exercises

1. Some sentences have a structure remarkably like the structure of paragraphs. Transform the sentences below into paragraphs, as in the following example:

Sentence
  1. A host of laughing children bestrode the animals,
    2. bending forward like charging cavalrymen, and
    2. shaking reins and whooping in glee.
          —Stephen Crane

Sentence into Paragraph
  1. A host of laughing children bestrode the animals.
    2. They bent forward like charging cavalrymen.
    2. They shook the reins and whooped in glee.

  1. It was really a lovely day,
    2. the first dandelions making suns,
    2. the first daisies so white.
          —D. H. Lawrence

  1. The boys ate warily,
    2. trying not to be seen or heard,

    3. the cornbread sticking,

    3. the buttermilk gurgling,

        4. as it went down their gullets.

—Katherine Anne Porter

1. The dentist began his work,

    2. probing into sensitive cavities,

    2. swabbing the tender area with a dulling liquid,

    2. his fingers pressing the gumline,

        3. searching for the exact spot to insert his needle,

           4. still hidden from the patient's cringing eyes.

    2. As the snow melted on the roof,

1. streams of clear, cold water rippled over the slanted, brown-glazed shingles and slid off the edge,

    2. forming a waterfall which splashed on the grey cement walk below.

1. The old woman prayed alone in the huge cathedral,

    2. her head covered by a dark shawl,

        3. making her round face wide and Slavic,

    2. her elbows leaning heavily on the pew in front of her,

    2. her thick hands cradling her chin and mouth,

        3. the fingers clasped about a wooden rosary,

        3. the large roughened knuckles bent away from the center,

           4. forming a basket with which to collect prayers before releasing them to heaven.

2. Using the kind of analyses illustrated in this section, analyze a few of the example paragraphs, numbering and indenting the levels. Be prepared to discuss the structure, ideas, and language of these paragraphs.

3. Select one or two paragraphs from your own reading and analyze them in the same manner, or bring them to class, put them on the board, and analyze and discuss them.

4. Write a few paragraphs of your own, beginning with narrative and descriptive paragraphs, and then move on to expository paragraphs. Try writing two-level as well as multi-level paragraphs.

Throughout this chapter, my assumption has been that one good way to learn to write effective paragraphs is to look carefully at the principles that other writers use to achieve their purposes and then to use these principles in your own writing. When you write, you are carried along by the movement of the prose, by the flow of ideas, by the logical, spatial, or temporal progression. Often you may have an intuitive sense of paragraph structure, but this is not enough. Good writers usually have a developed sense of form consciousness, and often they can be self-conscious about their writing when there is a need to be. Good writing is planned in such a way as to exploit all the resources of language—the sentence structure, the word choice, and the paragraph structure. Learning to write is in part learning to recognize and to use the best available resources of the language.

Achieving Coherence

The best way of achieving coherence in your writing is to develop your powers of consecutive thinking so that your paragraphs unfold in a logical, step-by-step manner. Sometimes, however, it may be helpful to your reader if you use **transitional devices** to make the relationship among the parts of your essay clear. You can achieve coherence by breaking your writing into logical units, but sometimes you need *connecting words and phrases to make the flow of your thoughts smooth and effortless.*

Careful writers use transitional words and phrases to show connections in thought. These coherence devices link words within a sentence, sentences within a paragraph, and sentences between paragraphs. The following are some typical examples:

Addition

Use connectives to suggest simple addition to the thought in the preceding sentence: *and, too, also, again, and then, moreover, further, indeed, in addition to, plus, likewise, besides, together, jointly.*

This is a wine to enjoy with your dinner. You will *also* enjoy its delicious flavor with fruit, cheese, and dessert after dinner is over.

Ask to visit several classrooms. *Also* make the most of parent–teacher conferences.

Series

Use transitional devices to link items in a series: *first, second, third; next, again, last; primarily, secondarily; in the first place, in the second place; finally, additionally, first and foremost, the former, the latter.*

At first, it may be Grand Prix's beautiful styling that captivates you the most. *The next time,* it may be Grand Prix's luxurious interior that charms you.

First we let blueberry pie dry on a dessert dish overnight. *Then* we washed it with Electrasol.

Pronoun Reference

Use a pronoun to refer to a noun, another pronoun, or a clause in the preceding sentence: *this, that, these, those, he, she, it, you, they, we, such, some, many, none.*

Welcome to *Hawaii. It* is a place as unique and varied as *its* flowers.

Some *people* dream of relaxing on a secluded island. *Others* dream of more lavish surroundings.

Repeated Word

Repeat a key word, or a word derived from the same root: *told/tell, arrived/arrival,   rare/rarity,   moisture/moistness/moisten/moist, depth/deep, mix/mixture/admixture/mixed.*

There are crippled *children* who want to walk so badly it hurts. *There are children* for whom even the simple act of moving a pencil becomes an agonizing test of determination. *There are children* whose courage in therapy would astonish you.

He *arrived* early. His *arrival* filled us with dread.

Synonyms

If the repetition of key words gets tiresome or if variety is needed, use a different word or phrase to refer to an element in the preceding sentence: *car/automobile, spectator/onlooker/observer/viewer, purchase/buy, join/unite/connect, exterior/outside, mere words/ nonsense.*

One of the hottest topics in public education today is *"back to the basics."* PTA meetings resound with debates on the *subject.*

It was a rare *caper,* planned to the second and full of acrobatic derring-do: thieves dropped in through the roof at San Francisco's De Young Memorial Museum and made off with several Dutch paintings, including Rembrandt's "The Rabbi," worth about a million dollars. Such elaborate *heists* are becoming increasingly common nowadays.

Whole-Part

Use a word or a phrase that names a whole in one sentence, and then use another word or a phrase that names a part of the whole: *television/picture tube, stereo/tuner, water/wave, flower/petal, book/chapter/section/paragraph, landscape/meadow.*

The roof on this house is made of a new kind of *nonwood. shingle.* The *edges* are thick and irregular.

The creosote *bush* is a wispy shrub. It has scraggly *branches* two to five feet high.

Class-Members

Name a general class in one sentence and a member of that class in another: *vehicle/car, sound/noise, fluid/water, fuel/coal/gas, fragrance/perfume, span of time/decade, place of worship/cathedral.*

> Supersoil is a superbly balanced *nutrient potting mix*. It contains rich *sphagnum peat, redwood, fir bark,* and *granite-based river sand.*

> In speed, power, and appetite, the *shark* is a formidable ocean predator. The little we know of this dangerous, unpredictable *fish* has been learned at a high cost in human life.

Emphasis

Use connectives to reinforce the thought in a previous clause or to give emphasis to that thought: *obviously, certainly, perhaps, surely, naturally, really, to be sure, in truth, very likely, undoubtedly, assuredly, without fail.*

> Add fresh taste and variety to your salad with country-fresh mushrooms. They're full of flavor and *surprisingly* low in calories.

> *Naturally*, a teething baby or even a small child cannot be expected to brush its own teeth. But you can—and must.

Comparison

Use connectives that reveal to the reader significant likenesses in thought: *equally important, similarly, in the same way, also, comparably, corresponding, equally, like.*

> Animal life on the desert is *like* life anywhere else. It is completely dependent upon plant life for sustenance.

The killer whale is one of the most dangerous marine animals. *Equally* dangerous is the moray eel.

Contrast

Connect sentences with linking devices that show contrast and that reveal to the reader significant differences in thought: *but, yet, however, still, nevertheless, on the contrary, on the other hand, in spite of, conversely, although, unlike, be that as it may.*

Until now, all bran cereals were made from wheat. *But* many people think corn tastes better.

Taking care of wood is a constant job. *Unlike* wood, vinyl siding takes care of itself.

Result

Use transitional devices when you want to show result: *consequently, therefore, thus, as a result, for this reason, on this account, it follows that, accordingly, hence, so, necessarily.*

The color of the roof is soft and muted. *So* it blends in naturally with the architecture and the surroundings.

No matter how many trash cans you buy, it always seems that there isn't enough room for the trash. *That's why* a Kitchen Aid trash compactor is so worth having.

Example

Use transitional words and phrases to introduce illustrations or examples: *for instance, for example, namely, that is, thus.*

The new cars are quieter than last year's models. You will be surprised, *for example,* by the almost complete absence of road noise and body vibrations.

Nouns which consist of two or more root words are called compound nouns. Often they are written as one word, but they can be written as two words. "Ice cream," *for instance,* is just as much of a compound as is "blueberry."

Parallel Structure

Repeat in the second clause a grammatical structure similar to that in a previous clause: *in the morning/in the evening, some things will never change/some things will always be the same.*

Have you ever seen a killer whale or a live shark up close? Have your children ever touched a real dolphin?

Come and watch Kabuki, a Japanese drama. Visit gilded palaces in Bangkok. Admire ancient temples in Malaysia.

Place

Use linking devices that indicate place or change of place: *here, there, above, under, near by, beyond, on the other side, opposite, adjacent to, in.*

Spend your vacation in *British Columbia.* Your American dollar's worth much more *there.*

Odors used to be an everyday problem *in my house* until I started using Lysol Disinfectant Spray every day. *In the bathroom,* Lysol doesn't just cover up odors, it eliminates them fast.

Time

Use connectives that indicate time or a change of time: *not long after, then, soon, now, after a short while, meanwhile, immediately.*

During the day, you can swim, sun, relax, and play. *At night,* you can watch a floor show.

When your cab pulls up in front of the London Hilton, you can expect a most gracious welcome from our doormen. *When* they open your cab door, they'll tip their hats and usher you in with a friendly smile.

Exercises

1. Analyze the following paragraphs. What methods are used to achieve coherence? Mark each paragraph in detail to illustrate the use of transitional devices (for example, put one line under pronouns and their antecedents, two lines under connectives, circle appropriate words and phrases, draw arrows, use squiggly lines, etc.). Then be prepared to discuss these paragraphs in class.

   a. Italians are convinced that it is good to be alive, and they spend considerable time and energy proving themselves right. With gusto, they sail on warm seas and chill lakes, bowl in the nearest back yard, race about sun-baked soccer fields or argue among themselves at a sidewalk café. But nothing reflects their enjoyment more than their cookery, which is as diverse as the nation's regions, as imaginative as the Italian character. Whether the cook presides in a swank hotel or an ancient farmhouse, the meal is likely to be superb. For, to an Italian, to eat is to live.
      —*Italy*, Life World Library

   b. For no other art do the Italians have more natural talent than they have for dramatic vocal music. The most extroverted and demonstrative people of the Mediterranean, they have since Dante and Petrarch spoken a language that is the most melodious in the world. Furthermore, the Italians seem peculiarly blessed with throats which naturally emit sweet, free-flowing sounds. Perhaps this is because they have been essentially a pastoral people free from many of the tensions of urban life—even when living in cities.
      —*Italy*, Life World Library

   c. Another farsighted practice of the English was to bring along their women. This made for a more homogeneous society than that of the French and Spanish colonies, in which men took native wives. And it also meant the family unit was to provide a solid core for a racially well-knit people, who early indicated that they had come to stay. For the next 300 years, as the descendants of these early settlers pushed westward across the continent, building the nation, it was the presence of the women and of the unit that provided stability and permanence to the new communities. It was they who demanded schools, religion, and order. It was their presence that encouraged a cultural uplift and broke down some of the rough-house tendencies of the masculine frontier. While the Spanish and French ranged over vast stretches of land, unhampered by any family ties, except momentary domesticity with occasional native women, the English stayed close to home. The result was a family type of frontier, characterized by small farms, that remained much more compact, more easily defended, and permanent in nature.

—*The New World,* American Heritage

2. Select an article from your reader or from a magazine. Identify the words and phrases that are used as explicit transitions *from paragraph to paragraph*.

Introductory Paragraphs

Have formal introductions gone out of style? According to some writers, they have. Because of television and the mass media, readers are impatient with long and formal introductions. They want you to get right to the point.

But even if you decide to keep your beginning paragraphs brief and informal, you must not forget that in your opening paragraphs, you make a commitment to your readers that you are expected to fulfull.

What should you do in your opening paragraph or paragraphs? At the very least, give your readers some idea of what you are going to write about, state your purpose, and indicate your plan of development. If your subject is a difficult one, you might also want to include a preliminary explanation.

Introductory paragraphs, then, should lead into the subject. But they should do more. They should also arouse the curiosity and interest of your readers and create the proper tone.

In considering strategies for your opening paragraphs, it might be helpful to ask yourself the following questions:

1. *Who are my readers?*
2. *Do they have any knowledge of my subject?*
3. *Do they have any interest in my subject?*
4. *How can I best gain their attention?*
5. *Is my purpose to present my readers with new ideas or information, to persuade them to take a certain course of action, or to entertain them?*
6. *How can I best convey to my readers my own interest in and attitude toward my subject?*

Experienced writers use a number of strategies in their opening paragraphs. Here are a few you may want to try.

Begin With Descriptive Details

Staring from the poster, they looked like a nightmare of what might be, that terrifying day when the street gangs take over the city, any city. Some of them wore leather vests over bare chests. Others had on Arab headdresses. A few, their faces painted harlequin colors, wore baseball uniforms and carried bats. Massed as far as the eye could see, all looked menacing, and the threat was underscored by the text above the picture: "These are the Armies of the Night. They are 100,000 strong. They outnumber the cops five to one. They could run New York City. Tonight they're all out to get the Warriors."

That Paramount ad was chillingly effective, bringing into 670 theaters around the country thousands of youths keen to see *The Warriors*—and eager for trouble. Since the film opened on Feb. 9, three young men have been killed by *Warrior*-inspired fights, and other brawls have broken out at moviehouses in several cities. More than a half a dozen theaters have dropped the film entirely; others are hiring some muscle of their own, which Paramount will pay for. In Washington, D.C., two full-time guards were on duty last week at the Town Downtown and will stay there until *The Warriors* finishes its run. Not since Stanley Kubrick's *A Clockwork Orange* opened in 1971 has a movie generated such anxiety about the seeming power of a film to engender gang violence in those who see it.

—"The Flick of Violence," *Time*

Begin With An Anecdote

Nearly five years ago I sat in the courtyard of a household in the village I call Tudu, Niger, haranguing the head of the household in an attempt to determine the year his first son was born. His replies were desultory as I sought to find out whether the son was older or younger than other men whose ages I knew fairly well. In the middle of this important but tedious part of demographic data collection, the man's daughter-in-law came out of her hut with an infant in her arms. She hurried over to me, and with tears running down her cheeks, her body shaking with sobs, she placed the baby in my lap and pleaded, "Ladi just stopped breathing in her sleep. Can you do anything?" Ladi—her stomach distended, the bones of her arms and legs like fragile spindles—was dead, and Ladi's mother, in spite of her question, knew that there was nothing I could do. At that moment my inability to help in a tangible way, as well as the needlessness of Ladi's death, ignited my anger and frustration at the effects of the Sahelian drought.

The drought in West Africa south of the Sahara was due to four straight years of poor rainfall—from 1970 to 1973—each year worse than the one before. The drought was reported to the United States and Europe in terms of thousands of deaths, hundreds of thousands made homeless, the encroaching Sahara, and somber declarations of international relief aid for the region.

—Ralph H. Faulkingham,
"Where the Lifeboat Ethic Breaks Down," *Human Nature*

Begin With a Quotation

"We cannot tolerate the Cubans to go swashbuckling unchecked in Africa, the Middle East and other areas, nor can we tolerate the Cubans of the Orient to go swashbuckling in Laos, Kampuchea or even in the Chinese border areas. Now some people in the world are afraid of offending them, even if they do something terrible. These people wouldn't dare take action against them."

So said China's Vice Premier Teng Hsiao-p'ing last week, puffing on a Panda cigarette as he aimed an unmistakable rebuke at what Peking considers the jelly-bellied Western response to adventurism

by the Soviets and their clients. Teng also gave the fullest explanation
yet of the motives behind China's two-week-old "punitive" invasion
of its southern neighbor, Viet Nam. In an effort to placate
international alarm, he repeated assurances that the operation "will
be limited in degree and will not last a long time," perhaps no longer
than China's four-week invasion of India in 1962. There were reports
at week's end, in fact, that the Chinese were considering a cease-
fire and might begin pulling back this week.

—"Suck Them In and Out-Flank Them," *Time*

Begin With the Thesis Statement

A revolution was spinning out of control. With nonviolent protests
and uncommon discipline, the people of Iran had ended the
tyranny of the Shah. Their rewards was not freedom but chaos, as
the forces united around Ayatullah Ruhollah Khomeini last week
showed the first dread signs of schism. Suddenly, guns were
everywhere, in every hand, as self-styled "freedom fighters" liberated
weapons from police stations and army barracks. In Tehran, Tabriz
and other cities, sporadic fighting raised the death toll for the week
to an estimated 1,500. A bewildering motley of forces was involved:
troops loyal to the Shah, ethnic separatists, *mojahedeen* (literally,
crusaders) who backed the new government of Prime Minister Mehdi
Bazargan, and, ominously, Marxist *fedayeen* (sacrificers) who felt
that the revolution had not moved far enough to the left.

—"Guns, Death, and Chaos," *Time*

Begin With a Question

Is it possible that a cigar-shaped spaceship descended over the tiny
town of Aurora, Texas (pop. 237), and crashed into Judge J. S.
Proctor's windmill? And that a tiny spaceman was buried in the Aurora
cemetery?

That was the tale sent to newspapers in nearby Dallas and Fort
Worth one April day in 1897 by a local correspondent named S. E.
Hayden. It was generally ridiculed at the time, and most citizens of
Aurora still scoff. "Hayden wrote it as a joke and to bring interest

to Aurora,'' says Etta Pegues, 86. ''The railroad bypassed us, and the town was dying.''

—''Close Encounters of a Kind,'' *Time*

Begin with a Figure of Speech

Like fast-approaching storm clouds, the consequences of the political turmoil that shut down Iran's oil fields became clearer last week, presaging a period of trouble and uncertainty for Western nations. Higher fuel prices and some scarcities are inevitable in the U.S. President Carter warned that though the situation created by the Iranian cutoff is ''not critical'' yet, it ''certainly could get worse.'' He said that the difficulties might be manageable if Americans ''honor the 55-mph speed limit, set thermostats no higher than 65° and limit discretionary driving.'' Otherwise, the President added, ''more strenuous action'' would be needed to curb fuel use.

—''The Price of Stormy Petrol,'' *Time*

Begin with a Cryptic Statement

Winnipeg is jumping. Airline reservations to the frostbitten Canadian city (pop. 560,000) have been booked for months. Hotels are full up too. The cause of this midwinter madness: the last solar eclipse over the continental U.S. until 2017. On Monday, Feb. 26, the moon will slip between the earth and sun, and progressively blot out the solar disc along a so-called path of totality that begins in the Pacific Ocean west of Washington State, cuts northeast over Canada, then darts off and away toward Greenland.

—''A Matter of Night and Day,'' *Time*

Begin with an Analogy

From Florida to Maine there is a war. Between man and man, fish and bird, wave and sand. The battle rages and storms over the coast. Yet the battlefield is strangely quiet. Grasses bend softly in the wind. Herons stalk silently through shallow waters. This war is being fought in the narrow green-and-tawny band of salt marsh that stretches along our eastern shore.

For millenniums there could be no final victory or defeat. Nature's contending forces stayed in balance. The rising sea stole from the marshland, and the marshland rebuilt its defenses. The marsh grass died and, decaying, nourished the animal life of the estuaries. Fish warred on fish and the birds on them, but all at last fell in the battle, and, in dissolution, fed the grass roots. The circle closed, and the battle was joined again.

Now, however, we humans can impose a final decision in this immemorial war of the wetlands along all our coasts. We even have it in our power to obliterate the battlefield. And if we do, will that be victory or defeat? Are we about to conquer nature, or about to conquer ourselves?

The salt marshes are disappearing before the onslaught of factories, dump and fill, homes with a seaward view. As chemicals and sewage pollute the wetlands, the encroachment of industrialists and developers is also the route of oyster dredgers, clammers, crabbers, sportsmen, and lovers of nature.

—Stephen W. Hitchcock,
''Can We Save Our Salt Marshes?''
National Geographic

Concluding Paragraphs

The concluding paragraph should conclude. Nothing could be so obvious or so simple. Yet inexperienced writers often have a difficult time concluding their essays. When they run out of something to say, they just stop.

If your writing is to have any effect on your readers, it ought to have an appropriate ending. If your essay is relatively short, you might end it with the most important point. If your essay is relatively long, you might repeat the main points you made in the body of your paper. If your ideas are difficult, you might want to summarize in your concluding paragraph what you have said in the body of your paper. In brief, you want to leave your readers with the feeling that your essay is complete.

Here are some suggestions for concluding your essays:

1. *End with the most important point of your essay.*
2. *Repeat the main points of your essay.*
3. *Present your reader with a summary of your main ideas.*
4. *Conclude with a call for action.*
5. *End with a question.*

6. *Conclude with a prediction or forecast.*
7. *Give your reader an opinion, based on your previous discussion.*
8. *Discuss the broader implications of your subject.*
9. *End with an anecdote.*
10. *Conclude with a striking example.*

The following are a few examples of concluding paragraphs.

End with a Restatement of Your Main Points

The rules that govern the act of kissing, in short, are complex and varied. The human kiss has evolved a long way from its probable origins in the sniff of animal recognition and the warmth of human bonding. It can be a reflexive gesture of greeting or deference, or a carefully planned sign of personal feeling. The first deep kiss, a passionate kiss from one's beloved, the last kiss exchanged between close friends or relatives, the happy kisses for a newborn baby—all evoke powerful emotions that are remembered for life. The simple kiss carries complex meaning, which poets will continue to praise, scientists will continue to explain, and all of us will continue to practice.

—Leonore Teifer, "The Kiss," *Human Nature*

End with a Generalization

Nothing in the universe has more grandeur than the infinity of the human mind. Even pea-sized computers capable of forecasting the movement of the galaxies are not more wondrous than the mysterious human creature that produced them. The ultimate frontier is not geographical or spatial but intellectual.

—Norman Cousins, "The Conquest of Pain," *Saturday Review*

End with a Quotation

Sir Richard Livingstone, late vice-chancellor of Oxford, once wrote that "true education is the habitual vision of greatness"—the study of great individuals, great events, and great art and literature. Teachers of English should demand greatness in what their students read and aim for greatness in what their students write. To do less is to condemn the next generation to mumbling mediocrity.

    Edward T. Hall, "Why Americans Can't Write," *Human Nature*

Exercises

1. Discuss the following introductory paragraphs in class. What method is used to begin each paragraph or set of paragraphs? Do they arouse your interest? Why or why not? How do they lead into the body of the paper?

> a. The China-Viet Nam War wilted like a frostbitten blossom last week. China's 100,000 or so infantry and armored troops arrested their languid advance 15 to 20 miles inside the Viet Nam border, wheeled, and began a gradual, piecemeal withdrawal. Vietnamese artillery and front-line units of the 70,000-man-strong border defense force put on a show of hot pursuit but coolly refrained from any real, obstructive attack. Judging from the ferocity of each side's victory claims, it seemed safe to conclude that neither side had won—or lost.
>
>   "Windup of a No-Win War," *Time*

> b. "Maps speak, and through the language of a map speaks the mind of a society," wrote Barbara Aziz (August 1978). Aziz skewered any lingering beliefs a citizen might have that maps are somehow independent of the people who create them. A 20th-century sophisticate, after all, is likely to regard a Rand-McNally atlas or an *Encyclopedia Britannica* geographical sketch as revealed truth.
>
>   But, as Aziz has demonstrated, geographic reality is culturally determined: "Maps, like language, select certain features and ignore others, and like language, maps are cultural expressions of elements significant to a society."
>
>   "Maps and the Mind," *Human Nature*

> c. Seething gases and liquids mask its rocky core. Its frigid atmosphere consists mostly of hydrogen and helium. Great cyclones and hurricanes swirl in its turbulent sky, with brilliant red and orange clouds constantly merging and breaking apart in ever changing patterns. Often the

turbulence creates trails of sinuous white vapors thousands of miles long. The awesome, forbiddingly beautiful world is that of Jupiter, a planet so large it could swallow more than 1,300 earths.

"Intimate Glimpses of a Giant," *Time*

d. Skimming down a steep, snow-covered road at Camp David in Maryland's lovely Catoctin Mountains, Jimmy Carter was enjoying the brisk air of an afternoon in the woods when the tip of one of his thin skis caught beneath a crust of rough ice. The President of the United States went down hard. The consequences of this tumble were clearly visible when he returned to snow-paralyzed Washington the next day: an ugly purple bruise the size of a silver dollar over his right eye, several bright red scratches on his cheek, a puffy lip and a slight limp. It took the deftest ministrations of his makeup woman to hide the wounds before public appearances.

The bruising of the President did not stop all week. Despite Carter's efforts to appear decisive and determined in his handling of the nation's affairs, he kept encountering hidden obstacles. And as his standing in U.S. public opinion polls once again sank, world events seemed conspiring to prove his frequently repeated assertion that "the United States cannot control events within other nations."

"Carter: Black and Blue," *Time*

e. What if it were possible to cut heating costs to a fraction of the current rate? Wouldn't this be worthwhile—particularly if it could be done without spending billions for solar retrofits and insulation, and if the final result would be a healthier, more satisfying heat like that provided by a fireplace or an old-fashioned potbellied stove? I believe we could do it if we would remember that regardless of the problem that faces us, it makes no sense to ignore human nature. In this case, the problem under discussion is the transaction between human beings and a variety of heat sources.

There is an abundance of data on the thermal requirements of heating buildings and none on heating people. We heat buildings in order to heat people (and even that job is often done rather badly). We behave like the mythical primitive who burned down his house in order to cook his pig.

Edward T. Hall, "Let's Heat People Instead of Houses," *Human Nature*

f. In ten summers of rewarding work at Aphrodisias, a great ruined city of the Greco-Roman age in Turkey's Anatolian uplands, I have learned that past and present often merge. For example, as we excavated the city's agora, or marketplace, we came upon some 300 fragments of inscribed stone panels. Fitted together like a giant jigsaw puzzle, they proved to be exactly what Americans find posted in neighborhood supermarkets today—a table of fixed prices.

In A.D. 301, runaway inflation had threatened to destroy the economy of the Roman Empire. To deal with this situation so closely paralleling that of our own era, the Emperor Diocletian froze all prices. It was his edict, and the prices he established, that we discovered in the agora of Aphrodisias. The roster of items is exhaustive, including commodities as varied as melons and marble, kerchiefs and cattle. Violations of the edict drew severe penalties, even death.

Kenan T. Erim, ''Aphrodisias: Awakened City
of Ancient Art,'' *National Geographic*

g. A man in bright orange trousers asked me to close my eyes and hold his hand. I did as he said. In my other hand he put one end of a forked plastic rod. He held the other side. Then he told me to breathe deeply, clear my mind, and think only of water. The rod pointed into the sky, but as we walked slowly across the grass it was pulled down as if by a magnet. I opened my eyes and saw the rod pointing directly to the ground in front of the fire hydrant on the green in Danville, Vermont.

Dowsing, also called divining, witching, wishing, or striking, is the process of discovering hidden objects by means of a divining rod. Many dowsers claim that the practice goes back to Biblical times, citing the story in Numbers of Moses striking a rock with his rod and water spurting forth. Some say that the Chinese relied on it for the placement of their houses. The image of a man pacing the earth with a divining rod in hand is certainly part of American folklore, but it is an imported rather than native-born practice. The first clear-cut account of dowsing is a report on German mining by Georgius Agricola in *De Re Metallica*, published in 1556. From Germany it spread to the rest of Europe and finally to the United States.

Nancy Hechinger, ''Discovering Human Nature,''
Human Nature

2. Bring to class at least three closing paragraphs from current magazine articles. Be prepared to discuss the techniques used for concluding the respective articles.

3. Write three introductory paragraphs, using one of the methods previously discussed.

4. Write three different types of concluding paragraphs, making sure to leave your reader with a sense of completeness.

Revising Paragraphs in Relation to Purpose and Audience

In strict logical terms, your paragraphing ought to contribute to the unity of the whole composition. Each paragraph ought to have a unity of its own. But it is quite possible that because of considerations of purpose or audience or kind of writing (for example, if you are writing an ad or a news story), you will want to go back after you have finished your writing and change the length of your paragraphs or change your overall organizational pattern. I am not suggesting that you write one- or two-sentence paragraphs, although at times a one-sentence paragraph might be very effective. I am suggesting, however, that you might learn something from advertisers about paragraphing, about the psychology of audiences, and about readability.

Short paragraphs can help you achieve emphasis in your writing. They are easy to read and to follow. However, in essay writing, an excess of short paragraphs might become tiresome. Sometimes long paragraphs are necessary to make a long, involved point. They can also give your reader the effect of reason and deliberation.

To illustrate these ideas more concretely, I'd like to take you through the stages of rewriting and reparagraphing a magazine ad to show you how copywriters skillfully adapt their copy to their purposes and audiences and to suggest paragraphing strategies that can be adapted for different purposes and audiences.

The ad I have chosen is a Suntory Royal Whiskey ad that appeared in the November 14, 1977, issue of *Time* magazine. The general audience is that of *Time* magazine, and the specific audience is Scotch drinkers. The purpose of the ad is to persuade Scotch drinkers to buy Suntory Royal Whiskey rather than Scotch. The dominant mode is process analysis. The copy reads as follows:

SUNTORY ROYAL.
SLIGHTLY EAST OF SCOTCH.

1

For over 50 years, we've been making our Suntory Whiskies just the way the very best Scotches are made.

2

To create Suntory Royal
we begin with fine barley malt
and clear mountain water.
Patiently we smoke the grain
over rich Scottish peat.

3

The mash is then distilled
in real copper pot stills. With
tedious, painstaking control.

4

To let it age and mellow,
we store the distillate in
genuine white oak barrels,
delicately steeped in sherry.

5

After ageing, the mature
whiskies are drawn from the
barrels and carefully married
according to time-honored
tradition.

6

We then store the blend
again, allowing the subtle
richness of the flavors to become one magnificent taste.

7

No, our Suntory Royal is
not Scotch.

8

And although it is made
the very same way, from the

very same ingredients, it still
retains a unique character
all its own. Smoother, lighter
and more distinctive.

9

Suntory Royal may be
close to Scotch, but it's still
about 10,000 miles apart.

This ad consists of nine paragraphs, each ranging in length from one to two sentences. Paragraph 1 contains one sentence. Paragraph 2 contains two sentences. Paragraph 3 contains a sentence and a prepositional phrase punctuated as a sentence. Paragraphs 4, 5, 6, 7, and 9 contain single sentences. Paragraph 8 consists of a complete sentence and a series of adjectival modifiers punctuated as if it were a complete sentence.

Paragraph length is interesting. Paragraph 1 consists of nineteen words; paragraph 2 has twenty-three words; paragraph 3, thirteen; paragraph 4, nineteen; paragraph 5, seventeen; paragraph 6, eighteen; paragraph 7, seven; paragraph 8, twenty-eight; paragraph 9, fourteen. Paragraphs 7 and 8 provide just enough variety in sentence length to keep the copy from getting monotonous. The other paragraphs are approximately the same length. If you look at the shape of the paragraphs in the overall plan, you will see that they are balanced and pleasing to the eye.

The mode of development is process analysis. But if you look closely at the way the stages of the process are organized into paragraphs, you wonder if the copywriter knows what he or she is doing. The ingredients of the product are listed in the second paragraph. But rather than separating the stages of making this whiskey into separate paragraphs or perhaps grouping all of the stages into a single paragraph, the writer puts the first stage of the operation in the second paragraph. Also, curiously, the writer switches person, from *we've* and *we* to *the mash*, to *we*, to *the mature whiskies*, to *we*. Doesn't this advertiser know how to write process copy? If you were to switch from the first person to the third or from the second to the third in writing a process essay, your instructor would probably mark you down for changing the point of view. However, this is not the description of a scientific process, but the use of process analysis *in the service of persuasion.* So the writer is deliberately breaking the conventions of process writing for a particular purpose.

If you were to follow the conventions of process analysis in rewriting this ad, you might use the first person almost exclusively. *The effect would be to put the emphasis on the maker of the product,* as in the following rewritten version:

For over 50 years, *we*'ve been making our Suntory Whiskies just the way the very best Scotches are made.

To create Suntory Royal *we* begin with fine barley malt and clear mountain water. Patiently *we* smoke the grain over rich Scottish peat.

We then distill the mash in real copper pot stills. With tedious, painstaking control.

To let it age and mellow, *we* store the distillate in genuine white oak barrels, delicately steeped in sherry.

After ageing the whiskies, *we* draw the mature whiskies from the barrels and carefully marry them according to time-honored tradition.

We then store the blend again, allowing the subtle richness of the flavors to become one magnificent taste.

No, our Suntory Royal is not Scotch.

And although it is made
the very same way, from the
very same ingredients, it still
retains a unique character
all its own. Smoother, lighter
and more distinctive.

Suntory Royal may be
close to Scotch, but it's still
about 10,000 miles apart.

You could also write the ad in the third person. *The effect would then be to put the emphasis on the product*, as in the rewritten version below:

For over 50 years, *Suntory Whiskies* have been made just the way the very best Scotches are made.

Fine barley *malt* and clear
mountain *water* are used to create
Suntory Royal. The *grain* is
smoked over rich Scottish peat.

The *mash* is then patiently
distilled in real copper pot
stills. With tedious, painstaking control.

So that it can age and mellow,
the *distillate* is stored in genuine
white oak barrels, delicately
steeped in sherry.

After ageing, the mature
whiskies are drawn from the
barrels and carefully married
according to time-honored
tradition.

The *blend* is then stored again,
allowing the subtle richness of
the flavors to become one magnificent taste.

No, Suntory Royal is not Scotch.

And although it is made
the very same way, from the
very same ingredients, it still
retains a unique character
all its own. Smoother, lighter
and more distinctive.

Suntory Royal may be
close to Scotch, but it's still
about 10,000 miles apart.

But the copywriter decided to switch back and forth between
the first person and the third, to emphasize both the maker of the
product and the product itself. Think for a moment about the strategies involved. Suntory Royal is made in Japan, not Scotland. It is
not Scotch whiskey, but according to the advertiser it's better than
Scotch. How can you convey this idea to the reader? *By stressing
both the process and the character of the makers of Suntory Royal.*
In other words, the advertiser is combining an ethical appeal with a
logical appeal. If Scotch drinkers trust the manufacturer, they will
buy the product. If they understand how well the product is made,
they will buy the product. So the shift from the pronoun *we*, which
stresses the manufacturer, to the nouns *(mash, whiskey)* that stress
the process is calculated.

The language of the ad reinforces the organizational strategies.
Adjectives such as *fine, rich, best, genuine, magnificent, unique,*
and *distinctive* emphasize the quality of the product. Adverbs such
as *patiently* and *delicately* and adjectives such as *tedious* and
painstaking stress the care that the manufacturer takes in making
the product. The line "patiently we smoke the grain over rich Scottish
peat" thus directs the reader to the patience of the manufacturer
in smoking the grain and to the process of smoking the grain.

If the advertiser had decided to follow the conventions of writing a scientific process, with logical paragraphing and a logical development of the ideas, the result would be something like the following:

> For over 50 years, Suntory
> Whiskies have been made just
> the way the very best Scotches
> are made, with barley malt
> and clear mountain water.
>
> To begin with, the grain
> is smoked over Scottish peat.
> Then the mash is distilled
> in copper pot stills. So that
> it can age and mellow, the dis-
> tillate is stored in white
> oak barrels steeped in sherry.
> After ageing, the mature whisk-
> ies are drawn from the barrels
> and blended. The blend is then
> stored again, allowing the fla-
> vors to become one.
>
> No, Suntory Royal is not
> Scotch. And although it is made
> the very same way, from the
> very same ingredients, it still
> retains a character all its own.
>
> Suntory Royal may be made
> like Scotch, but it's actually
> better.

Notice the difference in tone and in purpose in this version of the ad. Instead of nine paragraphs, there are four. The first paragraph consists of a single, long sentence of twenty-five words, which combines the first two sentences of the original. This paragraph lists the ingredients used in making the product. Paragraph 2 contains five sentences, for a total of sixty-one words. Each sentence in this paragraph enumerates a stage in the process. Paragraph 3 contains twenty-eight words. It stresses the quality of the process. Paragraph 4 contains eleven words. It makes the comparison with Scotch explicit.

You will notice that this version combines all of the sentence fragments into grammatically correct sentences, sticks to the third person, and neutralizes the language by taking out most of the emotion-laden and impressionistic diction. The result is a more scientific tone in which the emphasis is more on the process than on the character of the manufacturer.

I hope that this analysis reveals the importance of a self-conscious awareness of paragraphing and of organizational patterns. The extent to which many writers neglect organizational strategies is surprising. Unlike advertisers, many writers prefer to stress the uniqueness of a piece of writing rather than its conventionality. But advertisers have discovered that certain organizational conventions work better than others, that paradigms are important because they have a psychological reality, and that structure, rather than being constricting, can bring the writer freedom. The more structures you have available, the freer you are. Freedom depends on choices.

Exercises

1. Bring to class some very short magazine ads. Be prepared to discuss the mode of development and the paragraphing in relation to the writers' purposes.

2. Rewrite a short magazine ad, using different methods of paragraphing for each rewritten version.

3. Rewrite a news story, regrouping the paragraphs into new thought divisions.

4. Bring to class other examples of writing in which the writer paragraphs for other than logical reasons.

5. Bring to class an essay that uses paradigmatic structure (for example, comparison, classification, exemplification, process, cause and effect, and so forth).

Style:
The
Sentence

Chapter 11

Style: The Sentence

It is almost impossible to separate the rhetoric of a sentence from its grammatical form. Grammatical constructions have rhetorical consequences, and good writers usually have a firm grasp of grammatical principles, even though they cannot always bring this knowledge to conscious awareness. For this reason, I would like to put our discussion of the sentence on a firm grammatical basis.

Almost all writers know that sentences tend to fall into patterns that can be called "basic sentence patterns." These sentence patterns are *minimal grammatical structures* consisting of a few words and cast in an active, declarative form. Some linguists call these sentences "kernel sentences." The term is certainly interesting, suggesting the core or the essential part of something. It is a good term to describe the basic sentence types. Simply by examining the sentences you read in books and in magazines, you will notice that certain patterns recur with some frequency. Despite your increasing linguistic sophistication, you will find that it is still useful to work with these patterns.

Basic Sentence Types

The following sentences may be considered basic sentence types:

Subject-Verb
The slaves revolted.
Tension mounted.
Tastes differ.
Prices rose.
TV can talk.

Subject-Verb-Object
Death can unite a family.
Dracula wears dentures.
Education makes a difference.
Cars clogged the streets.
Some plants will eat insects.

Subject-Verb-Indirect Object-Object
We'll give the devil his due.
He offered her fame.
Joan gives her family trouble.
Children ask everyone questions.
Money can't buy you love.

Subject-Verb-Object-Objective Complement
He named his daughter Sandy.
Joan considered Jan neurotic.
His friend elected him secretary.
Van Gogh painted the sky orange.

Subject-Linking Verb-Noun
Loyalty is a virtue.
Posters were a weapon.
Their fears were legitimate.
Tokyo is many things.

Subject-Linking Verb-Adjective
The landscape is flat.
The weather was cold.
IBM is punchy.
The cup is empty.
Order seemed assured.

You are probably already familiar with most of these patterns, and you can write them quite easily. More interesting, perhaps, is their rhetorical effect. The sentence base, in its most concise form, is stark and striking. Because it is so striking, it can be used to emphasize:

Progress was slow.

Because it is so concise, it can present ideas clearly and directly:

Practice makes perfect.

Standing alone, it takes on an aphoristic quality:

Boys will be boys.

Exercises

1. Using the basic sentence types as models, compose five sentences for each of these pattern types:

    a. subject-verb
    b. subject-verb-object
    c. subject-verb-indirect object-object
    d. subject-verb-object-objective complement
    e. subject-linking verb-noun
    f. subject-linking verb-adjective

2. Discuss the basic sentence types in the following sentences:

    a. Factories proliferated.
    b. Sleeping Beauty takes Nytol.
    c. Skylab is falling.
    d. Planes crossed the alps.
    e. Reaction was strong.
    f. Audiences grew restless.
    g. Everyone imitated the Americans.
    h. Sonic booms are unsound.
    i. Not all whales are large.
    j. Marie Curie discovered radium.

Expansion by Modification

It should be obvious that these basic sentence types can be made more complex by making a few transformations. In English, these transformations constitute stylistic choices. These stylistic changes are many and varied, but most involve some sort of syntactic change. There is no need to go into complicated rules of grammar to learn how to make these changes. You already know intuitively how to make many of them. But you can exert a more conscious control over these processes with just a little effort.

One important means of transforming basic sentences into more complex sentences is by modification. **Modification** is *the process of supplying additional information about a word or word group to which the modifier is attached.* A modifier usually comments on, qualifies, or limits the word that it modifies. A modifier may be a word, a phrase, or a complete clause.

One way of expanding the basic sentence types is by adding **adjective modifiers** to a noun in the base sentence:

Adjective Modifiers
The *black* smoke poured out the chimney.
A *velvety* mold covers the walls.
The farmer picked the *golden, ripe* fruit.
The *decrepit old* house was abandoned.

Another way you can expand the basic sentence types is by adding **participial modifiers:**

Participial Modifiers
Chanting rhythmically, they file through the streets.
Picasso has a *fragmented* iris.
Broken hearts will mend.
The child, *kicking* and *screaming,* irritated the visitors.
Bruised and *battered,* he awaited the enemy.

A third way you can expand basic sentence patterns is to add **relative clauses** as modifiers of the noun:

Relative Clause Modifiers
All that *glitters* is not gold.
I like people *who are thoughtful.*
We admired the car *which he recently bought.*
Everything *that I am* I owe my parents.

A fourth way you can expand the sentence base is to add to the noun **prepositional phrase modifiers:**

Prepositional Phrase Modifiers
Paris is the central jewel *of the French crown.*
A sense *of humor* is important.
The explanation *in this book* is confusing.
The car *by the side of the road* has been abandoned.

Just as you can expand basic sentence types by adding modifiers to the noun, you can also expand them by *adding modifiers to the verb.*

For example, you can add a single **adverb** to the base:

Adverb Modifier
Golden ages *never* last long.
Summer is *here.*
Lately I can't sleep.
He *usually* eats breakfast.
The cost is *surprisingly* low.

You can add a **prepositional phrase:**

Prepositional Phrase Modifier
Immigrants poured *into America.*
Balloons bob *in the wind.*
He drove the car *into the ditch.*
In the morning, he watches television.
At first, I was afraid.

Or you can include a **subordinate clause:**

Subordinate Clause Modifier
Whales do not breathe *while they are under water.*

Take things *as you find them.*
If it is grape season, the gutters will be purple with leavings.
The alarm sounded *while she was sleeping.*

Expansion by Substitution

Another way of expanding the basic sentence types is by *substituting* words, phrases, or clauses for nouns in noun positions.

You can substitute a **gerund** for a noun:

Gerund Substitute
Facing a shark always takes courage.
Jan's *singing* drove me crazy.
Destroying the rain forest could upset the climate all over the world.
Shoveling snow is difficult.

You can put an **infinitive** or **infinitive phrase** in place of a noun.

Infinitive Substitute
We can't afford *to run* out of ideas.
Bullfrogs like *to croak.*
To act that way is unforgiveable.
He would have liked *to have believed* her.

Or you can substitute a **complete clause** for a noun:

Clause Substitute
Nostalgia isn't *what it used to be.*
What he did surprised me greatly.
You can believe *whatever she tells you.*
It depends upon *how they react.*

The rhetorical effect of expanded sentence types is not too much different from that of the minimal sentence types. Like minimal sentence types, expanded sentence types can be clear, concise, striking, forceful, direct, and aphoristic.

Exercises

1. Compose ten expanded sentences, using a different kind of modifier in each base.

2. Combine the following bases, changing one sentence in each set into a modifier (adjective, relative clause, participial phrase, prepositional phrase) in the other sentence. For example:

> Cinderella has a foot.
> The foot is dirty.
> Cinderella has a *dirty* foot.

    a. The widow kneels silently.
       The widow is wearing her grief like a cloak.

    b. The French people sometimes refer to their country as a hexagon.
       The French people greatly admire mathematical elegance.

    c. Her eyelashes waved at the world every time she blinked.
       Her eyelashes were heavy.
       Her eyelashes were false.

    d. The puppy had a long, skinny tail.
       The tail was in the shape of a parenthesis.

    e. The brook gurgled by.
       It was splashing and splattering.

    f. The moon peered down on the black world below.
       It was like the eye of a cyclops.

    g. *Sumō* calls itself the national sport.
       Sumō is the oldest form of Japanese wrestling.

    h. The raindrops fell against the window.
       They were tapping rhythmically against the glass.

    i. His hair formed waves.
       The waves were down the back of his head.

j. Her hands sat quietly in her lap.
   They were thin and transparent.

3. Combine the following sentences so that the second sentence in each
   set becomes a gerund, an infinitive, or a subordinate clause when embedded in the first. For example:

   Insomnia cures something.
   Someone is snoring.
   Insomnia cures *snoring.*

   a. He asked me something.
      I should leave at once.

   b. Something is forbidden.
      Someone carries firearms.

   c. I hate something.
      I get up early.

   d. Something is no easy task.
      Someone is a doctor.

   e. We just got a report.
      The president was assassinated.

   f. It is understandable.
      You are irritated about the economy.

   g. Something can change the ecology of a whole region.
      Someone is damming a river.

   h. The evidence convicted him.
      The jury considered the evidence.

   i. I have read something.
      Hank Aaron broke Babe Ruth's home-run record.

   j. Something is an active process.
      Someone is reading photographs.

4. Make one sentence into an adverbial modifier (adverb, prepositional phrase, subordinate clause). For example:

> It is summer.
> The heat is unbearable.
> The heat is unbearable *in the summer.*
> *or*
> *When it is summer,* the heat is unbearable.

a. It is autumn.
   The leaves begin to fall.

b. You smoke too much.
   You will get cancer.

c. We will meet.
   The bridge crosses the river.

d. She spoke the words.
   Then there was a dead silence.

e. He promised not to do it.
   He did it.

Expansion by Coordination

A third way of expanding the basic sentence types is by *coordination.* Because you employ coordination so often in everyday speech, it seems rather foolish to suggest that this is another sophisticated way that good writers have of manipulating sentences. Yet coordination is in fact an important way of transforming basic sentence patterns. It is important to learn something of grammatical coordination because it is basic to understanding the rhetorical concepts of parallelism and antithesis.

The Parallel Sentence

Parallelism is a special kind of coordination. It is *the process of linking two or more grammatical units using similar grammatical forms.* You can join *two* words in parallel structure:

You cannot serve God and
  Mammon.
Climate and landscape play an important role in the formation of
every civilization.

You can join a *series* of words or phrases in parallel order:

Apples,
peaches,
pears,
plums—he arranged them all in pleasing piles.

Suddenly he stopped,
  jumped straight up, and
  arched the ball toward the basket.

Or you can join *complete sentences* in parallel structure:

Insects cannot close their eyes; they sleep with them open.

The mountains are behind, and the thirsty plains lie ahead.

An apple a day keeps the doctor away. . . .
An onion a day keeps everybody away.

If you link two or more words, phrases, or clauses together without a conjunction, this has the effect of speeding up the line, affording
economy of expression, and achieving emphasis and climax:

I came, I saw, I flunked.
Whole armies, whole fleets vanished.

If, however, you join words, phrases, and clauses with many
connectives, this has the effect of slowing up the line:

The muddy groundswell lifts and breaks and falls and slides away.
  —John Gould Fletcher, *The Groundswell*

The raisins and almonds and figs and apples and oranges and
chocolates and sweets were now passed about the table and Aunt
Julia invited all the guests to have either port or sherry.
  —James Joyce, "The Dead"

Linking grammatical constructions with many conjunctions can be a means of emphasis because each word or phrase is presented to the mind in such a way that each word stands out. In addition, it can be a source of prose rhythm.

If you set forth words, phrases, or clauses in such a way that the final item in the series gains in force and intensity, the result is a parallel series ending in a climax:

> He who loses money loses much;
> he who loses a friend loses more;
> he who loses his nerve loses all.

> Because of a nail a horse was lost,
> because of a horse a battle was lost,
> because of a battle a war was lost, and
>   all for the want of a horseshoe nail.

The principle of expressing parallel ideas in parallel structures can be applied to grammatical constructions of all kinds:

> Sharks will swallow anything: sea turtles,
>   birds,
>   fish,
>   lobsters,
>   horseshoe crabs,
>   garbage,
>   coal,
>   people.

> But if thought corrupts language;
> language can also corrupt thought.
>   —George Orwell, *Politics of the English Language*
> Rainbows,
> halos,
> coronas—these are born of the action of atmospheric components
>   on light.

Parallel structure has a variety of uses in writing. It can be used to organize parallel ideas. It can be used to catalog a sequence of ideas in serial order. It can be employed to develop a climactic order of ideas. It can be used to secure balance and harmony. And it can be a source of prose rhythm.

Exercises

1. Write five sentences using words or phrases in a series.

2. Write five sentences using subordinate clauses in a series.

3. Compose five parallel sentences using independent clauses in a series.

4. Discuss the effect of the parallel structure in the following sentences and phrases:

   a. The Roman empire had many virtues and many vices.

   b. The river deepens and slows and loses its clarity.

   c. There were paintings everywhere—on store fronts, inside factories, and in private houses, where they sometimes decorated the rooms from floor to ceiling.

   d. Without the atmosphere no animal or plant, bird or fish, tree or blade of grass could exist.

   e. The world is coming to an end—repent and return those library books.

   f. In the trunks of trees, in dead limbs, in weathered fence posts, and in the wooden structures that man builds, myriad insects dig, bore, and tunnel, carving out nests and nurseries for their young.

   g. Whether they're Contemporary or Moroccan, Rya or Oriental, handmade or machine-made, the great classic rugs are wool.

The Antithetical Sentence

The **antithetical sentence** is *a special type of parallel sentence in which contrasting ideas are juxtaposed in balanced or parallel structures.* Antithesis, like parallelism, is a form of coordination, and the rules of coordination also apply to antithesis.

In contructing antithetical sentences, you can juxtapose *words* and *phrases:*

> *War:* 2,485,321; *Peace:* 0.
>
> Use *soft* words and *hard* arguments.
>
> Easy *come*, easy *go*.

Or you can link complete *clauses* or *sentences:*

> As there are valleys on land,
> so there are valleys under the sea.
>
> If a free society cannot help the many who are poor,
> it cannot save the few who are rich.
>
> —John F. Kennedy

In joining two or more clauses or sentences, you can use conjuctions or conjunctive adverbs:

> The spirit is willing, *but*
> the flesh is weak.
>
> Hope for the best *and* prepare for the worst.
>
> Jesus was a fisher of men, *not* a keeper of the aquarium.

Or you can simply juxtapose two or more sentences by means of punctuation:

> Moths spin cocoons;
> butterflies do not.
>
> What time you go to sleep is your business.
> What time you wake up is ours.

Order is comic;
chaos is tragic.

—John Updike

Antithesis is based upon the principle of contrast. By using antithesis, a writer can convey his or her ideas more clearly because of the emphasis afforded by the contrast. Thus, good can be contrasted with evil, love with hate, virtue with vice, peace with war, cowardice with bravery, and so forth. For example, in the graffiti

Make love, not war.

Plant flowers, not bombs.

the effect of the antithesis is to emphasize the idea that people should do something constructive, not destructive, in the modern world. Thus, life (love, procreation, conservation) is contrasted to death (hate, destruction, war).

Antithesis, like parallelism, is invaluable in achieving an effective prose style. It can be used to emphasize, to clarify, to sharpen an effect, to express a contradiction, to intensify ideas, or to discriminate between opposing ideas. Because antithesis is founded upon such a deep principle of human nature, you will find it in proverbs, maxims, wise sayings, dialogues, and formal debates.

Exercises

1. Pick out the word or words that form the basis of the antitheses in the following sentences. What effect do the antitheses have in relation to the meaning?

   a. The atmosphere is clearly not a calm ocean of air, but a tossing, unquiet sea.

   b. Do as I say; not as I do.

   c. There are no separate oceans; there is only the sea, single and all-encompassing.

d. For every mountain that is obliterated from the earth, a new one comes into being.

e. You can't control the purity of your tap water, but you can control the purity of your drinking water.

f. He that cannot obey, cannot command.

g. Every leaf, every flower, every garland is carved by hand.

h. Man proposes; God disposes.

i. Neither a borrower nor a lender be.

—Shakespeare

j. One man sows, and another reaps.

2. Compose five antithetical sentences.

The Cumulative Sentence

Thus far we have seen that the basic sentence types are the foundation of an effective style. But to achieve a mature style, you need to draw upon other stylistic principles, such as modification, substitution, and coordination, to expand your stylistic resources.

   In addition to these stylistic types, another important sentence type is the cumulative sentence. The *cumulative sentence* is a particular sentence type first described and discussed by Francis Christensen. According to Christensen, the **cumulative sentence** is *one that begins with a sentence base.* The base contains the main subject and the main verb together with any *bound modifiers* (modifiers such as articles, adjectives, participles, and prepositional phrases that cannot be freely moved about in the sentence). Then to that base are added *free* or *sentence modifiers* in the form of phrases and clauses. These phrases and clauses are usually set off by commas, and they can be freely moved to other positions in the sentence without distorting the essential meaning of the sentence. For example:

Slowly and laboriously, the car climbed up the hill.

The car, slowly and laboriously, climbed up the hill.

The car climbed up the hill, slowly and laboriously.

In the cumulative sentence, the main idea is stated in the sentence base, and the subordinate or qualifying ideas are stated in the free modifiers.

The following student sentence is a good example of the cumulative sentence.

    1 Her hands sat quietly in her lap,
      2 thin and nearly transparent with age, (A + A)
      2 the blue veins forming ridges from the wrists to the knuckles, (Abs)
        3 jutting from the wasted flesh, (VP)
      2 the crooked, skinny fingers bent around each other in her clasp, (Abs)
        3 like the claws of a bird clutching a tree limb. (PP)

This sentence begins with a base clause ("Her hands sat quietly in her lap"). This base clause is followed by a sequence of free modifiers (numbered and indented for visual effect) that add concrete details to the base. The modifiers labeled 2 are parallel to each other, but subordinate to the base clause (level 1). They add descriptive details to the base. The modifiers labeled 3 are subordinate to the level 2 modifiers immediately above them. Sentence elements are coordinate when they show similarity of structure of parallel ideas. Sentence elements are subordinate if they give evidence of subordination of ideas. There is a deductive movement in the sentence from the more general statement of the base to the less general and more specific descriptive details in the modifiers. The symbols in parentheses are shorthand terms to describe the grammatical nature of the modifiers (A + A, adjectives in a series; AC, adjective cluster; Abs, absolute construction; VP, verbal phrase; PP, prepositional phrase; RC, relative clause; SC, subordinate clause).

The cumulative sentence often begins with the sentence base, but there are variations on the basic pattern, as the following student sentences illustrate.

It may begin with free modifiers, followed by the sentence base, to which are added other modifiers:

> 2 As the snow melted on the roof, (SC)
> 1 streams of clear, cold water rippled over the slanted, brown-glazed shingles and slid off the edge,
>> 2 forming a waterfall which splashed on the grey cement wall below. (VP)

> 2 Stone naked, (AC)
>> 3 except for our skimpy underwear, (PP)
> 1 we stood like stalagmites,
>> 2 our feet anchored to the floor of the cavernous room, (Abs)
>> 2 our bodies shooting upwards. (Abs)

It may begin with a series of free modifiers, with the sentence base suspended until the very end:

> 2 Making a low, thunderlike rumble that progresses to a shriek as it barely clears the barn, (VP)
> 2 rattling every window in the house, (VP) and
> 2 terrifying the cattle, (VP)
> 1 the huge jet roars over the house.

> 2 Into the darkened room, (PP)
> 2 like a silver arrow, (PP)
> 1 the light filtered.

The cumulative sentence seems to be more fluid, more natural than some of the other sentence types. In the cumulative sentence, the ideas seem to run along easily, almost as if one were thinking aloud or engaging in a free-flowing conversation. In fact, the style of the cumulative sentence is very much like the style of spoken prose, in which the speaker makes a point, amplifies it, and then expands, limits, or illustrates it by successive phrases and clauses.

Although the cumulative sentence is perhaps more common in narrative and descriptive prose, it can be used very effectively in expository prose as the following example illustrates:

1 The cumulative sentence in unskillful hands is unsteady,
  2 allowing a writer to ramble on, (VP)
    3 adding modifier after modifier, (VP)
      4 until the reader is almost overwhelmed, (SC)
        5 because the writer's central idea is lost. (SC)

The above sentence, like the narrative sentence examples, begins with a sentence base ("The cumulative sentence in unskillful hands is unsteady"). Added to the base are four free modifiers (levels 2, 3, 4, 5), each one subordinate to the modifier above it, each one expanding the main idea in the sentence base.

It is relatively easy to write a cumulative sentence. Begin with a base:

1 Dark specks moved on the horizon,

Add a modifier:
  2 gliding across the ocean like white seagulls across the sky,

Add another modifier:
  2 their features slowly coming into view—

Add several more modifiers, making them subordinate to the previous modifier or modifiers:

    3 white sails,
    3 inverted v-shaped hulls,
    3 tall masts.

—Student sentence

The cumulative sentence is an especially good sentence to use in narratives because it enables the writer to enrich a sentence with concrete, specific detail. But it has other rhetorical uses also. It can be used in expository prose to define a topic, to limit it, to expand it by means of examples, or to qualify it in some way. It can also be an excellent source of prose rhythm.

Exercises

1. Compose ten cumulative sentences using the following base clauses:

   a. The fire raged.
   b. April had come again.
   c. The door began to open slowly.
   d. The music began.
   e. The sky outside was changing.
   f. The dentist began his work.
   g. The speaker approached the podium.
   h. The aroma was tantalizing.
   i. He released the ball.
   j. The clouds floated by.

2. Compose five original cumulative sentences. In at least one or two sentences, add as many free modifiers as possible to the base.

3. Bring to class five cumulative sentences and analyze their structure and their effectiveness.

4. Bring to class a paragraph composed almost exclusively of cumulative sentences. Then analyze the sentences and discuss their purpose and effectiveness.

I think it should be clear by now from our discussion of the grammar of the sentence that almost every sentence in English presents the writer with innumerable choices. Many beginning writers, however, are almost completely unaware that they have syntactic stylistic options and that these options have rhetorical consequences. Too often, writers concentrate more on word choice, assuming that the sentence structure will somehow take care of itself. Careful writers are able at times to choose deliberately, weighing their alternatives. At the very least, they can go back and revise their sentences after they have written them. Sentence style consists of using minimal grammatical patterns and of transforming these basic patterns into more complex patterns.

Summary Exercises

1. Write an essay in which you analyze the style of graffiti. Be sure that in your analysis, you show how the sentence structure is used to make a point.

2. Write an essay in which you do a stylistic analysis of proverbs.

3. Write an essay in which you do a stylistic analysis of advertising slogans and headlines.

4. Identify the sentence types in the following passages and discuss their use:

   a.   Soon afterwards they retired, Mama in her big oak bed on one side of the room, Emilio and Rosy in their boxes full of straw and sheepskins on the other side of the room.
   The moon went over the sky and the surf roared on the rocks. The roosters crowed the first call. The surf subsided to a whispering surge against the reef. The moon dropped toward the sea. The roosters crowed again.
   The moon was near down to the water when Pepe rode on a winged horse to his home flat. His dog bounced out and circled the horse yelping with pleasure. Pepe slid off the saddle to the ground. The weathered little shack was silver in the moonlight and the square shadow of it was black to the north and east. Against the east the piling mountains were misty with light; their tops melted into the sky.
   —John Steinbeck, ''Flight''

   b.   It came on great oiled, resilient, striding legs. It towered thirty feet above half of the trees, a great evil god, folding its delicate watchmaker's claws close to its oily reptilian chest. Each lower leg was a piston, a thousand pounds of white bone, sunk in thick ropes of muscle, sheathed over in a gleam of pebbled skin like the mail of a terrible warrior. Each thigh was a ton of meat, ivory, and steel mesh. And from the great breathing cage of the upper body those two delicate arms dangled out front, arms with hands which might pick up and examine men like toys, while the snake neck coiled. And the head itself, a ton of sculptured stone, lifted easily upon the sky. Its mouth gaped, exposing a fence of teeth like daggers. Its eyes rolled, ostrich eggs, empty of all expression save hunger. It closed its mouth in a death grin. It ran, its pelvic bones crushing aside trees and bushes, its taloned feet clawing damp earth, leaving prints six inches deep wherever it settled its weight. It ran with a gliding ballet step, far too poised and balanced for its ten tons. It moved into a sunlit area warily, its beautifully reptile hands feeling the air.

—Ray Bradbury, "A Sound of Thunder"

c.   None of them knew the color of the sky. Their eyes glanced level, and were fastened upon the waves that swept toward them. These waves were of the hue of slate, save for the tops, which were of foaming white, and all of the men knew the colors of the sea. The horizon narrowed and widened, and dipped and rose, and at all times its edge was jagged with waves that seemed to thrust up in points like rocks. Many a man ought to have a bathtub larger than the boat which here rode upon the sea. These waves were most wrongfully and barbarously abrupt and tall, and each froth-top was a problem in small-boat navigation.

—Stephen Crane, "The Open Boat"

d.   We observe today not a victory of party but a celebration of freedom—symbolizing an end as well as a beginning—signifying renewal as well as change. For I have sworn before you and Almighty God the same solemn oath our forebears prescribed nearly a century and three-quarters ago.

The world is very different now. For man holds in his mortal hands the power to abolish all forms of human poverty and all forms of human life. And yet the same revolutionary beliefs for which our forebears fought are still at issue around the globe—the belief that the rights of man come not from the generosity of the state but from the hand of God.

We dare not forget today that we are the heirs of that first revolution. Let the word go forth from this time and place, to friend and foe alike, that the torch has been passed to a new generation of Americans—born in this century, tempered by war, disciplined by a hard and bitter peace, proud of our ancient heritage, and unwilling to witness or permit the slow undoing of those human rights to which this nation has always been committed, and to which we are committed today at home and around the world.

Let every nation know, whether it wishes us well or ill, that we shall pay any price, bear any burden, meet any hardship, support any friend, oppose any foe to assure the survival and the success of liberty.

—John F. Kennedy, inaugural address, 1961

e. To everything there is a season, and a time to every purpose under heaven:
   2. A time to be born, and a time to die; a time to plant, and a time to pluck up that which is planted;
   3. A time to kill, and a time to heal; a time to break down, and a time to build up;
   4. A time to weep, and a time to laugh; a time to mourn, and a time to dance;
   5. A time to cast away stones, and a time to gather stones together; a time to embrace, and a time to refrain from embracing;
   6. A time to get, and a time to lose; a time to keep, and a time to cast away;
   7. A time to rend, and a time to sew; a time to keep silence, and a time to speak;
   8. A time to love, and a time to hate; a time of war, a time of peace.
   —Ecclesiastes, chapter 3, King James Version of the Bible.

f. The Devil (mortified): Senior Don Juan: you are uncivil to my friends.

   Don Juan: Pooh! Why should I be civil to them or to you? In this palace of lies a truth or two will not hurt you. Your friends are the dullest dogs I know. They are not beautiful: they are only decorated. They are not clean: they are only shaved and starched. They are not dignified: they are only fashionably dressed. They are not educated: they are only college passmen. They are not religious: they are only pew-renters. They are not moral: they are only conventional. They are not virtuous: they are only cowardly. They are not artistic: they are only lascivious. They are not prosperous; they are only rich. They are not loyal, they are only servile; not dutiful, only sheepish; not public-spirited, only patriotic; not courageous, only quarrelsome; not determined, only obstinate; not masterful, only domineering; not self-controlled, only obtuse; not self-respecting, only vain; not kind, only sentimental; not social, only gregarious; not considerate, only polite; not intelligent, only opinionated; not progressive, only factious; not imaginative, only superstitious; not just, only vindictive; not generous, only propitiatory; not disciplined, only cowed; and not truthful at all—liars every one of them, to the very backbone of their souls.

   —George Bernard Shaw, *Man and Superman*

Style:

Word Choice

Chapter 12

Style: Word Choice

Whether or not you write extensively, you are still faced constantly with the problem of choosing between two or more words. Quite often, you make your choices unconsciously, but the choice still has to be made. Many students have an intuitive feeling for language, but the problem is using words effectively in writing. Communication of some kind can be carried on with a small or imprecise vocabulary, and such communication can at times be moderately effective. But to have a small number of words at your disposal is to limit your resources, and intelligent choices among words cannot be made unless you have a store of words from which to choose.

"But I don't know much about words," one student protested, and then proceeded to write an imaginative and original paper about diction.

No Experience

While I'm thinking to myself, "What dialect? I haven't had any experience with dialect!" a sudden but not uncommon wail is heard through the hall. "Ay-un, kin I borrrr-oww you-ur pi-unk le-o-tards?" (TRANSL: Ann, can I borrow your pink leotards?) "Whaaaaa?" is the extremely nasal and immediate reply. "Pi-unk le-o-tards, do ye-u hay-ave iny I kin way-er?" Ignoring another "Whaaaaa?" the Voice goes on to implore, "Tha-ey hay-ave te-u be pi-unk, I cay-n't way-er bu-lack ones. I'ull wash they-um ou-oot ay-und ever-y-th-yang. Pu-lease?" The resultant reply from down the hall is very long and very unintelligible, but it doesn't daunt the seeker-of-leotards. "Way-ell, tha-ey cay-un be ao-paque whe-ite wuns. Way-ell?" Then, just as suddenly as it began, it is over. How can I concentrate on dialects with such interruptions?

Dialect, dialect, it's driving me bananas! A friend wanders in, momentarily halting my leap from the window.

"Hi. Yeah, well . . . watcha doin'?"

"Uh. Nothin' . . . Inglish . . ."

"Uh . . ."

"Well, I can't write anything, ya know?"

"Um . . . yeah . . . I know . . ."

"Um . . ."

"Ya know what I mean?"

"Um . . ."

After another half-hour or so of mutual commiseration, the friend wanders out and once again I am left without an idea in my head.

Before I can really get into some deep thinking on the subject, my mother calls. And while "discussing" money matters with her I hear another conversation in the background. "Oh, you sweet wittle baby-kins," my sister croons to the dog. "You is such a good wittle doggie-poo. Yes, um is de sweetest . . ." etc., etc. After hanging up, still nothing—except homesickness for my doggie-poo. I try thinking of something other than dialect, such as jargon, slang, idioms. Nothing!

Turning on the TV with the desperate hope of finding inspiration, I hear some impeccably dressed newscaster intone the words, "And this, just in. A usually reliable Pentagon source, who declined to be identified, has vigorously denied suggesting that published speculation, admittedly based on fragmentary and unconfirmed reports not available to the press, regarding allied troop movements in or near unspecified areas of Indochina and purportedly involving undisclosed numbers of South Vietnamese, Cambodian, Laotian, and perhaps American armed personnel is false, although he cautioned that such published speculation could be dangerously misleading and potentially divisive." The mind is boggled! And the sad truth being that a boggled mind with no experience with the subject might as well abandon all hope of an English paper.

If you are like this student, you have had considerable experience with diction, but you cannot always bring this knowledge to conscious awareness. Therefore, perhaps you need more formal approaches to word choice and vocabulary study.

Much of the traditional advice offered for enlarging your vocabulary is sound:

1. Buy a good dictionary and use it frequently.
2. Obtain a good thesaurus.
3. Try to bring new words into your writing and conversation.
4. Read widely in literature of all kinds.
5. Read aloud passages of unusual force and beauty.

Exercises

1. Write an essay, similar to the student essay on dialects, in which you transcribe as accurately as you can the speech of friends, relatives, acquaintances, radio or television newscasters, and the like, and place these transcriptions into a coherent narrative.

2. Bring to class five new words in the context of a short passage from a magazine ad, a newspaper, or a book, and discuss their meanings, their effectiveness in context, and their possible origins.

In addition to these more traditional ways of developing your vocabulary, another way of enlarging your vocabulary and increasing your sensitivity to language is by formal study, and it is with the formal study of words that we will be primarily concerned in this chapter.

Denotation and Connotation

Choose words for their literal as well as for their suggested meanings. The **denotation** of a word is *its literal or dictionary meaning.* The **connotation** of a word is *the sum total of its suggested or associative meanings.* Denotations are emotionally or morally neutral, while connotations convey an attitude toward their referents. Words have meanings beyond those in the dictionary. For example, if you look up the word *house* in the dictionary, you will find that the word refers to "a building or shelter that serves as living quarters for people." Then if you look up the related word *home*, you will notice that one of its primary meanings is "a family's place of residence." The **dictionary meaning** of these words is called their *denotative* meaning. In addition to their literal meanings, these words also evoke feelings and emotions and various associations. The word *house* seems to be the more neutral of the two words. You seldom hear or read about someone defending a house, but books and movies are filled with stories about people defending their homes. The movie *Straw Dogs* is one example. So the word *home* seems to carry with it stronger connotations than the word *house*. In fact, each of the following synonyms for the words *house* and *home* has slightly different meanings and different connotations from the others:

habitation	residence	retreat
abode	homestead	haunt
dwelling	hearth	nest
lodging	fatherland	quarters
domicile	country	hiding place

The first step in using a word in your writing, then, is to be sure that you understand its basic meaning, its referential meaning. If you do not, look it up in the dictionary. The second step is to consider its context, since the context of a word is also an important determinant of its meaning. Notice, for example, the difference in meaning in the words *house* and *home* in the following contexts:

People make houses.
People construct houses.
People make homes.
People construct homes.
People build houses, families make homes.

A third step is to consider the associated meanings of the word you are using. Would a reader be offended by the word, indifferent to it, aroused by it, or persuaded by it? Consider, for example, the differences in connotation of the following sentences, achieved by the substitution of a single word:

It's not much, but it's my *home.*
It's not much, but it's my *habitation.*
It's not much, but it's my *dwelling.*
It's not much, but it's my *residence.*
It's not much, but it's my *domicile.*
It's not much, but it's my *lodging.*
It's not much, but it's my *quarters.*
It's not much, but it's my *hiding place.*

Many connotations are individual and personal and depend on the writer's past experiences with the word and with the idea or thing to which the word refers. For example, for some people the word *snake* has unpleasant associations. For others, the words *country, patriotism, communism, fascism, totalitarianism, social-ism, left wing, right wing, radical, liberal, conservative, Republican,* and *Democrat* have emotional overtones. In addition to any personal meanings and associations that words might have for us, there are some meanings and associations that are shared with people as a group. If you were brought up in a certain country and lived in a particular state, or city, or neighborhood, you would hold in common with the people there certain attitudes, beliefs, and feelings about words and about the things to which they refer. But more often than not, the connotation of a word is less fixed than its denotation.

Exercises

1. Explain the differences in denotation and connotation of the following sets of words:

   a. exist, be, subsist, live, vegetate, prevail, pass the time
   b. confusion, disarray, jumble, mess, turmoil, ferment, disturbance, uproar, rumpus, fracas, disorder
   c. crowd, gathering, throng, multitude, rabble, mob, horde

d. child, brat, kid, urchin, youngster, tot, youth

e. spit, sputter, splutter, drool, drivel, slaver, slabber, slobber

f. meal, repast, spread, banquet, feast, feed

g. hard, rigid, stubborn, stiff, firm, starchy, unbending, unyielding, inflexible

h. sea, ocean, main, briny deep, waters, deep, high seas

i. woman, skirt, lady, broad, female, the fair sex, chick, dame

j. fat, corpulent, plump, stout, portly, burly, well-fed, fleshy, pudgy, paunchy, chubby

2. Make up sentences illustrating as accurately as possible one of the following sets of words. Use your dictionary if necessary.

a. rash, incautious, imprudent, heedless, careless, reckless, wild, foolhardy

b. loathe, dislike, resent, detest, hate, abhor, disgust, scorn

c. vain, conceited, self-assured, self-satisfied, pretentious

d. friend, acquaintance, intimate, associate, buddy, bosom pal, comrade, chum, sidekick

e. fondness, love, affection, tenderness, attachment, passion, rapture, adoration, enchantment

3. Discuss the differences in connotation of the following proper names:

a. Lulu, Lucile, Matilda, Agatha, Maggie, Percy, Elmer, Hugh, Jud, Edgar, Francis, Henry

b. Gloria, Ruby, Christy, Stella, Laura, Sylvia, Robin, Scarlet

c. Josephine/Josie, Marian/Mary, Robert/Bob, William/Will, Susan/Sue, Stephen/Steve, Katherine/Cathy, Thomas/Tom

d. Jennifer, Elizabeth, Roberta, Florence, Alicia, Madeline, Melanie, Emily

e. Achilles, Atlas, Hercules, Alfred, Atilla, Merlin, Casanova, Richard, Leonardo, Hero, Aristotle

4. Write an essay in which you discuss the denotative and connotative meanings of words in a letter to the editor or in a magazine advertisement.

5. Discuss the differences in connotation of the following brand names:

   a. Tide, Duz, Lux, All, Rinso, Cheer, Oxydol, Cold Power

   b. Winston, Camels, Lucky Strike, True, Kent, Salem, Viceroy, L&M, Virginia Slims, Marlboro

   c. Duster, Dart, Cheyenne, Pinto, Mustang, Charger, Continental, Imperial, Monarch, Jaguar, Rabbit, Bug

   d. Colgate, Aim, Pepsodent, Crest, Close-up, Pearl Drops, McCleans, Strike, Gleem

   e. Ivory, Palmolive, Dove, Joy, Downy, Borax, Clorox, Purex

6. Write five sentences in which you use the same word in each sentence, each time changing the connotation slightly.

Some categories of words seem to have the power to produce an immediate reaction in people. One category is words pertaining to everyday living such as *mother, father, home, marriage, bride, groom, divorce, widow,* and *God.* Another category is abstract words, such as *honor, virtue, pride, patriotism, truth, love, justice, valor, respect, duty, piety, freedom,* and *liberty.* A third category consists of proper names, especially the names of people who are in the public eye and who stir up emotional reactions: for example, Andrew Young, Ayatollah Khomeini, Castro, and Arafat. A final category is taboo words. Taboo words, especially profane and obscene words, shock and offend many people. They may be used to create attention, to discredit someone, to provoke confrontations, and to provide a kind of catharsis for the user.

Exercises

1. Give ten examples of emotion-laden words with which you are familiar and discuss their effects on you and the reasons for their effects.

2. What obscene words do you find offensive? Why do you find them offensive?

3. What makes a word obscene or taboo? Are people's attitudes toward taboo words changing? Is there a context in which obscenity might be justified?

4. Discuss the use of euphemisms that people employ to avoid mentioning the blunter taboo words.

Concrete and Abstract Words

Use concrete words to present a vivid picture to the reader's mind. **Concrete words** refer to *actual, specific things in experience.* More than any other words, concrete words bring us closest to immediate sensation. They appeal to the reader's sense of touch, taste, smell, sight, or hearing. They can be especially effective in narrative and descriptive writing, as the following student sentences illustrate:

> The teakettle sat on the stove boiling, the water rumbling against the metal sides, the steam rising in puffs through the top, disappearing into the air only moments after its escape, blowing a shrill whistle as I ran to lift it from the fire.

> About noon, Mom sliced up thick, uneven chunks of homemade bread, covering them with slabs of pink ham and wedges of creamy cheese; then she set out tumblers of foamy milk and clinking glasses of cola.

Not all writing can be concrete, nor does it necessarily have to be. But even in expository writing, you can be very concrete in your choice of supporting details, in your examples, and in your illustrations.

Abstract words *are words that refer to qualities (hot, cold, good, bad), relationships (existence, quantity, order, number), and ideas (curiosity, inquiry, judgments, brief, credulity).* They tend to be Latinate words and are usually, but not necessarily, longer and more complex than Anglo-Saxon words.

Abstract words are frequently used to express complex ideas. They can give fine distinctions to thought, and they are often used to convey technical or specialized ideas. They are often learned words, words found more in written than in spoken English. If you are going to engage in any serious discussion of ideas from law, science, medicine, psychology, philosophy, or politics, you will make some use of abstract words. You must be careful, however, in using abstract words. If you do not use them carefully, your writing can become vague, obscure, and inaccurate, as in the following passage taken from a student theme:

> Loneliness is an appalling ordeal, encasing its victim in a desolate world. If he is to survive, the individual must learn to cope with his dilemma. To dispossess this perplexity requires the careful observance of the sufferer's habitat, recreation, and thoughts.
>
> The victim of loneliness must use the eyes of Argus when choosing his environmental habitat. He should try to find a location in the midst of a mass of extroverts. Their gregarious characteristics might draw the victim into their circle, curing him of his problem. If this desired location cannot be found, his abode should be in the approximate area of a center of communal entertainment. This will, in all likelihood, give him a temporary reprieve from the torment of his plight. Under no circumstances should the individual choose a secluded dwelling. Seclusion only adds to the pain, driving him deeper into the depths of his despair.

Phrases such as "appalling ordeal," "dispossess this perplexity," "the sufferer's habitat," "environmental habitat," and the like obscure rather than advance this writer's thought. Not only does the misuse of the abstract words obscure the writer's full meaning, but these words also make the writing seem stuffy and affected. Do not, then, indulge in a fondness for abstract words for their own sake. When you do use them, try to use them with some clarity and precision. Your main task as a writer is actually to combine the abstract with the concrete. If you have been operating at a very high level of abstraction in your writing, you will want to narrow down occasionally and give some concrete illustrations.

General and Specific Words

Choose general words to express general ideas. Use specific words to supply exact details.

A **general word** is *one that applies to many things, to a collectivity, to the whole.* Any word that takes in a group of particulars, in which these particulars are thought of as parts of a whole, is a general word. If, however, a word refers to only a few of these particulars, to the parts, the word is specific. A **specific word** is *one that applies to particular, unique, and distinctive things.* A specific word calls forth a distinct mental image. Thus, the word *clothing* is general, but the term *yellow striped pants* evokes a specific image.

General and specific words should not be confused with abstract and concrete words. A general word is not necessarily an abstract word, nor is a concrete word necessarily specific. For example, the word *dog* is a general word because it can refer to many animals, but it is obviously not abstract. On the other hand, neither is it very specific, although it is concrete. To make the idea to which the word *dog* refers specific, you would want to make the word more particular. For instance, the words *cur, mutt,* and *hound* call forth much more distinct mental images than does the word *dog.* Usually, when your instructors ask you to make your writing more concrete, they want you to be both concrete and specific.

It is often pointed out that the terms *general* and *specific* are relative. A word may be specific in relation to one word, yet general in relation to another. Words specify in varying degrees. In writing, the context often indicates whether a word is being used in a general sense or in a particular sense. *Athlete* is more general than *fighter,* but *fighter* is more general than *Muhammad Ali. Fragrance* is more definite than *odor. Bird* is more general than *thrush; thrush* is more general than *robin.* In your writing, you want to be sure that you are aware of the difference. At times you will want to use general terms, but other times you may want to choose a more vivid and precise word to present the mind of your readers with a more definite picture.

Exercises

1. What is the purpose of the abstract words in the following sentences? What happens to the meaning if concrete words are substituted for the abstract words? Why do the writers of these sentences use abstract words instead of concrete words?

    a. Today's L&M is rich, mellow, distinctively smooth.

    b. Volvo gives you luxury, quality, and a sense of elegance that other so-called luxury cars can't match.

    c. Winston gives me real taste and real pleasure; in my book, that's the only reason to smoke.

    d. Armstrong carpets give you the easy elegance and warmth of rich autumn hues.

    e. Through the years, V.O. has stood apart as a whiskey uncompromising in quality, with a tradition of craftsmanship that has made it The First Canadian in smoothness.

2. Discuss in class your attitudes toward abstract words such as *truth, honor, courage, patriotism, virtue, love,* and *loyalty.* Cite specific experiences in the use of these words, avoidance of them, attempts to articulate them, and so forth.

3. Rewrite the following sentences. Substitute specific concrete details for the more abstract and general words (for example: general—*It was a cold morning;* concrete—*It was twenty degrees below zero*).

    a. We went shopping to get some food.
    b. He walked down the street in an unsteady manner.
    c. They tried to get money from him by dishonest means.
    d. The dishes fell to the floor with a loud noise.

e. The dog gave a high, excited bark.

f. He looked at her in an angry way.

g. She had a funny expression on her face as she talked.

h. Slowly he departed from the room.

4. Describe a scene, an event, or an experience using abstract words. Then describe the same scene using concrete words.

5. Paraphrase the following proverbs, eliminating the concrete and specific diction, including the figures of speech:

a. A stitch in time saves nine.

b. A rolling stone gathers no moss.

c. A new broom sweeps clean.

d. When the cat's away, the mice will play.

e. Every cloud has a silver lining.

f. A bird in the hand is worth two in the bush.

g. You can't teach an old dog new tricks.

h. Birds of a feather flock together.

i. Barking dogs never bite.

j. Still water runs deep.

Figurative Language

Use figures of speech to increase concreteness and to secure vividness in your writing. One student began a paper about an experience she had while working in the library with this vivid figure of speech:

> Maybe I shouldn't write on this particular topic, but at the moment it is the only thing on my mind. The experience is too fresh and disturbing. It lingers like a grease burn from a popcorn popper, stinging and irritating my thoughts.
>
> —Patti

Not only did the grease-burn comparison effectively convey her feelings about her experience in a way that few abstractions could, but also it was interesting. It captured my attention. It made me want to read on.

The **figurative meaning** of a word is *based on a comparison of unlike things.* To illustrate this, let us look at a couple of examples:

> The leopard cannot change his spots.
> When the wolf comes in the door, love creeps out the window.

In the first sentence, the leopard is obviously not a leopard but a metaphor for man. The spots of the leopard symbolize the ways of men, so the figurative meaning of the statement is that men cannot change their ways. In the second statement, the wolf is a metaphor for poverty, and the meaning of the proverb is that if young people marry before they have enough money to support themselves, their love will not last very long.

The **literal meaning** of a word is *its dictionary meaning,* its usual and customary meaning, as opposed to its figurative meaning. The literal meaning of the word *dog* is "a domesticated carnivorous mammal, having four legs." But you can call an unattractive person "a dog," as in the sentence "I went out last night with a real dog," and it is obvious that the statement is not literally true. Or you can use the word *dog* or the related word *cur* to refer to a miserable, contemptible person, as in the expression "You cur," and it is apparent that you are not speaking literally. When you transfer the reference of a word so that it covers other meanings and includes new associations, you are writing figuratively.

Three common figures of speech used by prose writers are the *simile,* the *metaphor,* and *personification.*

A **simile** is *a direct comparison in which two things, essentially unlike, are likened to one another.* The comparison is made explicit by the use of *like* or *as.* Similes can be used to express feelings as well as ideas, as the introductory paragraph from this student theme on the generation gap indicates:

> I have a problem which is eating away on my insides *like acid on a car battery.* Putting it down on paper won't solve anything, but it will make me calm down.
>
> —Christine

The figurative comparison of the student's problem with acid that eats away on a car battery captures the turbulence of the student's feelings in a way that literal language cannot.

Here is another example from a student theme of an effective use of similes to describe a wheat harvest:

> This weekend we took a short trip to the country and the countryside was beautiful. To begin with, the day was a beautiful day, such a blue sky, blue *like a lake on a clear day.* The grass was a kelly green which seemed to boast of a freshness that belongs only to the country.
>
> The wheat, *like golden waves,* shimmering in the sun, promised a bountiful harvest for the farmers. Seeing the wheat waving in the wind brought back old memories of the farm and of the yearly wheat harvest. Dad used to let me ride in the wheat bin of the combine, and I can still (very plainly) see the grasshoppers hopping and jumping to keep on top of the rising mound of golden grain that was pouring into the bin from an overhead spout, *resembling water being forced from an old-fashioned pump.*
>
> You know, I think wheat is the most beautiful crop that is grown on a Nebraskan farm. It always seems to be promising so much, *like a treasure chest full of golden coins.*
>
> —Shirley

The simile is such a natural form of expression that it is common in folk speech, where it draws its comparisons from everyday objects, animals, and events:

as fit as a fiddle	as blind as a bat
as steady as a rock	as strong as a horse
as clean as a whistle	as alike as two peas in a pod
as stiff as a board	like water off a duck's back
as stiff as a poker	like a bolt from the blue

A **metaphor** is *an implicit comparison in which two unlike things are likened to each other without the uses of* like *or* as. A metaphor can make abstract ideas concrete. It can describe, clarify, delineate, and point out logical relationships between things. It can also reveal attitudes and feelings and make judgments about the subject of the metaphor.

In the following passage from a student paper, the student uses a series of metaphors, combined with the vulture simile, to give her impressions of the gluttonous behavior of her friends one evening when they were dining out. The figurative language seems to capture the experience much better than an objective description of the scene might.

> Dinner tonight was a festival for gluttons. The people at the table where I was sitting were *ravenously* hungry, and we attacked our food *like vultures gleefully chomping on freshly killed meat.* We were gluttonous, sucking up our food, and when that was gone, scrounging for food at other tables. We were *snow cleaners*, inhaling a constant stream of victuals and seemingly exhaling it somewhere else so we could inhale more. We were *guerrilla fighters*, sneaking our *spoils of war* slyly (usually from the *jungle* of a neighboring table) so that we wouldn't have to share them with our *fellow fighters.* We were *Roman banqueters*, rolling in an *orgy* of good food, boisterous conduct, and riotous table manners. Even after exhausting the supply of food from every source possible, we clamored for more. We were insatiable and uncouth, and Emily Post would have been mortified!
>
> —Lynn

Like the simile, the metaphor is also a natural form of expression in everyday speech:

the apple of my eye	bury the hatchet
know the ropes	at the crossroads
in a nutshell	dark horse
sit on the fence	bone of contention
pull up stakes	nothing to sneeze at

Personification is *attributing to inanimate objects and abstractions, human qualities.* It is closely related to metaphor. In fact, personification is sometimes called personal metaphor. The tendency to ascribe life to inanimate objects seems to be universal.

> Truth has a good *face*, but bad *clothes*.
> Walls have *ears*.
> Love is *blind*.

Exercises

1. Write five sentences in which you use original figures of speech.

2. Discuss the use of figurative language in the following passages:

   a. Wit is a lean creature with a sharp inquiring nose, whereas humor has a kindly eye and comfortable girth. Wit, if it be necessary, uses malice to score a point—like a cat it is quick to jump—but humor keeps the peace in an easy chair. Wit is a better voice in a solo, but humor comes into the chorus best. Wit is as sharp as a stroke of lightning, whereas humor is diffuse like sunlight. Wit keeps the season's fashions and is precise in the phrases and judgments of the day, but humor is concerned with homely eternal things. Wit wears silk, but humor in homespun endures the wind.
   —Charles Brooks, "On the Difference Between Wit and Humor"

   b. The high gray-flannel fog of winter closed off the Salinas Valley from the sky and from all the rest of the world. On every side it sat like a lid on the mountains and made of the great valley a closed pot. On the broad, level land floor the gang plows bit deep and left the black earth shining like metal where the shares had cut. On the foothill ranches across the Salinas River, the yellow stubble fields seemed to be bathed in pale cold sunshine, but there was no sunshine in the valley now in December.
   —John Steinbeck, "The Chrysanthemums"

3. Pick out the figures of speech in the following sentences. What is being compared? Are the figures of speech effective?

   a. Ring and your room steward appears like a genie.

   b. The Mitsubishi Clean Air Engine is a pure engineering jewel.

   c. The Sheraton-Waikiki, like a gigantic ship of sail, stands poised on the crest of Waikiki Beach.

   d. Your air-conditioned room is a sunburst of Polynesian color.

e. The whirling, clattering helicopters, with the flexibility of humming birds, carry their passengers across green canyons and over the clawing fingertips of mountains from desert to rain forest.

f. Roads became black bands snaking their way through the fields.

g. The walrus is a relative of the seal with the wrinkled skin of an old oak.

h. These islands look like a strand of jade green beads splashed down in the middle of a cobalt blue sea.

i. Hawaii has magnificent beaches, blue-mirrored lagoons, high, wind-whipped cliffs that tumble majestically into the sea.

j. The starfish has a spokelike design.

4. Rewrite the passage from Steinbeck using literal language.

5. Select a brief prose passage almost completely lacking in figurative language. Then rewrite the passage using figurative language.

Doublespeak

Doublespeak is *the use of language to obscure the truth.* Increasingly, critics of contemporary culture are pointing out that when politicians, corporate executives, or advertisers deliberately distort language for their own gain, they are also distorting values. Consequently, the general public ought to be aware of the verbal techniques used to "overload our verbal circuits." These techniques include the use of jargon, meaningless abstractions, euphemisms, slogans, clichés, and so forth.

For example, advertisers attach adjectives such as *amazing, sensational, revolutionary, bold,* and *proud* to products as though these words had concrete referents. But what do these words really mean? Can the latest look in clothing, for example, really be called revolutionary?

More alarming, perhaps, than the use of meaningless abstractions is the use of euphemisms to hide the truth. A **euphemism** is *the substitution of a softened or less explicit expression for a more offensive one.* For example, during the Vietnam War, some government officials used euphemisms to hide from the American public the extent of the United States involvement in Vietnam. In the early stages of the war, despite the presence of United States troops in Vietnam, the word *troops* was never used. Instead, the United States was supposedly employing "advisers," and our role there was "indirect" and "political" rather than military. To soften public reaction to the waging of the war, apologists for the war used such words and expressions as "antipersonnel device" for gun, "routine improvement of visibility" for defoliation and crop destruction, "technical errors" for bombing errors in which civilians were killed, and "harassment and interdiction" for artillery fire. Slogans such as "waging the peace," "peace with honor," and "conducting a peace-keeping action" were also used to present the war in Vietnam in a more favorable light.

Both government deception (from the secrecy involving the U-2 affair in 1960 to the Watergate conspiracy) and corporate deception (lying in advertising; doubletalk used by corporate executives who give bribes and kickbacks to foreign officials) have occasioned a great deal of public distrust and have diminished confidence in the government and in the business community. The best way to react to doublespeak is to avoid it in your own language by using words, insofar as you are able, with truth, candor, and precision, and to insist upon a similar use of language on the part of government officials, public figures, and advertisers.

Exercises

1. Bring to class examples of gobbledygook from your textbooks or some other source. Discuss the stylistic features that make the writing gobbledygook and then try to rewrite the passage in clearer language.

2. Bring to class some recent advertisements that use jargon, slogans, clichés, or meaningless abstractions to make a point.

3. Examine the language of advertisements and discuss those which actually tell something about the product and those which merely influence us to buy.

4. Some critics argue that sometimes euphemisms are necessary to make events (jobs, death, and so forth) more bearable. Discuss.

Dialects

In its broadest sense, the word **dialects** refers to *varieties of language based on geographical, educational, or social differences, and writing conventions.* Dialects based on geographical differences are called *regional dialects.* Those based on educational or social differences are called *social dialects.* And those based on writing conventions are called *functional dialects.*

All students have a right to whatever language skills and conventions are necessary to enable them to carry on the tasks of the everyday world and to ensure them a moderate degree of success and happiness. But there is disagreement among scholars and speakers of nonstandard dialects about the best possible means to these goals. Must everyone learn to write in the standard dialect?

Whatever may be true of spoken dialects, there is no doubt that written conventions are very rigid and codified. The student who insists upon using the less formal conventions of spoken English in writing will find himself under a great handicap if he wishes to get a job that demands formal writing skills. Most employers would find the following student sentences unacceptable:

It take a femail to have children.
Then there were some black who escape the cruelty of the white man.
Whites says that blacks are not human beings.
The police claimed to have heard they reply, "Shoot it out."
That was all that happen no conversation no nothing.
So, White Americans, watch out of what you say or do concerning the Black Race.
He was young and dress in today fashion.

To me seems like the Mexican-American find themselves in an
alien environment.
He taken it.
Very slowly the man what up and pickup the red rose as she
had just dropped on a mudded of water.

The dialect features in these sentences are characteristic of those
found in many nonstandard social dialects: omission of the plural
marker on nouns, omission of the possessive marker, omission of
tense markers, a different use or the omission of the auxiliary, spelling
errors, and so forth. Whereas in certain kinds of writing dialect features would be perfectly acceptable, in more formal writing, such
as professional writing or business writing, dialect features could interfere with clarity and effectiveness of expression.

To use dialect features to report spoken conversation or to use
them in writing that is personal or expressive (as in diaries, journals,
or autobiographies) is perfectly acceptable, and perhaps even desirable,
as the following student paper illustrates:

Mama

Well she was born in a log cabin, in the back woods, black woods
of Mississippi. She drank moonshine and chewed tobacco. Raised
thirteen children all by herself. Never looked much like a lady. You
see, she was too busy providing and raising her babies. Spent her
evening sitting in her rocking chair. Never had much of nothing,
but was always willing to share.

I'm talking about Mama, my mama.

Education she didn't have none. Never had a sick day in her
life. She was as good and strong as any man who ever lived. You
better believe she was. Now look here. When papa died, she swore
on the good book up and down on it that she would not love nobody
else. Made sure we were in church every Sunday. Papa would of
wanted it that way, that was what she would always say.

Yes, I'am talking about Mama, yea!! I am talking about the
lady who raised me.

Every once and a while when Mama would get depressed, she
would go to the closet and get Pa's guitar. She would sit herself
down in her rocking chair, start humming and strumming. This was

Ma's way of letting off steam. In plain old english we could see, that Ma was doing her thing.

Ma is a very emotional woman. She gets very mad if someone ever tries to do us harm in any way. For example: A school teacher gave my little brother a hard time in his school and in a flash she was on the scene to straighten things out.

She always told us to stick together no matter what instances occurred. Because we would need each other one day as we grew older.

We always appreciated the things she done for us. We never gave her a hard time as we were going through our life cycles.

Till this day, Ma is the same as she was before taking care of her children as she has always have done. And I love her deeply because, without her I wouldn't of been here now. Mom thanks!!!!

—Larry

The repetitions, the fragments, the use of punctuation, and other features are characteristic more of the spoken than the written dialect in this student paper. You can almost "hear" the writer intoning the phrases:

> I'm talking about Mama, my mama.
> Never looked much like a lady.
> Raised thirteen children all by herself.
> Yes, I'am talking about Mama, yea!!!

To criticize such a highly personal paper as this would be to criticize the writer's self-image. Nor is there a need to, since the language is perfectly suited to the subject and the mode of discourse. But to use these same conventions in more formal writing would be inappropriate. All students, then, should be encouraged to do some kinds of writing in their own dialects, but they should also be given an opportunity to master the conventions of the standard dialect.

Exercises

1. Point out the dialect features in the following student sentences. Do they interfere with communication? Are they expressive? Appropriate? Inappropriate?

   a. The one room school house is no longer use because the childrens are now bused to a town twenty miles away.
   b. My grandfather used to set on his front porch and tell us of the old times.
   c. He stopped and look at the young girl whom dress in all red.
   d. With this kind of things happening, almost every city is a danger spot.
   e. Today only one city has a majority of black.
   f. Many solution are so simple that they are overlook.
   g. The music at this point liven up.
   h. His only recognition come through sports.
   i. Since you are not knowing much about the campus, I will give you a first hand ride through.
   j. When I first saw he, I could hardly believe it.

2. Write a personal narrative using your own regional or social dialect features.

3. Write a narrative in which you try to capture the language use and dialects of someone you know.

Summary Exercises

1. Discuss the word choice in the following ads. What effect is achieved by the word choice? Consider the denotation and connotation of words, abstractions, concreteness, specificity or lack of specificity, jargon, clichés, figurative language, dialect features, and so forth.

   a. Arandas captures a True Sunrise for those who are into the real McCoy, the legit, the right on, coming clean, on the level, straight goods, Simon Pure in the Grove, and all kinds of sweet vibrations.

Taste the Sun! Pour 1½ ounces Arandas Tequila (White or new Oro) and 4 oz. orange juice into a tall ice-filled glass. Stir. Add ¾ oz. grenadine (more or less) and a squeeze of fresh lime; then drop the lime wedge right in. Now you have a True Sunrise . . . and nothing can outshine it.

b.   *Cobra bites man.* Both live. And once bitten, there is no known cure except a long, quick drive down a snakelike road where Cobra II can show off its rack-and-pinion steering. Not to mention the slithering four-speed stick shift, and 2.3 litre engine. And with front/rear spoilers, black louvered back lite and quarter windows, hood scoop, sporty tires, wheels (car shown with optional aluminum wheels), and stripes, this is one snake that doesn't have to shed its skin. So if you're looking for some snake-bite remedy, see your local Ford Dealer.

c.   You have to go beyond moisturizing to deter premature aging.
      You must have noticed a woman's skin can often look older than it should.
      For this kind of needless aging, new Ultra Vera can be a real deterrent.
      First, it has an abundance of moisture elements to shelter your skin from the dryness that may cause little lines.
      But Ultra Vera goes beyond that.
      You see, contrary to what many women believe, just moisturizing isn't enough to keep your skin youthful-looking.
      That's why Ultra Vera Facial Lotion is formulated with aloe vera and UV screen.
      Consider the legendary aloe vera gel. It's not by chance aloe has been regarded throughout history as nature's gift to skin beauty. Cleopatra herself is said to have relied on it.
      As for our UV screen, a PABA derivative, many dermatologists recommend it to help block out ultra-violet rays. Make no mistake, continual exposure to these rays even in ordinary daylight can wither your skin and add years to the way it looks. Ultra Vera lets you guard against that.
      So why limit yourself to just moisturizing? Use Ultra Vera every day, alone or under makeup. It's a big step toward attaining that priceless asset. Ageless-looking skin.

d.   *This Smuggler Coat Does Everything But Stop Bullets.* Like it stops chicks, for instance, dead in their tracks. Only who's got time for chicks when you got a little business to attend to.

Like lining your pockets with maybe 12 boxes of Cuban cigars, 6 gross Swiss watches, one case good Scotch, 2 snow leopard skins, one German P-38 and 2 solid gold bricks.

Which with a little imagination you can do easy with this coat.

Or take that big collar.

Most guys see it as maybe a pain in the neck, what with keeping it down so it don't mess up your hair.

But any guy sees past his nose sees himself in an open boat in a sudden twister up the Florida Keys, with collar up high to protect the back of his head from taking an awful dousing.

Same goes for the icy blast of a Labrador northeaster down from Fundy.

Or the cold hard stare of a U.S. agent at customs.

There's just about nothing this coat won't do for you when the going gets rough.

Find yourself caught in a tight squeeze on the back of a truck in between a shipment of Picassos and a bunch of Greek vases and you can sleep through the whole night's events and shake off the wrinkles in the AM because the coat's 100% texturized Dacron polyester.

e.   *Kama baba, kama mwana.* Through his father, a son's eyes are opened to the world. He learns about pride at his father's side. The pride of being black, of being a man.

He learns, too, about pride in his culture and that this beautiful natural is the outward expression of that pride.

And nothing grooms and conditions a proud natural better than Afro Sheen. Afro Sheen makes the difference you can see in your hair. Your natural takes on new body, lustrous and alive. Afro Sheen, the complete product for father . . . for son . . . and for you . . . naturally.

Imitation and Style

Chapter 13

Imitation and Style

A number of important artists and writers down through the years have attested to the value of imitation as *one* way of achieving an original style. "The imitation of other artists," contends Lewis Mumford, "is one of the means by which a person enriches and finally establishes his own individuality, and on the whole such imitation is more promising than an icing of originality that hardens too quickly." "The originals are not original," wrote Ralph Waldo Emerson. "There is imitation, model and suggestion to the very archangels, if we knew their history." Vincent Van Gogh, the painter, complained that "we painters are always asked to compose of ourselves. . . . Heaps of people do not copy; heaps of others do—I started it by chance and I find that it teaches me things."

Some writers are very specific as to the manner in which they began to use imitation. "I began to compose by imitating other authors I admired," stated William Dean Howells, "and I worked hard to get a smooth, a rich, classic style." Robert Louis Stevenson confessed that "whenever I read a book or passage that particularly pleased me . . . in which there was either some conspicuous force or some happy distinction in the style, I must set myself to ape that quality. . . . That, like it or not, is the way to learn to write." Somerset Maugham is very explicit about his methodology, in his autobiography, *The Summing Up:*

> I studied Jeremy Taylor's *Holy Dying*. In order to assimilate his style, I copied out passages and then tried to write them down from memory.
>
> Later the prose of Swift enchanted me. I made up my mind that this was the perfect way to write and I started to work on him in the same way as I had done with Jeremy Taylor. . . . As I had done before, I copied passages and then tried to write them out from

memory. I tried altering words or the order in which they were set. . . .

The work I did was certainly very good for me. I began to write better.

The improvement of style can be achieved by creative imitation. This approach to style assumes that in assimilating the best features of a writer's style, you will produce writing that in time will come to rival the model itself. You can best do this by following a sequence of steps that may be described as follows:

1. *Select a short passage from a writer's work that seems to have excellencies of style and that seems to be relatively complete in itself.*

2. *Read the model carefully, preferably aloud at first to get the full impact, in order to get an overview of the dominant impression.*

3. *Analyze the model carefully, noting the sentence length, the sentence types, and the word choice.*

4. *Then do either a close or loose imitation of the model by selecting a subject that differs from the model's but is suitable for treatment in the model's style.*

Ideally, you will follow these steps exactly as outlined. In practice, however, there may be considerable overlapping.

Model Analysis 1

In order to exemplify one method of using models for imitation, I would like to analyze a few short selections so as to present at least one workable approach to improving style.

The model I have chosen for analysis is the introductory paragraph of the short story "The Eighty Yard Run," by Irwin Shaw. The passage describes an eighty yard run made in a scrimmage by Darling, the main character in the story. Ironically, this run is the

climax in Darling's football career as well as in his life. The rest of
the story follows his declining fortunes as his wife gradually takes
over the dominant position in the marriage. Because the story is told
by means of a flashback, which begins with the second paragraph,
the opening paragraph is relatively complete in itself, and thus it
makes a suitable model for imitation.

> The pass was high and wide and he jumped for it, feeling it
> slap flatly against his hands, as he shook his hips to throw off the
> halfback who was diving at him. The center floated by, his hands
> desperately brushing Darling's knee as Darling picked his feet up
> high and delicately ran over a blocker and an opposing linesman in
> a jumble on the ground near the scrimmage line. He had ten yards
> in the clear and picked up speed, breathing easily, feeling his thigh
> pads rising and falling against his legs, listening to the sound of cleats
> behind him, pulling away from them, watching the other backs
> heading him off toward the sidelines, the whole picture, the men
> closing in on him, the blockers fighting for position, the ground he
> had to cross, all suddenly clear in his head, for the first time in his
> life not a meaningless confusion of men, sounds, speed. He smiled
> a little to himself as he ran, holding the ball lightly in front of him
> with his two hands, his knees pumping high, his hips twisting in
> the almost girlish run of a back in a broken field. The first halfback
> came at him and he fed him his leg, then swung at the last moment,
> took the shock of the man's shoulder without breaking stride, ran
> right through him, his cleats biting securely into the turf. There
> was only the safety man now, coming warily at him, his arms crooked,
> hands spread. Darling tucked the ball in, spurted at him, driving
> hard, hurling himself along, his legs pounding, knees high, all two
> hundred pounds bunched into controlled attack. He was sure he was
> going to get past the safety man. Without thought, his arms and
> legs working beaufitully together, he headed right for the safety man,
> stiff-armed him, feeling blood spurt instantaneously from the man's
> nose onto his hand, seeing his face go awry, head turned, mouth
> pulled to one side. He pivoted away, keeping the arm locked, dropping
> the safety man as he ran easily toward the goal line, with the
> drumming of cleats diminishing behind him.

The passage describes the climactic momemt in a scrimmage,
just as the halfback is breaking away for a long, broken-field run.

As you read, you are caught up in the intense excitement of the action. The narrative movement is vivid, conveying a sense of rapid motion and dynamic action. The descriptive details are sharp and intense.

The paragraph consists of ten sentences. Sentence 1 contains thirty-three words; sentence 2 has thirty-seven words; sentence 3, eighty-six words; 4, forty words; 5, thirty-nine words; 6, sixteen words; 7, twenty-six words; 8, twelve words; 9, forty-one words; 10, twenty-seven words. The shortest sentence is 8, with twelve words; the longest sentence is 3, with eighty-six words. The total number of words in the paragraph is 357. The average number of words per sentence is 35.7. Most of the sentences are relatively long. Sentence length seems to contribute to the overall effectiveness of the passage in two ways: first, it gives variety to the sentences, and second, it lends rhythmic movement to the prose. Notice the difference in effect that is achieved by breaking up sentence number 3, the longest sentence in the paragraph, into shorter sentences:

> He had ten yards in the clear. He picked up speed. He breathed easily. He felt his thigh pads rising and falling against his legs. He listened to the sound of cleats behind him. He pulled away from them. He watched the other backs heading him off toward the sidelines. The whole picture was suddenly clear in his head. It was not a meaningless confusion of men, sounds, speed. The men were closing in on him. The blockers were fighting for position. He had to cross the ground.

Not only is the sense of vivid and intense action lost in this version, but this rendering also completely distorts the writer's purpose, which is to show that all these activities are taking place simultaneously. The rewritten version destroys the simultaneity and gives the impression of a sequence of separate actions.

In a preliminary reading of the selection, you seem to perceive the dynamic action and the descriptive details as being sharp and intense. To support this intuition, you naturally tend to look closely at what the verbs and verbals are doing. Yet when you make a word count, you find that of the twenty-six main verbs in the passage, only eleven are concrete and specific (*jumped, smiled, shook, headed, diving, tucked, stiff-armed, floated, swung, spurted, pivoted*). And of the twenty-eight present participles, approximately half are concrete and particular (*brushing, twisting, hurling, breathing, rising, pounding, biting, pumping,* and so forth). On the basis of the evidence, you are forced to conclude either that earlier intuitions were inaccurate or that Shaw is using other strategies to achieve his purpose. To offset the less specific verbs and verbals, Shaw uses a large number of manner adverbs to depict action and to add concreteness to the description:

> *Adverbs*
> feeling it slap *flatly* against his hands
> his hands *desperately* brushing Darling's knee
> picked his feet up *high*
> *delicately* ran over a blocker and an opposing lineman
> breathing *easily*
> all *suddenly* clear in his head
> his knees pumping *high*
> holding the ball *lightly* in front of him
> his cleats biting *securely* into the turf
> coming *warily* at him
> his arms and legs working *beautifully* together
> feeling blood spurt *instantaneously* from the man's nose
> seeing his face go *awry*
> ran *easily* toward the goal line

In addition, although many of the participles are somewhat general, because they are present participles, they increase the sense of rapid motion felt by the reader. The *-ing* ending helps to create this vivid sense of movement. And finally, the movement of the verbs is strengthened by the fact that there are few auxiliaries to slow the action. The burden of the action is carried directly by the main verbs: *stiff-armed, floated, spurted, pivoted,* and so forth.

 With the exception of sentence 8, the predominant sentence type is the *cumulative sentence:*

1

> 1 The pass was high and wide and
> 1 he jumped for it,
>   2 feeling it slap flatly against his hands, (VP)

3 as he shook his hips to throw off the halfback who was diving at him. (SC)

2

1 The center floated by,
   2 his hands desperately brushing Darling's knee as Darling picked his feet up high and delicately ran over a blocker and an opposing lineman in a jumble on the ground near the scrimmage line. (Abs)

3

1 He had ten yards in the clear and picked up speed,
   2 breathing easily, (VP)
   2 feeling his thigh pads rising and falling against his legs, (VP)
   2 listening to the sound of cleats behind him, (VP)
   2 pulling away from them, (VP)
   2 watching the other backs heading him off toward the sidelines, (VP)
      3 the whole picture, / , all suddenly clear in his head, for the first time in his life not a meaningless confusion of men, sounds, speed. (Abs)
         4 the men closing in on him, (Abs)
         4 the blockers fighting for position, (Abs)
         4 the ground he had to cross. (Abs)

4

1 He smiled a little to himself as he ran,
   2 holding the ball lightly in front of him with his two hands, (VP)
   2 his knees pumping high, (Abs)
   2 his hips twisting in the almost girlish run of a back in a broken field. (Abs)

5

1 The first halfback came at him and
1 he fed him his leg, then swung at the last moment, took the shock of the man's shoulder without breaking stride, ran right through him,
   2 his cleats biting securely into the turf. (Abs)

6

1 There was only the safety man now,
  2 coming warily at him, (VP)
    3 his arms crooked, (Abs)
    3 hands spread. (Abs)

7

1 Darling tucked the ball in, spurted at him,
  2 driving hard, (VP)
  2 hurling himself along, (VP)
    3 his legs pounding, (Abs)
    3 knees high, (Abs)
      4 all two hundred pounds bunched into controlled attack. (Abs)

8

1 He was sure he was going to get past the safety man.

9

  2 Without thought, (PP)
  2 his arms and legs working beautifully together, (Abs)
1 he headed right for the safety man, stiff-armed him,
  2 feeling blood spurt instantaneously from the man's nose onto his hand, (VP)
  2 seeing his face go awry, (VP)
    3 head turned, (Abs)
    3 mouth pulled to one side. (Abs)

10

1 He pivoted away,
  2 keeping the arm locked, (VP)
  2 dropping the safety man as he ran easily toward the goal line, (VP)
    3 with the drumming of cleats diminishing behind him. (Abs)

The cumulative sentences lend a sense of rapid motion to the prose and advance the action.

Another interesting stylistic feature that Shaw employs to convey rapid movement is the deliberate omission of conjunctions between the main verbs. This is one technique that may be used to speed up the action in a narrative.

> The first halfback *came* at him and he *fed* him his leg, then *swung* at the last moment, *took* the shock of the man's shoulder without breaking stride, *ran* right through him, his cleats biting securely into the turf.
> Darling *tucked* the ball in, *spurted* at him, driving hard, hurling himself along. . . .
> . . . he *headed* straight for the safety man, *stiff-armed* him, feeling blood spurt instantaneously from the man's nose. . . .

Imitation Exercises

Once you go through this kind of analysis, you can then do imitation exercises based on the principles discovered in the models chosen for study. One kind of exercise would consist of writing sentences of varying levels, beginning naturally enough with two-level narrative or descriptive sentences and then adding more complex levels. Within each sentence, the use of participial phrases and absolute constructions would be stressed. So also would the use of active verbs, manner adverbs (those that relate how an action is completed), and present participles. The omission of conjunctions between verbs might be emphasized in a few sentences, as would variety in the length of sentences. Finally, the choice of vivid and precise words appealing to the senses would also be suitable for imitation.

More important, however, the sentences chosen for imitation should be part of a larger unit so that you might see the effect that a stylistic technique has in a particular context. The most useful approach is to begin with a close imitation of the model, putting your own ideas and experiences into the structure of the whole. Then, at the same time that you are attending to the stylistic principles within the individual sentences as well as within the paragraph, you are also attending to the manner in which content interacts with form to produce a mature style.

The following student paper is a good example of a close imitation based on the Shaw model.

Close Imitation

(Situation: A grease monkey has only four cars left to lube before
he can leave the gas station. He hopes to finish before the other
shop workers.)

    The Cadillac was long and wide and he jumped for its underside,
feeling the suspension with his hands, as he shook his feet to throw
off the piece of bubble gum sticking to him. The manager floated
by, his finger desperately shaking at Ernie's face as Ernie picked his
feet up high and delicately ran over a hydraulic lift and a spare tire
in a jumble on the floor near the storage rack. He had three cars in
the clear and picked up speed, sighing despondently, feeling his greasy
overalls rising and falling against his legs, listening to the sound of
tune-ups behind him, pulling away from them, watching the
alignment boys heading him off toward closing time, the whole
picture, the men trying to finish before him, the other lube specialists
fighting for the grease gun, the cars he had to finish, all suddenly
clear in his head, for the first time in his job not a meaningless
confusion of grease monkeys, machines, speed. He smirked a little
to himself as he worked, holding the grease gun tightly in front of
him with his two grubby paws, his legs stretching high, his hips
twisting in the almost clumsy style of a bull in a china shop. The
first car came to him and he filled it with grease, then swung at
the last moment, took the shock of several more drops of grease on
his face without breaking stride, walked right over some more, his
tennis shoes slipping wildly on the slick concrete floor. There was
only the Volkswagen left now. Ernie approached it warily, his arms
crooked, legs spread. Ernie shoved the grease gun out, spurted at
the "bug," driving hard, hurling himself along, his heart pounding,
arms high, all one hundred twenty pounds stretched into an awkward
attack. He was sure he was going to finish before the tune-up man.
Without thought, his arms and legs working somewhat together, he
headed right for the oil pan, knocked the plug off, feeling hot oil
spurt instantaneously from the spout onto his head, seeing the
manager's face go awry, head turned, mouth pulled to one side in
an obscenity. Ernie pivoted away, keeping the arms forward, dropping
the grease gun as he ran for his own car, with the thunder of boots
diminishing behind him.

—Bruce

Contrary to what you might think, this kind of imitation is not mere copying, nor is it merely slavish imitation. This kind of assignment demands a high degree of skill. It demands a sensitivity to style and structure, a feeling for the nuances of language, and a knowledge of what type of content goes best with what type of structure.

Here is another student imitation that uses the same style but a different subject matter.

Close Imitation

The toy was pink and cuddly and he clutched it, feeling it squash within his chubby hands, as he wobbled to free himself from his mother's confining grasp. His brother scurried by, his arm jarringly knocking Jamie's shoulder as Jamie swerved to his left and desperately avoided a hard plastic horse and an imposing red wagon in a heap on the living room floor. He had five feet in the clear and became a bit steadier, gurgling loudly, feeling his terry-cloth pajamas stretch around his fat tummy, listening to the encouraging cheers behind him, venturing away from them, unconscious of the restraining relatives heading him into the center of the room, the entire picture, the thrust of the starting push, the relatives reaching with unneeded hands, the soft carpet he had to cross, all new and amazing in his mind, for the first time in his life not a distorted view of people and things from a crawling position. He grinned a little as he stepped, clinging to the toy frantically with his fat little palms, his head wobbling up and down, his pink bottom wiggling in the humorous fashion of a bouncing baby. The first aunt came at him and he shoved her with his bent elbow, then stumbled at the last moment, crashed to the floor, struggled to regain his footing by raising his bottom first, his determination exhibited in his serious little face. There was only an uncle now, squatting in the center of the floor, his arms cocked, his eyes busily watching. Jamie still clung to the toy, toddled toward his uncle, giggling repeatedly, hurling himself along, his legs pumping, free arm flopping for balance, all 19 pounds wobbling forward across the living room. Without thought, his arms and legs working awkwardly, he headed straight toward his uncle, arm flying, knocking his uncle off balance with the slightest brush, his uncle's startled eyes gawking at the tiny child. He waddled past, arm still swinging, then reaching for a huge hand, the safety of his daddy, with excited cheers from the gallery behind him.

—Jeanne

A second kind of useful exercise is based on a looser imitation of the model. In this type of exercise, you are asked to model your sentences on those of the original, but in any order and in varying lengths. The following is an example of a student imitation which uses a looser form of imitation.

Loose Imitation

The lively notes of the piano began and so did her action, as the three criticizing judges watched, their pencils poised, ready to deduct points. She executed a step-kick-lunge with great ease, her hands and arms reaching upward in perfect time to the smooth music filling the room. Now halfway through the first run of the pattern, she felt her black leotard stretch over her arched body, listening for the cue to continue with a quick front roll, breaking into a high leap, cartwheel, and back roll. She landed lightly on her knees and pointed toes, thinking of what was to come next. The second run, her easiest, was performed with grace and speed. She smiled as she rose to her toes, ran three short steps, did a high hitch kick, toes pointed, a cat leap, then going right into a step-hop, right toe pointed straight back. Next came four leaping steps and a pose, her right hand ending its movement high above her head, her eyes following its path. Abruptly she raised both hands, held a handstand and somersaulted into a flat position on the mat, her arms above her head, then quickly rolled a complete turn and sat up, her back arched, her knees bent. Straightening her right knee, then her left, she stood and turned. Without thought, her arms and legs keeping perfect time to the music, she executed her final run, sliding her right leg to her left, hopping left, sliding her left leg to right, then pivoting abruptly, her hands at the small of her back. Three swift turning steps followed, then two perfect cartwheels, her knees straight, her legs directly over her head, her exhibition ending exactly with the music in a lunge, her back arched, her head proudly held high, her heart pounding with success.

—Linda

Exercises

1. Using the Irwin Shaw model, do either a loose or a close imitation in which you depict a subject in motion (for example, a skier, a swimmer, a basketball player, a skater, an animal, a robot). Use cumulative sentences, with an extensive number of free modifiers. Use active participles, manner adverbs, and active verbs. Choose words that appeal to the senses.

1. The *periodic sentence* is the inverse of the cumulative sentence. The following passage uses both kinds of sentences. Do an imitation of this selection, but first analyze and discuss in class the sentence structure, the use of repetition and restatement, the images, the sound devices, and the rhythm of the prose.

Some Things Will Never Change

"Some things will never change. Some things will always be the same. Lean down your ear upon the earth, and listen.

"The voice of forest water in the night, a woman's laughter in the dark, the clean, hard rattle of raked gravel, the cricketing stitch of midday in hot meadows, the delicate web of children's voices in bright air—these things will never change.

"The glitter of sunlight on roughened water, the glory of the stars, the innocence of morning, the smell of the sea in harbors, the feathery blur and smoky buddings of young boughs, and something there that comes and goes and never can be captured, the thorn of spring, the sharp and tongueless cry—these things will always be the same.

"All things belonging to the earth will never change—the leaf, the blade, the flower, the wind that cries and sleeps and wakes again, the trees whose stiff arms clash and tremble in the dark, and the dust of lovers long since buried in the earth—all things proceeding from the earth to seasons, all things that lapse and change and come again upon the earth—these things will always be the same, for they come up from the earth that never changes, they go back into the earth that lasts forever. Only the earth endures, but it endures forever.

"The tarantula, the adder, and the asp will also never change. Pain and death will always be the same. But under the pavement trembling like a pulse, under the buildings trembling like a cry, under the waste of time, under the hoof of the beast above the broken bones of cities, there will

be something growing like a flower, something bursting from the earth again, forever deathless, faithful, coming into life again like April."
—Thomas Wolfe, *You Can't Go Home Again*

Model Analysis 2

The second model chosen for analysis is taken from a novel by Virginia Woolf entitled *To the Lighthouse*. Like the Irwin Shaw passage, it is relatively complete in itself, and it also is an interesting model for imitation. Its style and structure contrast nicely with that of the Irwin Shaw passage.

> The house was left; the house was deserted. It was left like a shell on a sandhill to fill with dry salt grains now that life had left it. The long night seemed to have set in; the trifling airs, nibbling, the clammy breaths, fumbling, seemed to have triumphed. The saucepan had rusted and the mat decayed. Toads had nosed their way in. Idly, aimlessly, the swaying shawl swung to and fro. A thistle thrust itself between the tiles in the larder. The swallows nested in the drawing room; the floor was strewn with straw; the plaster fell in shovelfuls; rafters were laid bare; rats carried off this and that to gnaw behind the wainscots. Tortoise-shell butterflies burst from the chrysalis and patterned their life out on the windowpane. Poppies sowed themselves among the dahlias; the lawn waved with long grass; giant artichokes towered among the roses; a fringed carnation flowered among the cabbages; while the gentle tapping of a weed at the window had become, on winter's nights, a drumming from sturdy trees and thorned briars which made the whole room green in summer.

This model describes the desolation of an abandoned house. Unlike the intense excitement conveyed by the movement of the prose in the Shaw passage, however, the prose in this passage seems to be static. The tone is somber.

This paragraph consists of ten sentences. Sentence 1 has eight words; sentence 2 contains twenty-one words; sentence 3, twenty words; 4, eight words; 5, six words; 6, nine words; 7, ten words; 8, thirty-three words; 9, fourteen words; 10, fifty-six words. The shortest sentence is 5, with six words. The longest sentence is 10, with fifty-six words. The total number of words in the paragraph is 185. The average number of words per sentence is 18.5, in marked contrast to the 35.7 words per sentence of the Shaw passage. The sentences, therefore, have good variety in length.

In reading this passage, you seem to perceive the action and the descriptive details as static. To support this intuition, you naturally look at how the verbs are used. A careful analysis reveals that of the twenty-four main verbs in the passage, four are static verbs *(was, was, seemed, seemed)*; three are in the passive voice *(was deserted, was strewn, were laid bare)*; five are in the past perfect tense *(had left, had rusted, had decayed, had nosed, had become)*; and twelve are in the past tense, active voice *(swung, thrust, nested, fell, carried, burst, patterned, sowed, saved, towered, flowered, made)*.

The static nature of the description can be accounted for in part by the static verbs, but the verbs in the passive voice and the verbs in the past perfect tense work more or less in the same fashion as the static verbs. The static verbs (the verb *to be* and the verbs of appearance) are followed by predicate adjectives or some kind of complement that moves back toward the subject and comments on it. The past participal forms of the verb following the auxiliary *was (were)* work in the same manner, as kinds of adjectivals moving back toward the subject. Similarly, the main verbs after the auxiliary *had* (in the past perfect tense verbs) act like adjective complements and refer to the subject. The result is that the forward motion of the prose is impeded, and the effect is static. The following scheme illustrates this point:

Static Verbs

the *house* was *left*

it was *left* like a shell on a sandhill

the long *night* seemed *to have set in*

the trifling *airs* seemed *to have triumphed*

Passive Voice Verbs

the *house* was *deserted*

the *floor* was *strewn* with straw

rafters were *laid bare*

Past Perfect Tense Verbs

life had *left* it

the *saucepan* had *rusted*

the *mat* [had] *decayed*

toads had *nosed* their way in

the gentle *tapping* of a weed . . . had become . . . a *drumming*

In addition, there is a large number of verbs, adjectives, and adverbials, which through their meaning give the sense of desolation and aimlessness:

Verbs
the swallows *nested* in the drawing room
the plaster *fell* in shovelfuls
tortoise-shell butterflies . . . *patterned* their life out on the windowpane

Adjectives
the *long* night
the *trifling* airs
the *clammy* breaths

Adverbials
idly
aimlessly
to and fro

Besides these words, the use of reflexive pronouns referring back to the subject adds to the static nature of the description:

Reflexives

a *thistle* thrust *itself*

poppies sowed *themselves* among the dahlias

There is some movement carried by the active verbs (*swung, thrust, nested, carried, burst, patterned,* among others), but these stand in stark contrast to the static verbs and reinforce the somber tone. The word choice in general conveys this sense of desolation and futility. The plants and flowers, which at first seem to impart life to their surroundings and add color, are growing wild. Everything is overgrown, random, and the plants are prickly or thistly:

long grass
poppies . . . among the dahlias
a fringed carnation among the cabbages
giant artichokes among the roses

In sharp contrast to the cumulative sentences that convey action in the Shaw passage, most of the sentences in this model are balanced sentences, or sentences that give the sense of being balanced:

1

1 The house was left;
1 the house was deserted.

2

1 It was left like a shell on a sandhill to fill with dry salt grains now that life had left it.

3

1 The long night seemed to have set in;
1 the trifling airs,
  2 nibbling, (VP)
1 the clammy breaths,
  2 fumbling, (VP)
    3 seemed to have triumphed.

4

1 The saucepan had rusted and
1 the mat [had] decayed.

5

1 Toads had nosed their way in.

6

  2 Idly, (Adv)
  2 aimlessly, (Adv)
1 the swaying shawl swung to and fro.

7

1 A thistle thrust itself between the tiles in the larder.

8

1 The swallows nested in the drawing room;
1 the floor was strewn with straw;
1 the plaster fell in shovelfuls;
1 rafters were laid bare;
1 rats carried off this and that to gnaw behind the wainscots.

9

1 Tortoise-shell butterflies burst from the chrysalis and patterned
  their life out on the windowpane.

10

1 Poppies sowed themselves among the dahlias,
1 the lawn waved with long grass;
1 giant artichokes towered among the roses;
1 a fringed carnation flowered among the cabbages;
  2 while the gentle tapping of a weed at the window had become,
    / , a drumming from sturdy trees and thorned briars which made
    the whole room green in summer.(SC)
  3 on winter's nights, (PP)

The coordinate and balanced structures combine with the static verb structures to convey a desolate picture of the abandoned house. The cumulative sentences in the Shaw passage move the action forward. The balanced sentences in this passage impede the action and force the movement backwards, as base clause piles up upon base clause, giving no sense that the prose is going anywhere.

    One final stylistic feature in the Virginia Woolf passage is the use of sound devices to give a sense of parallelism and balance. Its effect is similar to that of the syntactic parallelism:

Sound Parallelism
the *s*waying *sh*awl *s*wung to and fro
a *thi*stle *thr*ust *it*self be*t*ween the *t*iles in the larder
the floor was *str*ewn with *str*aw
the *l*awn waves with *l*ong grass
a *f*ringed carnation *f*lowered among the cabbages

The net result of all these stylistic devices is to convey a strong sense of desolation and futility. The somber tone is felt strongly as a single impression.

Imitation Exercises

As with the analysis of the Shaw model, once you go through this analysis you can do an imitation using balanced sentences, static verbs, verbs in the passive voice, and words that convey a desolate tone.

The following student imitation, based on the Virginia Woolf passage, is a good illustration of how one student handled the assignment.

Close Imitation

The ship was abandoned; the ship was forsaken. She was left like a wreck in a junkyard now that her usefulness had ended. The long day seemed to have its effect on her; the hot sun, burning, the humid air, corroding, seeming to have conquered. Her hull had rotted and her bow caved in. Fish had ambled their way in. Idly, purposelessly, the tattered flag flapped to and fro. Seaweed made its way between the boards in the hull. Some doves made nests in the ballroom; the floor was covered with debris; part of the ceiling had fallen in; the rafters were now exposed; rats had long ago deserted the corroding shell. Gray-colored seagulls tiptoed noiselessly among musty life jackets and then flapped aimlessly about the upper deck. Coral had attached itself to her bottom; crustaceans implanted themselves among the coral; a gray shape glided past in silence; while the gentle movement of a wave at the hull had become, on a still summer's day, a pounding which echoed from the bow to the stern.

—Jackie

The student imitation reprinted below follows the model in some detail, but in a looser fashion.

The church was empty; the church was abandoned. It resembled an old deserted ship, alone and forsaken. The pages of the hymn books in the pews had corroded and their covers rotted. Mice transported bits and pieces of the pages to nibble between the walls. Dark brown moths implanted themselves in the tattered cloth chairs near the altar, never to escape. Doves nested in the corners of the church, piling dried sagebrush together for a haven. The gloomy fall day appeared to be a sign of winter approaching, the damp brisk air rattling, the gray sky emerging through the broken stained-glass windows. The organ was enveloped in a network of mildew and moss, collecting slowly, spreading like a cancer over the keyboard. Cacti were springing up here and there on the earth visible through cracks in the floorboards. An ocotillo growing near the doorway fastened itself to a piece of dead wood; while the soft thumping of a bottlebrush tree, dwarfed against the giant church door, carried, on these fall afternoons, a pleasing scent to counteract the foul air inside the church. Loudly, continuously, a large, rusty bell above the doorway of the church repeated its mournful sound.

—Scott

Exercises

1. Write an imitation of the Virginia Woolf passage in which you describe a deserted mine, a ghost town, a cemetery at night, an antique shop, a junk shop, an abandoned house, or some other, similar subject. Try to achieve a dominant impression of desolation. Do either a loose or a close imitation. Use balanced sentences, with a sequence of coordinate clauses. Intersperse these with short sentences of single clauses that when combined with the coordinate sequences give the impression of being coordinate with them. Use static verbs, verbs in the passive voice, or verbs that give the sense of being static. Choose words whose meaning conveys desolation, futility, or the tone you want to achieve. If you like, use

sound devices such as alliteration that will give a sense of parallelism and balance.

2. At the end of the chapter on the sentence, there are three excellent selections that use balance and parallelism effectively: Kennedy's inaugural address, the selection from Ecclesiastes, and the passage from *Man and Superman*. Choose one of these passages, analyze it in class, and then do an imitation, using the style of the original.

3. Choose a short passage using parallel structure, by a writer you admire. Then do an imitation of that passage.

Model Analysis 3

The final model chosen for analysis is taken from Mark Twain's *Autobiography*.

The Farm

As I have said, I spent some part of every year at the farm until I was twelve or thirteen years old. The life which I led there with my cousins was full of charm and so is the memory of it yet. I can call back the solemn twilight and mystery of the deep woods, the earthy smells, the faint odors of the wild flowers, the sheen of rainwashed foliage, the rattling clatter of drops when the wind shook the trees, the far-off hammering of woodpeckers and the muffled drumming of wood-pheasants in the remoteness of the forest, the glimpses of disturbed wild creatures scurrying through the grass—I can call it all back and make it as real as it ever was, and as blessed. I can call back the prairie, and its loneliness and peace, and a vast hawk hanging motionless in the sky with his wings spread wide and the blue of the vault showing through the fringe of their end-feathers. I can see the woods in their autumn dress, the oaks purple, the hickories washed with gold, the maples and the sumachs luminous with crimson fires, and I can hear the rustle made by the fallen leaves as we plowed through them. I can see the blue clusters of wild grapes hanging amongst the foliage of the saplings, and I remember the taste of them and the smell. I know how the wild blackberries looked and how they tasted; and the same with the pawpaws, the hazelnuts, and the persimmons; and I can feel the thumping rain upon my head of hickory-nuts and walnuts when we were out in the frosty dawn to scramble for them with the pigs, and the gusts of wind loosed them and sent them down. I know the stain of blackberries and how pretty it is, and I know the stain of walnut hulls and how little it minds soap and water, also what grudged experience it had of either of them. I know the taste of maple sap and when to gather it, and how to arrange the troughs and the delivery tubes, and how to boil down the juice, and how to hook the sugar after it is made; also how much better hooked sugar tastes than any that is honestly come by, let bigots say what they will.

This passage is written in the form of a reminiscence. Twain uses the order of memory to organize the descriptive details. The first two sentences announce the subject, the memories of a man who lived on a Missouri farm when he was twelve or thirteen years old:

As I have said, I spent some part of every year at the farm until I was twelve or thirteen years old. The life which I led there with my cousins was full of charm and so is the memory of it yet.

The subsequent sentences add concrete and sensory images, detailing the memories of the farm.

The predominant sentence type is the *parallel series.* The structure of the sentences is relatively simple, each one beginning with a similar kind of base ("I can call back," "I can see." "I can hear," "I can feel"). Then to the base is added a *catalog* of sights, sounds, smells, and tastes of things found on a Missouri farm. The following are examples of the sentence structure, presented in graphic form.

1 I can call back
   2 the solemn twilight and mystery of the deep woods,
   2 the earthy smells,
   2 the faint odors of the wild flowers,
   2 the sheen of rainwashed foliage,
   2 the rattling clatter of drops when the wind shook the trees, the far-off hammering of woodpeckers and the muffled drumming of wood-pheasants in the remoteness of the forest,

    2 the snapshot glimpses of disturbed wild creatures scurrying
      through the grass—
  1 I can call it all back and make it as real as it ever was, and as
    blessed.

  1 I can call back
    2 the prairie, and
      3 its loneliness and peace, and
    2 a vast hawk hanging motionless in the sky with his wings spread
      and
      3 the blue of the vault showing through the fringe of their end-
        feathers.

  1 I can see
    2 the woods in their autumn dress,
      3 the oaks purple,
      3 the hickories washed with gold,
      3 the maples and the sumachs luminous with crimson fires, and
  1 I can hear
    2 the rustle made by the fallen leaves as we plowed through them.

  1 I can see
    2 the blue clusters of wild grapes hanging amongst the foliage of
      the saplings, and
  1 I remember
    2 the taste of them and the smell.

  1 I know
    2 how the wild blackberries looked and
    2 how they tasted; and
    2 the same with
      3 the pawpaws,
      3 the hazelnuts, and
      3 the persimmons; and
  1 I can feel
    2 the thumping rain upon my head of
      3 hickory-nuts and
      3 walnuts
        4 when we were out in the frosty dawn to scramble for them
          with the pigs, and

4 [when] the gusts of wind
   5 loosed them and
   5 sent them down

1 I know
  2 the stain of blackberries and
  2 how pretty it is, and
1 I know
  2 the stain of walnut hulls and
  2 how little it minds soap and water,
  2 also what grudged experience it had of either of them.

1 I know
  2 the taste of maple sap and
  2 when to gather it, and
  2 how to arrange
    3 the troughs and
    3 the delivery tubes, and
  2 how to boil down the juice, and
  2 how to hook the sugar after it is made;
  2 also how much better hooked sugar tastes than any that is honestly come by, let bigots say what they will.

In a passage that uses a cataloging technique to convey a sequence of sensory experiences, you would expect the sentences to be fairly long, and your expectations are fulfilled. The shortest sentence contains twenty-one words. The longest sentence is eighty-five words. The average sentence length is 43.5 words. So the *sentence length* is effective in achieving Twain's purpose. The following scheme illustrates the variety in sentence length:

Sentence 1	22 words
Sentence 2	21 words
Sentence 3	85 words
Sentence 4	38 words
Sentence 5	42 words
Sentence 6	26 words
Sentence 7	62 words
Sentence 8	37 words
Sentence 9	59 words

The word choice is predominantly concrete and specific, with some use of imagery and figurative language. The vocabulary is too extensive to permit an exhaustive sampling, but the following examples are representative:

Images of Sight
the snapshot glimpses of disturbed *wild creatures scurrying* through the *grass*

a vast *hawk hanging motionless* in the *sky* with his *wings spread wide*

the *blue* of the *vault* showing through the *fringe* of their *end-feathers*

the *oaks purple*
the *hickories* washed with *gold*
the *maples* and the *sumachs luminous* with *crimson fires*
the *blue clusters* of wild *grapes* hanging amongst the *foliage* of the *saplings*

Images of Sound
the *rattling clatter* of drops when the wind shook the trees
the *far-off hammering* of woodpeckers
the *muffled drumming* of wood-pheasants in the remoteness of the forest

the *rustle* made by the fallen leaves as we plowed through them

Images of Smell
the *earthy smells*
the *faint odors* of the *wild flowers*
the *smell* . . . of *wild grapes*

Images of Taste
the *taste* of *maple sap*
[taste] of hooked *sugar*
[taste] of *wild blackberries*

Tactile Images of Touch
the *thumping rain* upon my head of *hickory nuts* and *walnuts*
the *frosty dawn*
the *gusts* of *wind*

Figures of Speech
the far-off *hammering* of woodpeckers
the muffled *drumming* of wood-pheasants
the *snapshot* glimpses of disturbed wild creatures
the blue of the *vault*
the woods in their autumn *dress*
the hickories *washed* with gold
the maples and the sumachs *luminous* with *crimson fires*
the thumping *rain* upon my head of hickory-nuts and walnuts

The effect of the concrete and specific images and the figures of speech is to allow the reader to share the sensations and vivid experiences of a Missouri farm experienced by the writer.

Imitation Exercises

The Mark Twain passage lends itself well to the imitative method. Following this model, you would want to write a short reminiscence of your own, using parallel sentences with series of words and phrases in balanced constructions. The word choice should be concrete and specific, using images that appeal to the senses and figures of speech that present a vivid picture to the reader's mind.

The following student imitation follows fairly closely Mark Twain's model.

The Farm

Until I was thirteen or fourteen, I spent at least a week or more on the farm each year. The life there with my cousins was delightful and I still have memories of it yet. I can call back the brilliant sunlight and the expanse of the open farmland, the earthy smells, the pleasant aroma of cut alfalfa, the glistening of dew-drenched foliage, the crinkle and flap of corn leaves in the wind, the far-off roar of a tractor in the field and the sound of a single truck raking and grinding the gravel as it passed, and the split-second glimpses of prairie dogs scurrying across the pasture into their underground shelters—I can call it all back and see it as real as the day I was there. I can call back the farmland, and its apparent loneliness and peace, and a hen pheasant safely leading her brood of chicks through the tall brush in search of food. I can see the farmland in its summer dress, the corn green, the pastures brown from the scorching heat, the wheat golden ripe and ready for harvest, and I can hear the rustle of the tall grass and weeds as we plowed through them. I can see the pink clusters of wild plums hanging amongst the foliage of the brush down in the bottoms, and I can remember the sweet taste of the jelly we made from them. I know how the wild mulberries looked and how they tasted; and the same with the strawberries, the raspberries, and the cherries; and I can feel the thud of over-ripe peaches hitting my shoulder as we passed under the trees, as the wind loosened them and caused them to fall. I know the stains of raspberries and strawberries and how red they are, and I know only too well how they resist soap and water. I know how to irrigate, and when this job should be done, and how to arrange the plastic dams and siphon tubes, and when enough water has been applied, and how long it will be before water is to be added again; also how much better it is to irrigate than to farm dry land, let bigots say what they will.

—Jim

Here is another student paper that uses the same model, with an unusual choice of subject matter:

The Morgue

I seldom mention it, but while I was in the Army I spent two years in Japan working in a mortuary. The life in death which I led with my sergeants, the embalmers, Japanese morgue attendants, and physical anthropologists was full of charm and so is the memory of it yet. I can call back the ominous midnights and the mystery of the deep dark preparation room, the smell of embalming fluid, mingling with the faint odor of perking coffee from the front office, the rattling clatter of the doors and windows when the wind shook them, the faroff sound of a refrigerator motor starting up, the sound of a plane flying over which sounded exactly like the back door sliding open, the snapshot glimpses of disturbing shadows I swore were scurrying across the floor as I looked up. I can call it all back and make it as real as it ever was, and as frightfully blessed. I can call back the identification room with its tables of bones and their loneliness and peace, and a vast skeleton hanging motionless in a cabinet with its arms dangling and the green of the cabinet showing through its yellowish white ribs. I can see the Japanese morgue attendants in their work uniforms, white jackets with white trousers stiff with starch, their hands in red plastic gloves, their heads in white dome caps, making them look incongruously like Santa's elves working around a gigantic doll, and I can still hear their laughter as they scrubbed, stuffed, and stitched. I can see the sponge with different sized needles hanging on the wall, and I remember the purpose of each needle and its feel. I know how the viewing chapel looked and how it smelled, and the same with the casket room, the carpenter shop, and the embalming room, and I can feel the dull slap on my buttocks caused by the motion of the corpse's hand as I worked nervously trying to lift the legs in order to take the body off the draining braces at two in the morning, and I can feel the gust of wind I made as I ran like hell down the long dark hall. I know the stain of blood and how undistinguished it looks, and I know the stain of embalming fluid and how little it minds soap and water, also how hard it is to scrub to get rid of either of them. I know the look of a dead body and how to embalm it, and how to arrange the hoses and tubes, and how to start the fluid, and how to stop the flow when it is complete, also how much better cremated remains are than those that aren't, let the Pope say what he will.

—Dale

In writing an imitation, you need not use the same subject as in the original model. In fact, part of the challenge is to put your own ideas into different kinds of styles and structures, as both the previous student papers and this one illustrate.

The Dorm

As many others can say, I spent nine months one year in a dorm when I was 17 or 18 years old. The existence which I led there with the other dormies was fascinating and so are the memories of it yet. I can call back the noisy nights and the scariness of the dark halls, the perfume smells, the faint odors of popcorn, the piles of freshly washed clothes in the laundry room, the scrambling clatter of feet when the alarm clocks pierced the air, the nearby hammering on doors and the muffled roar of stereos in the adjoining rooms, the snapshots of funny friends clowning in the halls—I can call it all back and make it as real as it ever was, and as pleasing. I can call back the lounge, and its furniture and terrible acoustics, and a small TV hanging immobile on the wall with its antennas spread wide and the orange of the wall showing through the maze of its wires and cords. I can see the coeds in their fall wardrobes, the coats bright, the brunettes striking in golds, the blondes and the redheads glowing in greens, and I can hear the whistles from the freshman guys as we walked past them. I can see the long lines of hungry students waiting on the stairs of the cafeteria, and I remember the taste of the food and the smell. I know how the desserts looked and how they tasted; and the same with the salads, the meats, and the vegetables; and I can feel the clunking upon my tray of knives and forks when we went over in the early morning to grab for them among the early risers, and the press of classes rushed us and sent us on. I know the drape of fishnet and how pretty it is, and I know the problems of thumbtack holes and how hard they are to cover, also what frustrating experiences I had with them. I know the taste of rum in coke and when it is safe to drink it, and how to conceal it and get it to the room, and how to hide the bottles, and how to keep it a secret after it is hidden; also how much better drinks in your room taste than in any legal place, let the regents say what they will.

—Christy

Exercises

1. From your own experience, write a reminiscence similar to Twain's, using the rhetoric of the series. Use concrete imagery, sensory details, and figures of speech.

2. The use of light is interesting in the following description by James Baldwin. Pick out the images, such as "pale end-of-winter sunlight," and discuss them. What other images does Baldwin use to create a certain impression of the kitchen? Discuss Baldwin's use of word repetition, parallelism, and the series to reinforce the description. What effect does the grammatical structure have? Then write a description of a room using the Baldwin passage as a model. Focus on one or two details; the smell (floral, musty, damp), the colors, the clutter or order of the objects in the room, and so forth.

The Kitchen

Their mother, her head tied up in an old rag, sipped black coffee and watched Roy. The pale end-of-winter sunlight filled the room and yellowed all their faces; and John, drugged and morbid and wondering how it was that he had slept again and had been allowed to sleep so long, saw them for a moment like figures on a screen, an effect that the yellow light intensified. The room was narrow and dirty; nothing could alter its dimensions, no labor could ever make it clean. Dirt was in the walls and the floorboards, and triumphed beneath the sink where roaches spawned; was in the fine ridges of the pots and pans, scoured daily, burnt black on the bottom, hanging above the stove; was in the wall against which they hung, and revealed itself where the paint had cracked and leaned outward in stiff squares and fragments, the paper-thin underside webbed with black. Dirt was in every corner, angle, crevice of the monstrous stove, and lived behind it in delirious communion with the corrupted wall. Dirt was in the baseboard that John scrubbed every Saturday, and roughened the cupboard shelves that held the cracked and gleaming dishes. Under this dark weight the walls leaned, under it the ceiling, with a great crack like lightning in its center, sagged. The windows gleamed like beaten gold or silver, but now John saw, in the yellow light, how fine dust veiled their doubtful glory. Dirt crawled in the gray mop hung out of the windows to dry.

—James Baldwin, *Go Tell It on the Mountain*

The kind of imitation I am advocating is not "mere copying" or slavish imitation, but *imitation based on a thorough understanding and assimilation of the principles* of a writer's style. There are formal principles in all writing that recur from one writer to another, and it is valuable to learn something about these principles. Imitation may not make you a James Joyce, a Mark Twain, or a Virginia Woolf. Only natural ability will. But it can help you to achieve an effective and pleasing style.

Summary Exercises

1. Analyze in class the following selection from *The Yearling*, by Marjorie Kinnan Rawlings. Discuss the sentence structure, word choice, imagery, and figures of speech. Then, for a subsequent assignment, do an imitation in which you depict some subject in motion.

Two Bears

Two male bears were moving slowly ahead down the road, a hundred yards distant. They were on their hind legs, walking like men, shoulder to shoulder. Their walk seemed almost a dance, as when couples in the square dance move side by side to do a figure. Suddenly they jostled each other, like wrestlers, and lifted their forepaws, and turned, snarling, each trying for the other's throat. One raked his claws across the other's head and the snarls grew to a roar. The fighting was violent for a few moments, then the pair walked on, boxing, jostling, harrying. The wind was in Jody's favor. They could never smell him. He crept down the road after them, keeping his distance. He could not bear to lose sight of them. He hoped they would fight to a finish, yet he should be terrorized if one should end the fight and turn his way. He decided that they had been fighting for a long time and were exhausted. There was blood in the sand. Each attack seemed less violent than the others. Each shoulder-to-shoulder walking was slower paced. As he stared, a female walked out of the bushes ahead with three males following her. They turned silently into the road and walked on in single file. The fighting pair swung their heads a moment, then fell in behind. Jody stood until the procession passed from sight, solemn and ludicrous and exciting.

2. The following selection from "The Lagoon" by Joseph Conrad has some interesting characteristics of style: the tone (somber, brooding, heavy, still), the position of the conjoined adjectives after the noun, the use of alliteration and other sound devices, and the use of negatives. After reading and analyzing this passage, do the following exercises:

   a. Do a statistical count in which you give the total number of words in the passage, the number of words in each sentence, and the average sentence length.

   b. Isolate those sentences with sound devices and underline the sounds that are repeated.

   c. Discuss the use of the conjoined adjectives in this passage. What is the effect of their position after the noun?

   d. Discuss those characteristics of style that support the tone in this passage.

   e. Make a list of all the adjectives in the passage. Do they fall into certain semantic clusters? Discuss their use in the passage. Make similar lists for the adverbs, verbs, and nouns. What characteristics do these words have?

   f. Discuss the use of imagery and figures of speech in this passage.

   g. Do an imitation of this model, choosing a subject that lends itself to a somber tone.

The Lagoon

The Malay only grunted, and went on looking fixedly at the river. The white man rested his chin on his crossed arms and gazed at the wake of the boat. At the end of the straight avenue of forests cut by the intense glitter of the river, the sun appeared unclouded and dazzling, poised low over the water that shone smoothly like a band of metal. The forests, sombre and dull, stood motionless and silent on each side of the broad stream. At the foot of big, towering trees, trunkless nipa palms rose from the mud of the bank, in bunches of leaves enormous and heavy, that hung unstirring over the brown swirl of eddies. In the stillness of the air every tree, every leaf, every bough, every tendril of creeper and every petal of minute blossoms seemed to have been bewitched into an immobility perfect and final. Nothing moved on the river but the eight paddles that rose flashing regularly, dipped

together with a single splash; while the steersman swept right and left with
a periodic and sudden flourish of his blade describing a glinting semicircle
above his head. The churned-up water frothed alongside with a confused
murmur. And the white man's canoe, advancing upstream in the short-lived
disturbances of its own making seemed to enter the portals of a land from
which the very memory of motion had forever departed.

3. Analyze the following passage by James Joyce. Then do a free association
   or a surrealistic imitation, playing around with words, experimenting with
   language.

> In long lassoes from the Cock lake the water flowed full, covering
> green-goldenly lagoons of sand, rising, flowing. My ashplant will float away.
> I shall wait. No, they will pass on, passing chafing against the low rocks,
> swirling, passing. Better get this job over quick. Listen: a four-worded
> wavespeech: seesoo, hrss, rsseeiss ooos. Vehement breath of water amid
> seasnakes, rearing horses, rocks. In cups of rocks it slops: flop, slop, slap:
> bounded in barrels. And, spent, its speech ceases. It flows purling widely
> flowing, floating foampool, flower unfurling.
>
> Under the upswelling tide he saw the writhing weeds lift languidly
> and sway reluctant arms, hising up their petticoats, in whispering water
> swaying and upturning coy silver fronts. Day by day: night by night: lifted,
> flooded and let fall. Lord, they are weary: and, whispered to, they sigh.
> Saint Ambrose heard it, sigh of leaves and waves, waiting, awaiting the
> fullness of their times, *diebus ac noctibus iniurias patiens ingemiscit.* To
> no end gathered: vainly then released, forth flowing, wending back: loom
> of the moon. Weary too in sight of lovers, lascivious men, a naked woman
> shining in her courts, she draws a toil of waters.
>
> Five fathoms out there. Full fathom five thy father lies. At once he
> said. Found drowned. High water at Dublin bar. Driving before it a loose
> drift of rubble, fanshoals of fishes, silly shells. A corpse rising salt-white
> from the undertow, bobbing landward, a pace a pace a porpoise. There he
> is. Hook it quick. Sunk though he be beneath the watery floor. We have
> him. Easy now.
>
> —James Joyce, *Ulysses*

Revising and Editing

Chapter 14

Revising and Editing

You have probably read enough about making movies to realize that although film directors may follow a script closely, much of their important work is done after the shooting, in the editing of the film. At this time, they must arrange the individual shots or scenes in a desired order. The result is a version of the film called a **rough cut.** In making a rough cut, film directors or editors may reject certain shots or rearrange them. While doing this, they may focus on organization and transitions, but they will also consider other aspects of the composing process. Then they must prepare a final version of the film called the **fine cut,** in which the film is virtually ready for approval. So important is the process of editing (or revision) in making films that the Russian film director V. I. Pudovkin has flatly asserted that "the foundation of film art is editing."

Writers generally agree with Pudovkin about the importance of editing or revision in the art of composition. Thomas Huxley maintained that he wrote essays a half-dozen times before he could "get them into proper shape." Robert Louis Stevenson vehemently declared: "When I say writing, O, believe me, it is rewriting that I have chiefly in mind." Yet many student writers believe that the main task of writing is complete once they have put the last word down on paper.

Despite time-honored advice given by professional writers and artists about the importance of revision, however, very few students revise their work. Perhaps they make a few mechanical corrections after they have finished the first draft, but **revision** is more than correcting mechanical errors. At its best, it is *making improvements in the original paper by rearranging and reorganizing ideas* (and, if need be, entire paragraphs), *rephrasing sentences, deleting extraneous material, and adding completely new material.* It often requires *a total reconception of the subject and of the writer's approach to the subject.* Some writers make a distinction between revision and editing or proofreading. **Revision,** in this sense, refers to *reconstructing a theme, improving weak passages, adding new material,* whereas **editing** or **proofreading** refers to *correcting grammatical errors, rewriting misspelled words, and changing punctuation.* Both revising and editing are necessary for a finished piece of work.

In the beginning stages of learning to write, it may be difficult for you to cultivate the habit of self-criticism. Yet this is exactly what you must do if you want to be a good writer. Until you learn how to check your own work for proper organization and development of ideas, as well as for mechanical correctness, no matter how diligent you may be in writing your paper, the final result may be a paper that is incoherent, digressive, and a waste of your valuable time and that of the instructor. Never mind that in the process of composition you seemed suitably inspired, filled with the satisfaction that often results when the words come easily, almost unbidden from your mind. *Good writing often demands rewriting.*

After you have finished your first draft, therefore, *get to work immediately and read your paper.* Some writers recommend that you wait at least several days to let your work cool, and this is good advice. But be realistic. If you are taking several classes, or if your schedule prevents your being able to put your work aside for a while, or if you are the kind of person who procrastinates, who puts off even the first draft until the very last minute, you should read your work immediately. Reading your work after several days have gone by, however, does have this advantage—it allows you to become somewhat detached and dispassionate in your appraisal of it, so that in rereading it, it is almost as if you were reading someone else's work. Then you can bring to your criticism a kind of objectivity that you seldom get in the actual process of composing.

If it is at all possible, after you have handwritten your first draft, *type your paper.* You will find it amazing the degree to which problems in organization and in mechanics stand out after you have typed your paper. In a handwritten paper, your sentences and paragraphs are spread over several pages, so that it is difficult sometimes to take them in as a unit. In a typewritten paper, however, your sentences and paragraphs can usually be taken in at a glance.

Whether you decide to type your paper or to write it out in

longhand, after you have finished the first draft, *read your paper aloud.* This is fairly traditional advice, but it does work. Quite often, in reading your paper aloud, your ear will detect some problem that your eye may overlook. By reading your paper aloud, you can test, first of all, the logical flow of ideas. You can determine if the ideas connect with each other, if the pieces fit together, if the thrust of the essay is what you really want. You can literally *hear* the effect of the writing as it impinges on your consciousness. You can detect obscure passages, badly punctuated sentences, repetitive phrases, and monotonous expressions. You can also detect wordiness, the lack of grammatical correctness, and awkward combinations of words.

Revision Checklist

As you read, ask yourself certain pertinent questions, beginning first of all with *questions pertaining to the paper as a whole:*

1. Do I have a suitable introduction? Is it interesting and appropriate? Will it make my readers want to read on?

2. Do I have a clearly defined thesis sentence, or is my main idea at least implicit in my introduction?

3. Does my introduction clearly indicate my plan of development?

4. Is the body of my paper arranged according to some convenient plan? Are the successive steps easy to follow? Are there transitions from one part to another?

5. Have I used supporting details in such a way that they strengthen the general ideas in the body of the paper?

6. Is my evidence appropriate, and is my reasoning sound? Have I considered possible objections?

7. Does my conclusion follow logically from all that has gone before? Is it free from new or irrelevant material?

8. Is my conclusion effective? Does it leave my readers satisfied?

9. Is my paper as a whole clear? Have I included as many details as are necessary? Have I remembered that my audience may know little or nothing about my subject and that it is my responsibility to fill in the gaps?

10. Have I maintained a consistent point of view, or have I shifted unaccountably from one person to another, from one viewpoint to another?

11. Do I have an appropriate title? Does it reveal a close relationship to my central idea?

12. Finally, have I kept the commitment I implicitly made to my reader in my opening sentences?

After you have examined your paper as a whole, *consider the individual paragraphs:*

1. Is each paragraph logically developed?
2. Does it function well in the plan of the paper as a whole; for example, as a support for a general idea or as a means of going from one part of the essay to another?
3. Does it observe the rules of unity and coherence?
4. Is it punctuated properly?
5. Does it have good (that is, grammatical and effective) sentences?

Consider next the individual sentences, both isolated from the context and in the context of the sentences nearest to them:

1. Are my sentences varied in form?
2. Are my sentences varied in length?
3. Is each sentence clear and complete in itself?
4. Are the modifiers close to the words they modify?
5. Is there agreement between the subjects and the verbs?
6. Are subordinate ideas grammatically subordinated?
7. Are coordinate ideas properly coordinated?

8. Is each sentence properly punctuated?
9. Can some of the sentences be written more concisely?
10. Does each sentence relate logically and stylistically to the sentences around it?

Then, within the context of each sentence, *consider the word choice*, and ask yourself:

1. Is my wording clear and accurate?
2. Is it appropriate in context?
3. Is it free from jargon and trite or stale expressions?
4. Does it generally follow the conventions of language? That is, is it formal when it should be formal, idiomatic when it should be idiomatic, conversational when it is appropriate that it be so?
5. Is it free from vagueness or from unwarranted generalities?
6. Can I find a better word or phrase than the one I am currently using?

Finally, go through the entire essay and check for *mechanical correctness,* asking the following questions:

1. Have I checked all doubtful spellings? Words I habitually misspell? Hyphens? Capitals? Apostrophes?

2. Is my puncutation both correct and appropriate? Commas? Dashes? Semicolons? Colons? Periods?

3. Are quotations properly credited and enclosed in quotation marks? Are ellipses and interpolations properly marked?

4. Is my manuscript neat and clean? Few or no blotted or crossed-out lines?

5. Does this paper honestly represent my best effort?

A revision checklist can be very helpful in assisting you to read and revise your own work. But in addition to keeping a revision checklist, you may want to keep a record of your chronic faults.

You will discover that many of the weaknesses in your writing are caused by the same recurring types of faults. The following are suggestions for correcting some of the kinds of errors that recur in student writing.

Wordiness

Improve sentences and paragraphs that are needlessly wordy. Notice that this kind of advice is not necessarily the same as that which encourages you to write simply and directly. There are times when complex ideas should be expressed in complex grammatical structures. Nor is the injunction to avoid wordiness merely a matter of asking you to cut down on the length of a statement or a passage.

One type of wordiness you will want to avoid in your writing is **tautology,** *the needless repetition of the same meaning in different words.* For example, in the following student sentence, the words *carelessly discarded* are not necessary to make out the sense of the sentence:

> Among the increasing tons of *carelessly discarded* litter befouling the country's beautiful scenery are hundreds of thousands of beer cans.

Since the word *litter* means "trash that has been carelessly discarded," the phrase *carelessly discarded* is a tautology that should be eliminated.

Similarly, in the following student sentence, there is no need to use the word *necessary* before the word *prerequisites.* The word *prerequisites* contains the meaning of "necessary."

> I don't think I have the *necessary* prerequisites for graduation.

Another type of wordiness you will want to avoid is **redundancy,** that is, *using more words than are absolutely necessary.* Quite often, redundancy is the result of padding or of an inability to see how words work. In the revision process, therefore, you will want to cut out the padding.

For example, in the following student sentence, the word *today* can be substituted for the phrase "in this day and age" since both mean the same thing. The substitution immeasurably improves the sentence.

> *In this day and age,* a bachelor's degree is becoming commonplace.
> *Today,* a bachelor's degree is becoming commonplace.

Some kinds of wordiness are so obvious that they should be relatively easy for you to spot:

> Dates with persons of the opposite sex, *be they male or female,* can be classified in many ways.

You can improve this sentence merely by deleting the phrase "be they male or female," since this information is already contained in the words *persons of the opposite sex.*

Other kinds of wordiness may not be as obvious, but with a little practice you will be able to spot these as well. The following student sentence is grammatically correct, but the revised version, which is less wordy, is much more effective:

> As long as *there are pressures from parents to force students to try and obtain* a college degree, *there will be the problem of the overcrowding of disinterested students* in the universities.
> As long as parents pressure students to get a college degree, uninterested students will crowd the universities.

In revising your paper to eliminate wordiness, sometimes you may want to combine several sentences within a paragraph, as in the following student example:

> Have you ever had the misfortune to own a misconceived piece of junk better known as a late-model car? Well, if you have or do own one of these lifelong lemons and want to sell or unload it, please listen close. If you follow the following steps, you can be successful.

The rewritten version is not only more concise, but it is also more effective:

> If you own a late-model car which is a lemon and if you want to unload it, follow these simple steps and you will be successful.

Jargon

Improve sentences that contain jargon. Jargon is characterized by the following:

1. *Using several words when one word will do:*

exhibits a tendency	tends
in an efficient manner	efficiently
make inquiry regarding	inquire
a not inconsiderable number	many
resembling in nature	like
reach a decision	decide
render operative	fix
causative factor	cause

2. *A preference for abstract nouns ending in* -tion, -ity, -ment, -ness, -ance, -ative, -ate, -ous, -cy, -ist, *and the like:*

utilization	dentition
nullity	pertinacity
apportionment	exigency
credulousness	diplomatist
discountenance	parsimonious

3. *Excessive use of words with Latin or Greek prefixes:*

abnegation	debriefing
circumspect	upgrade
contravene	antitechnology
nonpreferential	bioelemetric
intrazonal	dishabituate

4. *The use of stock phrases:*

in the final analysis
other things being equal
from the point of view of
within the framework of
in the event that

5. *The substitution of euphemisms for less explicit or offensive terms:*

terminal living	dying
mortician	undertaker
defensive maneuver	retreat
mild irregularity	constipation
bathroom tissue	toilet paper
loan expert	pawnbroker
senior citizens	old people
underprivileged	delinquent
criminally assaulted	raped
liquidation	assassination

6. *The overabundant use of clichés:*

lock, stock, and barrel	one and all
as thick as thieves	a grievous error
all to the good	null and void
blank amazement	safe and sound
pick and choose	fair and square

7. *The extensive use of the passive voice rather than the use of the more direct active voice:*

Job opportunities may be increased by higher education.
Higher education may increase job opportunities.

Competitive activities should be avoided.
Avoid competitive activities.

The report has been solicited by the committee.
The committee has solicited the report.

Almost all of these characteristics of jargon, of course, need qualifying. Occasionally, a long phrase such as *along the lines of* might be more appropriate for your purpose than *like*. You can't always avoid abstract nouns, especially if you need to refer to the special vocabulary of a particular discipline or profession. Latin and Greek prefixes often add flexibility to the language. Stock phrases such as "with reference to" sometimes enable your thoughts to flow more smoothly than do single words, and aid the rhythm of your sentence. It might be necessary occasionally to use euphemisms to avoid offending your audience, especially if you are dealing with death or bodily functions. Sometimes clichés add intensity to the language. Finally, there are times when you can't avoid the passive voice, especially when you don't know the agent of the action in your sentences.

Here are some guidelines that you may want to keep in mind in revising your sentences to avoid jargon.

> *Substitute short words for long words.*
> *Avoid an excessive use of abstractions.*
> *Substitute Anglo-Saxon words wherever possible for those of Latin or Greek origin.*
> *Eliminate clichés and stock phrases.*
> *Take out the euphemisms.*
> *Change the passive voice to the active voice, unless you have a particular reason for using the passive voice.*

Clearly, all of these guidelines must be modified in relation to your purpose, your audience, and the occasion. But much of the writing that you do will be of the kind that emphasizes economy of language for a general audience.

Shift in Point of View

Improve passages in your writing that contain unnecessary or illogical shifts in point of view. Illogical shifts in point of view may be the result of moving from one person or number to another, from one subject to another, or from one voice or tense to another.

Avoid illogical shifts in person and number. Notice how, in the following student theme, the writer shifts confusingly from *pilot* to *he* to *you* to *one.* I have included the pronoun *you* in places where it is understood.

A Preflight Inspection of Aircraft

A preflight inspection of an aircraft is a must before every flight. If the *pilot* does not make a preflight inspection, *he* will not know if the aircraft is fit for flight. *He* will be endangering the passengers' lives as well as his own. There are several checkpoints *one* must inspect in making a preflight check.

The first checkpoint is the cockpit. In the cockpit, *you* should first turn the main switch on and check the fuel gauges and the generator light, then turn the main switch off. Also, *you* should make sure the ignition switch is off and the fuel valve is on.

The second checkpoint is the rudder. *One* should check the rudder for proper movement and do the same for the elevator. Then *you* should disconnect the tail tie-down.

At checkpoint three, [*you* should] look for lumps or cracks in the wing. Also, [*you* should] check the flaps and ailerons for proper movement.

Checkpoint four is in the front of the wings. There *you* should check the main wheels for proper inflation. *One* should also make sure that the airspeed static source is not clogged.

Checkpoint five is the cowling. At this checkpoint, *you* should check the oil level and fill if necessary. Next [*you* should] make sure the propellor is free of nicks and cracks and that it is attached securely. Then [*you* should] check the carburetor for cleanliness and the fuel supply for quantity and contamination. In addition, [*you* should] make certain the tire is properly inflated.

Checkpoint six is at the end of the left wing. At this checkpoint, *one* should remove the pilot tube covering and check the pilot tube for stoppage. [*You* should] check also the stall warning vent for interference.

A *pilot* should make this preflight inspection before every flight so it becomes a habit. If *he* does not, *he* may get off the ground, but *he* might never come down.

You can improve this paper by rewriting it, keeping consistently to the same person and number, as in the following revision:

A preflight inspection of an aircraft is a must before every flight. If you do not make a preflight inspection, you will not know if the aircraft is fit for flight. You will be endangering the passengers' lives as well as your own. There are several checkpoints you must inspect in making a preflight check.

The first checkpoint is the cockpit. In the cockpit, you should first turn the main switch on and check the fuel gauges and the generator light, then turn the main switch off. Also, you should make sure the ignition is off and the fuel valve is on.

The second checkpoint is the rudder. You should check the rudder for proper movement and you should do the same for the elevator. Then you should disconnect the tail tie-down.

At checkpoint three, you should look for lumps or cracks in the wing. Also, you should check the flaps and ailerons for proper movement.

Checkpoint four is in the front of the wings. There you should check the main wheels for proper inflation. You should also make sure that the airspeed static source is not clogged.

Checkpoint five is the cowling. At this checkpoint, you should check the oil level and fill if necessary. Next you should make sure that the propellor is free of nicks and cracks and that it is attached securely. Then you should check the carburetor for cleanliness and the fuel supply for quantity and contamination. In addition, you should make certain the tire is properly inflated.

Checkpoint six is at the end of the left wing. At this checkpoint, you should remove the pilot tube covering and check the pilot tube for stoppage. You should check also the stall warning vent for interference.

You should make this preflight inspection before every flight so it becomes a habit. If you do not, you may get off the ground, but you might never come down.

There are other problems in this student paper, of course, but keeping consistently to the same person and number improves the paper considerably.

Avoid illogical or confusing shifts in subject, as in the following example:

The new cars are not very comfortable, but you can drive in relative safety.

In this sentence, there is a shift from talking about the comfort of new cars to talking about *your* driving them in relative safety. You can correct this by keeping to the same point of view:

> The new cars are not very comfortable, but they are relatively safe.

Avoid also confusing shifts in voice (from active to passive or from passive to active). The following student paragraph shifts awkwardly from the active to the passive voice:

> Still another ad shows an endless amount of sand, sunlight, and heat. Then the camera is zoomed in and is focused on a can of underarm deodorant. The announcer's voice then explains that X deodorant will keep you dry.

You can rewrite this paragraph and make it more effective by changing the passive-voice verbs to the active voice:

> Still another ad shows an endless amount of sand, sunlight, and heat. Then the camera zooms in and focuses on a can of underarm deodorant. The announcer's voice then explains that X deodorant will keep you dry.

Avoid, finally, awkward shifts in tense where such shifts are not clearly warranted, as in these student sentences:

> The pitcher *came* up quickly and *tries* to strike out the batter.
> Laura *asks* the doctor about her brother's condition but *received* an evasive answer.
> She *goes* her way silently and no one *took* notice of her.
> By getting back to town late, they *missed* the sale and thus *lose* the opportunity to buy the TV.

You can make these sentences clearer and more effective by sticking to one particular tense:

> The pitcher *came* (comes) up quickly and *tried* (tries) to strike out the batter.

Laura *asked* (asks) the doctor about her brother's condition but *received* (receives) an evasive answer.

She *went* (goes) her way silently and no one *took* (takes) notice of her.

By getting back to town late, they *missed* (miss) the sale and thus *lost* (lose) the opportunity to buy the TV.

Revising the Whole Theme

In addition to revising your paper along the lines suggested thus far, you may need to make more extensive changes in your paper, in keeping with your original intention, your organizational plan, and your audience. Some of the questions in the revision checklist that pertain to the paper as a whole would be appropriate here. Remember that to revise is not merely to make superficial changes in your paper or simply to recopy it. It is rather to see your work again with a new vision, to improve it over your first effort.

The following student paper is a good example of a revision that goes beyond making a few mechanical changes. The paper is an analysis of an ad for Lindsay olives that appeared in *Sunset* magazine. The picture depicts a young boy dressed in the manner of a character from a Charles Dickens novel. He gazes longingly at a huge sandwich which is in the foreground of the picture. The sandwich has layers of ham, salami, and cheese, with olives generously sprinkled about. The text reads as follows:

The Oliver Twist
from Lindsay!

(It beats the Dickens out of ordinary sandwiches.)

Great Expectations! Feed a family of four with fun and frivolity. It's easy! Just slice, hollow and butter a loaf of round bread. Then pile on slices of ham, salami, cheese and anything else your family loves in a sandwich. Add pimiento pieces, lettuce and fresh onion rings. Now sprinkle a generous handful of Lindsay Ripe Pitted Black Olives between the layers. They add a special nutlike mellow flavor—plus added color and excitement. That's the Oliver.

Now the Twist: Press your sandwich to blend the ingredients together. Slice, serve and enjoy! That's the Oliver Twist from Lindsay—a Dickens of a great sandwich!

An olive is just an olive . . . unless it's a Lindsay.

Now here is the student paper, which was written in response to an assignment to analyze an ad and evaluate its effectiveness in relation to its intended audience.

With Oliver Twist (or possibly his literary first cousin, David Copperfield) gazing longingly in the background at a huge sandwich called "The Oliver Twist," Lindsay foods presents a clever ad in the December 1978 edition of *Sunset* magazine. By using heavy literary allusions, a little alliteration, and sophisticated manipulation of puns, the ad is successful in presenting and marketing Lindsay olives.

The ad is rich in literary allusions, both visually and textually. The sanwich itself, made of round bread suggests a by-gone era to the world of 24 slice one pound loaves, as well as forming the triangle base that eventually leads the eye to the waif in the background, heavily reminiscent of Oliver Twist asking for "some more."

The literary allusions are continued in the text. The headline mentions Oliver Twist, the secondary headline recalls the author, Dickens, and *Great Expectations* (another Dickens work) leads off the body copy. These references appeal to the more learned audience as they would be unintelligible to anyone not familiar with Dickens, they also form the base for the sophisticated use of puns.

By far the most successful stylistic device is the use of puns. The primary headline develops the frame of mind needed for the two major plays on words. The Oliver Twist, we are told, "beats the Dickens out of ordinary sandwiches." The use of literary allusions, but especially the puns, causes the audience to keep reading. *Great Expectations* is another play on words as it parallels the reader's anticipation as well as continues the literary theme. After detailing the process of making the sandwich (appropriately called the Oliver), the audience is told there's a "Twist"—completing the second major point. The pun cycle is completed with Dickens again being used in a different wordplay.

The simple expository sentences, heavy in parallelism, are

momentarily suspended with a strong alliterative "f" causing a sense of frivolity. This sense of frivolity causes the reader to continue.

By appealing to a literary audience, developing a general sense of frivolity, and by using sophisticated puns, the Lindsay ad causes the reader to finish the ad and envision himself using the product. These are features of a successful ad.

This paper is good in parts, but it certainly needs more than the correction of mechanical and grammatical errors. These consist primarily of a lapse in spelling or editing *(sanwich)*, a run-on sentence ("These references appeal to the more learned audience as they would be unintelligible to anyone not familiar with Dickens, they also form the base for the sophisticated use of puns"), and a dangling modifier ("After detailing the process of making the sandwich, appropriately called the Oliver, the audience is told there's a "Twist"—completing the second major point").

What this student has failed to do is to develop and explain his ideas fully, especially in the fourth and fifth paragraphs. He needs to give more examples, explain them, and quote from the text. Finally, he needs to rewrite some sentences that are awkward or in which the meaning is not too clear.

The following is a revised version of this paper.

With Oliver Twist (or probably his literary first cousin, David Copperfield) gazing longingly in the background at a huge sandwich called "The Oliver Twist," Lindsay foods presents a clever ad in the December 1978 edition of *Sunset* magazine, the magazine of western living. The ad uses literary allusions, puns, alliteration, and parallel structure to sell Lindsay olives.

The ad is rich in literary allusions. The waif in the background of the illustration is heavily reminiscent of Oliver Twist, a character in the Dickens novel of the same name. The sandwich itself is made of a round bread that could have been made in the nineteenth century. The sandwich is cut into two pieces and arranged in the shape of a triangular wedge that leads the reader's eye to the young boy who is looking hungrily at the sandwich.

The literary allusions are continued in the text. The headline, which reads "The Oliver Twist from Lindsay," is a reference not only to the sandwich, but also to the character Oliver Twist, in the Dickens novel. The next line ("It beats the Dickens out of ordinary sandwiches") is a play on the word *dickens* and an allusion to Charles Dickens. The opening line of the copy ("Great Expectations!") refers literally to what the reader could expect from a can of Lindsay olives and is an allusion to the title of another of Dickens's novels. The ad concludes with two more allusions: to Oliver Twist ("That's the Oliver Twist from Lindsay") and to Charles Dickens ("a Dickens of a great sandwich!").

By far the most successful stylistic device is the use of puns. "The Oliver Twist," we are told, "beats the Dickens out of ordinary sandwiches." The puns on the words *Oliver Twist* and *Dickens* can be understood in at least two senses. Oliver Twist is the name of the sandwich and the name of the young boy in the Dickens novel. The word *dickens* refers to Charles Dickens, and it is also a mild oath. Other puns similar to these can be found in the lines "That's the Oliver," "Now the Twist," "That's the Oliver Twist," and "a Dickens of a great sandwich."

Alliteration is used effectively in the line "Feed a family of four with fun and frivolity." The alliteration (the "f" sounds) seems to reinforce the playful tone of the ad.

Finally, the parallel structure combines with the word choice to convey a concrete, descriptive picture of the "makings" that go into the sandwich: "Just slice, hollow, and butter a loaf of round bread"; "Then pile on slices of ham, salami, cheese and anything else your family loves in a sandwich"; "Add pimiento pieces, lettuce, and fresh onion rings."

The reader of *Sunset* magazine is probably a person who has some education and money for leisure living, since the contents of the magazine have to do with food, outdoor living, and travel. Such a reader would be delighted by the allusions to Charles Dickens, by the playful language, and by the alliteration and parallelism. These stylistic devices, combined with the illustration, make for a very effective selling appeal.

Exercises

1. Before turning in your next composition, bring it to class. Then read your paper aloud to the class. The other members of the class should criticize it, using the revision checklist and offering constructive suggestions for revision.

2. As an in-class project, exchange papers with one of your classmates and make suggestions on the paper for revision.

3. Ask your instructor to put one of your themes on an overhead projector or an opaque projector and then have the class analyze it and offer constructive criticism.

4. Discuss in class the problems in the following student essays, and suggest ways of improving these essays.

Doodles

People who doodle during passive periods often reveal more about themselves than they do about their artistic ability. Although doodling is merely a means of relieving nervous tensions, it often times is a graphic manifestation of an individual's unconscious mind. Therefore, doodles in fact, can be insights to an individual's personality, thoughts, and even sexual attitudes.

Generally speaking, a person's personality is determined by the way in which the individual acts and reacts. People who do not outwardly express themselves through actions and verbal communication may do so through doodling. People with different personalities will doodle in a different manner. For example, a person who is meek and timid might doodle with thin lines and unattached figures. The thin line indicates that the person is very frail and afraid to bear down when faced with perplexing problems. Also, meekness can be equated with an inferior feeling about themselves. Thus, an inability to assert a solid position in a particular situation or circumstance. The unconnected configuration is also a sign of meekness. This type of figure illustrated an inability to cope with any task which is too hard to complete. Rather than attack the problem at its base the timid person would rather let it drop with the excuse of being too difficult. Other doodles that might indicate meek personalities are: unshaded squares and geometric figures; indicating emptiness and loneliness, and circles; which relates to a continuous fear of inferiority.

On the other hand, in a strong, dominating personality the doodles change radically in the opposite direction. A person with this type of personality is most often very sure of intended actions and will usually see a problem through to the very end. Their doodles are usually bold, precise, and definite in shape and size. Such doodles are objects, and depending upon artistic ability, closely resemble the object as it appears in real life. The objects might include human caricatures; indicating a positive relationship with others, animals, and a three-dimensional-objects; indicating solidity of thought and firmness of mind.

A person's thoughts can also be interpreted by analyzing their casual scribblings. By looking at their doodles it is possible to determine what mood or state of mind the person was in at that particular time. For example, if the doodles are made up of cross-hatched lines or a series of broken-line designs this could show an existant state of confusion in the mind of the individual. Moods of happiness, sadness, and loneliness can also be seen in the doodles of the individual. Doodles which might indicate happiness are quick, curly, and generally take the form of flower-like sketches. A person might unknowingly draw this type of doodle while speaking to someone whom they haven't seen in a long period of time. Sadness can also be a factor in determining the type of doodle which is produced at that particular instant. For example, a mood of sadness can be linked with small circular-like objects; denoting emptiness and a sense small and unimportant. Other doodles which also seem to indicate sadness are first names of an actual person. Such a case might involve the departure or break-up of friends or lovers. The sad individual might write the other person's name over and over, thus showing an actual mood of sadness because the other person has left. In most cases, loneliness is a factor of sadness and, therefore, the doodles are similar to those of sadness.

In most cases, doodles can reveal the sexual attitude or tendency of an individual. A person who is pre-occupied with the thought of sex will doodle in a very distinct manner. All the doodles will indicate sexual body parts and sexual ideas. Those doodles which might be equated with sexual thoughts are short straight lines, rounded objects, circular objects with depth, and the intersection of circles and lines. Logically, the circular and rounded objects indicate the female body, and the straight-line objects represent the male body. All of these types of doodles might indicate the desire to take part in sexual relationships. Although this is not a positive means of determining sexual attitudes it does, in fact, give a good indication of it.

In conclusion, by analyzing the doodles of an individual it is possible to determine certain aspects of that individual's character at a particular time. Doodles often leave a picture of the mood a person was in while drawing them. Doodles can determine a person's personality, thoughts, and sexual attitudes.

How To Survive Loneliness

Loneliness is an appalling ordeal, encasing its victim in a desolate world. If he is to survive, the individual must learn to cope with his dilemma. To dispossess this perplexity requires the careful observance of the sufferers habitat, recreation, and thoughts.

The victim of loneliness must use the eyes of Argus when choosing his environmental habitat. He should try to find a location in midst a mass of extroverts. Their gregarious characteristics might draw the victim into their circle, curing him of his problem. If this desired location can not be found, his abode should be in the approximate area of a center of communal entertainment. This will, in all likelihood, give him a temporary reprieve from the torment of his plight. Under no circumstances should the individual choose a secluded dwelling. Seclusion only adds to the pain, driving him deeper into the depths of his despair.

When the pangs of loneliness strike, the victim must find some way to salve his feelings. People are the only balm which can truly help this attack. If no people can be reached, a movie or play could prove helpful. He should show discretion in picking his subject, making sure not to choose one that would bring an old memory to surface. This memory would only be likely to increase his pain. To become a Bacchanalian is another route. It is not as desirous as the others because of an unwanted self-reproach which accompanies such indulgences. This self-reproach can cause a more serious problem than the symptom it was to have cured. It occurs the individual should abandon this means immediately.

The person afflicted with loneliness will find, in the long run, only he can find his own cure. No lasting results can be achieved unless the individual convinces himself that loneliness is just a state of mind. He should start by telling himself that he is equal to the next man. This has a tendency to lower the barriers separating him from others. It is only when those barriers of the difference are lowered can loneliness be uprooted and expelled. The suffering individual should not, at any time, feel sorry for himself. If he should start feeling this way, it will increase his feeling of isolation, causing him to slide further into desolation.

If an individual is to defeat his loneliness, he must meet it head on. There are an infinite number of ways a person may vie with this feeling. I have shown you the three that have helped me the greatest in my struggle with this adversary. It is through these eternal battles that I found that a careful regulation of habitat, recreation, and thoughts prove effective as a nemesis of loneliness.

Don't Be Fooled by Advertisements

Don't be fooled into thinking advertisements are innocent. They will stoop to any means to manipulate your mind. The diabolical weapons of the advertiser include slanted language, inferences, sly use of connotation, generalization with no supporting fact and claims that certain things will happen after buying their product. Our best defense against these diabolical weapons is objective analysis.

"It could well be the world's most wanted car," is the opening statement of an advertisement for 1972 Cadillac. Look at how extremely general and shallow the statement is. General, in the sense that it could be applied to any car. Shallow, in the sense that it doesn't say anything specific. A classic example of generalization without factual foundation. Working upon the assumption that the reader has accepted this primary statement we proceed. "Some want it for the way it looks . . . its beauty of line and form." Line and form are used for their connotative meanings. These words are used in description of art like great paintings and sculpture. An example of the sly use of connotation is seen here. It is ridiculous to equate a mass produced car with a sculpture of Michelangelo. A parallel statement appears later in the advertisement. "The finest of the automaker's art." The word "art" is used to deceive reader into thinking each car is tediously worked upon like a sculpture of Michelangelo. The word "achievement" is important to look at as well. It has a connotation of something that has been accomplished successfully, especially by means of exertion, skill, practice or perseverance. It reinforces the art connotation very well. "Some for what it says about them to others." This phrase exhibits a terrible lack of specifics. What does it say to others? Instead of answering the question in words, the advertiser cleverly uses a picture. Above the picture of the car, appears a group of affluent people at an expensive restaurant. A faint image of a flower appears over the scene. The importance of the restaurant scene is it shows what image you will, supposedly, produce if you own a Cadillac. The importance of the flower is it has a connotation of beauty and elegance. Owning a Cadillac is no indication of how elegant and affluent you are. If a person has 8,000 dollars he or she can own a Cadillac. This is regardless of how beautiful or affluent they may be. An illustration of how things will happen if you buy our product is seen here. "Some for its resale value, traditionally highest of any car in the land." Strange, recently, on television, I heard Skylark had the highest resale value. Factual information seems to be lacking in this claim. "Some for what it represents in driving peace of mind." Peace of mind has the connotation of inner contentment, calm and serenity. Driving a Cadillac doesn't remove the fears and dangers of driving. These factors exist no matter what type of car you're driving. Peace of mind is a phrase people love to hear because of what it implies. Mrs. Merritt, a well-known figure, once said, "If you put things into nice language, you can make anything sound nice." Cadillacs don't produce peace of mind in driving but by using the nice phrase "peace of mind" they are tricked into accepting it. "It could well be everything you've ever wanted in an automobile." Does the form look familiar? It should, they are using the same ambiguity they used to begin the advertisement to end it. The statement infers Cadillac is everything you've ever wanted in a car. However, by using the word "could" the company has completely detached itself from all liability. Meaning, that if their car isn't what you wanted you can't hold it against them because they said "it could be everything you've ever wanted," not it *is* everything you've ever wanted. Appearing at the bottom of the page is an article about how GM is progressively reducing exhaust emissions was because of government action. Don't believe they care more about the consumer than their profits. If they did care they would have taken more action earlier and on a much larger scale.

Now for an overall look at the advertisement. The language is sophisticated to express the prestige of the car and appeal to the class of people who buy it. The word "some" is used over and over again. There are two reasons behind it. The first reason is because it has a connotation of individualism. Knowing the society stresses rugged individualism, the advertiser wants to make you feel like one. This advertisement used language usage integrated with visual suggestion fantastically. Advertisements are extremely subversive. I urge the reader to really consider the points I have made. The next time you see an advertisement don't automatically swallow it hook, line and sinker, use objective analyzation!!!!

The Research Paper

Chapter 15

The Research Paper

The research paper should be a logical outgrowth of the kinds of papers you have been doing all semester. For example, if for a particular classroom assignment you are asked to go to your book of essays and read two articles about the same subject and to discuss the point of view taken by each writer about his or her subject, as soon as you begin to analyze and evaluate the ideas in each article, synthesize them, and come to some kind of conclusion about what you have read, you are in effect laying the foundation for a research paper. For a typical 500-word theme, you might be asked to write a comparison and contrast paper about what you have read. If in your paper you support your ideas by including a few footnotes based on the two articles you were required to read, you are in effect writing a miniature research paper.

But the word *research* suggests not a 500-word theme, but an "extended" investigation or inquiry into some particular subject. So if you add to the two articles a few books and several more articles and you read, analyze, evaluate, and synthesize the ideas from these sources into a coherent discourse, then you will have written a research paper about the different points of view concerning your subject.

In most of the papers you do in a composition course, you do not have time to do more than scratch the surface of a topic. But the research paper encourages you to think long and deeply about some subject.

The process of writing a research paper breaks up into steps something like the following: (1) choosing a general subject, (2) limiting the subject and formulating a thesis, (3) finding material and making a tentative bibliography, (4) evaluating your material and taking notes, (5) making a rough outline, (6) writing the paper, (7) documenting it, and (8) making the bibliography. Needless to say, there may be considerable overlapping in these steps.

Choosing a General Subject

In chapter 1, we discussed places where you can go to get general subjects to write about: the table of contents of magazines such as *Time* or *Newsweek,* the dictionary, the alphabetically arranged subject index or table of contents of a textbook or an essay anthology, the subject heading of the card catalog in the library, periodical indexes such as the *Reader's Guide to Periodical Literature,* and a good encyclopedia. Obviously, you should first select a subject you would enjoy reading about and writing about. But a second consideration is choosing a subject about which there is sufficient information.

The following topics were compiled by the library staff of Arizona State University. Each topic was researched by a member of the staff to be certain that there were sufficient library resources (books, periodicals, newspapers, government documents, and so forth) to enable students to complete their research. It may be, of course, that you will not find many of these subjects interesting, but at least you have a starting place.

Advertising	Migrant laborers
Astrology	Minorities
Camping	Nutrition
Censorship	Organic gardening
Conservation	Overpopulation
Consumer protection	Pollution
Demonology	Propaganda
Divorce	Riots in the United States
Drug abuse	Transplantation of organs
Earthquakes	War crimes
Gambling	Wildlife conservation
Ghettos	Women's liberation

Limiting the Subject and Formulating a Thesis

As you consider the subjects listed above, you will soon realize that each is too broad for a relatively short research paper (between ten and fifteen typed pages, double-spaced). Therefore, you need to limit your subject, to make clearer your approach to the subject, to tell the reader more precisely what you intend to cover. You can begin by dividing the subject into its parts. For example, you can divide the subject of censorship as follows:

censorship
   books
   films
   newspapers

Or better yet, you can formulate a thesis sentence that will express clearly and precisely your central idea. Your thesis sentence will provide a frame of reference so that when you begin to do your research, you can frequently return to it to get your bearings. Your thesis sentence will be the working idea of your paper.

The following thesis sentence was formulated by a student after she had become interested in the general subject of demonology:

My thesis is that devil worship does exist in the modern world, that it has become quite widespread in the '60s and '70s, and that there are a number of reasons for this new interest in devil worship and in the occult.

It is possible, of course, that after you have formulated your thesis you will want to change your mind about it and qualify it or discard it completely after you begin your research. But the formulation of a thesis sentence will give your research a particular direction, it will enable you to limit your subject, and it may even suggest to you an organizational plan when you finally begin to write your paper.

Finding Your Material and Making a Tentative Bibliography

Assuming now that you have chosen a general subject that interests you and you have formulated a thesis statement, your next step is to go to the library and find your material. Go first to an encyclopedia article and read it. You will find the encyclopedias in the reference room of the library. By reading the article, you will be able to get an overview of your subject. The article will also contain key ideas and some terms you can use later on in your searching. In addition, it may contain a brief bibliography at the end of the article, which you can copy down and use to begin your research.

Your next step is to go to the card catalog in your library. The card catalog will usually have three cards for each book: one under the *author's last name,* one under the *title,* and a third under the *subject.* In addition to information about the author, the title, and the subject, each card will have a *call number* in the upper left corner, which tells you where the book is located.

From the card catalog, begin to compile your bibliography. Jot down on 3×5 cards the bibliographical material you will need to conduct your reading. Put the information on your card in the same form that you will use in your bibliography. For example, the author's last name comes first, then his first name, followed by a period. Next comes the title of the book, underlined, followed by a period. The place of publication, followed by a colon, comes afterward; then the name of the publisher, followed by a comma; and finally the date, followed by a period.

The following are examples of an author card, a title card, and a subject card for one book.

Author Card

```
             Rudhyar, Dane, 1895--
 BF             The lunation cycle. A key to the under-
 1701        standing of personality.
 R778        Wassenaar, Netherlands, Servire;
             distributed by Llewellyn Publications,
             St. Paul: Minn. [1967]

             Bibliography of the author's work:
             p. 157-158.

          1. Astrology    I. Title

 BF 1701.R778              133.5              68-117119
```

Title Card

```
                    The lunation cycle

              Rudhyar, Dane, 1895--
    BF             The lunation cycle. A key to the under-
    1701       standing of personality.
    R778       Wassenaar, Netherlands, Servire;
              distributed by Llewellyn Publications,
              St. Paul: Minn. [1967]

                  Bibliography of the author's work:
                  p. 157-158.

                  1. Astrology    I. Title

    BF 1701.R778              133.5              68-117119
```

Subject Card

```
                        ASTROLOGY

              Rudhyar, Dane, 1895--
    BF             The lunation cycle. A key to the under-
    1701       standing of personality.
    R778       Wassenaar, Netherlands, Servire;
              distributed by Llewellyn Publications,
              St. Paul: Minn. [1967]

                  Bibliography of the author's work:
                  p. 157-158

                  1. Astrology    I. Title

    BF 1701.R778              133.5              68-117119
```

A typical entry on your card will look like this:

> Lindsey, Hal. *Satan Is Alive and Well on Planet Earth*. Grand Rapids, Mich.: Zondervan Publishing House, 1972.

The bibliographical form for books usually follows this format:

One Author
Hopkins, Jerry. *Elvis: A Biography*. New York: Warner Paperback Library, 1972.

Two Authors
Shulman, Arthur, and Roger Youman. *The Television Years*. New York: Popular Library, 1973.

Three or More Authors
Burns, Robert E., et al. *Episodes in American History*. Lexington, Mass.: Ginn and Co., 1973.

An Edited Book
Wise, Herbert H., ed. *Professional Rock and Roll*. New York: Collier Books, 1967.

A Book in Several Volumes
Gosse, Edmund. *English Literature an Illustrated Record*. 4 vols. New York: Grosset and Dunlap, 1908.

After you have put the bibliographical material about books that you need on separate 3×5 cards, do the same with articles. Go first to the *Reader's Guide to Periodical Literature*, which indexes hundreds of periodicals containing articles of general interest. This guide lists the author's name, the title of the article, the source, and the number of pages. For any particular piece of information, you can look under the subject, the author, or the title.

Then put the appropriate bibliographical information for magazine articles on your 3×5 cards, just as you did for books. The author's last name comes first, then his first name, followed by a period. Next comes the title of the article in quotation marks, followed by a period. The name of the magazine, underlined (or italicized) comes next, followed by a comma, the volume number, then the month and the year in parentheses, followed by a comma, and finally the page numbers, followed by a period.

Typical entries on your 3×5 bibliography cards will look like this:

Signed Article
Lardner, John. "Devitalizing Elvis," *Newsweek* (16 July 1956), 59.

Anonymous Article
"All About That Soviet Wheat Deal," *U.S. News & World Report* (9 October 1972), 28–30.

In addition to the *Reader's Guide to Periodical Literature*, you may need to consult other indexes, such as the *Book Review Digest*, the *Biography Index*, the *Education Index*, and the *Social Sciences and Humanities Index*, for information pertaining to your paper. Almost every major discipline has its own indexes that you might want to consult. You can find these reference sources in the card catalog under such specialized subject names as anthropology, linguistics, literature, philosophy, political science, psychology, and so forth. The librarian will be happy to show you where these reference books may be found.

Other important reference sources you will want to consult are dictionaries and encyclopedias such as the *Oxford Classical Diction-*

ary, the *Oxford English Dictionary*, the *Congressional Record*, the *Encyclopedia of Educational Research*, the *Encyclopedia Britannica*, and *Bartlett's Familiar Quotations*.

Finally, at times, you will undoubtedly want to use *The New York Times Index* as well as indexes from newspapers from all parts of the country. Many of these, however, may be on microfilm. A typical bibliographical entry from a newspaper will look like this on your card:

Signed Article
May, George O. "An Analysis of the Problem of Taxation." *The New York Times*, 9 May 1937, Sec. 4, p. 8.

Unsigned Article
"Presley Termed a Passing Fancy." *The New York Times*, 17 December 1956, Sec. 5, p. 28.

Evaluating Your Material and Taking Notes

Now that you have built up a fairly good bibliography, look up a few of the most interesting references. You might start with the magazine articles, then the newspaper articles, and then books. Read the articles and/or books carefully. As you read, take notes on 5×8 note-cards. Notice conflicting points of view, clashes of authority, knowledge of the field, unsupported or sweeping generalizations, facts, and the use of supporting details. Notice contradictory statements, disagreements, and lines of reasoning. Remember that the notes you take will become the rough material of your paper.

At the top of each notecard, put a brief description of the contents of the card, for example, "Devil Worshippers Turn to Christianity." Then, when you are finished your note-taking, you can sort the cards by categories. The result will be a kind of rough organization of your material. At the bottom of the last notecard dealing with a particular reference source, put the name of the author, the title, the volume number, the page, and so forth in footnote form.

On the card itself, put specific facts and quotable words or passages. At times, jot down these facts in outline form. At times, when the author's exact words are not required, paraphrase them. Quote the exact words of the writer if she or he has said something extremely well, or concisely, or if she or he is a particularly important authority on the subject. Be sure to enclose exact words in quotation marks. Other times, summarize the author's ideas, and from time to time record your own comments about what you are reading. As you jot down specific ideas about what you have read, be sure to put the page numbers from the original articles or books in the appropriate places on the notecards.

The following are typical examples of a notecard that uses the paraphrasing method and one that quotes the author's exact words.

The Paraphrase

<u>Murder</u> <u>linked</u> <u>to</u> <u>devil</u> <u>worshippers</u>

In Switzerland, an ex-priest, who had become a member of a religious cult, and his mistress were charged with the murder of a young girl. The reason for the murder, the killers later stated, was that the young girl had been physically and sexually possessed by the devil. p. 146

Henry Ansgar Kelly, "Death of the Devil?" <u>Commonweal</u>, 6 Nov. 1970, p. 146.

The Direct Quote

Reasons for the renewed interest in Satan

"The Satanic Age started in 1966. That's when God was proclaimed dead, the Sexual Freedom League came into prominence, and the hippies developed as a free sex culture." p. 29

Hal Lindsey, Satan Is Alive and Well on Planet Earth (Grand Rapids, Mich.: Zondervan Publishing House, 1972), p. 29.

In the process of taking notes, you may discover references to other books and articles about your subject. If you think them important, add these to your list and read them.

Making a Rough Outline

After you have finished your reading and your note-taking, organize your cards so that you can make an outline from them. Many teachers and students feel that an outline is an artificiality that simply does not take into account the way people actually compose. But a rough outline need not be complex or detailed. If you have been careful in formulating your thesis, it can provide you with a guide for making the simplest kind of tentative outline. At the very least, such an outline will suggest the main divisions of your paper.

For example, the student who did her research paper on devil worship and the occult worked up this simple outline:

Devil Worship in Modern Times

I. Introduction

   Devil worship does exist in the modern world, it has become widespread in the '60s and '70s, and there are reasons for this new interest in devil worship and the occult.

II. Body

   A. Devil worship does exist in the modern world.

   B. It has become widespread in the '60s and '70s.

   C. There are reasons for this new interest in devil worship and the occult.

III. Conclusion

   A. Some speculate that a Second Coming is at hand.

   B. Others see the birth of a new consciousness.

The form that your outline will take will in some measure be determined by the nature of your material, but in general the organizational plan of a research paper will not differ markedly from that of a shorter theme. The pattern may be logical or chronological, a division into parts or classes, comparison or contrast, or a pattern that deals with origins or causes. Each subject will suggest its own organizational plan.

Writing the Paper

Your reading has been done; your notes have been taken; your outline is finished. You are ready to begin writing. In your introduction, state your thesis, your purpose, and the scope of your paper. After you have done this, proceed with the body of the paper. You can use your outline as a guide, but do not hesitate to depart from the outline if new ideas or a slightly different organizational plan occurs to you as you are writing. Keep your notecards nearby and refer to them as the need arises. Everything you have learned previously about the writing of themes should be brought to bear on the writing of this paper: the use of a suitable introduction; the arrangement of the body of your paper according to some plan; the use of supporting details to strengthen the general ideas in the paper; the maintenance of a consistent point of view; an effective conclusion; and finally (as it relates to the paper as a whole), a check to see that you have kept the commitment you made to your reader in the opening sentences.

As you write, you may have to reword your notes so that the ideas fit smoothly into the body of your paper. At times, of course, your original paraphrase or a quotation can be copied exactly as is. As you go along, keep your thesis clearly in mind, checking back from time to time to be sure that your paper is progressing in a logical manner.

When you use a direct quotation, try to incorporate it gracefully into your text. Remember to put direct quotations in quotation marks. When your paper warrants a footnote, put it in the appropriate place in your text, numbering the footnotes consecutively throughout the paper. Finally, after you have finished the body of the paper, try to make your conclusion as natural as possible. Do not just stop. You may want to summarize or to comment on the significance of the ideas, but at this point you do not want to include any new ideas not warranted by what has gone before.

Documenting the Paper

Since the purpose of the research paper is to present the results of an investigation into some subject of importance or personal interest, you should give proper credit for your sources. You need not give credit, of course, to ideas that are common property, but any information that you get from an author should be footnoted if the ideas are original with him or her.

This, of course, brings up the idea of originality. In learning to write a research paper, you will be primarily concerned with learning a method. The success of your paper, therefore, will be determined by the extent to which you are able to integrate the ideas derived from your reading into a reasonable and coherent whole. As for originality, your paper will be original to the degree that you can arrange the material from your reading into a clearly focused, well-thought-out paper that moves toward a particular goal.

I have said that in documenting your paper, you should insert a number in your text just after the part you wish to footnote. Raise the number a little above the line (like this: [1]). This number will refer the reader to a similar number, followed by the appropriate footnote information, either at the bottom of the page (properly called "footnotes") or at the end of the paper (properly called "notes").

If you use footnotes, draw a line from margin to margin under the last line of your text. Then, under this line, type the footnotes, single-spaced, in the same order as they appear on that particular page.

The footnote information for books is usually arranged as follows:

1. Put the first name of the author first, then the last name, followed by a comma.

2. After this, place the title of the work, and underline (or italicize) it.

3. Then enclose the place and date of publication in parentheses, followed by a comma.

4. Finally, include the page number, followed by a period.

Representative examples of footnotes, including some variations, will look like this:

One Author
   [1] Ulric Neisser, *Cognitive Psychology* (New York: Appleton, 1967), pp. 232–233.

Two Authors
   [2] R. E. L. Masters and Jean Houston, *The Varieties of Psychedelic Experience* (New York: Holt, Rinehart and Winston, 1969), p. 61.

More Than Two Authors
   [3] Richard Young, et al., *Rhetoric: Discovery and Change* (New York: Harcourt Brace Jovanovich, 1970), p. 72.

A Book of Several Editions
⁴ Kenneth Burke, *Counter-Statement*, 2nd ed. (Los Altos, Calif.: Hermes Publications, 1953), pp. 141–142.

An Edited Book
⁵ Gyorgy Kepes, ed., *Structure in Art and Science* (New York: George Braziller, 1965), p. 7.

A Translation
⁶ Karl R. Popper, *The Logic of Scientific Discovery*, trans. Julius and Lan V. Fried (London: Hutchinson and Co., 1959), p. 31.

A Work in Several Volumes
⁷ William R. Parker, *Milton*, II (Oxford: Clarendon Press, 1968), p. 640.

The footnote information for articles may be arranged as follows:

1. Put the first name of the author first, then the last name, followed by a comma.

2. After this, place the name of the article, followed by a comma, in quotation marks.

3. Then write the name of the journal or magazine, underlined (or italicized), followed by a comma.

4. Next put the volume number, the month and year enclosed in parentheses, followed by a comma.

5. Finally, put the inclusive page numbers, followed by a period.

The following are a few examples of footnotes for articles, including variations.

Article from a Professional Journal
⁸ Robert M. Gorrell, "Structure in Thought," *College English*, 24 (May 1963), 592–594.

Article from a Weekly Magazine
  [9] Hennig Cohen, "Why Isn't Melville for the Masses?" *Saturday Review* (16 Aug. 1969), 19–20.

Article from a Monthly Magazine
  [10] Irving Howe, "James Baldwin: At Ease in Apocalypse," *Harper's* (Sept. 1968), 93–97.

Newspaper Article
  [11] David Hapgood, "The Diploma: A Meaningless, If Powerful, Piece of Paper," *Los Angeles Times*, 3 Aug. 1969, Sec. F, p. 1.

Signed Encyclopedia Article
  [12] Arthur Knight, "Motion Pictures," *The World Book Encyclopedia*, 13 (1970), 716.

Unsigned Encyclopedia Article
  [13] "Bilingualism," *Encyclopedia Britannica*, Micropaedia 2 (1974), 17.

Book or Film Review
  [14] Linda Wolfe, "Free and Nervous," rev. of *The New Chastity and Other Arguments Against Women's Liberation*, by Midge Decter, *Saturday Review* (21 Oct. 1972), 72–74.

Editorial
  [15] "Survival of a Free Society," Editorial, *The New York Times*, 7 June 1970, Sec. 4, p. 16, cols. 1–2.

Interview
  [16] Joyce Roberts, personal interview with Charles Manson, Phoenix, Arizona, 10 July 1971.

Essay in a Collection
  [17] Lancelot L. Whyte, "Atomism, Structure, and Form," in *Structure in Art and Science*, ed. Gyorgy Kepes (New York: George Braziller, 1965), p. 20.

In documenting your paper, you will undoubtedly cite your authorities more than once. Rather than citing such references fully each time, you will want to use certain abbreviations.

To cite the same author and title used immediately before, use the last name of the author and the page number. You may also use "ibid." (Latin for "in the same place"), followed by the page number, when only one reference is cited in the previous note; but current practice is to avoid cumbersome Latin words or phrases that irritate some readers.

Whyte, p. 19.
Ibid., p. 19.

To cite the same author and title used on a different page, use the last name of the author and the page number:

Kepes, p. 7.

To cite the same author for whom you may have used two or more books or articles, cite the title of the book or article:

Structure in Art and Science, p. 20.
"Structures in Thought," p. 492.

Making the Bibliography

After you have documented your paper, if during your research you have made a separate bibliographical entry for each of your sources (see beginning of this chapter), you need only to arrange your cards in alphabetical order and copy their contents. Below is a typical example of a completed bibliography:

Bibliography

"All About That Soviet Wheat Deal." *U.S. News & World Report* (9 Oct. 1972), 28–30.
"Bilingualism." *Encyclopedia Britannica*, Micropaedia 2 (1974), 17.

Burns, Robert E., et al. *Episodes in American History.* Lexington, Mass.: Ginn and Co., 1973.

Gorrell, Robert M. "Structure in Thought." *College English,* 24 (May 1965), 592–594.

Gosse, Edmund. *English Literature an Illustrated Record.* 4 vols. New York: Grosset and Dunlap, 1908.

Hopkins, Jerry. *Elvis: A Biography.* New York: Warner Paperback Library, 1972.

Knight, Arthur. "Motion Pictures." *The World Book Encyclopedia,* 13 (1970), 716.

Lardner, John. "Devitalizing Elvis." *Newsweek* (16 July 1956), 59.

May, George O. "An Analysis of the Problem of Taxation." *The New York Times,* 9 May 1937, Sec. 4, p. 8.

"Survival of a Free Society." Editorial, *The New York Times,* 7 June 1970, Sec. 4, p. 16.

Whyte, Lancelot L. "Atomism, Structure, and Form," *Structure in Art and Science.* Edited by Gyrogy Kepes. New York: George Braziller, 1965.

Wise, Herbert H., ed. *Professional Rock and Roll.* New York: Collier Books, 1967.

Wolfe, Linda. "Free and Nervous." Review of *The New Chastity and Other Arguments Against Women's Liberation,* by Midge Decter. *Saturday Review* (21 Oct. 1972), 72–74.

At this point, you have finished the rough draft of your research paper. All that remains to be done is to read your paper carefully and to revise it, if revision is necessary. In the revision process, you may feel that you have to expand portions of your paper or cut out some material, as well as revise for grammatical correctness. (See the chapter on revision.) But primarily, you will be concerned with making sure that your paper has a good introduction, a clear statement of your thesis, sufficient and appropriate supporting details, proper organization and unfolding of the ideas, and a suitable conclusion.

The Final Form

Your finished paper will have four or five parts: the title page, a table of contents, the paper itself, the notes (if you do not use footnotes), and the bibliography. The title page will contain the title on one or two lines, your name on a separate line, preceded by the word *by*, the title of the course, the name of the school, and the date, each on a separate line. The table of contents should be carefully numbered, lettered, and indented. The paper should be typed neatly, double-spaced throughout, with the pages numbered at the top, in the middle or in the right-hand corner. The bibliography should be arranged alphabetically by author, or by title if the author is unknown.

When you hand in your paper, it may look something like the following student paper.

Devil Worship in Modern Times

That devil worship existed in the past there is no doubt. Volumes have been written about devil worship in the Middle Ages alone. But does devil worship still exist in what many of us presume to be an enlightened, scientifically sophisticated age? My thesis is that devil worship does exist in the modern world, that it has become quite widespread in the '60s and '70s, and that there are a number of reasons for this new interest in devil worship and in the occult.

That devil worship (and interest in the occult) does exist in the modern world and that it has become quite widespread in the '60s and '70s can be substantiated quite easily. For example, Marcello Truzzi, in the *Sociological Quarterly*, recounts the claim of a New York bookstore that its occult sales have zoomed 100 percent in the past three years (1969–1971). Truzzi also reports that after forty years of poor sales, over two million Ouiji boards were sold in 1961, outdistancing the sale of Monopoly. Both *Time* magazine and *The Wall Street Journal* relate that a mystical renaissance is everywhere, according to Truzzi. But the most startling figures of all are that the Church of Satan in San Francisco claims 7,000 contributing members. This figure does not include people who occasionally come to a service.[1]

I could continue to quote from general sources and give statistical figures about this new interest in devil worship and related activities, but instead I will give some specific examples that perhaps will illustrate my thesis more dramatically.

In Switzerland, an ex-priest, who had become a member of a religious cult, and his mistress were charged with the murder of a young girl. The reason for the murder, the killers later stated, was that the young girl had been physically and sexually possessed by the devil.[2] In Kanab, Utah, a twenty-eight-year-old man was arrested for the murder of a young couple, whom he later buried in a shallow grave. A witness stated that he claimed the devil made him commit this act.[3] More recently, an article in *Newsweek* related that citizens around Strunk Lake, Nebraska, believed that several gruesome killings in the area had been committed by members of a local Satanic cult. These citizens further believed that a house in nearby McCook, Nebraska, served as the scene of many ritualistic Satanic ceremonies. Their evidence included the ritualistic, mutilated remains of animals and the body of a dead baby found in a pit nearby.[4]

Television entertainer Flip Wilson may grin and jokingly say, "The devil made me do it." But Mike Warnke and Johnnie Todd, former devil worshippers who have turned to Christianity, believe that joking about the devil is serious business. They led lives, they claimed, that were almost ruined by the devil. Warnke and Todd revealed that their involvement in Satanism included "mocking the Christian faith during rituals," indulging in sex orgies, and "controlling drug traffic in their areas."[5]

Warnke, who was once the high priest in the Church of Satan of Southern California, is now the president of an antioccult ministry called the Alpha Omega Outreach. He has turned his life over to Jesus Christ, he says, and he is out to win the 1,000 souls for Christ that he formerly had converted for Satan. The one thing lacking that is necessary to hold these Satanic followers together in a meaningful relationship, he proclaims, is forgiveness. The absence of forgiveness has made itself evident in the appalling number of suicides among witches and Satanists and their commitment to mental institutions and violent wards of hospitals.[6]

Johnny Todd, like Warnke, searched for something more fulfilling than Satanism. Yet Satanism was a natural thing for Todd to turn to before he embraced Christianity because Todd's whole family "did nothing but practice witchcraft." But Todd got to the point where he "couldn't even look himself in the face, because his eyes were so full of hate."[7] That is when he found Christ and forgiveness, said Todd.

Allegiance to Satan also has its commercial overtones, but underneath it all is a deadly seriousness. In Hollywood, a dancer who is known as Princess Leda Amun Ra, every evening in a nightclub called the Climax, dances a salute to Satan. The Princess covers her chalk-white skin with black feathers. Her stark black hair and mad eyes, ringed with black smudges, call attention to her face. Gold fishnet loosely hangs over her bare breasts. Her dance is a tribute to Satan and to lust. The Climax is a haven for members who come not only to see the Princess dance, but also to view old vampire films and to make convulsive movements before a twenty-foot Satan's head. The Princess herself, it is reported by residents who live in her Hollywood Hills neighborhood, is as bizarre as the members of the Climax club. One story has it that she lies out by her pond with a fullgrown black swan, screaming, "I will conceive by this swan."[8]

If these antics by followers of Satan seem bizarre, the actual ceremonies and ritualistic services held to worship the devil are even more so. The services vary from sect to sect, but most contain sexual activities and aberrations, drug trips, and sometimes human sacrifice. About the use of human scarifices in devil worship, Hal Lindsey, in his book, *Satan Is Alive and Well on Planet Earth*, states categorically that

> There has never been a society or culture that got into occult practice that didn't break out into sacrifices (whether animal or human). I have known of little children who have been offered. There was a nine month old baby boy sacrificed in the Church of Satan in Berkeley.[9]

As if "mere killing" is not enough, some of the cults engage in cruel and unusual treatment. Commander Bob Vernon of the Los Angeles Police Force encountered one case in which a part of the ceremony required the skinning of a dog without killing it. Vernon related that it was a very careful job and one of the most pitiful sights he'd ever seen.

One of the most complete accounts of a service devoted to the worship of the devil is that of a ritual held in El Sereno, California. According to the news reporter who attended the service, the ceremonies began as a naked girl (supposedly a virgin) draped herself over a black cloth on a table. Participants then dimmed the lights and lit black candles. Everyone present then took off their clothes and sprinkled ashes on the floor. Then someone covered a Raggedy Ann doll with wine, cursed it, and stabbed it in the heart. Afterwards, the participants placed walnuts on the virgin's chest, along with bunches of purple grapes. Then someone set yellow marigolds in her hair and painted a blood red cross on her body. After this was done, the leader read a Catholic mass backwards, while the others chanted hymns, begging Satan for a gift of money. When the chanting was over, the members fell to the floor in various sexual couplings. Their backs soon bore a host of red scratches. During this time, a wooden cross was burned to ashes, before which the individuals later bowed. Strange movements, which passed for dancing, became visible, and as it grew lighter, the Satanists got dressed and left. Only the naked girl on the altar remained . . . apparently sleeping.[10]

These examples illustrate better than any statistics might that devil worship and interest in the occult are increasing today. But why in this "Age of Reason" is Satanism gaining so many advocates? In a book called *The Flight from Reason*, James Webb suggests that in the past many people embraced Satanism in times of rapid change and social revolution. During such times, people are faced with the destruction of values and relationships which lie deep in the psyche. As a consequence, they become filled with fears and anxieties and turn to a world beyond, as represented by the occult.[11] Some critics feel that Webb's argument is just as relevant to our time as to past ages.

A complementary reason that people are turning to Satan and to the occult, according to Gorony Rees, is that the turn of the twentieth century has witnessed the death of God and the triumph of science. These two things gave birth to an astonishing variety of sects and movements dedicated to the idea that the only real world is the world beyond. So the widespread interest in Satanism is a response to one of the most powerful of human needs, the need for contact with and control over a world beyond the world of the senses.[12]

Commander Vernon, of the Los Angeles Police Force, comments:

I know there is a spiritual hunger among people today. Many of them have gone to a church and haven't found the answer to that hunger. Someone comes along and offers them a feeling of belonging, a sense of being loved by a group, and they fall for it. There are other reasons, of course, but the longing for acceptance and a place in the world is what I see as being a very important part of the insane direction many are taking into the supernatural.[13]

Anton LaVey, the high priest of the First Church of Satan in San Francisco, offers this explanation for the renewed interest in Satan:

The Satanic Age started in 1966. That's when God was proclaimed dead, the Sexual Freedom League came into prominence, and the hippies developed as a free sex culture.[14]

Henry A. Kelly, in his article the "Death of the Devil?" offers probably the shortest and most commonsensical reason for the renewed interest in Satanism: "diabolical possession is caused by a belief in diabolical possession."[15] T. K. Oesterreich supplements Kelly's explanation with one of his own:

In all periods of transition when a people's highest faith weakens and is threatened with destruction, and before the somewhat higher, new forms have as yet definitely developed, the more primitive, old beliefs emerge from the lower depths of the popular mind.[16]

What does all of this renewed interest in Satan and the occult portend? To the religious, perhaps that the second Coming is at hand. But to the nonreligious, that we seem to have entered a new stage in the evolutionary process, the beginning perhaps of a new consciousness.

Notes
[1] Marcello Truzzi, "The Occult Revival as Popular Culture: Some Random Observations on the Old and the Nouveau Witch," *Sociological Quarterly*, 13 (Winter, 1972), 16–36.

[2] Henry Ansgar Kelly, "Death of the Devil?" *Commonweal* (6 Nov. 1970), 146.

[3] "Murder Suspect Blamed Devil, Witness Testifies," *The Arizona Republic*, 11 Nov. 1973, p. A-15, cols. 7–8.

[4] "Nebraska Gothic," *Newsweek* (26 Nov. 1973), 37.

[5] Gene Luptak, "Devil Worshippers Turn to Christianity," *The Arizona Republic,* 18 Nov. 1973, p. B-1, cols. 6–8.

[6] Luptak, p. B-1, cols. 1–3.

[7] Luptak, p. B-1, cols. 1–2.

[8] Tom Burke, "Princess Leda's Castle in the Air," *Esquire,* 73 (March 1970), 104–111.

[9] Hal Lindsey, *Satan Is Alive and Well on Planet Earth* (Grand Rapids, Mich.: Zondervan Publishing House, 1972), p. 18.

[10] Trudy Taylor, "Witchcraft Is Everywhere," *Los Angeles Free Press,* 28 Sept. 1973, p. 5.

[11] Quoted in Gorony Rees, "Making Friends with Darkness," *Encounter,* 39 (Aug. 1972), 58.

[12] Rees, p. 56.

[13] Lindsey, p. 26.

[14] Lindsey, p. 29.

[15] Kelly, p. 148.

[16] Traugott Konstantin Oesterreich, *Possession Demonaical and Other Among Primitive Races, in Antiquity, the Middle Ages and Modern Times,* trans. D. Ibberson (New York: University Books, 1966), p. 170.

Bibliography

Bell, L. Nelson. "Recognize Your Enemy." *Christianity Today* (19 July 1968), 21–22.

Burke, Tom. "Princess Leda's Castle in the Air." *Esquire,* 73 (March 1970), 104–111.

Kelly, Henry Ansgar. "Death of the Devil?" *Commonweal* (6 Nov. 1970), 146–149.

Lindsey, Hal. *Satan Is Alive and Well on Planet Earth.* Grand Rapids, Mich.: Zondervan Publishing House, 1972.

Luptak, Gene. "Devil Worshippers Turn to Christianity." *The Arizona Republic,* 18 Nov. 1973, pp. B-1 – B-2, cols. 1–5.

Marty, Martin E. "Satan: Alive and Relevant?" *Christian Century* (10 Jan. 1973), 55–56.

McCasland, S. Vernon. *By the Finger of God.* New York: The Macmillan Co., 1951.

"Murder Suspect Blamed Devil, Witness Testifies." *The Arizona Republic,* 11 Nov. 1973, p. A-15, cols. 7–8.

"Nebraska Gothic." *Newsweek* (26 Nov. 1973), 37.

Oesterreich, Traugott Konstantin. *Possession Demonaical and Other Among Primitive Races, in Antiquity, the Middle Ages and Modern Times.* Translated by D. Ibberson. New York: University Books, 1966.

Rees, Gorony. "Making Friends with Darkness." *Encounter,* 39 (Aug. 1972), 56–58.

Roscoe, Judith. "Church of Satan." *McCalls* 97 (March 1970), 74–75, 133–36.

"Speak of the Devil," *Newsweek* (1 Jan. 1973), 39.

Taylor, Trudy. "Witchcraft is Everywhere." *Los Angeles Free Press,* 28 Sept. 1973, p. 5.

Truzzi, Marcello. "The Occult Revival as Popular Culture: Some Random Observations on the Old and the Nouveau Witch." *Sociological Quarterly,* 13 (Winter 1972), 16–36.

—Toni Konopisos

This paper has a very simple organization. In the opening paragraph, the student introduces her subject (devil worship and the occult) and states her thesis ("My thesis is that devil worship does exist in the modern world, that it has become quite widespread in the '60s and '70s, and that there are a number of reasons for this new interest in devil worship and in the occult.") Then, in successive paragraphs she takes up each point in turn, beginning first with a few quotations and statistics supporting the idea that devil worship is not just a thing of the past, but that it exists in the modern world and is increasing in popularity. After this, to dramatize her point, she narrows down and gives specific instances of people and events related to devil worship. In the last section of her paper, she cites reasons for the renewed interest in devil worship and in the occult, and she concludes by speculating upon the meaning of it all.

Since she began with a clearly defined thesis, in the writing of the paper all she had to do was to follow her notecards dealing with specific incidents of devil worship and work them into a logical progression and then do the same with the material dealing with the reasons for the devil worship. Since her cards were grouped together according to a central idea, it was relatively easy for her to sort them out and leaf through them, incorporating the specific examples into a progressive pattern. As she did this, she sometimes copied her paraphrases verbatim, putting in the notes as she went along, or she reworded the material from her cards to make it fit the context of her paper, or she quoted directly from a particular author.

This kind of paper is not too different, then, from the traditional theme. One obvious difference, of course, is that the process of invention comes about through research and from external sources. But the selection of a topic, the limitation of that topic, the formulation of the thesis, and the arrangement of ideas are the same steps you would use in writing a 500-word theme.

The Inductive Research Paper

An alternative to the deductive approach to writing the research paper is the inductive approach. The inductive research paper is the kind of paper in which you will be asked to consider some idea, event, personality, or topic about which differing opinions, attitudes, or perspectives may be found, to gather source materials relating to these ideas, events, or personalities, to classify them, and to come to some sort of conclusion about them. Your conclusion will be the thesis of your paper. The process is essentially inductive, but you may want to present your conclusions deductively, in the form of a thesis statement and supporting details in the actual writing of your paper.

For example, one student got interested in the critical furor that accompanied the CBS television special "The Guns of Autumn," a program that dealt with hunting and gun control in the United States. She wanted to trace the varying critical responses to that program. What were the different points of view toward hunting and gun control, she asked herself, and more specifically, what were the critical reactions to the CBS program? Were certain critics receptive or hostile to the CBS program? Why? What was the point of view of the program? Was it biased? Or was there an attempt to be as objective as possible? What was the basis of the acceptance or rejection of the point of view taken in the CBS special? How would you classify the positions taken for or against the program?

At this time she had a focal point, but no real thesis. So she went to sources such as the *Reader's Guide to Periodical Literature*, which indexes hundreds of periodicals, got some information there about the program, and then began to read in newspapers and magazines what different critics had to say about the program. Her task essentially was to gather the individual accounts, look for signs of differences of opinion among them, classify them, treat each classification as objectively as possible, and then come to some sort of conclusion about them, a conclusion that was not emphasized in the descriptions of each.

Then she made a rough outline, formulated an introductory statement, and wrote her paper. The result was the following paper.

The Guns of Autumn

I. Introduction
    A. The CBS program, "The Guns of Autumn," attracted strong and varied responses.
    B. The major emphasis in this paper is on a survey of these critical responses.
II. The pro-hunting reaction was predictably strong.
    A. Pro-hunting factions defended hunting as big business.
    B. Some pro-hunting groups gave game management as a justification for hunting.
    C. Pro-hunting supporters blocked much of the commercial advertising for the program.
III. The anti-hunting reaction was also predictably strong.
    A. Anti-hunting factions countered the game management arguments.
    B. Many critics likened hunting to warfare.
IV. The non-partisan reaction to the program varied.
    A. The United Fund was an innocent victim because of a public-service announcement.
    B. The general public reacted predictably both for and against the program.
V. Conclusion
    A. CBS tried to present the opposing viewpoints as fairly as possible.

    B. Nevertheless, CBS did effectively present a controversial issue for public discussion and debate.

The Guns of Autumn

Early this fall, CBS televised a controversial documentary entitled "The Guns of Autumn." Irv Drasnin wrote, produced, and directed this ninety-minute video essay about hunting and the need for some form of gun control in the United States. CBS newsman Dan Rather narrated the program. The program attracted strong and varied responses because some critics were questioning the legitimacy of hunting as a sport, and others the need for gun control legislation. Even before its nationwide airing on September 5, 1975, reactions to the forthcoming program had already reached sizable proportions. So vigorous were the reactions of special interest groups prior to air time that a second documentary, to be called "Echoes of the Guns of Autumn," was planned.

My major purpose in this paper will be to survey the varying critical responses to the program and to try to determine just who had the strongest feelings about this program and why. The critical responses can be broken down into three categories: the pro-hunting reaction, the anti-hunting reaction, and (for lack of a better term) the non-partisan reaction.

My sources are primarily newspapers and magazines because they provided immediate reactions to the program and because they seem to represent the reaction of a greater part of the population. Other sources include books and, of course, the television program itself.

The pro-hunting reaction to the program was predictably strong. Many pro-hunting factions defended hunting as a sport and a big business. Those who have financial interests in guns and hunting equipment naturally were not eager to have hunting presented in what they considered to be a detrimental light. Irv Drasnin, the producer of the show, in an interview which appeared in the *Christian Science Monitor*, remarked that a representative of the National Shooting Sports Foundation told him that even if the show was objective, he would consider it anti-hunting.[1] After all, hunting is a two billion dollar a year industry in the United States. A half billion alone goes for guns and ammunition.[2] Information I was able to obtain from television about "Echoes of the Guns of Autumn" indicated that private game preserves received seventeen and a half million dollars last year in hunting fees and licenses.[3] In numerical terms, hunters represent a considerable portion of the population. Hunters are estimated to number twenty million in the United States or approximately ten percent of the entire population.[4]

Some pro-hunting groups gave game management as a justification for hunting. They argued that hunting is beneficial to game management. For example, "the Wildlife Society recognizes 'sport hunting as one legitimate and desirable use of wildlife resources.' The Izaak Walton League says, 'hunting should be a valuable management tool.' The American Forestry Association believes in hunting as a 'tool of management by owners of large forest and rangeholdings.' Such documentaries [as "The Guns of Autumn"] can only swell the 'killing animals is wrong' psychology that has grown so rapidly in the United States of late, and this societal attitude may be reaching a point of ecological counter-productivity."[5]

Critics who supported the game management theory as a justification for hunting reached strongly to "The Guns of Autumn." Robert Thomas, in an article in *The Arizona Republic,* protested that "shooting preserves got a black eye in a recent CBS film, 'Guns of Autumn,' but preserves, when properly managed, can be a needed addition to hunting recreation."[6] John Russo, the chief of game management for the Arizona Game and Fish Department, agreed. "Hunting is the game manager's most important tool for complete and controlled management," he declared.[7]

So strong were the feelings of the hunting advocates against CBS airing "The Guns of Autumn" that pro-hunting supporters blocked much of the commercial advertising for the program. Lost advertising revenues due to the success of the campaign against CBS were estimated to be $100,000.[8] Before the program was even aired, the National Rifle Association obtained the names of the advertisers for "The Guns of Autumn." By broadcast time, all of the scheduled companies except the Block Drug Company had withdrawn their commercials.[9] This incident showed how effectively organizations such as the National Rifle Association could organize its members and supporters for a protest.[10]

The anti-hunting reaction was also predictably strong. Anti-hunting factions countered game management arguments by contending that nature follows the law of the survival of the fittest in weeding out the sick and the aged animals, but that man aims for the biggest and strongest.[11] There is no doubt that a tremendous number of strong and healthy animals are killed annually—2 million deer, 100,000 elk, 17,000 bear, 11 million ducks, and 1½ million geese.[12] And as CBS graphically demonstrated the once solitary contest between the hunter and these animals has come more to resemble modern warfare, complete with walkie-talkie, than a sport.

This comparison of hunting with modern warfare is not accidental. Many critics have likened hunting to warfare. For example, the anthropologist Lionel Tiger, in a fairly recent book entitled *The Imperial Animal*, has argued that *"organizing predatory violence* has always been a male monopoly, whether practiced against game animals or those enemy humans defined as 'not men' (and hence also a kind of prey animal). This is the important step in the move toward human warfare."[14]

Closely allied to the idea of hunting as modern warfare is the connection of hunting with assassination. Although the connection between these two ideas is slight, the relationship of all of these ideas to gun control legislation is important. For example, the two recent attempts (September 5 and September 22, 1975) on President Gerald Ford's life has increased public reactions against hunting and for gun control legislation. And, of course, the CBS program "The Guns of Autumn" itself brought angry reactions against hunting and for some form of gun control legislation. As *Time* magazine reported: "CBS and the Block Drug Company combined to make the unlikeliest gunfighters since Batman and Robin. Together they stood off the one-million strong National Rifle Association and its allies, the firearms manufacturers and game-preserve associations. That is more than Congress has been able to accomplish."[15]

Non-partisan reactions to the program varied. The United Fund was an innocent victim because of a public service announcement. Because CBS had lost a number of advertisers for "The Guns of Autumn," regular commercial time was filled with public service announcements. One announcement was a plea to aid the United Fund. Because some viewers thought that the United Fund was one of the sponsors of the program, they reacted strongly. According to one newspaper account, "angry television viewers in at least twelve cities, including Phoenix and Tucson, have told the United Fund they won't contribute this year because they thought the charity sponsored a controversial CBS hunting documentary. . . ."[16] Complicating the gun control issue for the United Fund was the fact that the Young Women's Christian Association and the Urban League, both local United Fund agencies, sanctioned gun control.[17] "If you're angry at CBS News," said Charles Collingwood, the narrator of the follow-up program, "Echoes of the Guns of Autumn," "that's one thing, but don't blame the United Fund."[18]

The general public reacted predictably both for and against the program. Many offered a variation on the theme, "We may hate people like Cleveland Amory [the president of the Fund for Animals], but some of what they are saying is true. Some forms of hunting are more cruel and the endangered species list continues to grow which means . . . don't put a bad name on hunting but look for better management."[19] Other opinions concerned individual hunters. "To picture us all [hunters] as cruel and ruthless is unfair. . . . It is not the "Guns of Autumn" that gives us the bad image, but the type of jerk we all know from time to time. There [are] people who indeed have some kind of cruel streak in them and unfortunately they sometimes fancy themselves hunters."[20] Finally, Henry Mitchell, of the *Washington Post*, felt compelled to comment, "The show is neither anti-hunting nor pro-hunting. . . ."[21] Supposedly, CBS was trying to be as objective as possible.

Both "The Guns of Autumn" then, as well as the companion program "Echoes of the Guns of Autumn" elicited reactions not only from formal organizations, clubs, and journalists, but also from the general public as well. Richard Salant, the CBS News president, observed that "never in all my years of broadcasting have I seen such an outpouring of reaction preceding an airing."[22]

The evidence seems to suggest that CBS did try to present the opposing viewpoints about hunting and gun control as fairly as possible. On the one hand, hunters viewed the pursuit of game as a natural part of their heritage. They saw nothing cruel or inhumane about something which seemed a part of nature. On the other hand, conservationists objected to the slaughtering of game for the sake of personal gratification. Whatever may have been true of hunting in the past, they declared, today because some forms of hunting are unnecessarily cruel and because hunting threatens to make some species of animals extinct, hunting should be severely limited. The CBS program effectively presented controversial issues for public discussion and debate. Both environmental and gun control issues were effectively brought before the public as well as the morality of killing animals, along with the deeper implications of killing, assassination, and warfare. Whether the program will continue to spur discussion and debate remains to be seen, but for a time "The Guns of Autumn" will press on the consciences of many.

Notes

[1] Arthur Unger, "CBS Won't Alter Friday's Controversial Look at Hunting," *Christian Science Monitor*, 4 Sept. 1975, p. 26, cols 1–4.

[2] John J. O'Connor, "The Guns of Autumn Hunted and Hunters," *The New York Times*, 14 Sept. 1975, Sec. 2, p. 25, cols. 1 and 2.

[3] Judith Betz, personal notes on "Echoes of the Guns of Autumn," 28 Sept. 1975.

[4] Robert N. Butler and Myrna I. Lewis, *Aging and Mental Health* (Saint Louis: The C. V. Mosby Company, 1973), p. 5.

[5] Kevin Phillips, " 'Guns of Autumn' Misses Bull's Eye But Still Scores," *TV Guide* (27 Sept. 1975), A-3 and A-4.

[6] Robert Thomas, "Bird Shooting Vitalizing," *The Arizona Republic*, 21 Sept. 1975, p. D-12, col. 1.

[7] "Role of Hunter Aids Game Growth," *The Arizona Republic*, p. D-12, col. 2.

[8] "Intimidated Advertisers," *Des Moines Register*, 10 Sept. 1975, p. 6-A, cols. 1 and 2.

[9] "Gunfight," *Time* (22 Sept. 1975), 73.

[10] "Intimidated Advertisers," p. 6-A, cols. 1 and 2.

[11] Judith Betz, personal notes on "Guns of Autumn," 5 Sept. 1975

[12] Gregg Kilday, "Hunting, Less Sport Than Harvest," *Los Angeles Times*, 5 Sept. 1975, part IV, p. 22, cols. 1 and 2.

[13] Kilday, part IV, p. 22, cols. 1 and 2.

[14] Lionel Tiger and Robin Fox, *The Imperial Animal* (New York: Holt, Rinehart, and Winston, 1971), p. 213.

[15] "Gunfight," p. 73.

[16] "United Fund Blamed for Hunting Show," *The Arizona Republic,* 29 Sept. 1975, p. A-5, cols. 3–6.

[17] "United Way Official Discounts Impact of Show on Gun Control," *The Arizona Republic,* 8 Oct. 1975, p. C-5, cols. 1 and 2.

[18] "United Fund Blamed for Hunting Show," p. A-5, cols. 3–6.

[19] J. Leo King, Editorial Commentary, "Some Are Jerks!" *The Arizona Republic,* 28 Sept. 1975, p. A-7, col. 1.

[20] J. Leo King, p. A-7, col. 1.

[21] Henry Mitchell, "Ready, Aim, Misfire," *Washington Post,* 5 Sept. 1975, p. B-1, col. 1 and B-11, cols. 1–5.

[22] Phillips, pp. A-3 and A-4.

Bibliography

Butler, Robert N., and Myrna I. Lewis, *Aging and Mental Health.* Saint Louis: The C. B. Mosby Company, 1973.

"Guns Issue Hurts Drive for United Way." *The Arizona Republic,* 7 Oct. 1975, p. B-1, cols. 1–3.

"The Gun Thugs." *The New York Times,* 7 Sept. 1975, Sec. 4, p. 16, col. 2.

"Gun-buff Judge Tough on Robbers." *The Arizona Republic,* 28 Sept. 1975, p. A-9, cols. 5–8.

"Gunfight." *Time* (22 Sept. 1975), 73.

"Intimidated Advertisers." *Des Moines Register,* 10 Sept. 1975, p. 6-A, cols. 1 and 2.

Kilday, Gregg. "Hunting, Less Sport Than Harvest." *Los Angeles Times,* 5 Sept. 1975, part IV, p. 22, cols. 1 and 2.

King, J. Leo. Editorial Commentary. "Some Are Jerks!" *The Arizona Republic,* 28 Sept. 1975, p. A-7, col. 1.

Lamson, Edward W. Editorial Commentary. "Weed Out Slob Hunters." *The Arizona Republic,* 3 Oct. 1975, p. A-7, cols. 1 and 2.

Mann, E. B. "Our Endangered Tradition: 'By Their Words Ye Shall Know Them.'" *Field and Stream* (Aug. 1975), 30 and 32.

———— "Our Endangered Tradition: Do Gun Laws Work?" *Field and Stream* (June 1975), 107–108.

Mitchell, Henry et al. Editorial Commentary. " 'Guns of Autumn' in Hot Crossfire." *The Arizona Republic*, 11 Sept. 1975, p. D-6, cols. 3–6.

———— "Ready, Aim, Misfire." *Washington Post*, 5 Sept. 1975, p. B-1, col. 1 and p. B-11, cols. 1–5.

O'Connor, John J. "The Guns of Autumn Hunted and Hunters." *The New York Times*, 14 Sept. 1975, Sec. 2, p. 25, cols. 1 and 2.

Phillips, Kevin. " 'Guns of Autumn' Misses Bull's Eye But Still Scores." *TV Guide* (27 Sept. 1975), A-c and A-4.

"Role of Hunter Aids Game Growth." *The Arizona Republic*, p. D-12, col. 2.

Samson, Jack. Editorial Commentary. *Field and Stream* (July 1975), 4.

Tiger, Lionel, and Fox, Robin. *The Imperial Animal.* New York: Holt, Rinehart, and Winston, 1971, p. 213.

Thomas, Robert. "Bird Shooting Vitalizing." *The Arizona Republic*, 21 Sept. 1975, p. D-12, col. 1.

———— " 'Guns' Stirs Furor." *The Arizona Republic*, 7 Sept. 1975, p. D-10, cols. 2 and 3.

Unger, Arthur. "CBS Won't Alter Friday's Controversial Look at Hunting." *Christian Science Monitor*, 4 Sept. 1975, p. 26, cols. 1–4.

"United Fund Blamed for Hunting Show." *The Arizona Republic*, 29 Sept. 1975, p. A-5, cols. 3–6.

"United Way Official Discounts Impact of Show on Gun Control." *The Arizona Republic*, 8 Oct. 1975, p. C-5, cols. 1 and 2.

Wheeler, Norma. Editorial Commentary. "Was Squeaky's Action Really an Anti-gun Ploy?" *The Arizona Republic*, 20 Sept. 1975, p. A-7, col. 6.

—Judith Betz

Notice how this approach to the research paper differs in some respects from that of the other research paper:

1. It begins with a *focal point*, not with a subject or thesis per se. The **focal point** is *an idea, event, personality, or any-*

thing about which differing opinions, attitudes, or perspectives may be found.

2. The actual **subject** of the paper is *the variety of opinions, attitudes, perspectives, or interpretations surrounding the focal point.*

3. In most cases, the **thesis** will be *a specific formulation of the idea that a better or more complete understanding of _____ can be obtained by observing certain opinions, attitudes, or perspectives about some focal point.*

4. The **source materials** will necessarily be limited, in terms of *media, availability of material, and subject, and the limitations of the sources must be strictly indicated to enable the reader to judge the validity of the conclusions.*

5. The approach is essentially inductive, analytical, and classificatory.

Your choice of a focal point and a subject will determine in large part a good deal of the success of your paper. In choosing a focal point, you should consider, among other things, your *interest* in the material and the *amount of material* available to you about the subject. In addition, you would want to choose a subject about which there are varying opinions or perspectives. The following focal points will give you some idea of how you might go about getting a topic of your own:

1. Reactions to some kind of controversial issue or subject such as those presented on CBS's *Guns of Autumn* or *Helter Skelter.*

2. Critical reactions to any segment of a television program such as CBS's *60 Minutes, The Dick Cavett Show,* or *The David Susskind Show.*

3. Differing critical opinions about some aspect of a major novel, story, poem, or play.

4. Reviews and critical reactions to best sellers and movies such as *Helter Skelter* and *Coming Home.*

5. A survey of opinions about the conclusion of *Huckleberry Finn* in critical books and essays.

6. A survey of critical comments about movies such as *The Deer Hunter, Apocalypse Now, The Warriors.*

7. Attitudes about disco music, jazz, rock, or some other kind of music.

8. Magazine views of Jackie Kennedy as First Lady, grieving widow of President Kennedy, newly married to Onassis, widow of Onassis, and so forth.

9. Attitudes toward controversial or interesting public figures as depicted in newspapers, magazines, and books.

10. Critical reactions to public events such as the capture and trial of Patty Hearst, the murder of Sharon Tate, The Three Mile Island, and so forth.

11. Differing points of view given in books, newspaper articles, or magazine articles for supporting or opposing behavioral modification, abortion, nuclear energy, and so forth.

12. A review of the attitudes of participants or nonparticipants in some particular war in American history (for example, the Civil War, the war in Vietnam).

In the event you decide to write about one of these topics, your focal point will be some topic such as The Three Mile Island, Jackie Kennedy, or *The Warrior* but your subject will be the varying opinions, attitudes, and perspectives about these movies, books, events, people, ideas, or things.

Once you have chosen your focal point and your subject, you go through the usual steps of locating your material, making a tentative bibliography, evaluating your material and taking notes, writing the paper, documenting it, and so forth.

PROCESS AND THOUGHT IN COMPOSITION

A Reference Handbook

Grammar Review

Chapter 16

Grammar Review

Although the emphasis in composition is primarily on connected stretches of writing, nevertheless, because these larger units are composed of sentences, you should have a basic knowledge of the grammar of the sentence. The principles of grammar that are of importance are those that concern words and those that concern word relationships.

Parts of Speech

The traditional grammarians listed and defined eight parts of speech. The structuralists classified fifteen or more. The transformationalists did not concern themselves with classifying words. Yet for compositional purposes, it is useful to know some of the basic terms of grammar.

My own preference is for transformational grammar, but since the transformationalists did not deal with many of the topics that are of interest to the composition student, I will here attempt to pick and choose from the various grammars.

The Noun

Nouns name things. They name persons, animals, places, objects, and abstract ideas. It is true that the other parts of speech can name things, too, but we usually associate the naming function with nouns. Here are some examples of nouns:

Cheryl	stone	honesty
woman	cactus	love
girl	desert	infinity
armadillo	sand	pride
scorpion	stream	courage

You learn to recognize nouns because they appear in certain positions in English sentences:

> *Sunflowers* bloom in the *spring.*
> *Hurricanes* form at *sea.*
> The *Babylonians* and the *Hittites* built *temples* to *eagles.*

They pattern with articles, demonstrative pronouns, and possessive pronouns (what the structuralists called *determiners*):

an *alcoholic*	this *fact*	your *telephone*
a *Buick*	these *cars*	my *troubles*
the *world*	that *threat*	her *eyes*

Nouns take characteristic inflectional endings to form plurals and possessives:

SINGULAR	PLURAL	POSSESSIVE
bell	bells	bell's
cargo	cargoes	cargo's
city	cities	city's
fiesta	fiestas	fiesta's
knife	knives	knife's

They also have characteristic derivational endings:

white + ness	whiteness
natural + ist	naturalist
play + er	player
music + ian	musician

There are two main kinds of nouns: common nouns and proper nouns. *Common nouns* name members of a class of things:

> *Insects* thrive in warm weather.
> Botany is the study of *plants.*

Proper nouns name particular members of a class of things. They always begin with capital letters:

The *Milky Way* has a graceful, pinwheellike form.
Switzerland owes much to its glaciers.

The Pronoun

Pronouns take the place of nouns or noun phrases. *Personal pronouns* indicate the speaker *(I, my, mine, me, we, our, ours, us)*, the person spoken to *(you, your, yours)*, and the person spoken about *(he, his, him, she, her, hers, it, its, they, their, theirs, them)*.

Pronouns have four forms, as indicated:

NOMINATIVE	OBJECTIVE	POSSESSIVE	POSSESSIVE
I	me	my	mine
we	us	our	ours
you	you	your	yours
he	him	his	his
she	her	her	hers
it	it	its	its
they	them	their	theirs

These pronouns appear in the following positions in sentences:

I dislike smoking. *(nominative)*
Tell *me* the truth. *(objective)*
Did you receive *my* letter? *(possessive)*
That book is *mine.* *(possessive)*

Reflexive pronouns are personal pronouns that combine with the nouns *self* and *selves* to form compounds:

The forest *itself* is a shelter.
I'd rather do it *myself.*

Relative pronouns introduce relative clauses and refer to some antecedent in the sentence. The relative pronouns are *who, whose, whom, which,* and *that.*

Shakespeare is the writer *who* wrote *Romeo and Juliet.*
I remember the day *that* the earth stood still.
The sound of bells is a sound *which* I like to hear.

Interrogative pronouns ask questions. The interrogative pronouns are *who, whose, whom, which,* and *what.*

Whose car has a new paint job?
What are we having for supper?

Indefinite pronouns are pronouns that do not specify or identify their antecedents. These are some of the most common indefinite pronouns:

some	any	everybody	one
someone	anyone	everyone	another
somebody	anybody	everything	each
something	anything	either	both
nobody	nothing	neither	many

The Adjective

Adjectives describe, limit, qualify, or specify the nouns that they modify:

The roadrunner walks with a *clownish* gait.
Lightning is a *violent, fearsome* thing.

You learn to recognize adjectives because of their positions before nouns, as in the sentences above, and because they can often be distinguished by various suffixes: *-able, -ous, -full, -less, -ic, -er, -est.*

The bells in the *historic* town of Taxco have been ringing for more than two hundred years.

Your family will love the *delicious* taste of orange juice.

Most adjectives have different inflectional forms: positive (plain form), comparative, and superlative. Here are a few examples:

POSITIVE	COMPARATIVE	SUPERLATIVE
brave	braver	bravest
lively	livelier	liveliest
simple	simpler	simplest
good	better	best
many	more	most

Many adjectives attain their comparative and superlative meanings by using *more* or *most:*

POSITIVE	COMPARATIVE	SUPERLATIVE
hopeful	more hopeful	most hopeful
circular	more circular	most circular
hesitant	more hesitant	most hesitant
squalid	more squalid	most squalid

The Adverb

Like adjectives, *adverbs* can qualify, limit, or add details to words. But the words they modify are verbs, adjectives, or other adverbs:

> Some fish can swim *backward*.
> The trip was *unexpectedly* short.
> The Yankees played *unusually* well.

Some adverbs modify complete clauses or sentences:

> Rivers carry silt into the sea *constantly*.
> *Certainly* I would prefer to read.

Adverbs are usually classified according to meaning; there are adverbs of *time, place, manner, degree* or *extent,* and *negation:*

> The plane will arrive *soon. (time)*
> Put the package *there. (place)*
> Alpine flowers grow very *slowly. (manner)*
> San Francisco was *almost* destroyed by an earthquake in 1906. *(extent)*
> I am *not* sick, but I am very tired. *(negation)*

Adverbs seldom can be identified by derivational endings. The only suffix of note is the *-ly* of manner adverbs:

generously	wildly
gracefully	carefully
suddenly	entirely

Although they do not have as many derivational forms as adjectives, adverbs also have three degrees of comparison: positive, comparative, and superlative. But most adverbs form their comparative and superlative degrees by using *more* or *most:*

POSITIVE	COMPARATIVE	SUPERLATIVE
slowly	more slowly	most slowly
loudly	more loudly	most loudly
wildly	more wildly	most wildly

A few adverbs, however, form their comparatives and superlatives by adding *-er* and *-est:*

POSITIVE	COMPARATIVE	SUPERLATIVE
soon	sooner	soonest
early	earlier	earliest
late	later	latest

Qualifiers

Qualifiers are words that pattern in sentences with adjectives and adverbs. Traditional grammarians classified these words as adverbs, but they seem not to function in English sentences in the way that adverbs do.

Some typical examples of qualifiers are words such as the following:

very	rather	really
quite	real	more
too	pretty	somewhat

These qualifiers pattern in sentences in similar ways:

The Arizona sun can be *very* hot.
The Arizona sun can be *quite* hot.
The Arizona sun can be *pretty* hot.

The Verb

Verbs express action, occurrence, condition, or existence. Other parts of speech can show action, too; for example, the noun *reaction* shows action of some kind. Other parts of speech can show existence; for instance, the adjective *happy* depicts a state of being, or existence. Nevertheless, these are the characteristics usually associated with verbs.

Spiny lizards *scuttle* over the rocks.
To all appearances, our earth *hangs* solidly in the heavens.
She *is* our family doctor.
Does life *exist* on other planets?

Besides identifying verbs by characteristics of meaning, you can identify verbs by their inflectional endings. Verbs have an unmarked form and four marked forms, with the endings *-s, -ed, -ed* or *-en,* and *-ing:*

PLAIN	THIRD PERSON SINGULAR	PAST TENSE
turn	turns	turned
mend	mends	mended
drive	drives	drove
know	knows	knew

PAST PARTICIPLE	PRESENT PARTICIPLE
turned	turning
mended	mending
driven	driving
known	knowing

These forms provide the basis for conjugating verbs.

To conjugate a verb, you list the various forms and put them into a paradigm:

PRESENT TENSE

Singular	*Plural*
I walk	we walk
you walk	you walk
he, she, it walks	they walk

PAST TENSE

Singular	*Plural*
I walked	we walked
you walked	you walked
he, she, it walked	they walked

FUTURE TENSE

Singular	*Plural*
I shall walk	we shall walk
you will walk	you will walk
he, she, it will walk	they will walk

PRESENT PERFECT

Singular	*Plural*
I have walked	we have walked
you have walked	you have walked
he, she, it has walked	they have walked

PAST PERFECT

Singular	*Plural*
I had walked	we had walked
you had walked	you had walked
he, she, it had walked	they had walked

FUTURE PERFECT

Singular	*Plural*
I shall have walked	we will have walked
you will have walked	you will have walked
he, she, it will have walked	they will have walked

Besides these forms of the verb, there are *progressive forms* that emphasize the idea of ongoing action. The progressive tenses of verbs are formed with the verb *be* and the present participle:

PRESENT TENSE

Singular	*Plural*
I am walking	we are walking
you are walking	you are walking
he, she, it is walking	they are walking

PAST TENSE

Singular	*Plural*
I was walking	we were walking
you were walking	you were walking
he, she, it was walking	they were walking

FUTURE TENSE

Singular	*Plural*
I shall be walking	we shall be walking
you will be walking	you will be walking
he, she, it will be walking	they will be walking

PRESENT PERFECT

Singular	*Plural*
I have been walking	we have been walking
you have been walking	you have been walking
he, she, it has been walking	they have been walking

PAST PERFECT

Singular	*Plural*
I had been walking	we had been walking
you had been walking	you had been walking
he, she, it had been walking	they had been walking

FUTURE PERFECT

Singular	*Plural*
I shall have been walking	we shall have been walking
you will have been walking	you will have been walking
he, she, it will have been walking	they will have been walking

Tense

The *present tense* indicates action going on in the present time *(I run)*. The *past tense* indicates action in the past *(I ran)*. The future tense indicates action that will take place in the future *(I shall run)*. The *present perfect tense* indicates completed action at the time of the assertion *(I have run)*. The *past perfect tense* indicates completed action in the past *(I had run)*. The *future perfect tense* indicates that the action will have been completed before some future time *(I shall have run)*.

Voice

Verbs can be in the *active* or the *passive* voice. If the subject performs the action of the verb, the verb is active. If the subject receives the action of the verb, the verb is passive.

> The cook *baked* the fish. *(active)*
> The fish *was baked* by the cook. *(passive)*

The passive voice is formed by using the appropriate form of the auxiliary *be* with the past participle of the verb. The following paradigm gives only the third person singular of each tense:

Present	he *is* asked
Past	he *was* asked
Future	he *will be* asked
Present perfect	he *has been* asked
Past perfect	he *had been* asked
Future perfect	he *will have been* asked
Present progressive	he *is being* asked
Past progressive	he *was being* asked

Mood

There are three moods: the *indicative,* the *subjunctive,* and the *imperative.* The first expresses a statement of fact. The second expresses a condition, wish, doubt, or uncertainty. The third expresses a command or entreaty.

> Some people *dream* of money. *(indicative)*
> If my car *were* here, I could leave early. *(subjunctive)*
> Please *visit* me soon. *(imperative)*

The subjunctive is seldom used by modern writers. When it is used, it often takes the form of the verb *were* and the conditional word *if* to express a hypothetical action.

Two-Part Verbs

A *two-part verb* is a verb followed by a particle. The particle looks like a preposition, but unlike the preposition, it can be freely moved about in a sentence, and it doesn't take an object:

> The student *looked up* the reference.
> The student *looked* the reference *up*.

The Auxiliary

In traditional grammar, the *auxiliary* was classified with the verbs as a "helping verb." The structuralists classified it as a functional word that patterns with verbs, as in the expression *can go*.

There are several kinds of auxiliaries: the *modal auxiliaries (may, might, can, could, shall, should, do, did, will, would,* and *must),* the *perfect aspect auxiliaries (have, had),* and the *progressive aspect auxiliaries* (forms of the verb *be*).

> Sharks *will* swallow anything. *(modal)*
> The sea *can* build as well as destroy. *(modal)*
> The best snake charmers *have* always lived in the East. *(perfect aspect)*
> I *am* losing patience. *(progressive aspect)*

Aspect

Aspect is a category of the verb indicating primarily the nature of the action performed in regard to the passage of time. There are two aspect categories: progressive and perfect.

The *progressive aspect* is that form which is used to convey the idea of ongoing action. It is formed with the connecting verb *be* and the present participle, which ends in *-ing:*

> She *is* leav*ing.* *(present progressive)*
> She *was* leav*ing.* *(past progressive)*

The *perfect aspect* is that form which is used to convey the idea of completed action. It is formed with the word *have* (and its variants *has* and *had*) and the past participle, which ends in *-ed* or *-en:*

> I *have* eat*en.* *(present perfect)*
> He *has* eat*en.* *(present perfect)*
> He *had* eat*en.* *(past perfect)*

The progressive and perfect aspects can be combined to form various tenses, as in these examples:

> She *has been* leav*ing.* *(present perfect progressive)*
> She *had been* leav*ing.* *(past perfect progressive)*

Both the progressive and the perfect aspects can combine with the modal auxiliaries to form tenses:

> I *will be* eat*ing.* *(future progressive)*
> He *will have been* eat*ing.* *(future perfect progressive)*

The Preposition

Prepositions show spatial, temporal, and logical relationships between the nouns or pronouns that follow them and some other word in the sentence:

> *In* the desert, water is life itself.
> The concert will begin *at* eight o'clock.
> Birds can escape *by* air.

These are some commonly used prepositions:

above	below	for	since
across	beneath	from	through
after	beside	in	to
against	between	into	under
along	beyond	like	until
among	by	of	up
around	concerning	off	upon
at	down	on	with
before	during	over	within
behind	except	past	without

Some prepositions are groups of words which have the force of a single word:

by means of	with respect to
in spite of	on account of
instead of	in reference to
out of	according to

A *prepositional phrase* is a group of words in which a preposition is followed by a noun or noun substitute. The word following the preposition is called the object of the preposition:

> The turtle looks *like a lump of mud.*
> *In a total eclipse*, the entire sun is obscured.

There are two prepositional phrases in the first example above: "like a lump" and "of mud." The objects of the respective prepositions are *lump* and *mud.* In the second sentence, the noun *eclipse* is the object of the preposition *in.*

Do not confuse prepositions with particles or adverbs, words which often have identical forms. Prepositions always take objects:

> Look *up! (adverb of direction)*
> Look the reference *up. (particle)*
> Look *up* the reference. *(particle)*
> Look *up* the street. *(preposition)*

The Conjunction

Conjunctions join words, phrases, and clauses. Like prepositions, they show spatial, temporal, and logical relationships.

There are three kinds of conjunctions: *coordinating, correlative,* and *subordinating:*

> Diamonds *and* gold are the earth's most dazzling prizes. *(coordinating)*
>
> *Either* moist, juicy pineapple *or* ripe, red strawberries will make your mouth water. *(correlative)*
>
> *When* you give, you also receive. *(subordinating)*

The coordinating conjunctions are *and, but, or,* and *nor.* The correlative conjunctions are *either . . . or, neither . . . nor, both . . . and, not only . . . but also, whether . . . or.* The following is a list of some frequently used subordinating conjunctions:

after	because	so that	when
although	before	than	whenever
as	if	though	where
as if	in order that	unless	wherever
as long as	since	until	while

Coordinating conjunctions join items of equal grammatical rank and importance:

> Few substances look less alike than *coal* and *diamonds*.

Subordinating conjunctions join items of unequal grammatical rank and importance:

> *If too many climb aboard*, the boat will sink.

The Sentence Connector

Sentence connectors, like conjunctions, can join independent clauses. Traditional grammarians called them conjunctive adverbs. Here is a partial list:

accordingly	however	similarly
also	indeed	still
besides	likewise	then
consequently	moreover	therefore
furthermore	nevertheless	thus

In current usage, sentence connectors are preceded by a semicolon when they join two independent clauses:

> I prefer to stay home tonight; *besides*, I have a cold.
> Streams run; *however*, glaciers merely crawl.

The Article

Articles limit the words they modify. *A* and *an* are indefinite articles, having the general meaning of *any:*

> Bring me *a* chair to stand on.
> Give me *an* envelope.

The is a definite article:

> Bring me *the* chair in the corner.

The article *a* is used before words beginning with a consonant. The article *an* is used before words that begin with a vowel:

a masterpiece	an idea
a seagull	an only child
a leaf	an eagle

Some grammarians group articles, demonstrative pronouns, and possessive pronouns in a single class called *determiners:*

ARTICLES	DEMONSTRATIVES	POSSESSIVES
a	this	my, your
an	that	his, her
the	these	its, our
	those	their

Their reasoning is that all of these words can pattern with nouns and noun phrases in similar ways:

an iguana	a fishing fleet
this iguana	that fishing fleet
these iguanas	those fishing fleets
your iguana	his fishing fleet
our iguana	her fishing fleet

Exercises

1. List the parts of speech in the following sentences. Use a separate column for each category.

   a. Swarms of insects filled the air.
   b. The world's energy is running out.
   c. Erosion builds, but it also destroys.
   d. Gold is very beautiful.
   e. Kick up your heels.
   f. Ensenada is the home of Mexico's largest fishing fleet.
   g. His car collided with an oil truck.
   h. You're reading this through a glass.
   i. Visit this unspoiled Pacific island.
   j. Who called for me?

2. Give the plural and possessive forms of the following nouns: *book, piece, bus, sheep, city, monkey, studio, tomato, loaf, tooth, antenna.*

3. Write the comparative and superlative forms of the following adjectives and adverbs: *good, bad, perfectly, slow, easy, often, brave, lucky, little, cool.*

4. Give the principal parts of the following irregular verbs: *break, do, buy, go, lie* (recline), *raise, rise* (ascend), *sit* (rest), *set* (place), *hit, meet, slide, win.*

5. Give the principal parts of the following regular verbs: *work, play, believe, drop, submit.*

The Sentence

A *sentence* is a structured string of words containing a subject and a predicate. The subject and predicate can be single words or several words:

> Maps/speak.
> The Mayan civilization/flourished for nearly 2000 years.

Sentences are classified by purpose and by structure. According to purpose, sentences may be categorized as declarative, interrogative, imperative, and exclamatory.

A *declarative sentence* makes a statement:

> The basic fare is forty cents.

An *interrogative sentence* asks a question:

> Do galaxies evolve?

An *imperative sentence* expresses a command, a request, or an entreaty:

> Take time out to stretch on the soft white sands of Micronesia.

An *exclamatory sentence* expresses strong feeling or emotion:

> It's a shark! Let's get out of here!

According to structure, sentences are traditionally classified as simple, compound, complex, or compound-complex.

A *simple sentence* is one that has a subject and a verb.

The old explains the new.

A *compound sentence* contains two or more subjects and verbs, and it coordinates two or more simple sentences:

You touch a bowl of jelly, and the whole thing will jiggle.

A *complex sentence* contains at least two clauses, one of which is subordinate:

Lobsters shed their shells as they grow.

A *compound-complex sentence* contains at least two independent clauses and one or more dependent clauses:

Our excitement grew in the ninth inning, and everyone stood up when Reggie Jackson hit a home run.

Exercise

Classify each of the following sentences according to purpose and structure.

a. In her dream, her son was calling for her.
b. Do we live more than once?
c. Help me!
d. Americans across the country fume behind their steering wheels while they wait for gasoline.
e. The Japanese telecast in stereo sound, but the Americans do not.
f. Germany turns out the best Super 8 cameras.
g. Solar energy won't come of age until it's competitive in price.
h. Let us fly you to Acapulco.
i. Are the rich happy?
j. Cave diving is risky recreation.

Basic Sentence Patterns

Every sentence consists of at least two parts, a *subject* and a *predicate.* These are the essential parts of all sentences:

It works.
Time flies.

Some sentences have a third part, called a complement. A *complement* completes the meaning of the subject or the object.

There are five kinds of complements: *the direct object,* the *indirect object,* the *objective complement,* the *predicate nominative,* and the *predicate adjective:*

Clothes screen *heat. (direct object)*
The computer saved *us* hours of work. *(indirect object)*
Her boss considered her an *asset. (objective complement)*
Love is the *answer. (predicate nominative)*
The sea is *old. (predicate adjective)*

There are six basic sentence patterns, five of which correspond to the five kinds of complements listed above:

Subject-verb
Most snakes can swim.
Times change.

Subject-verb-object
Money begets money.
Silence gives consent.

Subject-indirect object-object
His friend gave him the answers.
The salesperson showed me two suits.

Subject-object-objective complement
She called him a phony.
The police labeled the crime a felony.

Subject-linking verb-predicate noun
Corn is the only American grain.
Poverty is no sin.

Subject-linking verb-predicate adjective
Art seems timeless.
The miniskirt now seems ugly.

Exercises

1. Pick out the complements in the following sentences and tell what kind each is.

   a. The symbol of dowsing is a forked branch.
   b. Nature wastes nothing.
   c. Beggars can't be choosers.
   d. Knowledge is power.
   e. The bones of most birds are hollow.
   f. You can't teach an old dog new tricks.
   g. Still water runs deep.
   h. My cousin bought me a dictionary.
   i. Her boyfriend thought her a kook.
   j. No answer is also an answer.

2. Write six sentences to illustrate each of the basic sentence patterns.

Noun Phrases and Verb Phrases

The simplest kind of noun phrase that can combine with a verb to form a simple sentence is the noun by itself, such as the word *leaves* in the sentence "Leaves decay." Usually the noun has an article (or determiner) paired with it to form a simple noun phrase: *the wind, this day, my stereo.* Besides the article, the most common noun modifiers are adjectives: *golden apples, purple sky, azure water.* Prepositional phrases also combine with nouns to form noun phrases: *cheese on rye, the king of Siam, pheasant under glass.*

There are other ways of expanding noun phrases which we will consider later. But these are a few of the most basic ways:

> this summer
> crushed velvet
> the right spot
> an island for two
> the greatest show on earth

Just as the noun phrase is an expansion of a single noun (or pronoun), the verb phrase is an expansion of a single verb. The verb itself can take an auxiliary or several auxiliaries: *did* imagine, *are* thinking, *have* contemplated, *must have been* dreaming. To the main verb, you can add a single adverb: *never* fear, drive *carefully*, *frequently* drive. Prepositional phrases can also combine with the verb to form verb phrases: arise *in the morning*, sleep *until noon*, think *about you*. And as you have already seen, verbs can take complements: painted the table *brown*, considered the woman *a saint*, is *a good lawyer*. These complements are considered part of the verb phrase.

There are other ways of expanding the verb phrase, but these are some of the most basic:

> can be delightful
> kick up your heels
> treat you royally
> getting yourself in hot water
> can go camping in style
> always cooking up something new

Exercises

1. List the noun phrases and the verb phrases in the following sentences. Make a separate column for each.

   a. You can appreciate the difference.
   b. Some people set their sights very high.
   c. In the jungles, the fighting continues.
   d. Are we, as individuals, helpless in the face of inflation?
   e. With hunger in his eye, an abstract painter goes realist.

2. Write five sentences. Then underline the noun phrases in each. Write five more sentences and underline the verb phrases in each.

Expanding Sentences by Coordination

Compound sentences are formed by combining two or more sentences. The process of combining two or more sentences into one sentence is called the *conjunction transformation:*

| The earth may be cooling off.
It may be getting hotter. | The earth may be cooling off,
or it may be getting hotter. |

When sentences are conjoined, they may be punctuated with a semicolon or with a comma and a conjunction:

| Moths spin cocoons.
Butterflies do not. | Moths spin cocoons;
butterflies do not. |

| The ideas are old.
The technology is new. | The ideas are old, *but* the technology is new. |

If two or more sentences have parts in common, the common elements that appear in each sentence can be deleted:

| *The fish* grabbed the sea gull.
The fish pulled it beneath the water.
The fish drowned it. | The fish grabbed the sea gull, pulled it beneath the water, and drowned it. |

The result of deleting the identical noun phrases that appear later in the sentence is a series of parallel verbs.

Conjoined sentences with identical grammatical structures can be reduced to simple sentences with compound subjects or compound predicates:

| Robin *failed the driving test.*
Her brother *failed the driving test.* | Both *Robin* and *her brother* failed the driving test. |

| *Most drivers* obey traffic laws.
Most drivers stop at stop signs. | Most drivers *obey traffic laws* and *stop at stop signs.* |

Not all compound subjects and predicates, however, can be formed by deleting identical grammatical structures. Some are formed by joining the subjects or predicates directly:

Two and *two* are four.

Sarah, Mary, and *Alice* met in New York.

Exercise

Combine the following sentences into compound sentences or sentences with compound subjects or predicates:

a. The player limped off the field.
   He collapsed on the sidelines.
b. The waiter took my order.
   He handed me a bill.
c. I took your advice.
   I studied harder.
d. You like horror films.
   I like horror films.
e. We hated the movie.
   You liked it.

Expanding Sentences by Subordination

Adverbial clauses are formed by joining two or more sentences so that one sentence becomes a subordinate clause with the addition of a subordinate conjunction:

The horned lizard squirts blood from its eyes. The horned lizard is disturbed.	The horned lizard squirts blood from its eyes *when it is disturbed.*

There is a close connection between sentences that contain adverbial clauses and compound sentences:

If Carl said that, then he is wrong.
Carl said that; *then* he is wrong.

Because it is raining, I will stay home.
It is raining; *therefore,* I will stay home.

Although I would rather stay home, I must go.
I would rather stay home, *but* I must go.

Unless you go, I will be mad.
You go, *or* I will be mad.

This connection can be partially explained by assuming that sentences that contain adverbial clauses and their compound-sentence counterparts both come from underlying sentences:

Carl said that. ⎫
He is wrong. ⎭   If Carl said that, he is wrong.

Carl said that. ⎫
He is wrong. ⎭   Carl said that; then he is wrong.

Exercise

Combine the following sentences. Make one into an adverbial clause (for example: You are near a fire. Be careful. *When you are near a fire,* be careful).

a. The Raiders lost.
   Three players were hurt.
b. I am not an expert.
   I do like good food.
c. Your legs hurt.
   Then stop jogging.
d. You come at once.
   I shall be mad.
e. You were out.
   Someone called for you.

Expanding Sentences by Relativization

Relative clauses, and adjectival modifiers such as adjectives, participles, and prepositional phrases, are formed by combining two sentences. The relative-clause transformation makes one sentence into a relative clause:

All rocks contain some
minerals.   All rocks contain some
The minerals dissolve in   minerals *which dissolve in*
water.   *water.*

Notice that in order for a sentence to be relativized, there must be identical noun phrases in both sentences. One of the noun phrases is then replaced by a relative pronoun:

The magazine has been thrown away. You asked for *the magazine*.	The magazine *that you asked for* has been thrown away.
He is a singer. *He* entertains his audience.	He is a singer *who entertains* his audience.

There is a close relationship between adjectives and relative clauses. *Adjectives* come from relative clauses, which in turn come from complete sentences:

Mint has an odor. The odor is strong.	Mint has an odor *which is strong.*
Mint has an odor. The odor is strong.	Mint has a *strong* odor.

In traditional grammar, the *participle* is defined as a verbal adjective. It is a form of the verb used as an adjective to modify nouns. The participle can be a single word or a participial phrase:

> The *running* girl tripped over the skates.
> The child, *filled* with alarm, began to cry.

Like adjectives, participles are closely related to relative clauses. Both come from two or more complete sentences:

Rain carries salt. The salt is dissolved from the rocks.	Rain carries salt *that is dissolved from the rocks.*
Rain carries salt. The salt is dissolved from the rocks.	Rain carries salt *dissolved from the rocks.*

Participles take the following forms in English sentences:

PRESENT	PAST
asking	having asked
being asked	asked
	having been asked

These in turn can combine with other words to form participial phrases:

> I saw an old man *asking for food.*
> *Having asked for food,* the old man departed.
> *Being asked for food by the old man,* the woman said yes.
> *Asked for food,* the woman said yes.
> *Having been asked for food,* the woman could hardly refuse.

Since the *prepositional phrase,* when it modifies a noun or a pronoun, is adjectival (the whole phrase acts as a single adjective), it too is related to the relative clause:

> The flower withered.⎱   The flower *which is in the*
> The flower is in the vase.⎰   *vase* withered.
>
> The flower withered.⎱   The flower *in the vase*
> The flower is in the vase.⎰   withered.

Not all prepositional phrases are related to relative clauses. But when the prepositional phrase modifies a noun (unless it shows possession), a relative clause can always be substituted for it.

Appositives are nouns or noun substitutes, but like adjectives, they limit, describe, and explain other nouns:

> We spent the night in Flagstaff, *a city in northern Arizona.*
> Charlemagne, *a foreigner,* was never popular in Italy.

Although appositives are not considered to be verbals, nevertheless there seems to be a close connection between appositives and relative clauses:

> The thumb is a masterpiece of nature.⎱   The thumb, *which is an*
> The thumb is an anatomical work of art.⎰   *anatomical work of art,* is a masterpiece of nature.
>
> The thumb is a masterpiece of nature.⎱   The thumb, *an anatomical*
> The thumb is an anatomical work of art.⎰   *work of art,* is a masterpiece of nature.

What all of these grammatical structures have in common is that they modify nouns and they are related to relative clauses.

> TV shows *that depict violence* irritate censors. *(relative clause)*
> *Violent* TV shows irritate censors. *(adjective modifier)*

The child *who is sleeping* should not be disturbed. *(relative clause)*
The *sleeping* child should not be disturbed. *(participle)*

That book *which is on the desk* is torn. *(relative clause)*
That book *on the desk* is torn. *(prepositional phrase)*

Richard, *who is my friend*, married my girl. *(relative clause)*
Richard, *my friend*, married my girl. *(appositive)*

Exercise

In combining these sentences to form single sentences, make some sentences into relative clauses, some into adjectival, participial, or prepositional phrase modifiers, and some into appositives.

a. Dandelions form a setting.
   The setting is golden.
b. They ate its fruit.
   It has a red pulp.
c. A volcano sends out streams of rock.
   The streams are like molasses.
d. Tell Clara you want the dress.
   I returned it.
e. I dropped the jar.
   The jar was filled with honey.
f. He received the invitation.
   The invitation was from someone he didn't know.
g. The flood paralyzed the city.
   It caused the governor to seek emergency funds.
h. My friend was driving recklessly.
   He passed me like a bat out of hell.
i. Carol enrolled in Psychology 101.
   Psychology 101 is an interesting course.
j. Her home has an excellent view of the ocean.
   Her home is near San Francisco.

Expanding Sentences With Noun-Phrase Complements

Noun-phrase complements are noun substitutes. They are words or groups of words that can be used in nomitive positions in English sentences. Three important noun-phrase complements are the noun clause, the infinitive, and the gerund or gerundive.

In traditional grammar, a *noun clause* is one that can serve as the subject of a verb, the object of a verb, the object of a preposition, or a complement:

> *That he will appear* is certain. *(subject)*
> They said *that he will appear. (object)*
> I am not happy about *what you told me. (object of preposition)*
> Sand storms are *what we expect in the West. (complement)*

In traditional grammar, an *infinitive* is a verbal, a form of the verb with the word *to* in front of it. Here are some typical examples of the infinitive forms:

PRESENT	PAST
to ask	to have asked
to be asked	to have been asked

Like the noun clause, the infinitive can be used as a noun substitute:

> *To err* is human. *(subject)*
> She likes *to dance. (object)*
> *To eat* is *to live. (subject and complement)*

The *gerund* in traditional grammar is defined as a verbal noun. It has the following forms:

PRESENT	PAST
asking	having asked
being asked	having been asked

Notice that some of its forms resemble those of the participle. But the participle is an adjectival modifier. The gerund is a noun substitute. As a noun substitute, it functions in sentences the way nouns do:

Jogging is not much fun. *(subject)*
Seeing is *believing. (subject and complement)*
I do like *walking*, however. *(object)*
We were captivated by her *singing. (object of preposition)*

In transformational grammar, the noun clause, the infinitive, and the gerund are called *noun-phrase complements*. They come from complete sentences:

I know something. You like movies.	I know *that you like movies*.
My mother told me something. I should eat my dinner.	My mother told me *to eat my dinner*.
She likes something. She climbs mountains.	She likes *climbing mountains*.

In these examples, the second sentence of each pair is embedded in the first as a clause, an infinitive phrase, or a gerundive phrase. This is partially done by means of *complementizers*.

There are three kinds of complementizers: the clause complementizer *that*, the infinitive complementizer *for . . . to*, and the gerundive complementizer *'s . . . ing*. Here are some examples of sentences that use these complementizers:

That Bob smokes worries me.
It worries me *that* Bob smokes.
For Bob *to* smoke worries me.
Bob *'s* smok*ing* worries me.

Notice the close relationship that exists among these sentences. This relationship suggests what I have already pointed out—that complements come from two or more sentences. Their differences can be accounted for by the different complementizers. Complementizers enter sentences by means of transformations:

It worries me. Bob smokes.	*That* Bob smokes worries me.
It worries me. Bob smokes.	It worries me *that* Bob smokes.
It worries me. Bob smokes.	*For* Bob *to* smoke worries me.

It worries me. ⎫
Bob smokes. ⎭   Bob *'s* smok*ing* worries me.

What the traditional grammarians classify as noun clauses, infinitives, and gerunds are all related. They come from sentences, and then they are changed into clauses, infinitives, or gerunds by the appropriate complementizer:

It is astonishing. ⎫
Fossils exist at all. ⎭   It is astonishing *that fossils exist at all.*

Robins arrive X. ⎫
Robins greet worms. ⎭   Robins arrive *to greet worms.*

The leaves began X. ⎫
The leaves fade. ⎭   The leaves began *fading.*

Exercise

Combine the following sentences to form single sentences. Make some sentences into noun clauses, some into infinitives, and some into gerunds.

    a. It seemed obvious to me.
       He was safe at home.
    b. We stopped.
       We get gas.
    c. We shop at several stores.
       In this way we get the best deal.
    d. Jan has an irritating habit.
       She smokes cigarettes.
    e. I lost my driver's license.
       This was a great inconvenience.
    f. He pretended.
       He never saw me before.
    g. The fact sickens me.
       He has bad breath.
    h. Don't leave the lights on.
       It wastes electricity.
    i. Something is dangerous.
       Someone drives in heavy traffic.

Problems
in Grammar

Problems in Grammar

It is almost impossible to understand the compositional principles that govern the writing of sentences without some understanding of grammatical principles. The following are a few persistent problems in grammar that continue to be troublesome for many writers.

Subject/Verb Agreement

Make the verb agree with the subject in person and number:

> Disaster *movies* such as *The Poseidon Adventure are* my favorites. This *movie is* especially good.

If a phrase comes between the subject and the verb, do not make the verb agree with the noun in the phrase. Make the verb agree with the subject:

> UNACCEPTABLE   The paint *on these houses* are expensive.

Notice that the prepositional phrase comes between the subject and the verb. The verb *are* has incorrectly been made to agree with the noun *houses.* The sentence should read

> ACCEPTABLE   The *paint* on these houses *is* expensive.

Do not allow phrases such as *in addition to, including, as well as,* and *accompanied by,* which come between the subject and the verb, to affect the subject/verb agreement:

> UNACCEPTABLE   My arm, *as well as my leg,* were injured in the accident.
> ACCEPTABLE   My *arm*, as well as my leg, *was* injured in the accident.

Use a singular verb after words such as *each, every, everyone, anyone, someone, somebody, one, no one, everybody, either,* and *neither:*

> *Each* of them *is* anxious to leave.
> *Everyone was* irritated by the gasoline shortage.

Use a plural verb after a compound subject connected by *and:*

> A shirt *and* a tie *are* needed to get in.
> July *and* August *are* hot months.

Use a singular verb after singular subjects joined by *or, nor, either . . . or,* and *neither . . . nor:*

> *Neither* Ben *nor* Jane *has* the answer to the energy crisis.
> Lori *or* her friend *is* willing to help.

When you join two subjects, one of which is singular and the other plural, by *or* or *nor,* make the verb agree with the closer subject:

> Neither my truck nor my two *cars get* good gas mileage.
> Neither my two cars nor my *truck gets* good gas mileage.

Make the verb agree with the subject, even when the subject comes after the verb, especially in sentences beginning with *here, there,* and *where:*

> UNACCEPTABLE   There *was* five *people* in line before me.
> ACCEPTABLE   There *were* five *people* in line before me.

When a complement comes after the verb, make the verb agree with the subject, not with the complement:

> *Books are* my favorite recreation.
> My favorite *recreation is* books.

Use a singular verb after a collective noun that stands for a unit. Use a plural verb after a collective noun that stands for individuals:

> UNIT   The *team is* convinced it will win.
> INDIVIDUALS   A *majority are* opposed to gas rationing.

Use a singular verb after words denoting weights, measurements, amounts of money, and periods of time:

> *Thirty dollars is* a high price to pay for shoes.
> *Fifty minutes was* not enough time for the test.

Use a singular verb after nouns that are plural in form but singular in meaning:

> *Measles is* no longer a serious disease in many parts of the world.
>
> *Physics was* my most difficult subject in high school.

Use singular verbs after the nouns *kind* and *sort* and plural verbs after their plural forms:

> That *sort* of answer *bothers* me.
> These *kinds* of shoes are expensive.

Exercises

1. Pick out the correct form of the verb in parentheses:

   a. There (is, are) times when you'd like to get away from it all.
   b. It (is, are) television, not movies, that (distract, distracts) me.
   c. There (is, are) two groups of tourists who want to see the Grand Canyon.
   d. The President, accompanied by his aides, (is, are) going to China.
   e. Coffee and doughnuts (is, are) my weakness.
   f. Neither of the candidates (has, have) any appeal.
   g. The food in this chain of restaurants (is, are) awful.
   h. Everybody (was, were) concerned about the energy shortage.
   i. Neither Joan nor Jane (have, has) a job they really like.
   j. Twenty pounds (is, are) the correct weight.

2. Correct the errors in the following sentences:

   a. Each of your papers need revision.
   b. The sofa, as well as the chair, are in need of repair.
   c. The rest of these clothes goes to the Salvation Army.
   d. Neither she nor I were willing to apologize.
   e. Where's the papers that were due for today?
   f. Dan and his fiancée is coming over tonight.
   g. Odd jobs is his only source of extra money.
   h. A TV set or a stereo are given to the winners.
   i. Here is my plans for the new house.

j. Ten minutes aren't enough time.
k. Those kind of flowers don't grow well here.
l. The jury was not in their seats when the judge came in.

Noun/Pronoun Agreement

Make pronouns agree with their antecedents (words to which they refer) ***in person, number, and gender:***

PERSON	The *leopard* cannot change *its* spots. *(third person)*
NUMBER	*People* are known by the company *they* keep. *(plural number)*
GENDER	Nature meant *woman* to be *her* masterpiece. *(feminine gender)*

The first-person pronouns are *I, my, me, we, our,* and *us.* The second-person pronouns are *you* and *your.* The third-person pronouns are *he, him, she, her, it, they, their,* and *them.* All nouns are in the third person.

Use a plural pronoun to refer to two or more words joined by *and:*

Jan *and* Ellen will use *their* cars.
Books *and* stamps keep *their* value for many years.

Use a singular pronoun to refer to two or more words joined by *or* or *nor:*

Neither Jan *nor* Ellen will use *her* car.
Either Mike *or* Ted lost *his* notebook.

Use a singular pronoun to refer to words such as *each, either,* or *neither* when the gender is known:

Each of the applicants believed *she* would get the job.
Neither of the boys apologized for *his* actions.
Either of those girls will lend you *her* copy.

To avoid sexism in language, use two pronouns of different genders or a plural pronoun to refer to indefinite pronouns such as *nobody, anybody, somebody, everybody, no one, anyone, everyone,* and *any:*

ACCEPTABLE	*Everybody* thinks *their* children are bright.
ACCEPTABLE	*Anyone* who wants a class picture should bring *his* or *her* money tomorrow.

Their is acceptable in the first sentence above when a plural subject is meant. Otherwise, use *his* or *her.*

If the noun to which the pronoun refers could be either masculine or feminine, use either a plural noun or two pronouns of different genders:

SEXIST	The good *student* never worries about *his* grades.
ACCEPTABLE	Good *students* never worry about *their* grades.
ACCEPTABLE	The good *student* never worries about *his* or *her* grades.

Use a singular pronoun to refer to a collective noun such as *team, class, band, squad,* or *committee* if the noun refers to the group as a whole. If the noun refers to the individuals of a group, use a plural pronoun:

The *band* is playing *its* own compositions now.
The *class* took turns reading *their* papers aloud.

Use *who* to refer to people, *which* to refer to animals or things, and *that* to refer to persons, animals, or things:

Masseurs are *people who* knead people.
The marriage ceremony is a *knot which* is tied by your teeth.
Today is the *tomorrow that* you worried about yesterday.

When there are two possible antecedents for a pronoun, rewrite the sentence to make the antecedent clear and definite:

UNCLEAR	Mary told Kay that *she* should vote in the next election.
CLEAR	*You* should vote in the next election, Mary told Kay.

Rewrite sentences in which the antecedent of a pronoun is not expressed or in which the pronoun refers to an entire clause rather than to a single word:

UNCLEAR	You did not return my call *which* makes me very angry.
CLEAR	You did not return my call. Your *thoughtlessness* makes me very angry.

Rewrite sentences in which pronouns such as *you, they,* or *it* do not refer to a clear antecedent:

UNCLEAR	*They* don't allow smoking in this building.
CLEAR	Smoking is not allowed in this building.
UNCLEAR	*It* says on the ten o'clock news that there will be rain tomorrow.
CLEAR	The announcer on the ten o'clock news says that there will be rain tomorrow.

Exercises

1. Underline the antecedent and cross out the incorrect pronoun in the following sentences:

   a. Both Ray and Carl did (his, their) best.
   b. This is the boy (who, which) volunteered.
   c. Neither Ann nor Patricia would lend me (their, her) book.
   d. The committee was divided in (its, their) decision.
   e. Each of his sisters gave him (her, their) favorite recipe.
   f. Sue has a dog (who, that) loves to howl at midnight.
   g. If any girls are interested in swimming (you, she, they) should see the coach.
   h. If you find a pen and a notebook, take (it, them) to the front office.
   i. A cat or a dog will always defend (their, its) young.
   j. The jury has made (their, its) decision.

2. Supply the appropriate pronouns in the following sentences:

   a. Whenever a person is sick, _____ should go to a doctor.
   b. Everybody has a right to _____ opinion.
   c. Ask anyone where the Statue of Liberty is and _____ can tell you.
   d. If you drop a plate or a bowl, you'll have to pay for _____.
   e. Allan and his brother didn't eat _____ oatmeal.
   f. No one in _____ right mind would eat TV dinners.
   g. The class was ready to take _____ test.
   h. The entire faculty made _____ decision.
   i. As you enter the hotel, the first thing _____ see is the check-in desk.
   j. After a customer rents a car, _____ must return it.

3. Rewrite the following sentences to avoid vague pronoun references or to avoid sexism in language:

   a. The bus driver backed into my car, which irritated me very much.
   b. A good doctor always respects his patients.
   c. They say that gasoline will go up to two dollars a gallon.
   d. If nuclear energy is banned, they will have to develop new sources of energy.
   e. A criminal always gets what he deserves.

Dangling Modifiers

Avoid dangling modifiers. A dangling modifier is so called because it does not refer to some specific word in the sentence.

In the student sentence below, the dangling modifier confuses the reader. Who is entering the car? Is it "the condition of the interior"? One way to correct sentences that contain dangling modifiers is to supply a word to which the modifier can refer. The simple inclusion of the word *I* in the following sentence makes the meaning clear:

> UNCLEAR   *Upon entering the car*, the condition of the interior was impressive.
>
> CLEAR   Upon entering the car, *I* was impressed by the condition of the interior.

If you think of modifiers as reductions of complete sentences, you may gain a greater understanding of dangling modifiers. Take, for example, the following sentence:

> *Working for his father*, Ned learned much about cars. *(participial phrase)*

This sentence is derived from two underlying sentences:

> [Ned was] working for his father.
> Ned learned much about cars.

In the first sentence, if the words *Ned* and *was* are deleted, what remains is the participial phrase "working for his father." This phrase can then be positioned as a modifier in the second sentence to produce the sentence "Working for his father, Ned learned much about cars." There is no danger of confusion in this sentence because the modifier has a clear reference in the word *Ned.* This is an appropriate word for the participle to modify since the deleted subject of this phrase is also the word *Ned.*

But what is the relationship between the modifier and the main clause in this sentence?

> *Driving behind a truck*, a car hit me from behind.

If you reconstruct the two sentences from which this sentence is derived, you get

> [*I* was] driving behind a truck.
> A car hit me from behind.

The problem here is that the participle *driving* must go with the word *I*. But the word *I* has been deleted, and when the participial phrase combines with the main clause of the second sentence, the phrase is incorrectly made to modify the noun *car*.

To correct the dangling modifier, you have to include the word *I* somewhere in the new sentence. You can do this by making the dangling modifier into a dependent clause or by rewriting the main clause with *I* as the subject:

> As *I* was driving behind a truck, a car hit me from behind.
> Driving behind a truck, *I* was hit from behind by a car.

Dangling modifiers can be participles, gerunds, infinitives, or elliptical clauses:

> *Sitting behind the goalpost*, the football hit him in the head. *(dangling participle)*

> *By coming in early*, the work was completed before closing time. *(dangling gerund)*

> *To succeed in your new career*, three things are necessary. *(dangling infinitive)*

> *If adopted*, we hope the new energy plan will solve our problems. *(elliptical clause)*

We have already discussed the participle as a modifier, but notice that in the last three sentences, the problems are very similar to those discussed previously. A noun or pronoun subject has been deleted from each of the sentences from which the modifiers were derived. Without the deleted word, the modifier dangles. How might you correct these dangling modifiers? By putting in the deleted words:

> As *he was* sitting behind the goalpost, the football hit him in the head.
> By *your* coming in early, the work was completed before closing time.
> *For you* to succeed in your new career, three things are necessary.
> If *it is* adopted, the new energy plan will solve our problems.

Let's take a closer look at the gerundive, infinitive, and elliptical modifiers. Each of these modifiers is a reduction of a complete sentence.

The gerundive phrase "by coming in early" begins as a sentence:

> You were coming in early.

The sentence is then transformed into a gerundive phrase:

Your com*ing* in early

If the writer had inserted this phrase after the preposition *by,* there would have been no problem. But he erroneously deleted the word *your,* and this deletion causes the confusion. To put it briefly, anytime there is a dangling gerundive phrase, a possessive noun or pronoun must have been deleted. To correct the phrase, supply the missing word.

The sign of the gerund is a possessive form of a noun or pronoun and the suffix *-ing:*

the girl'*s* sing*ing*   her sing*ing*
the band'*s* march*ing*   its march*ing*
Ned'*s* play*ing*   his play*ing*

The infinitive phrase "to succeed in your new career" also begins as a sentence:

You succeed in your new career.

This sentence is then transformed into an infinitive phrase:

for you *to* succeed in your new career

As in the previous instance, here the writer erroneously deletes a part of the infinitive complementizer *(for)* and the noun subject *you.* Without the word *you* to relate to, the infinitive dangles. Infinitive complements always have the structure "for . . . to . . ." with the three dots standing for the subject and verb:

for Jack *to* go   *for* the boys *to* camp
for you *to* gossip   *for* him *to* work

To correct dangling infinitives, add the word *for* and an appropriate noun before the infinitive.

In the last example, the elliptical clause "if adopted" goes through this series of changes:

It is adopted
if it is adopted
if . . . adopted

To correct elliptical clauses, put in the words deleted from the original sentence.

Exercise

The following sentences contain dangling modifiers. Rewrite the sentences to correct them.

a. After seeing the film, strange images began to haunt my sleep.
b. If admitted, his tuition will cost him five hundred dollars a semester.
c. To sell this automobile, it must be advertised in the Want Ads.
d. While at the beach, sand got into my clothes.
e. Sitting on the steps, the speeding cars looked dangerous.
f. After talking with the dentist, my tooth continued to ache.
g. A boat suddenly appeared walking along the river.
h. By voting "no," the bill was defeated.
i. Since coming home, the town doesn't seem the same.
j. Being shy, going to a new school was terrifying.

Misplaced Modifiers

Place modifiers as closely as possible to the words they modify:

My aunt gave a chest to my sister *over fifty years old*.

Placing the modifier "over fifty years old" at the end of the sentence results in momentary confusion for the reader. Who or what is "over fifty years old"? The sister? The chest? This sentence can be corrected in two ways, both of which require moving the prepositional phrase close to the noun *chest:*

My aunt gave a chest *over fifty years old* to my sister.
My aunt gave my sister a chest *over fifty years old*.

Place single-word adverbs such as *only, nearly, almost,* and *just* close to the words they modify. Notice the difference in meaning suggested by the placement of a single word:

She *only* tasted the cheese.
(However, she didn't eat it.)

She tasted *only* the cheese.
(She didn't taste the other food.)

Do not place a modifier where it could refer confusingly to the words before it or to the words that follow it. Such a modifier is called a *squinting modifier.*

UNACCEPTABLE Because we finished our work *in one hour* we could go home.

The reader is not certain if the work was finished in one hour or if the workers could go home in one hour. One way to correct the problem is by punctuation. Another is by repositioning the modifier:

ACCEPTABLE Because we finished our work *in one hour,* we could go home.

UNACCEPTABLE Because we finished our work, we could go home *in one hour.*

Here is another example:

Anyone who goes downtown *occasionally* will notice the new streetlights.

In this situation, punctuation would be of little use. The sentence would still be ambiguous. The adverb must be moved to its proper place in the sentence:

Anyone who *occasionally* goes downtown will notice the new streetlights.
Anyone who goes downtown will *occasionally* notice the new streetlights.

Exercise

Correct the misplaced modifiers in the following sentences:

a. We only saw the end of the film.
b. Did you put the meat in the trashcan that was spoiled?
c. Jack discussed the accident he had in the bus.
d. She finished her talk on fishing in Canada.
e. As we looked around now and then we saw a deer.
f. Would you like to read this book on how to digest your food after dinner?
g. People who smoke constantly irritate others.
h. I got on a plane that was going to Chicago by mistake.
i. I turn on the television whenever I eat for entertainment.
j. You can see Bob cutting the lawn from the kitchen window.

Faulty Parallelism

Express parallel ideas in parallel structure:

> There's an energy crisis and
> > a food crisis and
> > any number of other crises.

> Many try, but
> few succeed.

> Swim,
> surf, and
> sail in the warm clear ocean.

In all of these sentences, the parallel ideas are expressed in similar grammatical constructions.

You cannot shift from one kind of grammatical construction to another in expressing parallel ideas. You must keep nouns with nouns, verbs with verbs, prepositional phrases with prepositional phrases, and so forth. In the sentence below, the comparison is faulty because a gerund is paired with a noun:

> *Opening* crabs is a harder job than *oysters*.

The comparison should not be between *opening* and *oysters*, but between *opening crabs* and *opening oysters*.

You can correct faulty parallelism in one of two ways. You can grammatically subordinate one of the parallel elements, if one of the ideas is subordinate:

> Fred is a figure of perfection and closely resembles a Greek god.
> Fred is a figure of perfection *who closely* resembles a Greek god.

Or you can rewrite coordinate elements that are supposed to be coordinate in form. In the following sentence, the words *television* and *walks* are incorrectly coordinated with the phrase "sitting on the porch."

> Some summer nights, people relax by *television*, *walks*, or *sitting on the porch*.

Television and *walks* are nouns. "Sitting on the porch" is a gerundive phrase. You can correct the faulty parallelism by putting the words *television* and *walks* in phrases:

> Some summer nights, people relax by *watching television, taking walks,* or *sitting on the porch.*

In the following student sentence, two adjectives are incorrectly coordinated with a verb phrase:

> The movie is *funny, heartwarming,* and *appeals to almost everyone.*

You can revise this sentence in two ways: by changing the verb phrase to an adjectival one or by adding a subject to the second verb phrase and making this phrase into a coordinate clause:

> The movie is *funny, heartwarming,* and *appealing.*

> The movie is funny and heartwarming, and *it* appeals to almost everyone.

Exercise

Rewrite the following sentences to correct faulty parallelism:

a. Good writers must know punctuation and how to spell.
b. My friend is considerate, friendly, and she gives help.
c. She thought that her dress was better than the other girls.
d. Hiking in the desert is different from anywhere else.
e. Jane was more interested in the movie than her date.
f. The car runs smoothly and quiet.
g. She likes hiking and to go jogging.
h. My boss caught me taking a smoke and on the telephone.
i. He was broke, disgusted, and had no job.
j. Carl prefers tennis to playing golf.

Run-on Sentence

Do not join sentences together with a comma or with no punctuation mark between them:

UNACCEPTABLE	We will take Flight 217 to New York, it is the quickest flight.
ACCEPTABLE	We will take Flight 217 to New York. It is the quickest flight.

| UNACCEPTABLE | It was late in the fourth quarter the score was six to nothing. |
| ACCEPTABLE | It was late in the fourth quarter. The score was six to nothing. |

The first kind of error indicated here, in which a comma is used between two sentences instead of a period, a semicolon, or a conjunction, is called a *comma splice* or *comma fault.* The second kind of error, in which no mark of punctuation is used between two sentences, is called a *period fault.* This latter sentence type is sometimes referred to as the *fused sentence.* However, I shall use the expression *run-on sentence* to cover both kinds of errors.

You can correct run-on sentences in a number of ways. You can use a period to separate the sentences:

| UNACCEPTABLE | Lori has never been interested in "girlish" games, give her a ball, a bat, or a tennis racket and she is perfectly happy. |
| ACCEPTABLE | Lori has never been interested in "girlish" games. Give her a ball, a bat, or a tennis racket and she is perfectly happy. |

You can use a semicolon in place of a comma, if the sentences are close in thought:

| UNACCEPTABLE | The process isn't really very hard, it just takes patience. |
| ACCEPTABLE | The process isn't really very hard; it just takes patience. |

You can insert a coordinate conjunction, usually with a comma, between the two sentences:

| UNACCEPTABLE | The bus stops just long enough for tourists to get one photograph then it takes them someplace else. |
| ACCEPTABLE | The bus stops just long enough for tourists to get one photograph, and then it takes them someplace else. |

Or you can make one sentence into a subordinate clause and embed it in the other sentence:

| UNACCEPTABLE | Sharon did not take that part-time job, she needed time for her studies. |
| ACCEPTABLE | Sharon did not take that part-time job because she needed time for her studies. |

Many run-on sentences are caused by adverbs such as *then, therefore, however, consequently, nevertheless,* and *furthermore* which the writer mistakes for conjunctions. When these words are used between independent clauses, they should come after a semicolon, or they should be capitalized to start a new sentence.

UNACCEPTABLE	It rained for most of the day, then it began to sleet.
ACCEPTABLE	It rained for most of the day; then it began to sleet.
ACCEPTABLE	It rained for most of the day. Then it began to sleet.

Exercise

Rewrite the following run-on sentences, separating the main clauses by a period, a semicolon, a coordinating conjunction, or a subordinating conjunction.

   a. We were an hour late, the concert had not started.
   b. The old man sat down under a tree, then he began to fish.
   c. Dan ate a whole box of candy no wonder he wasn't hungry.
   d. The story was boring, the acting was awful.
   e. The letter was unintelligible, none of us could understand it.
   f. At first I said I would go later I changed my mind.
   g. The store didn't have celery, however, it had plenty of lettuce.
   h. The road was slick we almost slid off the road.
   i. Yesterday I was ready to quit, today I will probably do so.
   j. The dress was one size too small, nevertheless, she tried it on.

Many handbooks advise the writer never to use commas between independent clauses, yet many professional writers deliberately violate this advice if the clauses are short, if they are parallel in structure, if they are antithetical, or if there is no chance that they will be misunderstood.

The following run-on sentences were taken from a variety of sources, including magazine advertising, *Time, Harper's, Psychology Today, Esquire,* and the *Saturday Review:*

Some can easily afford it, some cannot.
(antithetical)

They don't just wipe up, they clean up.
(antithetical)

Tire inflation pressures are important, so are lubricants.
(additive)

Most doctors agree, the best treatment for a patient with severe and permanent kidney failure is the surgical transplant of a healthy kidney from a donor. *(breaks the rule of short clauses)*

Abuse is not something we think about, it's something we do.
(antithetical)

Hit the beaches, beat the sandy traps.
(series)

Proverbs make extensive use of the run-on sentence. Perhaps the ideas in them are so familiar and the expressions are so succinct that there is little danger of their being misunderstood. Proverbs use very short phrases and balanced clauses:

Man proposes, God disposes.
The more you have, the more you want.

They use phrases and clauses in a series:

Hear no evil, see no evil, speak no evil.
Be civil to all, sociable to many, familiar to few.

And they make extensive use of antithesis:

Do as I say, not as I do.
United we stand, divided we fall.

Graffiti make frequent use of the comma fault:

Be nice to someone, kick a masochist.
I came, I saw, I flunked.

Advertising slogans use them almost as frequently:

Fly now, pay later.
Tide's in, dirt's out.

Run-on sentences, then, are not always inappropriate, even though they may be grammatically incorrect. Purists may condemn them, but I would suggest that you learn how to use them effectively, according to the guidelines given here. Then you'll have to determine when it is best to use them. Naturally, you will have to consider your audience, your purpose, and the occasion. Some readers may accept them; some may not. Know your readers and write accordingly. For example, there is no harm in using them in personal letters, but they may be inappropriate in business letters.

Sentence Fragment

Do not write a part of a sentence as if it were a complete sentence unless you have a good reason to do so. Sentence fragments do appear in the work of professional writers. They appear extensively in magazine advertising. But in the writing of students, they are almost always due to carelessness. To many teachers and editors, sentence fragments suggest ignorance.

Let's look at the concept of fragments, first from a traditional point of view and then from a nontraditional point of view. Sentence fragments are groups of words lacking a subject or a predicate. Others are modifiers that have been cut off from an independent clause:

> They look strong. Last long. *(subject omitted)*

> There are some things you never want to change. Like the feeling you get when you reel in that big one. *(modifier cut off)*

If the sentence fragment takes the form of a dependent clause, attach it to a previous clause or rewrite the clause as a complete sentence:

UNACCEPTABLE   Johnny Carson usually has several guests. While Dick Cavett often devotes his entire show to one guest.

ACCEPTABLE   Johnny Carson usually has several guests, while Dick Cavett often devotes his entire show to one guest. *(clause attached)*

ACCEPTABLE   Johnny Carson usually has several guests. Dick Cavett often devotes his entire show to one guest. *(clause rewritten as sentence)*

If the sentence fragment lacks a subject or a verb, supply the subject or verb, or tie the fragment to some previous or subsequent sentence:

UNACCEPTABLE	Drag racing is dangerous. Especially on city streets.
ACCEPTABLE	Drag racing is dangerous. It is especially dangerous on city streets. *(added subject and verb)*
ACCEPTABLE	Drag racing is dangerous, especially on city streets. *(modifier attached to main clause)*

For the past three years, I have been collecting examples of sentence fragments from both informal and formal writing, and I have found these kinds to be the most common:

The answer to a question
How did we do it? With an unusual engineering development.

Why do boxers like Ken Norton jump rope? To stay in good condition.

Predicate adjective
Each is a masterpiece. Realistic, yet delicate.

It's creamy. Positively luscious.

Appositive
I guess that's what makes a classic a classic. The ability to look completely different depending on how it's used.

We're all accustomed to high-impact, hard-hitting visual information. The kind only television can deliver.

Prepositional Phrases
They're shaped for kids' feet. With lots of room in the front.

People are taking it everywhere. On any kind of road, in any kind of weather, on every kind of trip.

Participial Phrase
Imagine golden yellow peaches. Bathing in a fresh stream of lightly sweetened real fruit juices.

We are waiting. Waiting for "someone else" to solve our energy problems.

Adverbial Clause
In the Polynesian Pacific, the wind can be a devil. Because the breezes seem to blow from all directions.

Years ago, everything was created one of a kind. Because everything was created by hand.

Subject Omitted
I like the way I look. Love the way I feel.

Never needs ironing.

Most of these sentences can be corrected simply by attaching the fragment to the main clause:

UNACCEPTABLE   It's creamy, Positively luscious.
ACCEPTABLE   It's creamy, positively luscious.

Exercise

In the sentences below, attach each sentence fragment to the main clause of the other sentence or rewrite it as a complete sentence.

a. Are there any hotels left in the world that still practice the fine art of attention to detail? Precious few.

b. Mustang is sporty and sleek. Inside and out.

c. Corn Bran is crispy. Even in milk.

d. It tastes the way lemonade was meant to taste. Delicious. Refreshing. Thirst quenching.

e. The colors are very special. Delicate shadings that look like they were created from nature's own sensitive palette.

f. The Spanish have a saying, *"Quidese con la uva."* Stick to the grape.

g. Chevy Monza is a thrill to drive. To take out on the open road and enjoy. To take into a corner and come out impressed.

h. Return to Los Angeles if you like. If you can bear the thought of coming back at all.

i. You scrub. Wax. Do a hard day's work every day.

j. Everything is compatible. Simpatico.

It must be admitted that in most of the sentence fragments we have looked at so far, there is little danger that the reader will misunderstand the writer's intention. Each fragment is placed so close to the sentence to which it is obviously related that the meaning is clear and evident.

Advertisers use fragments frequently and deliberately for easy reading and swift-moving copy:

> How does Webster's New Collegiate accomplish such a feat? With over 3,000 quotations from poets, comics, critics, and presidents. With over 24,000 phrases showing you how a word is used in context. And with scores of illustrations, charts, and tables.

> When you plan your visit to Colorado, make sure your trail takes you throughout the state. Up. Down. And all around.

Professional writers use them for emphasis or for special effects. In the following paragraph, taken from an article in *Time* (March 12, 1979), fragments are used in the opening paragraph to give the reader a sense of disorder and anarchy, of things coming apart:

> Revolution in Iran. A souring of the important U.S. special relationship with Saudi Arabia. A looming economic crisis, and soon, caused by oil shortages and runaway price boosts. A danger that much of the region might change its tilt away from the U.S. and toward the Soviet Union. A Middle East peace seemingly more elusive than ever. These are the troubles and threats that America faces in the so-called crescent of crisis—that great swath of countries running from the Horn of Africa through Egypt and across the Middle East to Afghanistan and Pakistan. Here, more than in any other area of the world, the U.S. has vital interests that are threatened by forces it has not been able to control, and all too often seems unable to influence.

In the first paragraph of an article titled "Interferon: Medicine for Cancer and the Common Cold?" taken from *Saturday Review* (November 25, 1978), the fragments are used to define and to emphasize:

> Interferon. A chemical that interferes. A mystery molecule made by the body itself to thwart the subversive intentions of invaders.
>
> Because the American Cancer Society (ACS) has announced the launching of a $2 million program to test it clinically, interferon is already being referred to as a "cancer drug"—which it may well prove to be. But those who have been studying interferon for its multiple other potential uses fear that, should it perform disappointingly in its cancer trials—if it is only marginally useful, for instance, as has been the case with so many other promising anticancer agents—then, as one scientist puts it, "Interferon may become a dirty word, because 'It was tried and didn't work.'"

And in this paragraph, also taken from *Saturday Review* (April 14, 1979), the fragments are used to freeze images in the reader's mind, images that are almost too frightening to contemplate:

> The first step into a children's cancer ward seems like a step into unreality. Images swim before you. A sign in boldface lettering, "Remove Prosthesis Before Being Weighed." Mothers weary, waiting. A teenager with no more hair than the fuzz of a newborn, a tiny girl with ribbons tied to the two or three strands that are left. They look like small-sized veterans of some long-ago war, wraiths returned in a bad dream. Your eyes register them but your mind refuses them; for they are children, you think, who are waiting for death. The first step into a children's cancer ward brings with it a queasy feeling of hopelessness, and there seems to be only one way of coping with it: leaving.

Fragments, then, can be very effective in both formal and informal writing. The advice I would give to the novice writer is to learn first the difference between a sentence and a fragment. Then learn how to use the fragment to achieve various effects. Finally, in using

fragments, always consider your audience, your purpose, and the occasion. Will your reader object to your using fragments? Can you achieve your purpose better by using fragments in this *particular* piece of writing, for this *particular* occasion, than you can by using complete sentences?

Punctuation

Chapter 18

Punctuation

Punctuation is the use of standardized marks to separate words into phrases, clauses, and sentences. Punctuation should be audience-centered. As you write, keep your readers in mind and try to determine where they will need the help of punctuation marks to follow your meaning or your emphasis. If you use too many punctuation marks, you may confuse your readers. If you use too few, you may make it difficult for them to see at a glance the words that go together and those that should be kept apart. A badly punctuated sentence or an unpunctuated sentence can mislead or confuse your readers.

The Period

Use a period at the end of a declarative sentence or one that is mildly imperative. A declarative sentence makes a statement:

> Good fences make good neighbors.
> Truth is stranger than fiction.

An imperative sentence expresses a *command, request,* or *entreaty:*

> Do not wear out your welcome.
> Never judge by appearances.

Put a period after abbreviations of titles, names, degrees, months, countries, states, and so forth:

TITLES	Dr., Mr., Ms., Mrs., Rev.
NAMES	H. G. Wells, Chas. Smith
DEGREES	Ph.D., M.A., B.S., M.D., D.D.S.
MONTHS	Sept., Oct., Nov., Dec.
STATES	Mass., Ill., Ariz., Ga., La.

| CITIES | N.Y., N.O., L.A. |
| MISCELLANEOUS | A.M., P.M., St., Ave. |

Question Mark

Put a question mark at the end of a direct question. There are two kinds of questions: the yes/no question and the *wh* question. The yes/no question is one that takes a simple yes or no for an answer:

> Did Shakespeare write *Romeo and Juliet?*
> Are you coming over tonight?

The *wh* question is one that cannot be answered by a simple yes or no. It is called a *wh* question because the questioning word usually begins with *wh* (*who, which, what, when, why;* but *how* is an exception):

> Who painted *The Starry Night?*
> What did she say to you?

Put a question mark in parentheses to express doubt:

> Plato's *Phaedrus* was written around 370(?) B.C.

Use a single question mark after a double question. The following sentence asks a question, and within that question is a quoted question:

> Who was the wise guy who cracked, "Did Adam and Eve have belly buttons?"

Exclamation Point

Use an exclamation point after expressions that show strong feeling or emotion:

> No! No! No! You shouldn't do that!
> Come here immediately!

Frequently, the words in your sentences will carry their own emphasis. Do not, therefore, use the exclamation point unless your expressions require unusual emphasis.

The Semicolon

Put a semicolon between independent clauses that are closely related:

> Drive with care; life has no spare.
> Keep Chicago clean; eat a pigeon a day.

Use a semicolon between independent clauses to show balance or contrast:

> Art is long; life is short.
> Walk on the grass; don't smoke it.
> People make mistakes; computers don't.

Put a semicolon between independent clauses joined by a sentence connector (also called a *conjunctive adverb* or *transitional expression*). A sentence connector is a word such as *therefore, however, nevertheless, accordingly, moreover, further-more, consequently, then, thus,* and *still:*

> You may be right; nevertheless, I'd like another opinion.
> We get along fine; however, we don't always agree.

Use a semicolon to show the main divisions in a series that is set off by commas:

> Among those receiving sports awards were Reggie Jackson, the right fielder of the New York Yankees; Pete Rose, the first baseman of the Philadelphia Phillies; Johnny Bench, the catcher of the Cincinnati Reds; and Vida Blue, the pitcher with the San Francisco Giants.

Do not use a semicolon in place of a colon:

WRONG   The following are the most popular singles for the month of June; "Reunited" (Peaches and Herb), "Love You Inside Out" (Bee Gees), "We Are Family" (Sister Sledge), "Goodnight Tonight" (Wings), and "In the Navy" (Village People).

RIGHT   The following are the most popular singles for the month of June: "Reunited" (Peaches and Herb), "Love You Inside Out" (Bee Gees), "We Are Family" (Sister Sledge), "Goodnight Tonight" (Wings), and "In the Navy" (Village People).

Do not use a semicolon in place of a comma. The exception is to show the main divisions in a series:

WRONG   For many years; we believed that chimps were smart enough to learn a language.

RIGHT   For many years, we believed that chimps were smart enough to learn a language.

WRONG   Ask a friend to balance a wooden pencil on the index finger of each hand; one hand at a time.

RIGHT   Ask a friend to balance a wooden pencil on the index finger of each hand, one hand at a time.

Exercises

1. Put in the appropriate end punctuation in the following sentences:

   a. Two heads are better than one
   b. What are we going to do tomorrow
   c. What a lousy day
   d. You never know what you can do until you try
   e. Who found the coin
   f. Liars should have good memories
   g. Never call me after midnight again
   h. Lend your money and lose your friend
   i. You didn't leave the water running, did you
   j. Stop in the name of the law

2. Supply semicolons where necessary in the following sentences:

   a. Old mailmen never die they just lose their zip.

   b. First build your house then think of your furniture.

   c. He who loses money loses much he who loses a friend loses more he who loses his nerve loses all.

   d. It is raining therefore, I will stay home.

   e. Get high on helium it's a gas.

f. Our instruction in writing was excellent nevertheless, we had some trouble with our first assignment in college.

g. Attending the meeting of the city council were Sam Sloane a salesman Charles Channing a lawyer Paula Perkins a clinical psychologist and Harriet Haynes a decorator.

h. Petty crimes are punished great ones are rewarded.

i. Rome wasn't built in a day the pizza parlors alone took several weeks.

j. If a man deceives me once, shame on him if he deceives me twice, shame on me.

The Comma

Put a comma in front of a conjunction (and, or, nor, but, for) ***that connects the two main clauses of a compound sentence:***

> A lawyer's advice may be expensive, but it will cost you more if you consult yourself.
>
> Experience keeps a dear school, yet fools will learn in no other.
>
> Sing before breakfast, and you'll cry before night.

Put a comma between introductory words, phrases, or clauses and the main clause:

> If life gives you lemons, make lemonade.
> When in doubt, don't.
> Overhead, the leaves rustled in the breeze.

Some writers suggest that if the introductory element is short, there is no need for commas. But if you get into the habit of punctuating introductory elements, you can increase ease of reading for your audience and prevent a misreading, as in the following sentence:

> CONFUSING   In addition to the socks she had mended two sweaters.
> BETTER   In addition to the socks, she had mended two sweaters.

Use a comma to separate words, phrases, and clauses in a series:

Eggs, sausage, bacon, and ham are foods you love to eat.

A dozen roses, a dozen golf balls, or cash—they're all tried and true gifts.

You cross the equator, pass the international date line, and steam through the Panama Canal.

The shopping is superb, the cuisine is gourmet, and the weather is sublime.

Some writers prefer to omit the final comma in a series (the comma before the conjunction). This is acceptable practice, provided that you are consistent. However, omitting the final comma can sometimes lead to ambiguity:

Sausage, ham, bacon and eggs are foods you love to eat.

Are bacon and eggs to be considered a single unit, or is each a separate item in the series?

Do not separate pairs of words, phrases, and clauses:

WRONG   Books, and friends should be few but good.

RIGHT   Books and friends should be few but good.

WRONG   By the bag, or by the box . . . your best candy buy is Brach's.

RIGHT   By the bag or by the box . . . your best candy buy is Brach's.

Set off nonrestrictive relative clauses with commas:

The novel is by William Faulkner, who wrote *The Sound and the Fury.*

The dislike of the Oakland Raiders by other teams, who consider them unnecessarily rough, is great.

The nonrestrictive clause acts as a kind of parenthetical element, containing information that is not crucial to the meaning of the main clause. The idea in the nonrestrictive clause is often a kind of after-thought or an interruption in the main flow of ideas. Paraphrasing the nonrestrictive clause is a good way to show these relationships:

ORIGINAL   My cousin, who lives in New York, is an actress.

PARAPHRASE   My cousin, and she happens to live in New York, is an actress.

PARAPHRASE   My cousin is an actress, and she lives in New York.

Do not enclose restrictive clauses with commas:

He that cannot obey cannot command.
A family who smokes together chokes together.
Blessed is he who expects nothing, for he shall never be disappointed.

In all of these sentences, the relative clause identifies, describes, or expands on the meaning of the noun it modifies. These sentences would make little sense and would have little relationship to the intended meaning of the original if you deleted the restrictive relative clause:

> He . . . cannot command.
> A family . . . chokes together.
> Blessed is he . . . , for he shall never be disappointed.

Use commas to set off appositives, nouns of address, and conjunctive adverbs:

> Welcome to Hawaii, a place as unique and varied as its flowers. *(appositive)*
> Julie, my best friend, called from New Orleans. *(appositive)*
> Laura, please don't get upset. *(noun of address)*
> Come in, Uncle Albert, and sit down. *(noun of address)*
> Nevertheless, I understand your position. *(conjunctive adverb)*
> I believe, moreover, that you lied to me. *(conjunctive adverb)*

Use commas to separate items in dates, addresses, and place names:

> July 4, 1776
> 125 Apache Boulevard, Phoenix, Arizona
> We travel occasionally to Juarez, Mexico.

Do not put commas between the subject and the predicate or between closely related parts of a sentence:

> WRONG   That last ball, should have been a strike.
> WRONG   She indicated, that she would arrive Wednesday.
> WRONG   The swing on the front porch, is broken.

Do not put a comma in place of a period between two sentences:

> WRONG   It takes all kinds of people to make a world, some are open-minded and some are bigoted.
> RIGHT   It takes all kinds of people to make a world. Some are open-minded and some are bigoted.
>
> WRONG   She walked very slowly, as I approached her, she picked up speed.
> RIGHT   She walked very slowly. As I approached her, she picked up speed.

Do not use an excessive number of commas in a sentence:

EXCESSIVE	Saturday, at ten o'clock, on Central Avenue, an old, battered truck struck a bright, red van and injured two, young children.
BETTER	Saturday at ten o'clock, on Central Avenue, an old battered truck struck a bright red van and injured two young children.

Exercises

1. Insert commas where necessary in the following sentences:

    a. If there were no clouds we would not enjoy the sun.
    b. Everybody complains about pollution but nobody wants to empty the wastebasket.
    c. For more than sixty centuries man has relentlessly scratched tunneled panned stripped dredged and blasted for gold.
    d. Swim surf and sail in the warm clear ocean.
    e. When the wolf comes in the door love creeps out the window.
    f. The house lonely and forlorn stood on the hill.
    g. He who hesitates is lost.
    h. Borrowed wives like borrowed books are rarely returned.
    i. Ann please call when your plane arrives.
    j. We left Phoenix on April 6 1972.
    k. Thomas Gray a professor at Cambridge wrote *Elegy in a Country Churchyard.*
    l. We thank you Susan for the lovely gift.
    m. Saturday August 21 1970 was an important day in my life.
    n. He felt moreover that she was right.
    o. Do as I say not as I do.

2. Supply commas for the nonrestrictive modifiers, but not for the restrictive modifiers:

    a. Golf which is a sport I really don't care for is her favorite sport.
    b. The story was written by Asimov who also happens to be a scientist.
    c. He travels the fastest who travels alone.
    d. A family that prays together stays together.
    e. I tried to get at the oranges that hung down into my neighbor's yard.

f. I ate the last piece of cake while you were at the store.
g. Tom who is my neighbor works in the library.
h. There were the keys dangling from the dashboard.
i. The car abandoned in an alley no longer had wheels.
j. That silver tray which almost everybody admires has been stolen.

The Colon

Use a colon to indicate that a series will follow:

Rum comes in three shades: white, gold, and dark.

We all know what a team needs to get somewhere: strong pitching, good hitting, a savvy manager, and plenty of speed and hustle.

Use a colon to introduce a formal statement or explanation:

There was no doubt about the outcome: he would be a ruined man forever.

Use a colon to introduce a quotation:

Pindar once wrote: "Hopes are but the dreams of those who are awake."

Use a colon to separate the hour from the minute in telling time:

My plane leaves at 9:00 P.M.

Use a colon after a formal salutation of a letter:

Gentlemen:
Dear Ms. Harris:

The Dash

Use a dash to indicate a sudden or abrupt break in thought:

He tried—and who could do more—to spare my feelings.
The desert—although not everyone will agree—is a place of beauty.

Use a dash after a summarizing series:

Deviled ham, chunky chicken, hearty roast beef—they all deliver that good, wholesome change of pace a great sandwich needs.

A basket of fruit, a fine natural cheddar—this is our pick for a really fresh dessert.

Use a dash to emphasize an important idea or to achieve suspense, climax, or irony:

For that rundown feeling—jaywalk.
The only way to stop smoking is to stop—no if's, and's, or butt's.
People are like beer cans—they crush when you step on them.

Use a dash in place of a comma to set off an appositive, if greater emphasis is needed:

No football player ever became great without practice—long, hard hours of practice.

Three things—imagination, patience, and fortitude—are necessary for success.

Use a dash instead of the more formal colon:

High schools used to recommend certain books for outside reading—*The Scarlet Letter, Moby Dick, The Grapes of Wrath,* and *A Tale of Two Cities.*

There are two objections to business monopolies—they eliminate competition and they fix prices.

The Ellipsis

Use the ellipsis mark (three periods separated by single spaces) to indicate that something has been omitted from quoted material:

ORIGINAL   For some people, the largest group, loneliness feels like desperation.

ELLIPTICAL   For some people . . . loneliness feels like desperation.

ORIGINAL   History, according to the accepted definition, began with writing, with recorded languages written on clay, stone, and papyrus, languages we have learned to decipher and to read, if not to speak.

ELLIPTICAL   History . . . began with writing, with recorded languages written on clay, stone, and papyrus. . . .

Notice that in the second example, the ellipsis comes at the end of a sentence. When the material to be omitted comes at the end of a sentence, add the ellipsis, but keep the period that ends the sentence. In other words, use four periods at the end of the sentence:

ORIGINAL   The Romans greeted everyone with a kiss—not just friends and relatives, but their cobblers, bakers, blacksmiths, and even tax collectors.

ELLIPTICAL   The Romans greeted everyone with a kiss. . . .

Use ellipsis marks to indicate that a series of numbers or a statement is incomplete or interrupted:

The odd numbers are 1, 3, 5, 7, 9. . . .
The speaker's voice droned on and on and. . . .

Parentheses and Brackets

Use parentheses to enclose ideas that explain, amplify, qualify, exemplify, or interpret:

The news that gets reported seems for the most part to be either bad (if something is really bad, it is good enough to report) or trivial.

The findings are that Americans (children and adults) watch between twenty-five and thirty hours of television a week.

Excessively wet kisses are unpopular (as the Danes say, "He is nice to kiss—when one is thirsty"); but a dry, tight kiss is usually regarded as either immature or inhibited.

Use parentheses to enclose cross-references:

(See page 762)
(See Appendix C)
The suicides and mental breakdowns of gifted people (see A. Alvarez's *The Savage God: A Study of Suicide*) are well known.

Use brackets to supply editorial explanations, comments, corrections, and omissions:

On the drawing, Michelangelo wrote: "Master Tommaso, if you don't like this sketch tell Urbino [Michelangelo's servant] in time for me to make another by tomorrow evening."

I was appalled to see the picture in your magazine of Dave Armstrong driving while holding his two-month-old baby in his lap ["Falling in Love with Four-Wheel-Drive," June 5].

"Unwarranted rises in oil prices mean more worldwide inflation and less [economic] growth. That will lead to more unemployment, more balance of payments difficulty, and [will] endanger stability. We deplore the [OPEC] decision."

Exercise

Insert dashes, colons, ellipses, parentheses, or brackets where needed in the following sentences:

a. Jones I think it was Jones called to say he would be late.
b. The legislature met in February actually in March.
c. You get a lot to like with a Marlboro filter, flavor, flip-top box.
d. New York is a city that moves to many rhythms the early morning jogger along the river, the ancient carriage clop-clopping through the park, and the jets crisscrossing the sky above.
e. Benjamin Franklin wrote "Fish and visitors stink after three days."
f. Gentlemen Please don't leave until 530 pm when the meeting is over.
g. Sign in reducing salon We Recycle Waists.
h. Patience long, long hours of patience is necessary to catch fish.
i. I can't remember all of the even numbers but to the best of my ability they are as follows 2, 4, 6, 8.
j. See Neumann's *Art and the Creative Unconscious.*
k. The article titled "The High Cost of Living" December 1973 contains many inaccuracies.

Quotation Marks

Use quotation marks to enclose the words of a speaker:

Again the answer was "Not guilty."

"Actually," says Dr. Marsh, "I doubt if you could drug a chicken. Their metabolic rate is too high."

Mother: "What's that?"
Child: "Fishy."
Mother: "Yes, and see him swimming?"

Use quotation marks to enclose quoted material:

As Gene Lyons wrote in *Harper's* magazine, "American students are not learning to write because nobody bothers to teach them how."

Like Heller's other novels, *Good as Gold* "is a book that takes large risks."

Chekhov, who was a doctor as well as a playwright, makes one of his intelligent characters say, "Lawyers merely rob you; doctors rob and kill you too."

Do not enclose indirect quotations in quotation marks:

Sigmund Freud, oddly enough, was among the more recent scholars to have contributed to the ridiculous notion that money can't buy happiness. Happiness, he said, is the adult fulfillment of childhood dreams, and children, he said, do not dream of money. Therefore, money does not buy happiness.

Use quotation marks to call attention to words as concepts:

Suppose a child must learn the category "bird." He or she must pay attention to features common to the class, such as wings, while ignoring color or size.

"Panic" is such a strong word that I was wondering whether to use it.

Some builders anxious to stimulate sales during slow periods will sometimes offer such "free" extras as self-cleaning ovens.

Use quotation marks for the titles of stories, songs, poems, magazine articles, essays, paintings, and so forth.
Titles of books, however, should be italicized or underlined.

In Cheever's short story "The Brigadier and the Golf Widow," Charlie Pastern and his wife build a bomb shelter in their garden.

Many of his best tunes, like "Fool's Gold," portray quite another character entirely.

Although Matthew Arnold's poem "Dover Beach" contains but one brief mention of personal affection, the primary theme is the power of love.

Use single quotation marks for quotations within quotations:

Theodore Roosevelt once wrote: "I am not sure that I understand 'Luke Havergal,' but I am entirely sure that I like it."

Sarah answered, "The salesman said to me, 'You will never find another new car at that price.' "

Punctuation and Quotation Marks

Put commas and periods inside quotation marks:

"It is perhaps as difficult to write a good life as to live one," said Lytton Strachey, author of *Eminent Victorians*.

Says Dr. V. I. Sarianich, "We've been trying to figure out the history of these people for years."

Put exclamation marks and question marks inside quotation marks if the quotation is an exclamation or a question; otherwise, put them outside:

"It's a catastrophe!" exclaimed Alfred Kahn, President Carter's chief inflation fighter.

"Save us! Save us!" shouted a Vietnamese refugee last week as Malaysian naval vessels towed two boats back out to sea.

"Is this for real?" she cried, and turned to her sister.

Can you imagine her saying, "You never help with the dishes"?

Put semicolons and colons outside quotation marks unless the punctuation mark is actually a part of the quotation:

Laura vowed, "You can be sure I'll meet you at 6:00 P.M."; but at 7:00 P.M. Laura still hadn't arrived.

I have only one reply to your comment that "Absence makes the heart grow fonder": "Out of sight, out of mind."

Exercise

Put in the proper punctuation along with quotation marks in the following sentences:

a. Sorry I'm late. I had to attend a seminar on acupuncture and I got stuck.
b. Kiwi is a four-letter word.
c. The politician droned on in the fields of sewage and pollution we can't afford to bury our heads.
d. Robert Frost wrote Stopping by Woods on a Snowy Evening.
e. She looked at him intensely and asked are you seeing someone else.
f. Marc asked the first person he met where is the French Quarter?
g. Small boy to playmate there's my mother at the scream door again.
h. This is a curious play Marian told her friend.
i. I think these new cars are roomy Helen said.
j. Would you go as far as the governor of Oregon who said I'd like to have you visit but please don't come to stay.

    k. Senator, the problem of getting rid of the radioactive waste products has not been solved yet, has it the reporter asked.

    l. American researchers use the term psychokinesis to describe psychic physical effects on both living and nonliving objects.

    m. When my two African friends told me the word for father in their tribal language was *dadi* I replied that the American word was similar.

The Apostrophe

Use an apostrophe followed by s *to form the possessive of a singular or plural noun not ending in* s:

child's	children's
man's	men's
woman's	women's
ox's	oxen's

Use an apostrophe without s *to form the possessive of a plural noun that ends in* s:

boys'	girls'
boxes'	ladies'
kings'	babies'

Use an apostrophe with s *or use the apostrophe alone to form the possessive of proper nouns ending in* s:

James's	James'
Burns's	Burns'
Jones's	Jones'

Singular common nouns ending in *s*, such as *boss*, add *'s*.

Use an apostrophe with s *to indicate the possessive case of indefinite pronouns:*

anybody's	everybody's
anyone's	someone's
one's	another's

Do not use an apostrophe, however, for possessive pronouns:

his	yours
hers	theirs
its	whose
ours	

Use an apostrophe to indicate that letters or figures have been omitted in contractions:

isn't	doesn't	class of '79
can't	I'll	best film of '60
o'clock	it's	hurricane of '53

Use an apostrophe with s to form the plural of letters, figures, and words that are referred to as words:

Don't forget to dot your i's.
Your 9's look like upside-down 6's.
You use too many *and*'s in your sentences.

Exercises

1. In the following sentences, put apostrophes only where they belong:

   a. Its seven oclock.
   b. I like its sleek lines.
   c. The car is his.
   d. If youre fired, you will receive a months salary.
   e. Ill accept no ifs or maybes for answers.
   f. The Smiths car is always parked in front of our house.
   g. Its not anybodys business.
   h. The doctors diagnosis stunned me.
   i. Do you believe in childrens rights?
   j. James guess is as good as anyones.
   k. The best film of 79 was *A Little Romance.*
   l. Hers are better than ours.

2. For each of the following words, write the possessive singular and plural forms (for example: *boy, boy's, boys'*).

   a. mat   f. creditor
   b. man   g. enemy
   c. lawyer   h. flowers
   d. reader   i. ambassador
   e. Jones   j. Picasso

Mechanics

Chapter 19

Mechanics

Capital Letters

Capitalize the first word of every sentence or group of words written as a sentence:

> Procrastination week has been called off.
> Beauty is in the eye of the beholder.
> Really? I never would have guessed.
> Tough luck. Perhaps you'll do better next time.

Capitalize the first word of each line of poetry (unless, of course, the line is from a poem in which the writer deliberately wants to avoid capitals):

> Tiger! Tiger! burning bright
> In the forests of the night. . . .

> Because I could not stop for Death,
> He kindly stopped for me. . . .

> My thoughts still cling to the mouldering past.

Capitalize the first word of a direct quotation (if the original begins with a capital letter):

> The doctor said gently, "Try to get some sleep."
> The newscaster made this announcement: "Skylab will fall into the Indian Ocean."

Capitalize proper nouns and proper adjectives:

> Cinderella, Oedipus, Laura, Hester
> Asia, Europe, Australia, Canada
> Middle Ages, Renaissance, Victorian Age
> Arizona State University, Museum of Modern Art

United Nations, American Embassy
Democratic party, Republican party
American cars, European clothes

Capitalize all titles that go in front of a proper name or that take the place of a proper name:

President Carter is losing his popularity.
The President is losing his popularity.

Senator Goldwater opposes recognizing Red China.
The Senator opposes recognizing Red China.

Do not capitalize a title if it does not substitute for the proper name:

WRONG He has been a College Professor for twenty-five years.
RIGHT He has been a college professor for twenty-five years.

Capitalize all words used to designate the deity:

God, the Messiah, the Supreme Being
Lord, Providence, the Holy Ghost
Savior, the Almighty, He, His, Him

Capitalize abbreviations of degrees, titles, and other capitalized words, including acronyms:

Ph.D., D.D.S., M.D., Jr., Sr.
USMC, UNESCO, NATO, NASA

Capitalize titles of magazines, books, plays, movies, chapter headings, and sections of a book:

Time, Psychology Today, Newsweek
Crime and Punishment, The Immense Journey
The American Dream, Antigone, King Lear
Alien, Picnic at Hanging Rock, Manhattan

Capitalize the names of holidays, the months of the year, and the days of the week:

Fourth of July, Christmas, Easter, Halloween
January, February, March, April, May
Sunday, Monday, Tuesday, Wednesday

Capitalize the names of points of the compass when they refer to geographical parts of the country or the world:

Admiral Byrd discovered the South Pole.
The oil crisis could cause a decline in the civilization of the Western world.
People are leaving the cold climate and settling in the South and in the West.

When these words refer to directions, they are not capitalized:

A cold wind came out of the northeast.
In New York, we lived on the west side of the park.

Exercise

Capitalize the words that should be capitalized in the following sentences:

a. he disliked english, but he liked latin.
b. I have classes on monday, wednesday, and friday because I work on tuesdays and thursdays.
c. professor garcia, my spanish professor, just returned from mexico.
d. one of wordsworth's best-known poems is *tintern abbey*.
e. mrs. adams called out: "please pick me up before dark."
f. sleeping beauty takes nytol.
g. the president will make his state of the union speech tonight.
h. the west is noted for its modern architecture.
i. mario puzo directed *the godfather*.

Italics

Italics are a special type of printing in which letters are slanted to the right to set off words or passages in a text. In typing, you can get a similar effect by underlining. In writing, draw a line under each word to be italicized.

Use italics to emphasize key words and expressions (quotation marks can also be used for this purpose):

Don't tell me that *she* is coming to the party?
That is *exactly* what I mean.
It's not *who* you love but *that* you love.

Use italics to call attention to a word as a word

(quotation marks can be used here, too):

> How do you spell *Mississippi?*
> You begin too many sentences with the word *and.*
> *Neat* is a much-used, general-purpose word.

Use italics for foreign words that have not yet been accepted as everyday English expressions. Consult a dictionary if you are in doubt.

> *au revoir*   *in medias res*
> *in absentia*   *fait accompli*

Use italics for titles of books, plays, magazines, movies, broadway shows, and so forth:

> *Catch-22, My Antonia, Prose Style*
> *Who's Afraid of Virginia Woolf?, Waiting for Godot*
> *Saturday Review, Atlantic, New Yorker*
> *Chorus Line, The Wiz, On the Twentieth Century*
> *Bloodline, Dracula, Rocky II, Superman*

Use italics for the names of trains, ships, planes, and the like:

> *Pioneer 10, Queen Elizabeth, Yankee Clipper*
> *U.S.S. Missouri, Apollo 8*
> *The City of New Orleans* (train)

Exercise

Put italics where necessary in the following sentences:

a. What does the phrase la dolce vita mean?
b. One of his best stories was printed in Harper's.
c. The word creed comes from the Latin word credere, which means to believe.
d. Chorus Line is one of the best broadway musicals I have seen in years.
e. The Sound and the Fury was made into a movie.
f. Does the Metroliner still carry passengers?

g. Frederico Fellini directed Amarcord.
h. Life magazine is back in print again.

Abbreviations

Abbreviations are shortened forms of words and phrases used to represent the complete forms. Abbreviations should follow the conventions set forth in dictionaries. In formal writing, few abbreviations are used. In scientific writing, technical writing, and some kinds of scholarly writing, many abbreviations are used. In ordinary writing, abbreviations are used moderately, in the following ways:

To name the days of the week and the months:

Mon., Tues., Wed., Thurs., Fri.
Aug., Sept., Oct., Nov., Dec.

To name organizations and government agencies:

NFL, AFL, MIT, NBC, CBS, AMA
FBI, IRS, HEW, CIA, NASA, AEC
OPEC, NATO, UNICEF, PLO, SALT

To name cities and states:

L.A., N.Y., S.F., N.O., Phil.
Calif., Ill., Mass., Ariz., Kans., Nebr.

To indicate names, titles, and degrees:

Mr., Messrs., Ms., Mrs., Jr., Sr.
Rev., Hon., Dr., St. (Saint), Msgr.
B.S., M.A., Ph.D., LL.D., D.D.S., M.D.

To indicate a large number of standard abbreviations:

i.e., e.g., etc., et al., vs., viz.
B.C., A.D., A.M., P.M., mph, mpg
O.K., G.I., TNT, TV, DDT, LSD, R.S.V.P.
anon., esp., intro., Ave., Inc., orig.
lbs., ft., no., amt., qt., vol., wt.

Exercises

1. Look up the following abbreviations in a good dictionary and write down their meaning:

   a. U.S.S.R.   f. cwt.   k. pseud.
   b. TNT   g. mgr.   l. P.S.
   c. Btu   h. rpm   m. mfr.
   d. anon.   i. hp   n. A.B.
   e. atty.   j. N.B.   o. AWOL

2. Change all of the abbreviations to words in the following sentences:

   a. The French Quarter in N.O. is an interesting place to visit.
   b. In the Olympics, the U.S. finished 1st in the 100-yd. dash.
   c. Eng. is my most difficult subject.
   d. There is a Main St. in many small cities in the United States.
   e. Meet me in front of the Federal Bldg. at 6:00 P.M.

3. Put abbreviations in place of the italicized words in the following sentences:

   a. *Doctor* Jones will lecture tomorrow at 6:30 P.M.
   b. The new *Chevrolet* Citation gets 24 *miles per gallon* in the city.
   c. The best coverage of sports is by the *American Broadcasting Company.*
   d. Los Angeles is often referred to as *Los Angeles.*
   e. Children watch too much *television.*

Hyphenation

The hyphen is a punctuation mark used to divide a word at the end of a line or to connect the parts of a compound word.

Use a hyphen to divide a word at the end of a line:

at-tic	back-lash	cou-pon
cir-cle	check-book	de-fense
hap-pen	furni-ture	la-ment

in-sult   ginger-bread   ma-jor
jour-nal   king-fish   pa-poose

Divide words between the prefix and the root:

anti-biotic	intro-duce	per-turb
bi-focal	trans-late	circum-scribe
ex-cavate	pan-orama	contra-dict
syn-thesis	auto-matic	un-concerned

Divide words between the root and the suffix:

king-dom	deriv-ation	woman-hood
prank-ster	secre-cy	mag-ic
riv-al	depend-ency	defeat-ist
diction-ary	sorc-ery	happi-ness

Do not divide words of one syllable:

WRONG   ben-ch, flu-sh, gra-sp
WRONG   hin-ge, my-th, pl-ate
WRONG   sai-nt, sei-ze, tr-ail

Divide compound words between the main parts of the compound:

COMPOUND WORD	HYPHENATED COMPOUND
pantyhose	panty-hose
airplane	air-plane
countdown	count-down
minibike	mini-bike
speedboat	speed-boat

Hyphenate compound numbers from twenty-one to ninety-nine:

twenty-two   thirty-three   forty-four

Hyphenate compound adjectives before a noun:

high-powered car	alien-looking beings
blue-gray eyes	fly-fishing lessons
time-consuming tactics	well-informed senator

Exercises

1. Consult a good dictionary. Then rewrite the following words as two separate words or as hyphenated words. If a word is all right as it is, simply recopy it.

   a. inlaws
   b. allinclusive
   c. anticommunist
   d. foulsmelling
   e. oldfashioned
   f. twothirds
   g. ninetynine
   h. reenter
   i. allpowerful
   j. cityhall

   k. selfmade
   l. hairstylist
   m. hitchhiker
   n. unAmerican
   o. icecream
   p. hotdog
   q. expresident
   r. flashbulb
   s. sodapop
   t. drivein

2. Check your dictionary to determine how the following words are divided into syllables:

   a. beware
   b. mileage
   c. troublesome
   d. disappear
   e. invalid

   f. reeducate
   g. coordinate
   h. precedes
   i. hypocritical
   j. hitchhiker

   k. logical
   l. proposition
   m. committee
   n. curious
   o. laser

Numbers

In formal writing, numbers are usually written out. In scientific writing, figures are frequently used. In informal writing, usage is divided. For such writing, the usual advice is to write out numbers that can be expressed in a word or two, but to use figures when the numbers are large.

Use figures to write dates and hours:

from 1936 to 1945   12:00 P.M.
between 1800 and 1900   6:15 A.M.
on January 1, 1980   9:45 P.M.

Use figures to write street numbers, but spell out the name of the street when the streets are numbered:

125 Apache St.   215 Fifth Ave.
2200 East Cairo Dr.   102 Forty-second St.

If, however, a word such as *North, South, East,* or *West* comes between the street number and the street name, and if there is no danger of misreading the address, then use figures instead of the street name:

CONFUSING   1016 16th St.
CORRECT   1016 Sixteenth St.
ACCEPTABLE   210 East 50th St.

Use figures to record sums of money, decimals, and percentages:

The shoes cost me $32.50.
Her grade point average was 3.5.
Living expenses rose by about 11.3 percent since January.

Use figures to record telephone numbers, volume numbers, chapter numbers, and page numbers:

My telephone number is 736–5234.
You will find an accurate description in volume I, chapter 5, page 17.

Express numbers in words when it is easy to do so; for large numbers, however, use figures:

one, three, five   first, second, third
32,320 students   2762 feet

If the figures are in round numbers, you may find it easier to write them out:

a thousand dollars   a hundred yards

Write out figures when they appear at the beginning of a sentence:

RIGHT   Fifty-two passengers got off the plane.
WRONG   52 passengers got off the plane.

Don't try to guess in writing Roman numerals. The following list of numbers will help to refresh your memory:

1	I	11	XI	30	XXX		
2	II	12	XII	40	XL		
3	III	13	XIII	50	L		
4	IV	14	XIV	60	LX		
5	V	15	XV	70	LXX		
6	VI	16	XVI	80	LXXX		
7	VII	17	XVII	90	XC		
8	VIII	18	XVIII	100	C		
9	IX	19	XIX	500	D		
10	X	20	XX	1000	M		

Exercise

Replace the figures in the following sentences with words:

a. My grade on the last test was 100.
b. 10 dollars is too much to spend on a tie.
c. For 12 months, she lived at 747 5th St.
d. Pick me up at 7:30 P.M.
e. 50,000 Frenchmen can't be wrong.
f. About 1000 new students enrolled in school in the fall.
g. Jody grew 3 inches taller this summer.
h. She is 7 years older than her husband.
i. I have 4 sisters and 2 brothers.
j. Tickets for the concert cost $10.

Spelling

Although it is true that the logical development of ideas is more important in writing than mechanics are, spelling is nevertheless important. Writers who habitually misspell words run the risk of confusing their readers and making their writing incoherent.

Writers who do misspell usually do not misspell a large number of words. (There are exceptions, of course.) Most so-called poor spellers misspell the same words over and over again. What can you do to improve your spelling?

1. *Master a few simple spelling rules.* Do not disdain memorization. Memorization and understanding should go together.

2. *Consult your dictionary frequently.* Notice how the dictionary spells each word and divides it into syllables.

3. *Proofread your writing carefully,* paying special attention to problems in spelling.

4. *Keep a notebook in which you put the words you frequently misspell.* Review these words regularly.

Spelling Rules

1. *The* ie *or* ei *Rule*

Put *i* before *e*, except after *c* or when pronounced like *a*, as in *neighbor* and *weigh:*

I BEFORE *E*	EXCEPT AFTER *C*	EXCEPTIONS
achieve	receive	either
relieve	deceive	neither
grief	conceit	leisure
chief	deceit	seizure
yield	receipt	foreign
wield	ceiling	sovereign

2. *The Final* e

Retain the final *e* before a suffix that begins with a consonant:

SILENT *E*	WITH SUFFIX	EXCEPTIONS
nine	ninety	truly
rude	rudeness	judgment
arrange	arrangement	argument
care	careful	awful
love	lovely	
move	movement	

Drop the final *e* before a suffix that begins with a vowel:

SILENT *E*	WITH SUFFIX	EXCEPTIONS
dine	dining	noticeable
grieve	grievance	courageous
admire	admiration	dyeing
fame	famous	hoeing
deplore	deplorable	canoeing
imagine	imaginary	mileage

3. *The Final* y

To form the plural of nouns ending in *y* preceded by a consonant, change the *y* to *i* and add *es:*

FINAL *Y*	*I* PLUS *ES*	PLURAL
lady	ladi + es	ladies
copy	copi + es	copies
story	stori + es	stories
fly	fli + es	flies

If a vowel comes before the final *y,* add *s:*

FINAL *Y*	PLUS *S*	PLURAL
monkey	monkey + s	monkeys
journey	journey + s	journeys
attorney	attorney + s	attorneys
chimney	chimney + s	chimneys

4. *Final Consonant*

For words of one syllable that end in a consonant preceded by a single vowel, double the consonant before a suffix that begins with a vowel:

hot	hott + est	hottest
plan	plann + ing	planning
drop	dropp + ed	dropped
man	mann + ish	mannish

For words of one syllable that end in a single consonant preceded by two vowels, do *not* double the final consonant before adding a suffix beginning with a vowel:

foam	foam + ed	foamed
reveal	reveal + ing	revealing
cool	cool + est	coolest

For words of one syllable that end in two consonants, do *not* double the final consonant before adding a suffix beginning with a vowel:

talk	talk + ing	talking
grasp	grasp + ed	grasped
strong	strong + est	strongest

For words of two or more syllables ending in a consonant, double the final consonant before a suffix beginning with a vowel *if the last syllable of the word is accented* and *if a single vowel precedes the consonant:*

regret	regrett + able	regrettable
allot	allott + ing	allotting
defer	deferr + ed	deferred

Both of these conditions must be met for this rule to hold true. These words do not meet both of the conditions:

obtain	obtain + ed	obtained
profit	profit + ed	profited
return	return + ing	returning

For words whose accent does not fall on the last syllable, do *not* double the final consonant before a suffix:

travel	travel + ed	traveled
enter	enter + ing	entering
benefit	benefit + ed	benefited

5. -cede *Words*

Spell words ending with the sound "seed" with *-cede:*

concede	precede	accede
recede	intercede	secede

There are four exceptions to this rule:

supersede	exceed
proceed	succeed

6. -ly *Suffix*

To form adverbs from adjectives ending in *l*, keep the *l* and add
-ly:

final	final + ly	finally
real	real + ly	really
accidental	accidental + ly	accidentally

7. -ful *Words*

When a word that ends in *ll* is used as a prefix or suffix in another
word, drop one *l:*

spite	spite + full	spiteful
fear	fear + full	fearful
fill	full + fill	fulfill

Exercises

1. Rewrite the following words, adding *ie* or *ei* where needed:

ch__f	p__ce	fr__nd
rec__pt	th__f	conc__ted
fr__ght	pr__st	n__ghbor
c__ling	rec__ve	for__gn
for__gn	dec__t	bel__f

2. Combine the following stems and suffixes. Review the rules for the
   final *e.*

type + ing	use + ing	improve + ment
care + ful	true + ly	excite + ing
use + less	write + ing	smile + ing
lone + ly	argue + ment	entire + ly
excite + ment	shine + ing	hope + ful
come + ing	extreme + ly	sincere + ly

3. Form the plural of the following nouns ending in *y* and the third-person
   singular of verbs ending in *y* (for instance, *reply, replies):*

worry	delay	berry
party	baby	study
employ	enjoy	journey
marry	carry	alley
memory	stay	turkey

4. Combine the following stems and suffixes. Remember the rules for doubling the final consonant.

propel + ed	wet + est	stir + ed
prefer + ence	plan + ing	prefer + able
happen + ing	refer + ing	steer + ing
excel + ing	reel + ed	develop + ed
benefit + ed	allot + ing	counsel + ing

5. Combine the following stems and suffixes:

total + ly	practical + ly	beauty + full
wonder + full	general + ly	sweet + ly
natural + ly	use + full	master + full

Bases, Prefixes, Suffixes

Familiarity with the elements that go to make up words can help you to avoid many spelling errors.

1. *Base (root or stem)*

The *base* of a word is the *main part* of a word. It cannot be subdivided into smaller units of meaning. There are two kinds of bases, free bases and bound bases. A *free base* is a stem that is a word by itself:

phone	sharp	green
ship	walk	live

A *bound base* is a stem that cannot stand alone as a complete word. It must be combined with prefixes, suffixes, or other bases:

alter-	nav-	neg-
tele-	vid-	magn-

You can combine bound bases with other word elements to get the following words:

alternative	navigate	negative
telephone	video	magnify

Compounding is the process of joining two or more bases to form a new word:

tele + graph	telegraph
cheese + burger	cheeseburger
over + pass	overpass

2. *Prefix*

A *prefix* is a word element *(morpheme)* that goes before the stem:

un-	im-	circum-
pre-	anti-	dis-

3. *Suffix*

A *suffix* is a word element that follows the stem:

-ly	-age	-y
-able	-ure	-ize

You can combine prefixes and suffixes with appropriate stems to get the following words:

unable	import	circumvent
prefix	antidote	disgrace
likely	shrinkage	noisy
teachable	failure	realize

Exercises

1. Write down the prefixes embedded in the following words. Then write down the meaning of each (for example: *advise*, prefix *ad*, meaning "to").

excavate	nonsense	convene
introduce	ambiguous	pervade
unconcerned	circumvent	proponent
bifocal	interfere	semifinal
contradict	avert	ultimate

2. Pick out the suffixes in the following words. What is the general meaning of each?

confidence	friendship	fortify
bookish	heritage	rivulet
favorite	assistant	donor
velocity	competent	dramatic
countless	humorist	realize

3. Write down the base or bases in the following words. Then write down the meaning of each.

audible	spectator	microphone
benefit	aqueduct	manuscript
finite	infidelity	vocation
liberate	transport	magnificent
patron	advent	tenacious

Homonyms

Homonyms are words that sound alike but that are different in meaning and often in spelling. They can cause trouble for the poor speller.

The following pairs of words are frequently confused. Know the differences in meaning and spelling.

We have *already* seen that movie.
They were *all ready* to go at seven.

She is *altogether* too advanced for this class.
My family was *all together* for Christmas.

The *capitol* building of Arizona has a copper dome.
He invested his *capital* in property.

He has *coarse* manners.
I could eat a three-*course* meal.

This week the election of the city *council* will be held.
My adviser gave me good *counsel.*

I get embarrassed by *compliments.*
These shoes *complement* your dress.

The list of words that follows was taken recently from a large sampling of student papers. Learn the differences in the meaning and spelling of these pairs.

accept/except	nob/knob
affect/effect	pain/pane
allusion/illusion	parish/perish
and/an	piece/peace
boarder/border	pitcher/picture
breaks/brakes	pored/poured
by/buy	principal/principle
coarse/course	revue/review
complement/compliment	right/write
creak/creek	see/sea
do/due	seen/scene
fore/for	sense/since
fowl/foul	sights/cites
here/hear	sum/some
latter/later	their/they're
maid/made	there/their
mined/mind	through/threw
no/know	to/too

Exercises

1. Use each word of the following pairs of homonyms in a separate sentence.

bare/bear	dye/die	pedal/peddle
boarder/border	fare/fair	weather/whether
cite/sight	led/lead	wave/waive
dessert/desert	minor/miner	stationery/stationary

2. What is the difference in meaning of the following pairs?

accept/except	quiet/quite	clothes/cloths
affect/effect	passed/past	principal/principle
choose/chose	formerly/formally	your/you're
all ready/already	council/counsel	lose/loose
who's/whose	brake/break	quite/quiet

Confusing Pairs

The following groups of words are responsible for a large number of spelling errors in student writing. Learn to use them correctly.

Than/then. Than is a conjunction. *Then* is an adverb.

> Joan sings better *than* Jane.
> *Then* I went to the movies.

Its/it's. Its is a possessive pronoun. *It's* is a contraction, meaning *it is.*

> I could tell it was a leopard by *its* spots.
> *It's* safer to wear seat belts.

To/too. To is a preposition, or it can be a part of an infinitive. *Too* is an adverb, meaning *also,* or a qualifier that patterns with adjectives.

> I'll send the tickets *to* you.
> If you want *to* swim, come over.
> The day is *too* hot for cutting the grass.

They're/their/there. They're is a contraction of *they are. Their* is a possessive pronoun. *There* is an adverb or a word used in a *there is, there are* construction.

> *They're* not for sale.
> *Their* nerves are on edge.
> Give me that book over *there.*
> *There* are several reasons for his behavior.

Advise/advice. Advise is a verb. *Advice* is a noun.

> I *advise* you to go to the dentist.
> I hope you take my *advice.*

Exercise

Rewrite the correct form of the word in parentheses in the following sentences:

    a. (Its, it's) too late to worry now.
    b. (There, their, they're) clothes are shabby.
    c. The movie was (to, too) long.
    d. Did you get a car (to, too)?
    e. (Its, it's) later (than, then) you think.
    f. (Its, it's) going to be a cold winter.
    g. This car gets better mileage (than, then) (its, it's) competitors.
    h. Come (to, too) your senses.
    i. She is prettier (then, than) ever.
    j. (There, their, they're) buying this house for an investment.

One Word or Two Words

Over the past few years, more and more students seem to be combining words that should be written as separate words and separating words that should go together. One reason for these errors may be a lack of knowledge about prefixes, suffixes, and bases. If you are having similar problems, check the spelling of such words in your dictionary and review the material on prefixes, suffixes, and bases.

Two words written as one:

alot/a lot	atleast/at least
alright/all right	socalled/so-called
maybe/may be	inspite/in spite

One word written as two:

where as/whereas	up set/upset
over come/overcome	all so/also
when ever/whenever	with out/without
no where/nowhere	my self/myself
any where/anywhere	its self/itself
to gether/together	in to/into
through out/throughout	pass time/pastime

Variant Spellings

Spelling takes effort. Student writers often get impatient with traditional spelling and look for economical ways to get to the point. Occasionally, they are influenced by shortened forms of words that they pick up from the media. There is nothing wrong with shortcuts, but if you decide to spell words in ways not indicated in the dictionary, it might be better to use these shortened forms in your less formal writing. In formal writing, they are usually unacceptable.

The following words keep recurring in student themes:

thru	tonite	tho
nite	lite	fore

These words are either clipped forms or alternate forms used to replace:

through	tonight	though
night	light	before

Look for these shortened forms in your own writing and replace them with conventional spellings.

(continued from page xvi)

Kate Mangelsdorf, "How I Compose." Reprinted by permission.

Ralph Nader, "The Safe Car You Can't Buy." From *The Nation*, April 11, 1959.

Human Nature article, "Second Look: Maps and the Mind." From "Second Look: Maps and the Mind," from *Human Nature*, January 1979. Copyright © 1978 by Human Nature, Inc. "Why Americans Can't Write." From "Why Americans Can't Write" in *Human Nature*, August 1978. Copyright © 1978 by Human Nature, Inc. Both reprinted by permission of the publisher.

Maria Oparnica, "Personal Methods of Composition." Reprinted by permission.

Psychology Today article, "The State of the Apes." Reprinted from *Psychology Today* Magazine. Copyright © 1974 by Ziff-Davis Publishing Company. Reprinted by permission.

Marjorie Kinnan Rawlings, *The Yearling*. Copyright © 1938. Reprinted by permission of Charles Scribner's Sons.

The Saturday Review article, "The Innate Grammar of Baby Talk," March 18, 1972. Reprinted by permission.

Shirley Rish, "The Composing Process" and "Environmentalist, Preservationist, and Conservationist." Both reprinted by permission.

Harry Wolcott Robbins and Roscoe Edward Parker, *Advanced Exposition*. Copyright © 1935. By permission of Prentice-Hall.

Edwin Arlington Robinson, "Richard Cory." From *The Children of the Night* by Edwin Arlington Robinson. Reprinted by permission of Charles Scribner's Sons.

Albert Rosenfeld, "Interferon: Medicine for Cancer & the Common Cold?" from *Saturday Review*, November 1978. Reprinted by permission of Saturday Review, Inc.

Bertrand Russell, "What I Have Lived For." In the *Autobiography of Bertrand Russell: 1872–1914*. Copyright © 1951, 1952, 1953 by Bertrand Russell. Copyright © 1967 by George Allen and Unwin Ltd. By permission of Little, Brown & Company in association with the Atlantic Monthly Press. From *A History of Western Philosophy*, copyright © 1945 by Bertrand Russell. Reprinted by permission of Simon & Shuster, Inc., New York.

John Ruskin, "The Stones of Venice." From *The Stones of Venice*. Copyright © 1970 by John Ruskin. An Everyman's Library edition. Published in the United States by E. P. Dutton & Company, Inc., and reprinted with their permission.

Susan Schiefelbein, "Children and Cancer," from *Saturday Review*, April 1979. Reprinted by permission of the Saturday Review.

George Bernard Shaw, *Man and Superman*. From *The Collected Works of Bernard Shaw*, Ayot St. Lawrence Edition, 1930. Reprinted with permission of The Society of Authors on behalf of the Bernard Shaw Estate.

Irwin Shaw, "The Eighty Yard Run." From *Mixed Company*, Collected Stories of Irwin Shaw. Copyright © Random House, Inc., and reprinted with permission.

Snowdrift shortening advertisement. From *What Every Good Cook Knows* in Effective Advertising Copy by Merrill DeVoe and published in 1956 by Macmillan, Inc. Reprinted by permission of Hunt-Wesson Foods, Inc.

Spanish olive advertisement. "Spanish Olives. How to Tell the Original." Reprinted with permission of the Spanish Olive Commission.

Steinway piano advertisement. Reprinted by permission of Steinway & Sons.

John Steinbeck, "Chrysanthemums" and "Flight." Both from *The Long Valley* by John Steinbeck. Copyright © 1938 by John Steinbeck. Copyright © renewed 1966 by John Steinbeck. Reprinted by permission of the Viking Press.

John Stidworthy, "Snakes of the World." From "Snakes of the World" by John Stidworthy. Copyright © 1971, 1974 by Grosset & Dunlap, Inc. Copyright © 1969 by the Hamlyn Publishing Group Ltd. Reprinted by permission of Grosset & Dunlap, Inc.

Suntory Royal Whiskey advertisement, "Suntory Royal. Slightly East of Scotch." Reprinted by permission of Suntory International.

Arandas Tequila advertisement. Reprinted by permission of Maidstone Importers, Inc.

Texaco advertisement. This advertisement provided by courtesy of Texaco Inc.

Timberland boot advertisement. Reprinted by permission of Timberland Co.

Leonore Tiefer, "The Kiss." From *The Kiss* by Leonore Tiefer, from *Human Nature*, July 1978. Copyright © 1978 by Human Nature, Inc. Used by permission of the publisher.

Time Magazine article, "Faces in the Crowd," June 24, 1974; "Guns, Death, and Chaos," February 26, 1979; "The Price of Stormy Petrol," February 26, 1979; "A Matter of Night and Day," February 26, 1979; "Carter: Black and Blue," March 5, 1979; "Suck Them In and Outflank Them," March 12, 1979; "Close Encounters of A Kind," March 12, 1979; "Intimate Glimpses of a Giant," March 12, 1979; "Searching for the Right Response," March 12, 1979; "The Flick of Violence," March 19, 1979; "Windup of a No-Win War," March 19, 1979. Reprinted with permission from TIME, The Weekly News Magazine; Copyright TIME, Inc.

(continued on page 624)

Index

(acknowledgments continued from page 618)

Mark Twain, "Mark Twain's Autobiography," Volume I. Copyright © 1942 by Clara Gabrilowitsch;
renewed 1952 by Clara Clemens Samossoud. Reprinted by permission of Harper & Row, Publishers,
Inc.

Olivia Vlahos, *New World Beginnings*. A selection
from *New World Beginnings* by Olivia Vlahos.
Copyright © 1970 by Olivia Vlahos. Reprinted by
permission of Viking Penguin Inc.

Webster's New Collegiate Dictionary advertisement. Reprinted by permission of G. & C. Merriam
Co., publishers of the Merriam Webster Dictionaries.

Whirlpool advertisement, from *Better Homes and
Gardens*, May 1979. Courtesy of the Whirlpool
Corporation.

Thomas Wolfe, "You Can't Go Home Again."
From *You Can't Go Home Again* by Thomas
Wolfe. Copyright © 1934, 1937, 1938, 1939, 1940
by Maxwell Perkins as Executor; renewed 1968 by
Paul Gitlin. Reprinted by permission of Harper &
Row, Publishers, Inc.

Virginia Woolf, *To the Lighthouse*. Published 1927
by Harcourt Brace Jovanovich, Inc. Reprinted by
permission. Also by permission from the Hogarth
Press Ltd. and the Literary Estate of Virginia Woolf.

Yamaha piano advertisement, from the *New
Yorker*, October 1972. Reprinted by permission of
Yamaha International Corporation.

New York Times article, "Kennedy Likened to Ben
Franklin." From *The New York Times*, January
1964. Copyright © 1964 by The New York Times.
Reprinted by permission.

Life Nature Library, *The Earth*. Courtesy of
Time-Life Books.

Y0-AGK-037

QUICK REFERENCE
GRAIN COOKING TABLE

1 cup uncooked grain, rinsed

Grain	Cups water	Tsp. Salt	Cooking time	Standing time	Cups Yield	Comments
Amaranth	1½	½	20 min.	—	2	Add salt after cooking
Pearl Barley	2⅔	1	40 min.	5 min.	3½	
Buckwheat (kasha)	2	1	12 min.	7 min.	3½	
Bulgar (medium grain)	2	¾	20 min.	5 min.	3 cups	
Job's Tears	3	½	1 hour + 40 min.	5 min.	3⅓	Discard discolored grains
Millet	2	½	30 min.	5 min.	4	
Whole Grain Oats	2	½	1 hour	10 min.	2½	
Quinoa	2	1	15 min.	5 min.	3½	Rinse grain very thoroughly before cooking
Rice, white long grain	2	1	20 min.	5 min.	3	Don't rinse
Rice, brown long grain	2¼	1	45 min.	10 min.	3½	Use ¼ cup more water for fluffier rice
Whole Grain Rye	2½	½	2 hours + 15 min.	10 min.	3⅓	
Teff	3	½	15 min.	—	3	Don't rinse
Whole Grain Triticale	2½	½	1 hour + 45 min.	10 min.	2½	Add salt only after cooking
Whole Grain Wheat	2½	½	2 hours	15 min.	2¾	Add salt only after cooking
Wild Rice	2½	¾	55 min.	10 min.	3⅔	

NOT FOR RESALE

THE

COMPLETE

WHOLE

GRAIN

COOKBOOK

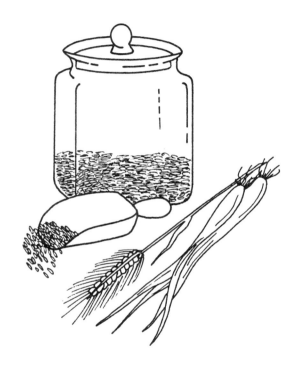

THE

COMPLETE

WHOLE

GRAIN

COOKBOOK

CAROL GELLES

DONALD I. FINE, INC.
NEW YORK

Copyright © 1989 by Carol Gelles

All rights reserved, including the right of reproduction in whole or in part in any form.
Published in the United States of America by Donald I. Fine, Inc. and in Canada by
General Publishing Company Limited.

Library of Congress Cataloging-in-Publication Data

Gelles, Carol.
  The complete whole grain cookbook / by Carol Gelles.
    p.   cm.
  Includes bibliographical references.
  ISBN 1-55611-155-X
  1. Cookery (Cereals)   I. Title.
TX808.G45   1989   89-45344
641.6′31—dc20   CIP

Manufactured in the United States of America

10 9 8 7 6 5 4 3 2 1

DESIGNED BY STANLEY S. DRATE/FOLIO GRAPHICS COMPANY, INC.

Contents

Acknowledgments

This book would have been impossible to complete without the help of many, many people: those who worked directly on the manuscript, others who provided technical information and advice, and, finally, all my friends and neighbors who tasted and critiqued the recipes.

My first thanks are to the worker bees: Holly Garrison, the best food editor a cookbook author could ever hope for, who was constantly there for me, checking up on all the details, bringing her creative talents to the project, and mostly for being such a good friend. And I can't neglect to mention Holly's husband, Gerry Repp, who cheerfully sat through endless meals consisting of one grain dish after another, and answered the phone a million times without once saying, "You again?" My parents, Charlotte and Ernest Gelles, who toiled for hours calculating the nutritional values for each and every recipe, and, of course, for just being all-around terrific parents and people. Roger Vergnes at Donald I. Fine, Inc., who worked to turn my manuscript into the book I had hoped for.

And thanks, too, to the tasters; above all, my sister, Sherry, who is a wonderful cook herself and who ate more grain dishes in a short period of time than anyone should ever have to. Her ideas and suggestions added so much. The entire chapter on millet, that most "difficult" of grains, should probably be dedicated to Danusia and Elliot Cohen, who were excellent tasters and good sports as well. Marie and Bob Riesel and Michele Pigliavento, who were my muffin and bread tasters. Paula Rudolph, Kevin Reed, Jesse, Erica and Leah Weissman, who were always so willing to come into the city on the spur of the moment for an impromptu tasting. The night staff at Proskauer Rose Goetz & Mendelsohn.

And thanks to the technical advisers: Rebecca Wood, who was very generous with her time, as well as contributing her recipe for injera. The many people at the Kansas Wheat Commission and

Kansas State University. The staffs at Arrowhead Mills and Eden Foods.

And, finally, very special thanks to all my good friends, who were always there to lend an ear and who kept the faith through all my "brilliant" ideas.

*To my mother and father
for their unending love and support.*

BUCKWHEAT	OATS

**LEGEND
TO
JACKET
GRAINS**

BASMATI BROWN RICE	SOFT GRAIN BROWN RICE
POT BARLEY	CORN
BASMATI WHITE RICE	ARTICULATED PEA
MILLET	QUIBOA

OAT BRAN	HARD WHEAT	AMARANTH	OATMEAL
TEFF	WHOLE GRAIN RYE	SOFT WHEAT	KASHA (ROASTED BUCKWHEAT)

Foreword

The idea for this book started about three years ago when I went on vacation with my friend, Lysa (Randy) Kraft. At her suggestion, we spent five days at the Norwich Inn & Spa in Connecticut which serves absolutely delicious food that emphasizes high complex carbohydrates, low sodium, and low fat. Of all the many wonderful dishes we enjoyed, whole-wheat berries and kasha salad were my very favorites.

As soon as I got home, I dashed to the nearest health-food store and scooped up grains from nearly every bin. I brought them home and only then did it hit me: here I was, sitting with a bunch of bags, all filled with good stuff, and I had no idea how to cook any of it. And so this book began.

When I started seeking cookbooks and other reference sources to help me understand and prepare my little collection of grains, I found that there wasn't a single, all-in-one reference book that answered even a small number of my questions. The need for one complete book on the subject, with the kinds of recipes I wanted to cook and eat, became obvious.

I chose to make the recipes in this book as specific as possible and included separate sections about things that I think are important. I was specific about amounts called for, pan sizes, and cooking times, so that even inexperienced cooks would have no difficulty following the recipes, and I could feel comfortable knowing that the results would be the same as mine. Old hands in the kitchen may prefer recipes that are less exact. They will undoubtedly take the liberty of just chopping up a small carrot instead of measuring out the half cup chopped carrot that I call for, for example, and will adjust the seasonings to suit themselves.

For the most part, the recipes also reflect the kinds of food that I enjoy (which is just about everything, come to think of it), and the seasonings are, more or less, to my taste. For example, as you use the book, you will find that I have a preference for spicy (although not fiery) food, and the first time you cook some of these foods you may want to start with just half the amount of these seasonings.

I believe that the recipes in this book will appeal to a large number of people with diverse tastes. I have tried to include things that will appeal both to the gourmet as well as to those who like simple, down-home food. Vegetarians are not neglected, nor are meat eaters. And parents will find lots of recipes that kids will like.

I strongly believe that grains are an important food for the future, and have great value as part of the human diet, monetarily, nutritionally, and simply as good food. So, it is my fondest hope that this book will awaken your interest (not to mention your taste buds) in this fascinating subject.

INTRODUCTION TO GRAIN COOKING: GETTING STARTED

◇

What Is Grain?
Grain Terminology
Milling
Buying Grains
Storing Grains
About Cooking Grains
Microwaving Grains
Alternate Cooking Methods
Freezing
Ingredients Used in These Recipes
Equipment
Nutritional Analysis
Health Tips
Vegetarian Recipes
Sprouting
Sources

What Is Grain?

Grains are grasses that bear edible seeds. Both the plant and the seed (kernel) are referred to as grain. Grains are also known as cereals (usually when referred to in nutritional terms). The seeds are the fruit of the grain, and, like all seeds, they are the vehicles of reproduction and are the part of the plant that contain the most nutrients.

Each kernel of grain is composed of four parts:

Outer husk or hull: This is the inedible seed covering, which is removed from grains that are intended for human consumption. In some grains, such as barley, the hull clings tightly to the grain and must be removed by grinding or pearling. Other grains, such as wheat, have hulls that are loosely attached and can be removed by threshing. Then there are some grains that are "naked" and don't have any hull at all. A grain that has had the outer hull removed is considered a whole grain if the bran and germ are still intact.

Bran: This is the protective covering on the grain and is several layers thick. The inner layers are called the aleurone layers. Bran is rich in B vitamins and minerals and is an excellent source of dietary fiber. It is the bran layer, plus the germ, that is removed from the grain when it is polished to produce "white" products such as white rice or pearled barley.

Germ: The germ is the embryo of the seed and is responsible for germination. It is this part of the kernel that produces the sprout; it is rich in enzymes, fat, and protein, as well as certain vitamins and minerals. Germ is also polished away when grains are refined.

Endosperm: This is the starchy center of the grain. It is high in carbohydrates and its purpose is to nourish the seed after it sprouts. White rice, pearled barley, and that part of the wheat that is made into white flour are all endosperms.

GRAIN KERNEL
(cross section)

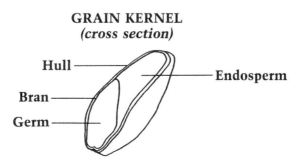

Hull —— Endosperm

Bran ——

Germ ——

Grain Terminology

Berry: The whole grain with just the outer hull removed. Whole grains that have loosely attached hulls and require very little mechanical processing (wheat, for instance) are called berries. Grains that have tightly attached hulls and need milling to remove them are called groats. It is not unusual to use the terms berry and groat interchangeably, since the product is still the whole grain with the bran and germ intact.

Bleached: After the endosperm has been ground into white flour, it can be treated chemically to make it even whiter. White flour is available bleached or unbleached.

Converted: This is a term used by the makers of Uncle Ben's rice and refers to a process in which the rice is steamed and then dried before the bran is removed. The process supposedly "seals in" more of the rice's nutrients.

Enriched: Because so many of the nutrients in grain are lost when the bran and germ are removed, many processors put vitamins back into the grains. This is especially true of long-grain white rice and breads. In the case of long-grain white rice, avoid rinsing before cooking or you will wash away the added vitamins.

Fiber: This is sometimes referred to as *roughage* or *bulk*, and is the cellular structure of the plant (*all* plants, as a matter of fact), which humans cannot digest. The fiber in grains is found primarily in the bran and the germ, those parts of the grain that are so often discarded during milling. There are two types of fiber: water insoluble and water soluble. Wheat bran is an insoluble fiber, and it is this type of fiber that provides bulk in the diet and is now thought to help prevent certain kinds of cancer and other less serious intestinal disorders. Oat bran, on the other hand, is water soluble, and it is this kind of fiber that is currently being studied for its ability to lower blood cholesterol. Both kinds of fiber are necessary in a healthy diet.

Flakes: When hulled grains are steamed and flattened between rollers, they are called flakes. The major advantage of flakes is that they cook faster than whole grains.

Flour: Finely ground hulled grains. Flour can be ground from the whole grain, including the bran and germ, but whole-grain flour does become rancid more quickly than flour made of just the endosperm (white flour).

Grits: Although the word hominy (which means hulled corn) comes to mind in connection with grits, grits are simply any coarsely ground, hulled grain. Any grain can be ground into grits.

Groat: A whole grain with only the outer hull removed. A groat differs from a berry in that its hull has been removed by polishing, a more abrasive process than threshing.

Meal: Very coarsely ground flour. Any grain can be made into meal.

Pearling: The process by which the outer hull is removed by grinding. For example, pot barley has been pearled until the hull is removed, but the bran is still intact. Further pearling will remove the bran and germ, resulting in pearl (or pearled) barley.

Polish: This is a term for both the process of grinding off the hull and also for a by-product of that process. Polish is a flour that still retains some of the bran and some of the wheat.

Rolled: The process of steaming grains and then pressing them between large metal rollers. Flakes tend to be thicker than those designated as rolled. For example, oat flakes are thicker than rolled oats.

Sprout: A young plant shoot. Sprouts are good sources of nutrition and can be eaten raw or cooked. Any grain or bean can be sprouted when the proper techniques are used. (See Sprouting, page 20.)

Threshing: The method used to separate the hull from the grain by beating, rather than by polishing or grinding.

Whole grain: Usually refers to a groat or a berry that has had neither the bran or germ removed. The term is also often used to describe products made with whole grains. Technically, it could also mean an unhulled grain.

Milling

Milling is the process of separating the various parts of the grain. It can start in the field when the grains are cut and put through a thresher, which, for grains with loose husks (wheat, rye, triticale, and hulless barley), will separate the grain from the husk very easily. Then all that remains to be done is to remove the debris and these grains are ready for further milling. Grains that have husks that adhere more tightly will have to be ground or pearled, a more abrasive process than threshing. These husking and sifting processes, as well as the further processing used to remove the bran and the germ, are correctly called decortication. Other milling processes will grind endosperm or whole grains into flour, steam and roll grain into flakes, or crack whole grain into pieces.

Occasionally you may note the term *stone ground* on a package. This means that the grain was ground with a stone mill rather than steel mill. Since stone grinders are gentler and more precise than steel grinders, they are less likely to overgrind the grain. And since there is also less chance of the germ being damaged by this method, stone-ground products will not become rancid as quickly as steel-ground products. Products that are stone ground will always say so on the package. They are also more expensive than steel-ground grains.

Buying Grains

The number of options you have when it comes to buying grains depends largely upon what kind of grain you want to buy. All of the popular grains are available, neatly packaged, at the supermarket. You can count on the fact that these grains have been pretty well picked over and cleaned before packaging.

However, if organically grown products are important to you, you might consider doing your grain shopping at a health-food store, where the selection will be wide and you will probably also have the option to buy in bulk. The advantage of buying in bulk is obvious: you save money, and you can also buy exactly what you need. If the health-food store is new to you, have a look around before you buy anything. Make sure that the general environment is clean and appetizing and that the storage bins are covered. Also, look carefully at the bin you are ready to buy from and make sure there are no insects moving around in the grain. (No store that I can think of would intentionally carry insect-laden grains, but even the best of stores can occasionally have a problem.)

If a health-food store is not available to you, then you can consider buying your grains from a mail-order source that is usually direct from the growers and/or distributors.

It is also possible, if you live in a rural area, to purchase grains directly from a feed mill. However, although these grains may be perfectly wholesome and edible, since they are not intended for human consumption they may not be very well cleaned. And, since picking out this extraneous material is a long and laborious task, you may decide it's better to go to conventional sources for your grains.

Seed houses are another possible source *that I would strongly advise against,* unless you are absolutely sure that the grains being sold are not treated with fungicides, pesticides, or other chemicals that would make them dangerous for human consumption.

Storing Grains

The germ of whole grains contain oils that can turn rancid, especially if the grain is improperly stored. Rancid foods give off a most unpleasant odor, and I generally use my nose to tell me whether or not a grain is still fresh and usable.

Ideally, all grains should be refrigerated to retard spoilage. This is especially true for whole-grain products, which tend to have a shorter shelf life than processed grains. Given that most people do not have endless refrigeration space, the next best thing is to place the grains in containers with tight-fitting lids and store them in a cool, dry spot. Even under ideal storage conditions, it is entirely possible that an insect egg or two may have found its way into your grain. By keeping each grain in a tightly sealed container, you can at least contain the infestation to that one grain.

Dampness is another enemy of grains, since they absorb moisture readily and can quickly turn moldly.

As a rule of thumb, whole-grain products should be stored at room temperature for no longer than one month. If you wish to store them for much longer, they should be refrigerated. Untoasted wheat and other grain germs, because they contain high levels of oil, should always be stored in the refrigerator. Toasted germs can be stored at room temperature.

About Cooking Grains

If the grains that are the basis for every single recipe in this book are not cooked properly, it's unlikely that the dish you are preparing will turn out successfully. There are so many variables in cooking grains that absolute cooking instructions are impossible. On the whole, I found the cooking instructions given on the packages of most grains to be very unreliable. I suggest that you follow my cooking instructions, regardless of what the package says. Here are a few of the major factors that figure into the perfectly cooked grain:

Type of cookware used: Grains should be cooked in a reasonably heavy saucepan with a tight-fitting lid. I used Farberware-brand cookware, which is comparable to the cookware most people own, for testing the recipes in this book. The lids, though certainly tight fitting, do allow a little steam to escape. If your pans have lids that fit tighter and don't allow any steam to escape, you may need a little less cooking water. Or you may need more water if your lids allow more steam to escape.

Temperature of cooking water: Although I call for the grains to be cooked in simmering water, our ideas of simmering may be slightly different. If your grains simmer more quickly than mine did, they will probably cook in a little less time, or at least the water will evaporate more quickly. It's always best to check near the end of cooking time to make sure the grains are not overcooking. Or the water may have evaporated, but the grains are still undercooked. In this case you will have to add a little boiling water and allow the grain to cook longer. If you are cooking at a lower simmer, then it may take a little longer for all of the water to be absorbed. In this case, you may find the cooked grain to be a little sticky.

Age of the grain: As grains grow older they also dry out. Freshly harvested grain may need less water to cook than grain that has been around a while. Unfortunately, there's no way of knowing how old your grain is, so if it has cooked the prescribed amount of time and you find that it is still undercooked, simply add a little boiling water and let it continue to simmer.

Personal preference: I prefer my grain the same way I do my pasta— al dente, or slightly chewy. If you like your grains softer, then you will require a little more water and a little more cooking time.

Bearing in mind these factors, here is the basic method for the preparation and cooking of all grains.

Sorting: If you've purchased loose grains, you may find that they are not as well cleaned as the popular packaged brands. So look them over and pick out any obvious foreign objects.

Measuring: Measure out the grains in a nested measuring cup (not a glass measuring cup that is intended for liquids), filling it to the top, then leveling it off.

Rinsing: For the most part, rinsing whole grains is optional. I feel that if the grain is not so small that it would fall through the strainer, and so long as it is not enriched, rinsing it to remove dust and debris is not a bad idea. However, some experts contend that rinsing washes away some of the valuable nutrients, so it's up to you.

If you choose to rinse, put the measured grain into a strainer and run it under cold tap water, then let it drain. Never rinse grains before storing them or they will mold. Rinse just before cooking.

I should note here that some grains require elaborate rinsing procedures. Specific directions for rinsing are given with those particular grains.

Cracked, rolled or other processed grains don't need rinsing.

Measuring the cooking liquid: Measure in a glass measuring cup, checking the measurement at eye level.

Adding salt: Each grain reacts a little differently to salt in the cooking water. Most grains cook well in salted water, and for those grains you can add salt to the saucepan when you add the water.

Some grains (amaranth, wheat berries, triticale, and Waheni brown rice) do not absorb liquid properly if it is salted, and they should be salted after cooking. The result of cooking these grains in salted water will be undercooked grains and only half of the liquid absorbed by the end of cooking time. Also, you will probably need to add less salt after cooking than if you were to add it before cooking for the same degree of saltiness. Needless to say, if you are watching your sodium intake, then cook the grains without adding any salt.

Adding the grain and simmering: When the water or other cooking liquid has come to a full boil, stir in the grain and then wait for the water to return to a boil. Reduce the heat so that the mixture is just simmering. Cover and start timing.

If you're cooking on an electric range, reduce the heat to low as soon as the grain is added, since the burner will remain hot long enough for the mixture to return to boiling.

On a gas range, keep the flame high until the water boils, then reduce the heat to the lowest possible setting, adjusting it upward until the mixture simmers.

The exact setting to achieve a simmer will vary from range to range, and even from one burner to another. What you are looking for is for the surface of the water to remain calm with just a few bubbles breaking the surface.

Sometimes gas ranges can't maintain a low enough flame for cooking grains at a simmer without going out. In that case, invest in an inexpensive simmering pad which will allow you to simmer at a higher temperature.

Checking for doneness: All things being equal, the grain should be cooked when almost all of the liquid is absorbed. There are three methods for determining if the grain is done:

1. Remove the lid and tilt the saucepan. If you don't see any water running out from the grain, then you can safely assume that it has evaporated. Let the saucepan stand, covered, on the cool burner for 5 to 10 minutes to allow any small amount of water that may be left on the bottom to be absorbed.
2. Lift the lid toward the end of cooking time. When holes appear between the grains, all of the water has been absorbed. (I prefer the first method of removing the pan from the heat, which is just before the holes appear, because then I am reasonably assured that the grain has not begun to stick to the bottom of the pan.)
3. Taste a few grains. Are they the consistency that you like? If so, the grain is ready, and you can simply drain off any water that remains in the pan.

Fluffing: Grain should not be stirred during cooking, because it will bruise the grains and make them sticky. After cooking, you can use a fork to fluff the grains, if you like, and you can also add salt to those grains that must have the salt added after cooking.

Microwaving Grains

Microwave instructions are given in the basic cooking directions for each grain.

Except for those grains that require very long cooking times, microwaving will not save a lot of time. It does, however, have the important advantage of producing consistent results, and all those varying factors of cooking grains on the stovetop are eliminated. In addition, many of the grains come out with a better texture

I usually recommend using the microwave only for cooking grains that will be needed, precooked, for a recipe. The microwave instructions in this book are for 600–700 watt microwave ovens. Smaller ovens will require longer cooking times.

Alternate Cooking Methods

Stove-top and microwave cooking methods are given with each grain in this book. However, for those who find themselves discouraged by the long cooking times required for some of the grains, here are some shortcut cooking strategies that work quite well:

Precooking: If the recipe you are planning to use calls for cooked grain, cook the grain a day or two in advance, and then follow the directions given for reheating it.

Slow cooker: This method is good for cooking grains that will be needed, precooked, for a recipe. Place both grain and liquid into a slow cooker (crock pot), and allow it to cook slowly during the day. When you get home at night, the grain should be cooked. (Please note that crock pots are no longer recommended for recipes that include meat.) You may find that grains cooked in a crock pot will absorb less liquid, so just drain off any excess.

Soaking: Following the general cooking directions, measure out the grain and the water and place them in the saucepan. Cover the pan and allow the grain to soak overnight or all day. Then cook for ⅓ less time than given in the general directions.

Pressure cooker: A pressure cooker will reduce the cooking time for grains, but you must be careful that you do not cook too much grain at one time. The starches given off during cooking can bubble up and clog the pressure gauge. Read the instructions that come with your pressure cooker, and call the manufacturer (nowadays, most manufacturers have telephone numbers for consumers to call with questions about their products) for specific information about cooking grains.

Freezing

I have found that cooked grains that have been frozen tend to become waterlogged and lose their al dente consistency. However, it is nice to have cooked grains on hand in the freezer, so you can try it and make the final judgment yourself. However, soups and stews that contain cooked grains freeze very well. For other dishes containing grains, here again it's a matter of personal preference as to whether or not you find the thawed and reheated grain dishes acceptable.

Ingredients Used in These Recipes

Eggs are always large.

Butter is always lightly salted.

Specific amounts of **salt** and **pepper** are given only as a guide. Feel free to alter them to suit your own taste.

Can sizes may be approximate. For instance, if the recipe calls for a 15-ounce can, and you have one that is 14 to 16 ounces, go ahead and use it.

Unless otherwise stated, **canned broths** are the ready-to-use variety, that come in can sizes of either 13¾ ounces or 14½ ounces.

Dried **herbs** are used in whole form, not ground.

Spices, when not specified as ground, are used whole, except for black pepper.

When the recipe calls for minced **garlic,** you can put the garlic through a press if you don't feel like mincing it.

Red-wine **vinegar** can be substituted in equal parts for any type of vinegar specified in a recipe.

Fresh **lemon juice** is always used in these recipes. Reconstituted lemon juice has a chemical flavor I don't like.

Fresh chopped **parsley** (either curly or flat) is always used. If necessary you can substitute 1 teaspoon of dried parsley for 1 tablespoon fresh parsley.

Scallions are also known as green or spring onions in certain regions.

Heavy cream and whipping cream are different terms for the same product.

Yeast: There are a number of recipes in this book that call for yeast. I almost always use the packets of active dry yeast that are usually sold in strips of three, but you can also use the little bricks of compressed (fresh) yeast, if you prefer.

Yeast is alive—a one-cell fungus—therefore it's important to use yeast by the expiration date on the package. When fed with the flour and sometimes the sugar that it is mixed with it, the yeast will begin to divide and to convert the carbohydrates in the flour into alcohol and carbon dioxide. It is this gas that gives dough its typical "yeasty aroma" and makes it swell and rise. (The alcohol will evaporate as the bread bakes.)

Most complete cookbooks devote at least one chapter, and lots of pictures, to the topic of baking with yeast. And by now there are undoubtedly videotapes available on the subject, too, so you can actually *see* what risen dough looks like, and how to knead, for instance. The old-fashioned direct approach is another way to learn this skill: ask a friend who has baked with yeast to show you how to do it.

Equipment

You probably already own most of the equipment necessary for preparing the recipes in this book. The following are what I consider essential for any well-equipped kitchen:

Good pots: For these recipes you will need a 2-quart saucepan with a tight-fitting lid (most of the grains are cooked in this size saucepan), a large skillet, a large saucepot (for soups and such) with a lid, a heavy 4-quart saucepan or a Dutch oven with a tight-fitting lid, and a double boiler (to prevent delicate sauces and other foods from overcooking). You can usually rig up a double boiler by resting a small pan into a larger one, but the real thing is best.

Sharp knives: They make the difference between easy work and hard labor. You can get along nicely with a 10-inch chef's knife (for chopping), a long serrated bread knife (for slicing breads), and a paring knife.

Measuring utensils: Use glass measuring cups for measuring liquids. Pour the liquid into the cup and then check the cup at eye level to make sure that the measurement is exact.
Use nested measuring cups for measuring dry ingredients. These metal or plastic cups are nested in four sizes: ¼ cup, ⅓ cup, ½ cup, and 1 cup; sometimes there are ⅛-cup or 2-cup measures, as well. To use these cups correctly, dip the measuring cup into the dry ingredient and lift out a generously full cup. Using a flat utensil, such as the back of a knife, level the top, returning the excess to the package or canister. When measuring brown sugar, press it firmly into the cup. Dry ingredients can also be spooned into the measuring cup if it's not possible to scoop them.
Remember that glass and nested measuring cups are not interchangeable. The general rule is that if it pours use the glass measuring cup. If it plops, or is dry, use the nested cups.
Standard measuring spoons are necessary for small amounts of either dry or liquid ingredients.

3 teaspoons	= 1 tablespoon
4 tablespoons	= ¼ cup
5 tablespoons plus 1 teaspoon	= ⅓ cup
8 tablespoons	= ½ cup
2 cups	= 1 pint
4 cups (or 2 pints)	= 1 quart

Simmering pad: In the old days this would have been an asbestos pad. Now it is a metal circle with a cardboardlike material inserted in the center. You insert this gadget between the flame and your pot if you find that you cannot adjust the heat source to maintain an even, slow simmer.

Mixing bowls: One large, one medium, and one small.

Colander: Essential for thorough draining.

Vegetable peeler: Although you can peel vegetables and fruits with a paring knife, this gadget saves time and, unless you're a real expert, doesn't waste as much of the flesh.

Strainer: A large one for rinsing grains before cooking.

Timer: Otherwise it's easy to forget when you put something on the stove or in the oven.

Spatulas: At least one rubber spatula for scraping mixtures out of bowls, and one wide metal spatula for turning pancakes and the like.

Wooden spoons: The professional cook's choice for stirring.

Whisk: For stirring ingredients that would otherwise lump; for use as a beater, if you don't own an electric mixer.

Grater: Preferably a four-sided grater that can shred as well as grate.

Oven thermometer: Preferably a mercury or a spring-type thermometer. The correct oven temperature can make the difference between an outstanding dish and a dismal failure. An oven thermometer will enable you to check the calibration of your oven.

Baking pans: For baked goods, especially cakes, muffins, and breads, it's important that you use the size pan called for, otherwise baking times will not be accurate.

Strongly Suggested Equipment

Blender and/or **food processor:** I use the blender for processing liquids and the processor for chopping and shredding.

Microwave oven: You will find the microwave is great for cooking and reheating grains. It is also incredibly helpful for small jobs such as melting butter and chocolate, bringing cream cheese and butter to room temperature, and heating milk.

Electric mixer: Either stand-alone or hand-held, an electric mixer will produce a much better baked product than one beaten with a spoon or a whisk, and it saves a lot of time and elbow grease, too.

Nonstick cookware: If you're watching your fat intake, this cookware is a god-send; it allows you to decrease the fat in your cooking significantly. It also minimizes sticking if you accidentally overcook your grain.

Pastry blender: Although you can cut shortening into flour with two knives, this gadget is much easier to use and much more efficient.

Garlic press: When you are too hurried to mince garlic by hand, a press (especially a self-cleaning one) makes quick work of this task.

Instant-read thermometer: If you're going to do much baking with yeast (this thermometer is wonderful for taking the temperature of the water in which the yeast is dissolved), or if you're just picky about exactly how done your meat is, this gadget is a dream come true. Just insert it into the food to get an accurate temperature reading within seconds. Don't leave the thermometer in the roast as it bakes or you will ruin the thermometer.

Steamer: Whether you select an Oriental bamboo steamer or a metal one, these are wonderful for reheating grains, as well as for cooking short-grain rice and vegetables to perfection.

Crock pot or **slow cooker:** See Alternate Cooking Methods on page 11.

Equipment That's Nice to Own, But Not Essential

For the most part, these are large, and sometimes expensive, single-use gadgets. If you do a lot of whatever it does (or if you have a lot of spare storage space) you might consider purchasing one or more of them:

Wok: You can certainly use a large skillet for stir-frying, but a wok does a better job. If you like lots of vegetables in your diet, all cooked tender-crisp, or if you intend to do much Oriental cooking, a wok is a good investment.

Rice cooker: In some parts of the world where rice is eaten every day and at almost every meal, owning a rice cooker is like owning a toaster. A rice cooker makes perfect rice every time with no fuss or bother, so if you eat a lot of rice you may want to consider buying one.

Waffle iron: Everybody loves waffles; they're a great way to enjoy many whole-grain products, and this book includes a number of recipes for them. Waffle irons come in various sizes, and nonstick coatings make waffles that stick to the iron a thing of the past.

Couscousiere: This is a rather large two-tiered pot. Holes in the top part allow you to cook the couscous over the stew. (Obviously, it cooks couscous better than anything else in the world.)

Tortilla press and comal: These are necessary for making authentic tortillas. If you have the press, you might as well have the comal (the cast iron griddle used for cooking tortillas) or vice versa.

Pizza-making equipment: If you just love homemade pizza, having a peel, which is a big wooden paddle used to slide the pizza in and out of the oven, may be an important item. A pizza wheel will cut very neat slices, but a sharp knife works almost as well. The stones that are used to line the oven will superheat it, which results in a very crisp crust, quickly. (Although, using these stones, I have occasionally ended up with a crust that was burnt to a crisp.) My method for preheating a baking sheet, as described in the pizza recipe on page 63, works just fine.

Pasta machine: There are two types of pasta machines available. One is hand cranked and will roll out the pasta dough and cut it into different widths. The second type is an electric machine that will mix, knead, and then extrude the dough into many different shapes. I suggest buying the less expensive hand-cranked model first in case the thrill of pasta making wears thin.

Bread-making machine: This is similar to the electric pasta machine and also very expensive. You put the ingredients into the machine and it mixes, kneads, proofs, and then bakes the bread all by itself. The quality of the bread it makes depends largely on the ingredients you put into it. Because I do so much baking in my work, I use one of these machines to mix and knead the dough, but then I shape it and bake the bread myself.

Grain mills: These appliances or attachments will grind your grains into flour. Most are fairly expensive and on the large side, but the obvious advantage is that you will always have fresh whole-grain flour when you want it. My feeling is that with so many fresh flours available, you probably don't need this machine unless you are a truly ardent baker. Many other kitchen appliances will do the same job. An unused spice or coffee grinder can be used; a blender will also do the job, but it's tedious to grind and sift out the flour, returning the coarse meal to the machine to be ground even finer.

Nutritional Analysis

The figures given for the nutritional content of the recipes in this book were calculated using "The Food Processor II" software developed by ESHA Research in Salem, Oregon. However, the figures for some of the more unusual grains were provided by Arrowhead Mills, Inc., of Hereford, Texas.

These calculations are for the estimated values of the ingredients. The figures can vary, depending on the brands used and variations in ingredients. In some cases, such as deep-fried foods, the amount of oil actually absorbed had to be approximated. But if you use these figures simply as guidelines, you should be able to find recipes that are compatible with your dietary goals.

Remember that nutritional figures given for these recipes (or any recipes, for that matter) have little or no meaning by themselves, but are imporant as part of a whole dietary program. Listed below are the United States Department of Agriculture's recommended dietary allowances for an average 26-year-old woman and man. If you have specific dietary restrictions, your needs will probably vary from the charts. Consult your physician or dietitian if you have any questions.

RECOMMENDED DIETARY ALLOWANCES			
RDA for: Jane Doe **Weight: 125 lbs**	**Age: 26 yrs 0 mo** **Height: 5 ft 4 in**		**Sex: Female** **Lightly active**
Calories	1973	Pyridoxine—B6	2.00 Mg
Protein	45.5 G	Cobalamin—B12	3.00 Mcg
Carbohydrates	286 G **	Folacin	400 Mcg
Dietary Fiber	19.7 G #	Pantothenic	7.00 Mg *
Fat—Total	65.8 G **	Vitamin C	60.0 Mg
Fat—Saturated	21.9 G **	Vitamin E	8.00 Mg
Fat—Mono	21.9 G **	Calcium	800 Mg
Fat—Poly	21.9 G **	Copper	2.50 Mg *
Cholesterol	300 Mg **	Iron	18.0 Mg
Vit A—Carotene	RE	Magnesium	300 Mg
Vit A—Preformed	RE	Phosphorus	800 Mg
Vitamin A—Total	800 RE	Potassium	3750 Mg *
Thiamin—B1	1.00 Mg	Selenium	125 Mcg *
Riboflavin—B2	1.20 Mg	Sodium	2200 Mg *
Niacin—B3	13.0 Mg	Zinc	15.0 Mg

* Suggested values; within recommended ranges
** Dietary goals   # Fiber = 1gram/100 kcal

RECOMMENDED DIETARY ALLOWANCES

RDA for: John Doe			Age: 26 yrs 0 mo		Sex: Male
Weight: 170 lbs			Height: 5 ft 10 in		Lightly active
Calories	2644	*	Pyridoxine—B6	2.20 Mg	
Protein	61.9 G		Cobalamin—B12	3.00 Mcg	
Carbohydrates	383 G	* *	Folacin	400 Mcg	
Dietary Fiber	26.4 G	#	Pantothenic	7.00 Mg	*
Fat—Total	88.2 G	* *	Vitamin C	60.0 Mg	
Fat—Saturated	29.4 G	* *	Vitamin E	10.0 Mg	
Fat—Mono	29.4 G	* *	Calcium	800 Mg	
Fat—Poly	29.4 G	* *	Copper	2.50 Mg	*
Cholesterol	300 Mg	* *	Iron	10.0 Mg	
Vit A—Carotene	RE		Magnesium	350 Mg	
Vit A—Preformed	RE		Phosphorus	800 Mg	
Vitamin A—Total	1000 RE		Potassium	3750 Mg	*
Thiamin—B1	1.32 Mg		Selenium	125 Mcg	*
Riboflavin—B2	1.59 Mg		Sodium	2200 Mg	*
Niacin—B3	17.5 Mg		Zinc	15.0 Mg	

*Suggested values; within recommended ranges
* *Dietary goals   # Fiber = 1gram/100 kcal

CALORIC CONTENT OF 1 CUP COOKED GRAIN

Grain	Calories
Amaranth	300
Pearled Barley	228
Whole Roasted Buckwheat	162
Bulgur	246
Job's Tears	194
Millet	135
Whole-grain Oats	264
Quinoa	171
White Rice	223
Brown Rice	232
Whole-grain Rye	171
Teff	266
Triticale	228
Whole-grain Wheat	276
Wild Rice	184

Health Tips

When calculating sodium values, I've assumed that the salt has also been omitted from precooked grains if they are called for in the recipe.

The health tips for each recipe are merely a guide to help you alter the recipes for your own special needs, and you can use any of the tips you want or need to. In many recipes in which the health tip is to reduce fat, I have not completely eliminated fat from the recipe. My feeling is that a little fat enhances flavor. If you feel that you want to reduce the fat even more, use skim milk where whole milk is called for, for example, and coat nonstick skillets and saucepans with vegetable-oil cooking spray.

There is one further health tip that applies to almost every recipe. Watch your portion size. Most recipes in this book provide more-than-ample serving sizes. Use your own good sense to determine whether or not you want to eat that much.

Vegetarian Recipes

Many of the recipes in this book are strict vegetarian (vegan) or lacto-ovo vegetarian. Other recipes include suggestions for vegetarian adaptations in the introduction or in the health tips. For instance, in many cases the only meat called for in a recipe will be the broth. For those recipes, it's easy enough to simply substitute vegetable broth.

You can make up a large quantity of the homemade vegetable broth given below and then freeze it in 1¾-cup portions, the standard substitution for a can of beef or chicken broth. If you prefer not to bother (although the result is well worth the effort), you can make a reasonably tasty facsimile from packets or cubes of dried vegetable broth.

——————— ◇ ———————

Vegetable Broth

12 cups (3 quarts) water
¼ head cabbage (about ½ pound)
4 medium carrots, peeled
4 ribs celery
3 medium leeks (both white and green parts), trimmed and well rinsed
3 medium parsnips, peeled
2 medium kohlrabi, peeled
2 white turnips, peeled
1 large tomato
1 large onion, peeled
1 small celeriac, peeled
1 bunch parsley
1 tablespoon lemon juice
¾ teaspoon salt

Place the water, cabbage, carrots, celery, leeks, parsnips, kohlrabi, turnips, tomato, onion, and celeriac in a large saucepot. Bring to a boil over high heat. Reduce heat and simmer, uncovered, for 1 hour and 45 minutes. Add parsley, lemon juice, and salt. Simmer for 30 minutes longer. Strain broth through a colander, pressing the vegetables with the back of a spoon to extract all of their essence before discarding.

Freeze broth in 1¾ cup portions.

MAKES ABOUT 5 CUPS.
CALORIES: 30   CHOLESTEROL: 0 mg   SODIUM: 95 mg   FIBER: 0g

Health tip:
Omit salt.
CALORIES: 30   CHOLESTEROL: 0 mg   SODIUM: 0 mg   FIBER: 0g

Sprouting

Sprouting is the process of soaking and draining whole grains until a shoot appears. Although all kinds of sprouts are generally available these days, even at the supermarket, it's still fun to make your own.

You will need a 1-quart jar, cheesecloth, and two rubberbands.

Place 3 tablespoons of whole grains into the jar (only use 2 tablespoons for the smaller grains, such as teff) and fill it half full with water. Let stand, uncovered, for about 8 hours, but not much longer, or until doubled in size. Drain off the water. (Although it won't look terribly appetizing, it's now rich in minerals and you can use this nutritious water for cooking or for watering your plants.)

Rinse the grains thoroughly in fresh water and drain well. Put the grains back in the jar. Cover the top of the jar with a piece of cheesecloth and fasten it with rubberbands. Lay the jar on its side in a spot that is dark, or at least dim. It's best if you elevate the back of the jar so that any excess water can drain off. Repeat this procedure three times a day until the grains have sprouted. It's important that during this time the grains are not too damp or too dry. If the grains are too wet they will rot (you'll know by the smell), and if they're too dry they will shrivel and die.

When the sprouts are about as long as the grain (this will take about three days, but the time can vary, depending on the temperature and even on the grain itself) they are ready to be eaten either raw or cooked.

Sources

Here are some addresses for sources of unusual and hard-to-find foods and equipment. They all do mail order.

Grains:

Arrowhead Mills
P.O. Box 2059
Hereford, TX 79045
Grains, cereals, beans

Deer Valley Farm
R.D. 1
Guilford, NY 13780
Grains, beans, baked goods, and health-food items (organic)

Eden Foods, Inc.
701 Tecumseh Road
Clinton, MI 49236
Grains, beans, baked goods, Japanese products, pastas, snacks, lima products from Belgium

Garden Spot Distributors
438 White Oak Road
New Holland, PA 17557
Grains, breads, beans, nuts, seeds, dried fruits, herbs, and health-food items

Walnut Acres
Penns Creek, PA 17862
Grains, beans, prepared foods, baked goods, equipment including grain mills)

Gourmet and Ethnic Foods and Equipment:

Balducci's
424 Sixth Avenue
New York, NY 10011
Unusual produce, meats, cheeses, Italian specialty foods

Dean and DeLuca
560 Broadway
New York, NY 10012
Fresh produce, grains, beans, herbs, cheeses, kitchen equipment

Kam Man Food Products
200 Canal Street
New York, NY 10012
Chinese products

Foods of India
121 Lexington Avenue
New York, NY 10016
Specialty rices, bulgur, spices, and Indian goods

Spice and Sweet Mahal
135 Lexington Avenue
New York, NY 10016
Specialty rices, bulgur, spices, and Indian goods

Maskal Forages, Inc.
1318 Willow
Caldwell, ID 83605
Teff Growers

Wild Rice:

Fall River Wild Rice
HC-01
Osprey Drive
Fall River Mills, CA 96028

Gibbs Wild Rice
10400 Billings Road
Live Oak, CA 95053

St. Maries Wild Rice
P.O. Box 293
St. Maries, ID 83861

PART

II

———— ◇ ————

MAJOR GRAINS:
THE CHOSEN ONES

———— ◇ ————

Wheat
Rice
Corn

I can't think of a single person who does not like at least some forms of wheat, rice, and corn, which may account for why these are the grains of choice for most cultures, both ancient and modern, and are the grains that feed the largest populations in the world today.

Initially, the determining factors for a so-called native grain that would become the diet staple for a particular civilization, were the climate and growing conditions. But as time went on, and trade routes became established and personal wealth grew, flavor and other considerations became more important. So, where barley was once the main grain of China, rye, the staple of Scandinavia, and oats, the native grain of both Scotland and Ireland, all of these countries now use more wheat or rice than they do those original grains. (The use of corn, incidentally, has never really caught on in Europe, with the exception of cornmeal for polenta in Italy.) The same is true of many of the other minor grains, as well. As the major grains became available, the wealthy would convert to them, abandoning the native grains as food for the poor. The poor, in turn, hoping to imitate the rich, would also abandon the old grain for new as soon as it was financially possible.

The most unfortunate part of this mass conversion was that in addition to adopting the new grains, processed grains eventually became a status symbol. When white flour and white rice became fashionable, for instance, many of the nutritional advantages of the grains were lost.

To some extent, the grain staple of a country or region is still determined by local growing conditions. For example, in northern India and China, where wheat grows well, the staple foods of these countries are bread in India and noodles in China. In the south, both countries use rice. The southwestern part of North America and Central America still base their diets on corn. But it is still the "big three" that dominate the scene for all developed countries.

I expect that most people in the United States are familiar with at least some form of these three grains. You would have to look far and wide to find someone who has never tasted white bread, long-grain white rice, or corn. On the other hand, the great majority of these people have probably never tasted wheat berries, short-grain rice, or corn bran.

This section includes recipes for many of the classic uses for these grains, as well as new uses for their less-familiar forms.

WHEAT
(Triticum)

I t is of little wonder that wheat is still referred to as the staff of
life, for it is the most widely grown and consumed grain in the
world. Although it is available in many forms, flour is the wheat
form most commonly used, usually for noodles, breads, and other
baked goods.

Wheat comes in hundreds of different varieties, but the types
used in the United States are red (really a reddish brown) and white
(really a golden color).

Hard and *soft* refers to the physical hardness of the wheat.
Technically, either hard or soft wheat can be high in gluten, a plant
protein which, when kneaded, develops elasticity that allows dough
to rise. As far as the consumer is concerned, hard wheat means the
high-gluten wheat that is generally used as bread flour, and soft
wheat is the low-gluten wheat used for pastry flour.

Durum wheat is a very hard spring wheat. It is used to make
semolina and semolina flour, which is important in pasta making.
Durum wheat is also used for making couscous.

Winter wheat, and spring wheat (sometimes called summer
wheat), refer to the time of year the wheat is planted. Spring wheat
tends to have a higher gluten content than winter wheat.

Types of Wheat Products Available

Whole-grain wheat (wheat berries): The whole kernel with just the
hull removed. When it is cooked, it can be used in the same manner
as rice, as a side dish or in salads.

Cracked wheat: This is exactly what the name implies: wheat
cracked into varying degrees of coarseness, generally coarse, medium, and fine. It can be made from red or white wheat and can be
distinguished from bulgur by the white uncooked center of the
cracked kernels. Cracked wheat still has the bran and germ intact
and so is high in fiber. If you cannot find cracked wheat, but have
access to wheat berries, you can make you own by placing the
berries in an electric blender container and processing until coarsely ground. Sift out the very fine flour, and the remaining coarse
pieces are cracked wheat.

27

Bulgur (bulghur or bulgar): Wheat berries that are pearled (the bran is removed), cooked (steamed), and dried. After drying, the berries are cracked into varying degrees of coarseness. Bulgur is uniform in color, differentiating it from cracked wheat. It requires less cooking time than cracked wheat, since it has already been cooked once. The fine grind is the one most commonly used for packaged mixes, such as tabouli (tabooli). The medium grind is the more common form of bulgur, and usually the one found in bins at health-food stores. Indian and Pakistani stores are more likely to carry four grinds. You can make your own bulgur by cooking wheat berries (see Basic Cooking Instructions), then spreading them in a single layer on a large baking sheet. Bake at 250° F for about an hour, or until completely dried. Cool, then process in a blender or food processor until broken into pieces. Place in a strainer to remove the particles that have been ground too finely.

Couscous: The bran and germ have been removed from durum wheat and the endosperm (the semolina) has been steamed, agglomerated (that means that the small pieces have been pressed together to make bigger ones), and dried. Couscous comes in fine, medium, and coarse grinds, but is most commonly available in a medium grind.

Wheat germ: As the name suggests, this is the germ (embryo) of the wheat. It is available raw, but the type with which we are most familiar has been toasted, sometimes with honey. Wheat germ has a high fat content and will turn rancid quickly unless stored in the refrigerator. (If the germ has been vacuum packed, it won't need refrigeration until after it has been opened.) Wheat germ is usually sprinkled on cereal or yogurt, or added to baked goods to boost the fiber and nutrition content.

Wheat bran (miller's bran/unprocessed wheat bran): The hard layer of the wheat kernel found under the hull. It is fiber rich and comes finely or coarsely ground. Wheat bran is valued for its high fiber content and is rarely used by itself, but rather as a nutrition booster in baked goods, cereals, meat loaves, and other cooked foods. Do not confuse pure wheat bran with breakfast cereals that have names that sound like they are purely bran. In addition to some wheat bran, these cereals also contain sugar, flavorings, and vitamin supplements. Pure wheat bran looks and tastes like sawdust.

Seitan: A meat substitute made of gluten (wheat protein), with a chewy consistency somewhere between a sponge and a rubber band. The flavor is bland, and it frequently comes packed in soy sauce. This is definitely an acquired taste.

Wheat flakes (rolled wheat): Steamed wheat berries, rolled flat, and is similar to oat, rye, and barley flakes.

Meals: A fine grind of wheat that is used for cereal.
FARINA: The endosperm of the wheat.
WHEATINA: The whole grain.
SEMOLINA: The endosperm of durum wheat.

Flour: The Finest Grind of Wheat

White flour is the ground endosperm. In addition, white flour can be bleached to be more visually appealing. Whole-wheat products are not bleached.

Graham flour: Flour made with the whole-wheat kernel. It has a coarser bran and always includes the germ. Extra germ is sometimes added.

Whole-wheat flour: The name implies that this is the ground whole-wheat kernel. In fact, usually some or all of the germ is removed to prolong shelf life. The term graham flour is often used to describe whole-wheat flour. There are no hard and fast rules about this.

Bread flour: It is usually unbleached and made of high-gluten wheat. As the name indicates, it is best for bread making.

Pastry flour: Flour made from low-gluten wheat that is best for cakes, pastry, and other tender baked goods. It can be made from either white or whole-wheat flour.

Cake flour: Bleached white pastry flour. If substituting for all-purpose flour: 1 cup plus 2 tablespoons cake flour equals 1 cup all-purpose flour.

All-purpose flour: This is the work horse of flours, and is a combination of high- and low-gluten flours. The proportions vary depending on the region where the milling is being done. All-purpose flour can be bleached or unbleached. All-purpose flour can be substituted for cake flour if it is sifted three times before measuring.

Self-rising flour: Flour that has had baking powder and salt added (about 1½ teaspoons baking powder and ½ teaspoon salt per cup). Available as both cake and all-purpose flour.

Semolina flour: Finely ground semolina that is primarily used in pasta making.

Texture and Flavor

The flavor of wheat is pleasing, but difficult to describe. It is mild and pleasant tasting, making it the perfect foil for anything the cook cares to cook or serve in it or with it.

The texture of the cooked whole-wheat berry should be slightly chewy and, for the most part, the berries should swell, but not burst, when they are cooked. The berries usually burst when they are cooked with too much water, and the results will be stickier than desirable. On the other hand, too little water will produce cooked berries that are a little too chewy. Cooked wheat berries should have a pleasant pop when you bite into them, which always reminds me of a whole cherry tomato.

Bulgur, cracked wheat, and couscous cook to a similar texture. They should be fluffy, not soggy or very sticky, and will not have the characteristic pop or chewiness of the cooked whole grain. Cooked cracked wheat is a little heavier and starchier than bulgur. This is because it has not been precooked and still retains its bran layer. Couscous is fluffier and drier than either bulgur or cracked wheat.

The germ is the most flavorful part of the grain. Its flavor is a cross between corn and pignoli nuts, which comes through best in its toasted form, which is also the form most commonly available. The texture is dry and crunchy.

Wheat bran is very dry, feather light, and extremely tasteless.

Wheat flakes cook into a delightful porridge, and can be added, uncooked, to baked goods for a crunchy consistency.

What I call "meals" are better known as hot breakfast cereals. The cooked texture is very soft and creamy. Cereal which has the bran intact will have some crunchy texture along with the characteristic creaminess. Cracked wheat and bulgur can also be cooked into cereal by using additional water and allowing longer cooking times.

The flavor of the different types of wheat flour will vary depending on the amount of processing that it has undergone. Graham flour will be the most flavorful, and white flour the least flavorful. The texture of the finished product in which they are used will, of course, vary depending upon the other ingredients used and the cooking method. The only certainty is that products made with a whole-wheat flour will be heavier than those made with white flour.

Compatible Foods, Herbs, and Spices

All wheat products have universally compatible flavors, and can be used for sweet or savory dishes. Of all the grains, wheat is certainly the most versatile in every way.

Availability

Whole-wheat berries, bulgur, cracked wheat, wheat bran, wheat flakes, wheat germ, and whole-wheat flour can almost always be found in health-food stores and through mail-order grain catalogs (see page 21).

Wheat meals (hot cereals), and sometimes bulgur, cracked wheat, and wheat germ, are carried by supermarkets in the cereals section.

Couscous, and sometimes bulgur and cracked wheat, can be found in the rice, health foods, or international foods sections of the supermarket.

All flours, with the exception of whole-wheat pastry flour and semolina flour, can usually be found at the supermarket with other baking products.

Couscous, semolina, semolina flour, bulgur, and cracked wheat can sometimes, but not always, be found in gourmet or specialty-food stores, and foreign-import stores. Check out Italian and Middle Eastern stores.

Nutritional Content

The more the wheat berry is processed, the more the nutritional qualities go down. Whole-wheat berries and cracked wheat, as well as wheat bran, wheat germ, and whole-wheat flour, are high-fiber foods. Bulgur, couscous, farina, semolina, and white flours have all been denuded of the bran and germ and so have insignificant fiber content.

Wheat germ is a good source of vitamin E, some protein and B vitamins, and fiber. When the germ is discarded, much of the nutritional value of the wheat goes with it.

The bran is the highest source of fiber in the wheat berry. It is also the source of many minerals, notably magnesium and phosphorous, and some B vitamins.

What remains of its nutritional profile once the wheat berry has lost its bran and germ, are starch, and some protein and B vitamins, a mere shadow of the original high-nutrition whole-wheat berry.

Substitutions

Whole-grain Wheat

Any groat or berry (triticale, rye, and oats) can be substituted for wheat berries, but check the other grains for flavor comparisons and cooking times.

Cooked short-grain brown rice: Has a crunchiness similar to the cooked whole-wheat berry.

Barley: Can also be used as a substitute for cooked whole-wheat berries.

Other acceptable substitutes (in order of preference): Job's tears (adjust cooking times).

Bulgur and Cracked Wheat

These two are absolutely interchangeable. Simply adjust cooking times.
Other acceptable substitutes (in order of preference):

Couscous: The perfect substitute for cooked bulgur or cracked wheat, but allowances must be made for the difference in cooking times before using raw couscous in recipes calling for raw bulgur or raw cracked wheat.

Brown rice: A suitable flavor substitute.

Buckwheat and millet: Both are fine texture substitutes, but each has an overpowering flavor that must be taken into consideration before making direct substitutions.

Cooked Couscous

Rizcous, a rice product, is a perfect substitute for couscous. Both cooked bulgur and cracked wheat are excellent substitutions.

Other acceptable substitutes (in order of preference): Millet (cooked by Method I) has a very similar texture, but the flavor will be significantly different. Cooked white rice is suitable, and cooked small pasta shapes are acceptable.

Seitan

Tofu (especially the pressed type) is the only substitute for seitan.

Wheat Flakes

Any grain flake can be interchanged for wheat flakes, but be sure and make flavor comparisons. (Incidentally, I am not referring to breakfast flakes, such as corn flakes.)

Flours

Most recipes for baked goods are a delicate balance between flour, liquid, fat, leavening agents, and sometimes sugar. To randomly substitute one kind of flour for another is simply inviting a baking disaster.

Yeast breads tend to be more forgiving of flour substitutions than delicate cakes and cookies. If you prefer using whole-wheat flour rather than the white flour called for in a recipe, I would suggest finding a similar reliable recipe that has been developed for the use of whole-wheat flour, rather than trying to do a conversion yourself.

Basic Cooking Instructions

Please read *About Cooking Grains* beginning on page 7.

The microwave methods that follow were tested in a 650-watt oven.

Whole-grain Wheat

Please note that salt must always be added *after cooking,* or the whole grain will not absorb the cooking water. Do not cook with broth.

Stove-top method:

> *2½ cups water*
> *1 cup whole-grain wheat, rinsed*
> *½ teaspoon salt*

In a 2-quart saucepan, bring water to a boil over high heat. Stir in wheat and return to boiling. Reduce heat and simmer, covered, for 2 hours, or until almost all of the liquid has been absorbed. Remove from heat and let stand, covered, for 15 minutes. Add salt and fluff with a fork.

MAKES 2¾ CUPS.

Microwave method:

Please note that salt must always be added *after cooking,* or the whole grain will not absorb the water. Do not cook with broth.

3 cups water
1 cup whole-grain wheat, rinsed
½ teaspoon salt

Place water in a 3-quart, microwave-safe bowl. Cover with waxed paper and microwave on high (100% power) for 5 minutes. Stir in wheat. Recover with waxed paper and microwave on high for 5 minutes. Microwave on medium (50% power), still covered with waxed paper, for 1 hour. Let stand 5 minutes. Stir in salt and fluff with a fork.

MAKES 2¼ CUPS.

Medium Bulgur or Cracked Wheat

Stove-top method:

2 cups water
¾ teaspoon salt
1 cup medium bulgur or cracked wheat (do not rinse)

In a 2-quart saucepan, bring the water and salt to a boil over high heat. Stir in bulgur or cracked wheat and return to boiling. Reduce heat and simmer, covered, for 20 minutes, or until almost all the liquid has been absorbed. Remove from heat and let stand, covered, for 5 minutes. Fluff with a fork.

MAKES 3 CUPS.

Microwave method:

1¾ cups water
¾ teaspoon salt
1 cup medium bulgur or cracked wheat (do not rinse)

Place the water and salt in a 3-quart, microwave-safe bowl. Cover with waxed paper and microwave on high (100% power) for 3 minutes. Stir in bulgur or cracked wheat. Recover with waxed paper and microwave on high for 3 minutes. Microwave on medium (50% power), still covered with waxed paper, for 30 minutes. Let stand 2 minutes. Fluff with a fork.

MAKES 3 CUPS.

No-cook method for fine bulgur:

> *1 cup fine bulgur (do not rinse)*
> *2 cups boiling water*
> *½ teaspoon salt*

Place the bulgur in a medium-size bowl. Stir in boiling water and salt. Cover tightly with plastic wrap and let stand for 20 minutes. Fluff with a fork.

MAKES 2½ CUPS.

Stove-top method for fine cracked wheat:

> *2 cups water*
> *½ teaspoon salt*
> *1 cup fine cracked wheat (do not rinse)*

In a 2-quart saucepan, bring the water and salt to a boil over high heat. Stir in cracked wheat and return to boiling. Reduce heat and simmer, covered, for 5 minutes, or until almost all of the liquid has been absorbed. Remove from heat and let stand for 10 minutes. Fluff with a fork.

MAKES 4 CUPS.

No-cook method for couscous:

> *1 cup couscous*
> *1¾ cups water*
> *½ teaspoon salt*

Place couscous in a medium-size bowl. Stir in boiling water and salt and let stand for 5 minutes. Fluff with a fork.

MAKES 2¾ CUPS.

Stove-top method for authentic couscous:

1½ cups couscous
⅔ cup water

Place couscous in a fine strainer. Rinse under cool water until all of the grains have been moistened. Turn into an 8×13-inch baking pan. Spread evenly in the pan and let stand for 20 minutes.

In a large saucepan (which should contain the simmering stew that you intend to serve with the couscous), place a steamer, strainer, or colander that fits well into the top of the pot. The bottom of the steamer should be above the stew, not in it.

Line the steamer with a double layer of cheesecloth. If you see steam escaping around the edge of the steamer, tape a doubled length of foil around the side of the pot. Bring the foil up and tuck it into the inside of the steamer, sealing the edges so that the steam is forced through the holes in the steamer and through the couscous.

Sift the couscous through your fingers to break up any lumps and place in the lined steamer. Steam, uncovered, for 20 minutes. Turn the couscous into the baking pan, then gradually stir the water into the couscous. Spread couscous evenly in the pan and let stand for 20 minutes.

Return couscous to the lined steamer and steam for 30 minutes more.

Reheating:

Wheat products can be reheated by lightly steaming or microwaving.

WHEAT RECIPES

(indicates easy recipes)*

———————— ◇ ————————

Cheese Straws *
Zucchini Sticks with Honey-Mustard Dipping Sauce
Wheat Berry Scampi *
Coq au Vin with Couscous
Spicy Pork with Lychees
Couscous with Moroccan Lamb Stew
Not Quite Spaghetti and Meat Sauce
Chicken-y Salad with Creamy Garlic Dressing *
Caesar Salad with Seitan Croutons
Tabouli *
Bulgur Tofu Salad *
Fruity Bulgur Salad *
Wheat Berry Tomato Salad *
Bulgur Chili
Broccoli with Wheat Flake Topping *
Kasha and Wheat Berries *
Wheat Berry Veggy Melt *
Couscous with Broiled Vegetables
Whole-Wheat Couscous with Lentils *
Brown Rice and Wheat Berries *
Bulgur Pea-laf *
Fresh Pasta
Fresh Pasta with Egg
Marinara Sauce *
Pesto *
Bolognese Sauce *
Puttanesca Plus Sauce *
Fettucini Alfredo *
The World's Best Pizza
Plain Old White Bread
Whole Wheat Bread
French Bread
Semolina Bread
Cornell Bread
Wheat-Germ Rolls
Delicious Pancakes *
Vanilla Waffles *
Apple Pie Waffles
Maple French Toast *
Whole-Wheat Biscuits *
Basic Muffins *
Pineapple Bran Muffins *
Orange Popovers

37

Basic Sweet Dough
Pecan Coffee Ring
Cream Puffs (Profiteroles)
Puff Pastry (Feuillete)
Puffy Apple Tarts *
Easy Napoleons *
Angel‑Food Cake
Whole Wheat Carrot Cake
Sour Cream Apple Cake
Yellow Cake with Vanilla Buttercream Frosting
Decadent Chocolate Cake
Jelly Roll Cake
Mim Jaffe's Butter Cookies *
My Famous Peach Pie

Cheese Straws

These are one of my favorite things to serve with a rich creamy soup. You can also serve them as hors d'oeuvres. If you don't want to make your own puff pastry, you can use prepared frozen puff pastry sheets, thawed. If you are not having a lot of company, you can halve the recipe and freeze the leftover puff pastry.

½ cup grated Parmesan cheese
1 teaspoon paprika
½ teaspoon chili powder
⅛ teaspoon ground red pepper
1 recipe puff pastry (page 81)

Preheat oven to 400°F.

In a medium-size bowl, toss together the Parmesan cheese, paprika, chili powder, and pepper.

Roll half of the pastry into an 8 × 18-inch rectangle. Sprinkle with one quarter of the cheese mixture. Turn over and sprinkle one-quarter of the cheese mixture on the second side of the pastry.

Cut into strips ½-inch wide (by 8-inches long), using a sharp knife or pizza wheel. Place one end of each strip in each hand. Twist in opposite directions to produce a candy-cane effect. Place on ungreased baking sheets. Roll out the second half of the dough and repeat. Bake 12 minutes or until completely puffed. Serve warm or room temperature.

MAKES 4 DOZEN.
CALORIES: 51   CHOLESTEROL: 11 mg   SODIUM: 47 mg   FIBER: 0 g

Health tip:
Eat just one.

———————— ◇ ————————

Zucchini Sticks with Honey-Mustard Dipping Sauce

The wheat germ makes these extra crunchy. I like to serve them at parties.

Zucchini Sticks:

⅓ cup flour
½ teaspoon salt
¼ teaspoon ground red pepper
2 eggs
1 tablespoon water
⅔ cup wheat germ (regular or honey crunch)
⅓ cup bread crumbs
4 to 5 cups zucchini sticks (3 × ½ × ½-inch)
Oil for frying

Honey-Mustard Dipping Sauce:

¼ cup sour cream
¼ cup plain yogurt
¼ cup mayonnaise
1½ tablespoons honey mustard

On waxed paper, stir together the flour, salt, and pepper.

In a shallow bowl, beat the eggs with the water.

On a separate piece of waxed paper, stir together the wheat germ and bread crumbs.

Dredge the zucchini in the flour mixture, dip in the egg, and then roll in the wheat germ.

Pour enough oil into a skillet to be ½-inch deep. Heat until the oil bubbles as soon as some bread crumbs are dropped in.

Fry the zucchini until golden on both sides. Drain on paper towels.

In a medium-size bowl, stir together the sour cream, yogurt, mayonnaise, and mustard. Serve with fried zucchini sticks.

SERVES 12 (makes 48 zucchini sticks and ¾ cup sauce).
CALORIES: 124   CHOLESTEROL: 40 mg   SODIUM: 178 mg   FIBER: 1 g

Health tip:
Omit the salt; use additional yogurt instead of the sour cream; and use reduced-calorie mayonnaise.
CALORIES: 95   CHOLESTEROL: 36 mg   SODIUM: 89 mg   FIBER: 1 g

———————— ◇ ————————
Wheat Berry Scampi

I'm a great garlic lover and this dish is right up my alley. It's an easy dish to prepare and a nice way to introduce people to cooked wheat berries.

½ cup butter
4 cloves garlic, minced
1½ pounds shrimp, peeled and cleaned
¼ cup chopped parsley
1 tablespoon lemon juice
¼ teaspoon pepper
2¾ cups cooked wheat berries

In a large skillet, melt the butter over medium-high heat. Add the garlic and sauté 30 seconds. Add the shrimp and sauté until the shrimp are just cooked through.

Stir in the parsley, lemon juice, and pepper. Stir in the wheat berries and cook, stirring until heated through.

SERVES 4.
CALORIES: 569 mg   CHOLESTEROL: 394 mg   SODIUM: 952 mg   FIBER: 3 g

Health tip:
Use ¼ cup unsalted margarine instead of ½ cup butter; omit the salt from the wheat berries.
CALORIES: 467   CHOLESTEROL: 332 mg   SODIUM: 399 mg   FIBER: 3 g

———————◇———————

Coq au Vin with Couscous

This is a stew that you can cook the couscous over, if you are using the semi-authentic cooking method; or you can just serve the no-cook couscous on the side.

3½ pound chicken, cut up
¼ cup flour
1 teaspoon salt
1 teaspoon paprika
¼ teaspoon pepper
⅛ teaspoon nutmeg
2 tablespoons butter
2 tablespoons oil
3 tablespoons warm brandy
1½ cups red wine
½ cup water
12 small white onions
1 package (10-ounce) fresh mushrooms, rinsed and bottom ends
    trimmed
2 tablespoons chopped parsley
½ teaspoon rosemary
¼ teaspoon thyme
1 cup couscous (steamed traditionally over the stew or soaked in
    boiling water according to package directions)

Rinse the chicken and pat dry.

On a piece of waxed paper or aluminum foil, stir together the flour, salt, paprika, pepper; and nutmeg. Dredge the chicken in the flour mixture.

In a large saucepan, melt the butter and oil over medium-high heat. Add the chicken and brown on all sides. Pour in the brandy and ignite.

After the flames have extinguished, stir in the wine, water, onions, mushrooms, parsley, rosemary, and thyme. Bring to a boil. Reduce heat and simmer, uncovered, 45 minutes or until the chicken is tender.

Serve over the couscous.

SERVES 4.

CALORIES: 765   CHOLESTEROL: 213 mg   SODIUM: 813 mg   FIBER: 11 g

Health tip:

Cook chicken without skin; omit butter and use only 1 tablespoon oil and cook in nonstick saucepan. Omit salt.

CALORIES: 636   CHOLESTEROL: 169 mg   SODIUM: 201 mg   FIBER: 11 g

Spicy Pork with Lychees

This dish is great. I like the combination of exotic and sweet and spicy flavors.

1 pork tenderloin (1½ pound)
1 can (20 ounce) lychees, in heavy syrup, undrained
3 tablespoons soy sauce
2 tablespoons mirin (a sweet rice wine available in Oriental grocery
  stores) or sherry
1 tablespoon cornstarch
1 tablespoon rice vinegar
1 tablespoon sugar
2 cloves garlic, minced
2 teaspoons minced ginger
1 teaspoon chili oil
3 tablespoons oil
1 cup sliced onion
2 cups cooked wheat berries

Thinly slice the tenderloin

Drain lychee nuts, reserving ⅓ cup of syrup. In a small bowl, stir together the soy sauce, mirin, cornstarch, vinegar, sugar, garlic, ginger, chili oil, and lychee syrup; set aside.

In a wok or large skillet, heat the oil over high heat. Add one third of the pork and stir-fry until cooked through. Remove from wok (or skillet) and cook the remaining 2 batches of pork and set aside. Add the onion and cook, stirring, until soft. Stir in the sauce mixture and cook, stirring, until thick. Return the pork to the skillet and add the lychees. Cook, stirring, until heated through. Add the wheat berries and cook, stirring, until heated through.

SERVES 6.
CALORIES: 607   CHOLESTEROL: 109 mg   SODIUM: 848 mg   FIBER: 4 g

Health tip:
Use low-sodium soy sauce and reduce oil to 2 teaspoons and cook in a non-stick skillet. Omit salt when cooking wheat berries.
CALORIES: 559   CHOLESTEROL: 100 mg   SODIUM: 431 mg   FIBER: 4 g

Couscous with Moroccan Lamb Stew

This is a stew typical of one that you would cook in the bottom of your couscousinere while you steam the couscous in the top. Follow the instructions for semi-authentic couscous and steam it over this stew.

3 tablespoons oil
2 cups chopped onion
3 cloves garlic, minced
1 teaspoon salt
½ teaspoon cinnamon
½ teaspoon ginger
¼ teaspoon clove
¼ teaspoon ground red pepper
3 cups water
2 tablespoons dark-brown sugar
2 pounds cubed lamb
2 cups cubed rutabaga or turnips
2 cups thickly sliced carrots
1 can (19 ounce) chick-peas, drained
½ cup mini pitted prunes
½ cup raisins
3 tablespoons lemon juice
2 cups cooked couscous

In a large saucepan, heat the oil over medium-high heat. Add the onion and garlic and cook, stirring, until onion is soft. Stir in the salt, cinnamon, ginger, clove, and red pepper until absorbed. Add the water and brown sugar; bring to a boil. Add the lamb and return to a boil. Reduce heat and simmer, covered, 1 hour. Add the rutabaga and carrots. Simmer, uncovered, 30 minutes. Add the chick-peas, prunes, and raisins. Simmer, uncovered, 30 minutes longer. Stir in the lemon juice. Serve over couscous.

SERVES 6.
CALORIES: 899   CHOLESTEROL: 185 mg   SODIUM: 517 mg   FIBER: 11 g

Health tip:
Reduce the oil to 2 teaspoons and cook in a nonstick saucepan; omit salt.
CALORIES: 879 mg   CHOLESTEROL: 185 mg   SODIUM: 178 mg   FIBER: 11 g

Not Quite Spaghetti and Meat Sauce

What a delicious treat! If you didn't mention that there was no meat in the meat sauce, no one would be any the wiser.

1 spaghetti squash (2 pound)
2 tablespoons olive oil
1 cup chopped onion
2 cloves garlic, minced
1 can (14½ ounce) whole peeled tomatoes, undrained
1 can (8 ounce) tomato sauce
1 tablespoon chopped parsley
1 bay leaf
1 teaspoon basil
½ teaspoon oregano
¼ teaspoon sugar
¼ teaspoon salt
⅛ teaspoon pepper
1 cup cooked bulgur

Preheat oven to 375°F.

Cut the squash in half, lengthwise. Scoop out and discard the seeds. Place, cut side down, in a baking dish. Bake 45 to 55 minutes, or until the squash is tender.

While the squash is baking, prepare the sauce. In a 3-quart saucepan, heat the oil over medium-high heat. Add the onion and garlic and cook, stirring, until the onion is soft. Stir in the tomatoes and break up with the back of a spoon. Stir in the tomato sauce, parsley, bay leaf, basil, oregano, sugar, salt, and pepper. Bring to a boil, reduce heat and simmer, uncovered, 20 minutes. Discard the bay leaf. Stir in the bulgur.

Remove the squash from the oven and, using a fork, separate the spaghetti-like strands as you scrape them from the shell. Place in a serving dish and top with sauce.

SERVES 4.
CALORIES: 243 CHOLESTEROL: 0 mg SODIUM: 837 mg FIBER: 12 g

Health tip:
Reduce oil to 2 teaspoons and prepare the sauce in a nonstick skillet. Omit the salt.
CALORIES: 204 CHOLESTEROL: 0 mg SODIUM: 570 mg FIBER: 12 g

———————— ◇ ————————

Chicken-y Salad with Creamy Garlic Dressing

My sister thinks this is really delicious—and I concur.

2 cups cubed cooked chicken
1½ cups cooked wheat berries
1 cup sliced celery
½ cup mayonnaise
3 tablespoons grated Parmesan cheese
1 tablespoon dijon mustard
1 tablespoon lemon juice
1 clove garlic, minced
⅛ teaspoon pepper

In a large bowl, toss together the chicken, wheat berries, and celery.

In a small bowl, stir together the mayonnaise, cheese, mustard, lemon juice, pepper, and garlic. Stir the dressing into the salad.

SERVES 4.
CALORIES: 432   CHOLESTEROL: 159 mg   SODIUM: 309 mg   FIBER: 5 g

Health tip:
Use ¼ cup reduced-calorie mayonnaise and ¼ cup plain yogurt instead of the mayonnaise. Omit salt from wheat berries.
CALORIES: 279   CHOLESTEROL: 66 mg   SODIUM: 237 mg   FIBER: 5 g

———————— ◇ ————————

Caesar Salad with Seitan Croutons

The seitan fries up to a soft crouton, but it has a slightly fishy flavor; if you want you can use plain bread croutons.

Oil for frying
½ cup diced seitan, blotted dry with paper towels
3 cloves garlic, divided
3 anchovies
½ teaspoon capers
1 egg yolk
½ teaspoon dry mustard
¼ teaspoon Worcestershire sauce
2 tablespoons olive oil
1 tablespoon lemon juice
1 teaspoon wine vinegar
1 small head romaine lettuce, torn into bite-size pieces
¼ cup grated Parmesan cheese

Pour enough oil into a medium-size skillet to be ½-inch deep. Heat until the oil bubbles as soon as a small piece of seitan is dropped in. Add 2 of the cloves of garlic and then the seitan. Cook the seitan until browned. Drain on paper towels and set aside. Discard garlic.

In a large bowl, mash the anchovies with the capers and the remaining garlic clove, until the mixture is a paste. Stir in the egg yolk, then the mustard and Worcestershire sauce. Stir in the oil, lemon juice, and vinegar.

Add the lettuce to the bowl and toss until coated with the dressing. Top with the seitan croutons and cheese and toss.

SERVES 4.
CALORIES: 99   CHOLESTEROL: 61 mg   SODIUM: 120 mg   FIBER: 1 g

Health tip:
Eat half a portion.
CALORIES: 100   CHOLESTEROL: 30 mg   SODIUM: 60 mg   FIBER: 1 g

---

◇

Tabouli

This is a traditional Middle Eastern salad. You can adjust the amount of mint to your own taste, but it's important that you use fresh, not dried, mint. You can use bulgur if cracked wheat is not available.

2 cups cooked fine-grain cracked wheat, cooled
1 cup chopped cucumber
1 cup chopped tomato
⅓ cup chopped parsley
¼ cup chopped scallion
2 tablespoons chopped mint
1 tablespoon olive oil
1 tablespoon vegetable oil
1 tablespoon lemon juice
½ teaspoon salt
¼ teaspoon pepper

In a large bowl, combine the cracked wheat, cucumber, tomato, parsley, scallion, and mint.

In a small bowl, stir together the oils, lemon juice, salt, and pepper. Pour over salad and toss.

SERVES 6.
CALORIES: 131   CHOLESTEROL: 0 mg   SODIUM: 360 mg   FIBER: 4 g

Health tip:
Use half the dressing and omit the salt.
CALORIES: 111   CHOLESTEROL: 0 mg   SODIUM: 5 mg   FIBER: 4 g

───────── ◇ ─────────
Bulgur Tofu Salad

This is a delicious, creamy salad. It complements anything you serve it with—or it can be eaten as a main dish.

1½ cups cooked bulgur
1 cup diced (¼-inch pieces) tofu
½ cup chopped celery
½ cup sliced radish
⅓ cup finely chopped red bell pepper
¼ cup sliced scallion
⅓ cup mayonnaise
3 tablespoons buttermilk
2 tablespoons chopped parsley
1 tablespoons chopped fresh dill
2 teaspoons distilled white vinegar
¼ teaspoon salt
⅛ teaspoon ground red pepper

In a large bowl, toss together the bulgur, tofu, celery, radish, red pepper, and scallion.

In a small bowl, stir together the mayonnaise, buttermilk, parsley, dill, vinegar, salt, and pepper. Pour over the salad and toss until combined.

SERVES 6.
CALORIES: 190   CHOLESTEROL: 7 mg   SODIUM: 313 mg   FIBER: 4 g

Health tip:
Use reduced-calorie mayonnaise; omit salt.
CALORIES: 134   CHOLESTEROL: 4 mg   SODIUM: 90 mg   FIBER: 4 g

───────── ◇ ─────────
Fruity Bulgur Salad

I like the fruity taste of the olive oil with the fruits in the salad. The Jerusalem artichoke adds just the right crunch, if you can't find them, use water chestnuts or jicama.

1½ cups bulgur
1 cup diced melon (cantaloupe or honeydew)
½ cup halved grapes
½ cup raspberries
½ cup chopped pecans
½ cup chopped Jerusalem artichoke

2 tablespoons vegetable oil
2 tablespoons olive oil
2 tablespoons lemon juice
1 teaspoon honey mustard
¼ teaspoon salt
⅛ teaspoon pepper

In a large bowl, toss together the bulgur, melon, grapes, raspberries, pecans, and Jerusalem artichoke.

In a small bowl, stir together the oils, lemon juice, mustard, salt, and pepper. Pour over salad and toss.

SERVES 6.
CALORIES: 331   CHOLESTEROL: 0 mg   SODIUM: 105 mg   FIBER: 10 g

Health tip:
Halve the dressing and omit salt.
CALORIES: 290   CHOLESTEROL: 0 mg   SODIUM: 10 mg   FIBER: 10 g

———————— ◇ ————————

Wheat Berry Tomato Salad

This salad is absolutely delicious. Like any salad with onion in it, it's best to make just before serving. If you want to make it in advance, leave out the onion and stir it in at the last minute.

2 cups cooked and cooled wheat berries
2 cups chopped tomatoes
½ cup chopped red onion
¼ cup loosely packed basil leaves
1 tablespoon olive oil
1 tablespoon vegetable oil
1 tablespoon red-wine vinegar
½ clove garlic, minced
½ teaspoon salt
¼ teaspoon pepper

In a large bowl, toss together the wheat berries, tomatoes, and onion.

Put the basil, oils, vinegar, garlic, salt, and pepper into a blender container. Cover and blend until smooth. Pour dressing over salad and toss.

SERVES 6.
CALORIES: 132   CHOLESTEROL: 0 mg   SODIUM: 362 mg   FIBER: 3 g

Health tip:
Omit salt.
CALORIES: 152   CHOLESTEROL: 0   SODIUM: 7 mg   FIBER: 3 g

———————— ◇ ————————

Bulgur Chili

The consistency of the bulgur lends a meat-like consistency to the chili. Serve this with chopped onion, shredded Cheddar, sour cream, sliced olives, or chilies for toppings.

1 cup water
¾ teaspoon salt, divided
½ cup medium or coarse whole-wheat bulgur
2 tablespoons vegetable oil
1 cup chopped onion
1 cup chopped green bell pepper
2 cloves garlic, minced
2½ tablespoons chili powder
2 teaspoons oregano
2 teaspoons paprika
1 teaspoon cumin
2 cans (14½ ounces each) whole peeled tomatoes, undrained
2 cans (16 ounces each) red kidney beans, drained

In a medium-size saucepan, bring the water and ¼ teaspoon of the salt to a boil. Add the bulgur, return to a boil. Reduce the heat and simmer 20 minutes or until the water is absorbed. Remove from heat and set aside.

In a large skillet, heat the oil over medium-high heat. Add onion, green pepper, and garlic and cook, stirring, until onion is soft. Add the chili, oregano, paprika, and cumin and stir until the oil is absorbed. Stir in the tomatoes and break up with the back of a spoon. Stir in the beans, bulgur, and remaining ½ teaspoon salt. Simmer, covered, 20 minutes or until heated through.

SERVES 6.
CALORIES: 272   CHOLESTEROL: 0 mg   SODIUM: 821 mg   FIBER: 18 g

Health tip:
Reduce oil to 2 teaspoons and cook in a nonstick skillet; omit salt.
CALORIES: 246   CHOLESTEROL: 0 mg   SODIUM: 555 mg   FIBER: 18 g

———————◇———————

Broccoli with Wheat Flake Topping

This is a quick and unusual side dish.

2 tablespoons butter
1 cup wheat flakes
¾ cup ready-to-serve chicken or vegetable broth (see page 19)
3 cups broccoli florets
2 tablespoons sunflower seeds

In a large skillet, melt the butter over medium-high heat. Add the wheat flakes, and cook, stirring, until the wheat flakes smell nutty. Remove from skillet and set aside.

Add the broth to the skillet and bring to a boil. Add the broccoli and cook, tossing, until the broccoli is tender-crisp. Add the wheat flakes and sunflower seeds and cook, tossing, 1 minute longer.

SERVES 4.
CALORIES: 174   CHOLESTEROL: 16 mg   SODIUM: 213 mg   FIBER: 5 g

Health tip:
Use 2 teaspoons unsalted margarine instead of the butter and cook in a nonstick skillet. Use low-sodium broth.
CALORIES: 156   CHOLESTEROL: 4 mg   SODIUM: 77 mg   FIBER: 5 g

◇

Kasha and Wheat Berries

I like the fluffy kasha mixed with the crunch of cashews and the chewiness of the wheat berries.

2¼ cups water
½ cup wheat berries (whole grain wheat)
½ cup whole-grain kasha
½ cup chopped cashews
3 tablespoons butter
½ teaspoon salt
⅛ teaspoon pepper

In a 2-quart saucepan bring the water to a boil. Stir in the wheat berries and return to a boil. Reduce heat and simmer 1 hour and 45 minutes. Stir in the kasha and return to a boil. Reduce heat and simmer 12 minutes. Stir in the nuts, butter, salt, and pepper.

SERVES 8.
CALORIES: 165   CHOLESTEROL: 12 mg   SODIUM: 171 mg   FIBER: 3 g

Health tip:
Omit salt and butter.
CALORIES: 127   CHOLESTEROL: 0 mg   SODIUM: 2 mg   FIBER: 3 g

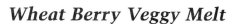

Wheat Berry Veggy Melt

You can prepare this casserole in advance, and instead of broiling the cheese at the last minute, you can bake the casserole at 375°F until the cheese is melted and the vegetable mixture is heated through.

2 cups cubed peeled butternut squash
1 cup sliced carrots
1 cup sliced yellow squash
2 cups cooked wheat berries
2 tablespoons chopped scallion
1 tablespoon soy sauce
2 cups shredded Monterey Jack cheese

Preheat the broiler.

Place the hubbard squash and carrots in a steamer over boiling water. Cover and steam 10 minutes. Add the yellow squash and steam 5 minutes longer, or until all the vegetables are tender.

In a 2-quart casserole, toss the vegetables with the wheat berries, scallion, and soy sauce. Sprinkle with the cheese and broil 5 minutes, or until the cheese is melted and browned.

SERVES 4.
CALORIES: 388   CHOLESTEROL: 52 mg   SODIUM: 844 mg   FIBER: 4 g

Health tip:
Use low-sodium soy sauce and only half the cheese. Cook wheat berries without salt.
CALORIES: 282   CHOLESTEROL: 26 mg   SODIUM: 355 mg   FIBER: 4 g

————— ◇ —————

Couscous with Broiled Vegetables

It's important that the vegetables are well browned in order to bring out their sweetness.

1 medium eggplant
2 medium yellow squash
1 large red onion
3 tablespoons olive oil
2 tablespoons vegetable oil
3 cloves garlic, minced
¼ teaspoon thyme
¼ teaspoon oregano
1¼ cups water
½ teaspoon salt
1 cup couscous
2 tablespoons lemon juice
2 tablespoons chopped parsley

Preheat the broiler.

Cut the eggplant and squash, lengthwise, into ½-inch thick slices. Cut the onion into ¼-inch slices.

In a medium-size bowl, combine the oils, garlic, thyme, and oregano. Place the vegetables in a single layer on baking sheets. Brush with the marinade. Broil until browned or slightly charred. Turn, brush with more marinade and broil until browned on second side. Separate the onion slices into rings. Slice the eggplant and squash into finger-size pieces; set aside.

In a 2-quart saucepan, bring the water and salt to a boil. Stir in the couscous and simmer 2 minutes. Stir in the vegetables and let stand 5 minutes. Stir in the lemon juice and parsley.

SERVES 6.
CALORIES: 244   CHOLESTEROL: 0 mg   SODIUM: 187 mg   FIBER: 11 g

Health tip:
Use only half the oil and brush the vegetables lightly before broiling; omit the salt.
CALORIES: 194   CHOLESTEROL: 0 mg   SODIUM: 9 mg   FIBER: 11 g

―――――◇―――――
Whole-Wheat Couscous with Lentils

The cinnamon and currants make this a very unusual dish.

½ stick cinnamon
6 whole cloves
2 tablespoons oil
½ cup chopped onion
1 clove garlic, minced
2¼ cups water
½ teaspoon salt
½ cup lentils
½ cup whole-wheat couscous
½ cup currants
2 tablespoons chopped parsley
2 tablespoons butter

Wrap the cinnamon and cloves in a piece of cheesecloth and tie with a string. Set aside.

In a 2-quart saucepan, heat the oil over medium-high heat. Add the onion and garlic and cook, stirring, until onion is soft. Add the water and salt, and bring to a boil. Add the lentils and spice sack, and return to a boil. Reduce heat and simmer 50 minutes.

Stir in the couscous and simmer 3 minutes. Remove from heat, let stand 5 minutes. Discard packet with spices. Stir in currants, parsley, and butter.

SERVES 4.
CALORIES: 282   CHOLESTEROL: 15 mg   SODIUM: 319 mg   FIBER: 8 g

Health tip:
Omit salt and butter, reduce oil to 2 teaspoons and cook in nonstick saucepan.
CALORIES: 192   CHOLESTEROL: 0 mg   SODIUM: 4 mg   FIBER: 8 g

—————— ◇ ——————

Brown Rice and Wheat Berries

The simplicity of the flavors make this an elegant side dish.

2¼ cups water
⅓ cup wheat berries (whole grain wheat)
⅓ cup long-grain brown rice
1 tablespoon butter
2 tablespoons pignoli
¼ cup chopped scallion
¼ teaspoon salt
⅛ teaspoon pepper

In a 2-quart saucepan, bring the water to a boil over high heat. Add the wheat berries and return to a boil. Reduce heat and simmer, covered, 1 hour.

Stir in the brown rice. Cover and simmer 50 minutes longer.

Melt the butter in a small skillet over medium heat 5 minutes before the rice is cooked. Add the pignoli and cook until lightly toasted. Stir in the scallion, and cook until softened. Stir the pignoli mixture into the rice along with the salt and pepper.

SERVES 4.
CALORIES: 170   CHOLESTEROL: 8 mg   SODIUM: 160 mg   FIBER: 3 g

Health tip:
Omit the salt and use unsalted margarine instead of butter; omit pignoli.
CALORIES: 130   CHOLESTEROL: 0 mg   SODIUM: 6 mg   FIBER: 2 g

—————— ◇ ——————

Bulgur Pea-laf

This is a lovely tasting pilaf. I used the pepper to bring out the flavor; you can use less.

2 tablespoons oil
1 cup medium or coarse bulgur
⅓ cup finely chopped onion
1 can (13¾ ounce) ready-to-serve chicken broth or
    1¾ cups vegetable broth (see page 19)
¼ cup water
1 cup frozen peas
2 tablespoons chopped parsley
¼ teaspoon pepper

In a 2-quart saucepan, heat the oil over medium-high heat. Add the bulgur and onion and cook, stirring, until the onion is soft and the bulgur smells nutty.

Add the broth and water, and bring to a boil over high heat. Reduce the heat and simmer, covered, 20 minutes. Stir in the peas, parsley, and pepper. Simmer 5 minutes longer, or until the peas are heated through.

SERVES 6.
CALORIES: 175   CHOLESTEROL: 0 mg   SODIUM: 231 mg   FIBER: 7 g

Health tip:
Use low-sodium broth; reduce oil to 1 tablespoon and cook in a nonstick saucepan.
CALORIES: 155   CHOLESTEROL: 0 mg   SODIUM: 37 mg   FIBER: 7 g

———————◇———————

Fresh Pasta

These noodles have a very lovely al dente consistency when cooked.

2 cups semolina flour
1½ cups all-purpose flour
1 teaspoon salt
1 cup warm water
2 tablespoons olive oil

In a large bowl, combine the semolina and all-purpose flours, and the salt. Make a well in the center.

Add the water and oil to the well. Using a wooden spoon, start mixing in small circles gradually making larger circles. Incorporate more of the flour as you mix, until you have mixed in as much of the flour as you can and are stirring big circles around the edge of the bowl.

Turn the dough, and any flour that has not been mixed in, onto a board and knead 10 minutes. Lift the dough and lightly flour the surface. Put the ball of dough down, cover with a bowl, and let stand 30 minutes.

Divide the dough into thirds and roll as thin as possible, using a lightly floured rolling pin. (I work on a wooden surface and roll until I can see the wood grain through the dough.) Or put through a hand-cranked pasta machine.

Cut the pasta to the width you desire: fettucini—¼-inch strips, linguini—⅛-inch strips, angel hair pasta—as thin as possible, lasagna—2 inches. (I find a pizza wheel works well for this job.)

Lay the cut pasta on a rack or a large surface to dry for at least one hour before cooking.

MAKES ABOUT 1¼ POUNDS DRIED PASTA.
CALORIES: 272   CHOLESTEROL: 0 mg   SODIUM: 358 mg   FIBER: 2 g

Health tip:
Omit salt.
CALORIES: 272   CHOLESTEROL: 0 mg   SODIUM: 3 mg   FIBER: 2 g

---

To cook fresh pasta: For each ½ pound of pasta you are cooking, use 4 quarts of boiling water with 1 tablespoon olive oil and 2 teaspoons of salt. Cook until al dente (the time will vary greatly according to how thickly you've cut the pasta and how long you've let it dry). Test the pasta for doneness frequently, by pulling one strand from the water and tasting it, starting about two minutes after you've added it to the water.

──────── ◇ ────────

Fresh Pasta with Egg

I'm torn as to whether I truly believe that homemade pasta is worth the time and effort. It is tastier, but I'm not convinced that it's that much tastier than the store-bought fresh pasta currently available. If you want to try your hand at it, the egg pasta is slightly firmer and more distinctive tasting than the pasta without eggs.

1¼ cups semolina flour
1 cup all-purpose flour
1½ teaspoons salt
4 eggs
1 tablespoon olive oil

In a large bowl, combine the semolina and all-purpose flours and the salt. Make a well in the center.

In a medium-size bowl, beat the eggs and olive oil until combined. Pour the egg mixture into the well in the flour.

Using a wooden spoon, start mixing the egg mixture in small circles gradually making larger circles. Incorporate more of the flour as you mix, until you have mixed in as much of the flour as you can and are stirring big circles around the edge of the bowl.

Turn the dough, and any flour that has not been mixed in, onto a board and knead 10 minutes. Lift the dough and lightly flour the surface. Put the ball of dough down, cover with a bowl, and let stand 30 minutes.

Divide the dough into thirds and roll as thin as possible, using a lightly floured rolling pin. (I work on a wooden surface and roll until I can see the wood grain through the dough.) Or put through a hand-cranked pasta machine.

Cut the pasta to the width you desire: fettucini—¼-inch strips, linguini—⅛-inch strips, angel hair pasta—as thin as possible, lasagna—2 inches. (I find a pizza wheel works well for this job.)

Lay the cut pasta on a rack or a large surface to dry for at least one hour before cooking.

MAKES ABOUT 1¼ POUNDS DRIED PASTA.
CALORIES: 219   CHOLESTEROL: 139 mg   SODIUM: 579 mg   FIBER: 1 g

Health tip:
Use the Fresh Pasta recipe without egg; omit salt.
CALORIES: 272   CHOLESTEROL: 0 mg   SODIUM: 3 mg   FIBER: 2 g

---

To cook fresh pasta: For each ½ pound of pasta you are cooking, use 4 quarts of boiling water with 1 tablespoon olive oil and 2 teaspoons of salt. Cook until al dente (the time will vary greatly according to how thickly you've cut the pasta and how long you've let it dry). Test the pasta for doneness frequently, by pulling one strand from the water and tasting it, starting about two minutes after you've added it to the water.

———————— ◇ ————————
Marinara Sauce

This is a very simple sauce that you can serve as is—or you can stir in meat or seafood.

2 tablespoons olive oil
1 cup chopped onion
3 cloves garlic, minced
1 can (28 ounce) Italian tomatoes, undrained
2 tablespoons tomato paste
2 tablespoons fresh chopped parsley
2 tablespoons fresh chopped basil or
    2 teaspoons dried basil
1 teaspoon sugar
½ teaspoon salt
¼ teaspoon pepper
⅛ teaspoon thyme

Heat the oil in a 3-quart saucepan, over medium-high heat. Add the onion and garlic and cook, stirring, until the onion is softened. Add the tomatoes with the juice, and break up the tomatoes with the back of a spoon.

Stir in the tomato paste, parsley, basil, sugar, salt, pepper, and thyme. Bring to a boil. Reduce heat and simmer, uncovered, 35 minutes.

SERVES 6.
CALORIES: 86   CHOLESTEROL: 9 mg   SODIUM: 398 mg   FIBER: 2 g

Health tip:
Use 2 teaspoons oil and cook in a nonstick saucepan; omit salt.
CALORIES: 59   CHOLESTEROL: 0 mg   SODIUM: 220 mg   FIBER: 2 g

———————— ◇ ————————
Pesto

I believe that hand-chopped pesto is the best possible version. You have a variety of textures that you lose when you prepare this in a blender. You can put any leftover pesto into an ice cube tray and freeze it, then use the cubes as desired.

2 cups packed basil leaves
⅔ cup pignoli
3 cloves garlic

1 cup grated Parmesan cheese
1 cup olive oil
½ teaspoon salt

Mince the basil, pignoli, and garlic. Put in a bowl and toss with the cheese; gradually stir in the olive oil and salt. Let stand at least one hour, but preferably overnight to mellow.
Food processor method: Put the basil into the processor container fitted with a steel blade. Cover and process until the basil is minced. Empty the basil into a medium-size bowl. Add the pignoli to the processor; cover and process until chopped. Add to the basil. Mince the garlic and toss with the basil. Add the cheese and toss. Gradually stir in the oil, then the salt. Let stand at least one hour.

SERVES 6.
CALORIES: 453   CHOLESTEROL: 10 mg   SODIUM: 438 mg   FIBER: 1 g

Health tip:
Use only half the oil and half the cheese; omit the salt.
CALORIES: 263   CHOLESTEROL: 5 mg   SODIUM: 312 mg   FIBER: 1 g

---

———————— ◇ ————————

Bolognese Sauce

This is a slightly creamy meat sauce, originating in the Bologna region of Italy. You can use any ground meat that you like or any combination of ground meats.

3 tablespoons olive oil
½ cup finely chopped onion
½ cup finely chopped carrot
½ cup finely chopped celery
1 pound ground meat (you can use beef, pork, or veal)
1 box (35 ounce) Pomi* fresh-strained tomatoes or tomato sauce
1 cup ready-to-serve beef broth
1 cup dry white wine
¼ cup chopped parsley
½ teaspoon salt
⅛ teaspoon nutmeg
½ cup heavy cream

Heat the oil in a 4-quart saucepan over medium-high heat. Add the onion, carrot, and celery and cook, stirring, until the onion is soft. Add the meat and cook until no longer pink. Stir in the

*Pomi brand is found in supermarkets or gourmet stores.

tomatoes, broth, wine, parsley, salt, and nutmeg. Bring to a boil. Reduce heat and simmer, uncovered, 2 hours. Stir in the cream.

SERVES 12.
CALORIES: 190   CHOLESTEROL: 46 mg   SODIUM: 200 mg   FIBER: 2 g

Health tip:
Reduce oil to 2 teaspoons and cook in a nonstick pot; use half-and-half for heavy cream; omit salt.
CALORIES: 145   CHOLESTEROL: 37 mg   SODIUM: 112 mg   FIBER: 2 g

———————— ◇ ————————

Puttanesca-Plus Sauce

The story goes that this is a quick sauce that the Italian "women of the evening" (puttanseca) would prepare after a night's work. It's an incredibly gutsy sauce, very salty and spicy—like the women it's named after. The plus in the sauce are the sun dried tomatoes. To tone it down, halve the amount of anchovies, garlic, sun-dried tomatoes, and capers.

> 3 tablespoons olive oil
> 6 anchovy fillets
> 3 cloves garlic, minced
> 1 can (14½ ounce) whole peeled tomatoes, undrained
> ⅓ cup water
> 3 tablespoons tomato paste
> Pinch crushed red pepper
> 1 cup chopped black olives
> 3 tablespoons chopped parsley
> 2 tablespoons chopped marinated sun-dried tomatoes
> 1 tablespoon capers

In a 2-quart saucepan, heat the olive oil over medium-high heat. Add the anchovies and cook, stirring, until the anchovies dissolve into a paste. Add the garlic. Stir in the tomatoes, and break up with the back of a spoon. Stir in the water, tomato paste and red pepper. Bring to a boil. Reduce the heat and simmer 15 minutes. Stir in the olives, parsley, sun-dried tomatoes, and capers. Simmer 10 minutes longer.

SERVES 6.
CALORIES: 134   CHOLESTEROL: 7 mg   SODIUM: 335 mg   FIBER: 2 g

Health tip:
Use 1 tablespoon oil and only 2 anchovies.
CALORIES: 89   CHOLESTEROL: 4 mg   SODIUM: 311 mg   FIBER: 2 g

---◇---

Fettucini Alfredo

I serve small portions of this dish because it is so rich. If you want to dress this up, toss in some proscuitto at the last minute.

1 cup heavy cream
¼ cup butter
Pinch nutmeg
½ pound fettucini, cooked just barely al dente and drained
⅔ cup grated Parmesan cheese
Freshly ground pepper

In a large skillet, bring the cream, butter, and nutmeg to a boil. Cook over high heat 2 minutes. Add the fettucini and toss. Add the cheese and pepper and continue tossing until the pasta is completely coated.

SERVES 4.
CALORIES: 451   CHOLESTEROL: 123 mg   SODIUM: 248 mg   FIBER: 1 g

Health tip:
Eat only a bite.

---◇---

The World's Best Pizza

In all modesty, I must say that I make the best pizza anywhere. The secret is using simple, basic ingredients that allow each flavor to shine. This recipe makes 4 individual pizzas, since these smaller ones are easier to manage than one large one. I entertain by making one and sharing it while the next one is in the oven.

Crust:

1 cup very warm water (105–115°F)
½ teaspoon sugar
1 package active dry yeast
2 to 2¾ cups all-purpose flour
⅓ cup semolina flour
1 tablespoon salt
1 tablespoon olive oil

Sauce:

> 2 tablespoons olive oil
> 1 cup chopped onion
> 1 can (14½ ounce) whole peeled tomatoes, undrained
> ¼ teaspoon salt

Topping:

> 6 cloves garlic, minced
> 1 or 2 packages (8 or 9 ounce) fresh mozzarella (it's important to the
> taste that you use the fresh type of mozzarella now available in the
> refrigerator case of your local supermarket or in gourmet stores),
> drained and shredded
> 1½ tablespoons olive oil

Optional toppings:

> Partially cooked sausage
> Fresh or dried herbs
> Pepperoni
> Sun-dried tomatoes
> Chopped onion
> Green bell peppers
> Mushrooms

In a glass measuring cup, stir together the warm water and sugar. Stir in yeast and let stand until ¼-inch of bubbly white foam forms on top. (This foaming is called *proofing*, and if it doesn't happen it means that for some reason or other the yeast has not been activated. Discard this batch and try again, double checking the date on the yeast package and the temperature of the water.)

In a large bowl, stir together 1½ cups of the all-purpose flour, the semolina, and salt. Stir in the yeast mixture and oil. Stir in ½ cup more flour to form a soft dough. Turn onto a floured board and knead in as much of the remaining flour as necessary to form a dough that is smooth and elastic (it is very important that the dough be very well kneaded).

Place in a greased bowl and cover with greased plastic wrap. Put in a warm, draft-free spot and let rise until doubled in bulk.

Prepare the sauce by heating the oil in a 2-quart saucepan. Add the onion and cook, stirring, until soft. Add the tomatoes with liquid, and break up the tomatoes with the back of a spoon. Stir in the salt. Bring to a boil, reduce heat and simmer, uncovered, 25 minutes.

Punch down the dough. Divide into fourths.

Remove racks from oven (unless you are using an electric oven, in which case you should leave one rack at the lowest possible rung). Preheat the oven to 450°F.

Place a large baking sheet on the floor of the oven (or the rack in the electric oven), with the rim of the baking sheet in the back of the oven.

On a well-floured surface, pat the one piece of dough as flat as possible. Make a fist and place the flattened dough on it. Then gently lift and spread your fingers to stretch the dough. When you have stretched the dough a little, start using both hands. When the center of the dough is quite thin, hold the dough with both hands, suspended in the air, and rotate the dough as you squeeze the edges, making them thin. You should have an 8-inch circle when you are finished.

Place on a flat baking sheet that has been well dusted with semolina or all-purpose flour.

Sprinkle the dough generously with one quarter of the garlic. Then spread one quarter of the sauce over the dough to within ½ inch of the border (you will be using only a thin layer of sauce). Sprinkle with one quarter of the cheese. (At this point you can add any topping that you like.) Drizzle with oil. (If you put on too much topping or cheese it will run off the edge of the pizza and burn onto the baking sheet—so don't be overly generous.)

Open the oven and transfer the pizza to the preheated baking sheet (you will probably have to use a jerking motion to convince the pizza to slide into the oven). Bake 7 to 10 minutes, or until the crust is browned and the cheese is melted.

To remove the pizza from the oven, slide the baking sheet you used to place the pizza into the oven under the cooked pizza and lift the pizza out (leaving the hot baking sheet in the oven for the next pizza).

Make 3 more pizzas out of the remaining dough, sauce and toppings.

SERVES 4.
CALORIES: 605   CHOLESTEROL: 44 mg   SODIUM: 1826 mg   FIBER: 5 g

Health tip:
Omit the salt and don't drizzle with additional oil; eat only half a pizza.
CALORIES: 281   CHOLESTEROL: 22 mg   SODIUM: 114 mg   FIBER: 3 g

—————— ◊ ——————

Plain Old White Bread

I gave my friend Michele Pigliavento half a loaf to taste. She called to ask what kind of bread it was—she couldn't believe that plain old white bread could taste so good.

½ cup very warm water (105–115°F)
1 teaspoon sugar
2 packages active dry yeast
5 to 5½ cups all-purpose flour, divided
1 tablespoon salt
1 cup milk
¾ cup water

In a glass measuring cup, stir together the warm water and sugar. Stir in the yeast and let stand until about ¼-inch of bubbly white foam forms on top. (This foaming is called *proofing,* and if it doesn't happen it means that for some reason or other the yeast has not been activated. Discard this batch and try again, double checking the date on the yeast package and the temperature of the water.)

In a large bowl, stir together 3 cups of the flour and the salt. Stir in the yeast mixture, milk, and water. Stir in 1½ cups more flour, to form a soft dough.

Turn onto a floured board and knead in enough of the remaining flour to make a dough that is smooth and elastic and no longer sticky. Place in a large greased bowl and cover with greased plastic wrap. Put in a warm, draft-free spot and let rise until doubled in bulk.

Punch down the dough and divide in half. Form into 2 8-inch loaves. Place in greased 8 × 4½ × 2¾-inch loaf pans. Cover with greased plastic wrap and let rise until doubled in bulk.

Preheat oven to 350°F. Bake 50 minutes of until loaf is browned and sounds hollow when tapped on the bottom. Remove from pans and cool on racks.

MAKES 2 LOAVES (14 slices each).
CALORIES: 89   CHOLESTEROL: 1 mg   SODIUM: 233 mg   FIBER: 1 g

Health tip:
Omit salt.
CALORIES: 89   CHOLESTEROL: 1 mg   SODIUM: 5 mg   FIBER: 1 g

———————— ◇ ————————

Whole Wheat Bread

I find this whole wheat bread to be especially good and light.

½ cup very warm water (105–115°F)
3 tablespoons sugar, divided
2 packages active dry yeast
3½ to 4 cups all-purpose flour, divided
3 cups whole-wheat flour
1 tablespoon salt
1½ cups milk
1 cup water
1 egg
3 tablespoons oil

In a glass measuring cup, stir together the warm water and 1 teaspoon of the sugar. Stir in yeast and let stand until about ¼-inch of bubbly white foam forms on top. (This foaming is called *proofing*, and if it doesn't happen it means that for some reason or other the yeast has not been activated. Discard this batch and try again, double checking the date on the yeast package and the temperature of the water.)

In a large bowl, stir together 1½ cups of the all-purpose flour, the whole-wheat flour, salt, and the remaining 2 tablespoons plus 2 teaspoons sugar. Stir in the yeast mixture, milk, water, egg, and oil. Stir in 1½ cups more all-purpose flour to make a soft dough.

Turn onto a floured board and knead in enough of the remaining 1 cup of flour to make a dough that is smooth and elastic and no longer sticky. Place in a large greased bowl and cover with greased plastic wrap. Put in a warm, draft-free spot and let rise until doubled in bulk.

Punch down the dough and divide in half; form into 2 9-inch loaves. Place in two greased 9 × 5 × 3-inch loaf pans.

Preheat the oven to 350°F.

Bake 45 minutes or until loaves are browned and sound hollow when tapped on bottom. Remove from pan and cool on racks.

MAKES 2 LOAVES (18 slices each).
CALORIES: 198   CHOLESTEROL: 13 mg   SODIUM: 367 mg   FIBER: 3 g

Health tip:
Omit salt.
CALORIES: 198   CHOLESTEROL: 13 mg   SODIUM: 12 mg   FIBER: 3 g

—————— ◇ ——————

French Bread

The French make their bread with a flour that is high in gluten—therefore I recommend using bread flour that contains more gluten than all-purpose flour. The typical crispy crust comes from steam in the oven during the first half of the baking. To duplicate this, I suggest tossing ice cubes in the hot oven so they will create steam as they melt.

½ cup very warm water (105–115°F)
1 teaspoon sugar
1 package active dry yeast
2¾ to 3½ cups bread flour, divided
2 teaspoons salt
¾ cup water
1 egg white, optional
6 ice cubes, divided

In a glass measuring cup, stir together the warm water and sugar. Stir in the yeast and let stand until about ¼-inch bubbly white foam forms on top. (This foaming is called *proofing*, and if it doesn't happen it means that for some reason or other the yeast has not been activated. Discard this batch and try again, double checking the date on the yeast package and the temperature of the water.)

In a large bowl, stir together 2 cups of the flour and the salt. Stir in the yeast mixture and the water. Stir in ½ cup more flour to make a dough that is easy to handle.

Turn onto a floured board and knead in enough of the remaining flour to make a dough that is smooth and elastic and no longer sticky. Place in a large greased bowl and cover with greased plastic wrap. Put in a warm, draft-free spot and let rise until doubled in bulk.

Punch down the dough and let rise until doubled in bulk again.

Grease a two-loaf French bread pan or baking sheet.

Punch down the dough and divide in half. Roll each half of the dough into a long thin loaf (about 15 inches long). Place in prepared pan and brush with egg white, if desired. Using a sharp knife, make 3 diagonal slashes. Cover with greased plastic wrap; let rise until doubled in bulk.

Preheat oven to 425°F.

Place pan into the oven and drop 2 ice cubes onto the oven floor (if you have an electric oven you may want to omit the ice cubes). Bake 5 minutes. Open oven and quickly throw in 2 more ice cubes.

Bake 5 minutes longer and add the remaining ice cubes. Continue baking until browned, about 25 minutes total. Cool on racks.

MAKES 2 LOAVES (about 16 slices each).
CALORIES: 88   CHOLESTEROL: 0 mg   SODIUM: 270 mg   FIBER: 1 g

Health tip:
Omit salt.
CALORIES: 88   CHOLESTEROL: 0 mg   SODIUM: 4 mg   FIBER: 1 g

◇

Semolina Bread

This bread is absolutely fabulous. It has a full flavor and great texture that is dense but not heavy. The secret to making it is to be patient. The first rising can take as long as 2½ hours or more. As long as your yeast has proofed (foamed), the bread will rise eventually.

½ cup very warm water (105–115°F)
½ teaspoon sugar
1 package active dry yeast
2 cups semolina
2 to 2½ cups all-purpose flour
2 teaspoons salt
1 cup milk
2 tablespoons butter, melted
1 egg white, optional
1 tablespoon sesame seeds, optional

In a glass measuring cup, stir together the warm water and sugar. Stir in the yeast and let stand until about ¼-inch bubbly white foam forms on top. (This foaming is called *proofing*, and if it doesn't happen it means that for some reason or other the yeast has not been activated. Discard this batch and try again, double checking the date on the yeast package and the temperature of the water.)

In a large bowl, stir together the semolina flour, ½ cup of the all-purpose flour, and the salt. Stir in the yeast mixture, milk, and butter. Stir in 1 cup more all-purpose flour to make a soft dough.

Turn onto a floured board and knead in enough of the remaining all-purpose flour to make a dough that is elastic and no longer sticky. Place in a large greased bowl and cover with greased plastic wrap. Put in a warm, draft-free spot and let rise until doubled in bulk, about 2 or more hours.

Punch down the dough and form into a round loaf, about 7

inches in diameter. Using a sharp knife, score the top of the bread. Place on a greased baking sheet, cover with greased plastic wrap and let rise until doubled in bulk.

Preheat oven to 375°F.

Beat the egg white lightly and brush on the loaf. Sprinkle with sesame seeds. Bake 40 minutes or until browned and crisp on top and bottom.

SERVES 18.
CALORIES: 112   CHOLESTEROL: 5 mg   SODIUM: 258 mg   FIBER: 1 g

Health tip:
Omit the salt; use unsalted margarine instead of butter.
CALORIES: 112   CHOLESTEROL: 2 mg   SODIUM: 17 mg   FIBER: 1 g

---

———————— ◇ ————————

Cornell Bread

I am including it in this book because, in addition to being delicious, it is very high in protein and healthy. It is my guess that the original formula for this bread was developed at Cornell University.

½ cup very warm water (105–115°F)
1 teaspoon sugar
2 packages dry yeast
1½ cups water
½ cup whole-wheat flour
½ cup nonfat dry milk
⅓ cup soy flour
¼ cup wheat germ
1 egg
3 tablespoons honey
2 tablespoons oil
1 tablespoon salt
5 to 6 cups all-purpose flour, divided

In a glass measuring cup, stir together the warm water and the sugar. Stir in the yeast and let stand until about ¼-inch bubbly white foam forms on top. (This foaming is called *proofing,* and if it doesn't happen it means that for some reason or other the yeast has not been activated. Discard this batch and try again, double checking the date on the yeast package and the temperature of the water.)

In a large bowl, beat together the water, whole-wheat flour, milk, soy flour, wheat germ, egg, honey, oil, and salt.

Beat in the yeast mixture, then 2½ cups of the all-purpose flour. Stir in 1½ cups more all-purpose flour. Turn onto a well-floured board and knead in as much of the remaining flour as necessary to make a dough that is no longer sticky.

Place in a large greased bowl and cover with greased plastic wrap. Put in a warm, draft-free spot and let rise until doubled in bulk, about 1 hour.

Punch down the dough and divide in half. Shape each half into a loaf and put into greased 8 × 4½ × 2½-inch loaf pans. Cover with greased plastic wrap and let rise until doubled in bulk.

Preheat the oven to 350°F for 20 minutes. Reduce heat to 325°F and bake 30 minutes longer, or until loaves are browned and sound hollow when thumped on the bottom.

MAKES 2 LOAVES (14 slices each).
CALORIES: 123   CHOLESTEROL: 7 mg   SODIUM: 238 mg   FIBER: 1 g

Health tip:
Omit salt.
CALORIES: 123   CHOLESTEROL: 7 mg   SODIUM: 10 mg   FIBER: 1 g

———————— ◇ ————————

Wheat-Germ Rolls

These rolls are very tasty and have a nice texture. I like to serve them to company at brunch, warm and with giant pats of butter.

½ cup very warm water (105–115°F)
2 teaspoons sugar
2 packages active dry yeast
3 to 4 cups all-purpose flour, divided
1½ teaspoons salt
1 cup water
½ cup Honey Crunch Wheat Germ

In a glass measuring cup, stir together the warm water and sugar. Stir in the yeast and let stand until about ¼-inch bubbly white foam forms on top. (This foaming is called *proofing*, and if it doesn't happen it means that for some reason or other the yeast has not been activated. Discard this batch and try again, double checking the date on the yeast package and the temperature of the water.)

In a large bowl, stir together 2 cups of the flour and the salt. Stir in the water and the yeast mixture. Stir in the wheat germ and ½ cup more flour.

Turn onto a floured board and knead in enough of the remaining flour as necessary to make a dough that is smooth and elastic and not sticky. Place in a large greased bowl and cover with greased plastic wrap. Put in a warm, draft-free spot and let rise until doubled in bulk, about 40 minutes.

Punch down the dough and form into 8 oval rolls. Place on 2 greased cookie sheets. Cover with greased plastic wrap and let rise until doubled in bulk.

Preheat the oven to 350°F. Bake the rolls 35 minutes or until browned and sound hollow when tapped on the bottom.

MAKES 8.
CALORIES: 206   CHOLESTEROL: 0 mg   SODIUM: 402 mg   FIBER: 3 g

Health tip:
Omit salt.
CALORIES: 206   CHOLESTEROL: 0 mg   SODIUM: 2 mg   FIBER: 3 g

——————— ◇ ———————

Delicious Pancakes

These are very thick and light pancakes just like the ones you see in the advertisements, but never seem to be able to make at home.

1½ cups self-rising flour
3 tablespoons sugar
1¼ cups milk
3 tablespoons butter, melted
2 eggs

In a large bowl, stir together the flour and sugar.

In a medium-size bowl, beat the milk, butter, and eggs together until completely combined. Stir the milk mixture into the flour until moistened. The batter will be thick and lumpy.

Heat a griddle or skillet until a drop of water dances across the surface before evaporating. Lightly grease the griddle and drop 2 rounded tablespoons of batter per pancake.

Cook until bubbles break on the surface of the pancake. Because the batter is so thick, you will have to cook on a low heat so that they cook through before they get too dark on the bottom. Turn and cook until browned on the other side.

MAKES 12.
CALORIES: 120   CHOLESTEROL: 46 mg   SODIUM: 217 mg   FIBER: 0 g

Health tip:
Use unsalted margarine instead of butter; scrambled-egg substitute; and 1-percent-fat milk.
CALORIES: 111   CHOLESTEROL: 1 mg   SODIUM: 202 mg   FIBER: 0 g

———————— ◇ ————————

Vanilla Waffles

These waffles smell so good as they cook that you'll hardly be able to wait for them to brown. Serve them with maple syrup or, if you feel really indulgent, topped with whipped cream and fresh berries.

2¼ cups self-rising flour
¼ cup sugar
1¾ cups milk
½ cup butter, melted
2 eggs
1 teaspoon vanilla extract

Heat the waffle iron.
In a large bowl, stir together the flour and sugar.
In a medium-size bowl, beat together the milk, butter, eggs, and vanilla. Stir the milk mixture into the flour until blended.
Pour about 1 cup of batter onto lightly greased, preheated waffle iron. Bake until golden and crisp.

MAKES 12 4-INCH WAFFLES
CALORIES: 188   CHOLESTEROL: 59 mg   SODIUM: 316 mg   FIBER: 1 g

Health tip:
Use unsalted margarine instead of butter and use scrambled-egg substitute.
CALORIES: 184   CHOLESTEROL: 4 mg   SODIUM: 266 mg   FIBER: 1 g

Apple Pie Waffles

These waffles are cinnamon-y and moist—a great candidate for à la mode.

1¼ cup all-purpose flour
1 cup miller's bran (fine grind)
¼ cup sugar
1 tablespoon baking powder
1½ teaspoons cinnamon
1 teaspoon baking soda
¼ teaspoon nutmeg
2 cups buttermilk
½ cup butter, melted
½ cup finely shredded apple
⅓ cup water
3 egg whites
¼ teaspoon salt

Preheat a waffle iron.

In a large bowl, stir together the all-purpose flour, bran, sugar, baking powder, cinnamon, baking soda, and nutmeg.

In a medium-size bowl, beat together the milk, butter, shredded apple, and water; set aside.

In another medium-size bowl, using clean beaters, beat the egg whites with the salt until stiff, but not dry.

Stir the milk mixture into the flour, then fold in the egg whites.

Spread 1¼ cups of batter onto the waffle iron. Bake until golden and crisp.

MAKES 12 4-INCH WAFFLES.
CALORIES: 170   CHOLESTEROL: 22 mg   SODIUM: 316 mg   FIBER: 4 g

Health tip:
Use unsalted margarine instead of butter. Omit salt.
CALORIES: 170   CHOLESTEROL: 1 mg   SODIUM: 236 mg   FIBER: 4 g

Maple French Toast

If, by any chance, you have some unsliced white bread left over, this is an ideal way to use it.

4 (1½-inch thick) slices white bread
4 eggs
¾ cup half-and-half
2 tablespoons maple syrup
2 tablespoons sugar
½ teaspoon vanilla extract
⅛ teaspoon salt
¼ cup butter, divided

Remove the crust from the bread. Cut each slice in half diagonally to form triangles.

In a medium-size bowl, beat the eggs, beat in the half-and-half, maple syrup, sugar, vanilla, and salt. Beat until the sugar is dissolved. Dip each piece of bread into egg mixture until soaked.

Melt 2 tablespoons of the butter in a 10-inch skillet, over medium-high heat. Place half of the bread triangles in the skillet. Cook until brown on bottom; turn and cook the second side until browned. Remove the finished pieces to a serving platter (the platter may be placed into the oven to remain warm). Melt remaining butter and cook remaining bread.

SERVES 4.
CALORIES: 359   CHOLESTEROL: 256 mg   SODIUM: 392 mg   FIBER: 0 g

Health tip:
Use milk instead of half-and-half; scrambled-egg substitute; and unsalted margarine instead of butter. Omit salt.
CALORIES: 333   CHOLESTEROL: 17 mg   SODIUM: 278 mg   FIBER: 0 g

———————— ◇ ————————

Whole Wheat Biscuits

These are the lightest most heavenly biscuits I've ever eaten.

1½ cups all-purpose flour
½ cup whole-wheat flour
2 tablespoons sugar
1 tablespoon baking powder
1 teaspoon salt
1½ cups heavy cream

Preheat the oven to 400°F.

In a large bowl, stir together the all-purpose flour, whole-wheat flour, sugar, baking powder, and salt.

Using a fork, gradually add the cream until a soft dough is formed. Place on a floured board and knead 10 to 12 times. Roll ½-inch thick. Using a 2½-inch biscuit cutter dipped in flour, cut biscuits. Place on ungreased cookie sheets and bake 15 to 18 minutes or until browned.

MAKES 12.
CALORIES: 185   CHOLESTEROL: 41 mg   SODIUM: 272 mg   FIBER: 1 g

Health tip:
Omit salt.
CALORIES: 185   CHOLESTEROL: 41 mg   SODIUM: 94 mg   FIBER: 1 g

———————— ◇ ————————

Basic Muffins

As the title indicates, these are basic muffins. It's up to you to dress them up. Stir in fresh or dried fruits, spices, nuts, or anything you can think of.

2 cups all-purpose flour
2 tablespoons sugar
1 tablespoon baking powder
½ teaspoon salt
1 cup milk
⅓ cup butter, melted
1 egg

Preheat the oven to 400°F. Grease 12 (2½-inch) muffin cups

In a large bowl, using a whisk, stir together the flour, sugar, baking powder, and salt. Set aside.

In a large bowl, beat together the milk, butter, and egg. Add the milk mixture to the flour all at once. Stir until dry ingredients are just moistened and remain lumpy.

Spoon into prepared baking tins, filling each cup about ⅔ full. Bake 20 to 25 minutes or until browned.

MAKES 12.
CALORIES: 148   CHOLESTEROL: 34 mg   SODIUM: 230 mg   FIBER: 1 g

health tip:
Omit salt; use unsalted margarine instead of butter.
CALORIES: 148   CHOLESTEROL: 20 mg   SODIUM: 104 mg   FIBER: 1 g

---

———————— ◇ ————————

Pineapple Bran Muffins

I asked a lot of people to taste these muffins for me (since I'm allergic to pineapple and couldn't taste them myself). My neighbors Marie and Bob Riesel said they were good, but just needed a little something. My friend Michele Pigliavento came up with the missing element—brown sugar. This version is very good.

1½ cups miller's bran (fine)
1 cup all-purpose flour
2 teaspoons baking powder
1 teaspoon baking soda
½ teaspoon salt
¾ cup buttermilk
1 can (8¼ ounce) crushed pineapple (syrup packed), undrained
⅓ cup firmly packed dark-brown sugar
¼ cup vegetable oil
2 egg whites

Preheat the oven to 400°F. Grease 12 3-inch muffin cups.

In a large bowl, stir together the bran, flour, baking powder, baking soda, and salt.

In a medium-size bowl, stir together the buttermilk, pineapple with syrup, brown sugar, oil, and egg whites until combined. Add the buttermilk mixture to the dry ingredients. Stir until just moistened.

Spoon into the prepared muffin cups and bake 20 minutes.

SERVES 12.
CALORIES: 135   CHOLESTEROL: 1 mg   SODIUM: 240 mg   FIBER: 2 g

Health tip:
Omit salt; use juice packed pineapple.
CALORIES: 131   CHOLESTEROL: 1 mg   SODIUM: 152 mg   FIBER: 2 g

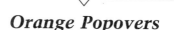

Orange Popovers

These come out best when made in a popover pan. If you are very fond of popovers, the investment is certainly worthwhile. To make regular popovers, just omit the orange rind and sugar.

1 cup milk
2 eggs
2 teaspoons sugar
1 tablespoon vegetable oil
½ teaspoon salt
1 teaspoon grated orange rind
1 cup sifted flour

Place the milk, eggs, sugar, oil, salt, and orange rind into the blender container (I prefer a blender to a processor for this). Cover and process until just blended. Add the flour, cover and process until smooth. Let stand 1 hour.

Preheat the oven to 425°F.

Place the popover pans in the oven for 5 minutes. (If you don't have popover pans use 6 custard cups—but they have to be deeper than they are wide. Put them onto a baking sheet for easier handling.)

While the pan is heating, process the batter in the blender just a few seconds to stir.

Remove the pans (or cups) from the oven and thoroughly grease each cup. Fill cups a little less than half full. Place in oven and bake 20 minutes, reduce heat to 350°F (don't open the door to peek at any time) and bake 15 minutes longer, or until puffed high.

SERVES 6.
CALORIES: 151   CHOLESTEROL: 75 mg   SODIUM: 220 mg   FIBER: .5 g

Health tip:
Omit salt.
CALORIES: 151   CHOLESTEROL: 75 mg   SODIUM: 43 mg   FIBER: .5 g

---◇---

Basic Sweet Dough

This is a very light and tasty dough. You can make it into raisin bread or monkey bread or any sweet yeast product you want.

1 cup milk
½ cup water
⅓ cup sugar
⅓ cup butter
4½ cups all-purpose flour
1 package active dry yeast
1½ teaspoons salt
2 eggs

In a 1-quart saucepan, over high heat, stir together the milk, water, and sugar. Bring to a boil and continue to boil 3 minutes, reducing the heat if the milk starts to boil over. Remove from the heat and stir in the butter. Let stand 30 minutes.

In a large bowl, stir together 2 cups of the flour, the yeast, and salt. Stir in the cooled milk mixture, then the eggs. Stir in 1¾ cups more of the flour.

Turn onto a floured board and knead in as much of the remaining ½ cups flour as necessary to make a dough that is just slightly sticky, about 7 minutes. (If you find that the dough is too sticky to knead and you've already used all the flour, just dust your hands with flour but don't add more to the dough. A soft dough is essential to a light and delicate crumb.) Place in a large greased bowl and cover with greased plastic wrap. Put in a warm, draft-free spot and let rise until doubled in bulk, about 1½ hours.

Punch down and allow to rise again, about 40 minutes.

Punch down the dough and use in your favorite recipes such as the coffee cake below.

MAKES DOUGH FOR 12 ROLLS OR PASTRIES.
CALORIES: 174   CHOLESTEROL: 34 mg   SODIUM: 219 mg   FIBER: 2 g

Health tip:
Use unsalted margarine instead of butter and omit salt.
CALORIES: 174   CHOLESTEROL: 24 mg   SODIUM: 18 mg   FIBER: 2 g

——————— ◇ ———————

Pecan Coffee Ring

There's something so homey and wonderful about having a cup of coffee and a slice (or three) of a good homemade coffee cake.

1 recipe sweet dough
3 tablespoons butter, melted
1 cup firmly packed brown sugar (dark or light)
1½ cups chopped pecans
1 teaspoon cinnamon
Icing (optional)
½ cup confectioners' sugar
1 tablespoon milk

Preheat the oven to 350°F. Grease a baking sheet.

On a lightly floured surface roll the dough into a 12 × 20-inch rectangle. Brush with the butter.

In a medium-size bowl, combine the sugar, pecans, and cinnamon. Sprinkle sugar mixture evenly over the dough. Roll into a log, starting at the long edge. Pinch the seams to seal. Bring the two ends together to form a ring and pinch to hold together. Place on prepared baking sheet.

Using a sharp knife or scissors, slice the dough from the outside of the ring ⅔ of the way to the center into 1-inch pieces, making sure that the center remains uncut. Take each 1-inch piece and twist onto its side, exposing the inside spiral. The pieces will lean slightly on each other.

Cover with greased plastic wrap and let rise until doubled in bulk. Bake 25 to 30 minutes or until golden. Remove from baking sheet and cool on rack.

If desired, glaze by stirring together the confectioners' sugar and water and drizzling over the cooled pecan ring.

SERVES 18.
CALORIES: 314   CHOLESTEROL: 39 mg   SODIUM: 241 mg   FIBER: 2 g

Health tip:
Use unsalted margarine instead of butter and have only a sliver. Omit salt from dough.
CALORIES: 314   CHOLESTEROL: 24 mg   SODIUM: 26 mg   FIBER: 2 g

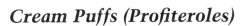

Cream Puffs (Profiteroles)

You can cut the tops off these little cream puffs and fill with sweet or savory fillings—simplest of all is sweetened whipped cream. This is a recipe for a small batch. If you're entertaining and want to make more, double the recipe.

¼ cup water
2 tablespoons butter
⅛ teaspoon salt
¼ cup flour
1 egg

Preheat the oven to 450°F. Grease a baking sheet.

In a small saucepan, bring the water, butter, and salt to a boil over medium-high heat. Remove from the heat and add flour, all at once, stirring vigorously. Reduce heat to low and cook, stirring constantly, 2 minutes. Cool 5 minutes.

Add the egg and stir until smooth and shiny.

Drop by rounded teaspoonsful at least 1 inch apart onto the prepared baking sheet. Bake 10 mintues. Without opening the oven door, reduce heat to 350°F and bake 15 minutes longer.

Remove puffs to wire rack and cool.

MAKES 12 SMALL PROFITEROLES.
CALORIES: 33 CHOLESTEROL: 22 mg SODIUM: 43 mg FIBER: 0 g

Health tip:
Use unsalted margarine instead of butter and omit salt.
CALORIES: 33 CHOLESTEROL: 17 mg SODIUM: 8 mg FIBER: 0 g

Puff Pastry (Feuillete)

This is absolutely the most wonderful pastry ever created. Keeping that in mind may help to overcome the fact that this is a long and involved recipe. Once made, though, puff pastry then becomes the base for very delicious and easy recipes. If you're not up to the challenge of homemade puff pastry, it can be purchased in the freezer department of your local supermarket.

1 cup butter, divided
1½ cups flour
½ cup, minus 1 tablespoon, ice water

Melt ¼ cup of the butter. In a large bowl, stir together the flour, water, and melted butter.

Shape into an 8 × 12-inch rectangle. Wrap in plastic wrap and refrigerate 10 minutes.

Place the remaining butter between 2 pieces of waxed paper. Roll into a 4 × 6-inch rectangle. Fold the butter into thirds and roll into a 4 × 6-inch rectangle again. Repeat this one more time (this process softens the butter to the necessary consistency).

Remove the dough from the refrigerator. Place on a lightly floured board. Place the butter in the center of the dough. Fold the left side of the dough over the butter, then fold the right side over to make a package with the butter enclosed in the center.

Roll, without pressing too hard, into a 8 × 18-inch rectangle. (If butter breaks through the dough, lightly pat the butter with flour until dry.) Fold one third of the dough toward the center (you now have two thirds of the dough in a double layer and one third in a single thickness). Fold the remaining one third of the dough over the double part to form 6 × 8-inch "book."

Roll the dough again into an 8 × 18-inch rectangle, dusting with flour if necessary. Fold into book. Wrap in plastic wrap and place into the refrigerator for 30 minutes. (You have now completed 2 turns.)

Remove the dough from the refrigerator and roll out and fold twice more (2 more turns). Wrap in plastic wrap and chill 30 minutes longer. Repeat once more and let chill at least 45 minutes more.

The dough is now ready to be rolled out for any of your baking needs, or if you prefer, you can freeze it for later use.

Recipe yield depends on what you are making with the pastry
Nutritional count is for the entire recipe. You can divide it into the number of servings according to your use.
CALORIES: 2304   CHOLESTEROL: 497 mg   SODIUM: 1551 mg   FIBER: 5 g

Health tip:
Use unsalted butter. (But it must be butter—no margarine!)
CALORIES: 2304   CHOLESTEROL: 497 mg   SODIUM: 25 mg   FIBER: 5 g

Puffy Apple Tarts

These are very delicious and very easy to make (once you've made the pastry).

2 large apples, peeled, cored, and thinly sliced
1 tablespoon lemon juice
½ recipe puff pastry (see page 81) or 1 sheet frozen prepared puff pastry, thawed
¼ cup apricot jam, put through a sieve and divided
2 tablespoons sugar, divided
1 cup whipped cream, if desired

Preheat the oven to 400°F.

In a medium-size bowl, toss the apples with the lemon juice. Set aside.

Roll the pastry into a 12 × 12-inch square. Cut into 4 6-inch squares. Place on ungreased baking sheet

Lightly brush each square with some of the apricot jam, to within 1 inch of the borders.

Arrange one quarter of the apple slices evenly over the jam in each square. Brush with remaining jam. Sprinkle each tart, including the pastry, with 1½ teaspoons sugar.

Bake 15 to 20 minutes or until the pastry is puffed and browned.

Cut into triangles and serve with whipped cream, if desired

SERVES 8.
CALORIES: 388   CHOLESTEROL: 51 mg   SODIUM: 101 mg   FIBER: 0 g

Health tip:
Skip the whipped cream. Have only half a serving.
CALORIES: 165   CHOLESTEROL: 16 mg   SODIUM: 52 mg   FIBER: 0 g

───────── ◇ ─────────

Easy Napoleons

I had dinner with my friend Holly Garrison one night and she made this exquisite simple dessert—simple if you already have made the puff pastry.

*½ recipe puff pastry (see page 81) or 1 sheet frozen prepared puff pastry,
thawed
1½ cups heavy cream
2 tablespoons sugar
1 pint fresh berries (if you're using strawberries, hull and halve them)
Confectioners' sugar*

Preheat oven to 375°F.
Roll the pastry dough into a 10 × 12-inch rectangle. Cut into 8 3 × 5-inch rectangles. Place on ungreased baking sheets and bake 10 to 15 minutes, or until lightly browned. Cool.
In a large bowl, beat the heavy cream with the sugar until stiff.
Split each piece of pastry in half, horizontal. This will give you a top and a bottom. Spread about ⅓ cup of the heavy cream mixture on the bottom half of each puff pastry. Top with some of the berries. Cover with top half (browned side up). Sprinkle generously with confectioners' sugar.

SERVES 8.
CALORIES: 244   CHOLESTEROL: 61 mg   SODIUM: 102 mg   FIBER: 0 g

Health tip:
Skip the puff pastry and whipped cream—just have fresh berries.

───────── ◇ ─────────

Angel Food Cake

Everyone who knows me, knows that I love white food—vanilla ice cream, milk, marshmallows; and Angel Food Cake is another one that I think is just great. If you are fond of almond flavoring you can add ½ teaspoon when you fold in the vanilla.

*1 cup cake flour
1 cup sifted confectioners' sugar
¼ teaspoon salt
12 egg whites, room temperature (about 1¾ cups)
½ teaspoon cream of tartar
¾ cup sugar
1 teaspoon vanilla extract*

Preheat the oven to 375°F.

Sift the flour, confectioners' sugar, and salt into a medium-size bowl, or onto a piece of waxed paper.

In a large bowl, beat the egg whites with the cream of tartar until foamy. Beat in the sugar 2 tablespoons at a time until the egg whites are stiff and glossy and all the sugar has been added.

Sift one quarter of the flour mixture over the egg whites and gently fold in, until completely combined. Continue folding in the remaining three quarters of the flour. Fold in the vanilla.

Gently spread the egg mixture into a 10-inch tube pan. Bake 35 minutes, or until browned. Cool upside down at least one hour. Run knife around edges and remove from pan.

Slice with serrated knife.

SERVES 10.
CALORIES: 150   CHOLESTEROL: 0 mg   SODIUM: 114 mg   FIBER: 0 g

Health tip:
Omit salt.
CALORIES: 150   CHOLESTEROL: 0 mg   SODIUM: 61 mg   FIBER: 0 g

───── ◇ ─────

Whole-Wheat Carrot Cake

This is a very moist, yummy, cake. If you want to dress it up you can frost it (try the frosting from the yellow cake, p. 87)

1 cup whole-wheat pastry flour
¾ cup all-purpose flour
2 teaspoons baking powder
1 teaspoon baking soda
1½ teaspoons cinnamon
¼ teaspoon nutmeg
¼ teaspoon salt
⅛ teaspoon clove
¾ cup raisins
½ cup chopped walnuts
⅔ cup corn oil
⅔ cup firmly packed dark-brown sugar
½ cup sugar
1 teaspoon vanilla extract
2 eggs
1½ cups shredded carrot

Preheat the oven to 350°F. Heavily grease and flour a 9 × 5 × 3-inch loaf pan.

In a large bowl, or on waxed paper, using a whisk, stir together the whole-wheat flour, all-purpose flour, baking powder, baking soda, cinnamon, nutmeg, salt, and clove. Add the raisins and nuts and toss.

In a large bowl, beat together the oil, brown sugar, sugar, and vanilla. Beat in the eggs, one at a time. Stir in the carrots, then the flour mixture, stirring until completely combined.

Pour into prepared pan and bake 1 hour, or until a wooden pick inserted in the center comes out clean. Cool in pan 10 minutes, then invert onto rack and cool completely.

SERVES 14.
CALORIES: 239   CHOLESTEROL: 30 mg   SODIUM: 164 mg   FIBER: 3 g

Health tip:
Omit salt.
CALORIES: 239   CHOLESTEROL: 30 mg   SODIUM: 126 mg   FIBER: 3 g

---

─────── ◇ ───────

Sour Cream Apple Cake

I wrote this recipe some time ago, but it's still my very favorite cake. It's light and moist with an unbelievable flavor.

2½ cups all-purpose flour
½ teaspoon baking powder
½ teaspoon baking soda
¼ teaspoon salt
¼ cup firmly packed light- or dark-brown sugar
½ teaspoon cinnamon
1 cup chopped nuts
1 cup butter, softened
2¼ cups sugar, divided
4 eggs
1 cup sour cream
1 teaspoon vanilla extract
3 cups coarsely chopped peeled apples

Preheat the oven to 350°F. Generously grease and flour a heavy bundt pan (light enamel bundt pans brown the outside of the cake too quickly) or 10-inch tube pan.

In a large bowl, or on a sheet of waxed paper, using a whisk, stir together the flour, baking powder, baking soda, and salt; set aside.

In a medium-size bowl, combine the brown sugar and cinnamon. Stir in the nuts; set aside.

In a large bowl, cream the butter with 2 cups of the sugar until light and fluffy. Beat in the eggs until combined.

Beat the flour mixture into the butter alternately with the sour cream, starting and ending with the flour. Beat in the vanilla.

In a medium-size bowl, toss the apples with the remaining ¼ cup sugar. Fold into the batter. Spoon half of the batter into the prepared pan.

Sprinkle the nut mixture over the batter. Top with the remaining batter and smooth with a spatula.

Bake 1 hour 10 minutes, or until a wooden pick inserted in the center comes out clean. Turn immediately onto a rack to cool.

SERVES 16.
CALORIES: 421   CHOLESTEROL: 89 mg   SODIUM: 194 mg   FIBER: 2 g

Health tip:
Use unsalted margarine instead of butter and omit the salt.
CALORIES: 421   CHOLESTEROL: 58 mg   SODIUM: 77 mg   FIBER: 2 g

———————— ◇ ————————

Yellow Cake with Vanilla Buttercream Frosting

This is a very easy cake to make. It's light and delicious with a frosting that's a real bowl licker. It's a perfect birthday, anniversary, or anyday cake.

Cake:

> 2¾ *cups all-purpose flour*
> 2 *teaspoons baking powder*
> ½ *teaspoon salt*
> ¾ *cup butter, softened*
> 1½ *cups sugar*
> 3 *eggs*
> 1 *teaspoon vanilla*
> 1½ *cups milk*

Frosting:

> ¾ *cup butter, softened*
> ½ *cup shortening*
> 1 *pound confectioners' sugar*
> 2 *tablespoons milk*
> 1 *tablespoon vanilla*

Preheat oven to 350°F. Grease and flour 2 9-inch round cake pans.

In a large bowl, or on waxed paper, using a whisk, stir together the flour, baking powder, and salt.

In a large bowl, cream the butter and sugar until light and fluffy. Beat in the eggs, one at a time, and beat until thoroughly combined. Beat in the vanilla.

Beat in the flour mixture, alternately with the milk, starting and ending with the flour.

Spread into the prepared pans. Bake 40 minutes, or until a wooden pick inserted into the center comes out clean.

Turn onto rack to cool.

In a large bowl, cream the butter and shortening. Beat in 1 cup of the confectioners' sugar. Beat in the milk and then the remaining confectioners' sugar, ½ cup at a time, beating well after each addition. Beat in the vanilla.

Fill and frost the cooled cake with the frosting. If you are making this cake more than 2 or 3 hours before serving, cover and store in refrigerator. Let return to room temperature before serving.

SERVES 12.
CALORIES: 640   CHOLESTEROL: 112 mg   SODIUM: 351 mg   FIBER: .5 g

Health tip:
Use unsalted margarine instead of butter and omit salt.
CALORIES: 640   CHOLESTEROL: 85 mg   SODIUM: 188 mg   FIBER: .5 g

---

———————— ◇ ————————

Decadent Chocolate Cake

This is a rich dense chocolate-y cake. You can fill and frost it with sweetened whipped cream, if you prefer. Holly Garrison gave me the recipe for this frosting and it is divine indeed.

Cake:

> *6 squares (1 ounce each) unsweetened chocolate*
> *2⅔ cups sifted all-purpose flour*
> *2 teaspoons baking powder*
> *1 cup butter, softened*
> *3 cups sugar*
> *4 eggs*
> *1 teaspoon vanilla extract*
> *2 cups milk*

Frosting:

1 cup sugar
1 cup heavy cream
5 ounces high quality semi-sweet chocolate
½ cup butter, cut into 6 pieces
1 teaspoon vanilla

Preheat oven to 350°F. Grease and flour 2 9-inch round cake pans.

In the top of a double boiler, over simmering water, melt the chocolate. Remove from heat and set aside.

In a medium-size bowl, or on waxed paper, using a whisk, stir the flour and baking powder together; set aside.

In a large bowl, cream the butter with the sugar until light and fluffy. Beat in the eggs until blended. Beat in the chocolate and vanilla.

Alternately add the flour and milk to the chocolate mixture, beating well after each addition. Pour into prepared pans.

Bake 35 to 45 minutes, or until a wooden pick inserted in the center comes out clean. Cool 10 minutes in the pan, then invert onto racks and cool completely.

Prepare the frosting by combining the sugar and cream in a 2-quart saucepan. Bring to a boil, over medium heat, stirring constantly. Reduce heat and simmer 5 minutes; remove from heat. Add the chocolate and stir until melted. Stir in the butter, 1 piece at a time, then stir in the vanilla. If necessary, chill until spreading consistency.

Fill and frost the chocolate layers with the frosting.

SERVES 12.
CALORIES: 676   CHOLESTEROL: 136 mg   SODIUM: 251 mg   FIBER: 2 g

Health tip:
Use unsalted margarine instead of butter. Have only half a piece.
CALORIES: 338   CHOLESTEROL: 51 mg   SODIUM: 75 mg   FIBER: 1 g

————————— ◇ —————————

Jelly Roll Cake

Jelly rolls are very versatile desserts. Obviously, you can fill them with jelly, but you can also use whipped cream or mousse or butter cream. Any way you serve it, this is a real delight.

6 tablespoons confectioners' sugar, divided
¾ cup all-purpose flour
1 teaspoon baking powder
¼ teaspoon salt
3 eggs
1 cup sugar
⅓ cup milk
1 teaspoon vanilla extract
1 jar (12 ounce) jelly or jam (any flavor you like)

Preheat oven to 375°F. Grease a 15½ × 10½ × 1-inch baking pan (jelly roll pan). Line with waxed paper and grease again.

Place 2 tablespoons of the confectioners' sugar into a strainer. Shake over the surface of a clean kitchen towel; set aside.

In a medium-size bowl, or on waxed paper, using a whisk, stir together the flour, baking powder, and salt; set aside.

In a large bowl, using an electric mixer, beat the eggs on high speed 5 minutes. Add the sugar and beat 3 minutes longer. Beat in the milk and vanilla.

Add the flour all at once and beat on low speed until just smooth. Pour into the prepared pan and spread evenly.

Bake 12 to 15 minutes, or until the cake springs back when gently pressed. Cool 2 minutes in pan, then turn onto prepared towel. Carefully peel off the waxed paper. Trim any uneven edges. Starting at the narrow end, roll up the cake and towel to form a 10-inch long log. Place, seam side down, onto a rack to cool.

Unroll the cake and spread with the jelly to within ½ inch of the edges. Reroll the cake, removing the towel. Place seam side down on a serving platter and sprinkle with the remaining confectioners' sugar.

SERVES 10.

CALORIES: 245   CHOLESTEROL: 63 mg   SODIUM: 114 mg   FIBER: 1 g

Health tip:
Use sugarless preserves and omit salt.
CALORIES: 165   CHOLESTEROL: 63 mg   SODIUM: 94 mg   FIBER: 1 g

Chocolate variation: Use 1 cup sifted flour instead of ¾ cup un-sifted and add 3 tablespoons unsweetened cocoa. Stir the cocoa into the flour, baking powder, and salt mixture. Follow directions as in jelly roll recipe.

Sponge Cake: Pour the batter into 2 8-inch round cake pans. Grease pan, line with waxed paper, and regrease. Bake 25 minutes or until the cake springs back when lightly touched. Run knife around the edge, then invert onto racks and peel off paper. Cool.

———————— ◇ ————————

Mim Jaffe's Butter Cookies

I told my friend Dori Bernstein that I didn't have a decent recipe for butter cookies. She said that her mother makes the best—and she was right. Here's the recipe.

1 cup butter, softened
½ cup sugar
2 cups plus 2 tablespoons all-purpose flour
1 teaspoon vanilla extract

Preheat oven to 350°F. Grease 2 or 3 baking sheets.

In a large bowl, cream the butter and sugar. Stir in the flour, then the vanilla.

Roll into 1-inch balls and press gently to flatten. Place on prepared baking sheets, about 1½ inches apart. Bake 15 to 20 minutes, until golden. Cool on racks.

MAKES 3 DOZEN.
CALORIES: 82   CHOLESTEROL: 13 mg   SODIUM: 43 mg   FIBER: 0 g

Health tip:
Use unsalted margarine instead of butter.
CALORIES: 82   CHOLESTEROL: 0 mg   SODIUM: 1 mg   FIBER: 0 g

Variations:

Thumb cookies: Press the ball of dough with your thumb to make a well (don't flatten the cookie). Fill the well with jelly or jam. Bake as directed.

Almond cookies: Mix ⅓ cup almond paste into the dough. Press a whole almond into the top of the ball, then flatten slightly. Bake 12 to 15 minutes.

Michelle's favorite: Press chocolate chips onto cookies

My Famous Peach Pie

This is one of my most requested dishes. The secret to this outstanding pie is to use very ripe, sweet peaches. If the peaches aren't delicious then the pie won't be either. I love the flavor of all-butter crusts. If you want a little extra flakiness, substitute ¼ vegetable shortening for ¼ cup of the butter.

Crust:

> 2 cups unbleached flour
> ¾ cup butter, cold but not too hard
> 4 to 5 tablespoons ice water

Filling:

> 3 pounds ripe peaches
> 1 tablespoon lemon juice
> ¾ cup firmly packed light- or dark-brown sugar
> 2 tablespoons flour
> ½ teaspoon cinnamon
> ¼ teaspoon salt
> Pinch nutmeg

Preheat oven to 425°F.

Put the flour in a large bowl. Using a pastry cutter or two knives, cut the butter into the flour until the mixture resembles coarse cornmeal.

Sprinkle the water over the flour mixture, one tablespoon at a time, and blend with a fork until the water has been incorporated. Then sprinkle with more water, using just enough to form a dough that will hold together. Divide dough into 2 pieces, one slightly larger than the other; set aside

Using a vegetable peeler, pare the peaches. Cut in half and discard the pits. Slice into medium wedges. Put the peach wedges in a large bowl and toss with the lemon juice. In a medium-size bowl, or on waxed paper, combine the brown sugar, flour, cinnamon, salt, and nutmeg. Add to the peaches and toss until combined; set aside.

Roll out the larger piece of dough, between 2 sheets of waxed paper, until 11 inches in diameter. Place in a 9-inch pie plate. Fill the pie with the peach mixture.

Roll the second piece of dough, between 2 pieces of waxed paper, until 10 inches in diameter. Peel off one sheet of waxed paper and turn the dough over the peaches. Peel off second piece of paper.

Gently press together the edges of the 2 crusts, then fold edges up and crimp.

Bake 45 minutes or until golden. Cool.

SERVES 8.

CALORIES: 414   CHOLESTEROL: 46 mg   SODIUM: 222 mg   FIBER: 4 g

Health tip:

Use unsalted margarine instead of butter; omit salt; and eat only ½ a piece.

CALORIES: 207   CHOLESTEROL: 0 mg   SODIUM: 6 mg   FIBER: 2 g

RICE
(Oryza sativa)

Rice is the staple grain for half of the earth's population, with a staggering number of varieties available worldwide. Until recently, the population of the United States has been eating just one kind of rice: long-grain white. It has only been within the last few years, maybe as the result of a new health awareness, that long-grain brown rice has gained any acceptance at all. As Americans become more adventuresome in matters of eating and more nutritionally aware, other more exotic rices are also making small gains in popularity. Some of these include the sweet rice that the Japanese use for sushi; basmati, an aromatic rice that is widely used in Indian cooking; and aborio, a short-grain white rice that the Italians use to make risotto.

For the most part, in the cultures and countries where rice is a staple, it is white rice that is valued (brown rice, although nutritionally superior, is still looked upon as food for the have-nots) and is used primarily as an accompaniment for other dishes, not as an ingredient. In Indonesia, for example, the Rijsttafel (which literally translates to mean "rice table") is a banquet at which 30 or more dishes and condiments are served that are intended to be eaten with plain rice.

China and other Asian countries eat greater portions of rice with each meal than the so-called main dish. The preferred rice in Asian cooking is sweet or glutinous rice, which is stickier and sweeter than long-grain rice. (It stands to reason that when using chopsticks, stickier is better.)

In the Orient and India, aging rice is a common practice. At one time, basmati was aged for five to seven years before it was deemed fit for consumption. Of course, at that point the rice was also laden with insects, and the merchant who offered raw rice that was not loaded with weevils would have been accused of trying to gyp his customers.

Rice was introduced to the United States in the mid-1700s. There are various accounts of how rice first arrived in this country, but the most commonly accepted version is that the captain of a ship from Madagascar presented rice to Henry Woodward, one of the founders of South Carolina. No matter what the origins were, the swampy land and free slave labor made rice growing in the U.S. a huge success, which is reflected in the number of southern dishes that are cooked with rice. Today rice is widely grown in Texas and California, as well as many southern states.

94

Types of Rice Available

Long-grain white rice: The hull, bran, and germ of the rice have been removed, leaving the starchy endosperm. The grains are long and thin and usually opaque, although converted rice, which has been specially precooked, has a more transparent quality. The different varieties of white rice are usually similar in shape, but they can range from pale yellow to pure white in color.

Long-grain brown rice: The hulled grain with the germ and bran intact. When buying brown rice, you will usually find green grains mixed in with the brown. Most long-grain brown rice are actually beige in color and fairly opaque. Uncle Ben's brand brown rice, although the box does not clearly state it, is "converted" like their white rice, so the grains are transparent. Aromatic brown rice, those varieties that are bred for specific flavors and other characteristics, come in a vast array of colors, from the standard brown to red and black.

Medium-grain rice: Not readily available in the United States, but if you do happen to find it, it is sold as brown or white rice. The taste and texture fall between those of long- and short-grain rice, and it is not as sticky as short-grain rice nor as fluffy as long-grain rice.

Short-grain white rice: There are two types available in this country. The first is known as glutinous, sweet, sticky, mochi, or pearl rice. It is almost as wide as it is long, and it is very opaque and white in color. It is important to rinse this rice thoroughly before cooking to remove talc and other agents used to enhance the whiteness. As the rice cooks, the grains become very starchy and sticky. This type of rice is also best cooked in a rice cooker or a steamer, rather than the usual method of simmering.

The second type of short-grain white rice is aborio, which is cooked in broth for risotto, and rarely eaten plain.

Short-grain rice is often used for rice cakes and in other dishes where its stickiness is used as a binding agent.

Short-grain brown rice: There are two types currently available and both are almost as wide as they are long. The regular short-grain brown rice has a transparent quality and has some green grains mixed in with the brown. The second type is a glutinous rice that is opaque and the color of unhulled sesame seeds or quinoa. Like glutinous white rice, the brown rice cooks best in a rice cooker or steamer. Neither of these rices are widely used.

Precooked (instant) rice: The rice grains are completely cooked and then dried. The consumer simply has to rehydrate the grains in boiling water and the rice is ready to be eaten. As you might suspect, much of the flavor and chewy texture are lost in this process. Precooked frozen rice is also available.

Rizcous: This product from Lundberg Family Farms is a quick cooking brown rice. It is cut into small pieces and when cooked closely resembles the texture and taste of couscous.

Rice mixes: These are available in many forms. Most are combined with dehydrated broth, vegetables, and herbs. Some are also combined with pasta and wild rice.

Puffed rice: The cooked grains are filled with air to puff them. This product is used as cold breakfast cereal.

Rice flakes: Made by cooking the rice and then rolling it flat. Rice flakes are similar to oat, rye, and barley flakes.

Rice meal: This is ground rice and it is sold as a hot breakfast cereal.

Rice flour: Finely ground rice that can be used for baking and to make rice noodles.

Rice-flour noodles or rice sticks: They come dried (you may be able to obtain fresh noodles in specialized Oriental markets) in varying widths. Rice noodles can be soaked (especially the thinest ones) or simmered. Cooked, they have a delightful chewiness and flavor. Or, you can deep-fry the noodles and watch them almost instantly puff up into an airy crisp nest.

Rice bran: The ground bran of the rice, recently reported to be as effective, (or more so) as oat bran in reducing blood cholesterol.

Texture and Flavor

Because each rice has its own distinctive flavor and texture, I am presenting them individually rather than by making generalizations.

Long-grain white rice: Packaged under familiar brand names, such as Carolina, this is the most common form of rice found in the

American home. The flavor is mild, and the texture is fluffy with a hint of stickiness.

Converted long-grain white rice: The "converted" refers to a process used by Uncle Ben's brand, which supposedly seals in nutrients by a pre-cooking process. The cooked rice has a pleasant chewiness and flavor, and the separate grains that Americans favor, and is less sticky and less fluffy than regular long-grain rice.

Basmati rice (Indian): Very white slender grains with an occasional opaqueness. As this rice cooks, the grains get very long. Cooked basmati is light and primarily fluffy, although individual grains may have a slight stickiness and chewiness. The texture has a fall-apart feeling in the mouth that is faintly similar to instant rice. It has a full flavor that is delicate and sweet, and a noticeably fragrant aroma.

Basmati rice (American): The grains are slightly larger, and the cooked rice a bit more yellow and woodier in flavor than the Indian variety. Both are lighter and fluffier than converted rice.

Jasmine rice: The whitest and, for my taste, the most delicate and delicious rice of all. It has the flavor of Indian basmati rice, but a firmer texture, and is not as fluffy or dry, but has a slight stickiness. I have found this to be the best of all of the white rices.

Aborio: The grains are usually partly transparent and partly opaque. Some brands have no opaqueness on the grains, and I find these less to my liking. Cooked aborio, like all short-grain white rices, is sticky. In risotto, the traditional use for aborio, the stickiness is encouraged by means of constant stirring as the rice cooks. The results are a creamy rice with the grains retaining just a little chewiness, with the rice taking on the flavor of whatever ingredients are cooked with it.

Glutinous rice: This is the stickiest rice of them all: It is used as the rice of choice in many Oriental cultures. The flavor is sweet and the grains have a soft chewiness.

Long-grain brown rice: When they are cooked, these long beige grains are fluffy with a very distinct grainy, and sometimes nutty, flavor. The differences in flavor among the various brown rices are not as noticeable as those in white rices. My own feeling is that long-grain brown rice lacks the pleasant chewiness found in short-grain brown rice. However, if fluffy is the quality you value in rice, and if you've avoided brown rice because you thought it might be heavy, try it and you may be pleasantly surprised.

Wild pecan rice: Given the rather exotic name, you might think that this long-grain brown rice would be exceptionally nutty with a distinct pecan flavor. What I found was a fairly typical, fluffy brown rice, that was not especially pecan flavored.

Waheni rice: A long reddish-brown rice with a texture more similar to wild rice than brown rice. The flavor, however, is more like plain brown rice.

Red rice: Although this is technically a long-grain rice, the grains are fairly short. The color of this rice is similar to waheni, a very reddish-brown, which leaches into the cooking water, but does not fade the color of the cooked rice very much. The texture is fluffy and the flavor is "meaty," rather like a strongly brewed tea with a hint of mushroom.

Black rice (Japonica): The grains of this rice are very long, and the color that leaches into the cooking water is purple, not black. Unlike most long-grain rices, this one is sticky, and the flavor is somewhat grasslike. This rice, which is from Thailand, is traditionally used for desserts, usually combined with coconut.

Short-grain brown rice: It has the grainy, nutty flavor of long-grain brown rice, but a denser, chewier texture. As well as being more pleasing, I find that this texture stands up well to any ingredient with which you choose to serve it.

Short-grain brown glutinous rice: Like its white counterpart, this rice is very sticky. The flavor is sweet and the texture is chewy.

Availability

Long-grain white and brown rices are universally available in supermarkets. Along with the white and brown rices, you will also find rice mixes, and, frequently, wild pecan rice, Texmati (or Calmati), and sometimes basmati rices.

Other rices and rice products can be found in specialty-food stores, Oriental stores, health-food stores, and through mail-order grain catalogs (see page 21).

Nutritional Content

Brown rice is a good source of fiber, B vitamins, vitamin E, iron, phosphorous, calcium, and potassium.

White rice contains considerably less of the vitamins than brown rice. Enrichment returns some of the B vitamins and iron, but not the fiber or vitamin E.

Home Remedy

As my grandmother always said, "Rice is binding." Here, then, is an old-fashioned remedy for diarrhea:

4 cups water
1 cup white rice

Bring water to a boil and stir in rice. Cover and simmer for 20 minutes. Drain the rice, reserving the water. Drink ½ cup of the rice water two times a day until the diarrhea is gone. (Eat the rice, too.)

Substitutions

You can interchange any type of long-grain white rice for another. Although the flavors and textures may vary somewhat, the cooking times are the same and the final results should be comparable. If using converted rice, use a little more water and cook about 5 minutes longer. Similarly, long-grained brown rices are interchangeable with the same comments given for white rice.

You can use short-grain brown rice for long-grain white or brown rice, but the cooking time will have to be longer if you are exchanging for white rice.

Wild rice can be substituted for brown rice, but it will require a little extra cooking time. Cooked wild rice can also be substituted for cooked white rice.

Bulgur can be used for short- or long-grain brown rice, but the cooking time will be shorter. For white rice, the cooking time will be shorter.

Couscous can be used in recipes calling for cooked rice or rizcous.

Cooked berries and groats can always be substituted for cooked rice.

Basic Cooking Instructions

Please read *About Cooking Grains* beginning on page 7.
The microwave methods that follow were tested in a 650-watt oven.

Stove-top method for white rice:

> *2 cups water*
> *1 teaspoon salt*
> *1 cup white rice*

In a 2-quart saucepan, bring water and salt to a boil over high heat. Stir in rice and return to boiling. Reduce heat and simmer, covered, for 20 minutes, or until almost all of the liquid has been absorbed. Remove from heat and let stand, covered, for 5 minutes. Fluff with a fork.

Please note, if cooking short-grain white rice, rinse raw rice thoroughly until water is no longer cloudy and runs clear. Do not rinse enriched long-grain white rice.

MAKES 3 CUPS REGULAR LONG-GRAIN WHITE RICE.
MAKES 3⅔ CUPS INDIAN BASMATI WHITE RICE.
MAKES 4 CUPS TEXMATI WHITE RICE.
MAKES 3 CUPS JASMINE RICE.
MAKES 3 CUPS SHORT-GRAIN WHITE RICE.

Steaming method for short-grain rice:

> *1 cup short-grain rice*
> *1½ cups water*
> *1 teaspoon salt*

Rinse the rice until the water is no longer cloudy. Place rice in a bowl filled with water. Let stand 30 minutes, then drain. Place rice, water, and salt in a 2-quart bowl. Place in a steamer with boiling water in the bottom. Cover the pot, but not the bowl, and steam for 30 minutes, or until the water is absorbed. Fluff with a fork.

MAKES 3 CUPS.

Microwave method for long-grain white rice:

2¼ cups water
1 teaspoon salt
1 cup long-grain white rice

Place the water and salt in a 3-quart, microwave-safe bowl. Cover with waxed paper. Microwave on high (100% power) for 3 minutes, or until water is boiling. Stir in rice. Recover with waxed paper and microwave on high for 4 minutes. Microwave on medium (50% power), still covered with waxed paper, for 15 minutes, rotating dish once, if necessary. Let stand for 2 minutes. Fluff with a fork.

MAKES 3 CUPS.

Stove-top version for converted long-grain white rice:

2½ cups water
1 teaspoon salt
1 cup converted long-grain white rice

In a 2-quart saucepan, bring the water and salt to a boil over high heat. Stir in rice and return to boiling. Reduce heat and simmer, covered, for 20 minutes. Remove from heat and let stand, covered, for 5 minutes. Fluff with a fork.

MAKES 3½ CUPS.

Microwave method for converted long-grain white rice:

Follow directions for regular long-grain white rice, but increase water to 2½ cups.

Stove-top method for brown rice:

2¼ cups waters
1 teaspoon salt
1 cup brown rice

In a 2-quart saucepan, bring the water and salt to a boil over high heat. Stir in rice and return to boiling. Reduce heat and simmer, covered, for 45 minutes. Remove from heat and let stand, covered, for 10 minutes. Fluff with a fork.

MAKES 3½ CUPS.

Microwave method for brown rice:

2½ cups water
1 teaspoon salt
1 cup brown rice

Place water and salt in a 3-quart, microwave-safe bowl. Cover with waxed paper and microwave on high (100% power) for 4 minutes, or until water comes to a boil. Stir in rice. Recover with waxed paper and microwave on high for 4 minutes. Microwave on medium (50% power), still covered with waxed paper, for 35 minutes, rotating dish once, if necessary. Let stand for 3 minutes. Fluff with a fork.

MAKES 3 CUPS.

Stove-top method for black and waheni rice:

Please note that salt must be added *after cooking* or rice will not absorb the cooking water. Do not cook in broth.

2 cups water
1 cup black or waheni rice
1 teaspoon salt

In a 2-quart saucepan, bring the water to a boil over high heat. Stir in rice and return to boiling. Reduce heat and simmer, covered, for 45 minutes. Remove from heat and let stand, covered, for 5 minutes. Stir in salt and fluff with a fork.

MAKES 3½ CUPS.

Stove-top version for red rice:

2¼ cups water
1 teaspoon salt
1 cup red rice

In a 2-quart saucepan, bring water and salt to a boil over high heat. Stir in rice and return to boiling. Reduce heat and simmer, covered, for 35 minutes. Remove from heat and let stand, covered, for 10 minutes. Fluff with a fork.

MAKES 3¾ CUPS.

Reheating

Rice can be reheated by lightly steaming or microwaving.

RICE RECIPES

(* indicates easy recipes)

———————— ◇ ————————

Stuffed Grape Leaves (Dolmas)
Pork-upines *
Mom's Tomato-Rice Soup *
Sizzling Rice Soup
Red Rice Soup *
Paella
Shrimp and Ham Jambalaya
Arroz con Pollo
Chicken Gumbo
Beef Heaven
Turkey–Brown-Rice Salad*
Chicken-Chutney Salad *
Warm Mexican Salad *
Warm Thai Beef Salad *
Lamb Curry and Rice Salad *
Mozzarella Salad with Sun-Dried Tomato Dressing
Randy's Party Rice Salad
Shredded Root Salad *
Molded Rice Salad *
Lazy Lady's Black Beans and Rice *
Dirty Rice
Hopping John
Fried Rice *
Nasi Goreng (Indonesian Fried Rice) *
Rice Pilau *
Creole Rice and Beans *
Beans, Greens, and Brown Rice *
Chris's Ratatouille Brown Rice
Brown Rice and Spinach *
Orange Rice with Almonds *
Nutty, Nutty Rice *
Basic Risotto
Risotto with Tomato and Basil
Risotto with Porcini Mushrooms
Sushi Rice *
Pecan Waffles
Rice-Bran Pancakes *
Blueberry-Bran Muffins *
Rice Pudding *
Black Rice Pudding

———————— ◇ ————————

Stuffed Grape Leaves (Dolmas)

This traditional Greek dish is a very popular appetizer, it can be eaten warm or cold. You can also serve these as part of an antipasto platter or increase the portion and use as a main course. Grape or vine leaves are available in most gourmet stores.

1 jar (16 ounce) grape or vine leaves, drained
¾ pound ground beef, lamb, or veal
⅓ cup finely chopped onion
¼ cup chopped walnuts
¼ cup uncooked rice
2 tablespoons chopped parsley
2 tablespoons currants
2 cloves garlic, minced
2 teaspoons chopped mint
¼ teaspoon ground cinnamon
¼ teaspoon salt
⅛ teaspoon pepper
1 can (13¾ ounce) ready-to-serve chicken broth
¼ cup fresh lemon juice

Carefully remove the grape leaves from the jar and unfold. Rinse under cold water and pat dry.

In a medium-size bowl, thoroughly combine the meat, onion, walnuts, rice, parsley, currants, garlic, mint, cinnamon, salt, and pepper.

Select the largest untorn leaves. Place one leaf, shiny side down, on the work surface. Place a rounded tablespoon of the filling in the center, near the stem. Fold the outer sides in toward the center, covering the filling. Roll toward the tip end to form a neat packet. Continue until all the filling has been used.

Arrange half of the unused leaves on the bottom of a 4-quart saucepan. Arrange the stuffed grape leaves, seam side down, as close together as possible over the leaves. Top with the remaining leaves. Pour the broth and lemon juice into the pot. Weight the leaves down with a heat-proof plate. Bring to a boil over medium heat. Reduce heat and simmer, covered, 1 hour.

Drain and serve warm, or chill in broth before serving.

SERVES 8.
CALORIES: 192   CHOLESTEROL: 38 mg   SODIUM: 398 mg   FIBER: 2 g

Health tip:
Omit salt and use reduced-sodium broth.
CALORIES: 192 mg   CHOLESTEROL: 38 mg   SODIUM: 55 mg   FIBER: 2 g

———————— ◇ ————————

Pork-upines

These make great appetizers at parties.

2 cups water
1¼ teaspoons salt, divided
½ cup short-grain white rice
1 pound ground pork
½ cup minced water chestnuts
3 tablespoons finely chopped scallion
2 tablespoons soy sauce
2 cloves garlic
1 teaspoon sugar
¼ teaspoon five-fragrance powder or ½ teaspoon ginger
⅛ teaspoon pepper

Bring the water and ¾ teaspoon of the salt to a boil in a 1½-quart saucepan over medium-high heat. Add the rice and boil 5 minutes. Drain, rinse with cool water, and separate the grains by sifting them through your fingers. Set aside.

In a large bowl, stir together the pork, waterchestnuts, scallion, soy sauce, garlic, sugar, remaining ½ teaspoon salt, five-fragrance powder, and pepper until thoroughly combined. Form into 24 balls (about 1-inch each).

Roll the balls in the rice (if necessary, separate the grains again). Place the pork-upines about 1 inch apart on a steamer. Place over boiling water and steam, covered, 20 minutes (you may need to make more than one batch).

MAKES 24.
CALORIES: 89   CHOLESTEROL: 19 mg   SODIUM: 421 mg   FIBER: 0 g

Health tip:
Use low-sodium soy sauce. Omit the salt.
CALORIES: 89   CHOLESTEROL: 19 mg   SODIUM: 70 mg   FIBER: 0 g

——————— ◇ ———————

Mom's Tomato-Rice Soup

As you go through this book you will find many of my mother's recipes. This soup is definitely one of the family's favorites. It's a perfect blend of sweet and tart. My mom always stirs the rice into the soup as it cooks, but I find that the rice tends to get too mushy (especially by the second day). I recommend using instant rice, and adding it to the serving bowl just before serving. That way the rice is never overcooked.

2 cans (29 ounces each) tomato puree
4 cups water
1 can (15 ounce) tomato sauce
⅓ cup sugar
¼ teaspoon salt
2 pounds flanken or short ribs
1 large onion, peeled
2 cloves garlic, peeled
Cooked instant or regular long-grain white rice

In an 8-quart sauce pot, stir together the tomato puree, water, tomato sauce, sugar, and salt. Add the flanken, onion and garlic. Bring to a boil. Reduce heat and simmer, uncovered, 2 hours. Discard the onion and garlic. Remove the beef and serve on the side.

Place 2 or 3 tablespoons cooked rice into each serving bowl; pour in hot soup.

SERVES 8.
CALORIES: 209   CHOLESTEROL: 4 mg   SODIUM: 428 mg   FIBER: 5 g

Health tip:
Omit salt.
CALORIES: 209   CHOLESTEROL: 4 mg   SODIUM: 302 mg   FIBER: 5 g

Sizzling Rice Soup

I love to order this soup in Chinese restaurants. I never thought I'd be able to make it at home. The recipe is not hard, but does require 2 days of cooking: day one to make the rice and the next day to fry the rice and serve the soup (you can make the soup on either day). If you want to make this a vegetarian dish, just omit the shrimp and use vegetable broth. You can make and dry the crusts in advance and then freeze them until needed.

Rice crust:

> *2 cups water*
> *1 cup long-grain white rice (not converted)*
> *1 teaspoon salt*

Soup:

> *2 cans (13¾ ounces each) ready-to-serve chicken broth or*
>   *3½ cups vegetable broth (see page 19)*
> *1 cup + 2 tablespoons water, divided*
> *1 tablespoon sherry*
> *1 teaspoon soy sauce*
> *½ pound medium shrimp, peeled, cleaned, and halved lengthwise.*
> *½ cup sliced baby corn*
> *⅓ cup straw mushrooms, halved lengthwise*
> *¼ cup sliced snow peas*
> *2 tablespoons cornstarch*
> *2 tablespoons thinly sliced scallion*
> *Oil for deep-frying*

To prepare the rice crust, place the water, rice, and salt in a 10-inch skillet. Bring to a boil over high heat. Reduce heat and simmer, covered, 1 hour and 45 minutes, or until a golden crust forms on the bottom.

Remove skillet from heat and scrape out any loose rice (reserve this rice for some other use), leaving the crust in the skillet. Using a metal spatula gently lift the crust from the pan. Don't worry if the crust breaks into pieces, but try to keep the pieces on the large side. Place the pieces on a baking sheet in a single layer and let them dry, uncovered, overnight.

To prepare the soup, add the broth, 1 cup of the water, sherry and soy sauce to a 3-quart saucepan. Bring to a boil. Add the shrimp, corn, mushrooms, and snow peas. Simmer 5 minutes.

In a small bowl, stir together the remaining 2 tablespoons water and cornstarch. Add to the soup and simmer, stirring until it is slightly thickened. Stir in scallion. Keep warm while you cook the rice crusts.

Pour enough oil for deep-frying into a wok or 2-quart saucepan. Heat until the oil bubbles as soon as a small rice crust is dropped in. Add the rice crusts, a few at a time, until crisp (this only takes a few seconds, you will see that the rice expands right away). Remove to a serving bowl.

Pour the soup into the bowl with the rice crusts and serve immediately.

SERVES 8.
CALORIES: 166   CHOLESTEROL: 10 mg   SODIUM: 747 mg   FIBER: 6 g

Health tip:
Use low-sodium broth; omit soy sauce.
CALORIES: 166   CHOLESTEROL: 10 mg   SODIUM: 423 mg   FIBER: 6 g

————————◇————————

Red Rice Soup

This is a creamy soup with a chewy texture from the rice.

2 tablespoons butter
½ cup thinly sliced leek (white part only)
2 cans (13¾ ounces each) ready-to-serve chicken broth or
    3½ cups vegetable broth (see page 19)
¾ cup red rice
¼ cup port or marsala wine
1½ cups half and half
¼ teaspoon cinnamon
Sliced scallion, for garnish

In a 3-quart saucepan, melt the butter over medium heat. Add the leeks and sauté until soft. Add the broth and bring to a boil. Stir in the rice. Reduce heat and simmer, uncovered, 40 minutes. Remove from heat.

Using a 1 cup measuring cup, scoop out as much rice as you can and put it into a blender container or food processor fitted with a steel blade. Cover and process until smooth. Stir the pureed rice soup into the remaining soup. Stir in the wine and then the half-and-half and cinnamon.

If necessary, reheat before serving. If desired, sprinkle with scallion before serving.

SERVES 6.
CALORIES: 237   CHOLESTEROL: 33 mg   SODIUM: 467 mg   FIBER: 1 g

Health tip:
Use buttermilk instead of cream and use low-sodium broth.
CALORIES: 179   CHOLESTEROL: 13 mg   SODIUM: 132 mg   FIBER: 1 g

---

——————— ◇ ———————

Paella

This is a classic Spanish dish. It is authentically prepared with a short-grain rice grown in the Valencia region of Spain. We are using aborio instead. Although paella has come to mean rice dish, its name comes from the shallow pan (paellera) traditionally used to cook it in. If you are feeling truly extravagant, stir in a cut up, cooked lobster when you add the mussels.

3 pound chicken
3 tablespoons olive oil
¼ pound chorizo, sliced
1 cup chopped onion
2 cloves garlic, minced
1½ cups aborio rice
1 can (13¾ ounce) ready-to-serve chicken broth
1½ cups water
½ cup dry white wine
¼ teaspoon saffron
12 clams
¾ pound shrimp, peeled and cleaned
12 mussels
1 cup peas, fresh or frozen
¼ cup chopped pimiento

Rinse the chicken and pat dry. Cut into pieces, separating the leg from the thigh, the wing from the breast, and then cutting the breasts into halves.

In a large saucepan, heat the oil over medium-high heat. Add the chicken and cook until well browned. Remove from pot. Add the chorizo and cook until no longer pink. Remove from skillet. Add the onion and garlic and cook, stirring, until the onion is soft. Add the rice and stir until the grains are coated.

Stir in the chicken broth, water, and wine. Add the saffron and chicken. Cook, covered, 25 minutes. Add the clams, cover, and cook 8 minutes. Add the chorizo, shrimp, mussels, peas, and pimiento and cook 8 minutes longer, or until all the shellfish have opened.

SERVES 6.
CALORIES: 524   CHOLESTEROL: 231 mg   SODIUM: 648 mg   FIBER: 2 g

Health tip:
Omit chorizo; cook the chicken without skin; and use low-sodium broth.
CALORIES: 497   CHOLESTEROL: 201 mg   SODIUM: 300 mg   FIBER: 2 g

—————— ◇ ——————

Shrimp and Ham Jambalaya

The only word I can use to describe this Creole dish is heavenly.

> 3 tablespoons butter
> 1 cup chopped onion
> 1/2 cup finely chopped celery
> 1/4 cup finely chopped green bell pepper
> 3 cloves garlic, minced
> 1 can (14 1/2 ounce) whole peeled tomatoes, undrained
> 1 can (13 3/4 ounce) ready-to-serve chicken broth
> 1/4 teaspoon thyme
> 1/4 teaspoon ground red pepper
> 1 cup long-grain white rice, not converted
> 1 pound large shrimp, peeled and cleaned
> 1 cup diced cooked ham
> 2 tablespoons chopped parsley

Melt the butter in a 3-quart saucepan, over medium-high heat. Add the onion, celery, green pepper, and garlic. Cook, stirring, until the onion is soft. Add the tomatoes and break up with the back of a spoon. Stir in the chicken broth, thyme, and pepper. Bring to a boil. Stir in the rice. Return to a boil, reduce heat and simmer, covered, 15 minutes. Stir in the shrimp, ham, and parsley. Simmer 15 minutes longer, stirring once, or until the shrimp are cooked through.

SERVES 4.
CALORIES: 499   CHOLESTEROL: 261 mg   SODIUM: 1315   FIBER: 3 g

Health tip:
Use 1 tablespoon unsalted margarine instead of the butter and cook in a nonstick skillet; use low-sodium broth and ham.
CALORIES: 422   CHOLESTEROL: 238 mg   SODIUM: 803 mg   FIBER: 3 g

Arroz con Pollo

This is a traditional Spanish chicken dish. I like to serve this with a delicious green salad and end the meal with one of my very favorite desserts—flan.

2 tablespoons vegetable oil
1 cup chopped onion
2 cloves garlic, minced
1 can (14½ ounce) whole peeled tomatoes, undrained
2 tablespoons chopped parsley
1 teaspoon oregano
1 teaspoon salt
¼ teaspoon pepper
1 bay leaf
3½ pound chicken, cut up
1¼ cups boiling water
1 cup converted long-grain white rice
½ cup sliced pimento-stuffed olives

In a 4-quart saucepan, heat the oil over medium-high heat. Add the onion and garlic and cook, stirring, until onion is soft. Stir in the tomatoes, parsley, oregano, salt, pepper, and bay leaf, breaking up the tomatoes with the back of a spoon. Add the chicken, bring to a boil. Reduce the heat and simmer, covered, 40 minutes. Add the water and bring to a boil. Stir in the rice, reduce heat and simmer 25 minutes. Stir in the sliced olives.

SERVES 4.
CALORIES: 524   CHOLESTEROL: 197 mg   SODIUM: 1422 mg   FIBER: 4 g

Health tip:
Omit salt. Cook the chicken without the skin. Reduce oil to 2 teaspoons and cook in a nonstick saucepan. Use only half the olives.
CALORIES: 421   CHOLESTEROL: 163 mg   SODIUM: 612 mg   FIBER: 4 g

Chicken Gumbo

This Louisiana specialty is usually thickened with either okra or file powder (ground sassafrass). I've used the okra because it's easier to obtain. Be sure that your roux (cooked flour mixture) is nice and brown before adding the tomatoes.

2 tablespoons butter
2 tablespoons vegetable oil
3 pound chicken; cut into eighths
⅓ cup flour
1 cup chopped onion
½ cup chopped green bell pepper
½ cup chopped celery
2 cloves garlic
1 can (14½ ounce) whole peeled tomatoes, undrained
3 cups water
1 can (13¾ ounce) ready-to-serve chicken broth
1 bay leaf
½ teaspoon Tabasco
2 cups sliced okra or
    1 package (10 ounce) frozen sliced okra
½ cup long-grain white rice (can be converted)
½ teaspoon salt

In a 4-quart saucepan, heat the butter and oil over medium-high heat. Add the chicken and cook until well browned all over.

Remove the chicken from the pot and set aside. Stir in the flour and cook, over low heat, stirring constantly, until well browned. Add the onion, pepper, celery, and garlic and cook, stirring, until the onion is softened. Stir in the tomatoes, and break up with the back of a spoon. Stir in the water and broth and bring to a boil. Return the chicken to the pot and add the bay leaf and Tabasco.

Return to a boil. Reduce heat and simmer, uncovered, 40 minutes. Stir in the okra, rice, and salt and simmer, uncovered, 25 minutes longer.

SERVES 4.
CALORIES: 470   CHOLESTEROL: 95 mg   SODIUM: 498 mg   FIBER: 4 g

Health tip:
Cook the chicken without the skin; omit the butter and cook in a nonstick saucepan; omit the salt; and use low-sodium broth.
CALORIES: 320   CHOLESTEROL: 15 mg   SODIUM: 239 mg   FIBER: 4 g

Beef Heaven

This is a very tasty Thai version of beef jerky. It's sold by street venders and is very popular. I've served it to company many times with very favorable responses.

1¼ pounds London broil
2 tablespoons coriander seeds
¼ cup soy sauce
¼ cup dark-brown sugar
¼ cup molasses
¼ teaspoon black pepper
Cooked glutinous rice

Thinly slice the beef (this may be easier if you freeze the meat until it is firm, not frozen), set aside.

Crush the coriander seeds in a mortar and pestle or put them in a plastic bag and pound with a hammer to break them up. Place in a large bowl. Stir the soy sauce, brown sugar, molasses, and black pepper into the bowl with the seeds. Add the meat and toss to coat completely. Let stand at least ½ hour.

Preheat the broiler. Lay the beef in a single layer (you may have to cook the beef in several batches) on wire racks. Place the racks in a shallow pan; brush the meat with marinade. Broil 3 minutes per side or until glazed.

Serve warm or room temperature with glutinous rice.

SERVES 4.
CALORIES: 312   CHOLESTEROL: 68 mg   SODIUM: 713 mg   FIBER: 1 g

Health tip:
Use low-sodium soy sauce and only half the marinade. Omit salt in rice.
CALORIES: 312   CHOLESTEROL: 68 mg   SODIUM: 466 mg   FIBER: 1 g

————————◇————————
Turkey–Brown-Rice Salad

Be sure that your rice is al dente so that the salad doesn't turn to mush when you add the dressing.

2 cups cooked and cooled brown rice (preferably short grain)
2 cups diced cooked turkey
1 cup chopped celery
1 cup diced avocado
¾ cup sliced black olives
½ cup chopped red bell pepper
⅓ cup sliced scallion
½ cup mayonnaise
¼ cup salsa (mild or hot)
¼ cup buttermilk
½ teaspoon salt

In a large bowl, toss together the brown rice, turkey, celery, avocado, olives, bell pepper, and scallion.

In a small bowl, stir together the mayonnaise, salsa, buttermilk, and salt. Add to the salad and toss to combine.

SERVES 6.
CALORIES: 390   CHOLESTEROL: 47 mg   SODIUM: 653 mg   FIBER: 6 g

Health tip:
Use reduced-calorie mayonnaise. Omit the salt.
CALORIES: 306   CHOLESTEROL: 41 mg   SODIUM: 294 mg   FIBER: 6 g

————————◇————————
Chicken-Chutney Salad

I wasn't sure whether to use mango or apple in this recipe, but after it received raves from my sister's co-workers, I decided to leave the mango in.

2 cups cooked and cooled long-grain white rice
    (preferably Indian basmati)
1½ cups cooked and cooled diced chicken
1 cup diced mango or nectarine or papaya
½ cup cooked peas
⅓ cup chopped cashews
¼ cup currants
2 tablespoons chopped coriander

⅓ cup unflavored yogurt
¼ cup chopped chutney
¼ cup mayonnaise
1 tablespoon fresh lime juice
¼ teaspoon grated lime rind
¼ teaspoon salt
⅛ teaspoon ground red pepper

In a large bowl, toss together the rice, chicken, mango, peas, cashews, currants, and coriander.

In a small bowl, stir together the yogurt, chutney, mayonnaise, lime juice and rind, salt, and pepper. Pour dressing over salad and toss until combined.

SERVES 4.
CALORIES: 475   CHOLESTEROL: 53 mg   SODIUM: 604 mg   FIBER: 4 g

Health tip:
Omit the salt and use reduced-calorie mayonnaise.
CALORIES: 411   CHOLESTEROL: 49 mg   SODIUM: 201 mg   FIBER: 4 g

───────◇───────

Warm Mexican Salad

This is rather like a shelless taco.

2 tablespoons oil
1 cup chopped onion, divided
3 cloves garlic, minced
½ pound ground beef
2 tablespoons chili powder
½ teaspoon cumin
½ teaspoon salt
1 cup mild salsa or taco sauce
2 cups cooked brown rice
1 cup chopped tomato
1 tablespoon white vinegar
4 cups shredded lettuce

In a large skillet, heat the oil over medium-high heat. Add ½ cup of the onion and the garlic and cook, stirring, until the onion is soft. Add the beef and cook, stirring, until browned. Stir in the chili, cumin, and salt. Stir in the salsa and bring to a boil. Reduce heat and simmer 10 minutes. Remove from heat and stir in the rice, tomato, vinegar, and remaining ½ cup onion. Serve on a bed of lettuce

SERVES 4.
CALORIES: 416 CHOLESTEROL: 51 mg SODIUM: 674 mg FIBER: 4 g

Health tip:
Reduce the oil to 2 teaspoons and cook in a nonstick skillet; omit the salt.
CALORIES: 376 CHOLESTEROL: 51 mg SODIUM: 407 mg FIBER: 4 g

──────── ◇ ────────

Warm Thai Beef Salad

This salad is a good example of the Thai cooking principle of balancing sweet and sour, hot and salty flavors.

¼ cup fresh lime juice
1½ tablespoons soy sauce
1 tablespoon vegetable oil
1 tablespoon sugar
2 cloves garlic
½ teaspoon salt
1 pound ground beef
1 teaspoon red pepper flakes
1½ cups cooked and cooled long-grain white rice (preferably jasmine)
½ cup chopped red onion
1 tablespoon fresh chopped coriander
2 cups shredded lettuce
½ cup chopped cucumber
½ cup chopped tomato

Put the lime juice, soy sauce, oil, sugar, garlic, and salt into a blender container. Cover and blend until smooth; set aside.

In a large skillet, cook the beef and pepper flakes until the beef is no longer pink. Stir in the rice, red onion, and coriander. Remove from heat. Pour on the dressing and toss until combined.

Serve on bed of lettuce and top with chopped cucumber and tomato.

SERVES 4.
CALORIES: 457 CHOLESTEROL: 99 mg SODIUM: 942 mg FIBER: 1 g

Health tip:
Omit salt.
CALORIES: 457 CHOLESTEROL: 99 mg SODIUM: 478 mg FIBER: 1 g

———————— ◇ ————————

Lamb Curry and Rice Salad

This is a delicious and unusual salad. I enjoy it especially in the summertime.

2 tablespoons vegetable oil
1½ cups chopped onion
2 cloves garlic, minced
2 teaspoons ground ginger
2 teaspoons ground coriander
1 teaspoon ground cinnamon
1 teaspoon ground cumin
1 teaspoon ground tumeric
¼ teaspoon salt
⅛ teaspoon ground cloves
⅛ teaspoon ground red pepper
1¼ pounds cubed lamb
1 cup water, divided
2 tablespoons white vinegar
2 cups cooked and cooled long-grain white rice
      (preferably jasmine or basmati)
1½ cups chopped tomato
4 cups shredded lettuce
2 tablespoons chopped scallion

In a 3-quart saucepan, heat the oil over medium-high heat. Add the onion and garlic and cook, stirring, until onion is soft. Stir in the ginger, coriander, cinnamon, cumin, tumeric, salt, cloves, and red pepper until absorbed by the oil.

Stir in lamb until coated with the spices. Stir in ½ cup of the water and bring to a boil. Reduce heat and simmer, tightly covered, 1 hour and 45 minutes. If the water seems to cook away, stir in ¼ cup more water at a time, as necessary. Chill.

Remove meat from the pot and shred. Return shredded meat to the pot, stir in the vinegar. Add the rice and tomato; toss until combined.

Line serving plates with lettuce, top with salad, and sprinkle scallion on top.

SERVES 4.
CALORIES: 622   CHOLESTEROL: 139 mg   SODIUM: 492 mg   FIBER: 4 g

Health tip:
Reduce oil to 2 teaspoons and cook in nonstick saucepan; omit salt.
CALORIES: 582   CHOLESTEROL: 139 mg   SODIUM: 97 mg   FIBER: 4 g

———————— ◇ ————————

Mozzarella Salad with Sun-Dried Tomato Dressing

This salad is a combination of many of my favorite ingredients. Its flavor is rich and has a great depth to it. You might consider serving this salad as an appetizer on plates lined with lettuce. You can omit the proscuitto and make this a vegetarian salad.

⅓ cup wine vinegar
2 tablespoons olive oil
2 tablespoons vegetable oil
4 sun-dried tomato halves (oil packed)
1 clove garlic, minced
½ teaspoon salt
2½ cups cooked and cooled wahini brown rice
8 ounces fresh mozzarella, cut into bite-size pieces
1 jar (6½ ounce) marinated artichoke hearts, drained and chopped into
      bite-size pieces
2 ounces thinly sliced proscuitto, chopped
¼ cup grated Parmesan cheese
2 tablespoons chopped fresh basil or
      ½ teaspoon dried basil
Freshly ground pepper

Place the vinegar, olive and vegetable oils, tomatoes, garlic, and salt into a blender container (a blender is better than a food processor for this recipe). Cover and blend until smooth; set aside.

In a large bowl, combine the rice, mozzarella, artichoke hearts, and proscuitto. Pour on the dressing and toss. Add the cheese, basil, and pepper; toss again.

SERVES 8.
CALORIES: 238   CHOLESTEROL: 21 mg   SODIUM: 511 mg   FIBER: 2 g

Health tip:
Use half the dressing; omit proscuitto and salt.
CALORIES: 196   CHOLESTEROL: 17 mg   SODIUM: 285 mg   FIBER: 2 g

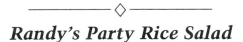

Randy's Party Rice Salad

Lysa (Randy) Kraft frequently serves this rice at buffets. There is never a grain left over. She suggests this recipe is as good warm as it is cool, and if you like, you can add diced chicken and serve it as a main course salad.

¾ cup olive oil
¼ cup Rose's Lime Juice
¼ cup mayonnaise
1 tablespoon dijon mustard
6 cups cooked and cooled long-grain white rice
2 cups sliced mushrooms
1 cup chopped red bell pepper
1 cup chopped zucchini
⅓ cup sliced scallion
⅓ cup toasted pignoli (place in dry skillet and cook, stirring, over low
    heat until browned)
¼ cup chopped fresh coriander or fresh basil or
    1 tablespoon dried
¼ teaspoon salt
¼ teaspoon pepper

In a small bowl, stir together the oil, lime juice, mayonnaise, and mustard; set aside.

In a large bowl toss together the rice and half of the dressing. Add the mushrooms, red pepper, zucchini, scallion, pignoli, and toss. Let stand ½ hour.

Add the chopped coriander or basil and remaining dressing and toss.

SERVES 12.
CALORIES: 298   CHOLESTEROL: 3 mg   SODIUM: 443 mg   FIBER: 1 g

Health tip:
Use only half the dressing and omit the salt.
CALORIES: 231   CHOLESTEROL: 1 mg   SODIUM: 22 mg   FIBER: 1 g

––––––––– ◊ –––––––––

Shredded Root Salad

I think this salad needs the extra chewiness that short-grain brown rice provides.

1½ cups cooked and cooled short-grain brown rice
1 cup shredded carrot
1 cup shredded parsnip
½ cup shredded jicama or daikon radish
2 tablespoons chopped parsley
2 tablespoons vegetable oil
1 tablespoon olive oil
1 tablespoon lemon juice
2 teaspoons cider vinegar
1 teaspoon spicy brown mustard
½ clove garlic, minced
¼ teaspoon salt
⅛ teaspoon pepper

In a large bowl, combine the rice, carrot, parsnip, jicama, and parsley.

In a small bowl stir together the vegetable and olive oils, lemon juice, vinegar, mustard, garlic, salt, and pepper. Pour the dressing over the salad and toss until combined.

SERVES 6.
CALORIES: 148   CHOLESTEROL: 0 mg   SODIUM: 245 mg   FIBER: 3 g

Health tip:
Omit the salt and use half the dressing.
CALORIES: 117   CHOLESTEROL: 0 mg   SODIUM: 19 mg   FIBER: 3 g

––––––––– ◊ –––––––––

Molded Rice Salad

Molding the rice salad makes a very festive presentation for company, but the salad is equally tasty just served in a bowl as is.

2½ cups water
1¼ teaspoons salt
1 cup converted long-grain rice
½ cup slivered almonds
½ cup mayonnaise
⅓ cup sliced pitted ripe olives

⅓ cup sliced pimiento-stuffed olives
2 tablespoons chopped scallion
2 tablespoons chopped parsley
2 tablespoons fresh lemon juice
1 teaspoon basil
¼ teaspoon pepper

Preheat oven to 350°F. Oil a 4-cup ring mold.

In a 2-quart saucepan, bring the water and salt to a boil over high heat. Add the rice and return to a boil. Reduce heat and simmer, covered, 25 minutes, or until the water is absorbed. Remove from heat.

While the rice is cooking, place the almonds in a baking dish, or on a piece of heavy-duty foil, and bake 10 minutes or until toasted. Remove from oven and cool.

When rice is cooked, stir the almonds, mayonnaise, sliced olives, scallion, parsley, lemon juice, basil, and pepper into the pot with the rice. Spoon into prepared mold and pack slightly. Chill at least 1½ hours.

Invert onto serving plate.

SERVES 6.
CALORIES: 320   CHOLESTEROL: 11 mg   SODIUM: 1177 mg   FIBER: 3 g

Health tip:
Omit the salt and use reduced-calorie mayonnaise. Use only half the olives.
CALORIES: 262   CHOLESTEROL: 5 mg   SODIUM: 729 mg   FIBER: 3 g

———————◇———————

Lazy Lady's Black Beans and Rice

Traditionally this soup is made with dried black beans, but I find that this short-cut version, with canned black beans, is just as delicious.

2 tablespoons olive oil
1½ cups chopped onion
1 cup chopped green bell pepper
2 cloves garlic, minced
⅔ cup water
2 bay leaves
½ teaspoon salt
½ teaspoon cumin
½ teaspoon sugar
¼ teaspoon black pepper
2 cans (16 ounces each) black beans, undrained
3 cups cooked long-grain white rice

Heat the oil in a 3-quart saucepan, over medium-high heat. Add the onion, green pepper, and garlic and cook, stirring, until the onion is soft. Stir in the water, bay leaves, salt, cumin, sugar, and pepper. Add the beans, with liquid, and stir. Bring to a boil. Reduce heat and simmer, uncovered, 1 hour. Discard bay leaves. Serve over rice.

SERVES 6.
CALORIES: 220   CHOLESTEROL: 0 mg   SODIUM: 708 mg   FIBER: 7 g

Health tip:
Omit salt; reduce oil to 2 teaspoons and cook in a nonstick saucepan.
CALORIES: 198   CHOLESTEROL: 0 mg   SODIUM: 264 mg   FIBER: 7 g

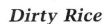

Dirty Rice

There's nothing pornographic about this rice, but rather, the word dirty refers to the typical brown-grey color from the liver and gizzards. I love the flavor of this dish freshly made, but when reheated, the liver flavor becomes overwhelming. I serve this as a side dish, but it certainly has enough protein in it to be a main course, if you like.

2 cups water
1 can (10½ ounce) double-strength chicken broth
¼ pound chicken gizzards, finely chopped
1 cup long-grain white rice
2 tablespoons vegetable oil or bacon fat
¾ cup finely chopped onion
½ cup finely chopped green bell pepper
½ cup finely chopped celery
½ pound chicken livers
¼ cup chopped parsley
¼ teaspoon salt
¼ teaspoon pepper

In a 3-quart saucepan bring the water and broth to a boil. Add the gizzards, reduce heat and simmer, uncovered, 30 minutes. Stir in the rice, return to a boil. Cover and simmer 15 minutes longer.

While the rice is cooking, heat the oil in a large skillet, over medium-high heat. Add the onion, green pepper, and celery. Cook, stirring, until onion is soft. Add the liver and cook, stirring, until only slightly pink in center. Remove liver from skillet and chop finely.

Stir the sautéed vegetables, liver, parsley, salt, and pepper into the rice. Simmer 5 minutes longer or until the liquid is absorbed.

SERVES 8.
CALORIES: 200   CHOLESTEROL: 206 mg   SODIUM: 335 mg   FIBER: 1 g

Health tip:
Use low-sodium broth; reduce oil to 2 teaspoons and cook in a nonstick skillet; reduce liver to ¼ pound.
CALORIES: 158   CHOLESTEROL: 117 mg   SODIUM: 112 mg   FIBER: 1 g

———— ◇ ————

Hopping John

This is a Southern dish traditionally served on New Year's. It always combines pork, black-eyed peas, rice, and onion. The type of pork used varies from person to person. I chose to use salt pork, but you can also use bacon or ham hocks.

1 cup dried black-eyed peas
¼ pound salt pork, blanched
1 cup chopped onion
3 cups water
1 teaspoon salt
Pinch red pepper flakes
1¼ cups long-grain white rice

Cover the beans with water and let stand 8 hours.

Remove and discard the rind from the salt pork and cut into ¼-inch pieces. In a 4-quart saucepan, cook the salt pork over medium-high heat until crisp and browned. Remove from skillet and set aside.

Add the onion to the skillet and cook, stirring, until soft. Add the water, salt, and pepper flakes to the pot. Bring to a boil. Drain the beans and add to the pot along with the reserved salt pork. Cover and simmer 1 hour.

Stir in the rice and simmer 20 minutes longer.

SERVES 8.
CALORIES: 215   CHOLESTEROL: 12 mg   SODIUM: 495 mg   FIBER: 8 g

Health tip:
Use half the salt pork and omit the salt.
CALORIES: 175   CHOLESTEROL: 6 mg   SODIUM: 116 mg   FIBER: 8 g

Fried Rice

This recipe is very flexible. You can use any vegetables that you have on hand. If you have broccoli, but no snow peas—no problem. You can also toss in diced cooked chicken, beef, duck, or shrimp and make this a main dish.

3 tablespoons vegetable oil, divided
1 egg, beaten
1½ cups bean sprouts (mung)
½ cup chopped snow peas
½ cup chopped onion
½ cup peas, or peas and carrots
⅓ cup sliced scallion
3 tablespoons soy sauce
2 cups cooked long-grain white rice

In a wok or large skillet, heat 1 tablespoon of the oil over high heat. Add the egg and cook until set (not stirring, as if you were making an omelet). Using a spatula or slotted spoon, lift the egg out of the wok or skillet, chop, and set aside.

Heat the remaining 2 tablespoons of oil in the wok (or skillet). Add the sprouts, snow peas, onion, peas, and scallion and cook, stirring, over high heat until the vegetables are tender-crisp. Stir in the soy sauce.

Add the rice and cook, stirring, until heated through. Stir in the reserved egg.

SERVES 6.
CALORIES: 163   CHOLESTEROL: 34 mg   SODIUM: 542 mg   FIBER: 2 g

Health tip:
Reduce the oil to 1 tablespoon and cook in a nonstick skillet. Use scrambled-egg substitute instead of egg. Used reduced-sodium soy sauce. Omit salt from rice.
CALORIES: 121   CHOLESTEROL: 0 mg   SODIUM: 140 mg   FIBER: 2 g

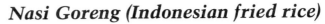

Nasi Goreng (Indonesian fried rice)

You can vary this recipe by stirring in any kind of cooked meat or vegetable when you add the rice. Originally I used a whole jalapeno and liked the result, but I toned it down for the less hearty. If you are feeling strong, use a whole seeded jalapeno. The dried shrimp paste and thick soy sauce are available in Oriental grocery stores.

> *1½ cups chopped onion, divided*
> *½ fresh jalapeno pepper, seeded or*
> *¼ teaspoon ground red pepper*
> *3 cloves garlic*
> *1 teaspoon dried shrimp paste or*
> *1 anchovy*
> *¼ teaspoon salt*
> *3 tablespoons vegetable oil, divided*
> *1 egg, beaten*
> *3 cups cooked long-grain white rice*
> *1 cup cooked vegetable or meat*
> *3 tablespoons thick soy sauce or*
> *2 tablespoons soy sauce plus*
> *1 tablespoon molasses*
> *Sliced tomato*
> *Sliced cucumber*

Put ¾ cup of the onion, pepper, garlic, shrimp paste or anchovy, salt, and 1 tablespoon of the oil into a blender container. Cover and blend until the mixture is smooth; set aside.

In a wok or large skillet, heat the remaining 2 tablespoons of oil over high heat. Add the egg and cook until set, stirring occasionally. Remove from skillet and chop; set aside.

Add the remaining ¾ cup onion to the skillet and cook, stirring, until softened. Add the mixture from the blender and cook, stirring, until boiling. Add the rice, vegetables, and chopped egg. Cook, stirring, until heated through. Stir in the soy sauce and cook, stirring, until completely combined.

Serve with sliced tomato and cucumber

SERVES 6.
CALORIES: 218 CHOLESTEROL: 35 mg SODIUM: 639 mg FIBER: 3 g

Health tip:
Use low-sodium soy sauce. Omit salt from rice.
CALORIES: 218 CHOLESTEROL: 35 mg SODIUM: 259 mg FIBER: 3 g

Rice Pilau

This is a traditional rice pilau, it goes especially well with curry.

2 tablespoons vegetable oil
1 tablespoon butter
1 cup chopped onion
½ cup chopped red bell pepper
1 clove garlic, minced
1 teaspoon salt
6 whole allspice
½ teaspoon curry powder
¼ teaspoon ground cumin
¼ teaspoon ground turmeric
⅛ teaspoon ground cinnamon
⅛ teaspoon ground red pepper
1 cup long-grain white rice (preferably basmati)
2 cups water
½ cup peas, fresh or frozen

In a 2-quart saucepan, heat the oil and butter over medium-high heat until the butter is melted. Add the onion, red pepper, and garlic and cook, stirring, until the onion is soft. Stir in the salt, allspice, curry, cumin, turmeric, cinnamon, and pepper until absorbed. Stir in the rice until coated. Add the water and bring to a boil. Reduce heat and simmer, covered, 15 minutes. Stir in the peas, cover and simmer 7 minutes longer, or until the water is absorbed.

SERVES 4.
CALORIES: 295   CHOLESTEROL: 8 mg   SODIUM: 696 mg   FIBER: 3 g

Health tip:
Omit salt; omit butter and reduce oil to 2 teaspoons, cook in nonstick saucepan.
CALORIES: 229   CHOLESTEROL: 0 mg   SODIUM: 5 mg   FIBER: 3 g

————————◇————————

Creole Rice and Beans

My friend Leah Weissman assisted me on this dish, and we both agreed it was terrific. The flavor of the vegetables comes through clearly, and the peppery taste wakes up your mouth.

2 tablespoons olive oil
1 cup chopped onion
1 cup chopped red bell pepper
½ cup chopped green bell pepper
½ cup chopped celery
1 can (14½ ounce) whole peeled tomatoes, undrained
1 can (8 ounce) tomato sauce
1 cup water
1 cup converted rice
1 can (16 ounce) pink beans or kidney beans, drained
¼ teaspoon salt
¼ teaspoon black pepper
⅛ teaspoon ground red pepper

In a 3-quart saucepan, heat the olive oil over medium-high heat. Add the onion, red and green peppers, and celery and cook, stirring, until the onion is soft.

Stir in the tomatoes and break up with the back of a spoon. Stir in the tomato sauce and water and bring to a boil. Stir in the rice, return to a boil. Reduce heat and simmer, covered, 20 minutes.

Stir in beans, salt, and black and red pepper. Simmer, covered, 10 minutes longer.

SERVES 12.
CALORIES: 129 CHOLESTEROL: 0 mg SODIUM: 293 mg FIBER: 4 g

Health tip:
Omit salt; reduce oil to 2 teaspoons and cook in a nonstick saucepan.
CALORIES: 116 CHOLESTEROL: 0 mg SODIUM: 250 mg FIBER: 4 g

Beans, Greens, and Brown Rice

Christine Koury is one of the most gifted food writers around. She developed this recipe and the next one. For this she suggests that you can experiment with the amount of vinegar you use, and you can substitute spinach or collards for the kale.

5 strips bacon, cut into 1-inch pieces
1 cup chopped onion
1 cup uncooked long-grain brown rice
2½ cups water
½ teaspoon salt
1 package (10 ounce) frozen chopped kale, unthawed
3 tablespoons white vinegar
¼ teaspoon red pepper flakes, crushed
1 can (15½ ounce) kidney beans, drained

In a 4-quart saucepan, cook the bacon over medium heat until browned. Remove the bacon from the pan with slotted spoon and set aside. Add the onion and cook, stirring, over medium-high heat until tender. Add the brown rice and cook, stirring, 1 minute.

Add the water and salt; bring to a boil. Reduce heat and simmer, covered, 30 minutes. Add the greens. Simmer, covered, 20 minutes longer, stirring occasionally until greens are defrosted and heated. Stir in the vinegar and pepper, then the beans. Simmer 5 to 10 minutes, or until beans are heated through, stirring occasionally. Stir in bacon just before serving.

SERVES 8.
CALORIES: 167   CHOLESTEROL: 8 mg   SODIUM: 300 mg   FIBER: 7 g

Health tip:
Reduce bacon to 2 slices and cook in a nonstick saucepan; omit salt.
CALORIES: 153   CHOLESTEROL: 3 mg   SODIUM: 129 mg   FIBER: 7 g

Chris's Ratatouille Brown Rice

If you want to make this dish a little heartier, you can stir in drained chick-peas or kidney beans. You can also make this into a casserole by putting the cooked rice mixture into a greased baking dish, sprinkling with 1 cup shredded Cheddar cheese, and baking 10 minutes at 350°F, or until heated through.

2 tablespoons vegetable oil
1 cup chopped onion
1 large clove garlic, minced
6 cups cubed eggplant (1¼ pounds eggplant)
4 cups sliced zucchini
¼ cup water
¼ teaspoon rosemary, crushed
½ teaspoon salt
2 cups cooked brown rice
3 cups chopped tomatoes

In a 5-quart saucepan, heat the oil over medium-high heat. Add the onion and garlic and cook, stirring, until the onion is soft. Stir in the eggplant, zucchini, water, and rosemary. Cover and cook over medium-low heat, stirring occasionally, for 30 minutes, adding more water if necessary.

Remove lid and simmer 15 minutes, stirring often or until thickened. Stir in the salt, then the rice and tomatoes. Cook, uncovered, 10 minutes over medium-low heat, or until heated through.

SERVES 8.
CALORIES: 134   CHOLESTEROL: 0 mg   SODIUM: 250 mg   FIBER: 5 g

Health tip:
Reduce oil to 2 teaspoons and cook in nonstick saucepan; omit salt.
CALORIES: 114   CHOLESTEROL: 0 mg   SODIUM: 10 mg   FIBER: 5 g

———————— ◇ ————————

Brown Rice and Spinach

This is a very simple and delicious way to prepare brown rice.

2 cups water
1 teaspoon salt
1 cup long-grain brown rice
1 package (10 ounce) frozen chopped spinach, unthawed
2 tablespoons butter
⅛ teaspoon nutmeg
⅛ teaspoon pepper

In a 2-quart saucepan, bring the water and salt to a boil over high heat. Stir in the rice and return to a boil. Reduce the heat and simmer 45 minutes. Add the spinach, butter, nutmeg, and pepper and simmer 10 minutes longer, or until all the liquid has been absorbed and the spinach is heated through. Stir.

SERVES 6.
CALORIES: 158   CHOLESTEROL: 10 mg   SODIUM: 431 mg   FIBER: 2 g

Health tip:
Omit the butter and salt.
CALORIES: 124   CHOLESTEROL: 0 mg   SODIUM: 43 mg   FIBER: 2 g

———————— ◇ ————————

Orange Rice with Almonds

I serve this very festive rice dish with game hens and other fancy poultry dishes.

½ cup slivered almonds
2¼ cups water
1 teaspoon salt
1 cup long-grain brown rice
2 tablespoons butter
2 tablespoons chopped scallion
1 tablespoon chopped parsley
1½ teaspoon orange rind

Preheat oven to 350°F. Place almonds in a baking dish or on heavy-duty foil. Bake 10 minutes, or until lightly browned. Set aside.

In a 2-quart saucepan, bring the water and salt to a boil. Stir in the rice and return to a boil. Reduce heat and simmer 45 minutes, or until the liquid is absorbed. Stir in the butter, scallion, parsley, orange rind, and almonds.

SERVES 6.
CALORIES: 212   CHOLESTEROL: 10 mg   SODIUM: 392 mg   FIBER: 2 g

Health tip:
Omit the butter and salt.
CALORIES: 178   CHOLESTEROL: 0 mg   SODIUM: 4 mg   FIBER: 2 g

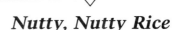

Nutty, Nutty Rice

Pecan rice is so named because the flavor of that rice is so "nutty." This recipe takes that quality and enhances it by stirring in chopped nuts to further emphasize the flavor. I think it's wonderful and highly recommend it as an easy to make but impressive side dish for company.

> *2 cups water*
> *1 teaspoon salt*
> *1 cup wild pecan rice or long-grain brown rice*
> *½ cup chopped pecans*
> *½ cup honey roasted macadamia nuts*
> *½ cup chopped cashews*
> *2 tablespoons butter*

In a 2-quart saucepan, bring the water and salt to a boil over high heat. Stir in the rice and return to a boil. Reduce heat and simmer, covered, 45 minutes, or until all the water has been absorbed. Stir in the nuts and butter.

SERVES 8.
CALORIES: 415   CHOLESTEROL: 8 mg   SODIUM: 299 mg   FIBER: 4 g

Health tip:
Omit the salt and butter.
CALORIES: 390   CHOLESTEROL: 0 mg   SODIUM: 8 mg   FIBER: 4 g

————————— ◇ —————————

Basic Risotto

It's important that you use aborio rice for risotto. It has a starchiness that is necessary to produce the creamy result associated with risotto. Risotto is a classic Italian dish, and once you have the technique to make a risotto, you can vary it to your heart's delight, stirring in almost any meat, fish, vegetable, or cheese you can think of.

1 can (13¾ ounce) ready-to-serve chicken broth or
1¾ cups vegetable broth (see page 19)
2¼ cups water
2 tablespoons butter or oil
2 tablespoons finely chopped onion or shallot
1 cup aborio rice
¼ cup grated Parmesan cheese, optional

In a 3-quart saucepan, heat the broth and water until simmering. Keep on low heat so that the liquids stay warm throughout cooking time.

While the broth is heating, melt the butter in a 2-quart saucepan over medium heat. Add the onion or shallots and cook until softened. Add the rice and cook 2 minutes, or until coated with the butter.

Add the broth to the rice mixture, ¼ cup at a time, stirring constantly, until the rice has absorbed the liquid. (You should make the next addition of liquid when you can draw a clear path on the bottom of the pot as you scrape through the rice with a wooden spoon. This will happen rather quickly at first and will take longer as you near the end of the cooking time.)

Stir in the cheese.

SERVES 6.
CALORIES: 172   CHOLESTEROL: 13 mg   SODIUM: 303 mg   FIBER: 1 g

Health tip:
Omit the Parmesan and use low-sodium broth; use 1 tablespoon of oil and cook in a nonstick skillet.
CALORIES: 143   CHOLESTEROL: 0 mg   SODIUM: 12 mg   FIBER: 1 g

———————◊———————

Risotto with Tomato and Basil

I think, in general, risotto is food of the gods. This risotto is divine. I forgot to peel the tomatoes before chopping, so I was left with little squares of tomato skin in the rice. I thought they added a little something—but you can feel free to peel the tomatoes before chopping.

> 1 can (13¾ ounce) ready-to-serve chicken broth or
>   1¾ cups vegetable broth (see page 19)
> 1¾ cups water
> 2 tablespoons butter
> ¼ cup finely chopped onion
> ½ clove garlic, minced
> 1 cup aborio rice
> 1½ cups chopped, seeded tomato (and peeled, if desired)
> ¼ cup grated Parmesan cheese
> 2 tablespoons chopped fresh basil or
>   1 teaspoon dried basil
> ¼ teaspoon salt
> ⅛ teaspoon pepper

In a 3-quart saucepan, heat the broth and water until simmering. Reduce the heat to low and keep liquid warm.

While the broth is heating, melt the butter in a 2-quart saucepan over medium heat. Add the onion and garlic and cook until the onion is soft. Add the rice and cook 2 minutes, or until coated with butter. Stir in the tomatoes.

Add the broth ¼ cup at a time, stirring constantly, until the rice has absorbed the liquid. (When you can draw a clear path through the rice by drawing a spoon along the bottom of the pot, the rice is ready for the next addition of liquid. This will happen quickly at first and take longer as you near the end of the cooking time.)

Stir in the cheese, basil, salt, and pepper.

SERVES 6.
CALORIES: 186   CHOLESTEROL: 13 mg   SODIUM: 396 mg   FIBER: 1 g

Health tip:
Use 1 tablespoon oil instead of butter and cook in a nonstick saucepan; use low-sodium broth; use only 2 tablespoons cheese; and omit the salt
CALORIES: 165   CHOLESTEROL: 1 mg   SODIUM: 49 mg   FIBER: 1 g

Risotto with Procini Mushrooms

This is the creamiest, richest rice dish I can ever remember eating (except rice pudding). Serve it to guests and watch them go into ecstasy. For a vegetarian version, use 2 tablespoons of butter or olive oil instead of the pancetta.

¼ cup chopped pancetta (2 ounces) or bacon
2 cups sliced porcini or cremiere mushrooms
⅓ cup heavy cream
2 tablespoons chopped Italian parsley
1 can (13¾ ounce) ready-to-serve chicken broth or
  1¾ cups vegetable broth (see page 19)
2¼ cups water
2 tablespoons butter or oil
2 tablespoons chopped shallots
1 cup aborio rice

In a medium-size skillet, cook the pancetta until crisp. Remove from skillet and drain. Add the mushrooms to the skillet and sauté until soft. Stir in the cream and boil, on high heat, until the cream is slightly thickened, about 3 minutes. Stir in the parsley and set aside.

In a 3-quart saucepan, heat the broth and water until simmering. Reduce heat to keep water just below simmering.

Melt the butter in a 2-quart saucepan, over medium heat. Add the shallots and cook until softened. Add the rice and cook 2 minutes or until coated with the butter.

Add the broth ¼ cup at a time, stirring constantly, until the liquid is absorbed. (When you can draw a spoon along the bottom of the pot and the path remains clear, you are ready for the next addition of liquid. This will happen quickly at first and will take longer as you near the end of the cooking time.)

Stir in the mushroom mixture.

SERVES 6.
CALORIES: 253   CHOLESTEROL: 32 mg   SODIUM: 396 mg   FIBER: 1 g

Health tip:
Use low-sodium broth and omit the cream; use 1 tablespoon oil instead of butter and cook in a nonstick saucepan.
CALORIES: 205   CHOLESTEROL: 8 mg   SODIUM: 165 mg   FIBER: 1 g

Sushi Rice

This most popular Japanese dish has gained wide acceptance in the U.S. The basis of sushi is cooked white rice (short- or medium-grain) flavored with vinegar and sugar. This rice is then topped with raw fish, or rolled in seaweed with fish or vegetable fillings. I don't recommend trying to serve raw fish at home, since many fish contain parasites that an untrained cook might not see. Sushi chefs, who are trained for many years, can usually, but not always, detect fish not fit for raw consumption. You can, however, create any kind of vegetable or cooked fish sushi at home. You can find the starred items in oriental grocery stores.

2 tablespoons rice vinegar*
1 tablespoon sugar
1 tablespoon mirin or sherry*
1 cup white sweet or glutinous rice*
2 cups water
1 teaspoon salt

In a small bowl, stir together the vinegar, sugar, and mirin and set aside.

Place the rice in a large bowl. Fill the bowl with cold water, stirring gently. Drain the rice into a strainer. Repeat the rinsing, stirring, and draining 5 more times. The water in the bowl should be fairly clear by the last rinsing. Let stand in strainer 15 minutes before cooking.

Bring the water and salt to a boil in a 2-quart saucepan. Stir in the rice and simmer, covered, 20 minutes. Let stand 5 minutes. Stir in the dressing. Cool to room temperature.

MAKES 3 CUPS. (Serves 6)
CALORIES: 120   CHOLESTEROL: 0 mg   SODIUM: 357 mg   FIBER: .5 g

Health tip:
Omit salt.
CALORIES: 120   CHOLESTEROL: 0 mg   SODIUM: 1 mg   FIBER: .5 g

———————— ◇ ————————

Pecan Waffles

The nuts give these waffles a delightful crunch. I served them with fruit syrup, and they were a real hit.

1¼ cups flour
¾ cup rice bran
1 cup finely chopped pecans
1 tablespoon baking powder
½ teaspon salt
1⅓ cups milk
⅓ cup pure maple syrup
⅓ cup vegetable oil
3 egg whites

Preheat the waffle iron.

In a large bowl, stir together the flour, bran, pecans, baking powder, and salt and set aside.

In a medium-size bowl combine the milk, maple syrup, and oil.

In a clean bowl, with clean beaters, beat the egg whites until stiff peaks form.

Stir the maple mixture into the flour until just combined. Fold in the egg whites.

Grease the waffle iron. Pour a generous 1 cup batter onto the waffle iron and spread evenly. Cook until browned, about 5 minutes.

MAKES 12 4-INCH WAFFLES.
CALORIES: 227 CHOLESTEROL: 4 mg SODIUM: 199 mg FIBER: 2 g

Health tip:
Omit salt; use 1-percent-fat milk.
CALORIES: 222 CHOLESTEROL: 1 mg SODIUM: 110 mg FIBER: 2 g

———————— ◇ ————————

Rice-Bran Pancakes

These pancakes are easy and light. Don't be discouraged by the grayish-brown batter.

1 cup all-purpose flour
½ cup rice bran
2 tablespoons sugar
2 teaspoons baking powder
¼ teaspoon salt
1¼ cup milk
¼ cup butter, melted
2 egg whites

In a large bowl, using a wire whisk, stir together the flour, rice bran, sugar, baking powder, and salt.

In a medium-size bowl, stir together the milk, butter, and egg whites. Add the liquid ingredients to the dry ingredients and stir until combined, but not smooth.

Heat a griddle until a drop of water dances across the surface before evaporating. Drop the batter onto the skillet ¼ cup at a time.

MAKES 12.
CALORIES: 110   CHOLESTEROL: 14 mg   SODIUM: 153 mg   FIBER: 1 g

Health tip:
Omit salt; use unsalted margarine instead of butter; and use 1-percent-fat milk.
CALORIES: 106   CHOLESTEROL: 1 mg   SODIUM: 81 mg   FIBER: 1 g

———————◇———————

Blueberry-Bran Muffins

These are very moist muffins, with just a hint of lemon.

1½ cups flour
1 cup rice bran
⅓ cup sugar
2 teaspoons baking powder
1 teaspoon baking soda
½ teaspoon salt
1¼ cups buttermilk
⅓ cup water
¼ cup butter, melted
2 egg whites
1 cup fresh or frozen blueberries, thawed
1½ teaspoons grated lemon rind

Preheat oven to 400°F. Grease 12 3-inch muffin cups.

In a large bowl, stir together the flour, rice bran, sugar, baking powder, baking soda, and salt.

In a medium-size bowl combine the buttermilk, water, butter, and egg whites. Stir in the blueberries and lemon rind. Stir the liquids into the dry ingredients until just combined.

Spoon into the prepared muffin cups and bake 20 minutes, or until browned on top. Remove from pan and cool on rack.

MAKES 12.
CALORIES: 156   CHOLESTEROL: 11 mg   SODIUM: 281 mg   FIBER: 3 g

Health tip:
Use unsalted margarine instead of butter. Omit salt.
CALORIES: 156   CHOLESTEROL: 1 mg   SODIUM: 173 mg   FIBER: 3 g

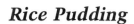

Rice Pudding

In my quest for the perfect white food, next to roasted marsh-mallows, rice pudding is one of my greatest passions. I've tried millions (okay maybe not millions) of recipes and none have been as creamy as this. You can stir in raisins before chilling, if desired.

1 cup water
½ cup long-grain white rice, not converted
¼ teaspoon salt
3 cups light cream
½ cup sugar
½ teaspoon vanilla extract
Cinnamon or nutmeg, optional

In a 1½-quart saucepan, bring water, rice, and salt to a boil over medium heat. Reduce heat and simmer, covered, 20 minutes.

Transfer to top of double boiler and stir in the cream and sugar. Cook, uncovered, over simmering water 1 hour, stirring often to separate the grains. (At the end of 1 hour the pudding will be a little liquid, but it will firm as it chills.) Stir in the vanilla. Chill. Sprinkle with cinnamon or nutmeg, if desired.

SERVES 6 (or 2 if you really love it).
CALORIES: 355   CHOLESTEROL: 79 mg   SODIUM: 138 mg   FIBER: 0 g

Health tip:
Use half-and-half instead of light cream, and eat only half a portion. Omit salt.
CALORIES: 139   CHOLESTEROL: 22 mg   SODIUM: 70 mg   FIBER: 0 g

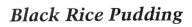

Black Rice Pudding

This is a very creamy, rich rice pudding. The black rice cooks up purple, and the finished pudding is a lovely lavender.

2¼ cups water
1 cup black rice
1½ cups half-and-half
¾ cup sweetened cream of coconut
¼ teaspoon rose water or vanilla extract
¼ teaspoon salt
1 cup heavy cream
½ cup chopped pistachios

In a 2-quart saucepan, combine the water and rice and bring to a boil. Reduce heat and simmer, covered, 55 minutes. Stir in the half-and-half and coconut cream. Slowly simmer 1 hour, stirring occasionally. Stir in the rose water or vanilla and salt. Chill completely.

In a large bowl, beat heavy cream until stiff. Fold in the rice and pistachios.

SERVES 12.
CALORIES: 285   CHOLESTEROL: 38 mg   SODIUM: 66 mg   FIBER: 1 g

Health tip:
Omit salt; use 2-percent-fat milk instead of half-and-half and only ½ cup heavy cream.
CALORIES: 216   CHOLESTEROL: 16 mg   SODIUM: 21 mg   FIBER: 1 g

CORN (MAIZE)
(Zea mays)

Originally the word corn was the generic name for all grains. Corn could mean barley, or wheat, or rye, or just any grain. When maize was introduced to the Old World, it was dubbed Indian corn. The settlers in the New World eventually dropped the word Indian and simply used the word corn to mean maize exclusively.

Corn is the only grain that is eaten fresh as a vegetable, and is also one of the few grains native to the Americas. It was corn that the Native Americans taught the settlers to plant that enabled the Colonists to survive during their first few years in the New World.

Types of Corn Available

There are many varieties of corn, each used for a different purpose.

Sweet corn (saccharata): This summertime favorite can be either yellow or white, or a combination of the two, and is eaten fresh.

Dent corn (indentata): So named because it develops a dent in the top as it drys. It is used mostly as animal feed. The small percentage used for human consumption is dried and ground into cornmeal or flour. It can be either yellow or white.

Flint or Indian corn: Because of its brightly colored, hard kernels, this corn is most commonly used for decoration.

Blue corn (Hopi corn): Yellow or white in color, it is used mainly for cornmeal and products made from cornmeal.

Pod corn: Each kernel of this corn has its own little husk. It is probably one of the earliest forms of corn and is not widely available.

Flour corn: This is an especially starchy corn that is favored by Native Americans who grow it for their own use. It is not widely available.

Popcorn: It has a low moisture content and the kernels explode when heated. It can be yellow, white, blue, or multicolored.

The varieties of corn are then processed into different grain products:

Frozen and canned corn: Sweet yellow corn, usually removed from the cob, is used almost exclusively for these products.

Cornmeal: Usually made from dent corn that is dried and ground into meal. Yellow and white cornmeal can be used interchangeably. Its most notable uses are for baking, breading, and to make cornmeal mush and polenta. Blue cornmeal is also available, but tends to turn what I consider to be an unappetizing purplish-gray when cooked.

Corn flour: Finely ground cornmeal that is not commonly used. It is available with or without the germ, but is more perishable if the germ is intact.

Hominy: It is also referred to as posole or pozole, or nixtamal, and broken hominy is sometimes called samp. Hominy is dried corn that has been soaked in either slaked lime or lye or wood ash to loosen the hulls. The hull and germ are then removed and the corn is dried. Hominy can be purchased both dried and canned, but neither form is too easily found, except in the South. Canned hominy is sometimes carried by Hispanic markets.

Grits: Dried hominy that has been ground. Grits is available in yellow or white and in coarse, medium, or fine grinds. It is most often used in souffles and baked goods, and as a hot cereal, but its most popular use in the southern part of the United States, where it is eaten as a side dish at nearly every meal with a pat of butter or gravy. Quick-cooking grits are also available.

Masa harina: Finely ground hominy that is used to make tortillas.

Corn bran: The bran of the corn, which is about the same as oat, rice, or miller's wheat bran. It is a good source of soluble fiber.

Corn germ: The germ of the corn can be used the same way as wheat germ, but it is not readily available or commonly used.

Other corn products include: corn starch, corn oil, corn syrup, and corn pasta.

Texture and Flavor

The flavor of fresh corn should be sweet, delicate, and not too starchy. It has long been said that to get the best-tasting corn, the water should be put on to boil before the corn is picked, for all too soon after picking its sugar begins to turn to starch. (It might be worth mentioning here that food engineers are growing corn in which this process has been retarded, thus making the corn stay sweet longer.) If the corn you buy is starchy and tasteless, it's probably because it has been off the stalk for too long. When buying corn, look for bright green husks that are firm and moist, and fresh-looking silk that has not dried out. Next, pull down part of the husk and examine the kernels. They should be plump and luminescent, right down to the tip of the cob. Otherwise the corn is simply too old to eat.

Baked products made with cornmeal will have a coarse and usually crumbly texture and some grittiness. Cooked cornmeal, such as polenta, has a slightly gritty mouth feel and a starchy flavor that may take some getting used to.

Cooked hominy has a very starchy consistency and a strange, faintly sour flavor. It cooks like, and has the texture of, cooked beans. Like cooked cornmeal, it may also be an acquired taste.

Hominy grits are bland, but have a slightly sour aftertaste. Neither hominy or grits tastes like corn. Their flavor is more or less nondescript, except for the sourness. Cooked grits have a grainy, not gritty, texture.

Products made from masa harina, which is also made from hominy, tend to have more of a corn flavor, with no hint of sourness. The texture is very slightly sandy.

Corn bran has only a hint of corn flavor and the consistency of all brans: sawdust.

Compatible Foods, Herbs, and Spices

Sweet corn complements the flavors of the minor and more unusual grains. It goes well with just about any meat or poultry and can be successfully combined with any herb or spice. The starchiness of corn makes it a bit repetitive to use solely with potatoes, rice, or pasta, although certain combinations of these can be wonderful if used as part of a larger recipe, such as corn chowder.

Cornmeal is mild in flavor and can also be used with just about everything. Assuming you like hominy, it also goes well with almost any food or flavor.

Availability

Sweet corn is available nearly all year, but it is always better when purchased during the peak growing months of June through September. Fresh local corn, especially when you buy it from the grower, or raise it yourself, can be quite out of this world. State-of-the-art freezing and canning techniques have made these forms of preserved corn very good and readily available any time of the year.

Yellow or white cornmeal, and quick-cooking or regular hominy grits are available in the cereals section of most supermarkets. Masa harina can often be found with flour and baking supplies. Look for popcorn with the other snacks.

If you have any trouble locating hominy, dried or canned, or masa harina, try a grocery store that caters to Hispanics.

Blue cornmeal and blue popcorn can usually be found in specialty-food stores and health-food stores.

Nutritional Content

Corn is not a great source of vitamins and minerals, although it is the only grain that contains vitamin A, and yellow corn supplies more of it than the white varieties. Corn has some B vitamins, calcium and iron, and protein, but it is low in lysine and needs to be eaten with complementary foods to be of any great nutritional value.

Substitutions

Corn is a very unique grain, and I can't imagine even one suitable substitute for it. However, you can use white, yellow, and blue corn products interchangeably, and frozen or canned corn can almost always be substituted for fresh.

Basic Cooking Instructions

The microwave methods that follow were tested in a 650-watt oven.

There are many methods for boiling sweet corn, but this is the one I happen to like best.

Stove-top method for fresh sweet corn:

12 ears fresh corn
Water
½ cup milk
1 tablespoon sugar
Butter, salt, and pepper

Shuck the corn and remove silk. Place in an 8-quart soup pot and cover with water. Stir in milk and sugar. Bring to a boil over high heat and continue to boil for 4 to 6 minutes, or until corn is tender. Drain and serve immediately with butter, salt, and pepper.

Microwave method for fresh sweet corn:

2 ears corn
Butter, salt, and pepper

Peel back husk, but don't remove it. Discard silk. Close husk and microwave on high (100% power) for 3 minutes. Turn corn over and microwave on high for 3 minutes longer. Let stand for 2 minutes. Remove husk and serve immediately with butter, salt, and pepper.

Alternate microwave method for fresh sweet corn:

Shuck corn and remove silk. Place a pat of butter on each ear of corn and wrap in plastic wrap. Microwave following directions above.

For four ears of corn, increase total cooking time to 14 minutes. Let stand for 3 minutes.

Stove-top method for hominy grits:

5 cups water
1 teaspoon salt
1 cup grits

In a 3-quart saucepan, bring the water and salt to a boil over high heat. Gradually stir in grits. Lower heat and simmer, covered, for 20 minutes, stirring frequently until thick.

MAKES 4¼ CUPS.

Microwave method for hominy grits:

2½ cups water
½ teaspoon salt
½ cup grits

Place the water and salt in a 3-quart, microwave-safe bowl. Cover with waxed paper and microwave on high (100% power) for 5 minutes, or until water boils. Gradually stir in grits. Recover with waxed paper and microwave on high for 3 minutes. Microwave on medium (50% power), still covered with waxed paper, for 10 minutes. Let stand for 3 minutes.

MAKES 2½ CUPS.

Stove-top method for quick-cooking grits:

4 cups water
1 teaspoon salt
1 cup grits

In a 3-quart saucepan, bring the water and salt to a boil. Gradually stir in grits. Cook for 5 minutes, stirring, until thick.

MAKES 4 CUPS.

Microwave method for quick-cooking grits:

2 cups water
½ teaspoon salt
½ cup grits

Place the water and salt in a 3-quart, microwave-safe bowl. Cover with waxed paper and microwave on high (100% power) for 5 minutes, or until boiling. Gradually stir in grits. Recover with waxed paper and microwave on high for 2 minutes. Microwave on medium (50% power), still covered with waxed paper, for 2 minutes longer.

MAKES 2 CUPS.

CORN RECIPES

(indicates easy recipes)*

———————— ◇ ————————

Zucchini-Corn Soup *
Best-Ever Cream-of-Corn Soup *
Crab and Corn Chowder
Posole and Shrimp Soup
Fried Catfish
Brunswick Stew
Veal Stew with Corn Wheels
Beef Tamales
Beef and Oriental Vegetables with Hoisin Sauce
Chili-Cheddar Baked Grits
Corn Puppies
Tortillas
Tostada Shell *
Bean Tostada *
Tortilla Chips *
Lite Tortilla Chips *
Fresh Tomato Salsa
Heuvos Rancheros
Nachos *
Puree-of-Pea-Grits Casserole
Polenta
Chicken Cacciatore
Torte di Polenta
Cornmeal Gnocchi with Gorgonzola Sauce
Hush Puppies
New Mexico Corn Salad *
Corn Relish
Succotash *
Better-Than-Canned Creamed Corn *
Skillet Corn *
Johnnycakes *
Can't-Eat-Just-One Corn Fritters
Cornmeal Mush *
Fried Cornmeal Mush *
Spoon Bread
Southern Corn Bread *
Northern Corn Bread *
Cream-of-Corn Bread *
Chestnut Corn-Bread Stuffing
Peppered Blue-Cornmeal Biscuits
Orange Corn-Bran Muffins *
Blue-Cornmeal Pancakes *
Corn-Bran Pancakes *
Indian Pudding
Crunchy Almold-Grits Pound Cake
Cornmeal-Shortbread Cookies

148

———————— ◇ ————————

Zucchini-Corn Soup

I find this soup rich and delicious. I serve it warm or cold.

2 tablespoons butter
¾ cup thinly sliced leek
2 cups shredded zucchini
1 can (13¾ ounce) ready-to-serve chicken broth or
    1¾ cups vegetable broth (see page 19)
1 can (17 ounce) corn kernels, undrained, divided
½ cup water
½ cup heavy cream

In a 3-quart saucepan, over medium-high heat, melt the butter. Add the leek and cook, stirring, until soft. Stir in the zucchini, broth, and all but ½ cup of the corn and water. Bring to a boil. Reduce heat and simmer, uncovered, 20 minutes.

Put half of the soup into the container of a blender or a food processor fitted with a steel blade. Cover and process until the vegetables are pureed. Pour into a bowl and puree the remaining soup. Return the pureed soup to the saucepan. Stir in the reserved ½ cup corn and the heavy cream. Cook over medium heat until heated through.

SERVES 6.
CALORIES: 176   CHOLESTEROL: 38 mg   SODIUM: 452 mg   FIBER: 2 g

Health tip:
Use buttermilk instead of the heavy cream; use low-sodium broth; and unsalted margarine instead of butter.
CALORIES: 115   CHOLESTEROL: 1 mg   SODIUM: 248 mg   FIBER: 2 g

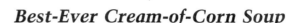

Best-Ever Cream-of-Corn Soup

My mom always made cream-of-corn soup by stirring milk into canned creamed corn. At the time, I thought that was delicious, but I see now that it doesn't hold a candle to this one. This recipe is based on the same principle of stirring milk into creamed corn.

¼ cup butter
¼ cup flour
1 cup half-and-half
2 cans (15 to 17 ounces each) whole-kernel corn, undrained
½ teaspoon salt
¼ teaspoon pepper
1 cup milk

Melt the butter in a 3-quart saucepan, over medium-high heat. Stir in the flour until absorbed. Gradually stir in the half-and-half. Add the corn with the liquid, salt, and pepper. Cook, stirring, until the mixture comes to a boil. Remove from heat.

Put 1 cup of the creamed corn into a blender container or food processor fitted with a steel blade. Cover and process until pureed. Pour the puree back into the saucepan. Stir in the milk. Cook until heated through.

SERVES 6.
CALORIES: 252   CHOLESTEROL: 41 mg   SODIUM: 637 mg   FIBER: 2 g

Health tip:
Use 1-percent-fat milk instead of the half-and-half and whole milk; omit the salt; use unsalted margarine instead of butter.
CALORIES: 217   CHOLESTEROL: 7 mg   SODIUM: 408 mg   FIBER: 2 g

─────── ◇ ───────

Crab and Corn Chowder

If you're not too fond of crab, or if you can't easily locate it, just leave it out. The soup is excellent even without the crab.

3 slices bacon, cut into 1-inch pieces
1 cup chopped celery
½ cup chopped onion
1 can (10¾ ounce) double-strength chicken broth
1 cup water
½ teaspoon salt
¼ teaspoon pepper
⅛ teaspoon thyme
2 cups peeled and diced new potatoes
2 cups corn kernels, fresh or frozen
6 ounces crab meat, fresh, frozen, or canned
1 cup half-and-half

In a 3-quart saucepan, over medium-high heat, cook the bacon until crisp and remove from pot. Add the celery and onion and cook, stirring, until the onion is soft.

Add the chicken broth, water, salt, pepper, and thyme. Bring to a boil and add the potatoes. Reduce heat and simmer 20 minutes. Stir in the corn, crab, and reserved bacon. Simmer 7 minutes. Stir in the half-and-half and cook until heated.

SERVES 6.
CALORIES: 216   CHOLESTEROL: 43 mg   SODIUM: 529 mg   FIBER: 4 g

Health tip:
Use only 1 slice of bacon for flavoring and cook the chowder in a nonstick saucepan. Use 1-percent-fat milk instead of half-and-half; omit salt; use low-sodium broth.
CALORIES: 168   CHOLESTEROL: 28 mg   SODIUM: 173 mg   FIBER: 4 g

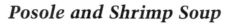

Posole and Shrimp Soup

This soup has a very delicate flavor, but you must be a fan of posole to really like it.

8 cups water
1 cup posole
2 tablespoons vegetable oil
1 cup chopped onion
1 cup chopped celery
1 can (14½ ounce) whole peeled tomatoes, undrained
1 bay leaf
1 teaspoon salt
¼ teaspoon ground red pepper
1 pound shrimp, peeled and cleaned

Put the water and posole in a large bowl and let stand, covered with aluminum foil, overnight.

In a 4-quart saucepan, heat the oil over medium-high heat. Add the onion and celery and cook, stirring, until the onions are soft. Add the posole with the soaking water and bring to a boil. Cover and simmer 2 hours. Stir in the tomatoes and break up with the back of a spoon. Add the bay leaf, salt, and pepper. Simmer, uncovered, 30 minutes.

Add the shrimp and simmer 5 to 7 minutes, or until the shrimp are cooked through. Discard the bay leaf.

SERVES 6.
CALORIES: 169   CHOLESTEROL: 115 mg   SODIUM: 435 mg   FIBER: 3 g

Health tip:
Omit the salt.
CALORIES: 169   CHOLESTEROL: 115 mg   SODIUM: 257 mg   FIBER: 3 g

———————— ◇ ————————

Fried Catfish

This recipe for fried catfish keeps the fish moist and delicious inside, and the cornmeal fries up to a very crispy crust. You can use this crust to make fried chicken as well.

4 catfish fillets (about 2 pounds)
¼ cup flour
1½ teaspoons seasoned salt
¼ teaspoon pepper
2 eggs
1 tablespoon water
1 cup cornmeal
Oil for frying

Rinse the fish and pat dry.

On a piece of waxed paper or aluminum foil, stir together the flour, seasoned salt, and pepper.

In a shallow bowl, beat the eggs with the water and set aside.

On a second piece of waxed paper or foil, put the cornmeal.

Dredge the fish in the flour, dip in egg, then coat with cornmeal.

In a large skillet, heat the oil until it bubbles as soon as some cornmeal is sprinkled into the oil.

Fry the fish until golden on both sides.

Drain on paper towels.

SERVES 4.
CALORIES: 548   CHOLESTEROL: 236 mg   SODIUM: 976 mg   FIBER: 3 g

Health tip:
Use an herb salt substitute for the seasoned salt.
CALORIES: 548   CHOLESTEROL: 236 mg   SODIUM: 177 mg   FIBER: 3 g

Brunswick Stew

This stew is thickened at the last minute with a flour wash. If you prefer a thin stew, just omit the flour and water step.

3 slices bacon, cut into 1-inch pieces
2 tablespoons vegetable oil
3½ pound chicken, cut into pieces
1½ cups chopped onion
2 cloves garlic, minced
1 can (14½ ounce) whole peeled tomatoes, undrained
2 cups plus 3 tablespoons water, divided
3 tablespoons chopped parsley
1 teaspoon salt
¼ teaspoon marjoram
1 package (10 ounce) frozen corn, undefrosted
1 package (10 ounce) frozen lima beans, undefrosted
3 tablespoons all-purpose flour

In a large saucepan, over medium heat, fry the bacon until crisp. Remove the bacon from the pot and drain.

Add the oil to the bacon fat in the saucepan. Brown the chicken on all sides. Remove from pot and set aside. (You may have to do this in more than one batch.)

Drain all but 2 tablespoons fat from the saucepan. Add the onion and garlic and cook, stirring, until soft. Stir in the tomatoes, breaking them up with the back of a spoon. Stir in 2 cups of water, parsley, salt, marjoram, and reserved bacon. Bring to a boil. Reduce heat and simmer, uncovered, 30 minutes. Stir in the corn and lima beans. Cook 20 minutes longer.

In a small bowl, stir together the remaining 3 tablespoons water with the flour until smooth. Gradually stir into the stew. Cook until thickened.

SERVES 4.
CALORIES: **613**   CHOLESTEROL: **201** mg   SODIUM: **1375** mg   FIBER: **10** g

Health tip:
Discard the chicken skin and omit the step for browning the chicken. Omit the oil; use only 1 slice of bacon for flavor and use 2 teaspoons of the bacon fat to sauté the vegetables; cook in a nonstick saucepot. Omit salt
CALORIES: **440**   CHOLESTEROL: **142** mg   SODIUM: **538** mg   FIBER: **10** g

—————— ◇ ——————

Veal Stew with Corn Wheels

I love the way whole chunks of corn on the cob look in a stew, but I must admit that they present a slight eating problem. So, if you prefer, you can use 2 cups of fresh or frozen corn kernels instead of the corn wheels.

2 tablespoons vegetable oil
1½ cups chopped onion
1 pound boneless veal, cubed
2 cups water
2 tablespoons flour
1 cup white wine
1 bay leaf
2 teaspoons sugar
½ teaspoon marjoram
½ teaspoon salt
¼ teaspoon thyme
⅛ teaspoon pepper
1 can (14½ ounce) whole peeled tomatoes, undrained
2 ears corn, cut into 1-inch wheels
2 cups fresh green beans, but into 1-inch pieces
¼ cup chopped parsley

Heat the oil in a 4-quart saucepan, over medium-high heat. Add the onion and cook, stirring, until soft.

Add the veal and brown slightly. Stir the water and flour together until there are no lumps, add to the pot with the wine, bay leaf, sugar, marjoram, salt, thyme, and pepper. Bring to a boil. Reduce heat and simmer 1 hour.

Add the tomatoes and break them up with a spoon, then add the corn and beans and return to a boil. Reduce heat and simmer 7 minutes, or until the corn and beans are cooked through.

SERVES 4.
CALORIES: 464   CHOLESTEROL: 155 mg   SODIUM: 565 mg   FIBER: 5 g

Health tip:
Reduce the oil to 2 teaspoons and cook in a nonstick saucepan; omit salt.
CALORIES: 424   CHOLESTEROL: 155 mg   SODIUM: 298   FIBER: 5 g

————— ◇ —————

Beef Tamales

If you don't have corn husks, you can prepare this dish in pieces of aluminum foil instead. Serve it with some Fresh Tomato Salsa (see page 163) on the side. If you cannot find corn husks, wrap the tamales in aluminum foil.

12 to 16 corn husks, fresh or dried (if you're using dried husks, soak them in warm water for 30 minutes)

Filling:

> *1 tablespoon vegetable oil*
> *¼ cup chopped onion*
> *2 cloves garlic, minced*
> *½ pound ground beef*
> *1 tablespoon masa harina*
> *½ cup taco sauce*
> *¼ teaspoon cumin*

Dough:

> *½ cup lard*
> *2 cups masa harina*
> *1 teaspoon salt*
> *1 cup warm ready-to-serve chicken broth*

Wash the husks and remove any cornsilk that may cling to them. Set aside.

In a medium-size skillet, heat the oil over medium-high heat. Add the onion and garlic and sauté until the onion is soft. Add the beef and cook until browned. Stir in the masa harina. Stir in the taco sauce and cumin and set aside.

In a medium-size bowl, beat the lard until fluffy using a mixer on low speed. Add the masa harina and salt and beat, on low speed, until completely combined. Add the broth to make a soft dough.

Spread the husks out on a board (they should be about 5 × 8-inches, if they are smaller, piece 2 or 3 husks together) Spread about 3 tablespoons of the dough onto the center of the husk, spread it to be about 4-inches square.

Spread about 1 rounded tablespoon of the filling in the center of the cornmeal square, leaving about a ½-inch border. Fold the husks in half lengthwise, making sure that the tamale has closed like a book, and press to seal the edges somewhat. Fold the corn husks again lengthwise, folding the part containing the tamale over the husk that is empty. You now have a package that has empty husks on top and bottom with a tamale in the middle. Fold the top and bottom empty husks over the tamale, forming a rectangular package. Tie a string around the package to hold it together.

Place the tamales in a steamer over simmering water. Cover and steam 1 hour. Serve immediately.

SERVES 4. (MAKES 12)
CALORIES: 434   CHOLESTEROL: 74 mg   SODIUM: 536 mg   FIBER: 5 g

Health tip:
Use vegetable shortening instead of lard; use ground chicken or turkey instead of beef; use low-sodium broth.
CALORIES: 373   CHOLESTEROL: 27 mg   SODIUM: 181 mg   FIBER: 5 g

---

———————— ◇ ————————

Beef and Oriental Vegetables with Hoisin Sauce

I'm not sure if canned baby corn really qualifies as a grain—but just in case it does, I want to cover all bets. Rice wine and hoisin sauce are available in Oriental markets.

¾ pound London broil
2 tablespoons soy sauce
1 tablespoon rice wine or dry sherry
1 tablespoon cornstarch
1 tablespoon hoisin sauce
2 teaspoons sugar
3 tablespoons vegetable oil, divided
2 cloves garlic, minced
1½ cups halved snow peas
1 cup sliced red bell pepper
⅓ cup sliced scallion
1 can (16 ounce) baby corn, drained

Place the steak in the freezer for 15 to 20 minutes so that the beef will be easier to slice. After the beef is chilled, thinly slice against the grain.

In a small bowl, stir together the soy sauce, rice wine (or sherry), cornstarch, hoisin sauce, and sugar. Set aside.

In a wok or large skillet, heat 2 tablespoons of the oil over high heat. Add the steak and cook, stirring, until browned. Remove from skillet.

Add the remaining 1 tablespoon oil to the wok or skillet. Add the garlic, snow peas, red peppers, and scallion. Cook, stirring, until tender-crisp. Return the beef to the skillet and add the baby corn.

Stir the soy sauce mixture and pour into the skillet. Cook, stirring, until the sauce is thickened and the mixture is warm.

SERVES 4.
CALORIES: 474   CHOLESTEROL: 76 mg   SODIUM: 853   FIBER: 3 g

HEALTH TIP:
Reduce oil to 1 tablespoon and cook in nonstick wok or skillet, using 2 teaspoons oil to cook the beef and 1 teaspoon oil for the vegetables; use low-sodium soy suace.
CALORIES: 415   CHOLESTEROL: 76 mg   SODIUM: 403 mg   FIBER: 3 g

———————◇———————

Chili-Cheddar Baked Grits

This is a very substantial dish, I like it as a side dish for brunch, but you can serve it as the main dish as well.

2½ cups water
1 cup milk
¾ cup grits
1 cup shredded sharp Cheddar cheese
¼ cup chopped canned chilies
1 teaspoon salt
½ teaspoon Worcestershire sauce
¼ teaspoon onion powder
¼ teaspoon dry mustard
Dash nutmeg
2 eggs

Preheat oven to 350°F. Grease a 2-quart casserole.

In a 3-quart saucepan, bring water and milk to a boil over high heat. Stir in grits. Cook, stirring, until mixture returns to a boil. Reduce heat and simmer, covered, 30 minutes.

Remove from heat and stir in the cheese until melted. Stir in the chilies, salt, Worcestershire sauce, onion powder, mustard, and nutmeg.

In a medium-size bowl beat the eggs and gradually stir into the grits mixture. Spoon into prepared casserole. Bake 1 hour and 10 minutes, or until baked through.

SERVES 4.
CALORIES: 299   CHOLESTEROL: 142 mg   SODIUM: 777 mg   FIBER: 4 g

Health tip:
Omit salt; use skim milk; use scrambled-egg substitute
CALORIES: 274   CHOLESTEROL: 33 mg   SODIUM: 262 mg   FIBER: 4 g

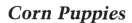

Corn Puppies

These are little corn dogs. They make great birthday party fare for your kids. They're easier to make than corn dogs because you don't have to fiddle with the popsicle sticks.

1 package (12 ounce) frankfurters, or cocktail franks
1 cup cornmeal
½ cup flour
1 teaspoon sugar
1 teaspoon baking powder
1 teaspoon salt
⅔ cup milk
2 eggs
Oil for deep-frying

Cut each frankfurter into 6 pieces (if using the whole).

In a medium-size bowl, stir together the cornmeal, flour, sugar, baking powder, and salt. In a separate bowl, beat the milk and egg. Stir the milk mixture into the dry ingredients

In a large saucepan, heat the oil until it bubbles as soon as some batter is dropped in.

Pierce a piece of frankfurter with a fork, dip into the batter until completely coated. Using a second fork, gently push the batter-coated puppy off the first fork and into the oil. Cook until golden on both sides. Drain on paper towel.

MAKES 42 PIECES

CALORIES: 66   CHOLESTEROL: 14 mg   SODIUM: 147 mg   FIBER: .5

Health tip: Eat just one.

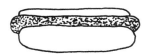

Tortillas

Tortillas are the base of many Mexican recipes. Most cookbooks call for 2 pieces of equipment for tortilla making: a tortilla press and a comal (a cast-iron tortilla cooker). I will assume that you don't have either piece of equipment (if you do have them you probably already know how to make tortillas). These homemade tortillas seem tougher than store bought, but they are tasty.

2 cups masa harina
1 teaspoon salt
1 cup plus 2 tablespoons warm water

Combine the masa harina and the salt in a large bowl. Make a well in the middle of the "flour" mixture and gradually add the water, mixing it into the flour using a wooden spoon. After you have stirred in the water, continue mixing the dough with your hands until the dough forms a ball. The final dough should be firm and hold together. If it is crumbly, it needs more water; if it is sticky, it needs additional masa harina. Cover with plastic wrap and let rest, at room temperature, 1 hour.

Form into 2-inch balls (you can vary the size of the ball according to how large you want your tortilla to be). If you have a tortilla press, you would flatten the tortillas in it now. If you do not have a tortilla press, place one ball of dough between 2 pieces of waxed paper. Roll into a 7-inch circle. Continue until all the dough has been rolled out.

Heat a heavy skillet (preferably cast iron). Cook the tortillas on the ungreased skillet 1 to 2 minutes per side or until blistery.

Stack the cooked tortillas, wrapped in a cloth or towel to keep them warm and away from the air, which would dry them out.

MAKES 8.
CALORIES: 126   CHOLESTEROL: 0   SODIUM: 267 mg.   FIBER: 3g

Health tip:
Omit the salt.
CALORIES: 126   CHOLESTEROL: 0   SODIUM: 25 mg.   FIBER: 3g

Tostada Shell

Tostadas are open-faced tacos. The tostada shells are easier to make because you don't have to worry about shaping them as they crisp. You can use the same toppings for tostadas as you would use to fill tacos.

Oil for deep-frying
8 tortillas, fresh or frozen and thawed

Heat the oil in a skillet large enough to hold the tortilla. When the oil is hot enough that it bubbles as soon as a small piece of tortilla is thrown in, fry 1 tortilla at a time until crisp. Drain on paper towels.

MAKES 8.
CALORIES: 95   CHOLESTEROL: 0 mg   SODIUM: 1 mg   FIBER: 2 g

Health tip:
Prepare these the same way you would for lite tortilla chips, but don't cut them into wedges (see page 00).
CALORIES: 66   CHOLESTEROL: 0 mg   SODIUM: 0 mg   FIBER: 2 g

Bean Tostada

This is a basic and easy recipe. You can dress it up by serving it with guacamole (you'll find a good recipe for it in the Job's Tears chapter), additional sour cream, salsa, sliced ripe olives, jalapenos, avocado, or anything you can think of.

1 can (16 ounce) refried beans
2 tablespoons sour cream
4 tostada shells (you can use homemade or
*   buy them packaged at the supermarket)*
1 cup shredded Cheddar cheese
1 cup shredded lettuce
½ cup chopped tomato
¼ cup chopped onion

Preheat the broiler.
In a medium-size bowl, stir together the beans and sour cream. Spoon one quarter of the bean mixture over each of the tostada shells. Sprinkle one quarter of the cheese over each shell. Place on a

baking sheet. Slide under broiler until cheese is melted and bean mixture is warm.

Place 1 tostada on each plate and top with one quarter of the lettuce, tomato, and onion.

SERVES 4.
CALORIES: 317   CHOLESTEROL: 33 mg   SODIUM: 633 mg   FIBER: 12 g

Health tip:
Use yogurt instead of sour cream.
CALORIES: 306   CHOLESTEROL: 30 mg   SODIUM: 633 mg   FIBER: 12 g

————— ◇ —————

Tortilla Chips

Homemade tortilla chips are totally irresible. Use them as a snack or eat them with Fresh Tomato Salsa (see page 163).

8 tortillas (homemade or packaged)
Oil for deep-frying
Salt, optional
Chili powder, optional

Cut each tortilla into 8 wedges. Heat the oil until it bubbles as soon as a small piece of tortilla is dropped in. Fry the tortillas, a few at a time, until they are crispy. Drain on paper towels. Sprinkle with salt or chili powder, if desired.

MAKES 64.
CALORIES: 20   CHOLESTEROL: 0 mg   SODIUM: 19 mg   FIBER: 2 g

Health tip:
Make lite tortilla chips (see p. 000).

————— ◇ —————

Lite Tortilla Chips

These are very tasty. They have a different type of snap from the fried variety.

6 corn tortillas (5-inch), frozen, thawed, or homemade
1 tablespoon vegetable oil
Salt, optional
Chili powder, optional

Preheat oven to 375°F. Lightly brush both sides of each tortilla with oil. Sprinkle with salt. Cut each tortilla into 8 wedges.

Place on an ungreased baking sheet and bake 10 minutes or until crisp. If desired sprinkle with chili powder.

MAKES 48.
CALORIES: 11   CHOLESTEROL: 0 mg   SODIUM: 14 mg   FIBER: 0 g

Health tip:
Omit salt.
CALORIES: 11   CHOLESTEROL: 0 mg   SODIUM: 0 mg   FIBER: 0 g

——————— ◇ ———————

Fresh Tomato Salsa

This is a delicious sauce that you can use as a dip, or as a sauce to top any Mexican dish. It's a little spicy as is, but you can vary that to your own taste.

2 medium tomatoes
¼ small green bell pepper, cut into chunks
¼ small onion, cut into chunks
⅛ lemon with the skin, cut into chunks
¼ teaspoon salt
½ small clove garlic
⅛ teaspoon ground red pepper

Peel the tomatoes by dipping them in boiling water for about 1 minute, then plunging them into ice water. Cool. Lift off skin using a paring knife. (If you have a gas range, you can place the tomato on a fork, hold it in the flame, rotating the tomato until the skin pops and splits in a few places, and lift off the skin.)

Cut half of one of the tomatoes into chunks and put in a blender container or food processor fitted with a steel blade. Add the pepper, onion, and the lemon to the blender or processor. Add the salt, garlic, and red pepper. Cover and process until pureed. Finely chop the remaining 1½ tomatoes and stir into the puree.

MAKES ABOUT 1½ CUPS. (per tablespoon)
CALORIES: 3   CHOLESTEROL: 0 mg   SODIUM: 23 mg   FIBER: 0 g

Health tip:
Omit salt.
CALORIES: 3   CHOLESTEROL: 0 mg   SODIUM: 1 mg   FIBER: 0 g

Huevos Rancheros

This is one of my favorite brunches. Start the meal with a spicy Bloody Mary and end it with Mexican coffee.

8 tortillas (5-inch), homemade or packaged
1 tablespoon vegetable oil
3 tablespoons butter
8 eggs
1 cup salsa (you can use any kind, mild or hot, or you can use
*   homemade Fresh Tomato Salsa, see p. 163)*
1 small avocado, sliced into 16 wedges

Preheat oven to 350°F.

Brush each tortilla with some of the oil. Place the tortillas in the oven to heat for 7 to 10 minutes, or until crisp.

While the tortillas are in the oven, melt 1½ tablespoons butter in a 10-inch, slope-sided skillet. Add 4 eggs to the skillet and cook until the whites are set, or to desired doneness. Place one egg on each of 4 tortillas and return to oven to keep warm. Melt the remaining 1½ tablespoons of butter in the skillet and cook the remaining eggs. Place one on each of the remaining tortillas.

Top each egg with 2 tablespoons salsa and 2 slices of avocado.

SERVES 4.
CALORIES: 488   CHOLESTEROL: 439 mg   SODIUM: 270 mg   FIBER: 11 g

Health tip:
Use unsalted margarine instead of butter and serve only 1 heuvos rancheros per person.
CALORIES: 244   CHOLESTEROL: 208 mg   SODIUM: 103 mg   FIBER: 11 g

Nachos

Nachos are a favorite appetizer in most Tex-Mex restaurants. You can make them with tortilla chips, but I prefer making it like a pizza on one whole tostada shell, then cutting it into wedges.

1 tostada shell (7-inch)
½ cup shredded Cheddar cheese
¼ cup sliced marinated jalapeno peppers

Preheat oven to 400°F.

Place the tostada shell on a baking sheet. Top with cheese, then sprinkle with pepper slices. Bake 5 minutes, or until the cheese is melted.

Place on serving plate and cut into 8 wedges, using a sharp knife or a pizza wheel.

SERVES 2.
CALORIES: 150   CHOLESTEROL: 30 mg   SODIUM: 425 mg   FIBER: 2 g

Health tip:
Use only ¼ cup Cheddar cheese.
CALORIES: 84   CHOLESTEROL: 15 mg   SODIUM: 337 mg   FIBER: 2 g

—————— ◇ ——————

Puree-of-Pea-Grits Casserole

The bacon can be omitted and you can make this into a vegetarian dish.

3 slices bacon
½ cup water
1 bouillon cube (chicken, beef, or vegetable)
1 package (10 ounce) frozen peas
3 eggs, separated
2 cups cooked grits

Preheat oven to 375°F. Grease a 2-quart casserole.

Cook the bacon in a large skillet, over medium-high heat, until crisp. Remove from skillet and drain on paper towels, crumble, and set aside. Add the water and boullion cube to the skillet and cook, stirring, until the cube dissolves. Add the peas and cook until just heated through.

Place the peas and cooking liquid into a blender container or a food processor fitted with a steel blade. Cover and process until pureed. Place into a large bowl and stir in the egg yolks, and then the grits.

In a clean bowl, using clean beaters, beat the egg whites until stiff. Fold into the grits mixture. Fold in reserved bacon. Spread into the prepared casserole.

Bake 45 minutes or until browned on top.

SERVES 6.
CALORIES: 165   CHOLESTEROL: 109 mg   SODIUM: 230 mg   FIBER: 4 g

Health tip:
Omit the bacon.
CALORIES: 123   CHOLESTEROL: 104 mg   SODIUM: 179 mg   FIBER: 4 g

◇

Polenta

My dog Poppy and I were in the park one day when we ran into my friend Lucia Sciorsci and her dog Topper. We were comparing notes on how awful the previous day had been. For me, no matter what I tried, my polenta had failed. So, here is Lucia's foolproof method for perfect polenta. It's only fair that I warn you that by the time the polenta is finished cooking you will have forearms that look like Popeye's.

8 cups water, divided
2 teaspoons salt
2½ cups yellow cornmeal

In a 4-quart saucepan, bring 5 cups of the water and the salt to a boil over high heat.

While the water is cooking, stir together the remaining 3 cups of water and the cornmeal (Lucia puts them in a jar and shakes it until combined). When the water comes to a boil, add the cornmeal, all at once, and stir like crazy until the cornmeal is completely combined with the water.

Reduce the heat so that the mixture is simmering and cook, stirring constantly, until the polenta pulls away from the side of the pot as it is stirred, about 30 minutes. (At this point, you can stir in any additions that you like, such as butter, cheese, sautéed vegetables, etc.). Pour the polenta into a bowl and let stand 2 minutes. Place a serving plate over the top of the bowl with the polenta and unmold the polenta onto the plate. Cut into wedges to serve (or you can put the cooked polenta into a greased container and chill it 2 or more hours, then slice for broiling, baking, or frying).

SERVES 8.
CALORIES: 157 CHOLESTEROL: 0 mg SODIUM: 533 mg FIBER: 3 g
Health tip:
Omit salt.
CALORIES: 157 CHOLESTEROL: 0 mg SODIUM: 1 mg FIBER: 3 g

Broiled Polenta: Slice the chilled polenta and place under the broiler until the polenta gets browned; turn and broil second side.

Fried Polenta: Slice the chilled polenta. Cook in a large skillet, with about ¼ inch of hot oil, until browned on both sides.

Chicken Cacciatore

Lucia mentioned that her favorite way to eat polenta is with Chicken Cacciatore, so here's my favorite recipe for it.

¼ *cup all-purpose flour*
½ *teaspoon salt, divided*
⅛ *teaspoon pepper*
3½ *pound chicken, cut into pieces*
2 *to 4 tablespoons vegetable oil, divided*
1 *cup chopped mushrooms*
¾ *cup chopped onion*
2 *cloves garlic, minced*
1 *can (16 ounce) whole peeled tomatoes in puree, undrained*
½ *cup dry white wine*
3 *tablespoons chopped parsley*
1 *teaspoon sugar*
1 *teaspoon oregano*
½ *teaspoon basil*
¼ *teaspoon thyme*

On a piece of waxed paper or in a medium-size bowl, combine the flour, ¼ teaspoon of the salt, and the pepper. Dredge the chicken in the flour, shaking off any excess.

In a 4-quart saucepan, heat 2 tablespoons of the oil over medium-high heat. Add the chicken and cook until browned on the bottom. Turn and brown on second side. (You may have to do this in batches and, if necessary, add the remaining oil to the saucepan.) Remove the chicken from the saucepan and set aside.

Add the mushrooms, onion, and garlic to the saucepan and cook, stirring, until the onion is soft. Add the tomatoes with the puree, breaking them up with the back of a spoon. Stir in the wine, parsley, sugar, oregano, basil, thyme, and remaining ¼ teaspoon salt. Return the chicken to the saucepan. Bring to a boil. Reduce heat and simmer, covered, 45 minutes.

SERVES 4.
CALORIES: 505   CHOLESTEROL: 197 mg   SODIUM: 675 mg   FIBER: 2 g

Health tip:
Remove the skin from the chicken before cooking; reduce oil to 1 tablespoon and cook in a nonstick skillet. Omit the salt.
CALORIES: 380   CHOLESTEROL: 141 mg   SODIUM: 346 mg   FIBER: 2 g

Torte di Polenta

This dish is similar to lasagna. If you prefer, you can just prepare the sauce and serve it over freshly cooked polenta, then pass the Parmesan cheese on the side.

Sauce:

> 1 pound ground beef
> 1 pound Italian sweet sausage
> 1½ cups chopped onion
> 1 cup sliced mushroom
> 3 cloves garlic, minced
> 1 can (14½ ounce) whole peeled tomatoes, undrained
> 1 can (8 ounce) tomato sauce
> 1 can (6 ounce) tomato paste
> ½ cup water
> 1 bay leaf
> 2 teaspoons basil
> 1 teaspoon sugar
> ½ teaspoon salt
> ¼ teaspoon oregano
> ¼ teaspoon thyme
> ⅛ teaspoon pepper
> 1 recipe polenta, chilled in an 8-inch loaf pan
> 1 cup shredded mozzarella
> ½ cup grated parmesan, divided

In a 4-quart saucepan, cook the beef, sausage, onion, mushroom, and garlic until the meats are cooked through and the onion is softened. Stir in the tomatoes, breaking them up with the back of a spoon, then the tomato sauce, tomato paste, water, bay leaf, basil, sugar, salt, oregano, thyme, and pepper. Simmer, uncovered, 40 minutes and set aside. Discard bay leaf.

Preheat oven to 350°F. Grease a 9 × 13 × 2-inch baking pan.

Remove the polenta from the loaf pan and cut into 20 slices. Line the bottom of the prepared pan with 10 slices of the polenta. Spoon the sauce over the polenta and sprinkle with the mozzarella and ¼ cup of the Parmesan. Top with the remaining 10 slices of the polenta; and sprinkle with the remaining ¼ cup of the Parmesan. Bake 40 minutes. Remove from oven and let stand 10 minutes before serving.

SERVES 10.

CALORIES: 492   CHOLESTEROL: 86 mg   SODIUM: 1350 mg   FIBER: 5 g

Health tip:

Drain any excess fat off after cooking beef and sausage; omit salt; use unsalted margarine instead of butter.

CALORIES: 480   CHOLESTEROL: 82 mg   SODIUM: 818 mg   FIBER: 5 g

———————— ◇ ————————

Cornmeal Gnocchi with Gorgonzola Sauce

I have read that the Roman's sometimes made their gnocchi of cornmeal, and although I have never seen a recipe for this, it sounded like a great idea. These gnocchi are on the large side. You can make them smaller by cutting them into smaller pieces before you shape them.

2 cups boiling water
1 teaspoon salt
½ cup white cornmeal
½ cup flour
¾ cup half-and-half
⅔ cup firmly packed gorgonzola (8 ounces)
1 tablespoon chopped parsley

In a 3-quart saucepan, bring the water and salt to a racing boil. Gradually stir in the cornmeal, making sure that the water never stops boiling and that the cornmeal doesn't lump. Reduce heat and simmer, stirring constantly, 5 minutes. Remove from heat and stir in flour. Set aside until cool enough to handle.

Divide the dough in half, and on a floured surface roll each half into a 30-inch rope. Cut into one ½-inch pieces. To shape the gnocchi, take one piece of dough and hold it against the floured handle of a wooden spoon (this should give the dough a crescent shape). Using the tines of a fork, score the outside of the crescent (it is easiest to do this while the dough is still on the spoon handle). The final result will be somewhat like a pasta shell.

Prepare the sauce by putting the half-and-half, gorgonzola, and parsley into a 1½-quart saucepan. Cook over medium heat, stirring until the gorgonzola has melted and the sauce has thickened. Keep warm until the gnocchi are cooked.

Bring a large pot of salted water to a boil. Drop the gnocchi into the water. (They will drop to the bottom of the pot. When they rise to the surface, they need just about 20 seconds extra before they are done.) Using a slotted spoon lift the cooked gnocchi out of the pot. Let them drain a few seconds, then put them into the sauce.

SERVES 8.
CALORIES: 210   CHOLESTEROL: 36 mg   SODIUM: 791 mg   FIBER: 2 g

Health tip:
Serve the gnocchi with tomato sauce instead of gorgonzola sauce.
CALORIES: 70   CHOLESTEROL: 0 mg   SODIUM: 186 mg   FIBER: 2 g

---

◇

Hush Puppies

Hush puppies and catfish are a perfect pair. These hush puppies are light and only mildly onion-y. If you like lots of onion flavor just add more.

> 1 cup cornmeal
> 1/3 cup flour
> 2 teaspoons baking powder
> 1 teaspoon salt
> 1 teaspoon sugar
> 3/4 cup milk
> 1 egg
> 1/3 cup finely chopped onion
> Oil for deep-frying

In a medium-size bowl, stir together the cornmeal, flour, baking powder, salt, and sugar.

In a medium-size bowl beat the milk, egg, and onion until completely combined. Stir the liquid mixture into the dry ingredients.

In a medium-size saucepan, heat the oil until bubbles form as soon as a small amount of batter is dropped into the saucepan. Drop the cornmeal batter by tablespoonsful into the hot oil. Fry until browned on both sides and the middle is cooked. Drain on paper towels.

MAKES 24.
CALORIES: 49   CHOLESTEROL: 10 mg   SODIUM: 123 mg   FIBER: 1 g

Health tip:
Omit salt, use 2-percent-fat milk
CALORIES: 48   CHOLESTEROL: 9 mg   SODIUM: 34 mg   FIBER: 1 g

———— ◇ ————

New Mexico Corn Salad

This salad is delicious. The taco sauce adds just a little zip to the dressing. You can jazz it up even more by using hot sauce instead of mild.

1 can (17 ounce) whole-kernel corn, drained
1 can (10 ounce) kidney beans, drained
1 cup sliced celery
½ cup chopped red bell pepper
½ cup chopped green bell pepper
⅓ cup chopped onion
3 tablespoons vegetable oil
3 tablespoons mild taco sauce
1 tablespoon cider vinegar
½ teaspoon chili powder
½ teaspoon salt
¼ teaspoon celery seeds
⅛ teaspoon pepper

In a large bowl, toss the corn, kidney beans, celery, red pepper, green pepper, and onion. In a small bowl, stir together the oil, taco sauce, vinegar, chili powder, salt, celery seeds, and pepper.

Pour the dressing over the salad and toss until combined.

SERVES 8.
CALORIES: 145   CHOLESTEROL: 0 mg   SODIUM: 247 mg   FIBER: 4 g

Health tip:
Use half the dressing and omit the salt.
CALORIES: 121   CHOLESTEROL: 0 mg   SODIUM: 110 mg   FIBER: 4 g

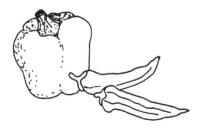

Corn Relish

I made this corn relish fairly plain, but you can add other vegetables to the recipe. Frequently, cabbage, zucchini, and/or green beans are added. If you don't want to spend the time cutting the kernels from the cob, you can use frozen corn.

1 cup cider vinegar
¾ cup sugar
1 teaspoon mustard seeds
½ teaspoon celery seeds
½ teaspoon turmeric
½ teaspoon salt
¼ teaspoon dill seeds
¼ teaspoon coarsely ground pepper
½ cup chopped green bell pepper
½ cup chopped red bell pepper
½ cup chopped celery
⅓ cup chopped onion
3 cups, packed, fresh corn kernels (5 to 6 ears), or frozen

In a 3-quart saucepan, bring the vinegar, sugar, mustard seeds, celery seeds, turmeric, salt, dill seeds, and ground pepper to a boil. Reduce heat and simmer 5 minutes.

Stir in the green and red pepper, celery, and onion. Return to a boil and simmer 10 minutes. Stir in the corn and simmer 10 minutes longer, stirring occasionally. Pack into sterilized jars.

MAKES 3⅓ CUPS. (16 SERVINGS)
CALORIES: 62   CHOLESTEROL: 0 mg   SODIUM: 75 mg   FIBER: 2 g

Health tip:
Omit salt.
CALORIES: 62   CHOLESTEROL: 0 mg   SODIUM: 9 mg   FIBER: 2 g

Succotash

This is a traditional American dish. It can be made with or without the cream, but I think the cream adds something special.

2 tablespoons butter
½ teaspoon sugar
½ teaspoon salt
¼ teaspoon pepper
1 package (10 ounce) frozen corn, unthawed
1 package (10 ounce) frozen lima beans, unthawed
¼ cup heavy cream

In a heavy 10-inch skillet, melt the butter over medium-high heat. Stir in the sugar, salt, and pepper. Add the corn and lima beans. Cook 5 minutes, stirring occasionally. Stir in the cream. Cook, stirring occasionally, until the liquid has almost completely evaporated, about 5 minutes.

SERVES 6.
CALORIES: 155   CHOLESTEROL: 24 mg   SODIUM: 152 mg   FIBER: 6 g

Health tip:
Omit the salt and the cream.
CALORIES: 121   CHOLESTEROL: 12 mg   SODIUM: 60 mg   FIBER: 6 g

---

Better-Than-Canned Creamed Corn

I find something wonderful about homemade creamed corn, because all the pieces of corn are whole and chewy instead of the canned variety where most of the kernels are mushed. Because canned whole-kernel corn is packed so differently from brand to brand, it's hard to determine how much liquid to expect. You can make this the consistency that you prefer by adding more or less half-and-half.

¼ cup butter
¼ cup flour
1 cup half-and-half, divided
2 cans (15 to 17 ounces) each whole-kernel corn, undrained
½ teaspoon salt
¼ teaspoon pepper

In a 3-quart saucepan, melt the butter over medium-high heat. Stir in the flour until absorbed. Using a wire whisk gradually stir in ½ cup of the half-and-half. Add the corn with the liquid, salt, and pepper. Cook, stirring, until the mixture comes to a boil. Stir in as much of the remaining ½ cup of half-and-half as necessary for your desired consistency. Cook, stirring, one minute longer.

SERVES 6.
CALORIES: 227   CHOLESTEROL: 36 mg   SODIUM: 617 mg   FIBER: 2 g

Health tip:
Use unsalted margarine instead of butter; omit the salt; use 2-percent-fat milk instead of half-and-half.
CALORIES: 195   CHOLESTEROL: 4 mg   SODIUM: 388 mg   FIBER: 2 g

———— ◇ ————

Skillet Corn

I absolutely love the way that the hot pepper sneaks up on you after you've started eating this. I think the contrast between the sweet, hot, and salty flavors is outstanding. you can omit the bacon and use 3 tablespoons butter, instead.

3 slices bacon
¼ cup chopped onion
2 cups fresh or frozen corn kernels
2 tablespoons maple syrup
⅛ teaspoon nutmeg
⅛ teaspoon ground red pepper

In a large skillet, cook the bacon until crisp over medium-high heat. Remove the bacon from the skillet and drain on paper towels, then crumble.

Discard all but 2 tablespoons of the bacon fat from the skillet. Add the onion and cook, stirring, until softened. Add the corn, maple syrup, and nutmeg. Cook, stirring, 5 to 7 minutes or until the corn is cooked and any accumulated liquid has evaporated. Remove from heat and stir in the pepper and reserved bacon.

SERVES 4.
CALORIES: 122   CHOLESTEROL: 4 mg   SODIUM: 89 mg   FIBER: 3 g

Health tip:
Use only 1 slice of bacon for flavor (or 2 teaspoons butter) and use a nonstick skillet.
CALORIES: 104   CHOLESTEROL: 1 mg   SODIUM: 38 mg   FIBER: 3 g

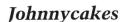

Johnnycakes

Recipes for johnnycakes range from very plain pancakes all the way to corn bread or cake. I've chosen to make them like pancakes. They're easy to make, but they are rather heavy. They taste very much like cereal, and should be served with maple syrup.

1 cup white cornmeal
1 teaspoon sugar
½ teaspoon salt
¾ cup boiling water
⅓ cup milk
1 egg

In a large bowl, stir together the cornmeal, sugar, and salt. Stir in the boiling water. In a medium-size bowl, beat the milk and egg until thoroughly combined. Stir into the cornmeal until blended.

Heat a griddle or slope-sided pan until a drop of water dances across the surface before evaporating. Grease lightly.

Drop by measuring tablespoonsful onto the heated griddle. Cook until browned on the bottom, then turn and cook the second side.

MAKES 32.
CALORIES: 20   CHOLESTEROL: 7mg   SODIUM: 36mg   FIBER: .5g

Health tip:
Omit the salt, use 2-percent-fat milk
CALORIES: 19   CHOLESTEROL: 7mg   SODIUM: 3mg   FIBER: .5g

——————— ◇ ———————

Can't-Eat-Just-One Corn Fritters

These fritters are slightly sweet with plenty of corn. I had a hard time stopping myself from eating the whole batch.

⅔ cup flour
½ cup yellow cornmeal
2 tablespoons sugar
1½ teaspoons baking powder
½ teaspoon salt
1 can (8¾ ounce) cream-style corn
1 egg
3 tablespoons milk
2 tablespoons butter, melted
1 can (8 ounce) whole-kernel corn, drained
Oil for deep-frying

In a large bowl, stir together the flour, cornmeal, sugar, baking powder, and salt.

In a medium-size bowl, beat the creamed corn, egg, milk, and butter until thoroughly blended. Stir in the corn kernels.

Stir the liquid ingredients into the dry.

Heat the oil in a saucepan, until bubbles form as soon as some batter is dropped into the saucepan. Drop the batter by measuring tablespoonsful into the oil. Fry until browned on both sides.

MAKES 24.
CALORIES: 77   CHOLESTEROL: 11mg   SODIUM: 128mg   FIBER: 1g

Health tip:
Omit salt and eat just one.
CALORIES: 77   CHOLESTEROL: 11mg   SODIUM: 84mg   FIBER: 1g

——————— ◇ ———————

Cornmeal Mush

If you've never tried this dish, you will find that it is exactly what the title says. It's very much like cooked farina with a corn flavor. You can serve it for breakfast, but it's really best when chilled and served as fried cornmeal mush.

5 cups water, divided
1 teaspoon salt

1½ cups cornmeal
3 tablespoons butter

Bring 4 cups of the water and the salt to a boil in a 2-quart saucepan.

In a medium-size bowl, stir together the cornmeal and the remaining cup of water. Using a whisk, stir the cornmeal mixture into the boiling water. Cook, stirring, about 10 minutes, until thick and cooked through. Stir in the butter.

SERVES 6.
CALORIES: 176   CHOLESTEROL: 15mg   SODIUM: 404mg   FIBER: 3g

Health tip:
Omit the salt; stir in only 1 tablespoon unsalted margarine instead of butter.
CALORIES: 142   CHOLESTEROL: 0 mg   SODIUM: 2 mg   FIBER: 3 g

$\diamond$

Fried Cornmeal Mush

This fried cornmeal mush has a crispy outside and a smooth and creamy inside. It tastes great with maple syrup.

1 recipe cornmeal mush (see page 176)
¼ cup flour
Oil for frying

Prepare the cornmeal mush according to recipe directions. Pour the warm mush into a greased 9 × 13-inch baking dish. Cover with plastic wrap and chill.

Cut the mush into 24 squares, about 2 inches each. Dredge each square in the flour.

Pour enough oil into a 10-inch slope-sided skillet to be ¼-inch deep. Heat it until the oil bubbles when a little flour is sprinkled into the skillet. Add the cornmeal squares a few at a time and fry on medium-high heat until golden on both sides.

SERVES 24.
CALORIES: 64   CHOLESTEROL: 4mg   SODIUM: 101mg   FIBER: 1g

Health tip:
Prepare the cornmeal mush using the substitutions suggested in the health tip for that recipe.
CALORIES: 55   CHOLESTEROL: 0mg   SODIUM: 0mg   FIBER: 1g

———————— ◇ ————————

Spoon Bread

Some people like spoon bread with a large pat of butter and plenty of salt and pepper; other people (include me in this group) like to serve it with syrup or powdered sugar.

1 cup yellow cornmeal
1 tablespoon sugar
1 teaspoon salt
2½ cups scalded milk, divided
3 tablespoons butter
3 eggs, separated
2 teaspoons baking powder

Preheat oven to 350°F. Grease a 2-quart casserole.

In a 3-quart saucepan, stir together the cornmeal, sugar, and salt. Gradually stir in 1½ cups of the milk. Cook over low heat, stirring constantly, until the mixture is very thick. Remove from the heat. Stir in the butter until completely melted.

In a medium-size bowl, lightly beat the egg yolks. Gradually beat in the remaining 1 cup of milk and add the baking powder. Stir the yolk mixture into the cornmeal.

In a large bowl, beat the egg whites until soft peaks hold. Stir one quarter of the egg whites into the cornmeal mixture. Fold in the remaining whites. Pour into the prepared dish. Bake 40 minutes, or until browned on top.

10.0SERVES6.
CALORIES: 244   CHOLESTEROL: 133mg   SODIUM: 597mg   FIBER: 2g

Health tip:
Use 1-percent-fat milk; omit salt; and use unsalted margarine for butter.
CALORIES: 224   CHOLESTEROL: 108mg   SODIUM: 201mg   FIBER: 2g

Southern Corn Bread

Traditionally, when Southerners prepare corn bread, it has little or no sugar. You can dress this corn bread up by stirring 1 to 2 teaspoons of your favorite dried herb into the batter, or stir in 1 cup shredded Cheddar and 1 can (3 ounce) chopped chilies, drained.

1¼ cups yellow cornmeal
¾ cup flour
1 tablespoon baking powder
2 teaspoons sugar
1 teaspoon salt
1¼ cups half-and-half
3 eggs
⅓ cup butter, melted

Preheat oven to 400°F. Grease a 9 × 9 × 2-inch baking pan.

In a large bowl, stir together the cornmeal, flour, baking powder, sugar, and salt.

In a medium-size bowl, beat the half-and-half, eggs, and butter until thoroughly combined.

Stir the liquid ingredients into the cornmeal mixture until completely combined. Pour into the prepared pan.

Bake 25 minutes, or until a wooden pick inserted in the center comes out clean. Cut into 12 squares.

SERVES 12.

CALORIES: 181   CHOLESTEROL: 75mg   SODIUM: 330mg   FIBER: 1g

Health tip:

Use milk instead of half-and-half; omit salt; use unsalted margarine instead of butter.

CALORIES: 157   CHOLESTEROL: 4mg   SODIUM: 126mg   FIBER: 1g

───────── ◇ ─────────

Northern Corn Bread

I like my corn bread sweet and moist—and this one is both.

1 cup all-purpose flour
1 cup yellow cornmeal
½ cup sugar
1 tablespoon baking powder
½ teaspoon salt
1 cup milk
2 eggs
⅓ cup butter, melted

Preheat oven to 400°F. Grease an 8 × 8 × 2-inch baking pan.

In a large bowl, stir together the all-purpose flour, cornmeal, sugar, baking powder and salt.

In a medium-size bowl, beat together the milk, eggs, and butter. Stir the liquid ingredients into the dry ingredients until just blended. Pour into prepared pan. Bake 25 to 30 minutes, or until top is golden. Cut into 12 pieces.

SERVES 12.
CALORIES: 183   CHOLESTEROL: 51mg   SODIUM: 235mg   FIBER: 1g

Health tip:
Use unsalted margarine instead of butter; use scrambled-egg substitute; omit salt.
CALORIES: 178   CHOLESTEROL: 3mg   SODIUM: 3mg   FIBER: 1g

Variations:

Corn Muffins: Place the batter for Northern Corn Bread into 12 greased 2½-inch muffin cups, filling each ⅔ full. Bake 15 to 20 minutes (in 400°F oven).
You can stir blueberries or apples into the batter before making the muffins, if desired.

MAKES 12.

Corn Sticks: Grease cast-iron corn-stick pan. Place in hot oven (400°F) as you prepare batter. Fill each corn-stick form ⅔ full. Bake 10 to 12 minutes, or until golden.

MAKES 24.

Cream-of-Corn Bread

I served this bread at Thanksgiving and it was a great hit. It bakes up to be very dense and moist.

1⅓ cups yellow cornmeal
1⅓ cups all-purpose flour
½ cup sugar
1 tablespoon baking powder
1 teaspoon salt
3 eggs
1 can (15 or 16 ounce) cream-style corn
1 cup milk
⅓ cup butter, melted

Preheat oven to 400°F. Grease a 9 × 9 × 2-inch baking pan.

In a large bowl, stir together the cornmeal, flour, sugar, baking powder, and salt.

In a medium-size bowl, beat the eggs, stir in the cream-style corn, milk, and butter until completely combined.

Stir the liquid ingredients into the dry ingredients until just blended. Pour into the prepared pan.

Bake 40 to 50 minutes, or until the top is golden and a wooden pick inserted in center comes out clean.

Cut into 12 pieces.

SERVES 12.
CALORIES: 241   CHOLESTEROL: 68mg   SODIUM: 431mg   FIBER: 2g

Health tip:
Reduce sugar to ¼ cup; use scrambled-egg substitute; use 1-percent-fat milk; omit salt; use unsalted margarine instead of butter.
CALORIES: 214   CHOLESTEROL: 34mg   SODIUM: 225mg   FIBER: 2g

———————— ◇ ————————

Chestnut Corn-Bread Stuffing

This recipe makes enough stuffing to fill a 6-pound roasting chicken. You can double the recipe for a turkey.

¼ cup butter
½ cup finely chopped celery
⅓ cup finely chopped onion
2 tablespoons chopped parsley
½ teaspoon poultry seasoning
¼ teaspoon sage
¼ teaspoon salt
¼ teaspoon pepper
⅛ teaspoon thyme
3 cups coarsely crumbled corn bread
3 slices white bread, cubed (I like the squishy type)
1 cup cooked and peeled chestnuts, chopped
1 egg
¾ cup chicken or vegetable broth (see page 19)

In a large skillet, melt the butter over medium-high heat. Add the celery and onion, and cook until the vegetables are softened. Stir in the parsley, poultry seasoning, sage, salt, pepper, and thyme. Stir in the corn bread, bread cubes, and chestnuts.

In a small bowl, beat the egg and broth until combined. Gradually pour the broth mixture over the corn-bread mixture, tossing constantly until the stuffing has absorbed the liquid.

Use this stuffing to fill the cavity of a roasting chicken, capon, or turkey.

SERVES 8 (makes 4 cups).
CALORIES: 229   CHOLESTEROL: 56mg   SODIUM: 365mg   FIBER: 5g

Health tip:
Use unsalted margarine instead of butter; omit salt.
CALORIES: 229   CHOLESTEROL: 41mg   SODIUM: 265mg   FIBER: 5g

Peppered Blue-Cornmeal Biscuits

Use white or yellow cornmeal if you can't get blue, or if you find that purplish food is unappealing. These biscuits are light and delicious, with an extra snap from the pepper.

1½ cups flour
½ cup blue cornmeal
2 teaspoons baking powder
1 teaspoon baking soda
1½ teaspoons medium-grind pepper
1 teaspoon salt
½ cup shortening
¾ cup buttermilk

Preheat oven to 425°F.

In a large bowl, stir together the flour, cornmeal, baking powder, baking soda, pepper, and salt.

Using a pastry cutter or two knives, cut the shortening into the flour mixture until it resembles coarse cornmeal.

Stir in the buttermilk until a soft dough is formed. Turn onto a floured board and knead 10 to 12 times. Pat ½-inch thick and cut with floured 2½-inch biscuit cutter. Place the biscuits on an ungreased baking sheet. Bake 12 minutes, or until lightly browned.

MAKES 12.
CALORIES: 123   CHOLESTEROL: 1mg   SODIUM: 317mg   FIBER: 1g

Health tip:
Omit the salt.
CALORIES: 123   CHOLESTEROL: 1mg   SODIUM: 140mg   FIBER: 1g

—————— ◇ ——————

Orange Corn-Bran Muffins

I like these muffins because the flavor is so subtle and delicate. The hint of orange is a perfect complement to the corn, and the amount of sweetness is just right.

1¼ cups all-purpose flour
¾ cup corn bran
½ cup cornmeal
2 teaspoons baking powder
1 teaspoon baking soda
½ teaspoon salt
¾ cup buttermilk
½ cup orange juice
⅓ cup firmly packed dark-brown sugar
¼ cup oil
2 egg whites
2 teaspoons grated orange rind
½ teaspoon vanilla extract

Preheat oven to 400°F. Grease 12 3-inch muffin cups.

In a large bowl, stir together the flour, corn bran, cornmeal, baking powder, baking soda, and salt.

In a medium-size bowl, stir together the buttermilk, orange juice, brown sugar, oil, egg whites, orange rind, and vanilla. Add the orange mixture to the dry ingredients and stir until just moistened.

Spoon into prepared cups and bake 20 minutes.

MAKES 12.
CALORIES: 158   CHOLESTEROL: 1mg   SODIUM: 241mg   FIBER: 2g

Health tip:
Omit the salt.
CALORIES: 158   CHOLESTEROL: 1mg   SODIUM: 152mg   FIBER: 2g

---◇---

Blue-Cornmeal Pancakes

These pancakes have a lovely flavor and a bit more consistency than traditional pancakes. You can use white or yellow cornmeal, if you prefer.

1 cup blue cornmeal
3 tablespoons sugar
½ teaspoon salt
¾ cup boiling water
½ cup milk
2 eggs
3 tablespoons butter, melted
¾ cup flour
1½ teaspoons baking powder

In a large bowl, stir together the cornmeal, sugar, and salt. Stir in the boiling water until all the cornmeal is moistened.

In a medium-size bowl, beat together the milk, eggs, and butter. Stir into the cornmeal mixture.

On a piece of waxed paper or in a medium-size bowl, stir together the flour and baking powder. Stir into the cornmeal mixture.

Heat a griddle or slope-sided skillet until a drop of water dances across the surface before evaporating. Drop about 2 tablespoons of the batter at a time to make 3-inch pancakes. Cook until bubbles on top start to burst. Turn and cook on second side.

MAKES 18.
CALORIES: 85 CHOLESTEROL: 29mg SODIUM: 114mg FIBER: 1g

Health tip:
Omit salt; Use 1-percent-fat milk and unsalted margarine.
CALORIES: 83 CHOLESTEROL: 23mg SODIUM: 41mg FIBER: 1g

———————— ◊ ————————

Corn-Bran Pancakes

Here's a great change from plain pancakes. These pancakes have the grittiness of the corn and the sweetness of maple syrup.

1 cup flour
¾ cup cornmeal
¾ cup corn bran
1 tablespoon baking powder
½ teaspoon salt
1⅓ cups milk
⅓ cup maple syrup
⅓ cup corn oil
2 egg whites

In a large bowl, stir together the flour, cornmeal, corn bran, baking powder, and salt.

In a medium-size bowl, beat the milk, maple syrup, oil, and egg whites until combined. Stir the liquid ingredients into the corn-bran mixture, until just moistened.

Heat a skillet until a drop of water dances across the surface before evaporating. Drop about ¼ cup batter per pancake. Cook, over medium heat, until bubbles burst on the surface. Turn and cook second side until browned.

MAKES 18.
CALORIES: 119   CHOLESTEROL: 2mg   SODIUM: 130mg   FIBER: 1g

Health tip:
Omit salt.
CALORIES: 119   CHOLESTEROL: 2mg   SODIUM: 71mg   FIBER: 1g

———— ◇ ————

Indian Pudding

This pudding is slightly gritty and pretty sweet. I like it best warm with lots of vanilla ice cream or whipped cream.

1 cup milk
½ cup cornmeal
3 cups scalded milk
2 tablespoons butter
3 eggs
½ cup molasses
¼ cup firmly packed light- or dark-brown sugar
1 teaspoon cinnamon
½ teaspoon ginger
½ teaspoon salt
½ cup light cream

Preheat oven to 325°F. Grease a 2-quart casserole.

In a 2-quart saucepan, stir together the milk and cornmeal. Stir in the scalded milk. Place over medium-high heat and cook, stirring frequently, until the mixture comes to a boil. Reduce heat and simmer until the mixture is thickened. Remove from heat and stir in the butter until completely melted.

In a medium-size bowl, beat the eggs. Beat in the molasses, brown sugar, cinnamon, ginger, and salt. Stir the egg mixture into the cornmeal mixture until completely combined.

Pour into the prepared casserole. Pour light cream on top, but do not mix in. Bake 1 hour to 1 hour and 15 minutes, or until a knife inserted in the center comes out clean. Let stand at least 15 minutes before serving. Serve warm or cool.

SERVES 8.
CALORIES: 258   CHOLESTEROL: 112mg   SODIUM: 255mg   FIBER: 1g

Health tip:
Use 2-percent-fat milk; use scrambled-egg substitute; omit the light cream; omit the salt.
CALORIES: 187   CHOLESTEROL: 99mg   SODIUM: 116mg   FIBER: 1g

Crunchy Almond-Grits Pound Cake

This is an absolutely perfect cake to have with a cup of coffee. It's dense and sweet with a crusty almond coating.

Almond crunch crust:

> ½ cup butter, softened
> 1 cup firmly packed light- or dark-brown sugar
> 1½ cups flour
> 1½ cups finely chopped almonds

Cake:

> ½ cup water
> ½ cup milk
> 3 tablespoons quick grits
> 1 cup butter, softened
> 2¼ cups sugar
> 6 eggs
> 1 teaspoon vanilla extract
> ½ teaspoon grated lemon rind
> 3 cups flour
> 1 teaspoon baking powder
> 1 teaspoon baking soda
> ½ teaspoon salt
> ½ cup sour cream

Preheat oven to 350°F. Grease a 10-inch tube.

Prepare the crust by creaming the butter and the brown sugar until light and fluffy. Add the flour and beat until crumbly. Stir in the almonds. Pat this mixture into the bottom and three-quarters of the way up the outer wall of the tube pan. Set aside.

In a 1½-quart saucepan, bring the water and milk to a boil. Gradually add the grits to the water, stirring constantly. Reduce heat and simmer 2 minutes. Remove from heat and set aside to cool.

In a large bowl, beat the butter with the sugar until light and fluffy. Beat in the eggs, one at a time, beating thoroughly after each. Beat in the vanilla and lemon rind.

Place the flour, baking powder, baking soda, and salt in a medium-size bowl, or on waxed paper, and stir with a whisk until completely combined. Set aside.

Stir the sour cream into the grits.

Add the dry ingredients to the butter, alternating with the grits, beating until smooth.

Spoon the batter into the prepared cake pan and bake 1 hour and 20 minutes, or until a wooden pick inserted in the center comes out clean. Cool on rack 5 minutes. Run knife around edges of the inner and outer tube, and turn onto rack to cool.

SERVES 16.

CALORIES: 567   CHOLESTEROL: 129mg   SODIUM: 325mg   FIBER: 3g

Health tip:

Use unsalted margarine instead of butter; omit salt.

CALORIES: 567   CHOLESTEROL: 71mg   SODIUM: 92mg   FIBER: 3g

Cornmeal-Shortbread Cookies

These buttery cookies just melt in your mouth. The cornmeal gives them a little extra flavor and slightly gritty texture. Everyone who tasted them loved them.

1½ cups flour
¾ cup white cornmeal
¾ cup superfine sugar
1 cup butter

Preheat oven to 325°F.

In a large bowl, stir together the flour, cornmeal, and sugar. Using a pastry cutter, or two knives, cut the butter into the flour until the mixture resembles coarse sand.

Using your hands, sift the mixture through your fingers, pressing the dough slightly so that each time you lift some of the dough, it starts to form larger and larger clumps. When the clumps start to hold together, turn onto a board and knead until the dough holds together and cracks when pressed down.

On a lightly floured board, roll the dough ¼-inch thick.

Cut into 1½-inch squares and place ½ inch apart, on ungreased baking sheets. If desired, press a design into each cookie using the dull edge of a cookie or aspic cutter.

Bake 12 minutes, or until the cookies are barely colored around the edges. Cool on racks.

MAKES 48.
CALORIES: 68   CHOLESTEROL: 10mg   SODIUM: 32mg   FIBER: .5g

Health tip:
Use unsalted margarine instead of butter.
CALORIES: 68   CHOLESTEROL: 0mg   SODIUM: 5mg   FIBER: .5g

THE MINOR GRAINS: FOR MAN OR BEAST?

◇

Barley
Buckwheat/Kasha
Millet
Oats
Rye
Wild Rice

The grains in this section are considered "minor" only in the sense that they constitute a small portion of the diet of mainstream America. In larger matters, such as world hunger, many of them are very major players.

Nutritionally, the so-called minor grains have it all over those in the major-grains category (wheat, rice, and corn), since they are almost always higher in protein, vitamins, and fiber than their more popular counterparts. The unrefined versions of the major grains rank about as high in nutrition as the minor grains, but it's rare when a whole major grain ever makes it to the American dining table. Usually by the time they get that far they've been hulled (bye-bye fiber), ground, and often bleached. Even rice is denuded of many of its finer nutritional properties before it hits the supermarket shelves.

Although the minor grains are known, albeit vaguely, to most Americans, their use has been largely stereotyped: Oats are for breakfast, and sometimes for cookies. Barley is for soup. Rye is for bread. Millet is for health nuts. Wild rice is for special occasions. Buckwheat had something to do with "Our Gang." Often they are even better known for their uss other than human consumption. Barley is used to make malt for beer. Millet is bird seed. Rye is used to make whiskey. Oats are for horses.

I think that many of the reasons these grains are neglected are understandable. Their flavors tend to be strong and require some getting used to. Barley is musky, millet is bitter, rye is a little sour, oats have a starchy consistency, buckwheat is overwhelming to some palates, and, although wild rice is wonderful, it's too expensive to eat very often.

Another reason these grains are ignored is that most of them take a long time to cook. For today's lifestyles, faster is better. Corn, for instance, heats or cooks in just moments, and white rice takes a mere 20 minutes from package to table. This is a far cry from any whole grain that can take from 1 to 2 hours to cook properly. Even when using a microwave oven, cooking times are still discouragingly long.

After reviewing the downsides of the minor grains, you may be inclined to wonder, why bother? The nutritional aspects alone, especially the dietary fiber in these unrefined or less-refined grains, should be motivation enough for moving away from preconceived notions, and at least *trying* them.

Most of us have heard about the blood cholesterol-lowering effects of oat bran, and wheat bran, it is now thought, reduces the risk of colon cancer. The claims that fiber will lessen your chances of a confrontation with heart disease, cancer, diverticulitis, hemorrhoids, and obesity, and will lead to an overall improvement in health, are well documented. Quite simply, unrefined and less-refined grains are excellent sources of crude dietary fiber, and that is reason enough to eat them.

On a less practical and more creative side, introducing new uses for grains into your diet offers a wide range of possibilities that are bound to enliven everyday meals. (Remember that it wasn't too long ago that the thought of eating cold pasta would have elicited a wide round of yucks.) The recipes that follow in this and Part IV offer many opportunities for interesting and sometimes even exciting alternatives to meat and potatoes.

BARLEY
(Horeium sativum vulgare)

Except for an occasional appearance in soups and stews, barley is sadly neglected. Its major uses are for animal feed and to make malt for beer.

The barley with which most of us are familiar is pearl or pearled barley (whole barley with the hull and bran removed), which is easily obtained in the supermarket.

Types of Barley Available

Unhulled barley: This is not particularly recommended, since it takes forever to cook and never does completely lose its toughness.

Pot or hulled or scotch barley: All of the hull (outer husk) and some of the bran has been removed by polishing (grinding off the tough hull). Pot barley is darker in color than pearl barley.

Hulless barley: New to the consumer market, this barley is cultivated so that its hull comes off more easily than pot or scotch barley, and so does not require polishing. It is a rich brown color and not quite as rounded in shape as pot or pearl barley.

Pearl or pearled barley: All of the hull, most of the bran, and some of the germ has been polished away, leaving a small rounded nugget that looks a lot like a seed pearl. (The pearl barley sold at the supermarket seems to me to be slightly lighter in color and slightly smaller than the pearl barley that I've found in health-food stores. The health-food-store variety also requires 5 to 10 minutes longer to cook.)

Barley grits: Toasted pot barley, broken into five or six pieces. Grits cook in less time than pot or pearl barley, and end up as a sort of sticky mixture that will remind you of cooked oatmeal and can be used the same way.

Barley flakes: Pearl barley that has been toasted and rolled into flakes, similar to the process that is used to produce rolled oats. Use barley flakes the same way that you would use rolled oats (baked goods, meatloaves, etc.). When cooked in water, barley flakes make a tasty hot cereal.

195

Barley flour: It can be substituted for up to 25 percent of the whole-wheat flour called for in recipes for baked goods. However, because barley flour is low in gluten, the finished product will have a slightly heavy consistency. If you have the proper equipment (a home grain mill, available in stores that carry highly specialized kitchen equipment), you can grind your own flour from toasted barley.

Barley malt: A sweet syrup, similar to molasses, that can be found in health-food stores. Unsulphured molasses may be substituted.

Texture and Flavor

Barley is usually found in recipes that are titled "hearty," such as "hearty" soups and "hearty" stews, or in so-called "winter" recipes. It has a pleasant earthy flavor. You can compare barley with beans for its ability to make the eater feel well fed. Its "toothiness" and the feeling of satiety that barley provides makes it the perfect grain for those who are looking for meat substitutes.

The texture of pearl barley will vary according to the amount of water in which it's cooked. It can range from a soft starchy porridge to a chewy separate grain that is similar to al dente–cooked pasta.

Pot and hulless barleys will be more chewy and take longer to cook than pearl barley.

Compatible Foods, Herbs, and Spices

Because of its distinct flavor, barley is compatible with meats that are also earthy and substantial, such as beef, pork, liver, lamb, and dark-meat fowl, such as duck or goose. Vegetables, beans, and nuts are also good cooked with barley. Barley's assertive taste can sometimes overwhelm the more subtle flavors of light-meat fowl (chicken and turkey), fish, and dairy products. Although barley would certainly be a suitable side dish for these foods, it is usually better if it is not actually cooked *with* them.

Barley can be enhanced by parsley, chives (or anything in the onion family, for that matter), bay leaf, fennel, garlic, anise, basil, caraway, cloves, pepper, rosemary, and thyme.

The thickening properties of barley are desirable for enriching soups and stews, and can be used to advantage in molded salads.

Availability

Pearl barley is available in supermarkets (look for it in the dried-bean section) and health-food stores, as well as through mail-order grain catalogs (see page 21). Pot barley, hulless barley, barley grits, barley flakes, and barley flour are available in health-food stores and mail-order catalogs.

Nutritional Content

Pot barley is a good source of fiber, niacin, thiamin, potassium, iron, phosphorous, and calcium. Pearl barley has less fiber than pot barley, and contains somewhat lower amounts of the other nutrients.

Home Remedy

Barley water, a liquid made from barley, lemon juice, and water, is frequently used as treatment for diarrhea, ulcers, and for the stimulation of breast milk.

3 cups water
2 tablespoons pearl barley
2 tablespoons lemon juice (optional)
2 tablespoons sugar (optional)

In a medium-size saucepan, boil the water and barley until reduced to 1½ cups. Strain through a sieve, discarding barley. If desired, stir lemon juice and sugar into barley water and simmer for 20 minutes.

Substitutions

Oat groats: They are similarly chewy with a flavor that is comparable to cooked barley, and have a slightly better nutritional profile. Use cooked oat groats in place of barley in salads or other dishes that call for already-cooked barley. However, the extreme starchiness of this grain does not make it the ideal choice for recipes in which the barley is cooked.

Brown rice: Either the short- or long-grain varieties may be substituted for barley, although I prefer to use the short-grain rice. This grain has a texture that is much like barley, but the flavor is more neutral. Substitute brown rice in recipes calling for either cooked or raw barley, but cook the rice about 5 minutes longer.

Wheat and triticale berries: Both of these grains have flavors that are comparable to barley, but take significantly longer to cook. I would not suggest substituting these berries in recipes calling for raw barley, but they do work well in recipes that call for cooked barley.

Other acceptable substitutes (in order of preference): Job's tears (allow longer cooking time); rye berries (same restrictions as wheat and triticale berries); white rice (allow shorter cooking time).

Basic Cooking Instructions

Please read *About Cooking Grains* beginning on page 7. *Note that all recipes in this section, unless otherwise noted, were tested with pearl barley from the supermarket.* If you like, you can substitute cooked pot or hulless barley for pearl barley in equal amounts. However, in recipes calling for uncooked barley, increase the liquid content by ½ cup and cook about 10 minutes longer.

I prefer to use the microwave oven for cooking plain barley, since it makes the cooked barley less sticky. The microwave methods that follow for cooking barley were tested in a 650-watt oven.

——————— ◇ ———————

Pot and Hulless Barley

Stove-top method:

> 2½ cups water
> 1 teaspoon salt
> 1 cup pot or hulless barley, rinsed

In a 2-quart saucepan, bring the water and salt to a boil over high heat. Stir in barley and return to boiling. Reduce heat, cover, and simmer for 1 hour and 20 minutes, or until almost all of the liquid has been absorbed. Remove from heat and let stand, covered, for 10 minutes. Fluff with fork.

MAKES 3¼ CUPS POT BARLEY.
 4¼ CUPS HULLESS BARLEY.

Microwave method:

> 3 cups water
> 1 teaspoon salt
> 1 cup pot or hulless barley, rinsed

Place the water and salt in a 3-quart, microwave-safe bowl; cover with waxed paper. Microwave on high (100% power) for 5 minutes, or until boiling. Stir in barley. Recover with waxed paper and microwave on high for 5 minutes. Microwave on medium (50% power), still covered with waxed paper, for 40 minutes, rotating dish once, if necessary. Let stand 5 minutes. Fluff with a fork.

MAKES 3 CUPS POT BARLEY.
3½ CUPS HULLESS BARLEY.

———————— ◇ ————————

Pearl Barley

Stove-top method:

2⅔ cups water
1 teaspoon salt
1 cup pearl barley, rinsed

In a 2-quart saucepan, bring the water and salt to a boil over high heat. Stir in barley and return to boiling. Reduce heat, cover, and simmer for 40 minutes. (If you are using barley from a health-food store, you may need to add 5 to 10 minutes of cooking time for a total of 45 to 50 minutes.) Remove from heat and let stand, covered, for 10 minutes. Fluff with a fork.

MAKES 3½ TO 3⅔ CUPS.

Microwave method:

2½ cups water
1 teaspoon salt
1 cup pearl barley, rinsed

Place the water and salt in a 3-quart, microwave-safe bowl. Cover with waxed paper. Microwave on high (100% power) for 5 minutes, or until boiling. Stir in barley. Recover with waxed paper and continue to microwave on high for 5 minutes. Microwave on medium (50% power), still covered with waxed paper, for 30 minutes, rotating dish once, if necessary. (If you are using barley from a health-food store, you may need to add 5 minutes of cooking for a total of 35 minutes.) Let stand 5 minutes. Fluff with a fork.

MAKES 3½ CUPS.

Reheating

Barley gets slightly dense when chilled, so it's best to steam it or reheat it in the microwave oven to restore its softer texture.

BARLEY RECIPES

*(*indicates easy recipes)*

———————— ◇ ————————

Mom's Mushroom-Barley Soup
Cock-a-Leekie
A Very Rich Lamb-and-Barley Soup
Lima-bean-and-Barley Stew
Basil-Split-Pea-Soup
Barley-and-Chick-pea Soup *
Beef-and-Barley Bourguignon
Chicken Livers and Barley *
Cholent
Duck Ragout
Zesty Meatloaf *
Veal, Sausage, and Barley Stew *
Stuffed Veal-Shoulder Roast
Clubhouse Barley-and-Ham Salad *
Progresso Salad *
Barley-Beet Salad with Honey-Mustard Dressing *
New-Fangled Mushrooms and Barley *
Good Old-Fashioned Mushrooms and Barley *
Winter-Vegetable-and-Barley Bake *
Leeks, Lentils, and Barley *
Barley and Bows *
Nancy Jane's Simple Barley Recipe *
Fiesta Barley and Beans *
Barley and Peas *
Crisp Vegetables and Barley
Barley Green *
Sweet Barley Bread
Barley-Potato Doughnut Holes
Yummy Barley-Date Bars
Spiced Barley-Raisin Cookies *

◇

Mom's Mushroom-Barley Soup

My mom makes the best soups in the world. This is one of them, and one of my favorites. Try to find dried Polish mushrooms, because they have an incredible intense flavor that adds much to the finished soup. If you can't find them, or are hesitant to buy them because of the price, substitute dried shiitake mushrooms.

1 ounce dried imported mushrooms (Polish mushrooms are best)
1 cup boiling water
4 quarts cold water
2½ pounds marrow bones
3 cups chopped carrot
2 cups chopped celery
1½ cups chopped onion
1 cup chopped parsnip
1 cup chopped celery root (also called celeriac)
¾ cup barley, rinsed
2 teaspoons salt
⅛ teaspoon pepper
1 bunch Italian parsley
1 bunch dill

Rinse the mushrooms under cold running water to remove any soil. Place in a medium-size bowl and pour boiling water over them. Let stand for 10 minutes, or until mushrooms are softened.

Reserve the soaking water, then finely chop mushrooms and place in an 8-quart soup pot, along with reserved soaking water. Add cold water, bones, carrot, celery, onion, parsnip, celery root, barley, salt, and pepper. Bring to a boil over high heat, then lower heat and cook at a slow boil, uncovered, for 2 hours. Add parsley and dill. Simmer 30 minutes longer. Discard bones. (Better yet, dig the mushy marrow out of the bones and spread it on fresh bread. Sprinkle with salt and enjoy, but don't tell your cardiologist that you did it.) You can discard the parsley and dill, but you may enjoy them, as I do, served as a side dish with the rest of the meal. Skim fat from the surface of the soup before serving.

SERVES 10.
CALORIES: 135   CHOLESTEROL: 3mg   SODIUM: 465 mg   FIBER: 10 g

Health tip:
Use only bones without marrow (soup-bone knuckles, for instance), since marrow adds lots of fat to the soup; omit salt.
CALORIES: 100   CHOLESTEROL: 2 mg   SODIUM: 32 mg   FIBER: 10 g

———————— ◇ ————————

Cock-a-Leekie

I've tried many recipes for this traditional Scottish soup (also called *cockie leekie*). Some are made with leeks and a cock (an old rooster). Some include veal, some prunes; some use barley, some use oats, and some don't use any grain at all. In my version, I prefer to cook the soup with the prunes, then serve the soup without them.

> *3-pound broiler-fryer chicken (It's unlikely that you will be able to obtain an old rooster, but if you can find a fowl, which is actually an old laying hen, you can use that, if you want to. You will have to cook the soup much longer in that case, and you may also have to adjust the amount of water, but you will also get a more intensely chicken-flavored soup.)*
> *3 medium-size leeks, cut into 1-inch pieces (both white and green parts)*
> *8 sprigs parsley*
> *1 bay leaf*
> *1 teaspoon salt*
> *¼ teaspoon crumbled thyme*
> *⅛ teaspoon pepper*
> *6 cups water*
> *2 tablespoons barley, rinsed*
> *¼ cup sliced leek (white part only)*
> *8 prunes*

Place the chicken, white and green slices of leek, parsley, bay leaf, salt, thyme, and pepper in a 4-quart saucepan. Add water and bring to a boil. Reduce heat and simmer, uncovered, for 1 hour.

Remove chicken from the pan. Strain the liquid into a 3-quart saucepan, discarding vegetables. Skim off fat. Stir barley, white slices of leek, and prunes into the broth. Simmer for 40 minutes. Pull skin from chicken and cut meat into large chunks. Add to broth and cook until heated through. Remove prunes before serving.

SERVES 6.

CALORIES: 255   CHOLESTEROL: 113 mg   SODIUM: 187 mg   FIBER: .5 g

Health tip:
Cook chicken without skin; omit salt.

CALORIES: 200   CHOLESTEROL: 50 mg   SODIUM: 120 mg   FIBER: .5 g

———————— ◇ ————————

A Very Rich Lamb-and-Barley Soup

To borrow a phrase from an advertising jingle, this is "a soup that eats like a meal," especially when it's served with bread (whole-grain, of course) and a side salad. The lamb-neck base gives the soup its incredible richness.

9 cups water, divided
2 pounds lamb necks
2½ tablespoons barley, rinsed
1½ cups chopped onion
1½ cups chopped celery
1 cup chopped carrot
2 parsnips, peeled
1 bunch Italian parsley
1 bunch dill
¾ teaspoon salt
⅛ teaspoon pepper

Place 6 cups of the water and lamb necks in a large soup pot. Bring to a boil over high heat. Lower heat and simmer, covered, for 45 minutes. Add remaining 3 cups water and barley. Bring to a boil, then lower heat and simmer, covered, for 15 minutes longer. Add onion, celery, carrot, and parsnips. Simmer, covered, for 45 minutes more. Add parsley and dill and continue to simmer, covered, for 30 minutes longer.

Remove pot from heat. Discard parsley and dill (or, better yet, set these aside to serve as a side dish with the soup) and remove lamb. Pull meat from the bones and return it to the pot, discarding bones. (Or, if you prefer, serve the lamb for dinner, along with the parsley and dill, and serve the soup meatless.) Add salt and pepper and stir the soup hard so that the parsnips break up and completely combine with the soup.

SERVES 6.
CALORIES: 302   CHOLESTEROL: 93 mg   SODIUM: 365 mg   FIBER: 4 g

Health tip:
Omit salt.
CALORIES: 302   CHOLESTEROL: 93 mg   SODIUM: 99 mg   FIBER: 4 g

————————— ◇ —————————

Lima-Bean-and-Barley Stew

This is definitely one of those hearty-type recipes frequently associated with barley. If you prefer a more "soupy" consistency, simply stir in boiling water as suggested. In either case, serve this very-filling dish with some of the beef in each portion.

12 cups water
1½ pounds oxtails or beef soup bones
1 cup dried baby lima beans, rinsed and picked over
2 cups chopped onion
1½ cups chopped celery
1 cup chopped turnip
½ cup barley, rinsed
1½ teaspoon salt
1 bay leaf
¼ teaspoon crumbled thyme
¼ teaspoon pepper
1 can (14½ ounce) whole peeled tomatoes, undrained
1 can (8 ounce) tomato sauce

Bring water to a boil in a large soup pot. Add oxtails and simmer, uncovered, for 45 minutes. Add lima beans and continue to simmer, uncovered, for 45 minutes longer. Stir in onion, celery, turnip, barley, salt, bay leaf, thyme, and pepper. Simmer, uncovered, 1 hour longer. As the stew cooks, stir in as much as 4 cups of *boiling* water if you want a more souplike dish. Stir in tomatoes and tomato sauce. Simmer for 15 minutes more. Remove bay leaf before serving.

SERVES 6.
CALORIES: 466   CHOLESTEROL: 68 mg   SODIUM: 928 mg   FIBER: 8 g

Health tip:
Omit salt.
CALORIES: 466   CHOLESTEROL: 68 mg   SODIUM: 395 mg   FIBER: 8 g

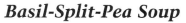

Basil-Split-Pea Soup

Fresh chopped basil, stirred into this soup at the last minute, gives the soup an unusual touch of flavor. If you don't fancy basil, then leave it out. The soup will still be good. And, if you *must* have smoked ham in your pea soup, add a ham bone or a couple of smoked hocks right at the beginning, or a little chopped cooked ham at the end.

14 cups water
1 package (16 ounce) dry split peas, rinsed and picked over
4 carrots, peeled
2 large parsnips, peeled
2 celery ribs
1 large onion, peeled
2 parsley roots (save tops for some other use)
½ cup barley, rinsed
¼ cup chopped celery leaves
1½ teaspoons celery salt
1 teaspoon salt
¼ cup chopped fresh basil (optional)

In a large soup pot, bring the water to a boil. Add split peas, carrots, parsnips, celery, onion, parsley roots, barley, celery leaves, celery salt, and salt. Reduce heat and simmer, uncovered, stirring occasionally, for 1¾ hours, or until peas have disintegrated. Discard vegetables, or chop them coarsely and serve as a side dish with the soup. Stir in basil just before serving.

SERVES 8.
CALORIES: 304   CHOLESTEROL: 0 mg   SODIUM: 717 mg   FIBER: 13g

Health tip:
Omit celery salt and salt.
CALORIES: 304   CHOLESTEROL: 0 mg   SODIUM: 33 mg   FIBER: 13 g

---◇---

Barley-and-Chick-Pea Soup

I usually prefer to make my soups from scratch. However, in some cases, this being one of them, a soup mix works beautifully to bring slow-simmered goodness to a quick and easy, meatless soup.

5 cups water
1 package (1.4 ounce) vegetable soup and recipe mix (Knorr)
1 can (10½ ounce) chick-peas (garbanzo beans), undrained
⅓ cup barley, rinsed

In a 3-quart saucepan, bring the water to a boil. Stir in soup mix, then beans and barley. Simmer 55 minutes.

SERVES 6.
CALORIES: 133   CHOLESTEROL: 0 mg   SODIUM: 431 mg   FIBER: 5 g

Health tip:
This is as healthy as it gets.

---◇---

Beef-and-Barley Bourguignon

This is an excellent version of a classic French recipe, and you don't have to follow it too exactly, either. For instance, you can use more or fewer mushrooms or onions, according to taste, or depending on how much or many of anything you happen to have on hand. Serve with bread and a green salad.

3 slices bacon, cut into 1-inch pieces
1 cup chopped onion
2 cloves garlic, minced
1 pound stewing beef, cut into 1-inch cubes
2–3 cups water
1 can (13¾ ounce) ready-to-serve beef broth
1 cup dry red wine
1 bay leaf
¼ teaspoon crumbled thyme
1 cup barley, rinsed
10 ounces small mushrooms, rinsed and left whole (or larger mushrooms, cut into quarters)
12 small white onions, peeled
¼ cup chopped parsley

In a large heavy saucepan or 4-quart Dutch oven, cook the bacon over medium-high heat until crisp. Remove bacon and drain on paper towels.

Add the chopped onion and garlic to bacon fat remaining in pot. Cook over medium-high heat until softened. Add beef cubes and cook, turning frequently, until richly browned on the outside. Add 2 cups of the water, broth, wine, bay leaf, and thyme. Bring to a boil. Reduce heat and simmer, uncovered, for 1 hour. Stir in barley and continue to simmer, covered, for 20 minutes. Add mushrooms, small onions, and parsley. Continue to simmer, uncovered, for 35 minutes longer. (If you want a more "saucy" consistency in the stew, add some or all of the remaining 1 cup water during the last 35 minutes of cooking time.) Remove bay leaf and stir in reserved bacon just before serving.

SERVES 4.
CALORIES: 487   CHOLESTEROL: 94 mg   SODIUM: 726 mg   FIBER: 10 g

Health tip:
Omit bacon; use a nonstick saucepan. Or use a nonstick skillet for softening onion and garlic and browning the beef, then transfer to the larger pan to finish cooking; use low-sodium beef broth.
CALORIES: 453 mg   CHOLESTEROL: 83 mg   SODIUM: 170 mg   FIBER: 10 g

$$\diamond$$

Chicken Livers and Barley

I automatically feel healthier when I eat liver, even though I know it's loaded with cholesterol. But liver also contains rich amounts of iron, vitamin A, phosphorous, potassium, and niacin, not to mention protein. For me, this is a delicious nutritious meal. Just add a salad.

3 tablespoons vegetable oil
1 cup chopped onion
1 pound chicken livers, rinsed and tough membranes removed
2 teaspoons white-wine Worcestershire sauce
½ teaspoon salt
¼ teaspoon pepper
⅛ teaspoon crumbled thyme
2 cups cooked barley
¼ cup chopped parsley

In a large skillet, heat the oil over medium-high heat. Add onion and cook, stirring occasionally, until softened. Add livers and cook, stirring and tossing, just until the centers are pale pink. Stir in Worcestershire sauce, salt, pepper, and thyme. Stir in barley and parsley. Cook, stirring occasionally, until heated through.

SERVES 4.
CALORIES: 369   CHOLESTEROL: 558 mg   SODIUM: 776 mg   FIBER: 3 g
Health tip:
If you are watching your cholesterol, perhaps you'd better skip this. Sodium watchers should omit salt.
CALORIES: 369   CHOLESTEROL: 558 mg   SODIUM: 73 mg   FIBER 3 g

———————— ◇ ————————

Cholent

In the Jewish religion you are not supposed to work on the Sabbath, so the ingredients for cholent are put together on Friday before Sabbath begins. Then the pot is covered tightly and put into the oven to bake for 24 hours at a low heat. Then, the moment that Sabbath ends, instant dinner! In earlier times, before people had ovens in their homes, the women would take their filled pots to the village baker on Friday evening and bring home the cooked meal on Saturday evening. This recipe assumes that most people would rather not bake overnight, and so I have shortened the process.

8 cups water
2 pounds beef flanken or lean short ribs
1 large onion, peeled and left whole
2 teaspoons salt
⅛ teaspoon pepper
1 cup dried beans, rinsed and picked over (I use navy beans, but it's not
    uncommon to find kidney beans or lima beans in this dish)
1 cup barley, rinsed
6 medium (about ¾ pound) red potatoes, scrubbed

Preheat oven to 325° F.

In a large, ovenproof soup pot or Dutch oven, place the water, beef, onion, salt, and pepper. Bring to a boil over high heat. Stir in beans, barley, and potatoes. Cover tightly and bake for 4 hours without stirring—or peeking.

SERVES 6.
CALORIES: 706   CHOLESTEROL: 84 mg   SODIUM: 776 mg   FIBER: 10 g
Health tip:
Omit salt.
CALORIES: 706   CHOLESTEROL: 84 mg   SODIUM: 73 mg   FIBER: 10 g

———— ◇ ————

Duck Ragout

Because it is a very rich dish, the ragout needs only a tart green salad to make it a complete meal.

4 slices bacon, cut into 1-inch pieces
4½-pound duck, cut into 8 pieces, visible fat removed
1½ cups chopped onion
½ cup chopped carrot
1 clove garlic, minced
½ cup dry red wine
1 cup water
¼ cup chopped parsley
1 bay leaf
¼ teaspoon salt
¼ teaspoon crumbled rosemary
⅛ teaspoon crumbled thyme
⅛ teaspoon pepper
1 package (10 ounce) frozen lima beans
½ cup barley, rinsed

In a large heavy saucepan or 4-quart Dutch oven, cook the bacon over medium-high heat until crisp. Remove bacon and drain on paper towels. Add duck to bacon fat in pan and cook over medium-high heat until browned on all sides. (You will probably be able to brown only three or four pieces of duck at a time.)

Remove duck from pan and discard all but 2 tablespoons of the fat. Add onion, carrot, and garlic to fat remaining in pan and cook over high heat, stirring until vegetables are softened. Stir in wine, scraping up any browned bits that cling to the bottom and side of the pan. Stir in water, parsley, bay leaf, salt, rosemary, thyme, and pepper. Return duck to pot. Cover and simmer for 45 minutes. Stir in lima beans and barley. Cover and simmer for 35 minutes longer. Stir in reserved bacon and simmer, covered, for 10 minutes longer, or until barley and duck are tender. Discard bay leaf and skim fat from surface before serving.

SERVES 4.
CALORIES: 1361 mg   CHOLESTEROL: 248 mg   SODIUM: 383 mg   FIBER: 9 g

Health tips:
This will never be a low-calorie dish, but you can cut down a little on the fat and salt content. Remove as much skin and fat as possible from the duck. Omit bacon and brown duck in 1 tablespoon oil in a nonstick skillet; omit salt.
CALORIES: 901   CHOLESTEROL: 124 mg   SODIUM: 60 mg   FIBER: 9 g

Zesty Meatloaf

If you're not too fond of barbecue sauce, you can use plain or spicy catsup as a substitute. I serve this with salad and a baked potato and it's always a hit.

Loaf:

> *1 pound ground veal or beef*
> *1 pound ground pork*
> *1 cup chopped onion*
> *¾ cup thick spicy barbecue sauce*
> *½ cup chopped green bell pepper*
> *½ cup barley flakes*
> *1 egg*
> *½ teaspoon salt*

Topping:

> *¼ cup apricot jam*
> *2 tablespoons thick spicy barbecue sauce*
> *1 tablespoon steak sauce (A-1)*
> *½ teaspoon dry mustard*

Preheat oven to 350°F.

In a large bowl, lightly and thoroughly combine the veal, pork, onion, barbecue sauce, bell pepper, barley flakes, egg, and salt. Shape meat mixture into a loaf measuring about 8 × 5 inches and set the loaf on a rack in a baking pan.

Stir together jam, barbecue sauce, steak sauce, and dry mustard in a small bowl. Spread over top and sides of meatloaf.

Bake for 1 hour and 15 minutes.

SERVES 6.
CALORIES: 472   CHOLESTEROL: 205 mg   SODIUM: 765 mg   FIBER: .5 g

Health tip:
Use 2 pounds ground veal and omit ground pork; omit salt and topping.
CALORIES: 400   CHOLESTEROL: 205 mg   SODIUM: 367 mg   FIBER: .5 g

───────── ◇ ─────────

Veal, Sausage, and Barley Stew

Tender veal, spicy sausage, and the chewy texture of barley are a wonderful combination.

1 tablespoon vegetable oil
1 cup chopped onion
½ pound Italian sausage, cut into 1-inch pieces
1 pound stewing veal, cut into 1-inch pieces
4 cups water
¾ cup barley, rinsed
1 large green bell pepper, cut into strips
½ teaspoon salt
⅛ teaspoon pepper

In a 4-quart saucepan, heat the oil over medium-high heat. Add onion and cook, stirring, until softened. Add sausage and cook, stirring occasionally, until no longer pink in the center. Stir in veal and water. Cover and simmer over medium heat for 45 minutes, stirring occasionally. Stir in barley, pepper strips, salt, and pepper. Cook, uncovered, for 40 minutes, or until veal and barley are tender.

SERVES 4.
CALORIES: 602   CHOLESTEROL: 148 mg   SODIUM: 709 mg   FIBER: 1 g

Health tip:
Omit sausage (but keep in mind that by doing so you will also be sacrificing a lot of flavor) and salt.
CALORIES: 365   CHOLESTEROL: 109 mg   SODIUM: 62 mg   FIBER: 1 g

———————— ◇ ————————

Stuffed Veal-Shoulder Roast

Veal shoulder has a lot of flavor, and when it's boned and stuffed can be quite out of this world. I often serve this roast for company, set on a big platter, surrounded by steamed baby vegetables. The pan juices have an exquisite flavor with not many calories, so be sure to pour the cooking juice into a sauce bowl and serve it on the side.

¾ cup cooked barley
⅓ cup finely chopped celery
¼ cup finely chopped onion
2 tablespoons chopped parsley
1 tablespoon snipped dill or
*   1 teaspoon dried dill weed*
¼ teaspoon crumbled tarragon
3-pound boneless veal shoulder
1 medium onion, sliced
1 cup sliced celery
1 cup sliced carrot
½ cup white wine or chicken broth
¼ teaspoon salt

Preheat oven to 325°F.

In a medium-size bowl, combine the barley, chopped celery, chopped onion, parsley, dill, and tarragon.

Cut veal shoulder, lengthwise, going almost all the way through the meat. Open the cut meat (like a book) and pound it to flatten. (Or, better yet, have the butcher do this for you.) Place barley mixture in the center of the flattened meat. Roll meat to enclose stuffing and tie in several places with string. (It's easiest to tie by starting in the center of the roll and working your way out to the ends. You can also use a few wooden picks to help keep the roll closed and the stuffing inside while you work.)

Place roast in a baking pan. Arrange sliced vegetables around roast. Pour wine over roast and sprinkle with salt. Cover tightly with foil and bake for 2 hours. Remove foil and continue baking for 1 hour longer.

Slice roast and serve with the vegetables and pan juices.

SERVES 8.

CALORIES: 506   CHOLESTEROL: 218 mg   SODIUM: 281 mg   FIBER: 1 g

Health tip:
Omit salt.

CALORIES: 506   CHOLESTEROL: 218 mg   SODIUM: 139 mg   FIBER: 1 g

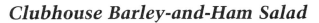

Clubhouse Barley-and-Ham Salad

I'm always so pleased with the way this salad tastes. The ingredients are just right and work so well together.

1½ cups cooked barley
1 cup ½-inch cubes cooked ham
1 cup cooked peas (thawed, if using frozen)
¼ cup chopped red bell pepper
¼ cup finely chopped pecans
2 tablespoons finely chopped scallion
1 tablespoon snipped fresh dill or
    1 teaspoon dried dill weed
⅛ teaspoon pepper
¼ cup mayonnaise

In a large bowl, toss the barley, ham, peas, bell pepper, pecans, scallion, dill, and pepper. Lightly mix in mayonnaise until thoroughly combined. Chill until serving time.

SERVES 6.
CALORIES: 259   CHOLESTEROL: 37 mg   SODIUM: 665 mg   FIBER: 3 g

Health tip:
Substitute chicken for ham; use reduced-calorie mayonnaise. Omit salt from barley.
CALORIES: 179   CHOLESTEROL: 4 mg   SODIUM: 100 mg   FIBER: 3 g

Progresso Salad

This salad is based on two excellent Progresso brand products: marinated olive salad and caponata. The olive salad is very vinegary, but if you enjoy food with a sharp flavor, add the olive salad without draining off the liquid in the jar.

2 cups cooked barley
1 jar (9¾ ounce) marinated olive salad, drained (see above)
1 can (4½ ounce) caponata
⅓ cup pignoli (pine nuts)
2 tablespoons mayonnaise
2 tablespoons sour cream
Lettuce, optional

In a large bowl, lightly toss the barley, olive salad, caponata, pignoli, mayonnaise, and sour cream until thoroughly combined. Chill until serving time. Serve on lettuce leaves, if you like.

SERVES 8. (Nutrition information not available for the Progresso appetizers.)
Health tip:
Use ¼ cup reduced-calorie mayonnaise instead of regular mayonnaise and sour cream. Sodium watchers: Beware!

Barley-Beet Salad with Honey-Mustard Dressing

Toss this salad shortly before serving time so that each vegetable retains its own pretty color, rather than turning a bright beet pink.

4 medium-size beets
1 cup cooked barley
½ cup sliced radish
12 snow peas, blanched in boiling water, rinsed in cold water, and cut in
*   half widthwise*
¼ cup sliced scallion, both white and green parts
2 tablespoons olive oil
2 tablespoons orange juice
1 tablespoon cider vinegar
2 teaspoons honey mustard
¼ teaspoon salt
Boston-lettuce leaves

Cook the beets until tender in boiling water, then peel and cut into julienne strips (you should have about 2 cups). Chill separately until ready to mix salad.

Combine the barley, radish, snow peas, and scallion. Chill until ready to mix salad.

In a small bowl, combine oil, orange juice, vinegar, honey mustard, and salt. Chill until ready to mix salad.

Just before serving, lightly toss beets and vegetables with dressing. Serve on lettuce leaves.

SERVES 4.
CALORIES: 146   CHOLESTEROL: 0 mg   SODIUM: 350 mg   FIBER: 4 g

Health tip:
Omit salt.
CALORIES: 146   CHOLESTEROL: 0 mg   SODIUM: 65 mg   FIBER: 4 g

——————◇——————

New-Fangled Mushrooms and Barley

This is my updated version of an old family recipe. For those who are more inclined toward the old ways, I've also included the old-fashioned recipe, which follows. Both go well as side dishes with roast chicken, or could be used as a main dish when served with a salad of watercress, endive, or arugula, dressed with a creamy vinaigrette.

¼ cup butter, divided
1 cup barley, rinsed
¼ cup finely chopped shallot or the white part of a scallion
1 cup (3 ounces) sliced shiitaki mushrooms
1 cup (3 ounces) sliced crimini or porcini mushrooms
1 cup (3 ounces) sliced white button mushrooms
1 can (13¾ ounce) ready-to-serve chicken broth or
    1¾ cups vegetable broth (see page 19)
1½ cups water
¼ teaspoon pepper
⅛ teaspoon salt
½ cup chopped pecans

Melt 2 tablespoons of the butter in a 3-quart saucepan over medium heat. Add barley and cook, stirring frequently, until barley is lightly browned, 5 to 7 minutes. Remove from pan and set aside. Add the remaining 2 tablespoons butter to pan. Melt over medium heat. Add shallot and cook, stirring, until softened. Add all three types of mushrooms and continue to cook, stirring, until softened. Stir in broth, water, pepper, and salt. Cover and bring to a boil. Stir in barley and simmer for 45 minutes, or until liquid has been absorbed and barley is tender. Stir in pecans.

SERVES 6.
CALORIES: 268   CHOLESTEROL: 21 mg   SODIUM: 318 mg   FIBER: 7 g
Health tip:
Use oil instead of butter; substitute water for broth; omit salt.
CALORIES: 270   CHOLESTEROL: 0 mg   SODIUM: 102 mg   FIBER: 7 g

─────────◇─────────

Good Old-Fashioned Mushrooms and Barley

This is one of the few uses for barley with which most people are familiar. It is also one of the easiest, and goes well with roasted anything, a nice change from potatoes and other starches.

2 tablespoons vegetable oil
1 cup chopped onion
½ cup chopped green bell pepper
2 cups sliced mushrooms
2⅔ cups water
1 cup barley, rinsed
1 teaspoon salt
¼ teaspoon pepper

Heat the oil in a 2-quart saucepan. Add the onion and green pepper and cook, stirring, over medium-high heat until softened. Add mushrooms and continue to cook, stirring, until softened. Stir in water and bring to a boil over high heat. Add barley, salt, and pepper. Return to boiling. Cover and simmer for 45 minutes longer, or until liquid has been absorbed.

SERVES 6.
CALORIES: 174   CHOLESTEROL: 0 mg   SODIUM: 358 mg   FIBER: 6 g
Health tip:
Use a nonstick saucepan and reduce oil to 1 tablespoon; omit salt.
CALORIES: 154   CHOLESTEROL: 0 mg   SODIUM: 10 mg   FIBER: 6 g

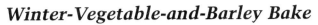

Winter-Vegetable-and-Barley Bake

I like this particular combination of winter vegetables. Each one has a natural sweetness that goes well with the other, and the sherry adds a nippy little taste surprise.

½ cup barley, rinsed
2 cups 1-inch cubes butternut squash
2 cups julienned carrot
1 cup julienned parsnip
1¼ cups boiling water
¼ cup dry or medium-dry sherry
2 tablespoons light- or dark-brown sugar
¾ teaspoon salt
⅛ teaspoon ground nutmeg
2 tablespoons butter

Preheat oven to 350° F.

Place the barley in a 2-quart casserole. Arrange squash, carrot, and parsnip over barley. Drizzle water and sherry over vegetables. Sprinkle evenly with brown sugar, salt, and nutmeg. Dot with butter.

Cover and bake for 1 hour, or until barley and vegetables are tender. Stir to combine vegetables with barley just before serving.

SERVES 6.
CALORIES: 159   CHOLESTEROL: 7 mg   SODIUM: 300 mg   FIBER: 7 g

Health tip:
Omit salt and butter.
CALORIES: 135   CHOLESTEROL: 0 mg   SODIUM: 10 mg   FIBER: 7 g

———————— ◇ ————————

Leeks, Lentils, and Barley

If you're fortunate enough to have leftovers of this delightful mixture, chill them and then toss with fresh chopped vegetables and your favorite Italian dressing to create a terrific salad.

2 tablespoons vegetable oil
3 cups thinly sliced leeks (white and light-green portions only)
1 can (13¾ ounce) ready-to-serve beef broth or
    1¾ cups vegetable broth (see page 19)
1 cup water
¾ cup lentils, rinsed and picked over
½ cup barley, rinsed
1 bay leaf
¼ teaspoon salt
¼ teaspoon pepper

Heat the oil in a large saucepan over medium-high heat. Add the leeks and cook, stirring, until softened. Add broth and water and bring to a boil. Stir in lentils, barley, and bay leaf. Cover and simmer for 40 minutes, or until liquid has been absorbed. Stir in salt and pepper. Remove bay leaf before serving.

SERVES 6.
CALORIES: 144   CHOLESTEROL: 1 mg   SODIUM: 312 mg   FIBER: 4 g

Health tip:
Use a nonstick skillet and reduce oil to 1 tablespoon. Use low-sodium broth; omit salt.
CALORIES: 144   CHOLESTEROL: 1 mg   SODIUM: 223 mg   FIBER: 4 g

———————— ◇ ————————

Barley and Bows

This wonderful combination of vegetables, pasta, and barley is based on an old German recipe called *kraut flekerl.* It is pleasantly peppery tasting and is usually served as a side dish. However, if it's sprinkled with confectioners' sugar it can also be served as dessert (believe me).

2 tablespoons vegetable oil
1 cup chopped onion
4 cups ¼-inch diced cabbage
1 tablespoon butter

1 cup cooked barley
½ cup cooked small bow ties or other small pasta
¾ teaspoon salt
½ teaspoon pepper

In a large skillet, heat the oil over medium-high heat. Add the onion and cook, stirring, until golden. Add cabbage and continue to cook, stirring, until wilted. Add butter, then stir in barley, bow ties, salt, and pepper. Cook stirring, until barley and bow ties are heated through.

SERVES 4.
CALORIES: 188   CHOLESTEROL: 1 mg   SODIUM: 437 mg   FIBER: 4 g
Health tip:
Use a nonstick skillet and reduce oil to 1 tablespoon; omit butter and salt.
CALORIES: 132   CHOLESTEROL: 0 mg   SODIUM: 14 mg   FIBER: 4 g

───────── ◇ ─────────

Nancy Jane's Simple Barley Recipe

I got this recipe from my friend, Nancy Jane Goldstein, who is an excellent cook and hostess. She serves this as a side dish at many of her company dinners.

2¾ cups vegetable broth (see page 19) or
    canned chicken broth
1 cup barley, rinsed
½ cup toasted almonds (place almonds on a baking sheet and toast in a
    350°F oven for 10 minutes, stirring occasionally)
⅓ cup chopped parsley
⅛ teaspoon pepper

Bring the broth to a boil in a medium-size saucepan. Stir in barley and cook for 50 minutes, or until liquid has been absorbed. Toss with almonds, parsley, and pepper.

SERVES 6.
CALORIES: 169   CHOLESTEROL: 0 mg   SODIUM: 343 mg   FIBER: 6 g
Health tip:
Use low-sodium broth.
CALORIES: 169   CHOLESTEROL: 0 mg   SODIUM: 139 mg   FIBER: 6 g

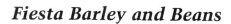

Fiesta Barley and Beans

You can vary this recipe to suit your own taste by choosing the kind of sauce you use. If you are wildly adventurous, try tomato-jalapeno pepper sauce. Those of a more conservative nature can use a mild taco sauce

2 tablespoons vegetable oil
½ cup chopped onion
½ cup chopped red or yellow bell pepper
½ cup chopped green bell pepper (or you can use 1 cup chopped green
    pepper and omit the red and yellow varieties altogether)
1⅓ cups water
1 cup tomato-jalapeno pepper sauce or mild taco sauce
¼ teaspoon ground cumin
⅛ teaspoon crumbled oregano
½ cup barley, rinsed
1 can (16 ounce) pinto or kidney beans, undrained

Heat the oil in a 2-quart saucepan. Add onion and bell peppers and cook, stirring, until softened. Stir in the water, sauce, cumin, and oregano and bring to a boil. Stir in barley and return to boiling. Cover and simmer for 40 minutes, stirring once or twice as barley approaches doneness. Stir in undrained beans. Simmer 5 minutes longer, or until beans are heated through.

SERVES 6.
CALORIES: 184   CHOLESTEROL: 0 mg   SODIUM: 302 mg   FIBER: 9 g

Health tip:
Use a nonstick saucepan and reduce oil to 1 tablesppon.
CALORIES: 164   CHOLESTEROL: 0 mg   SODIUM: 302 mg   FIBER: 9 g

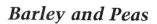

Barley and Peas

I love peas with starchy food. This is a simple, yet flavorfully impressive, side dish that goes well with almost anything, although I often find it extremely satisfying, just by itself, when I'm dining alone and too lazy or tired to fix anything more complicated.

1⅓ cups water
½ teaspoon salt
½ cup barley, rinsed
1 cup frozen peas
2 tablespoons finely chopped scallion
1 tablespoon butter

In a 1-quart saucepan, bring the water and salt to a boil. Stir in barley and return to boiling. Cover, reduce heat, and simmer for 40 minutes. Stir in peas, scallion, and butter. Cover and simmer for 5 minutes more, or until peas are heated through.

SERVES 4.
CALORIES: 129   CHOLESTEROL: 8 mg   SODIUM: 293 mg   FIBER: 6 g

Health tip:
Omit salt and butter.
CALORIES: 103   CHOLESTEROL: 0 mg   SODIUM: 21 mg   FIBER: 6 g

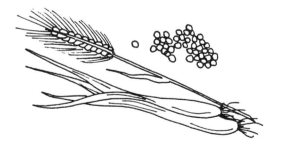

———————— ◇ ————————

Crisp Vegetables and Barley

Stirring the vegetables in during the last 15 minutes of cooking time keeps them bright and flavorful. This is a side dish that looks pretty and tastes good with roast chicken or other poultry.

3 tablespoons vegetable oil
1 cup barley, rinsed
2 cups chopped onion
1 can (13¾ ounce) ready-to-serve chicken broth or
*   1¾ cups vegetable broth (see page 19)*
¾ cup white wine
1 cup frozen peas
½ cup chopped zucchini
½ cup chopped yellow squash
2 tablespoons chopped roasted red peppers or pimiento
2 tablespoons chopped parsley
¼ teaspoon salt
¼ teaspoon pepper

In a 3-quart saucepan, heat the oil over medium-high heat. Add barley and cook over medium heat, stirring, until lightly browned, about 5 minutes. Stir in the onion and cook until soft. Stir in broth and wine. Lower heat and simmer, covered, for 30 minutes. Stir in peas, zucchini, yellow squash, red pepper, parsley, salt, and pepper. Cover and simmer for 15 minutes longer, or until liquid has been absorbed.

SERVES 8.
CALORIES: 191   CHOLESTEROL: 1 mg   SODIUM: 242 mg   FIBER: 6 g

Health tip:
Use a nonstick saucepan and reduce oil to 1 tablespoon; use low-sodium broth; omit salt.
CALORIES: 133   CHOLESTEROL: 1 mg   SODIUM: 21 mg   FIBER: 6 g

———————— ◇ ————————

Barley Green

You can use vegetables other than asparagus in this recipe, if you like. Try green beans, lima beans, or even chopped spinach.

1 can (10½ ounce) concentrated French onion soup or
    1¼ cups vegetable broth (see page 19)
1½ cups water or additional vegetable broth
1 cup barley, rinsed
½ pound fresh asparagus, cut into 1-inch pieces
¼ cup chopped parsley
¼ teaspoon pepper

In a 2-quart saucepan, bring the soup and water to a boil. Stir in barley, and simmer, covered, for 35 minutes, or until most of the liquid has been absorbed. Stir in asparagus, parsley, and pepper. Continue to simmer for 10 minutes more. Remove from heat and let stand for 5 minutes, or until remaining liquid has been absorbed.

SERVES 4.
CALORIES: 223   CHOLESTEROL: 2 mg   SODIUM: 644 mg   FIBER: 5 g

Health tip:
Substitute low-sodium beef broth for onion soup.
CALORIES: 223   CHOLESTEROL: 2 mg   SODIUM: 50 mg   FIBER: 5 g

———————— ◇ ————————

Sweet Barley Bread

Spread this slightly sweet bread with jam or butter (or both!) and enjoy it at coffee or tea time.

1¼ cups hot (105–115° F) water, divided
1 package dry yeast
2 cups all-purpose flour, divided
¾ cup barley flour
⅓ cup sugar
1½ teaspoons salt
¼ teaspoon anise seed or
    1½ teaspoons ground cinnamon
3 tablespoons barley malt or unsulphured molasses
2 tablespoons butter, softened
½ cup raisins

Grease a 9-inch-round layer-cake pan and set aside.

Place ½ cup of the water in a glass measuring cup, then stir in yeast (and a pinch of sugar, if you like, to encourage the yeast to activate). Let stand until about ¼ inch of white bubbly foam forms on top. (This foaming is called *proofing*, and if it doesn't happen it means that for some reason or other the yeast has not been activated. Discard this batch and try again, double checking the date on the yeast package and the temperature of the water.)

In a large bowl, stir together 1¼ cups of the all-purpose flour, barley flour, sugar, salt, and anise seed.

Combine proofed-yeast mixture and remaining ¾ cup water with barley malt. Stir into flour mixture, along with butter. Beat with an electric mixer at high speed for 5 minutes. Stir in ½ cup of the remaining all-purpose flour. Cover with greased plastic wrap and let rise in a warm spot, out of drafts, for 1 hour and 15 minutes.

Stir in the remaining ¼ cup all-purpose flour and raisins. Turn dough into prepared pan. With floured hands, pat dough into an even layer in the pan.

Cover with greased plastic wrap and let rise until dough reaches top of pan, about 1 hour and 15 minutes.

Preheat oven to 350°F.

Bake for 40 to 50 minutes, or until golden brown. Turn bread out of pan and cool on a wire rack. Cut into wedges to serve.

MAKES 1 LOAF (16 wedges).
CALORIES: 125   CHOLESTEROL: 4 mg   SODIUM: 213 mg   FIBER: 1 g

Health tip:
Omit salt; substitute unsalted margarine for butter.
CALORIES: 125   CHOLESTEROL: 0 mg   SODIUM: 37 mg   FIBER: 1 g

———————— ◇ ————————

Barley-Potato Doughnut Holes

If you like doughnuts, you'll really enjoy these. They are light, tasty, and have a slightly unusual flavor. Like most doughnuts, these are best when freshly made.

1 cup all-purpose flour
1 cup barley flour
1 tablespoon baking powder
½ teaspoon salt
½ teaspoon ground nutmeg
¼ teaspoon ground cinnamon
2 eggs
⅔ cup sugar
⅓ cup cold mashed potatoes (can be made from instant)
¼ cup butter, melted
1 teaspoon vanilla extract
½ cup milk
Oil, for frying
Granulated sugar, for coating doughnuts

In a medium-size bowl, combine the all-purpose flour, barley flour, baking powder, salt, nutmeg, and cinnamon. Stir with a whisk so that the flour mixture is light and well blended.

In a large bowl, beat eggs and sugar until light and fluffy, about 5 minutes. Beat in potatoes, then butter and vanilla. Mix dry ingredients into potato mixture, alternating with milk, until well blended.

Pour enough oil into a deep-fryer or large saucepan to measure about 2 inches deep. Heat oil to 375° F. Drop by rounded teaspoons into oil and fry until brown on each side. Drain on paper towels. Roll in granulated sugar to coat. Serve as soon after frying as possible.

MAKES ABOUT 4 DOZEN DOUGHNUTS.
CALORIES: 56 CHOLESTEROL: 14 mg SODIUM: 120 mg FIBER: .5 g

Health tip:
Use unsalted margarine instead of butter—and eat just one!
CALORIES: 56 CHOLESTEROL: 9 mg SODIUM: 40 mg FIBER: .5 g

———————— ◇ ————————

Yummy Barley-Date Bars

I often take these bars to food-photography sessions and everyone loves them, which I find flattering, since all of the people I work with are food professionals.

1 cup water
2 packages (8 ounces each) pitted dates
1 tablespoon lemon juice
1½ cups all-purpose flour
¾ cup firmly packed dark-brown sugar (light-brown sugar is okay, too, if that's what you have on hand)
¼ teaspoon salt
¾ cup butter
1½ cups barley flakes

Preheat oven to 350°F.
Grease a 13 × 9 × 2-inch baking pan.
In a 2-quart saucepan, combine the water, dates, and lemon juice. Bring to a boil over high heat. Reduce heat and simmer for 10 minutes, stirring occasionally, or until nearly all of the liquid has been absorbed. Stir hard with a wooden spoon until the dates are a fairly smooth paste.
In a large bowl, stir together the flour, sugar, and salt. With a pastry blender or two knives, cut butter into flour mixture until it resembles coarse cornmeal. Stir in barley flakes.
Press two-thirds of the barley-crumb mixture into the prepared pan, pressing down with the back of a measuring cup to make the layer firm and even. Spread the date mixture evenly over the crumb mixture. (This is a little tricky, since it is sticky and tends to lift some of the crumb mixture. To avoid this, spread with a rubber spatula, pressing down lightly. Spread in one direction at a time, and be careful each time you lift the spatula.) Sprinkle remaining barley-crumb mixture over date mixture.
Bake for 45 to 50 minutes, or until topping is lightly browned. Cool on a wire rack. Cut into 32 bars.

MAKES 32 BARS.
CALORIES: 109   CHOLESTEROL: 12 mg   SODIUM: 56 mg   FIBER: 1 g

Health tip:
Omit salt; use unsalted margarine instead of butter.
CALORIES: 109   CHOLESTEROL: 0 mg   SODIUM: 8 mg   FIBER: 1 g

——————— ◇ ———————

Spiced Barley-Raisin Cookies

These are cakelike cookies. They have a nice flavor-snap from the spices, and raisins give them a chewy sweetness.

¾ cup all-purpose flour
⅓ cup barley flour
1 teaspoon ground cinnamon
1 teaspoon baking soda
½ teaspoon salt
¼ teaspoon ground nutmeg
¼ teaspoon ground cloves
½ cup butter, softened
⅓ cup sugar
⅓ cup firmly packed light-brown sugar (dark-brown sugar is okay, too)
½ teaspoon vanilla extract
2 eggs
½ cup barley flakes
1 cup raisins

Preheat oven to 375°F.
Grease one or two cookie sheets and set aside.
In a small bowl, stir together the all-purpose flour, barley flour, cinnamon, baking soda, salt, nutmeg, and cloves.
In a large bowl, beat together the butter, sugar, brown sugar, and vanilla until creamy. Beat in eggs, then flour mixture. Stir in barley flakes and raisins. Drop by measuring tablespoonsful onto prepared cookie sheets.
Bake for 9 to 11 minutes, or until lightly browned. Remove from cookie sheets and cool completely on wire racks.

MAKES 2 DOZEN COOKIES.
CALORIES: 110   CHOLESTEROL: 28 mg   SODIUM: 119 mg   FIBER: 1 g

Health tip:
Omit salt; use unsalted margarine instead of butter.
CALORIES: 110   CHOLESTEROL: 17 mg   SODIUM: 45 mg   FIBER: 1 g

BUCKWHEAT
(Fagopyrum esculentum)

Buckwheat is not a grain (which is technically a grass seed), but rather the fruit of a plant related to rhubarb. But so many of its properties are similar to those of a true grain that I've gone ahead and included it, and referred to it as a grain, in this book.

When most people think of buckwheat, it is not the raw product that usually comes to mind. The so-called buckwheat with which most of us are familiar, and which is most readily available, is actually kasha, raw buckwheat that has been roasted. In its raw state, buckwheat is rather difficult to find. The reddish-brown grain you see in buckwheat bins is really kasha, and most recipes that call for buckwheat are actually calling for kasha.

Types of Buckwheat/Kasha Available

Whole buckwheat seed (raw): Dark brown in color; not recommended for eating, but very good for sprouting and making into flour.

Hulled buckwheat (raw): Greenish-khaki color; can be used in any recipe calling for kasha.

Whole kasha: Hulled buckwheat that has been roasted. It is especially suitable for salads, stews, or any recipe that would be best with distinct separate grains.

Coarse kasha: Similar to whole kasha, except that the grain has been cracked into a few pieces. The cooked pieces will not be quite as separate as whole kasha.

Medium kasha: Cracked into smaller pieces than coarse kasha, but can be used the same way.

Fine kasha: The smallest of the cracked kashas. The cooked consistency is stickier than the larger-cracked forms.

Buckwheat flour: Available as light or dark flour, the darker having a stronger buckwheat flavor. It is mainly used for making blini and other pancakes. Since buckwheat flour does tend to remain grainy with an unpleasant sandy mouth feel, I don't recommend it as a substitute for white or whole-wheat flours in breads and other baked goods.

Soda: Noodles made from buckwheat flour.

Texture and Flavor

Raw, unroasted buckwheat is shaped something like a round-cut diamond. It has a distinctive flowery flavor that will remind you of a blend of rosemary and green tea.

Kasha is probably one of the only grains from which you can get a sense of the flavor by smelling it before it's cooked. That's because the roasting has already brought out its aroma. It tastes slightly nutty, almost scorched, when it's warm, but loses this slightly burnt taste when it cools.

The consistency of cooked kasha is rather soft and fluffy, with an occasional piece of hull that will cling to the roof of your mouth like popcorn hull. The texture is especially nice when mixed with chewy foods.

When cooked with too much water, kasha becomes soggy and clumpy. Otherwise, it has a light mouth feel, and the feeling of satiety that it provides makes it a good choice for a meat substitute.

Compatible Foods, Herbs, and Spices

Because it has a strong taste, kasha works best in recipes with bland flavors that allow it to dominate. Most meats, game, and vegetables go well with kasha, and starchy foods, such as pasta and potatoes, are especially suitable companions.

Ginger, pepper, allspice, nutmeg, and other spices that hold their flavor tend to be more compatible with kasha than more delicate herbs.

Availability

Kasha is available in most supermarkets. (Try the foreign or gourmet food sections. Sometimes you can locate it with the rice, and other times with the cereal.)

Raw buckwheat, on the other hand, can only be found in some well-stocked health-food stores and from mail-order grain catalogs (see page 21).

Nutritional Content

Buckwheat is high in lysine, an amino acid that is found in very low amounts in true grains. But like true grains, buckwheat is high in B vitamins, protein, iron, and calcium.

Substitutions

The assertive flavor of kasha precludes a simple substitution with any other grain. However, you can substitute each form of kasha for another (fine kasha for whole kasha, etc.).

Whole-wheat flour can be substituted for buckwheat flour.

Basic Cooking Instructions

Please read *About Cooking Grains* beginning on page 7. *Note that all recipes in this section, unless otherwise noted, were tested with kasha, not buckwheat.*

When cooking kasha, always remember to remove it from the heat just as soon as most of the water has been absorbed and holes appear on the surface. Tilt the pan to determine that there is very little water left, then remove from the heat. The small amount of water that remains will be absorbed during a few minutes of standing time. (This vigilance will also prevent a difficult clean-up job, as the kasha and pot seem to be inseparable if the kasha is cooked until every last drop of water has been absorbed.)

Kasha cooks perfectly in a microwave oven, which also gives it a fluffier texture than the stove-top method. The microwave method that follows for cooking kasha was tested in a 650-watt oven.

Another method for cooking kasha involves coating the grains with egg and then drying them in a pot or skillet before adding liquid. Cooking the kasha this way will keep the grains fluffier and more separate than simple boiling.

The finer the grind of the kasha, the more like cereal the cooked product will be. For use in salads, whole or coarse kasha is a better choice than medium or fine grinds. But the finer grinds are good choices in recipes in which you want the kasha evenly distributed.

Stove-top method I:

2 cups water
1 teaspoon salt
1 cup whole kasha or buckwheat

In a 2-quart saucepan, bring the water and salt to a boil over high heat. Stir in kasha. Cover and simmer for 12 minutes, or until almost all of the water has been absorbed. Remove from heat and let stand for 7 minutes, or until all of the water has been absorbed. Fluff with a fork.

MAKES 3½ TO 3¾ CUPS.

Stove-top method II:

> *1 egg*
> *1 cup whole kasha or buckwheat*
> *2 cups boiling water*
> *1 teaspoon salt*

Beat the egg in a medium-size bowl. Add kasha and stir until all of the grains are coated with egg. Place coated kasha in a 2-quart saucepan and cook, stirring, until egg has dried. Stir in boiling water and salt. When water has returned to a boil, reduce heat, cover, and simmer for 10 minutes. Remove from heat and let stand 5 minutes. Fluff with a fork.

MAKES 3½ CUPS.

Microwave method:

> *1¾ cups hot tap water*
> *1 teaspoon salt*
> *1 cup whole kasha or buckwheat*

Place the water and salt in a 2-quart, microwave-safe bowl. Cover with waxed paper. Cook on high (100% power) for 3 to 5 minutes, or until boiling. Stir in kasha. Recover with waxed paper and cook for 15 minutes on medium (50% power), or until water has been absorbed. Let stand 5 minutes. Fluff with a fork.

MAKES 3¼ CUPS.

Reheating

Kasha remains soft after refrigeration and does not have to be reheated to be used in salads or other recipes. Should you want to reheat kasha, it can be microwaved, steamed, or baked.

BUCKWHEAT/KASHA RECIPES

*(*indicates easy recipe.)*

———————◇———————

Blini
Piroshki (miniature turnovers)
Delicious Knishes
Winter Lamb Stew *
Very Chicken-y Croquettes
Kasha-Potato Salad *
Waldorf-ish Buckwheat Salad *
Kasha Varniskas *
Kasha-Vegetable Strudel
Mushrooms Paprikash *
Kasha with Leeks and Endive *
Kasha with Brussels Sprouts and Bacon *
Boiled Soba
Zaru Soba (noodles in a basket)
Soba Noodles with Peanut Sauce
Buckwheat and Wild Rice Dressing *
Buckwheat Griddlecakes *
Low-cholesterol Buckwheat-and-Bran Muffins *
Buckwheat-Currant Brown Bread
Sweet Cheese Squares (kroopyenik) *

————— ◇ —————

Blini

These small buckwheat pancakes are a traditional Russian treat that is almost always eaten before Lent. The warm blini are first brushed with melted butter and then topped with such luxurious goodies as sour cream, caviar, red salmon roe, smoked sturgeon, smoked salmon, and pickled herring. Russian cooks figure on about 15 pancakes per person—unless someone is really hungry. (Don't forget a bottle of icy vodka!)

⅓ cup very warm water (105–115°F.)
1 package quick-rise yeast
3 tablespoons plus 1 teaspoon sugar, divided
1 cup all-purpose flour
1 cup buckwheat flour
½ teaspoon salt
⅓ cup butter
1⅔ cups milk, scalded (bubbles form around edge of the pot, but the
    milk should not actually boil)
3 eggs, separated
Melted butter
Sour cream
Caviar (the best you can afford)

Place the warm water in a glass measuring cup, then stir in yeast and 1 teaspoon of the sugar. Let stand until ¼ inch of white bubbly foam forms on top. (This foaming is called *proofing*, and if it doesn't happen it means that for some reason or other the yeast has not been activated. Discard this batch and try again, double checking the date on the yeast package and the temperature of the water.)

While the yeast is proofing, stir together both kinds of flour, salt, and remaining 3 tablespoons sugar in a large bowl.

Stir butter into scalded milk until nearly melted. Stir the milk mixture and the proofed-yeast mixture into the flour mixture. Beat in egg yolks. Cover and let rise in a warm spot, out of drafts, until doubled in bulk.

In a clean, grease-free, medium-size bowl, beat egg whites with clean beaters until stiff peaks form when beaters are lifted. Fold beaten egg whites into the risen batter. Cover with greased plastic wrap and let rise for an additional 30 minutes.

Heat a griddle or a large skillet until a few drops of water sprinkled on the hot griddle bounce about before evaporating. Butter the griddle *lightly.* (This is important, for if there is too much butter, the blini will have a somewhat unattractive gray appearance.) Drop batter by ¼ cupful onto the griddle. Cook until bubbles on top have broken. Turn and cook until second side is browned.

Brush cooked pancakes with melted butter and top with sour cream and caviar.

MAKES 16 BLINI.
CALORIES: 66   CHOLESTEROL: 28 mg   SODIUM: 66 mg   FIBER: .5 g

Health tip:
Omit salt; substitute unsalted margarine for butter; use 2-percent-fat milk.
CALORIES: 63   CHOLESTEROL: 26 mg   SODIUM: 31 mg   FIBER: .5 g

---

——————— ◇ ———————

Piroshki (miniature turnovers)

Like blini, piroshki is Russian in origin. You can fill them with almost anything you like. My grandmother used to favor chopped lung as a filling, but that's no longer available, so you'll have to settle for beef, poultry, or cheese mixtures, for instance, or the following vegetarian filling that I like very much.

Pastry Dough:

>   ¾ cup sour cream
>   ½ teaspoon baking soda
>   2½ cups all-purpose flour
>   1 teaspoon salt
>   ½ teaspoon baking powder
>   ½ cup butter, chilled
>   2 eggs, beaten

Filling:

>   2 tablespoons butter
>   1 cup finely chopped cabbage
>   ⅓ cup finely chopped onion
>   1 cup cooked kasha
>   ⅓ cup sour cream
>   ½ teaspoon salt
>   ¼ teaspoon pepper
>   1 egg, for glaze (optional)

Grease and flour two or three baking sheets and set aside.

To make the pastry dough, stir together sour cream and baking soda in a medium-size bowl. Set aside.

In a large bowl, stir together flour, salt, and baking powder. With a pastry cutter or two knives, cut in butter until mixture resembles coarse cornmeal.

Beat eggs into sour-cream mixture. Stir into flour mixture until completely combined. Turn onto a floured surface. Knead for 1 or 2 minutes, or until the dough is smooth and pliable. Form into a ball. Wrap in foil or plastic wrap and chill for 30 minutes while making filling.

To make filling, melt the butter in a large skillet over medium-high heat. Add cabbage and onion and cook, stirring, until vegetables are softened. Remove from heat and stir in cooked kasha, sour cream, salt, and pepper. Set aside.

Preheat oven to 400°F.

Roll dough into a rectangle measuring about 18 × 14 inches. Cut out 24 3-inch circles with a biscuit or cookie cutter. Or, if it's easier, cut the dough into 24 2½-inch squares. Brush around the edge of each circle, or square, with beaten egg. Place a level tablespoon of the filling in the center of each circle. Fold in half to form half moons (or triangles, if using squares of dough), then press the coated edges together with the tines of a fork to seal the pastries and make a decorative edge, as well. Prick the top with fork tines to vent steam.

Brush tops of dough with beaten egg; place on prepared baking sheets.

Bake for about 20 minutes, or until golden.

MAKES 24 PIROSHKI.

CALORIES: 121   CHOLESTEROL: 32 mg   SODIUM: 201 mg   FIBER: 1 g

Health tip:
Use unsalted margarine for butter.

CALORIES: 121   CHOLESTEROL: 22 mg   SODIUM: 40 mg   FIBER: 1 g

Delicious Knishes

Knishes are traditionally made with a mashed-potato or kasha filling. In my grandmother's house, large knishes were served for lunch or as a light meal with soup or a salad. Sometimes my mom makes "mini-knishes" and offers them as an appetizer when company comes.

Dough:

> ½ *cup cottage cheese*
> ½ *cup butter, softened*
> 1 *cup all-purpose flour*
> 1 *egg, beaten, for glaze (optional)*

Filling:

> ¼ *cup butter*
> ½ *cup finely chopped onion*
> 1½ *cups cooked fine or medium kasha*
> 1 *cup mashed potatoes (can be made from instant)*
> 1 *egg, beaten*
> ¼ *teaspoon pepper*
> ⅛ *teaspoon salt*

Grease and flour two or three baking sheets and set aside.

To make te dough, push cottage cheese through a fine strainer with the back of a spoon into a small bowl. Add butter and stir to combine. Stir in flour and chill for 15 minutes.

To make the filling, melt butter in a large skillet over medium-high heat. Add onion and cook, stirring, until softened. Remove from heat. Stir in kasha and mashed potatoes. Allow mixture to cool slightly. Stir in egg, pepper, and salt.

Preheat oven to 350 F.

Turned chilled dough out onto a floured surface. Roll dough into a rectangle measuring about 18 × 12 inches. (The dough will be very thin, so you may periodically have to lift it and add more flour to the work surface.)

To make 6 lunch-size knishes: Cut the dough into 6 squares measuring 6×6 inches. Place ⅓ cup of the kasha mixture in the center of each square. Brush around edges with beaten egg. Lift the four points of each square to meet over filling. Pinch the top together, then the seams, to secure the dough and seal the seams. Place on

prepared baking sheets in one of two ways: seam-side up, or seam-side down for a more conventional looking knish. Brush with beaten egg. Cut tiny vents in the dough with the tip of a knife, or prick with a fork to vent steam.
Bake for about 40 minutes, or until golden.

Makes 6 lunch-size knishes.
CALORIES: 395   CHOLESTEROL: 98 mg   SODIUM: 494 mg   FIBER: 3 g

Health tip:
Substitute unsalted margarine for butter; omit salt; substitute water for beaten egg used for sealing and glazing dough.
CALORIES: 395   CHOLESTEROL: 36 mg   SODIUM: 214 mg   FIBER: 3 g

---

To make 12 appetizer knishes: Cut dough into 12 4-inch squares (you'll have a little dough left over). Place 2 rounded tablespoonsful of filling in the center of each square. Follow directions above for folding and baking, reducing baking time slightly.

CALORIES: 190   CHOLESTEROL: 50 mg   SODIUM: 260 mg   FIBER: 1 g

Health tip:
Same as for lunch-size knishes.
CALORIES: 190   CHOLESTEROL: 18 mg   SODIUM: 107 mg   FIBER: 1 g

---

——————— ◇ ———————

Winter Lamb Stew

Although I enjoy this stew any time of the year, I like it the best on cold, blustery nights when I am joined for supper by two or three good friends. Serve the stew accompanied by chunks of crusty whole-grain bread in front of a cozy fire. A warm pie for dessert is all you need for an easy and memorable meal.

> 1 pound cubed stewing lamb
> 3 tablespoons all-purpose flour
> 3 tablespoons vegetable oil
> 2 cups water
> 1½ cups sliced celery
> 1 cup chopped onion
> 1 can (8 ounce) tomato sauce
> ½ teaspoon salt
> ⅛ teaspoon pepper
> 1 package (10 ounce) frozen cut green beans
> 2 cups cooked kasha (method II)

Dredge the lamb in flour. Heat oil in a 3-quart saucepan over medium-high heat. Add lamb and cook, turning, until browned on all sides. Add water, celery, onion, tomato sauce, salt, and pepper. Bring to a boil, then lower heat and simmer, uncovered, for 1 hour and 15 minutes. Stir in green beans and simmer for 45 minutes longer. (If you like your beans crisp, simmer the stew for 1 hour and 35 minutes, then stir in the beans and cook until heated through, 5 to 10 minutes.)

Serve stew over kasha.

SERVES 4.
CALORIES: 522   CHOLESTEROL: 104 mg   SODIUM: 133 mg   FIBER: 7 g

Health tip:
Reduce oil to 2 teaspoons and cook in a nonstick saucepan. Or, brown lamb in a nonstick skillet, transferring to the larger pan to finish cooking. Omit salt.
CALORIES: 453   CHOLESTEROL 104 mg   SODIUM: 467 mg   FIBER: 7 g

---

—————— ◇ ——————

Very Chicken-y Croquettes

I developed the recipe for these croquettes with my mother in mind, because they are one of her favorite foods. Mine, too

¼ cup butter
½ cup finely chopped celery
¼ cup finely chopped onion
¼ cup all-purpose flour
¾ cup chicken broth
2 tablespoons chopped parsley
1 teaspoon white vinegar
¼ teaspoon dry mustard
¼ teaspoon poultry seasoning
¼ teaspoon salt
¼ teaspoon pepper
1½ cups finely chopped cooked chicken
1 cup cooked fine kasha
¼ cup unflavored dry bread crumbs
¼ cup finely chopped pecans
Additional bread crumbs, for coating
Oil, for frying

Melt the butter in a 2-quart saucepan over medium-high heat. Add celery and onion and cook, stirring, until softened. Stir in flour until completely absorbed. Using a whisk, gradually stir in the broth. Cook, stirring constantly, until mixture comes to a boil. Stir in parsley, vinegar, mustard, poultry seasoning, salt, and pepper until well combined. Remove from heat. Stir in chicken, kasha, bread crumbs, and pecans. Place saucepan in the refrigerator until mixture is cold and slightly stiffened.

Form chilled croquette mixture into 8 patties. Roll patties in bread crumbs to coat.

Pour enough oil into a large skillet so that it measures about ¼-inch deep. Heat until oil bubbles when a few bread crumbs are sprinkled on the surface. Cook patties on both sides until appetizingly browned.

MAKES 8 CROQUETTES.

CALORIES: 227   CHOLESTEROL: 37 mg   SODIUM: 295 mg   FIBER: 1 g

Health tip:
Use low-sodium broth; substitute unsalted margarine for butter. Omit salt from kasha.

CALORIES: 227   CHOLESTEROL: 22 mg   SODIUM: 20 mg   FIBER: 1 g

—————— ◇ ——————

Kasha-Potato Salad

This is an absolutely yummy potato salad. The texture of the kasha contrasts so nicely with the crunchiness of the chopped vegetables and the chewiness of the potatoes. For a heartier salad, you can stir in a couple of chopped hard-cooked eggs.

1 pound (6 to 8) small waxy new potatoes
1 cup cooked whole or coarse kasha
½ cup finely chopped green bell pepper
2 tablespoons minced onion
⅓ cup mayonnaise
1 tablespoon water
2 teaspoons spicy brown mustard
1 teaspoon cider vinegar
½ teaspoon salt
¼ teaspoon pepper

Cook the potatoes in boiling water for 20 minutes, or until just tender when pierced with the tip of a knife. Drain and cool. Peel potatoes (or not) then slice into a large bowl. Add kasha, green pepper, and onion. Toss gently to combine.

In a small bowl, stir together the mayonnaise, water, mustard, vinegar, salt, and pepper. Gently toss salad with dressing until well combined.

SERVES 6.
CALORIES: 183   CHOLESTEROL: 7 mg   SODIUM: 369 mg   FIBER: 2 g

Health tip:
Use reduced-calorie mayonnaise; omit salt.
CALORIES: 178   CHOLESTEROL: 7 mg   SODIUM: 134 mg   FIBER: 2 g

---

———————— ◇ ————————

Waldorf-ish Buckwheat Salad

My version of a Waldorf Salad makes a complete light meal, and you can make it even heartier by stirring in chunks of cooked chicken.

3 cups cooked and cooled Kasha
1½ cups cored and chopped apple
1 cup seedless grapes, cut in half
⅓ cup raisins
½ cup radishes, sliced
½ cup diced celery
¼ cup pignoli (pine nuts)
¼ cup finely chopped scallion
½ cup plain yogurt
⅓ cup mayonnaise
1 tablespoon honey
½ teaspoon ground cinnamon

In a large bowl, toss together the kasha, apples, grapes, raisins, radishes, celery, pignoli, and scallion.

In a small bowl, stir together the yogurt, mayonnaise, honey, and cinnamon. Gently toss dressing and salad mixture until well combined.

SERVES 6.
CALORIES: 309   CHOLESTEROL: 12 mg   SODIUM: 270 mg   FIBER: 5g

Health tip:
Omit salt when cooking kasha; substitute reduced-calorie mayonnaise for regular mayonnaise, omit pignoli.
CALORIES: 205   CHOLESTEROL: 6 mg   SODIUM: 31 mg   FIBER: 5g

————◇————

Kasha Varniskas

This is the buckwheat dish with which I am most familiar. It's a very traditional Eastern European side dish that is good served with any kind of meat.

1 egg, beaten
¾ cup whole kasha
2 tablespoons vegetable oil
1 cup chopped onion
1½ cups boiling chicken broth or vegetable broth (see page 000)
¼ teaspoon pepper
1 cup uncooked bow-tie pasta

Stir the egg and kasha together in a small bowl. Heat a large skillet and cook the kasha mixture, stirring constantly, in the *dry* skillet until the egg has dried and the grains are separate. Remove from heat.

In a 2-quart saucepan, heat oil over medium-high heat. Add onion and cook, stirring frequently, until softened. Stir in the kasha mixture, broth, and pepper and bring to a boil. Simmer, covered, for 15 minutes.

While kasha is cooking, cook bow ties in boiling water for about 8 minutes, or until tender, and drain. Stir bow ties into kasha.

SERVES 8.
CALORIES: 159   CHOLESTEROL: 26 mg   SODIUM: 156 mg   FIBER: 2 g

Health tip:
Use low-sodium broth. Reduce oil to 2 teaspoons and use a nonstick saucepan. Or, cook onion in a nonstick skillet, transferring to the larger pan to finish cooking.
CALORIES: 159   CHOLESTEROL: 26 mg   SODIUM: 14 mg   FIBER: 2 g

————————◇————————

Kasha-Vegetable Strudel

Like all strudels, this one is rich and filling. Serve thin slices for a first course or side dish, or make the portions larger and accompany the strudel with a salad for a light meal.

¼ cup butter, divided
1 cup coarsely shredded zucchini
¾ cup coarsely shredded carrot
½ cup chopped onion
1½ cups cooked kasha (any type)
1 cup shredded Monterey Jack or Cheddar cheese
½ cup cottage cheese
1 tablespoon chopped parsley
½ teaspoon dried dill weed
¼ teaspoon salt
¼ teaspoon pepper
4 phyllo-dough sheets (17 × 12 inches), thawed as package directs
3 tablespoons dry unflavored bread crumbs

Preheat oven to 375°F.

In a large skillet, melt the butter over medium-high heat. Pour 2 tablespoons of the melted butter into a small bowl and set aside. Add zucchini, carrot, and onion to butter remaining in skillet and cook, stirring, until vegetables are softened. Remove from heat. Stir in kasha, cheeses, parsley, dill weed, salt, and pepper.

Remove thawed phyllo sheets from package (reseal package tightly so that remaining sheets won't dry out). Place one sheet on a work surface with a long side facing you. (Cover remaining two sheets of phyllo with a damp towel or plastic wrap to keep them from drying out.) Brush sheet lightly with reserved melted butter, then sprinkle with about 2 teaspoons bread crumbs. Place another phyllo sheet on top of the first. Brush with butter and sprinkle with bread crumbs as before. Repeat with remaining sheet of phyllo.

Spoon filling onto the stack of phyllo, 2 inches in from the long edge nearest you, leaving a 2-inch border at each side. (What you will have is a "log" of filling about 2 inches wide and 15 inches long.) Fold the two side edges in over the ends of the filling. Fold the 2-inch long edge near you over the log of filling. Start rolling the phyllo and filling away from you to the end of the dough, enclosing the filling in a neat, loglike package.

Place strudel on a baking sheet and brush top with any remaining butter.

Bake for 30 minutes, or until golden. Cut into slices to serve.

MAKES 4 MAIN-DISH SERVINGS.
CALORIES: 320   CHOLESTEROL: 61 mg   SODIUM: 721 mg   FIBER: 3 g

Health tip:
Use unsalted margarine instead of butter; omit salt.
CALORIES: 316   CHOLESTEROL: 27 mg   SODIUM: 513 mg   FIBER: 3g

———————— ◇ ————————

Mushrooms Paprikash

Paprikash is a Hungarian term and it means that the dish is flavored with paprika, usually lots of it, and cream. You can find real Hungarian paprika in specialty food stores. It is worth seeking out, for it has a lovely intense flavor, much more interesting than our domestic paprikas. The recipe that follows is an excellent side dish for plain roasted poultry or meat.

3 tablespoons vegetable oil
12 ounces mushrooms, rinsed, patted dry, and coarsely chopped
1 cup chopped onion
1 clove garlic, minced
2 tablespoons Hungarian or domestic paprika
¾ teaspoon salt
¼ teaspoon pepper
1 cup chicken broth or vegetable broth (see page 19)
¾ cup water
1 cup kasha
½ cup sour cream
2 tablespoons chopped parsley

In a 3-quart saucepan, heat the oil over medium-high heat. Add mushrooms, onion, and garlic. Cook, stirring, until vegetables are softened. Stir in paprika, salt, and pepper. Add broth and water and bring to a boil. Stir in kasha and return to boiling. Lower heat and simmer, covered, for 12 minutes. Remove from heat and let stand 5 minutes. Stir in sour cream and parsley.

SERVES 6.
CALORIES: 177   CHOLESTEROL: 6 mg   SODIUM: 308 mg   FIBER: 4 g

Health tip:
Reduce oil to 2 teaspoons and use a nonstick saucepan. Or, cook vegetables in a nonstick skillet, transferring to the larger pan to finish cooking. Use low-sodium broth; substitute plain lowfat yogurt for sour cream.
CALORIES: 102   CHOLESTEROL: 6 mg   SODIUM: 60 mg   FIBER: 4 g

Kasha with Leeks and Endive

Leeks and endive (not the lettuce, but rather those small oval heads that are light green in color and are often called "Belgian" endive, although much of it is grown in France), are both greatly under-utilized vgetables in this country. Leeks are part of the onion family, and look like a giant green onion. When cooked they are sweet and mellow. Endive has a slightly bitter, but nevertheless pleasing, taste, and they're both sure enough of themselves to stand up to the bold flavor of kasha.

1 can (13¾ ounce) ready-to-serve chicken broth or
*   1¾ cups vegetable broth (see page 19)*
¼ cup water
1 egg
1 cup kasha
⅛ teaspoon pepper
2 tablespoons butter
1½ cups thinly sliced leeks, both white and green parts
1 head endive, cut into 1-inch pieces

Combine chicken broth and water in a 2-quart saucepan and bring to a boil. Set aside.

Beat egg in a medium-size bowl. Stir in kasha to completely coat with egg. Cook the kasha in a *dry* 2-quart saucepan over medium-high heat, stirring, until egg is dried and grains are separate. Stir in hot chicken broth and water and pepper and bring to a boil. Reduce heat and simmer for 20 minutes. Remove from heat and let stand for 5 minutes. Turn into a serving bowl.

Melt the butter over medium-high heat in the same saucepan used to cook the kasha. Add leeks and cook, stirring often, until softened. Add endive and continue to cook, stirring, until wilted. Spoon leek-and-endive mixture on top of kasha to serve.

SERVES 8.
CALORIES: 129   CHOLESTEROL: 34 mg   SODIUM: 193 mg   FIBER: 3 g

Health tip:
Use low-sodium broth; substitute unsalted margarine for butter.
CALORIES: 128   CHOLESTEROL: 26 mg   SODIUM: 30 mg   FIBER: 3 g

———————— ◇ ————————

Kasha with Brussels Sprouts and Bacon

You can use frozen Brussels sprouts, if fresh are not available. Omit the bacon and use 2 tablespoons butter for a vegetarian dish.

2 slices bacon, cut into 1-inch pieces
1 cup chopped onion
1 pint Brussels sprouts, cut in half
½ cup chicken broth or vegetable broth (see page 19)
1 cup cooked coarse or medium kasha
1 teaspoon sugar
½ teaspoon white vinegar
¼ teaspoon salt
¼ teaspoon pepper

In a large skillet, cook the bacon until crisp. Remove bacon and drain on paper towels.

Discard all but 2 tablespoons of fat in skillet. Stir onion and Brussels sprouts into hot fat and cook over medium-high heat, stirring, until onions are softened. Stir in broth. Cover and cook for 5 minutes, or until sprouts are tender. Stir in kasha, sugar, vinegar, salt, and pepper and cook, stirring, until heated through.

SERVES 6.
CALORIES: 91   CHOLESTEROL: 24 mg   SODIUM: 301 mg   FIBER: 5 g

Health tip:
Use only 1 slice bacon and 1 tablespoon bacon fat. Use low-sodium broth; omit salt.
CALORIES: 86   CHOLESTEROL: 12 mg   SODIUM: 46 mg   FIBER: 5 g

Boiled Soba

The term soba in Japanese means buckwheat. The word also refers to a special type of Japanese noodle that is generally made of buckwheat. Although it's possible to make soba noodles at home, the process is very complicated. So, if you'd like to use the noodle recipes that follow, I suggest that you buy dried soba noodles, which you can find in Oriental grocery stores, and sometimes in health-food stores. However, if challenges excite you, you will find a recipe for homemade soba in "The Book of Soba," by James Udesky. The recipe that follows is the proper way to cook dried soba noodles, which, like other pastas, should be cooked al dente.

3 quarts water
1 package (8 ounce) dried soba noodles
1½ cups cold water, divided

Use a pot that is large enough to make sure that the noodles will not stick together as they cook. Bring 3 quarts of water to a fast boil. Stir in noodles so that the water continues to boil to some degree as you do so.

As the noodles cook, the water will start to bubble up, foam, and some scum will accumulate. At this point, stir in ½ cup cold water and reduce heat to medium. When the water bubbles up again, add another ½ cup cold water. Repeat this procedure once more, using the final ½ cup cold water. When the water boils for the fourth time, take out one noodle and test for doneness by biting into it to determine that it is still firm, but not uncooked, in the center. If noodles are not done, continue to boil, testing a strand every 30 seconds or so.

Drain noodles in a colander. Refill the cooking pot with cool water and add the cooked drained noodles. Swish the noodles around in the cool water, then drain again. The noodles are now ready to serve. If you are planning to use the noodles in a warm dish, place them in a strainer and dip them into boiling water for a minute or so just before serving to warm them. Drain again.

SERVES 4.
CALORIES: 209   CHOLESTEROL: 0 mg   SODIUM: 1 mg   FIBER: 2 g

Health tip:
None.

Zaru Soba (noodles in a basket)

Soba noodles are traditionally eaten in a hot broth, or cold with a dipping sauce. Both the dipping sauce and the hot-broth variation that follow use the following recipes for flavor base and the dashi (dipping sauce). (By the way, don't plan to whip this up just before the company arrives, because the flavor base needs at least 4 hours, preferably a day or two, for the flavors to develop.) Both of these recipes are standard for soba, but many variations exist. To learn more about soba, consult a Japanese cookbook.

This dish is so named because it is traditionally served in bamboo baskets (zaru). The Japanese products called for may be found in Oriental food stores.

Flavor Base:

> ⅓ cup Japanese soy sauce (Chinese soy sauce is too dark and salty)
> 1 tablespoon mirin (sweet rice wine)
> 2½ teaspoons sugar

Dashi:

> 2¼ cups water, divided
> 2 pieces giant kelp (kombu)
> 1 cup dried bonito flakes (hana-katsuo)
> 1 package (8 ounce) dried soba noodles,
>   cooked according to previous recipe
> 1 sheet nori (dried laver seaweed), optional
> 2 green onions (or to taste) thinly sliced on the diagonal
> 2 tablespoons (or to taste) grated daikon radish
> ½ teaspoon (or to taste) wasabi (green horseradish paste)

To make the flavor base, stir together the soy sauce and mirin in a small saucepan. Cook over medium heat until mixture is scalded (bubbles form around edge of pot). Reduce heat to low and gradually stir in sugar. Stir continuously until sugar is completely dissolved. Cook until mixture is scalded once again. Immediately remove from heat. Pour into a small bowl and let stand for at least 4 hours, or up to 2 days, to allow the flavors to develop. (Note: It is important that at no time is water allowed to come into contact with this mixture. Be sure that all utensils you use are dry, and if you choose to cover the sauce while it stands, use brown paper, cheesecloth, or some other porous material so that no condensation forms.)

To make dashi, place 2 cups of the water and kelp in a medium-size saucepan. Cook over medium heat until water shows the first signs of boiling, but does not actually boil. Remove from heat and pour in remaining ¼ cup water. Discard kelp. Stir in bonito flakes. Return to heat and bring to a boil. As soon as mixture boils, remove from heat and allow flakes to settle to the bottom of the pan. Strain mixture through cheesecloth and discard flakes. Stir base mixture into dashi and chill.

Place some of the chilled cooked noodles in a bamboo basket or serving plate for each person.

Toast the nori under the broiler until crisp, then crumble over noodles.

Stir as much of the scallion, radish, and wasabi as desired into the dashi. Divide sauce among 4 individual bowls, placing one on each basket or plate.

Eat by picking up some of the noodles with chopsticks and dipping into sauce.

SERVES 4.
CALORIES: 244   CHOLESTEROL: 0 mg   SODIUM: 1566 mg   FIBER: 6 g

Health tip:
Like so many Oriental dishes, this is low in fat and calories, but high in sodium, so you may want to use low-sodium Japanese soy sauce.
CALORIES: 244   CHOLESTEROL: 0 mg   SODIUM: 1358 mg   FIBER: 6 g

---

———— ◇ ————

Hot Soba Noodles in Broth

Here is another traditional recipe for preparing soba noodles.

One recipe for flavor base (see page 247)
Double recipe for dashi (see page 247)
1 package (8 ounce) dried soba noodles, cooked and reheated according
    to previous recipe
1 scallion, thinly sliced on the diagonal
2 teaspoons grated fresh ginger

Make the flavor base and stir it into the dashi. Heat until almost boiling.

Place warm noodles in four bowls. Pour broth over noodles and top each with a sprinkling of scallion and ginger.

SERVES 4.
CALORIES: 244   CHOLESTEROL: 0 mg   SODIUM: mg   FIBER: 6 g

Health tip:
Use low-sodium Japanese soy sauce.
CALORIES: 244   CHOLESTEROL: 0 mg   SODIUM: 1358 mg   FIBER: 6g

Soba Noodles with Peanut Sauce

This is really a Chinese recipe for noodles, but it's one that I like very much, and it seems to work just as well with the Japanese noodles.

1 package (8 ounce) dried soba noodles,
   cooked according to previous recipe
¼ cup chopped scallion
¼ cup smooth peanut butter
3 tablespoons dark Chinese soy sauce
1½ tablespoons Chinese red vinegar (available in Oriental grocery
   stores) or cider vinegar
1 tablespoon hot chili oil or Oriental sesame oil (both available in
   Oriental grocery stores)
1½ teaspoons sugar

In a large bowl, toss together the noodles and scallion.

Place peanut butter, soy sauce, vinegar, chili oil, and sugar in the container of an electric blender. Cover and blend until completely combined. Pour over noodles and toss.

SERVES 4.
CALORIES: 326   CHOLESTEROL: 0 mg   SODIUM: 775 mg   FIBER: 3 g

Health tip:
Use low-sodium Chinese soy sauce.
CALORIES: 258   CHOLESTEROL: 0 mg   SODIUM: 38 mg   FIBER: 3 g

————————— ◇ —————————

Buckwheat and Wild Rice Dressing

Try this instead of your traditional dressing at holiday time, or serve it as a side dish whenever you feel like something special and a little different.

4 slices bacon, cut into 1-inch pieces
1 tablespoon butter
1 cup chopped onion
1 cup sliced mushrooms
½ finely chopped celery
½ cup finely chopped green bell pepper
2 cups cooked wild rice
1¾ cups cooked kasha
1 can (8 ounce) water chestnuts, drained and chopped
¼ cup chopped parsley
¼ teaspoon ground sage
¼ teaspoon pepper

In a large skillet, cook the bacon until crisp. Remove bacon and drain on paper towels.

Discard all but 2 tablespoons of fat in the skillet. Add butter to fat and melt over medium-high heat. Add onion, mushrooms, celery, and green pepper and cook, stirring frequently, until vegetables are softened. Stir in wild rice, kasha, water chestnuts, parsley, sage, pepper, and reserved bacon. Cook, stirring, until heated through.

SERVES 12.

CALORIES: 59   CHOLESTEROL: 2 mg   SODIUM: 409 mg   FIBER: 2g

Health tip:
Use only 2 slices bacon and omit butter. Omit salt when cooking kasha.
CALORIES: 47   CHOLESTEROL: 1 mg   SODIUM: 128 mg   FIBER: 2 g

Buckwheat Griddlecakes

These light, but substantial, pancakes are sweet before you even add syrup. Try them for breakfast or brunch on a leisurely morning sometime soon.

1⅓ cups milk
⅓ cup butter, melted
2 eggs
½ teaspoon vanilla extract
1 cup all-purpose flour
⅓ cup buckwheat flour
3 tablespoons sugar
1 tablespoon baking powder
1 teaspoon baking soda
¾ teaspoon salt
Additional melted butter, for brushing skillet.

In a medium-size bowl, beat the milk, butter, eggs, and vanilla with a wire whisk until thoroughly combined.

In another medium-size bowl, stir both flours, sugar, baking powder, baking soda, and salt together until blended. Add milk mixture to flour mixture and stir just until blended. Do not over-mix. The batter should be lumpy. Let stand 5 minutes.

Heat a large skillet or griddle over medium heat until a few drops of water sprinkled in the hot skillet bounce about before evaporating. Brush skillet with a thin coating of melted butter. Immediately pour ¼ cup of the batter into the skillet for each pancake. (You should be able to make 3 or 4 pancakes at once in a large skillet. If you are particularly well coordinated, you may want to have more than one skillet going at a time.) Cook until bubbles break on top of cakes. Turn with a wide spatula and cook the second side until lightly browned.

MAKES 12 TO 14 PANCAKES.
CALORIES: 143   CHOLESTEROL: 55 mg   SODIUM: 360 mg   FIBER: 1 g

Health tip:
Use unsalted margarine instead of butter; substitute scrambled-egg substitute for eggs; omit salt.
CALORIES: 136   CHOLESTEROL: 0 mg   SODIUM: 180 mg   FIBER: 1 g

Low-Cholesterol Buckwheat-and-Bran Muffins

These muffins are moist and mouthwatering, but small, so you may want to eat a second one, and that's okay, because they're so good for you. Just don't forget to count the extra calories. (No food in the world is *that* perfect!)

¾ cup apple juice
½ cup plain nonfat yogurt
½ cup applesauce
1 cup morsels of wheat bran cereal (Kellogg's Bran Buds)
2 egg whites
1 cup all-purpose flour
⅓ cup buckwheat flour
¼ cup sugar
1 tablespoon baking powder
1 teaspoon baking soda
1½ teaspoons ground cinnamon
¼ teaspoon ground nutmeg

Preheat oven to 400°F.
Place paper liners in 16 muffin cups and set aside.
In a medium-size bowl, stir together the apple juice, yogurt, and applesauce. Stir in cereal. Set aside for 5 minutes. Stir in egg whites.
In a large bowl, stir together both flours, sugar, baking powder, baking soda, cinnamon, and nutmeg. Stir liquid mixture into flour mixture just until blended. Don't overmix. The batter should be lumpy. Divide batter evenly among muffin cups.
Bake for 15 to 18 minutes, or until a wooden pick inserted in the center of a few of the muffins comes out clean. Turn muffins out of pan to cool on wire racks.

MAKES 16 MUFFINS.
CALORIES: 85   CHOLESTEROL: 0 mg   SODIUM: 157 mg   FIBER: 2 g
Health tip:
None. These muffins are perfect just the way they are.

——————— ◇ ———————

Buckwheat-Currant Brown Bread

This bread will remind you of raisin-pumpernickel, but the texture is lighter. To serve, cut into thick slices, and cut the slices into halves or quarters. If you can afford the calories, spread generously with butter or cream cheese. Thinner slices may be lightly toasted.

½ cup very warm water (105–115°F)
2 packages dry yeast
½ teaspoon sugar
1 cup buckwheat flour
2 tablespoons unsweetened cocoa powder
1 tablespoon caraway seeds (optional)
2 teaspoons salt
1 teaspoon instant coffee granules
1 cup buttermilk
½ cup unsulphured molasses
2 tablespoons vegetable oil
½ cup dried currants
3 cups all-purpose flour, divided

Grease a 9 × 5 × 3-inch loaf pan and set aside.

Place warm water in a glass measuring cup, then stir in yeast and sugar. Let stand until ¼ inch of white bubbly foam forms on top. (This foaming is called *proofing*, and if it doesn't happen it means that for some reason or other the yeast has not been activated. Discard this batch and try again, double checking the date on the yeast package and the temperature of the water.)

While yeast is proofing, in a large bowl, stir together buckwheat flour, cocoa, caraway seeds, salt and coffee. Stir in buttermilk, molasses, oil, and proofed-yeast mixture. Stir until completely combined. Stir in currants, then 2¼ cups of the all-purpose flour.

Turn dough onto a heavily floured surface. Knead for about 7 minutes, using as much of the remaining flour as necessary to form a smooth, elastic dough that is still slightly sticky.

Place dough in a greased bowl. Cover with greased plastic wrap and let rise in a warm spot, out of drafts, until doubled in bulk. Punch down and knead again for 1 minute.

Shape dough into a loaf and place in prepared pan. Cover with greased plastic wrap and let rise until doubled in bulk.

Preheat oven to 350°F.

Bake for 50 minutes, or until top and bottom are browned. Turn loaf out of pan to cool on a wire rack.

MAKES 1 LOAF (20 servings).
CALORIES: 129   CHOLESTEROL: 0 mg   SODIUM: 228 mg   FIBER: 2 g

Health tip:
Omit salt.
CALORIES: 129   CHOLESTEROL: 0 mg   SODIUM: 15 mg   FIBER: 2 g

---------◇---------

Sweet Cheese Squares (kroopyenik)

You'll probably think of noodle pudding when you eat this traditional Russian dish that may be served as a side dish or dessert.

1 container (8 ounce) cottage cheese
1 package (3 ounce) cream cheese, softened
½ cup sugar
½ teaspoon grated lemon rind
3 eggs, separated
2 cups cooked whole kasha
½ cup golden raisins
¼ teaspoon salt

Preheat oven to 375°F.
Grease an 8-inch-square baking pan and set aside.
In a large bowl, beat the cottage cheese, cream cheese, sugar, and lemon rind until well combined. Beat in egg yolks. Stir in kasha and raisins.
In a grease-free, medium-size bowl, with clean beaters, beat egg whites with salt until stiff peaks form when beaters are lifted. Stir about one-quarter of the beaten whites into the cheese mixture. Fold in remaining whites. Spread batter into prepared pan.
Bake for 30 minutes, or until top is browned and a knife inserted in the center comes out clean. Cut into squares to serve.

MAKES 16 SQUARES.
CALORIES: 106   CHOLESTEROL: 47 mg   SODIUM: 190 mg   FIBER: 1 g

Health tip:
Omit salt.
CALORIES: 106   CHOLESTEROL: 45 mg   SODIUM: 157 mg   FIBER: 1 g

MILLET

(Panicum miliaceum)

It can safely be said that millet is "for the birds," since bird feed—(and cattle feed)—is its primary use in the United States. But in many parts of the world, mainly Africa, China, and India, millet is a dietary staple.

Millet is a sturdy grain, capable of flourishing in dry and underfertilized soil. The seed can even manage to survive in times of severe drought, only to sprout anew when the lightest rain falls.

Frankly, millet has its drawbacks. Because of a definite bitter taste and an odd starchiness when it is improperly cooked and served, millet is deliberately avoided in this country—even by grain lovers and health faddists. However, it can be absolutely delicious *when it is cooked properly with compatible foods.* Even if you've tried millet in the past and decided you didn't like it, you owe it to yourself to try it again—my way.

Not to be overlooked, of course, is millet's enviable nutritional profile and great versatility. Inexpensive millet can be used to extend or replace meat dishes, thereby cutting down on fat and calories, and its dense, moist texture adds a satisfying element to salads and vegetable dishes.

Types of Millet Available

Whole millet: The whole grain with the hull removed.

Millet meal: Whole millet, coarsely ground. It looks a lot like small hulled sesame seeds. Use it in breads and for cereal.

Millet flour: The whole grain, finely ground. Millet flour has no gluten, so it must be used in conjunction with gluten-containing flours when making yeast-baked goods. You can substitute millet flour for part of the whole-wheat flour (up to 25%) in baking, but the texture of the finished product will be heavier. Millet flour is sometimes referred to as *teff,* and is used to make *injera,* the national bread of Ethiopia.

Puffed millet: The whole grain, cooked and processed. Use as a breakfast cereal.

Texture and Flavor

Millet is small, round, and golden-yellow in color with a beady appearance that will remind you of mustard seeds. As it cooks, the grains swell and explode (like popcorn), exposing the starchy inside of the grain that has burst out of the tough bran layer.

Cooked millet has a consistency similar to cornmeal mush (dense and heavy), the difference being that you will occasionally find an undercooked grain (that will be slightly crunchy, but not unpleasantly so) and there will always be some empty bran left. The only way to eliminate the uncooked grains is to increase the amount of water and the cooking time. However, this will produce a sticky porridge that I would not recommend for the recipes in this chapter.

The bitterness of cooked millet can be mostly eliminated by sautéing the uncooked millet in oil or butter before adding boiling water (method I). Or it can simply be toasted in a dry skillet before cooking. I prefer the sauté method. Both of these procedures will also help to keep the grains separate as they cook.

Boiling millet (method II) will produce a sticky mixture that is excellent for holding together croquettes, or in other recipes where its binding properties are desirable.

Cooking millet in stewing liquid or soups, I have found, gives the finished dish a strange sort of starchiness. I found this undesirable, so most of the recipes that follow start with cooked millet. The preferred cooking method for the millet is included in each recipe.

Compatible Foods, Herbs, and Spices

Because of its inherent bitterness, it is best to use millet in dishes with strong flavors that are either compatible with, or will mask, this undesirable trait. Recipes that use any of the four basic flavor sensations; sweet, spicy, salty, or sour work well with millet. Subtle flavorings, such as delicate herbs, are not good choices. Most meats, fruits, and vegetables are fine served with millet.

Availability

There are many varieties of millet grown worldwide, but only one is available in the United States: pearl millet. The packages are labeled "whole millet," even though the grain has been hulled.

Millet is widely available in health-food stores and can be purchased through mail-order grain catalogs (see page 21). At this writing, I have not been able to find millet in any supermarket.

Nutritional Content

Although the millet is hulled (meaning the outer layer has been removed), the bran, with its fiber and vitamin content, remains.

Millet has a high nutritional profile when compared to other non-meat sources, in both the amount of protein and the amino-acid balance, which is pretty close to complete. It is also a good source of B vitamins, potassium, magnesium, phosphorous, and iron. Millet is naturally alkaline, which makes it good for the digestive tract, and it is touted to be the grain most likely to be tolerated by people who are allergic to other grains.

Substitutions

Because millet is not easily available, and because of the bitter aftertaste, to which some palates are more sensitive than others, you may want to substitute other grains for the millet in the recipes that follow.

Couscous: Cooked, it's texture is similar to cooked millet, and makes an excellent substitute. Couscous is available in most supermarkets.

Rizcous: A brown rice product is an excellent substitute. It can be found in gourmet stores.

Quinoa: The flavors and nutritional profile are similar, but the textures are not, so quinoa is not a suitable substitute for recipes in which the sticky consistency of millet is required (making croquettes, etc.). It has the same drawback as millet of only being available in health-food stores.

Brown rice: I prefer the short-grain variety because it has enough "toothiness" and flavor to work well in millet recipes. But because of textural differences, it is not possible to substitute brown rice—or any rice—when millet is used as a binding agent.

Cooked cornmeal: This is an excellent substitute for use in recipes where millet is used as a binding agent.

Other acceptable substitutes (in order of preference): White rice, bulgur, barley, and wild rice.

Basic Cooking Instructions

Please read *About Cooking Grains* beginning on page 7. The microwave methods that follow for cooking millet were tested in a 650-watt oven.

Stove-top method I:

> *1 tablespoon vegetable oil or butter*
> *1 cup millet, rinsed*
> *2 cups boiling water*
> *½ teaspoon salt*

Heat oil in a 2-quart saucepan. Add millet and cook over medium heat, stirring, until it is milky in appearance and some of the grains have browned. (The millet will make lots of crackling sounds at this point.) Stir in boiling water and salt. (Stand away from the pot because it will be giving off lots of steam.) Return to boiling, then cover and simmer for 30 minutes, or until all of the water has been absorbed. Remove from heat and let stand 5 minutes. Fluff with a fork.

MAKES 4 CUPS.

Stove-top method II:

> *2 cups water*
> *½ teaspoon salt*
> *1 cup millet, rinsed*

Bring the water and salt to a boil in a 2-quart covered saucepan. Stir in millet and return to boiling. Reduce heat and simmer, covered, for 30 minutes, or until all of the liquid has been absorbed. Remove from heat and let stand 5 minutes. Fluff with a fork.

MAKES 3 CUPS.

Microwave method I:

> *1 tablespoon oil or butter*
> *1 cup millet, rinsed*
> *1¾ cups hot tap water*
> *½ teaspoon salt*

In a 3-quart, microwave-safe casserole, stir together the oil and millet. Microwave on high (100% power), uncovered, for 2 minutes. Stir, then continue to microwave on high, uncovered, for 2 minutes longer. Stir in hot water and salt. Cover with waxed paper and microwave on high for 5 minutes. Microwave on medium (50% power), still covered with waxed paper, for 20 minutes. Let stand 4 minutes. Fluff with a fork.

MAKES 3½ CUPS.

Microwave method II:

1¾ cups water
1 cup millet, rinsed

Place the water in a 3-quart, microwave-safe casserole. Cover with waxed paper. Microwave on high (100% power), for 3 minutes. Stir in millet, recover with waxed paper, and microwave on high for 5 minutes. Microwave on medium, still covered with waxed paper, for 20 minutes. Let stand 4 minutes. Fluff with a fork.

MAKES 3¼ CUPS.

Reheating

Many of the recipes given here call for cooked millet. As long as you use freshly cooked millet, you will have moist, separate, fluffy (if cooked by method I) grains. If you have cooked the millet in advance and chilled it, you'll find that the grains are hard, dry, and clumpy. You can remedy this by microwaving or steaming the millet slightly to return it to its just-cooked consistency.

MILLET RECIPES
*(*indicates easy recipe.)*

———————◇———————

Codfish Cakes *
Sweet-and-Sour Milletballs *
Groundnut Stew *
Southwestern Beef Stew with Millet
Lamb Biriani with Onion Relish
California Salad *
Oriental Millet Salad *
Lightly Curried Millet Salad *
Italian Bean-and-Millet Salad *
Cheddar-Bacon Millet *
Autumn Casserole *
Eggplant-and-Chick-Pea Curry with Millet
Fried Corn Cakes
Bruncheon Spoon Bread
Orange-Flavored Millet-Meal Bread

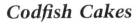

Codfish Cakes

I like these tasty little fish cakes for lunch or a light supper, served with tartar sauce and coleslaw.

1 cup cooked millet (method II)
1 cup cooked flaked cod
¼ cup chopped scallion, both white and green parts
2 tablespoons grated onion
2 tablespoons minced green bell pepper
1 egg
½ teaspoon salt
¼ teaspoon pepper
¼ cup dry unflavored bread crumbs
Oil, for frying

In a large bowl, thoroughly combine millet, cod, green onion, shredded onion, green pepper, egg, salt, and pepper. Shape into 8 patties.

Scatter bread crumbs on a piece of waxed paper. Carefully roll each patty in crumbs.

Pour enough oil into a large skillet so that it measures ⅛-inch deep. Heat over medium-high heat until a few crumbs brown quickly when sprinkled on the oil. Place 4 patties in skillet and cook until browned on one side. Turn and brown second side. Repeat with remaining patties.

MAKES 8 FISH CAKES.
CALORIES: 107   CHOLESTEROL: 34 mg   SODIUM: 192 mg   FIBER: 1g

Health tip:
Omit salt. Instead of frying cakes, bake on a greased baking sheet until appetizingly browned.
CALORIES: 61   CHOLESTEROL: 34 mg   SODIUM: 27 mg   FIBER: 1 g

———————◇———————

Sweet-and-Sour Milletballs

I use millet in this recipe as a meat extender. Serve these little balls plain as a hot appetizer, or as a main course served over additional millet or pasta.

1 pound lean ground beef (I use ground round)
1 cup cooked millet (any method)
2 cloves garlic, minced
¼ teaspoon salt
1 tablespoon oil
½ cup finely chopped onion
½ cup water
½ cup catsup
½ cup orange juice
⅓ cup firmly packed light or dark-brown sugar
2 tablespoons lemon juice
1 tablespoon white vinegar
2 teaspoons thick steak sauce (A-1)
3 gingersnaps
1 can crushed pineapple, drained

In a medium-size bowl, combine the ground beef, millet, garlic, and salt. Shape into 16 balls.

In a 3-quart saucepan, heat the oil over medium-high heat. Add onion and cook, stirring frequently, until softened. Stir in water, catsup, orange juice, brown sugar, lemon juice, vinegar, steak sauce, and gingersnaps. Simmer for 10 minutes. Stir in milletballs and simmer for 10 minutes longer, or until balls are cooked through. Gently stir in pineapple, and cook until heated.

MAKES 16 MILLETBALLS.
CALORIES: 124   CHOLESTEROL: 27 mg   SODIUM: 155 mg   FIBER: 1 g

Health tip:
Omit salt; use low-sodium catsup.
CALORIES: 124   CHOLESTEROL: 27 mg   SODIUM: 105 mg   FIBER: 1g

———————◇———————

Groundnut Stew

My friend, Paula Rudolph, served in the Peace Corps in Ethiopia. She said she frequently ate millet while she lived there, but didn't have a specific recipe to give me. So, in her honor, I've made up a probably-not-too-authentic African stew to serve with millet.

2 tablespoons vegetable oil
3½-pound chicken, cut into parts
¾ cup finely chopped onion
1¼ cups chopped tomato
1 can (13¾ ounce) ready-to-serve chicken broth
⅓ cup tomato paste
¼ cup peanut butter
¼ teaspoon crumbled thyme
¼ teaspoon salt
¼ teaspoon ground red pepper
2 cups cooked millet (method I)

In a large heavy saucepan or Dutch oven, heat the oil over medium-high heat. Add chicken and cook, turning, until browned. Remove chicken from pan. Add onion and cook, stirring frequently, until softened. Add tomato and cook, stirring frequently, until softened.

In a medium-size bowl, combine broth, tomato paste, peanut butter, thyme, salt, and red pepper and whisk until smooth. Stir this mixture into the onion mixture in the saucepan. (You may be tempted to taste the sauce at this point, but restrain yourself. It doesn't taste very good until it's fully cooked and mellowed. Then it's delicious.) Bring to a boil and return chicken to pan. Cover and simmer for 40 minutes, or until chicken is cooked through. Serve over millet.

SERVES 4.
CALORIES: 600   CHOLESTEROL: 198 mg   SODIUM: 813 mg   FIBER: 5 g
Health tip:
Omit salt and use low-sodium broth, cook chicken without skin.
CALORIES: 556   CHOLESTEROL: 164 mg   SODIUM: 221 mg   FIBER: 5 g

Southwestern Beef Stew with Millet

I like the complex flavors of this dish, mainly spicy with a hint of sweetness. Serve the stew with a salad, and maybe some corn-bread or biscuits, for a complete meal.

2 tablespoons vegetable oil
1 cup chopped onion
¾ cup chopped green bell pepper
2 cloves garlic, minced
1½ pounds stewing beef, cubed
1 can (14½ ounce) whole peeled tomatoes
1 can (8 ounce) tomato sauce
1 can (4 ounce) chopped mild green chilies, drained
2 tablespoons dark-brown sugar
2 teaspoons red-wine vinegar
1½ teaspoons ground coriander
1 teaspoon chili powder
½ teaspoon ground cumin
¼ teaspoon crumbled oregano
¼ teaspoon salt
3 cups cooked millet (method I)

In a large saucepan or Dutch oven, heat the oil over medium-high heat. Add onion, green pepper, and garlic and cook, stirring frequently, until vegetables are softened. Stir in beef, tomatoes, tomato sauce, chopped chilies, brown sugar, vinegar, coriander, chili powder, cumin, oregano, and salt. Bring to a boil. Reduce heat and simmer, covered, for 1 hour and 15 minutes. Uncover and cook for 30 minutes longer. (If the mixture starts to look too thick, or if it begins to stick to the bottom of the pot, stir in some extra water.) Serve over millet.

SERVES 6.
CALORIES: 388   CHOLESTEROL: 92 mg   SODIUM: 479 mg   FIBER: 4 g

Health tip:
Reduce oil to 2 teaspoons and cook in a nonstick saucepan. Or, cook onion, green pepper, and garlic in a nonstick skillet, transferring to the large saucepan to finish cooking. Use low-sodium tomato sauce and omit salt.
CALORIES: 362   CHOLESTEROL: 92 mg   SODIUM: 390 mg   FIBER 4 g

Lamb Biriani with Onion Relish

Curry is THE flavor that was made for millet. This dish is a real show-stopper and makes wonderful party food. There are a lot of ingredients, but the dish actually goes together very quickly once you have everything assembled.

Stew:

> 3 tablespoons ghee (clarified butter) or vegetable oil
> 1½ cups chopped onion
> 3 cloves garlic, minced
> 1 tablespoon minced fresh ginger or 2 teaspoons ground ginger
> 2 tablespoons curry powder
> 2 teaspoons ground coriander
> 1¼ teaspoons salt
> 1 teaspoon turmeric
> ½ teaspoon ground cinnamon
> 1½ pounds boneless lamb, cubed
> 2 cups chopped tomato
> ¾ cup water
> 2 tablespoons chopped fresh mint or 2 teaspoons dried mint flakes

Relish:

> 1 cup chopped onion
> 1 teaspoon salt
> 2 tablespoons water
> 1½ teaspoons tomato paste
> 1 teaspoon white vinegar
> 1 teaspoon paprika
> 1 teaspoon lemon juice
> ½ teaspoon sugar
> ¼ teaspoon ground ginger
> ⅛ teaspoon ground cumin
> ⅛ teaspoon ground red pepper
> 2 cups cooked millet (method I)

To make a stew, heat ghee in a large heavy saucepan or Dutch oven over medium-high heat. Add onion, garlic, and ginger and cook, stirring frequently, until onion is softened. Stir in curry, coriander, salt, turmeric, and cinnamon. Cook over low heat, stirring, for 1 minute. Add lamb and stir until coated with spice mixture. Stir in tomato, water, and mint and bring to a boil. Reduce heat and simmer, covered, for 1 hour. Uncover and simmer for 20 minutes more, or until lamb is tender.

While stew is cooking, make relish. Toss onion with salt in a medium-size bowl. Let stand 30 minutes. Transfer onion to a colander and rinse well. Drain thoroughly and turn back into bowl. Stir in water, tomato paste, vinegar, paprika, lemon juice, sugar, ginger, cumin, and red pepper.

Serve stew with millet and relish.

SERVES 6.
CALORIES: 538   CHOLESTEROL: 156 mg   SODIUM: 892 mg   FIBER: 4g

Health tip:
Use 2 teaspoons oil instead of ghee and cook in a nonstick saucepan. Or, cook onion, garlic, and ginger in a nonstick skillet, transferring to the larger pan to finish cooking. Omit salt.
CALORIES: 521   CHOLESTEROL: 139 mg   SODIUM: 92 mg   FIBER: 4g

————— ◇ —————

California Salad

If you like avocado, you'll enjoy this summery salad that combines the creamy sweetness of avocado and corn with the tartness of lime juice, and the nubbiness of cooked millet.

1½ cups cooked millet (method II)
1 can (7 ounce) whole-kernel corn, drained
1 cup chopped celery
1 small avocado, diced (1 cup)
½ cup chopped red bell pepper
1 tablespoon finely chopped scallion, both white and green parts
2½ tablespoons fresh lime juice
1 tablespoon olive oil
1 tablespoon vegetable oil
¼ teaspoon grated lime rind
¼ teaspoon celery seed
¼ teaspoon salt
⅛ teaspoon ground red pepper

In a large bowl, gently toss the millet, corn, celery, avocado, red bell pepper, and scallion until well combined.

In a small bowl, stir together the lime juice, olive oil, lime rind, vegetable oil, celery seed, salt, and ground red pepper. Pour over millet mixture and toss gently until completely combined.

SERVES 8.
CALORIES: 105   CHOLESTEROL: 0 mg   SODIUM: 140 mg   FIBER: 3 g

Health tip:
Omit salt.
CALORIES: 105   CHOLESTEROL: 0 mg   SODIUM: 73 mg   FIBER: 3 g

Oriental Millet Salad

I like spicy food, and this recipe is mildly so. Experiment with the amount of chili oil or hot sesame oil. If you're not crazy about spicy food, use plain Oriental sesame oil. (All of these oils, and the rice vinegar, by the way, can be found in Oriental grocery stores.)

2 cups cooked and cooled millet (Method I)
1 cup mung bean sprouts
½ cup coarsely chopped snow peas (about 16)
½ cup chopped canned water chestnuts
¼ cup chopped green onion, both white and green parts
2 tablespoons vegetable oil
1½ tablespoons soy sauce
1 tablespoon smooth peanut butter
1 tablespoon rice vinegar or white vinegar
½ teaspoon (or to taste) chili oil or hot
    sesame oil (plain Oriental sesame oil may be substituted)
1 clove garlic, minced

In a medium-size bowl, toss together the millet, sprouts, snow peas, water chestnuts, and scallion.

In a small bowl, combine the oil, soy sauce, peanut butter, rice vinegar, chili oil, and garlic. Pour dressing over millet mixture and toss until completely combined.

SERVES 6.
CALORIES: 115   CHOLESTEROL: 0 mg   SODIUM: 350 mg   FIBER: 2 g

Health tip:
Use low-sodium soy sauce. Omit salt from millet.CALORIES: 115   CHOLESTEROL: 0 mg   SODIUM: 98 mg   FIBER: 2 g

———————◇———————

Lightly Curried Millet Salad

I was thrilled with the way this exciting blend of vegetables and spicy curry dressing tasted after I prefected it.

2 cups cooked millet (method I)
1 cup chopped tomato
½ cup chopped cucumber
½ cup chopped green bell pepper
¼ cup sliced scallion, both white and green parts
2 tablespoons vegetable oil
1 tablespoon cider vinegar
1 teaspoon curry powder
¼ teaspoon ground cinnamon
¼ teaspoon ground coriander
¼ teaspoon paprika
⅛ teaspoon salt
⅛ teaspoon ground red pepper, or black pepper for a milder taste

In a large bowl, toss together the millet, tomato, cucumber, green pepper, and green onion.

In a small bowl, stir together the oil, vinegar, curry powder, cinnamon, coriander, paprika, salt, and pepper. Toss with millet mixture until completely combined.

SERVES 6.
CALORIES: 98   CHOLESTEROL: 0 mg   SODIUM: 136 mg   FIBER: 2 g

Health tip:
Omit salt.
CALORIES: 98   CHOLESTEROL: 0 mg   SODIUM: 4 mg   FIBER: 2 g

———————◇———————

Italian Bean-and-Millet Salad

Beans and millet together make this a very satisfying salad, so that it can also be served as a meal by itself, as well as a side dish.

2 cups cooked and cooled millet (method I)
1 can (10½ ounce) cannellini (white kidney beans)
*   or red kidney beans, drained*
½ cup chopped red onion
½ cup sliced black olives

¼ cup chopped parsley
1 tablespoon chopped cilantro (fresh coriander)
3 tablespoons lemon juice
1 tablespoon vegetable oil
1 tablespoon olive oil

In a large bowl, gently toss together the millet, beans, onion, olives, parsley, and cilantro.

In a small bowl, stir together the lemon juice, vegetable oil, and olive oil. Toss with millet mixture until completely combined.

SERVES 6 (as a side dish).
CALORIES: 152 CHOLESTEROL: 0 mg SODIUM: 285 mg FIBER: 6 g

Health tip:
Omit olives; rinse canned beans, which will remove excess sodium.
CALORIES: 129 CHOLESTEROL: 0 mg SODIUM: 45 mg FIBER: 6 g

—— ◇ ——

Cheddar-Bacon Millet

The texture of this dish—dense, sticky, and cheesy—makes it a good choice to serve with eggs. A nice change from fried potatoes or grits.

3 slices bacon, cut into 1-inch pieces
½ cup millet
1 cup boiling water
2 cups shredded Cheddar cheese
¼ cup chopped scallion, both white and green parts

In a 2-quart saucepan, cook the bacon until crisp. Remove bacon and drain on paper towels.

Remove all but 1 tablespoon of the fat in the pan. Add millet and cook, stirring, until browned and making crackling noises. Stir in boiling water. Bring to a boil, reduce heat, and simmer for 30 minutes. Stir in cheese, scallion, and reserved bacon. Cook, stirring, until cheese is melted.

SERVES 4.
CALORIES: 381 CHOLESTEROL: 69 mg SODIUM: 562 mg FIBER: 4 g

Health tip:
This dish is hopeless. Try another side dish.

Autumn Casserole

Try this sweet blend of millet, squash, nuts, and cranberries with the holiday turkey or ham.

1 cup cooked millet (method I)
1 cup ½-inch-diced butternut squash
½ cup chopped walnuts
½ cup apple juice or cider
¼ cup cranberries
2 tablespoons honey
2 tablespoons dark-brown sugar
1 teaspoon ground cinnamon

Preheat oven to 350° F.

Combine the millet, squash, walnuts, apple juice, cranberries, honey, brown sugar, and cinnamon in a 1½-quart casserole. Cover and bake for 35 to 40 minutes, or until squash is soft.

SERVES 6.
CALORIES: 147   CHOLESTEROL: 0 mg   SODIUM: 49 mg   FIBER: 2 g

Health tip:
Use half the amounts of honey and sugar. Cook millet without salt.
CALORIES: 128   CHOLESTEROL: 0 mg   SODIUM: 4 mg   FIBER: 2 g

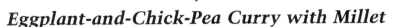

Eggplant-and-Chick-Pea Curry with Millet

Although I find this spicy curry delightful, if it's too hot for your taste, omit the ground red pepper.

3 tablespoons ghee (clarified butter) or vegetable oil
1½ cups chopped onion
2 large cloves garlic, minced
1½ tablespoons curry powder
1 teaspoon salt
½ teaspoon ground ginger
½ teaspoon ground turmeric
½ teaspoon ground cumin
½ teaspoon ground coriander
¼ teaspoon ground red pepper
1 large (about 1½ pounds) eggplant, unpeeled and cut into cubes
1 can (10½ ounce) chick-peas, undrained
2 medium tomatoes, diced
¾ cup water
¼ cup chutney, chopped
3 cups cooked millet (method I)

In a large heavy saucepan or Dutch oven, heat ghee over medium-high heat. Add onion and garlic and cook, stirring frequently, until softened. Stir in curry powder, salt, ginger, turmeric, cumin, coriander, and red pepper. Cook over low heat, stirring constantly, for 1 minute. Add eggplant, undrained chick-peas, and tomatoes, stirring until vegetables are coated with spices. Stir in water and bring to a boil. Lower heat and simmer for 40 minutes. Stir in chutney. Serve over millet.

SERVES 6.
CALORIES: 263   CHOLESTEROL: 17 mg   SODIUM: 501 mg   FIBER: 10 g

Health tip:
Use oil instead of ghee; omit salt.
CALORIES: 263   CHOLESTEROL: 0 mg   SODIUM: 14 mg   FIBER: 10 g

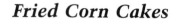

Fried Corn Cakes

Crunchy on the outside, creamy on the inside, these little cakes go nicely with a pot roast.

1 cup cooked millet (method II)
1 can (8¾ ounce) cream-style corn
1 egg, beaten
3 tablespoons flour
1 tablespoon sugar
¼ teaspoon salt
Oil, for frying

In a medium-size bowl, stir together the millet, corn, egg, flour, sugar, and salt until thoroughly combined.

Pour oil into a large skillet until it measures about ¼-inch deep. Heat the oil over medium-high heat until bubbles form when a drop of batter is put into the oil. Drop batter by heaping tablespoonsful into the hot oil. (These cakes spatter a lot while they're frying, so if you have a spatter shield, use it. Otherwise, be careful and stand back while you're frying.) Fry until browned on both sides. Drain on paper towels.

MAKES 12 CORN CAKES.
CALORIES: 81   CHOLESTEROL: 17 mg   SODIUM: 131 mg   FIBER: .5 g

Health tip:
Use scrambled-egg substitute instead of egg; omit salt.
CALORIES: 70   CHOLESTEROL: 0 mg   SODIUM: 67 mg   FIBER: .5 g

———————— ◇ ————————

Bruncheon Spoon Bread

I often serve this versatile casserole as a main dish for brunch or lunch with a salad. Other times I use it as an accompaniment for eggs. And I don't see why it couldn't be used as a replacement for a traditional turkey stuffing at Thanksgiving.

½ pound bulk breakfast sausage
¼ cup finely chopped onion
½ cup millet
1 cup boiling water
3 eggs, separated
1 cup shredded Vermont Cheddar cheese
1 can (4 ounce) chopped mild green chilies, drained
1 teaspoon baking powder

Preheat oven to 375°F.

Grease a 1½- or 2-quart casserole and set aside.

In a medium-size saucepan, cook the sausage over medium-high heat, stirring frequently, until it is no longer pink. Remove from skillet to a large bowl.

Pour off all but 2 tablespoons fat in the skillet. Add onion and millet and cook over medium-high heat until millet is browned and onion is softened. Add water and bring to a boil. Lower heat and simmer, covered, for 30 minutes, or until liquid is absorbed. Remove from heat.

In a medium-size bowl, beat egg yolks slightly. Beat in ½ cup of the millet mixture. Stir egg-yolk mixture back into pan with remaining millet mixture.

Add millet-and-egg mixture to cooked sausage, along with cheese and chilies. Stir until well combined. Stir in baking powder.

Beat egg whites in a clean, grease-free bowl with clean beaters until stiff peaks form when beaters are lifted. Stir one-quarter of the beaten egg whites into the sausage mixture. Fold in remaining egg whites. Spoon into prepared casserole.

Bake for about 45 minutes, or until top is golden. Serve immediately.

SERVES 6.
CALORIES: 291   CHOLESTEROL: 153 mg   SODIUM: 558 mg   FIBER: 3 g

Health tip:
Regular cornbread (see page 000) would probably be more healthful than this.

─────────◇─────────

Orange-Flavored Millet-Meal Bread

This bakes up into a large, impressive loaf. If you'd like to try the bread with a grain other than millet, substitute uncooked fine couscous, or even teff.

½ cup softened butter, divided
½ cup millet meal
3 cup all-purpose flour
1 teaspoon baking powder
1 teaspoon baking soda
1 teaspoon salt
1 cup sugar
2 eggs
½ cup orange juice
1 tablespoon grated orange rind
1 teaspoon vanilla extract
¾ cup milk

Preheat oven to 350°F.

Grease and flour a 9 × 5 × 3-inch loaf pan and set aside.

Melt 1 tablespoon of the butter in a medium-size skillet over medium-high heat. Add millet and cook, stirring, until lightly browned. Set aside.

In a medium-size bowl, stir together the flour, baking powder, baking soda, and salt and set aside.

In a large bowl, cream the remaining butter with sugar until light and fluffy. Beat in eggs, then orange juice, orange rind, and vanilla. Alternately beat in reserved flour mixture with milk until blended. Fold in reserved millet. Spoon into prepared loaf pan.

Bake for 1 hour, or until a wooden pick inserted in the center comes out clean. Cool on a wire rack before slicing.

MAKES 1 LOAF (16 slices).
CALORIES: 204   CHOLESTEROL: 43 mg   SODIUM: 276 mg   FIBER: 1 g

Health tip:
Substitute unsalted margarine for butter; omit salt.
CALORIES: 208   CHOLESTEROL: 27 mg   SODIUM: 93 mg   FIBER: 1 g

OATS
(Avena)

Oats are the only one of the so-called minor grains that are generally incorporated into everyday eating patterns in the American home. But, popular as oats may be for breakfast and for cookies, the bulk of the crop still goes to feed horses and other livestock.

Oats thrive in harsher climates, so it's not surprising that they are a staple in Ireland and Scotland. They are valued for their high nutrition profile and their filling and warming qualities.

Although this grain has always been a great favorite in the United States, what we know today about the health benefits derived from eating oat bran makes oats more popular than ever.

Types of Oats Available

Oat groats: The whole oat grain with the husk removed. It is suitable for use in salads, stews, and baked products, and is similar in size and shape to long-grain rice.

Irish or Scottish oats: Oat groats, sometimes toasted, that have been cut with steel blades into small pieces, and are often called steel-cut oats. Like rolled oats, they are used to make porridge (better known as oatmeal), but take longer to cook.

Rolled oats: The Quaker Oats Company has been calling this product "old-fashioned oats" for so many years, that the term is practically generic. Rolled oats are groats that have been steamed and rolled flat.

Quick-cooking rolled oats: Oat groats that have been steamed, rolled and then cut into pieces. They take less time to cook than the regular variety.

Oat flakes: Rolled oats, which have been steamed and then put through rollers to flatten them. They are similar to rolled oats, but the flakes are slightly thicker and require a longer cooking time, though not as long as Irish or Scottish oats.

Instant oatmeal: Oats that have been partially cooked and dried before being rolled. This cereal product does not require cooking, but is hydrated by letting it stand in boiling water until it is brought

275

to the familiar oatmeal consistency. Flavored instant oatmeal is also available. In my opinion, instant oatmeal is not a satisfactory recipe ingredient.

Oat bran: This is the highly touted outer covering of the hulled oat that is credited with being able to lower blood-cholesterol levels. (All oat products, except some oat flour, contain *some* oat bran.)

Oat flour: The whole oat or just the endosperm that has been ground. Although this product is readily available in health-food stores, it is also very simple to make at home. For each cup of oat flour, place 1¼ cups oatmeal (either regular or quick-cooking, but not instant since this contains ingredients other than just oats) in the container of an electric blender or food processor. Cover and process until all the large pieces have been reduced to flour. This flour will be slightly coarser than the flour you can buy, but it will be very fresh and you can make just what you need. *All the recipes in this chapter calling for oat flour were made with homemade flour, according to the directions above.*

Texture and Flavor

Oats come in many different forms, and each will give you a slightly different texture. Cooked oat groats (whole-grain oats with only the husk removed) are similar in size and shape to pignoli (pine nuts). Its color is a pale, yellow-beige.

Cooked groats are chewy, with individual grains that have a slightly starchy mouth feel. Although expected and pleasant in hot cereal, this starchiness is not desirable in salads, and can be removed by rinsing the cooked grains before they are mixed with other ingredients. But remember that in doing so you will also be sacrificing some of the B vitamins, which are water soluble.

The flavor of the oat groat is very delicate and mild, bordering on naturally sweet and definitely pleasant. The flavor is not at all "oatmealy." In fact, blindfolded, you might guess that you were eating brown rice, especially if the oats were rinsed.

If you like oatmeal, you will undoubtedly be thrilled with the Irish or Scottish variety, which is sometimes toasted before it is packaged, and cooks into a lovely thick porridge with a robust flavor.

All forms of oatmeal and oat flakes are basically grey-white in color and are thinly rolled. Oat flakes are somewhat thicker than oatmeal, and regular oatmeal is less broken up than the quick-cooking or instant varieties. Instant oatmeal often has salt (sodium-watchers beware) and wheat germ added. Flavored instant oatmeal also contains sugar, salt, and a variety of other flavoring agents. Check the list of ingredients on the package.

Irish oatmeal, oat flakes, and various other oatmeals have a distinctly starchy texture and a soft consistency. They all have a nutty delicate flavor.

Compatible Foods, Herbs, and Spices

The mild flavor of the oat groat makes this a grain that is compatible with any flavor. It goes well with all kinds of meat, vegetables, nuts, dairy products, and virtually any seasoning.

In America, oatmeal is traditionally used in sweetened dishes—especially cookies and streusel toppings—and is frequently coupled with milk.

Availability

Oat groats and oat flakes are available in health-food stores and through mail-order grain catalogs (see page 21).

Regular rolled oats, quick-cooking rolled oats and instant oatmeal are all available at the supermarket in the breakfast-cereals section.

Irish steel-cut oats are now in some supermarkets, and always in health-food stores, gourmet stores, and through mail-order grain catalogs.

You can find oat bran in some supermarkets, health-food stores, and grain catalogs.

Oat flour is available in health-food stores and through catalogs, and can also be easily made at home in a blender or food processor (see under Types of Oats Available).

Nutritional Content

The most exceptional nutritional advantage of oats has to do with the current findings that oat bran can lower LDL blood-cholesterol of levels. There are at least two kinds of cholesterol: high-density lipoprotein (HDL cholesterol), which is the good kind and acts like a magnet to prevent cholesterol from sticking to the walls of the arteries; and low-density lipoprotein (LDL cholesterol), which is the kind that sticks to your arteries and causes trouble.

More good news is that ALL oat products contain some bran. Oats are one of the few grains from which the bran and germ are not removed during processing. Naturally, you will need less pure oat bran (about ⅔ cup cooked oat bran per day) than oatmeal (about 2 cups cooked oatmeal per day) to achieve any significant cholesterol-lowering effects. And, of course, a healthier cardiovascular system will also depend upon your other eating habits (less saturated fat, the kind that is found in eggs, dairy products, meat, and many prepared foods) and regular exercise.

Lately oat bran is being incorporated into many commercial products, such as cookies, muffins, breakfast cereals, and breads. However, always read the ingredient list of every packaged food you buy to make sure that cholesterol-raising ingredients, such as hydrogenated or tropical (palm and coconut) oils are not also present, or only in limited amounts. (Ingredients, you know, must be listed in the order of their importance.)

Warning: Before you hasten into the kitchen, remember that introducing large portions of oat bran into your diet all at once can lead to severe digestive-tract disturbances, and although they are far from life threatening, can be very uncomfortable. Start your oat bran intake gradually, so that your body can become accustomed to it.

With the exception of the newly introduced super-grains, such as quinoa and amaranth, oatmeal is the grain leader in protein content. It also has good quantities of B vitamins, vitamin E, iron, calcium, and phosphorous.

Home Remedy

Uncooked oatmeal is an excellent remedy for acid indigestion. Start with a teaspoonful or so, and chew it slowly.

Substitutions

You can always used regular rolled oats and quick-cooking rolled oats interchangeably.

Brown rice: Its flavor and consistency make this a very satisfactory substitute in any recipe calling for cooked groats.

Bulgur: The flavor is comparable to oat groats, but the consistency is less chewy, and cooking times will vary greatly. Used cooked bulgur when cooked oats are called for, but not in recipes calling for uncooked groats.

Barley: The texture is similar to oat groats, but the flavor is slightly stronger.

Whole-wheat flour: May be substituted for oat flour.

Wheat, corn or rice bran: Can be substituted for oat bran, but remember that wheat bran does not have the beneficial cholesterol-lowering qualities of oat bran.

Other acceptable substitutes (in order of preference): Wild rice, white rice, wheat berries, triticale berries, and rye berries.

Basic Cooking Instructions

Please read *About Cooking Grains* beginning on page 7. For a richer-tasting cereal but not groats, substitute half of the water with milk.

The microwave methods that follow for cooking oats were tested in a 650-watt oven.

———————— ◇ ————————

Oat Groats

Stove-top method:

> *2 cups water*
> *½ teaspoon salt*
> *1 cup oat groats, rinsed*

In a 2-quart saucepan, bring the water and salt to a boil over high heat. Stir in groats and return to boiling. Reduce heat and simmer, covered, for 1 hour, or until almost all of the liquid has been absorbed. Remove from heat and let stand for 10 minutes. Fluff with a fork.

MAKES 2½ CUPS.

NOTE: You can reduce the water to 1¾ cups and the cooking time to 55 minutes for a chewier, less starchy grain.

Microwave method:

> *3 cups water*
> *1 cup oat groats, rinsed*
> *½ teaspoon salt*

Place the water in a 3-quart, microwave-safe bowl Cover with waxed paper and microwave on high (100% power) for 5 minutes. Stir in groats. Recover with waxed paper and microwave on high for 4 minutes. Microwave on medium (50% power), still covered with waxed paper, for 1 hour, rotating dish once, if necessary. Let stand 5 minutes. Stir in salt and fluff with a fork.

MAKES 2¾ CUPS.

———————— ◇ ————————

Irish Oatmeal

Stove-top method:

> *3 cups water*
> *½ teaspoon salt*
> *1 cup Irish oatmeal*

In a 2-quart saucepan, bring the water and salt to a boil over high heat. Stir in oatmeal and return to boiling. Reduce heat and simmer, uncovered, for 1½ hours.

MAKES 3 CUPS.

Microwave method:

> *3½ cups water*
> *1 teaspoon salt*
> *1 cup Irish oatmeal*

Place the water and salt in a 3-quart, microwave-safe bowl. Cover with waxed paper and microwave on high (100% power) for 5 minutes. Stir in oats. Recover with waxed paper and microwave on high for 4 minutes. Microwave on medium (50% power), still covered with waxed paper, for 20 minutes. Stir and let stand for 3 minutes.

MAKES 3½ CUPS.

Oat Flakes

Stove-top method:

> 2 cups water
> ¼ teaspoon salt
> 1 cup oat flakes

In a 1½-quart saucepan, bring the water and salt to a boil. Stir in oat flakes and return to boiling. Reduce heat and simmer, covered, for 15 minutes. Remove from heat and let stand 5 minutes.

MAKES 2½ CUPS.

Microwave method:

> 1¾ cups water
> ¼ teaspoon salt
> 1 cup oat flakes

Place the water in a 3-quart, microwave-safe bowl. Cover with waxed paper and microwave on high (100% power) for 4 minutes. Stir in salt and oat flakes. Recover with waxed paper and microwave on high for 3 minutes. Microwave on medium (50% power), still covered with waxed paper, for 8 minutes. Let stand 4 minutes. Stir well.

MAKES 2¼ CUPS.

Regular Rolled Oats

Stove-top method:

> 2¼ cups water
> ¼ teaspoon salt
> 1 cup old-fashioned rolled oats

In a 1½-quart saucepan, bring the water and salt to a boil. Stir in oats and return to boiling. Reduce heat and simmer, uncovered, for 7 minutes, stirring occasionally.

MAKES 1½ CUPS.

Microwave method:

>2 cups water
>¼ teaspoon salt
>1 cup old-fashioned rolled oats

Place water in a 3-quart, microwave-safe bowl. Cover with waxed paper and microwave on high (100% power) for 3 minutes. Stir in salt and oats. Recover with waxed paper and microwave on medium (50% power) for 5 minutes.

MAKES 1¼ CUPS.

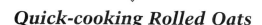

Quick-cooking Rolled Oats

Stove-top method:

>2 cups water
>¼ teaspoon salt
>1 cup quick-cooking rolled oats

In a 1½-quart saucepan, bring water and salt to a boil. Stir in oats and return to boiling. Reduce heat and simmer, uncovered, for 2 minutes, stirring almost constantly.

MAKES 1¼ CUPS.

Microwave method:

>2 cups water
>¼ teaspoon salt
>1 cup quick-cooking rolled oats

Place water in a 2-quart, microwave-safe bowl. Cover with waxed paper and microwave on high (100% power) for 3 minutes. Stir in salt and oatmeal. Recover with waxed paper and microwave on high for 1 minute.

MAKES 1¼ CUPS.

Reheating

Oats do not have to be reheated for use in salads and other recipes calling for cooked oats. They can be reheated by microwaving or steaming, if desired.

OATS RECIPES

(* Indicates easy recipe.)

———————— ◇ ————————

Oatsy Stuffed Mushrooms *
Creamy Cauliflower-and-Oats Soup *
Oats-Lentil-and-Chicken Soup
Roast and Groats
Veal, Chicken, or Turkey-Oats Schnitzel *
Oats and Kielbasa *
Spinach, Oats, and Turkey Loaf *
Spicy Oven-Baked Chicken *
Oats-and-Sardine Salad *
Crunchy Sprouts Salad *
Groats and Kidney Beans *
Pignoli-Oats Salad *
West Coast Pear-Watercress-and-Oats Salad *
Zucchini and Oat Groats *
Oats and Black Beans *
The World's Most Perfect Oatmeal *
Homemade Granola *
Extra-Good Oatmeal Pancakes *
Gingerbread Waffles
Bannocks *
Oatcakes *
Honey-Topped Biscuits *
Oat-Bran Muffins *
Betty-the-Baker's Oat-Bran Bread
Winter-Squash Bread
Irish-Oatmeal Soda Bread
Oatmeal Toasting Bread
Crunchy Irish-Oats Bread
Apple-Pear-Cranberry Crumble *
Bernice's Garbage
Oatmeal Brownies *
Prune-Filled Bar Cookies *
Giant Raisin-Oatmeal Cookies *
Plum Crumb Cake *

———————— ◇ ————————

Oatsy Stuffed Mushrooms

These are a nice accompaniment for broiled steaks or chops.
And they are wonderful as a hot appetizer.

18 medium mushrooms (about 12 ounces)
2 tablespoons butter
1 tablespoon minced shallot or the white part of scallion
1 tablespoon chopped parsley
⅛ teaspoon crumbled thyme
⅛ teaspoon salt
⅛ teaspoon pepper
1 tablespoon quick-cooking rolled oats
1 tablespoon oat bran

Preheat broiler.

Rinse the mushrooms briefly and pat dry on paper towels.
Remove stems from caps. Chop stems and set aside.

Melt 1 tablespoon of the butter in a medium-size skillet and
use to lightly brush mushroom caps. Set aside.

Add remaining 1 tablespoon butter to skillet. Add shallot and
cook over medium-high heat, stirring, until softened. Add reserved
chopped stems and cook over high heat, stirring and tossing, until
soft. Remove from heat and stir in parsley, thyme, salt, and pepper.
Stir in oats and oat bran.

Fill each mushroom cap with oats mixture. Place on broiler
pan. Broil mushrooms for about 5 minutes, or until browned. Serve
immediately.

MAKES 18 STUFFED CAPS.
CALORIES: 18   CHOLESTEROL: 3 mg   SODIUM: 26 mg   FIBER: 1 g

Health tip:
Use unsalted margarine instead of butter; omit salt.
CALORIES: 18   CHOLESTEROL: 0 mg   SODIUM: 2 mg   FIBER: 1 g

———————— ◇ ————————

Creamy Cauliflower-and-Oats Soup

I could eat this soup every day and never tire of it. It tastes very rich, but actually it's not, since it's pureed cauliflower and oats that give the soup its delightful creamy consistency.

1 tablespoon butter
1 cup sliced leek, both white and green parts
2 cups water
1 can (13¾ ounce) ready-to-serve chicken broth or
   1¾ cups vegetable broth (see page 19)
4 cups cauliflower florets
⅓ cup quick-cooking rolled oats
½ teaspoon salt
⅛ teaspoon ground red pepper
½ cup buttermilk

In a large saucepan, melt the butter over medium-high heat. Add leek and cook, stirring, until tender. Stir in water and chicken broth. Bring to a boil. Add florets, oatmeal, salt, and red pepper and return to boiling. Lower heat and simmer, covered, for 45 minutes. Remove from heat and set aside to cool slightly.

Measure 2 cups of the soup mixture into the container of a blender or food processor. Cover and process until smooth. Transfer to a large bowl. Continue processing, 2 cups at a time, until all of the mixture is pureed. Add the buttermilk. Reheat soup and serve immediately. Or chill the soup and serve it cold, but in that case you may have to add a little more salt, and possibly more red pepper, since chilling dulls flavors.

SERVES 6.
CALORIES: 80   CHOLESTEROL: 6 mg   SODIUM: 434 mg   FIBER: 2 g

Health tip:
Use low-sodium broth or water; omit salt.
CALORIES: 80   CHOLESTEROL: 6 mg   SODIUM: 50 mg   FIBER: 2 g

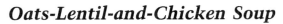

Oats-Lentil-and-Chicken Soup

If you serve this soup with the chicken in it, it becomes a whole meal. Or serve the soup as a first course and the chicken as part of the main course. Either way, this is a thick soup, so you may want to add a little more water, especially if you reheat any leftovers. By the way, turnip adds incredibly good flavor to a soup or stew, so don't be tempted to leave it out if you don't happen to have one or two in the crisper.

12 cups water, divided
3½ pound chicken, cut into quarters
2 cups shredded cabbage
1 cup chopped onion
1 cup diced carrot
1 cup diced turnip
1 cup lentils, rinsed and picked over
1 cup oat groats
¼ cup chopped parsley
1 teaspoon dried dill weed
1 teaspoon salt
⅛ teaspoon pepper

Place 10 cups of the water and chicken in a large soup pot. Bring to a boil over high heat. Reduce heat and simmer, uncovered, for 1 hour. Add cabbage, onion, carrot, turnip, lentils, and groats. Simmer, uncovered, for 45 minutes longer.

Remove chicken from pot and set aside. Stir in the remaining 2 cups water, parsley, dill, salt, and pepper. Simmer, uncovered, for 40 minutes. Reheat chicken in the soup, or remove it and serve as part of the main course.

SERVES 8.
CALORIES: 296   CHOLESTEROL: 43 mg   SODIUM: 327 mg   FIBER: 6 g

Health tip:
Remove skin before cooking chicken; omit salt.
CALORIES: 230   CHOLESTEROL: 23 mg   SODIUM: 238 mg   FIBER: 6 g

Roast and Groats

After the groats have cooked in this stew they are so full of flavor that they could convert a so-called grain-hater after the first bite. If you like, you can drain the extra liquid from the groats and serve it on the side like gravy.

1 tablespoon vegetable oil
1 cup chopped onion
1 can (14½ ounce) whole peeled tomatoes, undrained
1 can (12 ounce) beer
½ cup water
1 bay leaf
¼ teaspoon salt
⅛ teaspoon pepper
2½ to 2¾ pounds top round or chuck pot roast
1 cup oat groats

Heat oil in a large heavy saucepan or Dutch oven over medium-high heat. Add onion and cook, stirring, until softened. Stir in tomatoes, beer, water, bay leaf, salt, and pepper. Place beef in pot, spooning tomato mixture over top. Cover and simmer for 1½ hours. Add groats and continue to simmer, covered, for 1 hour longer. Discard bay leaf before serving.

SERVES 4.
CALORIES: 418   CHOLESTEROL: 91 mg   SODIUM: 573 mg   FIBER: 3 g

Health tip:
Omit salt.
CALORIES: 418   CHOLESTEROL: 91 mg   SODIUM: 229 mg   FIBER 3 g

———————— ◇ ————————

Veal, Chicken, or Turkey Schnitzel

Oat bran gives extra crunchiness to the breading on this schnitzel. Do the breading in advance, if that's more convenient, and refrigerate until cooking time. You can turn this into a veal, chicken, or turkey Parmesan by topping cooked schnitzels with tomato sauce and mozzarella cheese, and then baking in a 350°F. oven for 10 to 15 minutes, or until cheese has melted.

⅔ cup dry unflavored bread crumbs
⅓ cup oat bran
⅓ cup all-purpose flour
½ teaspoon salt
⅛ teaspoon pepper
3 egg whites
1¼ pounds veal, chicken, or turkey scallops, pounded thin
Oil, for frying

Combine the bread crumbs and oat bran on a piece of waxed paper. On another piece of waxed paper, combine flour, salt, and pepper.

Beat egg whites slightly in a wide shallow dish or pie plate. Dip both sides of each scallop into flour mixture, then into egg whites, then into crumb mixture, patting the crumbs on gently to help them adhere. Chill for 15 minutes, which helps to keep the coating in place.

Add enough oil to a large skillet to measure about ⅛-inch. Heat over medium-high heat until oil bubbles when some of the bread crumbs are sprinkled on it. Reduce heat slightly and cook scallops until browned on both sides.

SERVES 4. (nutritional values for veal)
CALORIES: 448   CHOLESTEROL: 195 mg   SODIUM: 415 mg   FIBER: 3 g

Health tip:
Omit salt.
CALORIES: 448   CHOLESTEROL: 195 mg   SODIUM: 281 mg   FIBER: 3 g

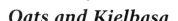

Oats and Kielbasa

This is one of those rare oats recipes not recommended for those who are concerned with lowering either their cholesterol or blood pressure. But it's good!

1 tablespoon vegetable oil
½ pound kielbasa (Polish sausage), chopped
¾ cup chopped onion
¾ cup chopped green bell pepper
¼ teaspoon crumbled thyme
2 cups cooked oat groats

In a large skillet, heat oil over medium-high heat. Add kielbasa, onion, bell pepper, and thyme. Cook, stirring frequently, until vegetables are softened. Add oats and cook, stirring, until heated through.

SERVES 4.

CALORIES: 263　CHOLESTEROL: 37 mg　SODIUM: 720 mg　FIBER: 3 g

Health tip:
Unfortunately, this is about as healthy as this recipe gets.

Spinach, Oats, and Turkey Loaf

It's the pesto sauce (that wonderful blend of fresh basil, pine nuts, oil, and garlic) that gives this loaf its fine flavor and moistness. You can make you own pesto (following the recipe on page 60) or you can buy it in the tomato-sauce section or refrigerator case at the supermarket. In order to keep the cholesterol count low, make sure that the ground turkey that you buy is low in fat, or grind your own in the food processor.

1 pound ground turkey
1 package (10 ounce) frozen chopped spinach, thawed and squeezed dry
⅓ cup quick-cooking rolled oats
¼ cup pesto sauce
2 tablespoons water
2 tablespoons oat bran
½ teaspoon salt
¼ teaspoon pepper

Preheat oven to 350°F.

In a medium-size bowl, combine the turkey, spinach, oats, pesto sauce, water, oat bran, salt, and pepper.

Shape turkey mixture into a loaf measuring about 8 × 4 inches in a baking pan. Or press into an 8 × 4-inch loaf pan. Bake for 1 hour, or until cooked through.

SERVES 4.

CALORIES: 305   CHOLESTEROL: 87 mg   SODIUM: 408 mg   FIBER: 3 g

Health tip:
Omit salt.

CALORIES: 305   CHOLESTEROL: 87 mg   SODIUM: 142 mg   FIBER: 3 g

――――――◇――――――

Spicy Oven-Baked Chicken

I like those little cheese-flavored fish-shaped crackers in my chicken coating, but you can use any cracker you happen to have around. This is a particularly nice work-day company dish. Prepare the chicken early in the day and then refrigerate it until baking time. Serve with a salad and maybe bread or rolls, an easy dessert, and that's it.

¼ cup sour cream
¼ cup mayonnaise
1 tablespoon liquid red pepper
1 tablespoon Worcestershire (Tabasco) sauce
½ teaspoon ground cumin
1 clove garlic, minced
1⅓ cups Cheddar-flavored fish-shaped crackers
½ cup oat bran
¼ teaspoon ground red pepper (optional)
3-pound chicken, cut into 8 parts, skinned

Preheat oven to 400°F.

Lightly grease a shallow baking pan that is just large enough to hold the chicken comfortably and set aside.

In a small bowl, stir together the sour cream, mayonnaise, liquid red pepper, Worcestershire sauce, cumin, and garlic. Set aside.

Place crackers in a 1-gallon plastic bag and finely crush with a rolling pin. Add oat bran and red pepper, if using, to bag. Shake until completely combined.

Liberally brush the chicken with sour-cream mixture. Place chicken pieces, one or two at a time, in the bag with the crumb mixture. Shake to coat completely. Place chicken pieces in prepared pan.

Bake for 40 to 45 minutes (a little longer if chicken has been refrigerated), or until browned and cooked through.

SERVES 4.
CALORIES: 680   CHOLESTEROL: 48 mg   SODIUM: 743 mg   FIBER: 2 g

Health tip:
Substitute plain yogurt for sour cream; use reduced-calorie mayonnaise.
CALORIES: 650   CHOLESTEROL: 40 mg   SODIUM: 743 mg   FIBER: 2 g

—————— ◇ ——————

Oats-and-Sardine Salad

Truthfully, I'm not all that wild about sardines, but I do like this salad—especially when I think how good it is for me. In addition to the well-known health benefits of oat groats, the sardines contain huge amounts of calcium (if you eat the tender little bones), and Omega-3 fatty acids that are now believed to protect against heart disease.

1 cup cooked oat groats, rinsed to remove any starchiness
½ cup chopped tomato
⅓ cup chopped cucumber
3 tablespoons chopped red onion
1½ tablespoons vegetable oil
1 tablespoon lemon juice
Lettuce leaves
1 can (3½ ounce) whole Maine or Norwegian sardines, drained

In a medium-size bowl, toss together the oats, tomato, cucumber, onion, oil, and lemon juice.

Line two luncheon plates with lettuce leaves. Top each with half of the oats mixture, then half of the sardines.

SERVES 2.
CALORIES: 301   CHOLESTEROL: 66 mg   SODIUM: 366 mg   FIBER: 3 g

Health tip:
Use sardines packed in water. Omit salt from oats.
CALORIES: 270   CHOLESTEROL: 60 mg   SODIUM: 215 mg   FIBER: 3 g

—— ◇ ——

Crunchy Sprouts Salad

Crunchy sprouts are simply beans that are sprouted, a combination of lentil sprouts, azuki-bean sprouts, and sweet-pea sprouts. You can find them in the produce section of a health-food store and sometimes at the supermarket. Other sprouts may be substituted.

1½ cups cooked oat groats, rinsed to remove any starchiness
1 package (3½ ounce) crunchy sprouts
½ cup chopped red bell pepper
½ cup chopped celery
¼ cup chopped scallion, both white and green parts
2 tablespoon chopped parsley
2 tablespoons vegetable oil
1½ tablespoon cider vinegar
¼ teaspoon salt
⅛ teaspoon pepper

In a medium-size bowl, gently toss the oats, sprouts, red bell pepper, celery, scallion, and parsley.
In a small bowl, stir together the oil, vinegar, salt, and pepper. Pour over salad ingredients and toss gently until well combined.

SERVES 6.
CALORIES: 154   CHOLESTEROL: 0 mg   SODIUM: 206 mg   FIBER: 2 g

Health tip:
Omit salt and use half the oil and half the vinegar in the dressing.
CALORIES: 144   CHOLESTEROL: 0 mg   SODIUM: 11 mg   FIBER: 2 g

—— ◇ ——

Groats and Kidney Beans

Because it contains oat groats, kidney beans, and cheese, this salad is packed with nutrition. (Vegetarians who do not eat cheese should simply leave it out.)

1 can (10½ ounce) kidney beans, drained
1 cup cooked oat groats, rinsed to remove any starchiness
½ cup diced Monterey Jack cheese
¼ cup sliced scallion, both white and green parts
¼ cup chopped mild green chilies (from a 4-ounce can)
3 tablespoons oil

1 tablespoon red-wine vinegar
½ clove garlic, minced
¼ teaspoon crumbled oregano

In a large bowl, gently toss together the kidney beans, oats, cheese, scallion, and chilies.

In a small bowl, stir together the oil, vinegar, garlic, and oregano. Pour over salad ingredients and toss gently until well combined.

SERVES 4.
CALORIES: 301   CHOLESTEROL: 26 mg   SODIUM: 698 mg   FIBER: 8 g

Health tip:
Omit cheese and cut dressing ingredients in half.
CALORIES: 195   CHOLESTEROL: 0 mg   SODIUM: 371 mg   FIBER: 8 g

——————— ◇ ———————

Pignoli-Oats Salad

Pignoli in case you're wondering, means pine nuts in Italian. Despite the ease of preparation, this salad draws raves in any language. The pine nuts look so much like cooked oat groats that you wouldn't know they were in the salad until you bit into one. Nice surprise.

2 cups cooked oat groats, rinsed to remove any starchiness
1½ cups chopped tomato
¼ cup sliced scallion, both white and green parts
¼ cup pignoli, raw or toasted (cook in a dry skillet, stirring, until they
    smell toasted)
2 tablespoons chopped parsley
1 tablespoon olive oil
1 tablespoon vegetable oil
1 tablespoon white-wine vinegar with shallots (or without shallots)

In a large bowl, toss together the oats, tomato, scallion, pignoli, and parsley.

In a small bowl, stir together the olive oil, vegetable oil, and vinegar. Pour over salad ingredients and toss until well combined.

SERVES 6.
CALORIES: 165   CHOLESTEROL: 0 mg   SODIUM: 74 mg   FIBER: 2 g

Health tip:
Use half the dressing ingredients.
CALORIES: 145   CHOLESTEROL: 0 mg   SODIUM: 3 mg   FIBER: 2 g

West Coast Pear-Watercress-and-Oats Salad

In true California style, this salad is a delightful mixture of fruits, nuts, vegetables, and, of course, grain—all good for you.

1½ cups cooked oat groats, rinsed to remove any starchiness
1 cup chopped fresh or canned pear
½ cup chopped walnuts
¼ cup chopped red onion
¼ cup orange juice
2 tablespoons olive oil
1 tablespoon balsamic vinegar
1 tablespoon lemon juice
2 teaspoons honey mustard
¼ teaspoon salt
⅛ teaspoon pepper
2 cups watercress (remove any tough stems)
1 head Belgian endive, cut into 1-inch pieces

In a large bowl, gently toss together the oats, pear, walnuts, and onion.

In a small bowl, stir together the orange juice, oil, vinegar, lemon juice, honey mustard, salt, and pepper until thoroughly mixed. Pour over oats mixture and gently toss until well combined.

Combine watercress and endive on a serving platter. Top with salad mixture.

SERVES 4.
CALORIES: 229   CHOLESTEROL: 0 mg   SODIUM: 339 mg   FIBER: 4g
Health tip:
Omit salt.
CALORIES: 229   CHOLESTEROL: 0 mg   SODIUM: 46 mg   FIBER: 4 g

◇

Zucchini and Oat Groats

Substitute yellow squash for all or part of the zucchini, if you like.

2 tablespoons vegetable oil
½ cup chopped onion
1 can (13¾ ounce) ready-to-serve chicken broth or
    1¾ cups vegetable broth (see page 19)
1 cup oat groats
2 cups chopped zucchini
¼ cup chopped parsley
¼ teaspoon pepper

In a 2-quart saucepan, heat the oil over medium-high heat. Add onion and cook, stirring frequently, until softened. Stir in broth and bring to a boil. Stir in oats. Cover and simmer for 45 minutes. Stir in zucchini, parsley, and pepper. Cover and simmer for 7 minutes longer, or until zucchini is tender-crisp.

SERVES 6.
CALORIES: 147   CHOLESTEROL: 0 mg   SODIUM: 208 mg   FIBER: 2 g

Health tip:
Use water or low-sodium broth.
CALORIES: 147   CHOLESTEROL: 0 mg   SODIUM: 20 mg   FIBER: 2 g

——————— ◇ ———————

Oats and Black Beans

This is a variation of a popular dish served throughout Latin America. Rice, not oat groats, is the usual grain combined with the beans, but because the oats have a consistency similar to rice, and a greater nutritional value, I tried substituting oat groats in this recipe and it worked beautifully.

¾ cup water
½ cup oat groats
1 can (15 ounce) Cuban black bean soup (Goya brand)
1 clove garlic, minced
1 bay leaf
½ teaspoon ground cumin
½ teaspoon salt
¼ teaspoon crumbled oregano
⅛ teaspoon ground red pepper
½ cup chopped onion
¼ cup chopped parsley

In a 1½–2-quart saucepan, bring the water to a boil. Stir in oats and return to boiling. Reduce heat, cover, and simmer for 30 minutes. Stir in bean soup, garlic, bay leaf, cumin, salt, oregano, and red pepper. Cover and simmer 20 to 25 minutes longer, or until most of the liquid has been absorbed. Remove bay leaf.

In a small bowl, stir together onion and parsley. Serve over oats and beans, to be stirred in just before eating.

SERVES 6.

CALORIES: 94   CHOLESTEROL: 0 mg   SODIUM: 545 mg   FIBER: 2 g

Health tip:
Omit salt.

CALORIES: 94   CHOLESTEROL: 0 mg   SODIUM: 367 mg   FIBER: 2 g

The World's Most Perfect Oatmeal

To me (and a lot of other people, I suppose) this means that rich creamy cereal that Mother would prepare when I was feeling ill. If you like a firmer oatmeal, reduce the water by ¼ cup.

1½ cups water
1½ cups milk
1 teaspoon salt
1⅓ cups regular rolled oats
2 tablespoons butter
½ cup half-and-half

In a medium-size saucepan, stir together water, milk, and salt. Stir in oats. Set over medium heat and bring to a boil, stirring occasionally. Reduce heat and simmer for 3 minutes. Remove from heat and let stand for 3 minutes.

At this point you have some choices. You can stir in the butter and half-and-half, or you can serve the cereal topped with butter and half-and-half.

SERVES 4.
CALORIES: 250   CHOLESTEROL: 39 mg   SODIUM: 639 mg   FIBER: 3 g

Health tip:
Omit salt, butter, and half-and-half—but then the oatmeal is not so perfect anymore.
CALORIES: 225   CHOLESTEROL: 13 mg   SODIUM: 67 mg   FIBER: 3 g

Homemade Granola

This homemade version of granola is every bit as good (and probably better) than any you can buy, even in a health-food store. Vary the recipe to suit your own taste. For instance: Use any nut instead of almonds; replace sunflower seeds with pumpkin seeds; omit sesame seeds; stir in as much or as many varieties of chopped dried fruit as you like.

¼ cup butter
3 tablespoons dark-brown sugar
2 tablespoons honey
2 cups regular rolled oats
½ cup chopped almonds
½ cup sunflower seeds
2 tablespoons sesame seeds
½ cup wheat germ
½ cup chopped dates

Preheat oven to 350°F.

Place butter in a 9 × 13-inch baking dish. Place baking dish in oven for 5 minutes to melt butter. Stir in brown sugar and honey until well mixed. Stir in oats, almonds, sunflower seeds, and sesame seeds. Bake for 15 minutes, stirring twice. Stir in wheat germ. Bake for 10 minutes longer, stirring once. Remove from oven and stir in dates. Cool and store in an air-tight container.

SERVES 12.
CALORIES: 238   CHOLESTEROL: 10 mg   SODIUM: 37 mg   FIBER: 5 g

Health tip:
Use unsalted margarine for butter.
CALORIES: 231   CHOLESTEROL: 0 mg   SODIUM: 8 mg   FIBER: 5 g

Extra-Good Oatmeal Pancakes

These pancakes are just about perfect: moist and satisfying with just the right combination of sweetness and saltiness. If you feel like boosting their dietary-fiber content, stir a little oat bran into the batter.

1 cup oat flour
1 cup all-purpose flour
3 tablespoons sugar
1 tablespoon baking powder
1 teaspoon salt
2 eggs
1¾ cups milk
⅓ cup butter, melted
Additional butter

In a large bowl, stir together both kinds of flour, sugar, baking powder, and salt.

In a medium-size bowl, beat the eggs. Beat in milk and butter. Stir egg mixture into flour mixture just until blended. Do not overbeat. The batter should be slightly lumpy.

Heat a large skillet over medium-high heat until a few drops of water sprinkled in the hot skillet bounce about before evaporating. Brush skillet lightly with melted butter. Pour ¼ cup batter for each pancake onto skillet. Cook until bubbles break on top of pancakes. Turn with a wide spatula and cook until second side is browned.

SERVES 6 TO 8.
CALORIES: 249   CHOLESTEROL: 91 mg   SODIUM: 569 mg   FIBER: 2 g

Health tip:
Omit salt; substitute scrambled-egg substitute for eggs; use 1-percent milk instead of whole milk; use unsalted margarine instead of butter.
CALORIES: 230   CHOLESTEROL: 26 mg   SODIUM: 275 mg   FIBER: 2 g

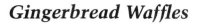

Gingerbread Waffles

One of these crisp little waffles for breakfast is filling enough to keep you going till lunch. They also freeze well and can be reheated in a toaster or microwave oven.

1 cup all-purpose flour
¾ cup oat flour
⅓ cup oat bran
⅓ cup sugar
1 tablespoon baking powder
2 teaspoons ground ginger
1 teaspoon ground cinnamon
½ teaspoon ground cloves
½ teaspoon salt
1⅓ cups milk
⅓ cup vegetable oil
3 egg whites

Preheat and grease a waffle iron as manufacturer directs.

In a large bowl, stir together both kinds of flour, oat bran, sugar, baking powder, ginger, cinnamon, cloves, and salt. Add milk and oil and stir just until blended. Do not overmix. The batter should be slightly lumpy.

In a clean, grease-free, medium-size bowl, beat egg whites with clean beaters until stiff peaks form when beaters are lifted. Fold egg whites into batter.

Spread half the batter into the prepared waffle iron. Bake until the steaming stops, about 5 minutes, or until browned. Repeat with remaining batter.

SERVES 8.

CALORIES: 250   CHOLESTEROL: 5 mg   SODIUM: 298 mg   FIBER: 2 g

Health tip:
Omit salt; use 1-percent milk.

CALORIES: 242   CHOLESTEROL: 2 mg   SODIUM: 165 mg   FIBER: 2 g

Bannocks

Strange as it may sound, these griddle cakes were originally used for communion bread. They can be made with either oatmeal flour or barley flour, or some combination thereof. Serve these anytime you need a plain cracker that is a bit unusual.

¾ cup oat flour
3 tablespoons hot water
1 tablespoon butter, softened
Pinch salt

In a large bowl, stir together the oat flour, water, butter, and salt. Knead on a floured surface until thoroughly combined. Roll out to a 6-inch circle. Cut into 8 wedges.

Heat a large skillet or griddle until a few drops of water sprinkled in the hot skillet bounce about before evaporating. Lightly grease skillet. Place bannocks in skillet and cook until lightly browned on each side. Cool on a wire rack.

MAKES 8.
CALORIES: 27   CHOLESTEROL: 4 mg   SODIUM: 12 mg   FIBER: 1 g

Health tip:
Use unsalted margarine instead of butter; omit salt.
CALORIES: 27   CHOLESTEROL: 0 mg   SODIUM: 0 mg   FIBER: 1 g

Oatcakes

These are not actually cakes, but crackers, which grow on you as you eat them. They make a healthy snack and are good with cheese and other spreads.

¼ cup oat flour
1 teaspoon baking powder
1 teaspoon sugar
½ teaspoon salt
2 tablespoons butter
1½ cups quick-cooking rolled oats
⅓ cup milk

Preheat oven to 375°F.
Grease two baking sheets and set aside.

In a medium-size bowl, stir together the oat flour, baking powder, sugar, and salt. Using a pastry cutter or two knives, cut butter into flour mixture until it resembles coarse cornmeal. Cut in rolled oats until the mixture forms balls. Then using a fork stir in milk.

On a lightly floured surfaced, roll dough out into a 10-inch circle. Cut into 2¼- or 2½-inch circles using a biscuit or cookie cutter. (If you don't have these, or can't find them, cut the dough into squares.) Place on prepared baking sheets.

Bake for 20 minutes, or until lightly browned.

MAKES 15 OATCAKES.
CALORIES: 54   CHOLESTEROL: 5 mg   SODIUM: 109 mg   FIBER: 1 g

Health tip:
Use unsalted margarine instead of butter. However, if the salt is omitted, the flavor of these cakes will suffer terribly. So sodium watchers would do better to skip this recipe.
CALORIES: 54   CHOLESTEROL: 1 mg   SODIUM: 27 mg   FIBER: 1 g

——————— ◇ ———————

Honey-Topped Biscuits

Every cook should have a good recipe for biscuits on hand. While most biscuits are simply a combination of all-purpose flour, shortening, and milk, these biscuits, made with generous amounts of oatmeal flour and oat bran, are as good for you and they are good to eat.

1 cup all-purpose flour
1 cup oat flour
¼ cup oat bran
1 tablespoon baking powder
1 teaspoon salt
⅓ cup butter
⅔ cup plus 2 tablespoons milk
2 tablespoons honey

Preheat oven to 425°F.

Grease a large baking sheet and set aside.

In a medium-size bowl, stir together both kinds of flour, bran, baking powder, and salt. Using a pastry cutter or two knives, cut butter into flour mixture until it resembles coarse cornmeal. Gradually stir in ⅔ cup of the milk to make a dough that is soft, but not sticky. If necessary, stir in as much of the remaining 2 tablespoons of the milk as needed.

Turn dough onto a lightly floured surface and knead 12 times. Roll out to a ½-inch thickness and cut into circles with 2- or 3-inch cookie cutters.

Bake for 12 to 15 minutes, or until lightly browned. Remove from oven and brush with honey.

MAKES ABOUT 12 BISCUITS.
CALORIES: 142   CHOLESTEROL: 16 mg   SODIUM: 312 mg   FIBER: 2 g

Health tip:
Omit salt; substitute unsalted margarine for butter.
CALORIES: 142   CHOLESTEROL: 2 mg   SODIUM: 97 mg   FIBER: 2 g

—————— ◇ ——————

Oat-Bran Muffins

If you're trying to lower your cholesterol, or even if you're not, one or two of these muffins make a great stick-to-the-ribs breakfast. They also freeze well and reheat nicely in a toaster oven or microwave.

1 cup all-purpose flour
¾ cup oat flour
½ cup oat bran
¼ cup sugar
2 teaspoons baking powder
1½ teaspoons ground cinnamon
1 teaspoon baking soda
¼ teaspoon ground nutmeg
¼ teaspoon salt
2 egg whites
½ cup buttermilk
½ cup milk
¼ cup butter, melted

Preheat oven to 400° F.

Grease 18 2½-inch muffin cups and set aside.

In a large bowl, stir together both kinds of flour, bran, sugar, baking powder, cinnamon, baking soda, nutmeg, and salt.

In a small bowl, beat the egg whites, buttermilk, milk, and butter just until blended. Stir egg mixture into flour mixture just until blended. Do not overmix. Batter should be lumpy. Spoon batter into muffin cups, filling two-thirds full.

Bake for 25 minutes, or until browned. Remove muffins from pan and cool on wire racks.

MAKES 18 MUFFINS.
CALORIES: 91 CHOLESTEROL: 8 mg SODIUM: 150 mg FIBER: 1 g

Health tip
Omit salt; use unsalted margarine instead of butter.
CALORIES: 91 CHOLESTEROL: 1 mg SODIUM: 102 mg FIBER: 1 g

———————— ◇ ————————

Betty-the-Baker's Oat-Bran Bread

My friend, Betty Boldt, owns a bakery in New York, and she sells a *lot* of this bread.

> 2 cups all-purpose flour
> 1 cup oat bran
> 1 cup quick-cooking rolled oats
> 2 teaspoons baking soda
> 2 teaspoons baking powder
> 1 teaspoon ground cinnamon
> 1 cup butter
> 1 cup buttermilk
> ½ cup honey
> 1 cup finely chopped apple or the fruit of your choice (Betty often uses
>   drained crushed pineapple, for instance)

Preheat oven to 325°F.

Heavily grease and flour a 9 × 5 × 3-inch loaf pan and set aside.

In a large bowl, stir together the flour, bran, oats, baking soda, baking powder, and cinnamon. Using a pastry cutter or two knives, cut butter into flour mixture until it resembles coarse cornmeal. Add the buttermilk and honey and stir just until blended. Do not overmix. Batter should be lumpy. Stir in apples. Turn batter into prepared pan.

Bake 60 to 70 minutes, or until a wooden pick inserted in the center comes out clean. Turn bread onto a wire rack to cool.

MAKES 1 LOAF (16 slices.)
CALORIES: 229 CHOLESTEROL: 32 mg SODIUM: 259 mg FIBER: 2 g

Health tip
Use unsalted margarine instead of butter.
CALORIES: 229 CHOLESTEROL: 1 mg SODIUM: 96 mg FIBER: 2 g

———— ◇ ————

Winter-Squash Bread

This is a moist, delicious bread that's good for breakfast, for a snack, or even dessert. Slice, wrap, and freeze any leftovers. Like most sweet breads, this one cuts best if you use a serrated knife.

Topping:

> 1½ tablespoons all-purpose flour
> 1½ tablespoons sugar
> ⅓ cup regular rolled oats
> 1 tablespoon butter

Bread:

> 2 cups ½-inch-cubes of peeled butternut squash, buttercup squash, or fresh pumpkin (You can also use 1 cup canned pureed pumpkin and skip the cooking, draining, and mashing. But since pumpkin is not as sweet as squash, you may want to add an extra tablespoon or two of sugar.)
> 1 cup sugar
> ½ cup vegetable oil
> ⅓ cup apple juice
> 2 eggs
> 1 cup all-purpose flour
> ½ cup oat flour
> ¼ cup oat bran
> 2 teaspoons baking soda
> ½ teaspoon baking powder
> ½ teaspoon salt
> ½ teaspoon ground cinnamon
> ½ cup chopped pecans

Preheat oven to 325°F.

Grease and flour a 9 × 5 × 3-inch loaf pan and set aside.

Prepare topping by mixing the flour, sugar, oats, and butter in a medium-size bowl until crumbly (I use my fingertips to do this) and set aside.

To make the bread, cook squash in a medium-size saucepan in boiling water until soft, about 12 minutes. Drain well. Turn into a large bowl and mash until smooth. Add sugar, oil, apple juice, and eggs. Beat until completely combined. Add both kinds of flour, bran, baking soda, baking powder salt, and cinnamon. Stir until well combined. Stir in pecans. Turn batter into prepared pan.

Bake for 1 hour, or until a wooden pick inserted in the center comes out clean. Turn bread onto a wire rack to cool.

MAKES 1 LOAF (16 slices).
CALORIES: 215   CHOLESTEROL: 28 mg   SODIUM: 185 mg   FIBER: 2 g

Health tip:
Use unsalted margarine instead of butter. Omit salt.
CALORIES: 212   CHOLESTEROL: 12 mg   SODIUM: 118 mg   FIBER: 2 g

Irish-Oatmeal Soda Bread

It's oatmeal that gives this almost-traditional soda bread extra moistness and a good dense consistency. If you like your soda bread a little on the sweet side, add 3 tablespoons of sugar when you stir the dry ingredients together.

1½ cups oat flour
1½ cups all-purpose flour
1 tablespoon caraway seeds
1½ teaspoons salt
1½ teaspoons baking soda
1½ teaspoons baking powder
½ cup raisins
1½ cups buttermilk

Preheat oven to 350°F.
Grease a baking sheet and set aside.
In a large bowl, stir together both kinds of flour, caraway seeds, salt, baking soda, and baking powder. Toss in raisins. Stir in buttermilk just until blended. Turn out onto a floured surface and knead for about 1 minute. Form into a 6-inch-round loaf. Place on prepared baking sheet.
Bake for 35 to 40 minutes, or until browned.

MAKES 1 LOAF (12 servings).
CALORIES: 141   CHOLESTEROL: 1 mg   SODIUM: 444 mg   FIBER: 2 g

Health tip:
Omit salt.
CALORIES: 141   CHOLESTEROL: 1 mg   SODIUM: 177 mg   FIBER: 2 g

Oatmeal Toasting Bread

When this bread is freshly baked, it is dense, chewy, and utterly delicious, but I like it even better when it's toasted and spread with a little sweet butter and jam.

1 cup boiling water
¾ cup quick-cooking rolled oats
½ cup water
½ cup milk
1 cup whole-wheat flour
½ cup oat bran
2 tablespoons sugar
2 teaspoons salt
1 egg
1 package yeast
2 to 3 cups bread flour or all-purpose flour

Grease two 8½ × 4½ × 2¾-inch loaf pans and set aside.

In a large bowl, stir together boiling water and oatmeal. Let stand 1 minute. Stir in the water and milk. Stir in whole-wheat flour, bran, sugar, and salt. Beat in egg, then yeast. Stir in 2 cups of the bread flour. Turn out onto a heavily floured surface and knead for 7 minutes, or until smooth and elastic, using only as much of the remaining 1 cup flour as necessary to make a smooth dough that is only slightly sticky.

Place dough in a greased bowl and cover with greased plastic wrap. Let rise in a warm spot, free from drafts, until doubled in bulk, about 1 hour. Punch dough down.

Form dough into two loaves and place in prepared pans. Cover with greased plastic wrap and let rise until doubled in bulk.

Preheat oven to 375°F.

Bake for 40 minutes, or until browned. Turn bread out onto wire racks to cool.

YIELD: 2 LOAVES (14 slices each).
CALORIES: 72   CHOLESTEROL: 8 mg   SODIUM: 138 mg   FIBER: 2 g

Health tip:
Omit salt.
CALORIES: 72   CHOLESTEROL: 8 mg   SODIUM: 6 mg   FIBER: 2 g

————— ◇ —————

Crunchy Irish-Oats Bread

It gives me a lot of satisfaction when I notice my dinner guests guiltlessly indulging in two or even three slices of my bread because they know it's good for them. This bread is particularly nice to serve when you are having a simple meal, such as a hearty soup, stew, or salad.

2 cups boiling water
¾ cup Irish or Scottish oats
1 package dry yeast
1 tablespoon sugar
3½ cups all-purpose flour, divided
1 cup oat flour
1 egg
2 tablespoons vegetable oil
2 tablespoons unsulphured molasses
2 teaspoons salt

In a large bowl, stir together boiling water and Irish oats. Let stand until the mixture cools to very warm (105–115°F). This can take as long as 15 or 20 minutes, so don't rush it. Stir in yeast and sugar. Let stand for about 10 minutes, or until foamy. Stir in ½ cup of the all-purpose flour. Place plastic wrap loosely over top of bowl. Let stand in a warm spot, out of drafts, for 8 to 12 hours or overnight.

Grease two 8½ × 4¼ × 2¾-inch loaf pans and set aside.

Stir oat flour, egg, oil, molasses, and salt into yeast mixture. Stir in 2 cups of the remaining all-purpose flour, then stir in as much of the remaining 1 cup flour as necessary to make a dough that is not too sticky to handle.

Turn dough onto a heavily floured surface. Knead for 10 minutes, using as much of the remaining flour as necessary to make a dough that is smooth and elastic. Place in a large greased bowl and cover with greased plastic wrap. Let stand in a warm spot, out of drafts, until doubled in bulk, about 2 hours.

Punch dough down. Form into two loaves and place in prepared pans. Cover with greased plastic wrap and let stand until doubled in bulk, 1 to 1½ hours.

Preheat oven to 350°F.

Bake for 35 to 45 minutes, or until top is brown and bottom is golden. Turn out of pans to cool on wire racks.

MAKES 2 LOAVES (16 slices each).
CALORIES: 84   CHOLESTEROL: 6 mg   SODIUM: 136 mg   FIBER: 1 g

Health tip:
Omit egg and salt.
CALORIES: 82   CHOLESTEROL: 0 mg   SODIUM: 1 mg   FIBER: 1 g

———————— ◇ ————————

Apple-Pear-Cranberry Crumble

A scoop of vanilla ice cream on top of this warm crumble is absolutely heavenly. (By the way did you know that you can almost always buy out-of-season cranberries frozen? You can also freeze them yourself. Just throw a bag or two of cranberries into the freezer to use like fresh all year.)

2 cups peeled cubed apple
2 cups peeled cubed pear
½ cup chopped fresh or frozen cranberries
½ cup sugar, divided
½ cup all-purpose flour, divided
1 tablespoon lemon juice
⅛ teaspoon ground nutmeg
3 tablespoons butter, divided
½ cup regular rolled oats

Preheat oven to 400°F.

In a 1½- to 2-quart casserole, toss together apples, pears, cranberries, ¼ cup of the sugar, 2 tablespoons of the all-purpose flour, lemon juice, and nutmeg until thoroughly combined.

In a small saucepan, melt 2 tablespoons of the butter. Add the oats and cook over medium heat, stirring constantly, until lightly browned. Stir in remaining 1 tablespoon butter until melted. Stir in remaining ¼ cup sugar, and remaining ¼ cup plus 2 tablespoons all-purpose flour until mixture is crumbly. Sprinkle over fruit mixture.

Bake for 30 minutes, or until hot and bubbly and topping is browned. Serve warm, cool, or chilled.

SERVES 6.
CALORIES: 238   CHOLESTEROL: 15 mg   SODIUM: 50 mg   FIBER: 4 g

Health tip:
Use unsalted margarine instead of butter.
CALORIES: 238   CHOLESTEROL: 0 mg   SODIUM: 9 mg   FIBER: 4 g

——————— ◇ ———————

Bernice's Garbage

My mother's friend, Bernice Gurtman, is a *great* baker. One day she came over to our house with some terrific cookies she'd just baked. When we asked what they were she said, "Oh, just some garbage I made." So they've been known as "garbage cookies" ever since. Of course, Bern's cookies didn't have any oats in them. That's *my* addition.

½ cup oat flour
½ cup all-purpose flour, divided
½ cup sugar, divided
¼ teaspoon baking soda
½ cup butter
1 egg, separated
⅓ cup quick-cooking rolled oats
½ cup apricot butter
½ cup chopped nuts

Preheat oven to 350°F.

In a large bowl, stir together both kinds of flour, ¼ cup of the sugar, and baking soda. Using a pastry cutter or two knives, cut butter into flour mixture until it resembles coarse cornmeal. Stir in egg yolk, then oats. Press into a 9 × 9-inch baking pan. Gently spread apricot butter to within ¼ inch of the edge.

In a clean, grease-free, medium-size bowl, beat egg white with clean beaters until foamy. Gradually beat in remaining ¼ cup sugar. Continue beating until white forms stiff peaks when beaters are lifted. Spread over apricot butter. Sprinkle with nuts.

Bake for 40 minutes, or until lightly browned. Cool on a wire rack and cut into squares.

MAKES 16 COOKIES.
CALORIES: 135   CHOLESTEROL: 14 mg   SODIUM: 69 mg   FIBER: 1 g

Health tip:
Omit salt; use unsalted margarine instead of butter.
CALORIES: 135   CHOLESTEROL: 2 mg   SODIUM: 28 mg   FIBER: 1 g

---

Oatmeal Brownies

This is not actually an attempt to "healthy-up" brownies, but rather a recipe for people who cannot easily tolerate wheat products. However, the brownies are also a tribute to a true friend, Lonnie Sterling, who sat through more than one multi-grain-course dinner while I was testing the recipes for this book. Lonnie, whose taste runs more to steak and fries, definitely appreciated these brownies I whipped up for dessert on one of these occasions, even though they do contain some oat flour.

2 squares unsweetened chocolate
½ cup butter
1 cup sugar
2 eggs
½ teaspoon vanilla extract
¾ cup oat flour
½ cup chopped walnuts

Preheat oven to 350°F.

Grease and flour (you can use oatmeal flour) an 8-inch-square baking pan and set aside.

Melt chocolate and butter in a medium saucepan over very low heat and set aside.

In a large bowl, beat the sugar and eggs until light and fluffy, about 5 minutes. Beat in reserved chocolate mixture and vanilla. Stir in flour and nuts until well combined. Turn into prepared pan.

Bake for 35 minutes. Place in refrigerator to cool. Cut into squares.

MAKES 16 BROWNIES.
CALORIES: 168   CHOLESTEROL: 41 mg   SODIUM: 58 mg   FIBER: 1 g

Health tip:
Use unsalted margarine instead of butter.
CALORIES: 168   CHOLESTEROL: 13 mg   SODIUM: 14 mg   FIBER: 1 g

———————◇———————

Prune-Filled Bar Cookies

You'll love the cakey bottom, crumbly topping, and moist, chewy centers.

¾ cup water
¼ cup sugar, divided
1 cup firmly packed pitted prunes
2 teaspoons lemon juice
¾ cup all-purpose flour
¼ cup firmly packed brown sugar
6 tablespoons butter
¾ cup quick-cooking rolled oats
⅓ cup chopped almonds

Preheat oven to 350°F.

Grease an 8-inch-square baking pan and set aside.

In a medium-size saucepan, combine water and 2 tablespoons of the sugar. Stir in prunes. Bring to a boil over high heat. Reduce heat and simmer for about 20 minutes, stirring occasionally, until almost all of the water has been absorbed. Stir in lemon juice.

Place prune mixture in the container of an electric blender or food processor. Cover and process until smooth and set aside.

In a large bowl, stir together the flour, brown sugar, and remaining 2 tablespoons sugar. Using a pastry blender or two knives, cut butter into flour mixture until it resembles coarse cornmeal. Stir in oats.

Press 1¾ cups of the oats mixture into prepared pan. Spread prune puree over oats mixture in pan. Stir almonds into the remaining oats mixture. Sprinkle over puree.

Bake for 45 minutes, or until topping is lightly browned. Cool on a wire rack. Cut into 12 bars.

MAKES 12 BAR COOKIES.
CALORIES: 188   CHOLESTEROL: 15 mg   SODIUM: 52 mg   FIBER: 3 g

Health tip:
Use unsalted margarine instead of butter.
CALORIES: 188   CHOLESTEROL: 0 mg   SODIUM: 5 mg   FIBER: 3 g

————————— ◇ —————————

Plum Crumb Cake

Besides being simple to make, you can also change this recipe to suit your mood or the season by substituting other fruits, such as peaches, apples, nectarines, etc. for the plums.

Cake:

½ cup butter
¾ cup sugar
3 eggs
1½ cups all-purpose flour
1 teaspoon baking powder
½ cup milk
1½ cups chopped ripe plums
1 teaspoon vanilla extract

Topping:

⅓ cup all-purpose flour
¼ cup sugar
¼ teaspoon ground cinnamon
2 tablespoons butter, melted
⅓ cup regular rolled oats

Preheat oven to 375°F.
Grease and flour an 8-inch-square baking pan and set aside.
To make the cake, cream butter and sugar in a large bowl until light and fluffy, about 5 minutes. Beat in eggs one at a time.
Stir together flour and baking powder. Add to butter mixture, alternately with milk, beating well after each addition. Stir in plums and vanilla. Pour into prepared pan.
To make topping, stir together flour, sugar, and cinnamon. Stir in butter until mixture makes fine crumbs. Stir in oats. Sprinkle over plums.
Bake for 50 minutes, or until a wooden pick inserted in the center comes out clean. Cool on a wire rack. Cut into 12 squares.

MAKES 12 CAKE SQUARES.
CALORIES: 276   CHOLESTEROL: 95 mg   SODIUM: 179 mg   FIBER: 2 g

Health tip:
Substitute unsalted margarine for butter; use scrambled-egg substitute for eggs.
CALORIES: 276   CHOLESTEROL: 34 mg   SODIUM: 104 mg   FIBER: 2 g

───────── ◇ ─────────
Giant Raisin-Oatmeal Cookies

These cookies are very crisp and sweet. If you think they may be too sweet, reduce the granulated sugar to ¼ cup.

⅓ cup all-purpose flour
¼ cup oat bran
½ teaspoon baking soda
½ teaspoon salt
1 cup raisins
½ cup butter
⅓ cup firmly packed brown sugar
⅓ cup sugar
2 tablespoons milk
1 teaspoon vanilla extract
1½ cups regular rolled oats

Preheat oven to 350°F.
Grease two baking sheets and set aside.
In a medium-size bowl, stir together the flour, bran, baking soda, and salt. Stir in raisins until well coated and set aside.
In another medium-size bowl, cream butter, brown sugar, and granulated sugar until light and fluffy, about 5 minutes. Beat in milk and vanilla. Beat in reserved flour mixture, then stir in oats. Shape dough into 1½-inch balls and place two inches apart on prepared baking sheets. Flatten slightly with the back of a spoon.
Bake 12 to 14 minutes, or until light golden. Allow cookies to cool on baking sheets for 5 minutes. Using a spatula, remove cookies from baking sheets to cool on wire racks.

MAKES 15 COOKIES.
CALORIES: 168   CHOLESTEROL: 17 mg   SODIUM: 155 mg   FIBER: 2 g

Health tip:
Omit salt; use unsalted margarine instead of butter.
CALORIES: 168   CHOLESTEROL: 0 mg   SODIUM: 41 mg   FIBER: 2 g

Chewy Oatmeal Cookie Variation:

Increase flour to ½ cup
Increase milk to ¼ cup

Follow instructions for crispy cookies, but decrease baking time by 2 minutes.

CALORIES: 175   CHOLESTEROL: 17 mg   SODIUM: 156 mg   FIBER: 2 g

Health tip:
Omit salt; use unsalted margarine instead of butter.
CALORIES: 175   CHOLESTEROL: 0 mg   SODIUM: 41 mg   FIBER: 2 g

RYE
(Secale cereale)

Rye is a grain that flourishes in cold, damp climates. For that reason it has become a staple in Russia, Scandinavia, and Eastern Europe, where it is valued more as flour rather than as whole grain.

Rye bread and pumpernickel are the most common uses of rye flour in this country. However, the rye breads that we are accustomed to eating are actually made with some combination of rye and wheat flours, since rye flour alone has very little gluten and bakes up into a loaf that is too dense, chewy, and strong flavored for the taste of most Americans.

Types of Rye Available

Whole-grain rye: The rye berry with just the outer hull removed.

Rye grits: Whole rye that has been cracked into pieces. Can be used as a cereal.

Rye flakes: Rye berries that have been steamed and then flattened between steel rollers. Suitable for cereal or to add to baked goods or meat loaves, or as a topping for casseroles. May be used the same way as barley flakes, oat flakes, or wheat flakes.

Rye flour: There is a choice of dark flour, medium flour, and light flour. The difference is that the dark flour is made from the whole grain, and the medium and light flours are made from rye that has had the bran and/or the germ removed.

Texture and Flavor

Rye flour and undercooked rye groats have a strong sour after-taste, but the flavor of rye itself is rather elusive. The flavor that comes to mind when most people think of rye bread is actually the flavor of caraway seeds that are baked in the bread. Properly cooked, rye berries are plump and chewy with a slight starchiness that can be rinsed off after cooking, but there will still be a faint sour after-taste.

Compatible Foods, Herbs, and Spices

The flavor of rye is compatible with just about any meat, cheese, herb, or spice.

Dill and caraway seeds are most often used with rye, but other seeds are also acceptable. Parsley and dill are the herbs of choice, but any other herb that you like would undoubtedly work well, too.

All vegetables, especially root vegetables, and all of the onion family, go well with rye.

Apple is the most suitable fruit to pair with rye, and although the orange flavor in Swedish limpa bread seems to be a good match, on the whole, the sour taste of rye does not lend itself to fruity or sweet dishes.

Nuts, like fruit, are not very compatible with rye in most cases.

Availability

Whole-grain rye, rye grits, and rye flakes are available in health-food stores and from mail-order grain catalogs (see page 21). Rye flour is more commonly available and can usually be found at the supermarket.

Nutritional Content

Like most grains, rye is a good source of B vitamins. It also contains iron, calcium, phosphorous, potassium, and fiber.

Substitutions

Triticale: Since triticale is a hybrid of wheat and rye, it is the best substitute in any recipe. But it is not as flavorful as rye and less sour. Cooking time is about the same. Triticale flour is an acceptable substitute for rye flour, but it can be hard to find and has less flavor character than rye flour.

Wheat: Wheat berries are similar to rye berries, but have a sweeter flavor. The cooking times are similar. Whole-wheat flour can be used instead of rye flour when making bread, but the loaves will not have the characteristic sourness and denseness that is such an important part of rye bread.

Oat groats: A fine substitute for rye in salads, but oat groats are a bit too starchy for cooking purposes.

Brown rice: It can be used as a substitute, but cooking times will vary greatly.

Other substitutes (in order of preference): White rice and cracked wheat.

Basic Cooking Instructions

Please read *About Cooking Grains* beginning on page 7.

The microwave methods that follow for cooking rye were tested in a 650-watt oven.

——————— ◇ ———————

Whole-grain Rye (rye berries)

Stove-top method:

> 2½ cups water
> 1 cup whole-grain rye
> ½ teaspoon salt

Bring the water to a boil in a 3-quart saucepan over high heat. Stir in rye and salt and return to boiling. Reduce heat and simmer, covered, for 2 hours and 15 minutes, or until most of the liquid has been absorbed. Remove from heat and let stand for 10 minutes.

MAKES 3⅓ CUPS.

Microwave method:

> 3 cups water
> 1½ teaspoons salt
> 1 cup whole-grain rye

Place the water and salt in a 3-quart, microwave-safe bowl. Cover with waxed paper and microwave on high (100% power) for 5 minutes. Stir in rye. Recover with waxed paper and microwave on high for 5 minutes. Microwave on medium (50% power), still covered with waxed paper, for 1 hour. Stir and let stand for 5 minutes.

MAKES 2¼ CUPS.

Rye Grits

Stove-top method:

> 2⅓ cups water
> 1 cup rye grits
> ½ teaspoon salt

In a 3-quart saucepan, bring the water to a boil over high heat. Stir in rye grits and salt and return to boiling. Reduce heat and simmer, covered, for 35 minutes, or until all of the liquid has been absorbed.

MAKES 2 CUPS.

Microwave method:

> 2 cups water
> 1 cup rye grits
> ½ teaspoon salt

Place the water in a 3-quart, microwave-safe bowl. Cover with waxed paper and microwave on high (100% power) for 4 minutes. Stir in grits and salt. Recover with waxed paper and microwave on high for 4 minutes. Microwave on medium (50% power), still covered with waxed paper, for 20 minutes, rotating dish once, if necessary. Let stand 5 minutes.

MAKES 1¾ CUPS.

Rye Flakes

Stove-top method

> 2 cups water
> 1 cup rye flakes
> ½ teaspoon salt

In a 3-quart saucepan, bring the water to a boil over high heat. Stir in rye flakes and salt and return to boiling. Reduce heat and simmer, covered, for 30 minutes, or until the mixture is a thick porridge.

MAKES 2½ CUPS.

Microwave method:

1¾ cups water
1 cup rye flakes
½ teaspoon salt

Place the water in a 3-quart, microwave-safe bowl. Cover with waxed paper and microwave on high (100% power) for 3 minutes. Stir in rye flakes and salt. Recover with waxed paper and microwave on high for 4 minutes. Microwave on medium (50% power), still covered with waxed paper, for 10 minutes, rotating dish once, if necessary. Let stand 4 minutes.

MAKES 2½ CUPS.

Reheating

Whole-grain rye does get tough when refrigerated, and gentle steaming or microwaving will restore tenderness. Otherwise, plan to use the rye shortly after cooking while the grain is still fresh and soft.

For use in salads, cool the cooked rye only to room temperature before adding to the other ingredients.

RYE RECIPES

(*indicates easy recipe.)

———————— ◇ ————————

Mom's Chopped Liver *
Franks, Rye, and Beans *
More-or-Less Stuffed Cabbage *
Eggs-in-a-Nest *
Savory Rye-Bread Pudding *
Open-Faced Reuben Sandwich *
Best-Ever Chicken Salad *
Tuna-and-Rye-Berry Salad *
Celeriac-Rye Salad *
Club Salad *
Ham-and-Cheese on "Rye" *
Rye and Mushrooms *
Classic Rye Bread
Pumpernickel Bread
Miami-Style Rye Bread
Raisin-Pumpernickel Bread *
Rye English Muffins
Crunchy Rye Bread
Dilled Rye-Beer Bread
Swedish Limpa Bread
Mini Rye-Soda Breads *
Garlic-Rye Crackers *
Rye Waffles

Mom's Chopped Liver

I managed to get the ingredients for my mother's chopped-liver recipe into cups and teaspoons (she uses handfuls of this and pinches of that) for my friend Holly Garrison's book, *Comfort Food*, because it is certainly one of my favorite comfort foods. I'm including it here because this really is the best chopped liver to be found anywhere. I like it on untoasted rye bread with a little extra "mayo" "schmeared" on the bread, and lots of iceberg lettuce. It tastes good, too, with garlic-rye crackers (see page 343).

¼ cup vegetable oil
2 cups chopped onion
1 pound chicken livers, rinsed and any fat or tough membranes
    removed
4 hard-cooked eggs, cut into quarters
⅓ cup mayonnaise
1½ teaspoons kosher (coarse) salt, or to taste
¼ teaspoon pepper

Heat the oil in a large skillet over medium-high heat. Add onion and cook, stirring frequently, until golden. Add livers and cook until they are no longer pink in the center, about 7 minutes. Remove from heat and let cool completely.

Place liver mixture and eggs in a food processor (or you can put it through a meat grinder). Process until liver and eggs are fairly smooth.

Scrape into a medium-size bowl. Stir in mayonnaise, salt, and pepper. Adjust seasonings to taste. Refrigerate until ready to serve.

SERVES 8 (2½ to 3 cups).
CALORIES: 265   CHOLESTEROL: 467 mg   SODIUM: 856 mg   FIBER: 0 g

Health tip:
Cholesterol watchers should not even *think* about this recipe. Sodium watchers should omit salt.
CALORIES: 265   CHOLESTERAL: 467 mg   SODIUM: 115 mg   FIBER: 0 g

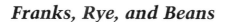

Franks, Rye, and Beans

I had to think twice about including a recipe for franks-and-beans in a grains cookbook. But the truth of it is that I love this combination, and I think most other people do, too. Adding rye berries (first simmered in beer) to this old favorite turned out to be truly inspired. If you like, you can serve the rye-and-beans, without the franks, as a side dish.

1 cup beer
¼ cup water
½ cup whole-grain rye, rinsed and drained
1 can (16 ounce) baked beans (vegetarian beans, pork-and-beans, or
    oven-baked beans)
1 tablespoon mustard
1 package (8 ounce) frankfurters, sliced

In a 1½-quart saucepan, bring the beer and water to a boil. Add rye berries and return to boiling. Reduce heat, cover, and simmer for 1 hour, or until the liquid has been absorbed. Stir in baked beans and mustard, then sliced frankfurters. Simmer, stirring occasionally, for 15 minutes.

SERVES 4.
CALORIES: 396   CHOLESTEROL: 35 mg   SODIUM: 1132 mg   FIBER: 10 g

Health tip:
Omit frankfurters.
CALORIES: 213   CHOLESTEROL: 8 mg   SODIUM: 552 mg   FIBER: 10 g

———————— ◇ ————————

More-or-Less Stuffed Cabbage

My sister invented this clever way to make a version of stuffed cabbage without the bother of separating the cabbage leaves and rolling them up with the filling. Her method is quick and easy, and you get the same wonderful flavors as you do when you make it the old-fashioned way.

1 pound lean ground beef
⅓ cup rye flakes
1 egg
¾ teaspoon salt, divided
½ teaspoon pepper, divided
2 tablespoons vegetable oil
1 cup chopped onion
1 large clove garlic, minced
3 cups coarsely shredded cabbage
1 can (14½ ounce) diced peeled tomatoes
1 can (8 ounce) tomato sauce
1 cup sauerkraut, well drained and firmly packed
⅓ cup firmly packed brown sugar

In a medium-size bowl, combine the beef, rye flakes, egg, ½ teaspoon of the salt and ¼ teaspoon of the pepper. Form into 16 balls measuring about 1½ inches. Set aside.

In a large heavy saucepan or Dutch oven, heat the oil over medium-high heat. Add onion and garlic and cook, stirring, until softened. Stir in cabbage and cook, stirring frequently, until wilted. Stir in the tomatoes, tomato sauce, sauerkraut, brown sugar, and remaining ¼ teaspoon salt and ¼ teaspoon pepper. Bring to a boil over high heat. Lower heat and add meatballs. Return to boiling, then reduce heat. Cover and simmer for 20 minutes.

SERVES 4.
CALORIES: 428   CHOLESTEROL: 151 mg   SODIUM: 1438 mg   FIBER: 6 g

Health tip:
Omit salt; rinse sauerkraut, decrease oil to 2 teaspoons and cook in a nonstick saucepan. Or, cook onion and garlic in a nonstick skillet, transferring to the larger pan to finish cooking. Reduce sugar to taste.
CALORIES: 386   CHOLESTEROL: 151 mg   SODIUM: 1038 mg   FIBER: 6 g

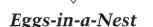

Eggs-in-a-Nest

I think this is the kind of breakfast that kids really like, and it's easy and fun to serve: a whole meal in one course. The amount of ingredients in this recipe will serve two, but you can make as many of these as you need. The leftover cutouts of rye bread can be dried out and used for bread crumbs.

2 slices rye bread, lightly toasted
2 tablespoons butter, softened
2 eggs
Salt, to taste
Pepper, to taste

Using a 3-inch biscuit cutter, cut a hole in the center of each slice of toast. Butter the toast on both sides, using about 1 teaspoon butter per side.

Heat a 10-inch skillet over medium heat. Turn toast over. Divide remaining butter in half and melt in the cut-out circles of the toast. Break an egg into the cut-out circle of each slice of toast. Sprinkle eggs with salt and pepper to taste. Cook until eggs are done as you like them.

SERVES 2.
CALORIES: 241   CHOLESTEROL: 239 mg   SODIUM: 726 mg   FIBER: 2 g

Health tip:
This breakfast is not a good choice for cholesterol watchers. Sodium watchers should omit salt and use unsalted butter.
CALORIES: 241   CHOLESTEROL: 239 mg   SODIUM: 244 mg   FIBER: 2 g

Savory Rye-Bread Pudding

Not long ago, I served this for lunch to a few friends and *everyone* asked for the recipe.

¼ cup butter
6 slices rye bread, cubed
½ cup shredded Cheddar cheese
3 eggs
¼ cup grated Parmesan cheese
½ teaspoon salt
½ teaspoon Worcestershire sauce
⅛ teaspoon pepper
2 cups milk, scalded (bubbles form around the edge of the pot, but the milk does not actually boil)

Preheat oven to 350°F.

Place the butter in a 2-quart soufflé dish. Place dish in preheated oven (or microwave) until butter melts. Swirl melted butter around dish to coat side and bottom. Add bread cubes and Cheddar cheese to soufflé dish and toss until well combined.

In a medium-size bowl, beat together egg, Parmesan cheese, salt, Worcestershire sauce, and pepper. Gradually beat in milk. Pour over bread mixture in soufflé dish.

Bake for 45 minutes. Serve immediately.

SERVES 4.
CALORIES: 410   CHOLESTEROL: 222 mg   SODIUM: 918 mg   FIBER: 3 g

Health tip:
Use unsalted margarine instead of butter; omit salt.
CALORIES: 410   CHOLESTEROL: 191 mg   SODIUM: 568 mg   FIBER: 3 g

Open-Faced Reuben Sandwich

I've always wondered who thought of this sort of strange combination of ingredients for a sandwich. After researching the matter, I discovered that it was an entry—in fact, the winner—of the first sandwich contest, sponsored by the Wheat Flour Institute.

2 slices rye bread
2 tablespoons Russian dressing, divided
¼ pound sliced corned beef, divided
½ cup sauerkraut, well drained
2 slices Swiss cheese, divided

Preheat broiler.

Place the bread on a baking sheet. Spread each slice with 1 tablespoon Russian dressing. Top each slice with half the corned beef, then half the sauerkraut, and, finally, one slice of cheese.

Place under broiler for about 2 minutes, or until cheese is melted and flecked with brown. Serve with sour pickles and potato chips.

SERVES 2.

CALORIES: 741   CHOLESTEROL: 143 mg   SODIUM: 3009 mg   FIBER: 6 g

Health tip:
Have a turkey sandwich instead!

Best-Ever Chicken Salad

I wouldn't feel that I had satisfactorily completed the rye section of this cookbook if I neglected the most familiar use for this grain, which is bread for sandwiches. After all, how would you serve corned beef if there was no rye? My mother makes great sandwiches on rye bread. She serves this salad on rye toast with lettuce and Russian dressing.

2 cups diced cooked chicken
½ cup chopped celery
⅓ cup mayonnaise
1 teaspoon grated onion
1 teaspoon white vinegar
¼ teaspoon salt
⅛ teaspoon pepper, or to taste

In a medium-size bowl, toss the chicken with celery.

In a small bowl, stir together mayonnaise, onion, vinegar, salt, and pepper. Pour mayonnaise mixture over chicken and celery and mix gently until well combined.

SERVES 4 (enough salad to make 2 huge sandwiches, 3 generous sandwiches, or 4 regular sandwiches).
CALORIES: 258   CHOLESTEROL: 69 mg   SODIUM: 300 mg   FIBER: 0 g

Health tip:
Use reduced-calorie mayonnaise; omit salt.
CALORIES: 174   CHOLESTEROL: 63 mg   SODIUM: 162 mg   FIBER: 0 g

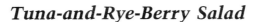

Tuna-and-Rye-Berry Salad

This salad is a nice alternative to a plain old tuna-salad sandwich, and the whole-grain rye (rye berries) stretch the tuna so that one can is enough for 2 or 3 generous-size servings.

1 cup cooked and cooled whole-grain rye
1 can (6¾ ounce) solid-white tuna, packed in oil and drained
½ cup chopped celery
¼ cup chopped red onion
1 tablespoon vegetable oil
1 tablespoon mayonnaise
1 tablespoon lemon juice

In a small bowl, place the rye, tuna, celery, and onion. Toss gently until well mixed.

Mix the oil, mayonnaise, and lemon juice in a cup. Pour over tuna mixture and toss until completely combined.

SERVES 3.
CALORIES: 265   CHOLESTEROL: 37 mg   SODIUM: 370 mg   FIBER: 2 g

Health tip:
Use low-sodium, water-packed tuna; substitute reduced-calorie mayonnaise for regular mayonnaise.
CALORIES: 172   CHOLESTEROL: 14 mg   SODIUM: 271 mg   FIBER: 2 g

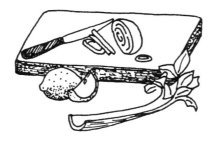

---◇---

Celeriac-Rye Salad

Don't be put off by the appearance of celeriac (also known as celery root and knob celery), as it is a rather unattractive root vegetable. Its white flesh, which tastes sort of like a turnip, is covered by brown knobby skin that is peeled away before it is cooked. (An honest produce man will tell you that if the root is any larger than his fist, it's not worth buying.) If you have never tried celeriac, this salad is a good place to start. It's important to use a good brand of extra-virgin olive oil in the preparation of the dressing. (I like the Colavita brand the best.)

1½ cups cooked and cooled whole-grain rye
1 cup cooked julienned celeriac
1 cup sliced celery
¼ cup sliced scallion, both white and green parts
2 tablespoons extra-virgin olive oil
2 teaspoons white-wine vinegar
1 teaspoon Dijon mustard
¼ teaspoon celery salt
¼ teaspoon celery seed
⅛ teaspoon pepper

In a large bowl, toss together the rye, celeriac, celery, and scallion.

In a small bowl, stir together the oil, vinegar, mustard, celery salt, celery seed, and pepper. Pour over salad ingredients and toss until thoroughly combined.

SERVES 4.

CALORIES: 186   CHOLESTEROL: 0 mg   SODIUM: 322 mg   FIBER: 4 g

Health tip:
Omit celery salt and reduce dressing ingredients by half.

CALORIES: 161   CHOLESTEROL: 0 mg   SODIUM: 155 mg   FIBER: 4 g

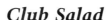

Club Salad

Like ham-and-cheese on rye, this salad is based on a sandwich that is almost always served on rye bread. The results are superb! (Needless to say, this salad is one terrific way to dispose of some of the remnants of the holiday bird.)

1½ cups cooked and cooled rye berries
1 cup diced turkey
1 cup chopped tomato
¼ cup chopped scallion, both white and green parts
3 slices bacon, cooked crisp and crumbled
¼ cup mayonnaise
1 tablespoon catsup
1 tablespoon India relish
1 tablespoon chopped parsley
¼ teaspoon salt
¼ teaspoon pepper

In a medium-size bowl, toss together the rye, turkey, tomato, scallion, and bacon.

In a small bowl, stir together the mayonnaise, catsup, relish, parsley, salt, and pepper. Spoon dressing over salad ingredients and toss until completely combined.

SERVES 4.

CALORIES: 262   CHOLESTEROL: 39 mg   SODIUM: 460 mg   FIBER: 2 g

Health tip
Substitute reduced-calorie mayonnaise for regular mayonnaise; omit bacon and salt.
CALORIES: 160   CHOLESTEROL: 31 mg   SODIUM: 220 mg   FIBER: 2 g

————— ◇ —————

Ham-and-Cheese on "Rye"

I couldn't resist developing this recipe because I liked the name so much. As it turns out, it tastes good, too.

1½ cups cooked and cooled whole-grain rye
3 tablespoons mayonnaise
1 tablespoon Dijon mustard
1 tablespoon snipped dill
¼ teaspoon pepper
1 cup ¼-inch-diced Muenster cheese with or without caraway seeds
1 package (5 ounce) ham, diced

In a medium-size bowl, combine the rye, mayonnaise, mustard, dill, and pepper. Top with cheese and ham.

SERVES 4.
CALORIES: 355   CHOLESTEROL: 57 mg   SODIUM: 817 mg   FIBER: 2 g

Health tip:
Use reduced-calorie mayonnaise.
CALORIES: 307   CHOLESTEROL: 54 mg   SODIUM: 814 mg   FIBER: 2 g

————— ◇ —————

Rye and Mushrooms

The combination of whole-grain rye and mushrooms is an excellent one, because their consistencies are so compatible. This is a very good side dish for hamburgers, roasts, and chops.

2 tablespoons butter
1 cup sliced white button mushrooms
1 cup sliced shiitake mushrooms
2 cloves garlic, minced
1 cup whole-grain rye, rinsed
1¾ cups water
½ cup grated Parmesan cheese
½ teaspoon salt
¼ teaspoon pepper

In a 2-quart saucepan, melt the butter. Stir in both kinds of mushrooms and garlic. Cook over medium heat, stirring, until softened. Add water and bring to a boil. Stir in rye. Cover and simmer for 1 hour. Stir in Parmesan cheese, salt, and pepper.

SERVES 6.
CALORIES: 196   CHOLESTEROL: 16 mg   SODIUM: 338 mg   FIBER: 6 g

Health tip:
Use unsalted margarine instead of butter; omit Parmesan cheese and salt.
CALORIES: 165   CHOLESTEROL: 0 mg   SODIUM: 7 mg   FIBER: 6 g

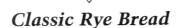

Classic Rye Bread

This is it! And better than you can buy at any bakery.

½ cup very warm water (105–115°F)
½ teaspoon sugar
1 package dry yeast
2 cups rye flour
1½ to 2 cups all-purpose flour
1 tablespoon caraway seeds (optional)
2 teaspoons salt
1 cup water

Grease an 8½ × 4½ × 2¾-inch loaf pan and set aside.

In a glass measuring cup, stir together the warm water and sugar. Stir in yeast and let stand until ¼ inch of white bubbly foam forms on top. (This foaming is called *proofing*, and if it doesn't happen it means that for some reason or other the yeast has not yet been activated. Discard this batch and try again, double checking the date on the yeast package and the temperature of the water.)

In a large bowl, stir together the rye flour, ½ cup of the all-purpose flour, caraway seeds, if using, and salt. Stir in yeast mixture and water. Stir in ⅔ cup more of the all-purpose flour to make a dough that is easy to handle.

Turn dough out onto a floured surface and knead in enough of the remaining all-purpose flour to make a dough that is smooth, elastic, and no longer sticky. Place dough in a large greased bowl and cover with greased plastic wrap. Set in a warm spot, out of drafts, until doubled in bulk, about 1 hour.

Punch dough down and form into an 8-inch loaf. Place in prepared pan. Cover with greased plastic wrap and let rise until doubled in bulk.

Preheat oven to 350°F.

Bake for 50 to 60 minutes, or until loaf is browned on top and bottom. Remove from pan and cool on a wire rack.

MAKES 1 LOAF (14 slices).
CALORIES: 102   CHOLESTEROL: 0 mg   SODIUM: 267 mg   FIBER: 3 g

Health tip:
Omit salt.
CALORIES: 102   CHOLESTEROL: 0 mg   SODIUM: 0 mg   FIBER: 3 g

Rye Bread Sticks

Use the above recipe for the dough, but omit caraway seeds. After the first rise, cut dough into 12 equal pieces. Roll into sticks about 12 inches long on a floured surface. Brush each stick with melted butter and roll in your choice of: coarse salt, dehydrated onion, caraway seeds, poppy seeds, or sesame seeds. Place on greased baking sheets, leaving 1½ inches around each bread stick. Cover with greased plastic wrap and let rise until doubled in bulk. Bake for about 18 minutes, or until golden.

MAKES 12 BREAD STICKS.

Rye Pretzels

Shape bread sticks into pretzel shapes after rolling in the topping of your choice. Bake as directed for bread sticks.

MAKES 12 PRETZELS.

Pumpernickel Bread

When I think of pumpernickel bread, a dark-brown loaf comes to mind, which is similar to rye bread, but that is actually a Russian black bread. True pumpernickel was supposedly developed by a German gentleman named Pumper Nickel. It is light in color with a dense chewy texture. This bread involves many steps (none of them very difficult), so it pays to make several loaves at once. (Extra loaves may be tightly wrapped and frozen.) Now, get out a BIG, BIG bowl to allow the dough plenty of room to rise.

3 cups water
¾ cup cormeal
2 tablespoons butter
2 tablespoons sugar

1 tablespoon salt
1 tablespoon caraway seeds
2 packages dry yeast
½ cup very warm water (105–115°F)
2 cups mashed potatoes (can be made from instant)
4 cups rye flour
2 cups whole-wheat flour
2 to 3 cups all-purpose flour

Grease four 8½ × 4½ × 2¾-inch loaf pans (or three 9-inch layer-cake pans) and set aside.

In a medium-size saucepan, stir together the water and cornmeal. Cook over medium heat, stirring constantly, until mixture is thick. Remove from heat. Stir in butter, sugar, salt, and caraway seeds. Let stand for about 40 minutes, or until lukewarm.

When cornmeal mixture has cooled to lukewarm, stir the yeast into warm water. Let stand until ¼ inch of white bubbly foam forms on top. (This foaming is called *proofing,* and if it doesn't happen it means that for some reason or other the yeast has not been activated. Discard this batch and try again, double checking the date on the yeast package and the temperature of the water.)

Stir potatoes into cornmeal mixture, then stir in proofed yeast. Stir in rye flour and whole-wheat flour. Stir in 1 cup of the all-purpose flour to form a dough that is stiff enough to handle.

Turn dough onto a well-floured surface. Knead in enough of the remaining 2 cups all-purpose flour to form a dough that is only very slightly sticky (or until you're too exhausted to continue kneading any longer).

Place dough in a very large greased bowl and cover with greased plastic wrap. Let stand in a warm spot, out of drafts, until doubled in bulk, about 1 hour.

Shape dough into four loaves and place in prepared loaf pans. (Or, if you want to make three round loaves, knead in a little extra flour, shape into rounds, and place in prepared layer-cake pans.) Cover with greased plastic wrap and let rise until doubled in bulk.

Preheat oven to 375°F.

Bake for 45 to 50 minutes, or until browned on top and bottom. Remove from pans and cool on wire racks.

MAKES 4 LOAVES (14 slices each) OR 3 ROUND LOAVES.
CALORIES: 113   CHOLESTEROL: 2 mg   SODIUM: 186 mg   FIBER: 2 g

Health tip:
Omit salt.
CALORIES: 113   CHOLESTEROL: 2 mg   SODIUM: 57 mg   FIBER: 2 g

——————— ◇ ———————

Miami-Style Rye Bread

"Miami-style" means that golden-fried onions are tucked in-side the loaf of rye bread before it is baked, adding their own special sweetness and flavor.

¾ cup very warm water (105–115°F)
½ teaspoon sugar
1 package dry yeast
1 cup rye flour
2 teaspoons caraway seeds
1 teaspoon salt
1 to 1½ cups all-purpose flour
2 tablespoons butter
½ cup finely chopped onion
1 teaspoon poppy seeds
1 egg white, for glaze (optional)
Additional poppy seeds (optional)

Grease an 8½ × 4½ × 2¾-inch loaf pan and set aside.

In a glass measuring cup, stir together the water and sugar. Add yeast and let stand until ¼ inch of white bubbly foam forms on top. (This foaming is called *proofing*, and if it doesn't happen it means that for some reason or other the yeast has not been activated. Discard this batch and try again, double checking the date on the yeast package and the temperature of the water.)

In a large bowl, stir together rye flour, caraway seeds, salt, and ¾ cup of the all-purpose flour. Stir in proofed-yeast mixture. Stir in ½ cup flour. Turn dough onto a floured surface and knead for 10 minutes using as much of remaining flour as necessary to form a dough that is no longer sticky. Place in a large greased bowl. Cover with greased plastic wrap. Set in a warm spot, out of drafts, until doubled in bulk, about 1 hour.

Melt the butter in a small skillet over medium-high heat. Add onion and cook, stirring, until golden brown. Stir in poppy seeds and set aside.

Punch dough down. Roll into an 8-inch square. Spread onion mixture over one side of the square to within 1 inch of the edges. Starting on the onion-side of the bread, roll dough into a log so that onion is tucked into the center of the bread. Pinch the seam and the ends to seal. Place seam side down on prepared baking sheet. Cover lightly with greased plastic wrap and let rise until doubled in bulk. (This will be a small loaf, so don't expect it to rise to the top of the pan.) Brush with egg white and sprinkle with poppy seeds, if you like.

Preheat oven to 375°F.

Bake for 40 minutes, or until browned. Remove from baking sheet and cool on a wire rack.

MAKES 1 LOAF (10 slices).
CALORIES: 117 CHOLESTEROL: 6 mg SODIUM: 239 mg FIBER: 3 g

Health tip:
Omit salt; substitute unsalted margarine for butter.
CALORIES: 116 CHOLESTEROL: 0 mg SODIUM: 9 mg FIBER: 3 g

————— ◇ —————

Raisin-Pumpernickel Bread (Russian Black Bread)

This is the dark-brown loaf that most people think of as being pumpernickel, but it's really a Russian black bread. If you prefer your bread plain, leave out the raisins.

½ cup very warm water (105–115°F)
½ teaspoon sugar
2 packages dry yeast
3 cups rye flour
1 cup whole wheat flour
1 cup morsels of wheat bran cereal (Kellogg's Bran Buds)
¼ cup unsweetened cocoa powder
2 tablespoons caraway seeds
1 teaspoon fennel or anise seeds (optional)
1 tablespoon salt
1½ cups water
⅔ cup unsulphured molasses
¼ cup butter, melted
2 teaspoons instant-coffee powder or granules
1 teaspoon white vinegar
1½ cups dark raisins
2 to 3 cups bread flour or all-purpose flour

Grease a baking sheet and set aside.

In a glass measuring cup, stir together the warm water and sugar. Stir in yeast and let stand until ¼ inch of white foam forms on top. (This foaming is called *proofing*, and if it doesn't happen it means that for some reason or other the yeast has not been activated. Discard this batch and try again, double checking the date on the yeast package and the temperature of the water.)

While yeast is proofing, in a large bowl, stir together rye and whole-wheat flours. Stir in cereal, cocoa, caraway seeds, fennel seeds, if using, and salt. Add water, molasses, melted butter, instant-coffee powder, vinegar, and proofed-yeast mixture. Stir in raisins and 1 cup of the bread flour. Turn dough onto a floured surface and knead in as much of the remaining bread flour as necessary to form a dough that is no longer sticky. Place in a large greased bowl. Cover with greased plastic wrap. Set in a warm spot, out of drafts, until doubled in bulk, about 2 hours. (As a point of interest, the last time I made this bread the dough didn't rise much at all, but just enough to assure me that the yeast was active. So, after two hours, I just proceeded with the recipe and the results were fine.)

Punch dough down and form into a round loaf. Place on prepared baking sheet. Cover lightly with greased plastic wrap. Let rise until doubled in bulk, about 1 hour. (Here again, the dough may not really double in bulk, but it will rise.)

Preheat oven to 350°F.

Bake for 1 hour, or until loaf sounds hollow when tapped, and the bottom is nicely browned. Remove from baking sheet to cool on a wire rack.

MAKES 1 LOAF (24 servings).
CALORIES: 183   CHOLESTEROL: 7 mg   SODIUM: 313 mg   FIBER: 6 g

Health tip:
Omit salt; use unsalted margarine instead of butter.
CALORIES: 183   CHOLESTEROL: 0 mg   SODIUM: 28 mg   FIBER: 6 g

---

◇

Rye English Muffins

Sixteen-year-old Jesse Weissman was my primary taster for these muffins. He loved them, but had a very legitimate criticism. He found (as did I) that the 3-inch muffin is just a little too small to remove easily from an ordinary toaster. If you can find a 4-inch-round cookie or biscuit cutter, use that, or toast the muffins in a toaster oven or under the broiler in your regular oven

1 package dry yeast
½ cup very warm water (105–115°F)
3 cups rye flour
1 tablespoon sugar
1 tablespoon caraway seeds

1½ teaspoons salt
1½ cups milk
¼ cup butter, melted
2 to 2½ cups all-purpose flour
Cornmeal

In a glass measuring cup, stir the yeast into water. Let stand until ¼ inch bubbly foam forms on top. (This foaming is called *proofing*, and if it doesn't happen it means that for some reason or other the yeast has not been activated. Discard this batch and try again, double checking the date on the yeast package and the temperature of the water.)

While yeast is proofing, in a large bowl, stir together the rye flour, sugar, caraway seeds, and salt. Stir in milk and melted butter. Stir in 1½ cups of the all-purpose flour. Turn dough onto a floured surface. Knead in as much of the remaining 1 cup all-purpose flour as necessary to form a dough that is fairly stiff and only barely sticky. Place dough in a greased bowl. Cover with greased plastic wrap. Set in a warm spot, out of drafts, until doubled in bulk. Punch dough down.

Generously sprinkle a work surface with cornmeal. Turn dough onto cornmeal and pat into a 12-inch circle. Using a 3-inch biscuit or cookie cutter, cut into 16 to 18 muffins. (Pat scraps together for an extra muffin, if you like.) Place muffins on aluminum foil or waxed paper, leaving 2 inches around each one. Cover lightly with greased plastic wrap and let rise until doubled in bulk.

Heat a large skillet or griddle until it is moderately hot and grease it lightly. Cook muffins a few at a time over medium heat until browned on both sides, about 7 minutes per side. (If your muffins seem to be browning much faster than this, reduce heat.) Cool muffins on wire racks, then split with a fork. The muffins are now ready to be toasted and enjoyed, or you may freeze them. No need to defrost before toasting.

MAKES 18 MUFFINS.
CALORIES: 151   CHOLESTEROL: 10 mg   SODIUM: 210 mg   FIBER: 3 g

Health tip:
Omit salt; use unsalted margarine instead of butter.
CALORIES: 151   CHOLESTEROL: 3 mg   SODIUM: 14 mg   FIBER: 3 g

———————◇———————

Crunchy Rye Bread

This bread is very dense and slightly sweet, with a hint of honey flavor. The combination of different flours and milk powder also makes it especially healthful.

½ cup very warm water (105–115°F)
½ teaspoon sugar
2 packages dry yeast
2 to 2½ cups all-purpose flour
1½ cups rye flour
½ cup cornmeal
½ cup soy flour
½ cup rye flakes
⅓ cup dry-milk powder
2 teaspoons salt
1 cup water
½ cup honey

Grease a baking sheet and set aside.

In a glass measuring cup, stir together the water and sugar. Stir in yeast and let stand until ¼ inch of white bubbly foam forms on top. (This foaming is called *proofing*, and if it doesn't happen it means that for one reason or other the yeast has not been activated. Discard this batch and try again, double checking the date on the yeast package and the temperature of the water.)

While yeast is proofing, in a large bowl, stir together ¾ cup of the all-purpose flour, rye flour, cornmeal, soy flour, rye flakes, milk powder, and salt. Stir in proofed-yeast mixture, water, and honey. Stir in 1 more cup all-purpose flour. Turn out onto a floured surface and knead in as much of the remaining all-purpose flour as necessary to make a dough that is no longer sticky. Place in a large greased bowl. Cover with greased plastic wrap. Set in a warm spot, out of drafts, until doubled in bulk, about 1½ hours.

Punch dough down and form into a round loaf. Place on prepared baking sheet. Cover lightly with greased plastic wrap and let rise until doubled in bulk.

Preheat oven to 350°F.

Bake for 40 minutes, or until loaf is browned on top and bottom. Remove from baking sheet and cool on a wire rack.

MAKES 1 LOAF (20 slices).
CALORIES: 124 CHOLESTEROL: 0 mg SODIUM: 219 mg FIBER: 3 g

Health tip:
Omit salt.
CALORIES: 124 CHOLESTEROL: 0 mg SODIUM: 6 mg FIBER: 3 g

Dilled Rye-Beer Bread

Dill is the favorite herb of many people, me included, so I'm especially fond of this light delicious bread. It's wonderful spread with butter or for sandwiches.

½ cup very warm water (105–115°F)
½ teaspoon sugar
1 package dry yeast
3 cups rye flour
2 to 2¼ cups all-purpose flour
1 tablespoon dried dill weed
1 tablespoon salt
1 teaspoon dill seed (optional)
1 can (12 ounce) beer, room temperature

Grease a 9 × 5 × 3-inch loaf pan and set aside.

In a glass measuring cup, stir together the water and sugar. Stir in yeast and let stand until ¼ inch of white bubbly foam forms on top. (This foaming is called *proofing*, and if it doesn't happen it means that for one reason or other the yeast has not been activated. Discard this batch and try again, double checking the date on the yeast package and the temperature of the water.)

While yeast is proofing, in a large bowl, stir together rye flour, 1 cup of the all-purpose flour, dill weed, salt, and dill seed, if using. Stir in proofed-yeast mixture and beer. Stir in ½ cup more of the all-purpose flour.

Turn dough onto a floured surface and knead in as much of the remaining ¾ cup all-purpose flour as necessary to make a dough that is no longer sticky. Place in a large greased bowl and cover with greased plastic wrap. Set in a warm spot, out of drafts, until doubled in bulk, about 1½ hours.

Punch dough down and form into a 9-inch loaf. Place in prepared pan. Cover lightly with greased plastic wrap and let rise until doubled in bulk, about 40 minutes.

Preheat oven to 350°F.

Bake for 40 to 50 minutes, or until loaf is browned on top and bottom. Turn out of pan and cool on a wire rack.

MAKES 1 LOAF (16 slices).
CALORIES: 144   CHOLESTEROL: 0 mg   SODIUM: 402 mg   FIBER: 4 g

Health tip:
Omit salt; use light beer.
CALORIES: 142   CHOLESTEROL: 0 mg   SODIUM: 2 mg   FIBER: 4 g

Swedish Limpa Bread

In Sweden, this bread is call *vortlimpor* and it's traditionally baked for Christmas. The common denominator in all limpa (sometimes spelled limpe) bread seems to be rye flour, some sweetening, and some form of orange. Variations include the use of beer, caraway seeds, malt, anise, and many types of flour. This recipe is by no means a truly authentic version, as I'm sure that "authentic," in this case, must mean whatever your Swedish mother put into *her* loaf.

½ cup very warm water (105–115°F)
½ teaspoon sugar
2 packages dry yeast
3 cups rye flour
3 to 3½ cups all-purpose flour
½ cup firmly packed light- or dark-brown sugar
2 teaspoons salt
1 teaspoon ground cardamom (optional)
1 cup orange juice
½ cup water
½ cup butter, melted
¼ cup honey
2 tablespoons grated orange rind

Grease two baking sheets and set aside.

In a glass measuring cup, stir together the warm water and sugar. Stir in yeast and let stand until ¼ inch of white bubbly foam forms on top. (This is called *proofing*, and if it doesn't happen it means that for some reason or other the yeast has not been activated. Discard this batch and try again, double checking the date on the yeast package and the temperature of the water.)

While yeast is proofing, in a large bowl, stir together rye flour, 1 cup of the all-purpose flour, brown sugar, salt, and cardamom, if using. Stir in proofed-yeast mixture, orange juice, water, butter, honey, and orange rind. Stir in 1¼ cups more all-purpose flour to form a dough that is easy to handle.

Turn dough out onto a floured surface and knead in as much of the remaining 1¼ cups all-purpose flour as necessary to make a dough that is no longer sticky. Place in a large greased bowl. Cover with greased plastic wrap. Set in a warm spot, out of drafts, until doubled in bulk, about 1 hour.

Punch dough down and form into two round loaves. Place on

prepared baking sheets. Cover lightly with greased plastic wrap and let rise until doubled in bulk.

Preheat oven to 350°F.

Bake for 40 to 50 minutes, or until loaves are browned on top and bottom. Remove from sheets and cool on wire racks.

MAKES 2 LOAVES (16 slices per loaf).
CALORIES: 128   CHOLESTEROL: 8 mg   SODIUM: 159 mg   FIBER: 2 g

Health tip:
Omit brown sugar and salt; use unsalted margarine instead of butter.
CALORIES: 128   CHOLESTEROL: 0 mg   SODIUM: 8 mg   FIBER: 2 g

———————— ◇ ————————
Garlic-Rye Crackers

Plan on serving these crisp little crackers soon after they're baked or store in a tightly covered container in the refrigerator. If necessary, you can recrisp them in the oven for a few minutes. These neat little crackers, which will remind you of melba toast, are great to serve with cheese, or are delicious to munch on as is.

2 tablespoons butter, very soft, but not melted
2 cloves garlic, minced
Herbs, as desired
4 very-thin slices rye bread (or you can use melba rye)

Preheat oven to 400°F.

In a small bowl, stir together butter and garlic. You can also stir in any herb that you like: thyme or basil, for instance.

Lightly brush each side of bread with a little of the butter mixture. Using a serrated knife, cut each slice into 8 wedges. Place wedges in a single layer on a baking sheet.

Bake for 5 minutes, then turn bread over and bake for 3 to 5 minutes longer, or until lightly browned and crispy. Remove from baking pans and cool on wire racks.

MAKES 32 CRACKERS.
CALORIES: 13   CHOLESTEROL: 2 mg   SODIUM: 23 mg   FIBER: 0 g

Health tip:
Use unsalted margarine instead of butter.
CALORIES: 13   CHOLESTEROL: 0 mg   SODIUM: 17 mg   FIBER: 0 g

———————◇———————

Mini Rye-Soda Breads

This recipe is actually a cross between Irish soda bread and scones. It is slightly denser than soda bread, and has the tenderness of a scone without the sweetness.

1 cup rye flour
1 cup all-purpose flour
½ cup raisins
1 tablespoon sugar
1 tablespoon caraway seeds
1 teaspoon baking soda
1 teaspoon baking powder
1 teaspoon salt
¼ teaspoon cream of tartar
¾ cup buttermilk
3 tablespoons melted butter

Preheat oven to 350°F.

Grease two baking sheets and set aside.

In a large bowl, stir together both kinds of flour, raisins, sugar, caraway seeds, baking soda, baking powder, salt, and cream of tartar. Stir in buttermilk and melted butter. Turn dough onto a floured surface and knead 12 times.

Cut dough into four equal pieces and shape each piece into a round loaf. Place on baking sheets. Using a sharp knife, cut an "X" in the top of each loaf.

Bake for 35 to 40 minutes, or until lightly browned. Remove from baking sheets and cool on wire racks.

SERVES 8.
CALORIES: 195   CHOLESTEROL: 12 mg   SODIUM: 470 mg   FIBER: 3 g

Health tip:
Omit salt; substitute unsalted margarine for butter.
CALORIES: 195   CHOLESTEROL: 1 mg   SODIUM: 172 mg   FIBER: 3 g

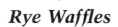

Rye Waffles

These waffles are not crispy, but they are delicious. They also freeze nicely and reheat well in the microwave oven (no small thing).

1 cup all-purpose flour
⅔ cup rye flour
⅓ cup honey-flavored wheat germ
¼ cup cornmeal
1 tablespoon baking powder
1 teaspoon salt
2 eggs, separated
1⅓ cups milk
½ cup butter, melted
⅓ cup honey

Preheat and grease waffle iron as manufacturer directs.

In a large bowl, stir together both kinds of flour, wheat germ, cornmeal, baking powder, and salt. Beat together egg yolks, milk, butter, and honey. Stir into flour mixture.

In a clean, grease-free, medium-size bowl, with clean beaters, beat egg whites until stiff peaks form when beaters are lifted. Fold whites into batter.

Pour about 1 cup of the batter into the waffle iron. Close and bake until steaming stops, about 5 minutes, or until well browned.

MAKES 12 SERVINGS

CALORIES: 202   CHOLESTEROL: 59 mg   SODIUM: 350 mg   FIBER: 2 g

Health tip:
Omit salt; use unsalted margarine instead of butter; substitute 1-percent milk for whole milk.

CALORIES: 195   CHOLESTEROL: 35 mg   SODIUM: 168 mg   FIBER: 2 g

WILD RICE
(Zizania aquatica)

Wild rice is not a rice, or even a grain, for that matter, but a seed from an aquatic grass native to the Great Lakes region of North America. However, I'm including it as a grain in this book because it's cooked and used in many of the same ways as most true grains.

Much of the wild rice available these days is cultivated in paddies, but some of it is still harvested by Native Americans, who gather the grain using canoes the same way they've been doing it for centuries.

Even using the tools and agricultural know-how of the twentieth century, wild rice remains a frustratingly difficult crop to grow and harvest, which is ultimately reflected in the price paid for it. Consequently, wild rice has long been considered a gourmet item to be served on *very* special occasions. More often than not it is mixed with less-expensive rices and eaten at less auspicious meals.

Types of Wild Rice Available

There is only one type of pure wild rice. It is never processed more than removing the hull. Its shape is similar to long-grain rice, but it is usually even longer. The color can range from medium-brown to almost-black, but most wild rice is dark brown.

Wild rice is graded into three categories:

Select: The grains are short, about ⅜ inch or less, are not uniform in size, and will most likely contain some broken grains.

Extra-fancy: The grains are about ½ inch long and uniform in size. Very few of the grains are broken.

Giant: The grains are about 1 inch long, uniform in size, and there are few, if any, broken grains.

As you might guess, the grade determines the price, with select being the least expensive and giant being the most expensive. Packages may be labeled with other terminology, such as "premium" or "finest quality," but you can pretty easily tell which grade you're buying by simply looking at the rice (most is sold in plastic bags or boxes with windows) and checking for size, uniformity, and breakage.

As far as taste and nutrition go, all grades of wild rice are about the same and can be used interchangeably.

The recipes in this chapter were tested with extra-fancy wild rice

Texture and Flavor

Wild rice has a distinct earthy, or woodsy, flavor that is best described as being reminiscent of a walk in the woods just after a rain storm. Some people also perceive a slight nuttiness to the taste, as well.

As it cooks, the grains burst open to reveal a grey-white interior. The texture is dense, a bit chewy, and extremely pleasant.

Compatible Foods, Herbs, and Spices

Wild rice goes especially well with other earthy foods, such as wild game, mushrooms, and beans. The flavor, though very distinct, is also very versatile, so it can also be used successfully with both subtle herbs and pungent spices

Meat, poultry, and fish are also good companions for wild rice, as well as dairy products, fruits, vegetables, and nuts. You can also combine wild rice with other starchy foods, especially white or brown rice.

If you find the flavor of wild rice a little too strong for your taste, or too expensive for your budget, you can subdue the flavor and lower the cost of a recipe by replacing part of the wild rice called for in these and other recipes with white rice.

Availability

Wild rice is now available in most supermarkets. Look in the gourmet-foods section if it is not with the rice. It is also sold in fancy-food stores, some health-food stores, and by mail-order from growers or distributors (see page 21).

Nutritional Content

It's rare when something that is so good is also good for you, but the nutritional profile of wild rice is very impressive. It has more protein and is higher in amino acids, lysine, and methionine than true grains. It is also high in fiber, since only the hull has been removed, and is also a good source of B vitamins, iron, phosphorous, magnesium, calcium, and zinc.

Substitutions

Wehani brown rice: This comes the closest to the flavor and consistency of wild rice, and can be used any time wild rice is called for. However, it's also expensive, and is even harder to find.

White rice: I prefer the flavor of long-grain white rice rather than brown rice as a substitute for wild rice. In recipes calling for raw wild rice, you will have to reduce the cooking time significantly.

Brown rice: Use either the short- or long-grain variety. The flavor of brown rice is close enough to wild rice to be compatible with recipes developed for wild rice. The cooking times are also similar.

Other acceptable substitutes (in order of preference): Oat groats, wheat berries, bulgur, and couscous.

Basic Cooking Instructions

Please read the section *About Cooking Grains* beginning on page 7.

Instructions are given for both 1 cup of wild rice and a 4-ounce package. I have also included instructions for cooking wild rice and brown or white rice together.

The microwave methods for cooking wild rice were tested in a 650-watt oven.

Stove-top method for 1 cup:

> *2½ cups water*
> *¾ teaspoon salt*
> *1 cup wild rice, rinsed*

Bring the water and salt to a boil over high heat in a 2-quart covered saucepan. Stir in rice and return to boiling.

Reduce heat and simmer, covered, for 55 minutes, or until most of the liquid has been absorbed. Remove from heat and let stand, covered, for 10 minutes. Fluff with a fork.

MAKES 2⅔ CUPS.

Stove-top method for 4-ounce package:

> *1½ cups water*
> *¼ teaspoon salt*
> *4-ounce package wild rice, rinsed*

Bring the water and salt to a boil over high heat in a 1½-quart covered saucepan. Stir in wild rice and return to boiling. Reduce heat and simmer, covered, for 55 minutes, or until most of the liquid has been absorbed. Remove from heat and let stand, covered, for 10 minutes. Fluff with a fork.

MAKES 2⅓ CUPS.

Microwave method for 1 cup:

2½ cups water
1 cup wild rice, rinsed
¾ teaspoon salt

Place the water in a 3-quart, microwave-safe bowl. Cover with waxed paper. Microwave on high (100% power) for 5 minutes. Stir in wild rice and salt. Recover with waxed paper and microwave on high for 5 minutes. Microwave on medium (50% power), still covered with waxed paper, for 45 minutes, rotating dish once, if necessary. Let stand 5 minutes. Fluff with a fork.

MAKES 3¼ CUPS.

Microwave method for 4-ounce package:

1½ cups water
4-ounce package wild rice, rinsed
¼ teaspoon salt

Place the water in a 2-quart, microwave-safe bowl. Cover with waxed paper. Microwave on high (100% power) for 3 minutes. Stir in wild rice and salt. Recover with waxed paper and microwave on high for 4 minutes. Microwave on medium (50% power), still covered with waxed paper, for 35 minutes, rotating dish once, if necessary. Let stand 5 minutes. Fluff with a fork.

MAKES 2 CUPS.

To Cook Wild Rice and Brown or White Rice Together

Wild rice and brown rice: Since the amounts and cooking times of wild rice and brown rice are similar, substitute as much brown rice as you like for wild rice. Add rinsed wild rice to the water when it boils and simmer for 15 minutes. Add brown rice and simmer for 45 minutes longer.

Wild rice and white rice: Simmer rinsed wild rice for 30 minutes after adding to boiling water. Add white rice and simmer for 25 minutes longer. Substitute as much white rice for wild rice as you like.

Cooking Note: Since many recipes call for wild rice to be cooked in a flavored broth, you should know that wild rice takes longer to cook in broth than it does in water. Also, use about ¼ cup less broth than water.

Reheating

Wild rice does not stiffen after refrigeration and so does not have to be reheated before adding it to a salad or other recipes that will be served chilled or at room temperature. Steam or reheat in the microwave oven, if desired.

WILD RICE RECIPES

*(*indicates easy recipe.)*

———————— ◇ ————————

Duck Bouillon with Wild Rice and Mushrooms
Chestnut-and-Wild-Rice Soup
An Omelet with Wild-Rice-and-Mushroom Filling*
Cajun Shrimp*
Creamy Scallops and Leeks with Wild Rice*
Inside-Out Beef Wellington
Wild Oxtail Stew*
Stuffed Cornish Game Hens*
Apple-and-Wild-Rice Stuffing*
Salade de Provence*
Tropical-Fruit-and-Wild-Rice Salad*
Wild Rice with Fennel and Endive*
Wild-Rice Slaw*
Mandarin-Orange-and-Wild-Rice Salad*
Black-White-and-Red Salad (with a Touch of Green)*
Summery Wild-Rice-and-Cucumber Salad*
An Elegant Fruit-and-Vegetable Salad*
Wild Rice and Pasta with a Creamy Tomato Sauce*
Lentils and Wild Rice*
White-and-Wild Rice*
Rice Trio with Peas*
Wild Rice with Summer Squash*
Southern-Style Wild Rice with Mushrooms*
Green Beans, Shiitake Mushrooms, and Wild Rice*
Wild Rice with Red and Yellow Peppers*
Wild-Rice Crêpes with Apricot Sauce

351

———————— ◇ ————————

Duck Bouillon with Wild Rice and Mushrooms

I can't think of a more elegant starter for a super-festive meal than this bouillon. The duck will not go to waste. Chill it and use it in salads and for sandwiches.

12 cups water
5-pound duck
2 medium leeks, trimmed and thoroughly rinsed
3 ribs celery
3 medium carrots, peeled
2 medium parsnips, peeled
1 large bunch parsley, rinsed
2 cups sliced mushrooms (I use shiitake mushrooms, but you can use
*   any exotic mushroom you like, or even cultivated white button*
*   mushrooms)*
¼ cup wild rice, rinsed
½ teaspoon salt

In an 8-quart soup pot, combine the water, duck (include the neck, heart, and gizzard, but not the liver), leeks, celery, carrots, and parsnips. Bring to a boil. Reduce heat and simmer, uncovered, for 1½ hours. Add parsley and simmer for 30 minutes longer.

Remove duck, giblets, and vegetables from pot. Place them in a colander and let the cooking liquid drip back into the pot. Continue to simmer for 30 minutes longer, or until soup is reduced to 8 cups. Skim off fat. (If you have the time, the best way to do this is to chill the soup in the pot overnight, then lift off the congealed fat and continue with the recipe the next day.)

Stir in mushrooms, rice, and salt. Simmer, uncovered, for 1 hour longer.

SERVES 6 TO 8.
CALORIES: 80   CHOLESTEROL: 5 mg   SODIUM: 177 mg   FIBER: .5 g

Health tip:
Omit salt.
CALORIES: 80   cholesterol: 5 mg   SODIUM: 0 mg   FIBER: .5 g

———————— ◇ ————————

Chestnut-and-Wild-Rice Soup

This soup was a great hit when I served it last New Year's Eve. It's creamy and has a slightly sweet flavor that my guests found unusual and delicious. The wild rice adds a slightly chewy element, even though the soup is pureed.

2 tablespoons butter
⅔ cup chopped onion
2 cans (13¾ ounces each) ready-to-serve chicken broth or
    3½ cups vegetable broth (see page 19)
1 cup water
1½ cups cooked peeled chestnuts (you can buy these in a can or a jar,
    already cooked and peeled, or you can do this yourself by baking or
    boiling the chestnuts until tender)
⅓ cup wild rice, rinsed
½ cup whipping cream
2 tablespoons dry or medium-dry sherry
¼ teaspoon salt

In a 4-quart saucepan, melt the butter over medium-high heat. Add onion and cook, stirring frequently, until softened. Add broth and water and bring to a boil. Add chestnuts and wild rice. Reduce heat and simmer, covered, for 1 hour and 15 minutes. Remove from heat to cool slightly.

Ladle about one-third of the soup mixture into the container of an electric blender or food processor. (I prefer the blender in this case.) Cover and process until soup is pureed, but the wild rice is still in visible pieces. Pour into a large bowl. Continue processing until all of the soup has been pureed.

Stir cream, sherry, and salt into soup. Reheat before serving.

SERVES 6.
CALORIES: 248   CHOLESTEROL: 38 mg   SODIUM: 337 mg   FIBER: 5 g

Health tip:
Use unsalted margarine instead of butter, and half-and-half instead of cream. Omit salt.
CALORIES: 205   CHOLESTEROL: 8 mg   SODIUM: 310 mg   FIBER: 5 g

———————— ◇ ————————

An Omelet with Wild-Rice-and-Mushroom Filling

Wild rice and mushrooms make this omelet-for-two very special. A bottle of champagne to accompany it wouldn't be a bad idea, either. (If you like, the rice-and-mushroom mixture can be used as a savory filling for the crêpes recipe given on page 377.) Although I've designated this recipe as easy, if you've never cooked an omelet before, a little practice may be necessary in order to produce a perfectly gorgeous omelet every time.

3 tablespoons butter, divided
½ cup sliced leek, white and light-green parts only
2 cups sliced mushrooms
⅔ cup cooked wild rice
3 tablespoons herb-and-garlic triple–cream cheese (Boursin)
6 eggs
6 tablespoons water
½ teaspoon salt
¼ teaspoon pepper
Snipped chives, for garnish (optional)

Melt 1 tablespoon of the butter in a large skillet over medium-high heat. Add leek and cook, stirring, until softened. Add mushrooms and cook stirring and tossing, until softened. Stir in wild rice and cheese and continue to cook, stirring, until rice is warm and cheese is melted. Set aside.

Break eggs into a medium bowl. Add water, salt, and pepper. Stir together with a fork until completely blended. *Do not beat the eggs.* Melt 1 tablespoon of the butter in a medium-size nonstick skillet over medium-high heat. When it is foamy, pour in half the egg mixture. As the edges set, tilt the pan and lift eggs with a pancake turner so that the uncooked egg can flow underneath. While the top is still moist, spoon half of the wild-rice filling over the left side of the omelet (if you're right handed, or over the right side of the omelet if you're left-handed). Lift the right (or left) side of the omelet up with the pancake turner and fold it over part of the filling. Tilt pan and turn omelet upside down onto a warm plate. Repeat with remaining butter, eggs, and filling. Scatter a few snipped chives over tops of omelets, if you like.

SERVES 2.

CALORIES: 469   CHOLESTEROL: 695 mg   SODIUM: 1485 mg   FIBER: 2 g

Health tip:

Omit salt. Cholesterol-watchers should skip this dish.

CALORIES: 469   CHOLESTEROL: 695 mg   SODIUM: 419 mg   FIBER: 2 g

—————— ◇ ——————

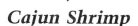

Cajun Shrimp

Lorraine Klein was one of my primary tasters for the recipes in this book. Although she says she's not too fond of seafood, she did have a second portion of this and thought it was divine.

1½ pounds jumbo shrimp, peeled and deveined
1 tablespoon plus 1 teaspoon Cajun seasoning or spicy seafood
    seasoning (or you can use spicy seasoned salt)
¼ cup butter, divided
½ cup chopped onion
½ cup chopped celery
2 tablespoons lemon juice
2 cups cooked wild rice

In a medium-size bowl, toss shrimp with seasoning. Melt 2 tablespoons of the butter in a large skillet over medium heat. Add shrimp and cook, stirring, until they turn pink and are just cooked through (there's almost nothing tougher than an overcooked shrimp), about 4 minutes. Remove shrimp from skillet and set aside.

Melt remaining 2 tablespoons butter in the same skillet, scraping up all the seasonings that cling to the bottom and side. Add onion and celery and cook, stirring frequently, until softened. Stir in lemon juice. Stir in wild rice and reserved shrimp and cook, stirring, just until heated through.

SERVES 4.

CALORIES: 325   CHOLESTEROL: 203 mg   SODIUM: 2412 mg   FIBER: 3 g

Health tip:

Use 2 tablespoons unsalted margarine instead of butter.

CALORIES: 273   CHOLESTEROL: 172 mg   SODIUM: 2322 mg   FIBER: 3 g

———————— ◇ ————————

Creamy Scallops and Leeks with Wild Rice

When I'm not writing cookbooks, I work as a food stylist for magazines and advertisers when they photograph food. Often I bring dishes that I've made to work with me to get the opinion of other food professionals. The day I brought this to a photography session for Parents Magazine, Abby Johnson, the associate food editor, liked it so much that she asked for the recipe. I consider that a very high compliment.

2 tablespoons butter
¾ cup sliced leek, both white and green parts
1½ cups sliced mushrooms
1 pound bay scallops (or sea scallops cut into quarters)
2 tablespoons chopped parsley
Pinch crumbled thyme
¼ cup dry white wine
½ cup heavy cream
⅛ teaspoon salt
Pinch ground red pepper
2 cups cooked wild rice

Melt the butter in a large skillet over medium-high heat. Add leek and cook, stirring, until softened. Add mushrooms and cook, stirring and tossing, until softened. Stir in scallops, parsley, and thyme. Cook, stirring, until scallops are opaque, about 3 minutes. Using a slotted spoon, remove the scallops and vegetables from skillet. Stir wine then cream into juices remaining in skillet. Bring to a boil over high heat and cook until the entire surface of the liquid is furiously bubbling and the cream has turn a light beige, 3 to 4 minutes.

Return scallops and vegetables to skillet. Stir in salt and red pepper. Cook, stirring, until scallops and vegetables are heated through. At this point you can stir the wild rice into the scallop mixture, or you can serve the scallop mixture on a bed of reheated wild rice.

SERVES 4.
CALORIES: 373   CHOLESTEROL: 93 mg   SODIUM: 516 mg   FIBER: 4 g

Health tip:
Omit salt and don't eat too much.
CALORIES: 373   CHOLESTEROL: 93 mg   SODIUM: 250 mg   FIBER: 4 g

Inside-Out Beef Wellington

Back in the days before we worried about cholesterol and saturated fat, beef Wellington starred at many important events. It was made with a whole beef tenderloin filet (the most tender and pricey part of the beef), which was spread with a pâté de foie gras, covered with puff pastry, and baked. The pastry was lightly browned and flaky, and the pâté-flavored beef was rare and juicy. More often than not, a brown sauce, made with wine and truffles, was served, too. It stands to reason that any recipe that was so popular and so enduring had to be out of this world, and lately this great recipe has enjoyed a comeback. My version of beef Wellington uses a less-costly boneless sirloin steak, and is stuffed with a mixture of wild rice and pâté. Keep the servings reasonably small and expect a lot of compliments.

2 tablespoons butter
2 tablespoons minced shallot or the white part of a scallion
1 cup cooked wild rice
⅓ cup of smooth creamy liver pâté you can afford (This is sometimes
  called a liver mousse. Any smooth, creamy pâté will work,
  and foie gras would be lovely! Just make sure you don't use a
  coarse dry pâté, such as a pâté de campagne, for the pâté
  must melt in this recipe.)
1 tablespoon chopped parsley
1¾ pound boneless sirloin steak, about 1½ inches thick
¼ teaspoon salt
⅛ teaspoon pepper

Preheat oven to 350°F.

Heat the butter in a small skillet. Add shallot and cook, stirring, until softened. Remove skillet from heat and stir in wild rice, pâté, and parsley. Set aside.

Working with a long, sharp knife, cut the steak almost in half, lengthwise. (Just imagine that you are cutting the steak into two thinner steaks. Place your hand flat on top of the steak and slice through the meat halfway down between your hand and the cutting surface. Leave about ½ inch uncut so that you can open the steak like a book.) Open the steak and sprinkle the cut surface with salt and pepper. Spread rice mixture over one half of the cut surface, then fold the other half over it, closing the steak back into its original shape. Fasten the cut edge with wooden picks or skewers.

Place the stuffed steak in a shallow roasting pan.

Bake for 40 minutes for rare, or longer for medium-done. Let stand 10 minutes before slicing.

SERVES 6.
CALORIES: 494   CHOLESTEROL: 129 mg   SODIUM: 334 mg   FIBER: 1 g

Health tip:
Omit salt and pâté; use unsalted margarine instead of butter.
CALORIES: 453   CHOLESTEROL: 101 mg   SODIUM: 91 mg   FIBER: 1 g

---

——————— ◇ ———————

Wild Oxtail Stew

There's an old saying that the meat is sweetest closest to the bone. So, even if you think you don't like oxtail, you owe it to yourself to try it, for the flavor of the meat is simply wonderful. Oxtail is difficult to eat. The best way is simply to pick the pieces up in your fingers and nibble the last bits of meat that cling to the bone. Or you can substitute lean short ribs for the oxtail.

2 tablespoons vegetable oil
2½ pounds oxtail (it will be cut in short lengths) or lean short ribs
1½ cups chopped onion
2 cloves garlic, minced
2 cups water
1 cup dry red wine
1 can (6 ounce) tomato paste
1 bay leaf
½ teaspoon crumbled marjoram
¼ teaspoon crumbled rosemary
1½ teaspoons salt
¼ teaspoon pepper
2 cups sliced carrot
¾ cup wild rice, rinsed

In a large heavy saucepan or Dutch oven, heat the oil over medium-high heat. Add oxtail pieces and cook, turning and adjusting heat, until well browned. Add onion and garlic and cook, stirring, until softened. Stir in water, wine, tomato paste, bay leaf, marjoram, rosemary, salt, and pepper. Bring to a boil. Lower heat and simmer, covered, for 1 hour. Stir in carrot and wild rice. Cover and simmer for 1 hour longer. Remove bay leaf before serving.

SERVES 4.
CALORIES: 740   CHOLESTEROL: 128 mg   SODIUM: 679 mg   FIBER: 5 g

Health tip:
Omit salt.
CALORIES: 740   CHOLESTEROL: 128 mg   SODIUM: 140 mg   FIBER: 5 g

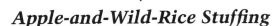

Apple-and-Wild-Rice Stuffing

Use this stuffing to fill a roasting chicken or 6 to 8 Cornish hens. Double the recipe to stuff a turkey. (And, although I haven't tried it, I expect that this would also be a wonderful filling for duck or goose.)

3 tablespoons butter
2 tablespoons minced shallot
1 cup chopped peeled apple (use a tart crisp apple, such as Granny
    Smith or McIntosh)
⅓ cup finely chopped celery
½ teaspoon salt
¼ teaspoon crumbled rosemary
¼ teaspoon crumbled thyme
⅛ teaspoon pepper
3 cups bread cubes (about 4 slices of white bread)
1 cup cooked wild rice
2 tablespoons chopped parsley

In a medium-size skillet, melt the butter over medium heat. Add shallot and cook, stirring, until softened. Add apple, celery, salt, rosemary, thyme, and pepper. Cook, stirring, until apple is softened. Remove skillet from heat. Stir in bread cubes, then wild rice and parsley, and toss gently until completely combined.
    (Nutrition information is based on ½ cup stuffing.)

MAKES 3½ CUPS.
CALORIES: 143   CHOLESTEROL: 15 mg   SODIUM: 428 mg   FIBER: 2 g

Health tip:
Omit salt; use a nonstick skillet, substituting 2 teaspoons unsalted margarine for butter.
CALORIES: 113   CHOLESTEROL: 0 mg   SODIUM: 142 mg   FIBER: 2 g

---------------◇---------------

Stuffed Cornish Game Hens

You can also use this elegant stuffing to fill a 3- to 4-pound broiler-fryer chicken. Or you can double the recipe for an even bigger bird. Just use the liver that comes with whatever poultry you're using when you make the stuffing.

2 slices bacon, cut into 1-inch pieces
½ cup chopped onion
⅓ cup chopped celery
Livers from hens, finely chopped
1 cup cooked wild rice
1 tablespoon chopped parsley
½ teaspoon salt
¼ teaspoon crumbled thyme
¼ teaspoon pepper
4 small or 2 large (total weight should be about 4 pounds) Cornish
    game hens
Additional salt and pepper

Preheat oven to 350°F.

In a medium-size skillet, cook the bacon until crisp. Remove bacon and drain on paper towels.

Add onion and celery to the bacon fat left in the skillet. Cook, stirring, until softened. Add liver and cook, stirring, just until cooked through. Remove from heat and stir in rice, parsley, salt, thyme, and pepper.

Skewer the skin at the neck end of the hens to close the opening. Place about ½ cup of the stuffing in the body cavity of each bird, then skewer the skin together to close the vent. (You can use wooden picks for this job.) Sprinkle hens with salt and pepper. Place in a roasting pan that is large enough to hold the hens comfortably.

Bake for 50 to 60 minutes, or until juices run clear when hens are pierced with a fork.

SERVES 4.
CALORIES: 345   CHOLESTEROL: 180 mg   SODIUM: 414 mg   FIBER: 2 g

Health tip:
Omit bacon and liver and use 2 teaspoons oil in a nonstick skillet to cook vegetables. Omit salt.
CALORIES: 322   CHOLESTEROL: 87 mg   SODIUM: 90 mg   FIBER: 2 g

Salade de Provence

Since the olives contribute so much to the character of this salad, I would advise you to make the effort to find an olive that is a little more unique than the canned supermarket variety. If you can get to a fancy-food store, you will undoubtedly find an interesting selection of bottled, canned and loose olives. Try and find a small French olive, such as a black Nicoise, that is usually oval and slightly tapered at one end. Or you could substitute small Greek or Italian olives. Most, if not all, of these olives will have pits, but that's life.

2 cups cooked and cooled wild rice
½ cup diced or crumbled goat cheese (I use part of a log of Montrachet)
⅓ cup small French olives (see above)
3 tablespoons Provence herb-flavored oil (or olive oil, plus ¼ teaspoon
    herbes de Provence or fines herbes)
1 tablespoon Cabernet-wine vinegar or red-wine vinegar
2 teaspoons lemon juice
2 teaspoons minced shallot
1 teaspoon Dijon mustard
Mixed salad greens (as many colors, flavor, and textures and you can
    find)

In a large bowl, toss the wild rice with cheese and olives.

In a small bowl, whisk together the oil, vinegar, lemon juice, shallot, and mustard until completely combined.

Pour dressing over rice mixture and toss gently until well mixed. Spoon onto a bed of mixed salad greens.

SERVES 4.

CALORIES: 268   CHOLESTEROL: 33 mg   SODIUM: 610 mg   FIBER: 3 g

Health tip:

Use a low-fat goat cheese and only half of the dressing.

CALORIES: 208   CHOLESTEROL: 26 mg   SODIUM: 352 mg   FIBER: 3 g

———————◇———————

Tropical-Fruit-and-Wild-Rice Salad

The impact this salad will have depends upon locating exotic fruits to put in it. I like to use a pink Hawaiian papaya, when I can find it, or otherwise I substitute a more ordinary papaya (peak season, May through September). Kiwifruit, from California or New Zealand, is available almost all the time. Finding a feijoa may give you a little trouble, but what you are looking for is a little dark-skinned fruit (the skin is similar to an avocado) that looks something like a kiwi. The feijoa is intensely aromatic, with a flavor that will remind you of a combination of pineapple, pear, and banana. The flesh is creamy-white and has a texture something like a pear.

1 cup cooked and cooled wild rice
1 cup diced papaya
1 kiwifruit, peeled and diced
1 feijoa, peeled and diced (if you can't find a feijoa, use another kiwi)
⅓ cup chopped pecans
1 tablespoon vegetable oil
2 teaspoons red-wine vinegar
¼ teaspoon salt

In a medium-size bowl, combine the wild rice, papaya, kiwifruit, feijoa, and pecans.

In a cup, mix together the oil, vinegar, and salt and pour over wild-rice mixture. Toss gently until well combined.

SERVES 4.
CALORIES: 186   CHOLESTEROL: 0 mg   SODIUM: 237 mg   FIBER: 4 g

Health tip:
Omit salt.
CALORIES: 180   CHOLESTEROL: 0 mg   SODIUM: 4 mg   FIBER: 4 g

—————— ◇ ——————

Wild Rice with Fennel and Endive

Fennel has a distinct licorice flavor that many people love, but some don't. If you fall into the second category, or can't find fennel, substitute celery.

¼ cup sliced almonds
2 cups cooked and cooled wild rice
1 cup sliced fennel
1 Belgian endive, cut into bite-size pieces
½ cup chopped dried fig
1 small red onion, thinly sliced
3 tablespoons olive oil
2 tablespoons lemon juice
1 tablespoon white-wine vinegar
½ clove garlic, minced
¼ teaspoon herbes de Provence or fines herbes
Leaf lettuce (optional)

Preheat oven to 350°F.
Place almonds on a baking sheet. Bake for 10 minutes, stirring once. Set aside.
In a large bowl, combine the wild rice, fennel, endive, fig, and onion.
In a small bowl, stir together the oil, lemon juice, vinegar, garlic, and fines herbes. Pour dressing over wild-rice mixture and toss gently until well combined. Serve over lettuce leaves, if you like, sprinkled with almonds.

SERVES 4.
CALORIES: 288   CHOLESTEROL: 0 mg   SODIUM: 238 mg   FIBER: 7 g

Health tip:
Use half the amount of dressing, diluting it with 1 tablespoon orange juice to make it go further.
CALORIES: 244   CHOLESTEROL: 0 mg   SODIUM: 38 mg   FIBER: 7 g

———————◇———————

Wild-Rice Slaw

Wild rice gives this fairly typical slaw a lot of body and infinitely more interest. The parsnip adds a lovely fresh flavor, so please don't be tempted to leave it out.

2 cups chopped cabbage
1 cup cooked and cooled wild rice
½ cup shredded carrot
½ cup shredded parsnip
¼ cup chopped parsley
¼ cup mayonnaise
¼ cup sour cream
¼ cup sliced scallion, both white and green parts
1 teaspoon white vinegar
½ teaspoon salt
¼ teaspoon pepper

In a large bowl, combine cabbage, wild rice, carrot, parsnip, and parsley.

In a small bowl, stir together mayonnaise, sour cream, scallion, vinegar, salt, and pepper. Pour over wild-rice mixture and toss gently until completely combined.

SERVES 6.
CALORIES: 136   CHOLESTEROL: 10 mg   SODIUM: 312 mg   FIBER: 3 g

Health tip:
Use ½ cup reduced-calorie mayonnaise instead of regular mayonnaise and sour cream; omit salt.
CALORIES: 96   CHOLESTEROL: 5 mg   SODIUM: 88 MG   FIBER: 3 g

———————— ◇ ————————

Mandarin-Orange-and-Wild-Rice Salad

Mandarin-orange sections look pretty in this salad, and their sweet-and-sour flavor contrasts nicely with the taste and texture of wild rice.

2 cups cooked and cooled wild rice
1 can (10 ounce) mandarin-orange sections, drained
½ cup chopped walnuts
2 tablespoons walnut oil or vegetable oil
2 tablespoons orange juice
1 tablespoon raspberry vinegar or cider vinegar

In a large bowl, toss the wild rice, orange sections, and walnuts.
In a cup, stir together the oil, orange juice, and vinegar. Pour over wild-rice mixture and toss gently until completely combined.

SERVES 6.
CALORIES: 197   CHOLESTEROL: 0 mg   SODIUM: 138 mg   FIBER: 3 g

Health tip:
Use half the amount of dressing.
CALORIES: 176   CHOLESTEROL: 0 mg   SODIUM: 5 mg   FIBER: 3 g

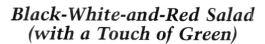

Black-White-and-Red Salad (with a Touch of Green)

This salad has just the right amount of crispy stuff and mushy stuff, all in the right flavors. It makes a good main-course salad, as well as a side salad.

1 can (19 ounce) cannellini (white kidney beans), drained
1½ cups cooked and cooled wild rice
1 cup chopped red bell pepper
¼ cup sliced scallion, both white and green parts
2 tablespoons olive oil
1 tablespoon vegetable oil
1 tablespoon cider vinegar
1 tablespoon lemon juice
2 teaspoons spicy brown mustard
1 clove garlic, minced
½ teaspoon salt
⅛ teaspoon pepper

In a large bowl, toss together the beans, wild rice, red bell pepper, and scallion.

In a small bowl, stir together the olive oil, vegetable oil, vinegar, lemon juice, mustard, garlic, salt, and pepper. Pour over wild-rice mixture and toss gently until completely combined.

SERVES 8 (as a side dish).
CALORIES: 140   CHOLESTEROL: 0 mg   SODIUM: 460 mg   FIBER: 6 g

Health tip:
Omit salt.
CALORIES: 140   CHOLESTEROL: 0 mg   SODIUM: 252 mg   FIBER: 6 g

Summery Wild-Rice-and-Cucumber Salad

Cucumber, dill, and radish are all fresh, summery flavors, and when you combine them with a light and creamy yogurt dressing, they're guaranteed to make you feel as "cool as a cucumber" on a hot day.

1½ cups chopped peeled or unpeeled cucumber
1 cup cooked and cooled wild rice
½ cup sliced radish
¼ cup sliced scallion, both white and green parts
⅓ cup plain yogurt
2 tablespoons mayonnaise
2 tablespoons snipped fresh dill or
  1 tablespoon dried dill weed
¼ teaspoon grated lemon rind
¼ teaspoon salt
⅛ teaspoon pepper

In a large bowl, combine the cucumber, wild rice, radish, and scallion.

In a small bowl, stir together the yogurt, mayonnaise, dill, lemon rind, salt, and pepper. Pour over wild-rice mixture and toss gently until completely combined.

SERVES 4.
CALORIES: 242   CHOLESTEROL: 4 mg   SODIUM: 866 mg   FIBER: 2 g

Health tip:
Use reduced-calorie mayonnaise instead of regular mayonnaise; omit salt.
CALORIES: 210   CHOLESTEROL: 2 mg   SODIUM: 65 mg   FIBER: 2 g

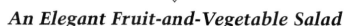

An Elegant Fruit-and-Vegetable Salad

I originally made this salad during a last-minute emergency. I had some leftover wild rice, so I threw in with it almost anything else I could find in the refrigerator, and, as so often happens in times of "food crises," it turned out to be great.

2 cups cooked wild rice
1 cup cooked asparagus tips (you can use the stems, too, if you like)
1 cup sliced celery
1 cup chopped apple
⅓ cup chopped red onion
2 tablespoons orange juice
2 tablespoons vegetable oil
1 tablespoon olive oil
2 teaspoons Dijon mustard
2 teaspoons lime juice
2 teaspoons balsamic vinegar
1 teaspoon honey
¼ teaspoon crumbled tarragon
¼ teaspoon salt

In a large bowl, combine the wild rice, asparagus, celery, apple, and onion.

In a bowl, stir together the orange juice, vegetable oil, olive oil, mustard, lime juice, vinegar, honey, tarragon, and salt. Pour over wild-rice mixture and toss gently until completely combined.

SERVES 8.
CALORIES: 115   CHOLESTEROL: 0 mg   SODIUM: 82 mg   FIBER: 3 g

Health tips:
Omit salt; use half of the dressing.
CALORIES: 000   CHOLESTEROL: 0 mg   SODIUM: 15 mg   FIBER: 3 g

———————— ◇ ————————

Wild Rice and Pasta with a Creamy Tomato Sauce

Although this sauce is easy to make, it's one of the best I've ever eaten. The wild rice mixed with the pasta adds a flavor and texture dimension that makes the finished dish as interesting as it is tasty. In making the sauce, I prefer to use Asiago, an Italian grating cheese with a more delicate flavor than Parmesan.

1 cup tubetti or other small pasta
2 tablespoons olive oil
1 cup chopped onion
2 cloves garlic, minced
1 can (14½ ounce) whole peeled tomatoes
2 tablespoons tomato paste
½ teaspoon salt
⅛ teaspoon ground red pepper
⅓ cup grated Asiago or Parmesan cheese
½ cup heavy cream
1 cup cooked wild rice

Cook the pasta according to package directions; drain.

In a medium-size saucepan, heat oil over medium-high heat. Add onion and garlic and cook, stirring, until softened. Stir in undrained tomatoes, tomato paste, salt, and red pepper. Bring to a boil, reduce heat, and simmer for 20 minutes. Stir in cheese, then cream. Simmer for 10 minutes longer, or until thickened.

In a large bowl, toss together the cooked pasta and wild rice. Pour sauce over wild-rice mixture and toss gently until well combined.

SERVES 8 (as a side dish).
CALORIES: 106   CHOLESTEROL: 23 mg   SODIUM: 348 mg   FIBER: 2 g

Health tip:
Omit salt; use half the cheese; substitute half-and-half for cream.
CALORIES: 134   CHOLESTEROL: 8 mg   SODIUM: 165 mg   FIBER: 2 g

───────── ◇ ─────────

Lentils and Wild Rice

I'm one of those people who think that everything tastes delicious, as long as it has lentils in it, and this recipe is no exception. After she tasted it, my sister Sherry observed that leftovers would probably make a lovely salad if they were dressed with a vinaigrette, and I'm sure she's right.

1 can (13¾ ounce) ready-to-serve beef broth or
  1¾ cups vegetable broth (see page 19)
¾ cup water
1 medium-size onion, peeled and left whole
4 cloves
½ cup wild rice, rinsed
½ cup lentils, rinsed and picked over
¼ cup sliced scallion, both white and green parts

In a 2-quart saucepan, bring the broth and water to a boil. Stud the onion with cloves and add to the broth along with rice. Bring to a boil. Reduce heat, cover, and simmer for 15 minutes. Stir in lentils. Cover and simmer for 35 minutes longer.
Discard onion and stir in scallion.

SERVES 6.
CALORIES: 121   CHOLESTEROL: 5 mg   SODIUM: 214 mg   FIBER: 3 g

Health tip:
Use low-sodium broth.
CALORIES: 121   CHOLESTEROL: 5 mg   SODIUM: 130 mg   FIBER: 3 g

White-and-Wild Rice

This is a homemade version of the rice mix you can buy in a box—and a lot better. I think that once you've tasted it you may never go back to the packaged version again.

2 tablespoons vegetable oil
1 cup chopped onion
1 can (13¾ ounce) ready-to-serve beef broth or
     1¾ cups vegetable broth (see page 19)
¾ cup water
⅓ cup wild rice, rinsed
⅛ teaspoon crumbled thyme
1 bay leaf
⅔ cup converted white rice
2 tablespoons chopped parsley

In a 2-quart saucepan, heat the oil over medium-high heat. Add onion and cook, stirring frequently, until softened. Stir in broth and water and bring to a boil. Stir in wild rice, thyme, and bay leaf. Reduce heat, cover, and simmer for 30 minutes. Stir in converted rice. Simmer, covered, for 25 minutes longer, or until all of the liquid has been absorbed. Remove bay leaf and stir in parsley.

SERVES 6.
CALORIES: 166   CHOLESTEROL: 0 mg   SODIUM: 208 mg   FIBER: 1 g

Health tip:
Use low-sodium broth.
CALORIES: 166   CHOLESTEROL: 0 mg   SODIUM: 30 mg   FIBER: 1 g

Rice Trio with Peas

I use a combination of wild, brown, and white rices in this dish. And even though it's very tasty, since the cooked long-grain brown rice looks about the same as the white rice. You may want to try and find a dark-brown rice, such as Wahani, and use that instead.

1 can (13¾ ounce) ready to-serve chicken broth or
    1¾ cups vegetable broth (see page 19)
¾ cup water
⅓ cup wild rice, rinsed
⅓ cup long-grain brown rice or Wahani rice
⅓ cup converted white rice
1 cup frozen peas
¼ cup grated Parmesan cheese
¼ cup chopped scallion, both white and green parts
2 tablespoons butter

In a 3-quart saucepan, combine the broth and water and bring to a boil. Stir in wild rice. Reduce heat, cover, and simmer for 10 minutes. Stir in brown rice, cover, and simmer for 25 minutes. Stir in white rice, cover, and simmer for 15 minutes. Stir in peas and simmer for 10 minutes longer, covered, or until all of the liquid has been absorbed. Remove pan from heat. Stir in cheese, scallion, and butter.

SERVES 6.
CALORIES: 171   CHOLESTEROL: 13 mg   SODIUM: 418 mg   FIBER: 1 g

Health tip:
Omit salt; use low-sodium broth. Use unsalted margarine instead of butter, and only 2 tablespoons cheese.
CALORIES: 159   CHOLESTEROL: 1 mg   SODIUM: 153 mg   FIBER: 1 g

Wild Rice with Summer Squash

Zucchini and yellow squash used to be summertime vegetable treats. Now they're both available all year, so you can enjoy this dish any time.

2 tablespoons vegetable oil
½ cup chopped onion
1 can (13¾ ounce) ready-to-serve chicken broth or
1¾ cups vegetable broth (see page 19)
¼ cup water
¼ teaspoon salt
½ cup wild rice, rinsed
½ cup converted white rice
1 cup sliced zucchini
1 cup sliced yellow squash
¼ teaspoon crumbled oregano
⅛ teaspoon pepper

In a 3-quart saucepan heat the oil over medium-high heat. Add onion and cook, stirring, until softened. Stir in broth, water, and salt and bring to a boil. Stir in wild rice and return to boiling. Reduce heat and simmer, covered, for 30 minutes. Stir in white rice and simmer, covered, for 15 minutes. Stir in zucchini, yellow squash, oregano, and pepper. Cover and simmer for 15 minutes longer.

SERVES 6.
CALORIES: 165 CHOLESTEROL: 0 mg SODIUM: 298 mg FIBER: 2 g

Health tip:
Reduce oil to 2 teaspoons and use a nonstock saucepan. Or, cook onion in a nonstick skillet, transferring to the larger pan to finish cooking. Use low-sodium broth; omit salt.
CALORIES: 145 CHOLESTEROL: 0 mg SODIUM: 108 mg FIBER: 2 g

Southern-Style Wild Rice with Mushrooms

Southerners almost never cook a starchy dish without some kind of bacon or pork flavoring, but you can leave it out and you'll still have a very delicious side dish.

3 slices bacon, cut into ½-inch pieces or
  2 tablespoons vegetable oil
½ cup chopped onion
½ cup chopped green bell pepper
2 cups sliced mushrooms
1 can (13¾ ounce) ready-to-serve beef broth or
  1¾ cups vegetable broth (see page 19)
¼ cup water
¼ teaspoon salt
½ cup wild rice, rinsed
½ cup brown rice

In a 3-quart saucepan, cook the bacon until crisp. Remove bacon and drain on paper towels.

Add the onion and green pepper to bacon fat in skillet. Cook, stirring, until vegetables are softened. Stir in mushrooms and cook, stirring and tossing, until softened. Stir in broth, water, and salt and bring to a boil. Stir in wild rice. Reduce heat and simmer, covered, for 20 minutes. Stir in brown rice. Cover and simmer for 45 minutes, or until most of the liquid has been absorbed. Remove from heat and let stand for 10 minutes. Stir in reserved bacon.

SERVES 8.
CALORIES: 112   CHOLESTEROL: 4 mg   SODIUM: 266 mg   FIBER: 2 g

Health tip:
Omit bacon; cook in a nonstick saucepan with 2 teaspoons of oil. Or, cook onion, green pepper, and mushrooms in a nonstick skillet, transferring them to the larger pan to finish cooking.
CALORIES: 98   CHOLESTEROL: 0 mg   SODIUM: 161 mg   FIBER: 2 g

––––––––––– ◊ –––––––––––

Green Beans, Shiitake Mushrooms, and Wild Rice

I first tasted green beans with shiitake mushrooms at the home of my friend, Holly Garrison, and loved the combination. In my adaptation for this book, I added wild rice and, if you'll forgive me, Holly, I think it's even better.

3 tablespoons butter
2 tablespoons minced shallot
1 cup sliced shiitake mushrooms
¼ cup beef or vegetable broth
2 cups green beans, cut into 1-inch pieces
1½ cups cooked wild rice

In a large skillet with a tight-fitting lid, heat the butter over medium heat. Add shallot and mushrooms and cook, stirring and tossing, until mushrooms are softened. Stir in broth. Add green beans, cover, and steam for 10 minutes, or until tender-crisp. Add rice and stir until heated through.

SERVES 6.
CALORIES: 122   CHOLESTEROL: 16 mg   SODIUM: 185 mg   FIBER: 3 g

Health tip:
Use 1 tablespoon unsalted margarine instead of butter and cook in a nonstick skillet.
CALORIES: 88   CHOLESTEROL: 0 mg   SODIUM: 39 mg   FIBER: 3 g

———————◇———————

Wild Rice with Red and Yellow Peppers

If you want to turn this beautiful dish into a full meal, sauté two chicken-breast halves until done, then cut them into strips, and stir them into the wild-rice-and-peppers mixture just before serving. Or, for a more au courant touch, grill the breasts (on a barbecue or under the oven broiler), and serve on top or alongside of the wild-rice-and-peppers mixture.

3 tablespoons butter
½ cup chopped onion
2 cloves garlic, minced
1 cup chopped red bell pepper
1 cup chopped yellow bell pepper
1 cup sliced zucchini
2 cups cooked wild rice
¼ teaspoon salt
⅛ teaspoon pepper

In a large skillet, heat the butter over medium-high heat. Add onion and garlic and cook, stirring frequently, until onion is softened. Add red bell pepper, yellow bell pepper, and zucchini and cook, stirring, until tender-crisp. Stir in rice, salt, and pepper and cook, stirring, until heated through.

SERVES 4.
CALORIES: 203   CHOLESTEROL: 0 mg   SODIUM: 506 mg   FIBER: 3 g

Health tip:
Reduce butter to 2 teaspoons and cook in a nonstick skillet; omit salt.
CALORIES: 163   CHOLESTEROL: 0 mg   SODIUM: 39 mg   FIBER: 3 g

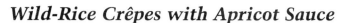

Wild-Rice Crêpes with Apricot Sauce

The slight chewiness and subtle flavor of wild rice in these delicate crêpes makes them a luxurious dessert treat. If you leave the sugar out of the crêpe batter, you could also serve these as savory crêpes and fill them with any wonderful mixture you like. For instance, you might want to try using the scallops-and-leeks mixture on page 356, serving it inside the crêpes instead of with wild rice.

Crepes:

> 1½ cups milk
> ¼ cup butter, melted
> ¼ cup sugar
> 2 eggs
> 1 cup all-purpose flour
> ⅔ cup cooked wild rice
> Oil, for greasing skillet

Sauce:

> ¾ cup apricot pouring fruit (This is a relatively new product. Look for it with the syrups or jellies and jams at the supermarket. If you can't find it, use apricot jam.)
> 2 tablespoons hazelnut or orange liqueur

To make the crêpes, combine milk, butter, sugar, and eggs in the container of an electric blender. Cover and blend until thoroughly combined. Add flour, cover, and blend until smooth. Stir in wild rice, cover, and blend until chopped. Let stand for 30 minutes.

Heat a 9-inch, slope-sided, nonstick skillet (the cooking surface should measure 5½ to 6 inches) until a drop of water sprinkled in the bottom of the pan bounces about before evaporating. Brush skillet very lightly with oil. Pour a scant ¼ cup of the batter into the skillet and swirl it around to cover the bottom. Cook until the underside of the crêpe is lightly browned, about 2 minutes. Turn crêpe over and cook until the second side is lightly browned. Remove crêpe by tilting the skillet over a piece of waxed paper. (The crêpe should simply fall out of the pan. If it doesn't, use a wide spatula to assist.) Repeat this procedure with remaining batter, greasing the pan occasionally. Stack crêpes with a piece of waxed paper between each. (This keeps them from sticking, and if you want to you can simply wrap the whole stack tightly and freeze until needed. Thaw crêpes just before using and reheat in the microwave or in a 325°F oven.)

To make sauce, combine pouring fruit and liqueur in the blender container. Cover and blend until smooth. Pour the sauce into a small saucepan to be heated gently just before serving.

To assemble, fold crêpes into quarters and divide among serving plates. Pour a little of the warm sauce over the crêpes and serve remaining sauce on the side.

MAKES 14 CREPES AND 1 CUP SAUCE.
CALORIES: 186   CHOLESTEROL: 42 mg   SODIUM: 53 mg   FIBER: 1 g

Health tip:
Use unsalted margarine instead of butter. Substitute 1-percent-fat milk for regular milk. Eat just one.
CALORIES: 181   CHOLESTEROL: 30 mg   SODIUM: 30 mg   FIBER: 1 g

IV

───◇───

UNUSUAL GRAINS AND BREAKFAST CEREALS: SOMETHING OLD, SOMETHING NEW, SOMETHING MANUFACTURED

───◇───

Amaranth
Job's Tears
Quinoa
Teff
Triticale
Breakfast Cereals

This group of grains ranges from the purest and least tampered with to totally man-made grains and grain products. I consider them to be unusual in a couple of respects. First, they are practically unknown to the general population. Second, most of them do not fit into any of the typical grain generalizations.

When we think of grain, certain qualities come to mind: Grains are starchy and filling with a flavor that is usually described as nutty. With the exception of triticale, the unusual grains have few of these qualities. Teff is seedlike and not at all starchy, although the flavor can be described as a bit like wheat. Amaranth and quinoa have a slippery texture, and the flavor of amaranth is more like a vegetable than like a grain. Job's tears seems closer to beans than grains in both taste and texture. And triticale, since it is a hybrid of rye and wheat, has the qualities of true grains. As for breakfast cereals, we all know that they frequently bear no resemblance to real food at all.

Amaranth and quinoa, which were originally grown in South America, have illustrious histories and similar properties. Both grains have the distinction of having been considered sacred by the Aztec and Inca civilizations. However, as a means of dominating both peoples, the Spaniards forced the Aztecs and Incas to abandon their sacred grains, and amaranth and quinoa fell into disuse for hundreds of years.

It was not until recently that any real interest has been focused on the two grains, and for this reason they have remained *pure* in the sense that agricultural scientists have not had the opportunity to experiment with their gene pools in an attempt to produce heartier or greater-yielding strains. Both amaranth and quinoa are small grains that have most of the bran and germ intact, and consequently most of their nutritional value. Both grains contain unusually high amounts of amino acids, lysine, and methionine, which are generally low in the more common grains.

Teff is another ancient grain. Like amaranth and quinoa, teff has been left virtually untouched by scientific hands. It is native to Africa and is the smallest of all grains. In its flour form, teff is the basis for *injera*, the staple bread of Ethiopia.

Job's tears is a newcomer on the American health-food scene, but it has been used for thousands of years in China and Japan, mainly for medicinal purposes and as a skin beautifier.

Triticale has the distinction of being the newest grain in the world. It is a hybrid of wheat and rye and was engineered by scientists seeking a grain that would be as hearty as rye and as appealing as wheat. It was also hoped that such a grain would have a nutritional value greater than either of the other two, and idealists of the sixties envisioned the grain making a significant dent in world hunger. Unfortunately, triticale is not as hearty as was hoped for, and has never gained anything like overwhelming acceptance. The end result is that much of it is used for animal feed.

Breakfast cereals have the rather sad history of having started out as a healthful product that evolved, in many instances, into nutritional nightmares. A disheartening number are loaded with sugar and saturated fats (palm and coconut oils), sugar, salt, and artificial colors. As a nutritionist, I certainly don't condemn the eating of cold cereals, especially since they do promote milk consumption, but if you're eating this type of cereal with the idea that you're getting a nutritious breakfast, read package labels carefully, or stick with the cooked cereals.

The whole grain scene is currently in a state of frenzied growth. In addition to amaranth, quinoa, Job's tears, and teff, we can look forward to sorghum (an African grain) and newer varieties of quinoa and amaranth making their debut at health-food stores in the near future.

AMARANTH

When Cortez conquered Mexico, the "savages" he found there were actually the advanced Aztec civilization, rich in culture and, more important to their conqueror, *gold!*

The Aztec's diet consisted mainly of corn, beans, and amaranth. The latter, they felt, made them strong (they were probably right about that, since amaranth has a higher protein profile than either of the other two) and they used it as part of their religious ceremonies, and even sent it as a tribute to their emperor, Montezuma.

In addition to stealing the Aztec's gold, the Spaniards also destroyed all the amaranth they could find and forbade the Aztecs from eating it. Eventually the Aztecs themselves cast out the grain from their lives, a real pity, since the nutritional loss was significant to a population who was by then poor and undernourished.

Types of Amaranth Available

Whole-grained amaranth: The whole grain, unhulled.

Amaranth flour: Whole-grain amaranth, finely ground.

Amaranth pasta: Pasta made from amaranth flour and whole-wheat flour.

Texture and Flavor

Amaranth is golden in color with an occasional dark grain, and is as tiny as a poppy seed. As it cooks, the grain becomes transparent, and a miniscule root sprout is visible. The texture will vary considerably depending on the amount of cooking water. If it is cooked according to package directions, the mixture will look like a thick, clear, cornstarch sauce with seeds in it. Cooked with less water, the grain has a mouth feel similar to a crunchy cornmeal mush. It may also remind you of caviar because you are so aware of the many, tiny, individual grains.

Amaranth's distinctive flavor is similar to the aroma of fresh corn silk, and is a taste that may take some getting used to. Stirring butter into cooked amaranth mellows the flavor considerably.

Heating amaranth in a skillet, with or without oil, will pop the grains and they will become little white puffs, which have a milder flavor than the boiled version. If you decide to try popped amaranth, do not be surprised to find that, like corn, it pops high and far, so you may want to have a lid handy to contain it. Popped amaranth can be eaten like popcorn, or used as a kind of miniature crouton in soup or in salads.

Compatible Foods, Herbs, and Spices

The cooked texture of amaranth makes it unsuitable for using in salads or as a vegetable dish. It is best when used in baked goods or, to take advantage of its crunch, stirred into smooth-textured dishes. Combining amaranth and other grains can add a fresh and unusual flavor. The same is true of amaranth flour. Substitute up to one fourth of amaranth flour for the all-purpose flour in most baked goods.

Adding cooked amaranth to some batters (pancakes or waffles, for instance) helps the finished product to retain moisture and gives it a wonderful lightness.

Availability

Amaranth is available in most health-food stores and through mail-order grain catalogs (see page 21). Because of its high nutrition profile, you will find that it has been added to many health-food products, such as breakfast flakes, cookies, breads, and pasta.

Nutritional Content

Because it is so small, amaranth is not hulled as most grains are, so the benefits of all the vitamins and fiber contained in the hull remain. It is one of the few grains that contains significant levels of lysine and methionine, which makes it a high-quality protein. Amaranth is also rich in calcium, iron, fiber, and phosphorous.

Substitutions

Except for teff, there are no substitutions for amaranth because of its unusual texture and flavor.

Teff: Similar to amaranth in many ways, although even smaller in size, and its flavor is milder. However, teff flour can be substituted for amaranth flour.

Basic Cooking Instructions

Please read *About Cooking Grains* beginning on page 000. Also note that when cooking amaranth, <u>salt must always be added *after* cooking</u>, or the grain will not absorb the water. Do not cook amaranth with broth.

Stove-top method:

> *1½ cups water*
> *1 cup amaranth*
> *½ teaspoon salt*

In a 1½-quart saucepan, bring the water to a boil. Stir in amaranth and return to boiling. Reduce heat and simmer, covered, for 20 minutes. Stir in salt.

MAKES 2 CUPS.

Microwave method:

> *1½ cups water*
> *1 cup amaranth*
> *½ teaspoon salt*

Place the water in a 2-quart, microwave-safe bowl. Cover with waxed paper and microwave on high (100% power) for 3 minutes. Stir in amaranth. Recover with waxed paper and microwave on high for 2 minutes. Microwave on medium (50% power), still covered with waxed paper, for 10 minutes. Stir in salt. Let stand for 4 minutes.

MAKES 2 CUPS.

Reheating

If you are going to set the cooked amaranth aside, be sure to place a piece of plastic wrap directly on the surface of the grain. Otherwise, when the air drys it out, which happens quickly, the grains cling together and harden into a skin that is tough and like plastic. Chilled amaranth stiffens considerably, and should be microwaved or lightly steamed to restore its soft texture.

AMARANTH RECIPES

*(*indicates easy recipe.)*

———————————◇———————————

Curried Fry Bites
Poor Man's Caviar
Chicken with Amaranth Dumplings
Spinach Quiche with an Amaranth Crust
Amaranth-Pasta Tonnato *
Creamy Mashed Potatoes and Amaranth *
Amaranth and Brown Rice *
Scallions and Amaranth *
Bacon-y Corn Bake *
Amaranth Popovers
Amaranth-Walnut Bread
Light-as-Air Amaranth Pancakes *
Amaranth-Mocha Bundt Cake

Curried Fry Bites

Serve these crunchy spicy appetizers with a dipping sauce of pureed chutney or sweet-and-sour duck sauce. Although I think these are best if eaten right after they are fried, you can make the appetizers in advance, if that's more convenient, and freeze them. Reheat in a 350° F oven for 20 minutes. You may also want to adjust the amount of red pepper given here to suit your own taste.

1 can (19 ounce) chick-peas, drained
1 egg
½ cup cooked amaranth
1 tablespoon curry powder
2 teaspoons chopped cilantro (fresh coriander)
1 clove garlic, minced
½ teaspoon salt
¼ teaspoon ground red pepper
¼ cup amaranth flour
¼ cup all-purpose flour
Oil, for deep frying

Place the chick-peas in the container of a food processor. Cover and process until smooth. Add egg and process until thoroughly combined. Add cooked amaranth, curry, cilantro, garlic, salt, and red pepper. Process until well blended. Add both flours and process again until well blended.

Pour enough oil into a deep-fryer or saucepan so that it measures about 2 inches deep. Heat oil until bubbles form when you drop in a bit of the batter. Drop batter by rounded measuring teaspoonsful into the hot oil. Fry until golden on both sides. (It's important that the oil not be too hot, otherwise the batter will brown too quickly on the outside, but the inside will remain uncooked. On the other hand, if the oil is too cool, the bites will be greasy.)

Remove with a slotted spoon and drain on paper towels.

MAKES 30 BITES.
CALORIES: 53   CHOLESTEROL: 7 mg   SODIUM: 39 mg   FIBER: .5gr

Health tip:
Omit salt.
CALORIES: 53   CHOLESTEROL: 7 mg   SODIUM: 10 mg   FIBER: .5 gr

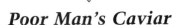

Poor Man's Caviar

The first time I tasted eggplant caviar was at the home of my friend, Robin Gallagher. I must tell you that I spent the entire afternoon glued to the spread, bread, and "caviar." I could not resist adding a little amaranth to my version of the spread and it doesn't hurt it one little bit. This is excellent when served with thinly sliced whole-grain or pumpernickel bread.

1 large (about 1½ pounds) eggplant
¼ cup olive oil
¾ cup finely chopped onion
½ cup finely chopped green bell pepper
3 cloves garlic, minced
1½ cups chopped tomato
⅓ cup cooked amaranth
3 tablespoons water
1 teaspoon white vinegar
1 teaspoon sugar
¼ teaspoon salt
¼ teaspoon black pepper

Preheat oven to 400°F.

Bake the eggplant for 1 hour, or until the outside is charred and the inside is fork-tender.

While eggplant is baking, heat oil in a large skillet over medium heat. Add onion, green pepper, and garlic and cook, stirring, until vegetables are slightly softened. Stir in tomato and cook over low heat, stirring occasionally, until the vegetables are very soft, about 15 minutes. Remove from heat and set aside.

Cut eggplant in half and scrape the flesh out of the shell. Discard shell and chop eggplant finely. Stir into mixture in skillet. Cook over medium heat, stirring occasionally, for 20 minutes. Stir in amaranth until completely blended. Stir in water, vinegar, sugar, salt, and pepper. Cook over medium heat, stirring, until thickened. Cool slightly, then chill until serving time.

MAKES 2¾ CUPS. Nutritional information based on 10 servings.
CALORIES: 95   CHOLESTEROL: 0 mg   SODIUM: 219 mg   FIBER: 3 g

Health tip:
Reduce oil to 1 tablespoon and cook in a nonstick skillet.
CALORIES: 59   CHOLESTEROL: 0 mg   SODIUM: 54 mg   FIBER: 3 g

――――――◇――――――

Chicken with Amaranth Dumplings

This is a thin stew, but very good, almost like a chicken soup with dumplings.

2 tablespoons oil
1 cup chopped onion
3 cups peeled and cubed butternut squash
1 cup sliced carrot
1 cup sliced celery
2 cups water
⅓ cup chopped parsley, divided
1 bay leaf
1 teaspoon salt, divided
⅛ teaspoon pepper
3½-pound chicken, cut into 8 pieces
⅔ cup all-purpose flour
¼ cup amaranth flour
½ teaspoon baking powder
3 tablespoons solid white vegetable shortening
½ cup milk

In a large heavy saucepan or Dutch oven, heat the oil over medium-high heat. Add onion and cook, stirring frequently, until softened. Add squash, carrot, and celery and stir until lightly coated with oil. Add water, ¼ cup of the parsley, bay leaf, ¾ teaspoon of the salt, and pepper. Bring to a boil, add chicken pieces, and return to boiling. Reduce heat and simmer, covered, for about 45 minutes, or until chicken is tender.

After chicken has been cooking for 30 minutes, prepare the dumplings. In a medium-size bowl, stir together both flours, baking powder, and remaining ¼ teaspoon salt. Cut in shortening with a pastry blender or two knives, until mixture resembles coarse cornmeal. Stir in remaining parsley. Stir in milk to form a soft dough.

Remove bay leaf from stew. Drop dumpling batter into the stew by measuring tablespoonsful. You should have about 8 dumplings. Cook, covered, for 10 minutes. Uncover pan and cook for 7 minutes longer.

SERVES 4.
CALORIES: 645   CHOLESTEROL: 201 mg   SODIUM: 851 mg   FIBER: 5 g

Health tip:
Omit salt; remove chicken skin before cooking.
CALORIES: 505   CHOLESTEROL: 180 mg   SODIUM: 293 mg   FIBER: 5 g

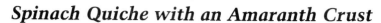

Spinach Quiche with an Amaranth Crust

The only thing that makes this different from a classic spinach quiche is the crust, which is crisp, golden, and definitely amaranth flavored. If you prefer, you can substitute Swiss cheese for the Gouda in the filling.

Crust:

> 1½ *cups all-purpose flour*
> ½ *cup amaranth flour*
> 1 *teaspoon salt*
> ¾ *cup butter*
> 4 *to 6 tablespoons ice water*

Filling:

> 4 *eggs*
> 2 *cups half-and-half*
> ½ *teaspoon crumbled tarragon*
> ½ *teaspoon salt*
> ¼ *teaspoon crumbled thyme*
> 1 *package (10 ounce) frozen chopped spinach, thawed and squeezed dry*
> 1 *cup shredded Gouda cheese*
> ⅓ *cup sliced scallion, both white and green parts*
> ¼ *cup grated Parmesan cheese*

Preheat oven to 400°F.

To make crust, in a large bowl, stir together both flours and salt. Cut in butter with a pastry blender or two knives, until the mixture resembles coarse cornmeal. Stir in ice water, 1 tablespoon at a time, until the dough forms a ball.

Roll dough between two sheets of waxed paper into an 11-inch circle. Fit into a 9-inch pie plate and crimp the edges. Weight the bottom of the crust with uncooked rice, dried beans, or pie weights. (By placing something heavy in the bottom of the pie shell you shouldn't have a problem with the pastry shrinking or puffing up as it bakes. The technical term for baking an unfilled pie shell is "baking it blind.") Bake for 15 minutes, or until lightly browned. Take pie crust out of the oven and remove weights. Reduce oven temperature to 350°F.

To make filling, beat the eggs in a medium-size bowl. Beat in half-and-half, tarragon, salt, and thyme. Stir in spinach, Gouda, scallion and Parmesan. Pour into baked crust. Bake for 35 to 45 minutes, or until a knife inserted in the center comes out clean.

SERVES 6.
CALORIES: 569   CHOLESTEROL: 246 mg   SODIUM: 954 mg   FIBER: 4 g

Health tip:
Omit salt; use unsalted margarine instead of butter; substitute scrambled-egg substitute for eggs. Use milk instead of half-and-half.
CALORIES: 497   CHOLESTEROL: 27 mg   SODIUM: 461 mg   FIBER: 4 g

———————— ◇ ————————

Amaranth-Pasta Tonnato

In Italian, tonnato means tuna, and it's an important ingredient in the lusty food served in the parts of those countries that surround the Mediterranean Sea. To me, it also means this simple and satisfying dish that I often prepare when I want a quick, substantial meal.

2 tablespoons olive oil
1 cup chopped onion
2 cloves garlic, minced
1 can (28 ounce) whole tomatoes in puree
2 tablespoons chopped parsley
1½ teaspoons crumbled oregano
1 teaspoon crumbled basil
½ teaspoon sugar
⅛ teaspoon crumbled thyme
⅛ teaspoon pepper
2 cans (7½ ounces each) tuna, drained
12 ounces amaranth pasta, cooked according to package directions and
  drained

In a 3-quart saucepan, heat the oil over medium-high heat. Add onion and garlic and cook, stirring frequently, until softened. Add tomatoes with puree, parsley, oregano, basil, sugar, thyme, and pepper. Bring to a boil, reduce heat, and simmer for 30 minutes. Add tuna to the sauce and cook, stirring, until heated through. Pour sauce over hot pasta.

SERVES 4.
CALORIES: 597   CHOLESTEROL: 15 mg   SODIUM: 628 mg   FIBER: 6 g

Health tip:
Reduce oil to 2 teaspoons and cook in a nonstick skillet.
CALORIES: 372   CHOLESTEROL: 10 mg   SODIUM: 419 mg   FIBER: 4 g

Creamy Mashed Potatoes and Amaranth

Mashed potatoes are a caloric splurge in which I rarely indulge. (The potatoes themselves are somewhat spartan, but if you want really delicious mashed potatoes, you can't be stingy with the butter.) I love the grainy texture that the amaranth adds to the smoothness of mashed potatoes and think it's a nice touch.

1 pound (about 3 medium-size) boiling potatoes, peeled and cut into
   quarters
¼ cup butter, divided
¼ cup finely chopped onion
⅓ cup half-and-half
2 tablespoons sour cream
½ teaspoon salt
¼ teaspoon pepper
⅓ cup cooked amaranth

In a 3-quart saucepan, cook the potatoes in boiling water for about 30 minutes, or until soft when pierced with a fork. Drain thoroughly.

While potatoes are boiling, melt 1 tablespoon of the butter in a small skillet. Add onion and cook over medium-high heat, stirring, until softened. Remove from heat and set aside.

Mash hot drained potatoes, in the saucepan, with remaining 3 tablespoons butter, half-and-half, sour cream, salt, and pepper. Stir in amaranth and cooked onion. Stir rapidly over low heat until potato mixture is hot.

SERVES 6.
CALORIES: 181   CHOLESTEROL: 28 mg   SODIUM: 283 mg   FIBER: 2 g

Health tip:
Use unsalted margarine instead of butter, and milk instead of half-and-half. Substitute plain yogurt for sour cream; omit salt.
CALORIES: 165   CHOLESTEROL: 2 mg   SODIUM: 23 mg   FIBER: 2 g

————— ◇ —————

Amaranth and Brown Rice

I think these two go well together, the crunchiness and flavor of the amaranth setting off the chewy blandness of the rice.

2¾ cups water
1 cup long-grain brown rice
¼ cup amaranth
1 teaspoon salt

In a 2-quart saucepan, bring the water to a boil. Stir in brown rice and return to boiling. Reduce heat, cover, and simmer for 30 minutes. Stir in amaranth. Cover and simmer for 20 minutes longer. Stir in salt.

SERVES 6.
CALORIES: 139   CHOLESTEROL: 0 mg   SODIUM: 359 mg   FIBER: 2 g

Health tip:
Omit salt.
CALORIES: 139   CHOLESTEROL: 0 mg   SODIUM: 3 mg   FIBER: 2 g

————— ◇ —————

Scallions and Amaranth

Since amaranth is dense and filling, it makes a nice side dish for simple meals without too many other accompaniments: a plain roasted chicken and a salad, for instance. You could even serve this for breakfast with scrambled eggs, if you like.

1½ cups water
1 cup amaranth
2 tablespoons butter
1 to 2 tablespoons chopped scallion
½ teaspoon salt

In a 1½-quart saucepan, bring the water to a boil. Stir in amaranth and return to boiling. Reduce heat and simmer, covered, for 20 minutes. Remove from heat and stir in butter, scallion, and salt. Serve immediately.

SERVES 4.
CALORIES: 218   CHOLESTEROL: 16 mg   SODIUM: 319 mg   FIBER: 2 g

Health tip:
Use unsalted margarine instead of butter; omit salt.
CALORIES: 218   CHOLESTEROL: 0 mg   SODIUM: 11 mg   FIBER: 2 g

————————◇————————
Bacon-y Corn Bake

Serve these squares instead of home-fried potatoes or grits fo
breakfast, brunch, or supper. This dish is also a nice accompani
ment at dinner.

4 slices bacon, cut into 1-inch pieces
1 cup cooked amaranth
½ cup milk
2 eggs
2 tablespoons butter, melted
½ cup whole-wheat flour
⅛ teaspoon pepper
1 can (8 ounce) whole-kernel corn, drained

Preheat oven to 350°F.
Grease an 8-inch square baking pan and set aside.
In a large skillet, cook the bacon until crisp. Remove bacon
from skillet and drain on paper towels. Reserve 2 tablespoons of th
bacon fat.
In a large bowl, stir together amaranth, milk, eggs, butter, an
reserved bacon fat until completely blended. Stir in flour and pep
per. Stir in reserved bacon and corn. Spread into prepared pan.
Bake for 30 minutes, or until a knife inserted in the cente
comes out clean. Cut into 9 squares. Serve warm.

SERVES 9.
CALORIES: 183   CHOLESTEROL: 57 mg   SODIUM: 148 mg   FIBER: 1 g

Health tip:
Eat only half a portion.

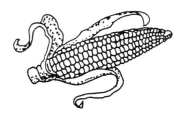

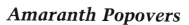

Amaranth Popovers

If you've never eaten a popover, you have a treat in store for you. A popover is a very airy muffin, and is so named because, as it bakes, the lightness of the batter causes it to pop over the side of the baking cup. To make certain that popovers "pop," it's important that the batter is poured into *hot*, heavily greased popover cups. The finished popover is somewhat hollow and a little doughy inside, and crisp and brown on the outside. The flavor of the amaranth flour in the popover recipe that follows is a delightful addition.

¾ cup sifted all-purpose flour
¼ cup sifted amaranth flour
½ teaspoon salt
2 eggs
1 cup milk
2 tablespoons melted butter

Preheat oven to 425°F.

Place a popover pan or 6 custard cups (whatever you use, they must be deeper than they are wide) on a baking sheet. Heavily grease each cup with vegetable oil, then place them in the oven to heat.

In a medium-size bowl, stir together both kinds of flour and salt. Set aside.

Place eggs, milk, and butter in the container of an electric blender. Cover and blend until thoroughly combined. Add the flour mixture. Cover and blend until smooth. Remove cups from oven. *Immediately* divide batter evenly among hot popover cups and return to oven.

Bake for 25 to 35 minutes. Remove from oven and pierce each popover with a knife or a fork to vent the steam inside them. Return to oven and bake for 5 minutes longer.

MAKES 6 POPOVERS.
CALORIES: 157   CHOLESTEROL: 85 mg   SODIUM: 253 mg   FIBER: 1 g

Health tip:
Omit salt; use unsalted margarine instead of butter.
CALORIES: 157   CHOLESTEROL: 75 mg   SODIUM: 43 mg   FIBER: 1 g

—————— ◇ ——————

Amaranth-Walnut Bread

If you like the flavor of butterscotch, use pecans instead of walnuts and substitute firmly packed brown sugar for the granulated sugar. However, the walnuts will give you a nuttier-tasting bread.

1⅓ cups all-purpose flour
1 cup ground walnuts
1 cup sugar
⅔ cup amaranth flour
2 teaspoons baking powder
1 teaspoon salt
1 cup milk
1 egg
⅓ cup butter, melted
1 teaspoon vanilla extract

Preheat oven to 350°F.

Grease a 9 × 5 × 3-inch loaf pan and set aside.

In a large bowl, stir together the all-purpose flour, nuts, sugar, amaranth flour, sugar, baking powder, and salt.

In a medium-size bowl, beat together the milk, egg, melted butter, and vanilla. Stir the milk mixture into the flour mixture until well combined. Turn batter into prepared pan.

Bake for 55 to 60 minutes, or until a wooden pick inserted in the center comes out clean. Turn bread out onto a wire rack to cool.

MAKES 1 LOAF (16 slices).
CALORIES: 185 CHOLESTEROL: 25 mg SODIUM: 219 mg FIBER: 1 g

Health tip:
Omit salt; use unsalted margarine instead of butter.
CALORIES: 185 CHOLESTEROL: 15 mg SODIUM: 58 mg FIBER: 1 g

———— ◇ ————

Light-as-Air Amaranth Pancakes

These pancakes are moist and light, not at all cakelike. And, they're good enough to eat without syrup (not that *I* ever do without!)

⅔ cup all-purpose flour
⅓ cup amaranth flour
2 tablespoons sugar
1½ teaspoons baking soda
½ teaspoon salt
1¼ cups buttermilk
¼ cup butter, melted
1 egg

In a large bowl, stir together both kinds of flour, sugar, baking soda, and salt.

In a medium-size bowl, stir together the buttermilk, melted butter, and egg until completely combined.

Add milk mixture to flour mixture and stir until blended. The batter should be lumpy.

Heat a large skillet until a few drops of water sprinkled into it bounce about before evaporating. Grease skillet lightly. Drop 2 tablespoonsful of batter for each pancake into the skillet. Cook until bubbles on top of pancake break. Turn and cook until lightly browned on the second side.

MAKES 16 PANCAKES.
CALORIES: 71   CHOLESTEROL: 21 mg   SODIUM: 192 mg   FIBER: 1 g

Health tip:
Omit salt; use unsalted margarine instead of butter.
CALORIES: 71   CHOLESTEROL: 14 mg   SODIUM: 105 mg   FIBER: 1 g

Amaranth-Mocha Bundt Cake

Mocha is a somewhat elusive flavor. A successful mocha-any-thing should not taste too much like chocolate nor too much like coffee, but a subtle blend of each. The first time I made this cake, I couldn't stop myself from cutting slices to munch on, and when I brought the cake to work (to save myself) everyone fell in love with it. I am always amazed that this cake can be so moist *and* feather-light. (Very often if something is described as moist, you can bet your bottom dollar that it is also as heavy as lead.)

1½ cups water
½ cup amaranth
½ cup semisweet chocolate morsels
3 tablespoons heavy cream
1 tablespoon instant espresso powder or
  1½ tablespoons regular instant-coffee granules
½ teaspoon vanilla extract
2 cups all-purpose flour
2 teaspoons baking powder
1 teaspoon baking soda
¼ teaspoon salt
1 cup butter
1¼ cups sugar
3 eggs

Preheat oven to 325°F.

Heavily grease and flour a Bundt pan and set aside.

In a 1-quart saucepan, combine the water and amaranth. Bring to a boil. Lower heat and simmer, covered, for 20 to 25 minutes, or until the liquid has been absorbed and the grain has the consistency of a thick sauce. Remove from heat and stir in chocolate morsels, cream, espresso, and vanilla. Set aside to cool to room temperature and don't worry if the ingredients separate.

In a medium-size bowl, stir together the flour, baking powder, baking soda, and salt.

In a large bowl, beat butter and sugar until light and fluffy, about 5 minutes. Beat in eggs. (The mixture may look curdled, but that's okay.)

Beat the flour mixture into the butter mixture alternately with the chocolate mixture, starting and ending with flour mixture. Turn batter into prepared pan.

Bake for 1 hour, or until a wooden pick inserted in the center comes out clean. Turn the cake onto a wire rack and cool. (Because his cake is so tender, it must be completely cool before slicing, and ven then you should use a serrated knife.)

MAKES 20 SERVINGS.

CALORIES: 233   CHOLESTEROL: 59 mg   SODIUM: 191 mg   FIBER: 1 g

Health tip:
Use milk instead of cream; omit salt; use unsalted margarine instead of butter; use scrambled-egg substitute instead of eggs.

CALORIES: 223   CHOLESTEROL: 30 mg   SODIUM: 102 mg   FIBER: 1 g

JOB'S TEARS
(Croix Lacryma-jobi)

Job's tears is a fairly recent entry into the American grair scene. However, it is an ancient grain, highly esteemed in Japan and China. In the Orient, it is valued for its reputed restorative powers It is also believed that consuming Job's tears will make the skir clear and beautiful.

Job's tears goes by many different names: *hato mugi* (the Jap anese name for it), *Juno's tears* (for the Roman goddess), *river grain* and *jobi*. (I've even seen it labelled pearled barley.) The "tears" refe: to the way the grain grows in clusters resembling tears.

Types of Job's Tears Available
Job's tears comes only as a whole grain with the outer husk removed.

Texture and Flavor
Job's tears can best be described as looking like a large pearl barley or a small white coffee bean. It is white and round and has a wide brown indentation that runs lengthwise down one side.

The taste and texture of Job's tears will vary a lot depending on the amount of water in which it is cooked, and the length of time it is cooked. I bring this up because I found that when I followed package directions, the grain had an uncooked flavor and texture that was not at all pleasing—at least to me. By adding half again as much water as called for and cooking the grain longer, it had a much more pleasant, beanlike flavor, and the texture was softer.

Cooked grains of Job's tears are separate and not at all starchy. Please note it is very important that when you rinse the grain before cooking, you also pick out and discard any grains that are tan, rather than white, in color. When the tan grains are cooked they have a very moldy flavor, which makes for a rather unpleasant surprise when you bite into one. (The major importer of Job's tears, Eden Foods, assures me that they are trying new methods of sorting to avoid having the tan grains in the package, so in the near future this may not be a problem. For now, there will always be a few grains that must be discarded.)

Compatible Foods, Herbs, and Spices

Because the flavor and texture of Job's tears is close to that of navy beans, it makes sense that any foods and flavors you would normally combine with the beans are also good with this grain. I think that as a rule of thumb strong flavors work best with Job's tears. Consider using beef, lamb, pork, and ham, rather than poultry or dairy products.

The crunchy texture of vegetables, especially raw or crisp-cooked, are an excellent contrast.

Strong spices and seasonings are, not surprisingly, my first choice to go with Job's tears: curries, chili, and Szechuan or Mexican foods are all good choices in which to include this grain. And since the grain also swells when it is cooked, it makes a good filler for soups and stews.

Availability

Job's tears can be found in health-food stores and through mail-order grain catalogs (see page 21).

Nutritional Content

Job's tears is high in protein, potassium, phosphorous, and magnesium, and it is a good source of dietary fiber.

Substitutions

Navy beans or any small white beans (cooked): You can use either canned or dry beans, substituting them in recipes calling for cooked Job's tears.

Barley: A suitable substitution when used in soups or sautés.

Starchy vegetables: Peas, lima beans, or potatoes can be substituted in stews.

Basic Cooking Instructions

Please read *About Cooking Grains* beginning on page 7.

Stove-top method:

1 cup Job's tears
3 cups water
½ teaspoon salt

Rinse and drain the Job's tears, then carefully pick through, discarding any grains that are tan in color.

In a 2-quart saucepan, bring water and salt to a boil over high heat. Stir in Job's tears and return to boiling. Reduce heat and simmer for 1 hour and 40 minutes, covered, or until almost all of the liquid has been absorbed. Remove from heat and let stand 5 minutes.

MAKES ABOUT 3⅓ CUPS.

Microwave method:

1 cup Job's tears
3½ cups water
½ teaspoon salt

Rinse and drain Job's tears then carefully pick through, discarding any grains that are tan in color.

Place the water and salt in a 3-quart, microwave-safe bowl. Cover with waxed paper and microwave on high (100% power) for 4 minutes. Stir in salt and Job's tears. Recover with waxed paper and microwave on high for 4 minutes. Microwave on medium (50% power), still covered with waxed paper, for 1 hour and 10 minutes. Let stand 5 minutes. Fluff with a fork.

MAKES A SCANT 3 CUPS.

Reheating

As Job's tears cool, the grain becomes more like its under-cooked version. It becomes harder, and develops an underlying flavor that I don't like. I recommend tasting the cold grain and making your own judgement about the flavor. Microwaving or steaming it will return the grain to a softer texture, but I think it is much better to use it freshly cooked.

JOB'S TEARS RECIPES

*(*indicates easy recipes.)*

———————— ◇ ————————

Job's Tex-Mex Bean Dip with Guacamole
Sesame Spread *
Escarole-Turkey Soup
Yellow-pea Soup *
Navarin with Job's Tears
Sausage and Tears *
Job's (Brings Tears to the Eyes) Chili
Job's Brussels Sprouts *
Curried Vegetables and Job's Tears
Indonesian Vegetables

───────◇───────

Job's Tex-Mex Bean Dip with Guacamole

You can serve the bean-dip by itself sometimes, or with the gaucamole, as I have done in this recipe. Serve dips with taco or tortilla chips, of course.

Bean Dip:

> *½ cup cooked Job's tears*
> *½ cup refried beans (I used Old El Paso brand with green chilies, onion, and garlic)*
> *2 tablespoons sour cream*
> *2 tablespoons mild or hot salsa*

Guacamole:

> *1 medium avocado, mashed (about 1 cup)*
> *2 tablespoons sour cream*
> *2 tablespoons minced scallion, both white and green parts*
> *1 tablespoon mayonnaise*
> *1 tablespoon chopped cilantro (fresh coriander)*
> *1 tablespoon lime juice*
> *⅛ teaspoon ground red pepper*

To make the bean dip, in a medium-size bowl, stir together the Job's tears, beans, sour cream, and salsa. Cover and chill until ready to serve.

To make the guacamole, in a medium-size bowl, stir together the avocado, sour cream, green onion, mayonnaise, cilantro, lime juice, and red pepper. (If you aren't serving this immediately, prevent it from turning brown by pressing a piece of plastic wrap directly on the surface. Or you can spread sour cream over the surface. Chill until needed, and stir well just before serving.)

MAKES 1 CUP BEAN DIP; 1⅓ CUPS GUACAMOLE.
Bean Dip per tablespoon:
CALORIES: 19   CHOLESTEROL: 8 mg   SODIUM: 47 mg   FIBER: 1 g

Health tip:
Substitute plain yogurt for sour cream. Omit salt from Job's tears.
CALORIES: 16   CHOLESTEROL: 7 mg   SODIUM: 34 mg   FIBER: 1 g

Guacamole per tablespoon:
CALORIES: 26   CHOLESTEROL: 1 mg   SODIUM: 6 mg   FIBER: 1 g

Health tip:
Substitute plain yogurt for sour cream and mayonnaise.
CALORIES: 19   CHOLESTEROL: 0 mg   SODIUM: 3 mg   FIBER: 1 g

Sesame Spread

This tastes very much like *hummus*, a tasty Middle Eastern concoction that is usually eaten with or spread on pita bread. Use this as a dip for raw vegetables or as a sandwich filler topped with salad in a pita bread. Tahini, a "butter" made from sesame seeds, is available in health-food stores in jars or in cans.

1 cup cooked Job's tears
⅓ cup tahini (see above)
2 tablespoons lemon juice
2 cloves garlic, minced
2 tablespoons water
2 tablespoons vegetable oil
1 tablespoon Oriental sesame oil
¼ teaspoon salt
¼ teaspoon ground cumin
⅛ teaspoon ground red pepper

Place Job's tears, tahini, lemon juice, garlic, water, vegetable oil, sesame oil, salt, cumin, and red pepper in the container of a food processor. Cover and process until smooth.

MAKES 1¼ CUPS.
CALORIES: 42   CHOLESTEROL: 0 mg   SODIUM: 37 mg   FIBER: 1 g

Health tip:
Omit salt.
CALORIES: 42   CHOLESTEROL: 0 mg   SODIUM: 1 mg   FIBER: 1 g

Escarole-Turkey Soup

You can use more escarole in this soup if you like it, or not as much, or not at all if you don't like it. The soup will still be good.

10 cups water
2 turkey wings (about 3½ pounds)
3 carrots, peeled
3 ribs celery
2 parsnips, peeled
1 tomato, stem removed
1 onion, peeled
¼ cup celery leaves
1 clove garlic
1 teaspoon salt
⅓ cup Job's tears, rinsed, drained, and picked over
1 small bunch parsley
1 small bunch dill
2 cups firmly packed chopped escarole

In a large soup pot, place the water, turkey wings, carrots, celery, parsnips, tomato, onion, celery leaves, garlic, and salt. Bring to a boil and stir in Job's tears. Reduce heat and simmer, uncovered, for 1 hour and 45 minutes. Add parsley and dill. Simmer for 25 minutes longer. Remove turkey and all the vegetables (you can serve these separately with the soup or after it as another course, if you like, or you can throw them out). Skim off all fat. Stir in escarole. Simmer for 5 minutes.

SERVES 8.

CALORIES: 65   CHOLESTEROL: 4 mg   SODIUM: 424 mg   FIBER: .5 g

Health tip:
Remove as much of the skin as you can from the turkey wings before cooking; omit salt.

CALORIES: 65   CHOLESTEROL: 1 mg   SODIUM: 157 mg   FIBER: .5 g

Yellow-Pea Soup

This is the kind of soup you can stand a spoon in, but you can add more water, if you like. Serve with croutons, if you like.

10 to 12 cups water
1 smoked pork hock (about 1 pound) or a ham bone
⅓ cup Job's tears, rinsed, drained, and picked over
1 package (16 ounce) yellow split peas
2 ribs celery
2 carrots, peeled
1 parsnip, peeled
1 celeriac, peeled (celery root)
1 teaspoon salt

Place 10 cups of the water, pork hock, and Job's tears in a large soup pot. Bring to a boil. Reduce heat and simmer, covered, for 30 minutes. Add split peas, celery, carrots, parsnip, celery root, and salt. Return to boiling. Reduce heat and simmer, uncovered, for 1½ hours, or until the peas have dissolved. If the soup is getting too thick for your taste, add up to 2 cups more water. Discard meat and vegetables.

SERVES 8.
CALORIES: 221   CHOLESTEROL: 3 mg   SODIUM: 409 mg   FIBER: 8 g

Health tip:
Use a fresh ham bone rather than a smoked one; omit salt.
CALORIES: 221   CHOLESTEROL: 3 mg   SODIUM: 19 mg   FIBER: 8 g

———— ◇ ————

Navarin with Job's Tears

Navarin is a French term meaning lamb stew. This one is thickened with Job's tears and is slightly sweet, just right for a cold night.

1½ pounds boneless lamb, cut into bite-size pieces
3 tablespoons all-purpose flour
¼ cup vegetable oil
1 cup chopped onion
2 cloves garlic, minced
6 to 8 cups water
½ cup dry vermouth
2 tablespoons tomato paste
1 bay leaf
1 teaspoon salt
¼ teaspoon crumbled thyme
⅛ teaspoon pepper
1 cup Job's tears, rinsed, drained, and picked over
2 cups sliced carrot
1½ cups diced rutabaga or turnip

Dredge the lamb in flour, shaking off any excess.

In a large heavy saucepan or Dutch oven, heat the oil over medium-high heat. Add lamb and cook, turning, until lightly browned. Stir in onion and garlic and cook, stirring, until softened. Stir in 6 cups of the water, vermouth, tomato paste, bay leaf, salt, thyme, and pepper, and bring to a boil. Stir in Job's tears, carrot, and rutabaga and return to boiling. Reduce heat and simmer for 1½ to 2 hours, or until lamb is tender. If the stew gets too thick for your taste, stir in as much of the remaining 2 cups water as necessary. During the last 45 minutes of cooking time, you will need to stir the stew from time to time to prevent it from sticking to the bottom of the pan. Remove bay leaf before serving.

SERVES 6.
CALORIES: 498   CHOLESTEROL: 100 mg   SODIUM: 475 mg   FIBER: 4 g

Health tip:
Reduce oil to 2 teaspoons and cook in a nonstick pan. Or, brown lamb in a nonstick skillet, transferring to the larger pan to finish cooking; omit salt.
CALORIES: 471   CHOLESTEROL: 100 mg   SODIUM: 120 mg   FIBER: 4 g

———————— ◇ ————————

Sausage and Tears

Serve this as either a main dish or a hearty side dish.

2 tablespoons vegetable oil
1 cup Job's tears, rinsed, drained and picked over
1 cup chopped onion
½ cup chopped green bell pepper
1 pound sweet or spicy Italian sausage (bulk sausage is preferable)
3 cups water
1 can (8 ounce) tomato sauce
¼ teaspoon salt
¼ teaspoon pepper

In a 2-quart saucepan, heat the oil over medium-high heat. Add Job's tears and cook, stirring, until the grain starts to crackle and pop. Add onion and green pepper and cook, stirring frequently, until vegetables are softened.

If you are using link sausage, discard casing. Add sausage to the pan and cook, stirring, until no longer pink. Stir in water, tomato sauce, salt, and pepper and bring to a boil. Reduce heat and simmer, covered, for 1½ hours.

SERVES 6.
CALORIES: 402   CHOLESTEROL: 64 mg   SODIUM: 1088 mg   fiber: 2 g

Health tip:
Reduce oil to 2 teaspoons and cook in a nonstick saucepan. Or, cook grain, onion, and green pepper in a nonstick skillet, transferring to the larger pan to finish cooking. Cook sausage separately and drain well before adding to other ingredients; omit salt.
CALORIES: 375   CHOLESTEROL: 58 mg   SODIUM: 999 mg   FIBER: 2 g

――――――― ◇ ―――――――

Job's (Brings Tears to the Eyes) Chili

Serve this chili with cold plain yogurt or sour cream to tame it
a little. Of course, you can adjust the spiciness to suit your own
taste.

3 tablespoons vegetable oil
1 cup chopped onion
½ cup chopped green bell pepper
½ cup chopped red bell pepper
3 cloves garlic, minced
2 tablespoons chili powder
1 teaspoon paprika
½ teaspoon ground cumin
½ teaspoon ground red pepper
½ teaspoon liquid red pepper (tabasco)
½ teaspoon salt
⅛ teaspoon ground cinnamon
1 can (14½ ounce) whole peeled tomatoes, undrained.
1 can (15 ounce) white beans (I use Goya brand Spanish Style)
1 cup cooked Job's tears
½ cup water

In a 3-quart saucepan, heat the oil over medium-high heat. Add
onion, green and red bell peppers, and garlic. Cook, stirring frequently, until vegetables are softened. Stir in chili powder, paprika,
cumin, ground red pepper, liquid red pepper, salt, and cinnamon.
Cook, stirring, for 30 seconds, or until spices have been absorbed
into the oil. Stir in tomatoes and break them up with the side of a
spoon. Stir in beans, Job's tears, and water. Bring to a boil. Reduce
heat and simmer, uncovered, for 20 minutes, stirring frequently.

SERVES 4.
CALORIES: 344   CHOLESTEROL: 0 mg   SODIUM: 560 mg   FIBER: 13 g

Health tip:
Reduce oil to 1 tablespoon and cook in a nonstick saucepan. Or, cook onion,
bell peppers, and garlic in a nonstick skillet, transferring to the larger pan to
finish cooking; omit salt.
CALORIES: 274   CHOLESTEROL: 0 mg   SODIUM: 208 mg   FIBER: 13 g

——————— ◇ ———————

Job's Brussels Sprouts

If you're not too fond of Brussels sprouts, you can use almost any vegetable you like better.

1 tablespoon butter
½ cup Job's tears, rinsed, drained, and picked over
1 can (13¾ ounce) ready-to-serve chicken broth or
    1¾ cups vegetable broth (see page 19)
1 pint Brussels sprouts, cut into quarters

In a 2-quart saucepan, melt the butter over medium-high heat. Add Job's tears and cook until the grains begin to crackle and pop. Stir in broth and bring to a boil. Reduce heat, cover, and simmer for 60 minutes. Stir in Brussels sprouts. Cover and simmer for 30 minutes longer.

SERVES 6.
CALORIES: 99   CHOLESTEROL: 5 mg   SODIUM: 233 mg   FIBER: 2 g

Health tip:
Use unsalted margarine instead of butter; use low-sodium broth.
CALORIES: 99   CHOLESTEROL: 0 mg   SODIUM: 46 mg   FIBER 2 g

——————— ◇ ———————

Curried Vegetables and Job's Tears

I usually like my vegetables cooked tender-crisp. Curries are the exception. In a good curry, the vegetables should be cooked until they're mushy.

1 tablespoon vegetable oil
3 tablespoons butter, divided
½ cup Job's tears, rinsed, drained, and picked over
1 cup chopped onion
3 cloves garlic, minced
2 tablespoons curry powder
1 teaspoon salt
½ teaspoon ground cumin
½ teaspoon ground turmeric
½ teaspoon ground ginger
⅛ teaspoon ground red pepper
3 cups water
2 cups cauliflower florets
2 cups green beans, cut into 1½-inch lengths
1 cup peas, fresh or frozen

Heat the oil and 1 tablespoon of the butter in a large heavy saucepan or Dutch oven. Add Job's tears and cook, stirring, until the grains start to crackle and pop. Add remaining 2 tablespoons butter. Stir in onion and garlic and cook, stirring frequently, until softened. Add curry powder, salt, cumin, turmeric, ginger, and red pepper. Cook, stirring, for 30 seconds, or until the spices have been absorbed into the oil. Add water and bring to a boil. Cover and simmer for 1 hour. Add cauliflower, green beans, and peas. Simmer for 45 minutes longer.

SERVES 8.
CALORIES: 137   CHOLESTEROL: 12 mg   SODIUM: 311 mg   FIBER: 3 g
Health tip:
Omit butter and cook in a nonstick saucepan. Or, cook onion and garlic in a nonstick skillet, transferring them to the larger pot to finish cooking. Omit salt.
CALORIES: 99   CHOLESTEROL: 0 mg   SODIUM: 45 mg   FIBER: 3 g

—————— ◇ ——————

Indonesian Vegetables

If you're not crazy about vegetables, but you do like spicy, exotic dishes, you'll think this recipe was created just for you. Vary the vegetables as much as you like. And there's probably no reason you couldn't stir in a few cooked shrimp if you like them.

4 shallots, peeled and cut in half (or use the white part of scallions)
2 cloves garlic, peeled
2 tablespoons white vinegar
1 tablespoon water
1 tablespoon coarsely chopped fresh ginger
2 teaspoons paprika
2 teaspoons sugar
1 teaspoon ground turmeric
1 teaspoon salt
¼ teaspoon ground red pepper
3 tablespoons vegetable oil
2 cups julienned carrot
1 cup julienned green or red bell pepper
1½ cup cooked Job's tears

Place the shallots, garlic, vinegar, water, ginger, paprika, sugar, turmeric, salt, and ground red pepper in the container of an electric blender. Cover and blend until the mixture becomes smooth and pasty. (You can use the food processor for this job, but, in this case, I think the blender works better.)

In a wok or large skillet, heat the oil over high heat. Add spice paste and cook, stirring, for 30 seconds. Add carrot and bell pepper and cook, stirring and tossing, until vegetables are tender-crisp. Stir in Job's tears and cook, stirring, until heated through.

SERVES 6.

CALORIES: 171   CHOLESTEROL: 0 mg   SODIUM: 569 mg   FIBER: 3 g

Health tip:

Use 2 teaspoons oil and cook in a nonstick skillet; omit salt.

CALORIES: 125   CHOLESTEROL: 0 mg   SODIUM: 125 mg   FIBER: 3 g

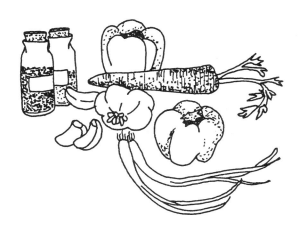

QUINOA

The history and fate of quinoa (pronounced KEEN-wa) is parallel to those of amaranth. It, too, was a sacred "mother grain" to the Incas of Peru. Like the Aztecs, the Incas were also forced to give up eating the grain believed to be the source of their strength by their Spanish conquerors. As time went by, the Incas themselves abandoned the grain.

Today quinoa is regaining some of its past glory, for nowadays both quinoa and amaranth are being touted as the "super-grains" of the eighties.

Although technically an herb, quinoa has an extremely impressive nutritional profile. The amount and quality of the protein this little grain provides is about as high, or higher, than any true grain.

Quinoa is also unique in that it has a built-in insect repellent called *saponin*. Since this substance is bitter and soapy tasting, it would also be a people repellent were it not easily rinsed from the grain in an alkaline water as part of the processing. (In addition to the rinsing it gets before packaging, quinoa should also be thoroughly rinsed before cooking.)

Types of Quinoa Available

Whole-grain quinoa: The grains have been rinsed to remove the saponins.

Quinoa flour: The whole grain that has been ground. If you cannot find the flour, you can easily make it at home. For each cup of flour, place ¾ cup whole-grain quinoa in the container of a blender or a food processor fitted with a steel blade. Cover and process until no whole grains remain and the quinoa is reduced to flour.

Pasta: Made from the quinoa flour, it comes in a variety of shapes and can be used in any recipe calling for pasta or noodles.

Texture and Flavor

Whole-grain quinoa comes in many varieties. The only one that is currently available is creamy beige in color and resembles unhulled sesame seeds in size and shape. The two brands of quinoa that I have found have slightly different characteristics. The Eden brand quinoa, as compared to the Ancient Harvest brand, is slightly

414

smaller, with a few black grains mixed in, and has less residual saponin. Ancient Harvest, on the other hand, has practically no dark grains, but does seem to retain more saponin and requires more rinsing. I found that these differences did not affect the cooked product one way or the other.

The flavor of cooked quinoa will depend largely on how much rinsing you do. The more you rinse, the milder the flavor. The first flavor of the grain is nutty, but the distinct aftertaste is bitter, similar to, but milder than, millet. However, I have been told that people who are fond of quinoa value the bitterness and prefer not to rinse too much of it away, as they feel the bitterness is what gives quinoa its character. My own preference is to rinse the quinoa fairly thoroughly to play down the bitterness. Toasting or sautéing quinoa before adding liquid will also cut down on the aftertaste.

In texture, quinoa is light and fluffy, with an almost melt-in-the-mouth quality. There is very little, if any, of the starchy chewiness usually associated with cooked grains.

As it cooks, quinoa changes from opaque to transparent, first becoming transparent at the edge with an opaque dot in the center. Fully cooked, quinoa is completely transparent and has a small white sprout, or rootlike tail, that surrounds the grain. One sure way to tell if quinoa is cooked is to make sure that the opaque dot is gone.

Compatible Foods, Herbs, and Spices

The flavor of quinoa, and even the bitter aftertaste, is mild. Therefore it can be used with any food or seasoning you choose. The best flavors for quinoa, like millet, are sweet, sour, salty, or spicy.

Availability

Health-food stores and mail-order grain catalogs (see page 21) are the most likely places to find quinoa. But a growing number of gourmet stores and some supermarkets carry it.

Nutritional Content

Quinoa is a veritable powerhouse of nutrition. It has a high percentage of protein, the highest of all grains, in fact. In addition, it has unusually high quantities of lysine, cystine, and methionine—the amino acids lacking in most true grains. All of this makes quinoa a good complement to other grains, as well as beans.

Substitutions

Cooked bean threads: They come the closest to quinoa in texture, and may be used, perhaps cut up, in place of cooked quinoa.

White rice: Can be substituted for quinoa, but the cooking time is almost twice as long and requires a bit more liquid. The texture is also chewier.

Brown rice: Its flavor is similar to quinoa, but the texture and cooking time are very different.

Other acceptable substitutes (in order of perference): Couscous, bulgur, and millet.

Basic Cooking Instructions

Please read *About Cooking Grains* beginning on page 7.

Stove-top method:

1 cup quinoa
2 cups water
1 teaspoon salt

Place the quinoa in a large bowl. Fill bowl with forcefully running cold water (the saponins are what create the sudsy bubbles). Drain the quinoa in a sieve. Put the quinoa back into the bowl and repeat the rinsing and draining for a total of five times.

In a 2-quart saucepan, combine water and salt. Bring to a boil over high heat. Add drained quinoa and return to boiling. Reduce heat and simmer, covered, for 15 minutes. Remove from heat and let stand 5 minutes. Fluff with a fork.

MAKES 3½ CUPS.

Microwave method:

1 cup quinoa
2 cups water
1 teaspoon salt

Place the quinoa in a large bowl. Fill bowl with forcefully running cold water (the saponins are what create the sudsy bubbles). Drain the quinoa in a sieve. Put the quinoa back into the bowl and repeat the rinsing and drain for a total of five times.

Place water in a 3-quart, microwave-safe bowl. Cover with waxed paper and microwave on high (100% power) for 4 minutes. Stir in quinoa and salt. Recover with waxed paper and microwave on high for 4 minutes. Microwave at medium (50% power), still covered with waxed paper, for 9 minutes. Let stand 4 minutes. Fluff with a fork.

MAKES 3 CUPS.

Reheating

Although quinoa clumps slightly as it cools, it can easily be broken up with a fork. Chilled quinoa does not have to be reheated before being used. Should you want to reheat it, steaming or microwaving works fine.

QUINOA RECIPES

(*indicates easy recipes.)

————— ◇ —————

Quinoa Eggdrop Soup *
Quinoa Pasta with Fresh Tomato Sauce *
Sesame Chicken with Quinoa and Broccoli
Quinoa Sloppy Joes *
Oriental Liver and Quinoa
Quinoa-and-Cucumber Salad with Cilantro Dressing *
Orange, Almond, and Quinoa Salad *
Quinoa-and-Pear Salad *
Simply Toasted Sesame Seeds and Quinoa *
Cheddar-Zucchini-Quinoa Bake *
Quinoa and Spanish-Style Beans *
Quinoa with Leeks and Asparagus *
Curried Peas and Quinoa *
Mexican Quinoa Stew *
Quinoa Kugel
Cranberry-Quinoa Quick Bread
Pecan-Quinoa Cookies *

Quinoa Eggdrop Soup

Any form of chicken soup is comfort food for me, and this one is no exception. Adding quinoa to eggdrop soup only makes it thicker and more satisfying.

1 can (13¾ ounce) ready-to-serve chicken broth or
    1¾ cups vegetable broth (see page 19)
1½ cups plus 2 tablespoons water, divided
¼ cup quinoa, rinsed five times (see Basic Cooking Instructions)
1 tablespoon cornstarch
2 eggs
2 tablespoons thinly sliced scallion, both white and green parts

In a 3-quart saucepan, bring chicken broth and 1½ cups of the water to a boil. Stir in quinoa and simmer 20 minutes.

In a small bowl, stir together remaining 2 tablespoons water and cornstarch. Gradually stir into the boiling broth.

Beat egg in the same small bowl and gradually stir into the boiling soup. Reduce heat and simmer until egg is completely cooked. Remove from heat and stir in scallion.

SERVES 6.
CALORIES: 65   CHOLESTEROL: 70 mg   SODIUM: 228 mg   FIBER: 1 g

Health tip:
Use reduced-sodium broth.
CALORIES: 65   CHOLESTEROL: 70 mg   SODIUM: 137 mg   FIBER: 1 g

───────── ◇ ─────────

Quinoa Pasta with Fresh Tomato Sauce

I cook this sauce for only 15 minutes, especially when I can use ripe, delicious, summertime tomatoes, at which point the tomato chunks are still intact and the sauce is quite thin. But you can continue cooking the sauce until it reaches the consistency you like. If the sauce is cooked with winter (tasteless) tomatoes, I usually add a tablespoon or two of tomato paste to bolster the tomato flavor.

4 large tomatoes
¼ cup olive oil
1 cup chopped onion
2 cloves garlic, minced
½ jalapeno pepper, minced or
     ⅛ teaspoon black pepper
¼ cup chopped fresh basil
¼ teaspoon salt
1 package (8 ounce) quinoa rotini or macaroni, cooked according to
     package directions and drained
Grated Parmesan cheese

Core the tomatoes and cut in half through the middle (not through the stem end) and squeeze out the seeds. Coarsely chop tomato halves.

In a 3- or 4-quart saucepan, heat the oil. Add onion, garlic, and jalapeno pepper and cook over medium-high heat, stirring frequently, until softened. Add chopped tomato, basil, and salt. Cook for 15 minutes, stirring occasionally. The sauce will be thin and the tomato pieces still quite visible. Cook longer if you prefer a thicker sauce.

Serve sauce over hot pasta, sprinkled with Parmesan cheese.

─────────────────────────────────

SERVES 4.
CALORIES: 389   CHOLESTEROL: 4 mg   SODIUM: 373 mg   FIBER: 5 g

Health tip:
Reduce oil to 1 tablespoon and cook in a nonstick saucepan. Or, cook onion, garlic, and jalapeno pepper in a nonstick skillet, transferring to the larger pan to finish cooking. Omit salt.
CALORIES: 277   CHOLESTEROL: 0 mg   SODIUM: 12 mg   FIBER: 5 g

Sesame Chicken with Quinoa and Broccoli

Made without the chicken, this casserole can be served as a side dish.

2 tablespoons sesame seeds
2 to 3 tablespoons vegetable oil
1 pound skinless, boneless chicken breast, cut into bite-size pieces
1 cup sliced onion
2 cloves garlic, minced
2 cups broccoli florets
1 tablespoon soy sauce
1 tablespoon mirin (a sweet rice wine available at Oriental grocery
    stores) or dry sherry
2 cups cooked quinoa
1 teaspoon Oriental sesame oil (or chili oil, for braver souls)

In a dry wok or large skillet, cook the sesame seeds over medium-high heat, stirring, until golden. Remove from pan and set aside.

Heat 2 tablespoons of the vegetable oil in the wok over medium-high heat. Add chicken and cook, stirring, until lightly browned and cooked through. Remove from wok and set aside. If necessary, add the remaining tablespoon of vegetable oil to the wok. Add onion and garlic and cook, stirring and tossing, until softened. Add broccoli and cook, stirring and tossing, until tender-crisp. Stir in soy sauce and mirin. Add reserved chicken and quinoa and cook, stirring, until heated through. Add sesame oil and reserved sesame seeds and toss to mix.

SERVES 6.
CALORIES: 225 CHOLESTEROL: 53 mg SODIUM: 443 mg FIBER: 3 g

Health tip:
Reduce vegetable oil to 2 teaspoons and cook in a nonstick skillet. Use reduced-sodium soy sauce. Omit salt when cooking quinoa.
CALORIES: 197 CHOLESTEROL: 53 mg SODIUM: 68 mg FIBER 3 g

Quinoa Sloppy Joes

This recipe started out as sautéed chicken with quinoa, but sometimes recipes have a mind of their own. This can be eaten like chili (with chopped raw onion and sour cream) or like Sloppy Joes (spooned onto a roll or a bun). Either way, the quinoa acts as a meat extender.

2 tablespoons vegetable oil
½ cup finely chopped onion
½ cup finely chopped green bell pepper
½ cup finely chopped red bell pepper
1 pound ground pork
1 cup water
½ cup bottled barbecue sauce
2 tablespoons light- or dark-brown sugar
1 tablespoon unsweetened cocoa powder
2 teaspoons white vinegar
½ teaspoon ground cinnamon
½ teaspoon salt
½ cup quinoa, rinsed 5 times (see Basic Cooking Instructions)

In a 2-quart saucepan, heat the oil over medium-high heat. Add onion and peppers, and cook, stirring frequently, until softened. Add pork and cook, stirring, until no longer pink. Stir in water, barbecue sauce, brown sugar, cocoa powder, vinegar, cinnamon, and salt. Bring to a boil. Stir in quinoa and return to boiling. Reduce heat and simmer, covered, for 15 to 20 minutes, or until all of the liquid has been absorbed.

SERVES 6.
CALORIES: 269 CHOLESTEROL: 54 mg SODIUM: 391 mg FIBER: 2 g

Health tip:
Omit salt. Use ground turkey instead of pork.
CALORIES: 211 CHOLESTEROL: 47 mg SODIUM: 239 mg FIBER: 2 g

—————— ◇ ——————

Oriental Liver and Quinoa

If you like liver, you'll love this. Be sure not to overcook the liver. Even if you think you like it well done, liver should be slightly pink in the center to taste its best. Otherwise it will be tough and dry. This is especially true for calves liver, which should be cooked more quickly than beef liver.

¾ cup water
3 tablespoons mirin (sweet rice wine available in Oriental grocery
    stores) or dry sherry
2 tablespoons Japanese soy sauce (Chinese soy sauce is too dark and
    salty for this dish)
1½ tablespoons cornstarch
1 teaspoon sugar
¼ to ½ teaspoon crushed red pepper
3 tablespoons vegetable oil, divided
1 pound beef or calves liver, cut into 1-inch-wide strips
2 cloves garlic, minced
1 tablespoon minced fresh ginger
2 cups cooked quinoa
⅓ cup sliced scallion, both white and green parts

In a medium-size bowl, stir together the water, mirin, soy sauce, cornstarch, sugar, and red pepper.

In a wok or large skillet, heat 2 tablespoons of the oil over high heat. Add liver and cook, stirring, until done as you like it. Remove liver from wok and set aside.

Heat the remaining tablespoon of oil; add garlic and ginger to wok and cook, stirring, for 30 seconds. Stir in soy-sauce mixture and cook, stirring, until mixture comes to a boil. Return liver to wok and toss until strips are coated with sauce. Add quinoa and scallion and cook, stirring and tossing, until heated through.

SERVES 4.
CALORIES: 340   CHOLESTEROL: 547 mg   SODIUM: 943 mg   FIBER: 3 g

Health tip:
Use reduced-sodium soy sauce; reduce oil to 2 teaspoons and cook in a non-stick skillet. Cook quinoa without salt.
CALORIES: 290   CHOLESTEROL: 547 mg   SODIUM: 294 mg   FIBER: 3 g

———————◇———————

Quinoa-and-Cucumber Salad with Cilantro Dressing

The dressing for this salad is very tart, so you can reduce the lime juice accordingly, if you like. If you're an avocado lover, this is the perfect salad in which to include one: small, very ripe, and cut into cubes.

2 cups cooked and cooled quinoa
2 cups chopped peeled and seeded cucumber
¼ cup sliced scallion both white and green parts
¼ cup firmly packed cilantro (fresh coriander) leaves
2 tablespoons olive oil
2 tablespoons vegetable oil
2 tablespoons lime or lemon juice
⅛ teaspoon salt
⸱⅛ teaspoon ground red pepper (optional)

medium-size bowl, toss together the quinoa, cucumber, a n.
e cilantro, both oils, lime juice, salt, and red pepper in the container of an electric blender. Cover and blend until cilantro is finely chopped. Pour dressing over salad and toss until well combined.·

SERVES 4.

CALORIES: 224   CHOLESTEROL: 0 mg   SODIUM: 445 mg   FIBER: 4 g

Health tip:
Omit salt; cut dressing ingredients in half.

CALORIES: 161   CHOLESTEROL: 0 mg   SODIUM: 3 mg   FIBER: 4 g

◇

Orange, Almond, and Quinoa Salad

I find this particular combination of citrus fruit, nuts, quinoa, and a slightly sweetened dressing to be an exquisite combination of refreshing flavors and textures.

½ cup slivered almonds
2 juicy oranges
2 cups cooked and cooled quinoa
½ cup chopped green bell pepper
⅓ cup chopped red onion
1 tablespoon olive oil
3 tablespoons orange juice
1 teaspoon cider vinegar
1 teaspoon honey
½ teaspoon dry mustard
Lettuce leaves

Place almond slivers in a small dry skillet. Cook over medium heat, stirring almost constantly, until slivers are lightly browned and really smell "toasty." Remove from heat and set aside.

Grate enough of the rind from one of the oranges to make about 1 teaspoon. Set aside. Using a small sharp knife or a vegetable peeler, remove the rind from both oranges, as well as the bitter white pith just beneath it. Cut oranges into ¼-inch slices and remove any seeds with the tip of the knife. Reserve any orange juice that accumulates when you slice the oranges to use in the dressing. This is most easily accomplished if you slice the oranges in a shallow dish, such as a pie plate.) Set orange slices aside.

In a large bowl, toss together the quinoa, green pepper, red onion, and toasted almond slivers.

In a small bowl, stir together the olive oil, reserved orange juice, vinegar, honey, mustard, and grated orange rind. Pour dressing over salad and toss until well combined.

Line four salad plates with lettuce leaves. Place orange slices over lettuce, then top with salad.

SERVES 4.
CALORIES: 262   CHOLESTEROL: 0 mg   SODIUM: 319 mg   FIBER: 7 g

Health tip:
Cook quinoa without salt.
CALORIES: 262   CHOLESTEROL: 0 mg   SODIUM: 12 mg   FIBER: 7 g

—————— ◇ ——————
Quinoa-and-Pear Salad

I enjoy this salad for lunch. Sometimes I stir in some cottag(
cheese for extra protein.

1 can (8½ ounce) pears in syrup
1½ cups cooked and cooled quinoa
½ cup chopped walnuts
¼ cup golden raisins
1 tablespoon vegetable oil
1 tablespoon honey
1 tablespoon lemon juice
¼ teaspoon ground cinnamon
⅛ teaspoon ground ginger
⅛ teaspoon ground nutmeg

Drain pears, reserving 2 tablespoons of the juice. Chop pear
coarsely.

In a medium-size bowl, toss together the pears, quinoa, wal
nuts, and raisins.

In a small bowl, stir together the reserved pear syrup, oil
honey, lemon juice, cinnamon, ginger, and nutmeg. Pour dressin(
over salad and toss until well combined.

SERVES 4.
CALORIES: 275   CHOLESTEROL: 0 mg   SODIUM: 236 mg   FIBER: 5 g

Health tip:
Cook quinoa without salt; omit oil.
CALORIES: 250   CHOLESTEROL: 0 mg   SODIUM: 7 mg   FIBER: 5 g

—————— ◇ ——————
Simply Toasted Sesame Seeds and Quinoa

Do not be deceived by the few ingredients in this recipe, and
the ease of preparation, as it is an absolutely perfect blend of flavors
and textures.

2 tablespoons hulled sesame seeds
2 cups cooked quinoa (it should still be warm)
2 tablespoons butter

Place the sesame seeds in small skillet. Cook over medium
h ɛ, stirring, until seeds turn golden. Remove from heat.

In a medium-size bowl, combine quinoa, butter, and sesame seeds, stirring until butter is melted.

SERVES 4.
CALORIES: 167   CHOLESTEROL: 16 mg   SODIUM: 356 mg   FIBER: 3 g

Health tip:
Cook quinoa without salt; use unsalted margaine instead of butter.
CALORIES: 167   CHOLESTEROL: 0 mg   SODIUM: 9 mg   FIBER: 3 g

Cheddar-Zucchini-Quinoa Bake

I usually serve this with roast chicken, for which it is the perfect side dish. You might also serve it as the main dish for a meatless meal.

3 tablespoons butter, divided
2 cups coarsely shredded zucchini
2 cups cooked quinoa
2 cups shredded Cheddar cheese
⅛ teaspoon pepper
⅓ cup unflavored bread crumbs

Preheat oven to 350°F.
Grease a 1½-quart casserole and set aside.
In a large skillet, melt 2 tablespoons of the butter over medium-high heat. Add zucchini and cook, stirring frequently, until softened. Stir in quinoa, cheese, and pepper. Spoon into prepared casserole.
Melt remaining 1 tablespoon butter in a small pan. Stir in bread crumbs. Sprinkle crumbs over casserole.
Bake for 30 minutes, or until heated through and crumbs are golden.

SERVES 4.
CALORIES: 275   CHOLESTEROL: 56 mg   SODIUM: 500 mg   FIBER: 2 g

Health tip:
Use unsalted margarine instead of butter. Cook quinoa without salt.
CALORIES: 275   CHOLESTEROL: 0 mg   SODIUM: 255 mg   FIBER: 2 g

———————— ◇ ————————

Quinoa and Spanish-Style Beans

You can make this dish as snappy as you like by adding more ground red pepper.

1 tablespoon vegetable oil
½ cup chopped onion
½ cup chopped green bell pepper
1 cup water
1 can (15 ounce) pink beans, undrained (I use Goya brand pink beans
    prepared Spanish style)
½ cup quinoa, rinsed 5 times (see Basic Cooking Instructions)
2 tablespoons chopped cilantro (fresh coriander)
¼ teaspoon salt
⅛ teaspoon ground red pepper

In a 2-quart saucepan, heat the oil over medium-high heat. Add onion and green pepper and cook, stirring frequently, until softened. Stir in water and bring to a boil. Stir in beans and quinoa. Return to boiling. Reduce heat and simmer, covered, for 20 to 25 minutes, or until quinoa is completely transparent and tender. Remove from heat and stir in cilantro, salt, and red pepper.

SERVES 6.
CALORIES: 166   CHOLESTEROL: 0 mg   SODIUM: 92 mg   FIBER: 5 g

Health tip:
Omit salt.
CALORIES: 166   CHOLESTEROL: 0 mg   SODIUM: 4 mg   FIBER: 5 g

—————— ◇ ——————

Quinoa with Leeks and Asparagus

This is a delightful dish to serve in the spring, when both asparagus and leeks are at their best and in good supply.

2 tablespoons vegetable oil
1 cup sliced leek, white and light-green parts only
½ cup quinoa, rinsed 5 times (see Basic Cooking Instructions)
1 cup chicken or vegetable broth, heated to boiling
1 cup asparagus pieces and tips
¼ teaspoon salt

In a 2-quart saucepan, heat the oil over medium-high heat. Add leek and quinoa and cook over medium heat, stirring, until quinoa starts to crackle (it will not have started to brown at this point) and leeks are very soft. Stir in broth and bring to a boil. Reduce heat and simmer, covered, for 10 minutes. Stir in asparagus and salt and simmer, covered, for 5 to 10 minutes longer, or until the liquid has been absorbed and asparagus are tender crisp.

SERVES 4.
CALORIES: 170   CHOLESTEROL: 1 mg   SODIUM: 335 mg   FIBER: 3 g

Health tip:
Reduce oil to 2 teaspoons and cook in a nonstick saucepan. Or, cook leek and quinoa in a nonstick skillet, transferring to the larger pan to finish cooking. Use low-sodium broth and omit salt.
CALORIES: 170   CHOLESTEROL: 1 mg   SODIUM: 116 mg   FIBER: 3 g

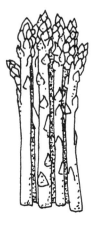

———————◇———————

Curried Peas and Quinoa

If you've read very far into this book, you know that I like spicy curry very much. If you're not quite as fond of mouth-tingling foods as I am, you may want to omit the red pepper.

¼ cup butter
½ cup chopped onion
3 cloves garlic, minced
1 teaspoon fresh ginger, minced
1 tablespoon curry powder
½ teaspoon ground coriander
½ teaspoon salt
¼ teaspoon turmeric
¼ teaspoon ground cumin
⅛ teaspoon ground red pepper
1 package (10 ounce) frozen peas
1¼ cups chicken or vegetable broth
½ cup quinoa, rinsed 5 times (see Basic Cooking Instructions)

In a 3-quart saucepan, melt the butter over medium-high heat. Add onion, garlic, and ginger and cook, stirring frequently, until softened. Stir in curry powder, coriander, salt, turmeric, cumin, and red pepper. Cook 30 seconds, stirring, until spices have been absorbed. Stir in peas and broth. Cover and simmer for 15 minutes. Add quinoa and return to boiling. Cover and simmer for 15 to 20 minutes longer, or until liquid has been absorbed and quinoa is transparent and tender.

SERVES 6.
CALORIES: 172   CHOLESTEROL: 21 mg   SODIUM: 459 mg   FIBER: 4 g

Health tip:
Use 2 tablespoons unsalted margarine instead of butter. Omit salt and use low-sodium broth.
CALORIES: 139   CHOLESTEROL: 0 mg   SODIUM: 64 mg   FIBER: 4 g

Mexican Quinoa Stew

This recipe started out as a side dish, but after it was cooked it
te more like a stew, since all of the liquid is not absorbed by the
uinoa. So, add a loaf of bread, a simple salad, and call it dinner.

2 tablespoons vegetable oil
½ cup quinoa, rinsed 5 times (see Basic Cooking Instructions)
½ cup chopped onion
1 clove garlic, minced
1 can (14½ ounce) Mexican-style stewed tomatoes or plain stewed
*   tomatoes, undrained*
1 can (15 ounce) whole-kernel corn, undrained
¼ teaspoon ground cumin
¼ teaspoon ground red pepper
¼ teaspoon salt
Shredded Monterey Jack cheese (optional)

In a 2-quart saucepan, heat the oil over medium-high heat. Add
quinoa, onion, and garlic and cook, stirring, until quinoa starts to
rackle (it will not have started to brown at this point) and onion is
oftened. Add tomatoes and corn, cumin, red pepper, and salt, and
ring to a boil. Reduce heat and simmer, covered, for 20 minutes, or
ntil quinoa is transparent and tender. Remove from heat and let
tand 5 minutes. If you like, sprinkle with cheese just before serv-
ng.

ERVES 4.
ALORIES: 260   CHOLESTEROL: 0 mg   SODIUM: 550 mg   FIBER: 5 g

Health tip:
Reduce oil to 2 teaspoons and cook in a nonstick saucepan. Or, cook quinoa,
nion, and garlic in a nonstick skillet, transferring to the larger pan to finish
ooking. O:nit salt and cheese.
ALORIES: 208   CHOLESTEROL: 0 mg   SODIUM: 417 mg   FIBER: 5 g

Quinoa Kugel

This fabulous kugel recipe is a variation of an old family favorite that my mother got originally from a cookbook published by her local chapter of The National Council of Jewish Women called "Dining Out at Home." I didn't think that my mother's recipe could be improved upon until I tried it using quinoa noodles, which are *much* more flavorful than ordinary wide noodles. This is as delicious served cold as it is warm.

Pudding:

> *1 package (8 ounce) quinoa flat noodles*
> *4 eggs*
> *½ cup orange juice*
> *½ cup sugar*
> *½ teaspoon vanilla extract*
> *¼ teaspoon salt*
> *1 cup cottage cheese*
> *½ cup sour cream*
> *½ cup milk*
> *2 cups chopped peeled apple*
> *1 cup golden raisins*

Topping:

> *½ cup apricot jam*
> *¾ cup crushed corn flakes*
> *3 tablespoons, melted*
> *1 tablespoon sugar*
> *½ teaspoon ground cinnamon*

Preheat oven to 350°F.

Grease a 9 × 13 × 2-inch baking dish and set aside.

To make the pudding, first cook noodles according to package directions. Drain and set aside.

In a bowl, beat eggs. Beat in orange juice, sugar, vanilla, and salt. Beat in cottage cheese, sour cream, and milk. Stir in noodles, apples, and raisins. Pour noodle mixture into prepared baking dish. (The custard will be quite thin.)

To make the topping, in a small saucepan heat jam until melted and pour over pudding mixture. (The jam may also be heated in a small bowl in a microwave oven.)

In a medium-size bowl, stir together crushed corn flakes, butter, sugar, and cinnamon. Sprinkle over top of kugel.

Bake for 1 hour, then cool for 1 hour before cutting into squares. Serve warm or at room temperature.

SERVES 15.
CALORIES: 246   CHOLESTEROL: 70 mg   SODIUM: 161 mg   FIBER: 2 g

Health tip:
Use scrambled-egg substitute instead of eggs; plain yogurt instead of sour cream; and unsalted margarine in place of butter. Use skim milk.
CALORIES: 227   CHOLESTEROL: 3 mg   SODIUM: 149 mg   FIBER: 2 g

———————— ◇ ————————

Cranberry-Quinoa Quick Bread

This sweet bread has a very grainy (in the best sense of the word!) texture to it: dense inside with a crisp crust. It tastes good just as it is, but if fat and cholesterol are no problem for you, smear it with cream cheese or butter and serve it with a cup of good coffee.

1¼ cups sugar, divided
1½ cups chopped cranberries
½ cup butter, slightly softened
2 eggs
1½ cups all-purpose flour
¾ cup quinoa flour
1 teaspoon baking soda
1 teaspoon baking powder
½ teaspoon salt
¼ cup milk

Preheat oven to 350°F.
Grease a 9 × 5 × 3-inch loaf pan and set aside.
In a medium-size bowl, combine ¼ cup of the sugar and cranberries. Set aside for 15 minutes.
In a large bowl, cream butter with remaining 1 cup sugar until light and fluffy, about 5 minutes. Beat in eggs.
In a medium-size bowl, stir together both kinds of flour, baking soda, baking powder, and salt. Add to the butter mixture alternately with milk. Stir in cranberries. (The mixture will be thick.)

Turn into prepared pan, smoothing top. Bake for 50 to 60 minutes, or until a wooden pick inserted in the center comes out clean. Turn loaf out of pan and cool on a wire rack.

MAKES 1 LOAF (16 slices).
CALORIES: 186   CHOLESTEROL: 42 mg   SODIUM: 198 mg   FIBER: 1 g

Health tip:
Use unsalted margarine instead of butter; omit salt.
CALORIES: 186   CHOLESTEROL: 42 mg   SODIUM: 89 mg   FIBER: 1 g

———————— ◇ ————————

Pecan-Quinoa Cookies

I was skeptical about how a cookie would taste made with quinoa flour. The answer is: absolutely great!

½ cup butter, slightly softened
3 tablespoons sugar
½ teaspoon vanilla extract
½ cup ground pecans
½ cup all-purpose flour
⅓ cup quinoa flour
Confectioners' sugar

Preheat oven to 300°F.
Grease one or two baking sheets and set aside.
In a large bowl, cream the butter and sugar until light and fluffy. Beat in vanilla, then pecans. Beat in both flours until well combined.
Roll batter into 1-inch balls. Place on prepared baking sheets and bake for 15 to 20 minutes, or until bottoms are lightly browned.
Place confectioners' sugar in a plastic bag. Carefully drop warm cookies into bag and shake to coat them with sugar. Cool on wire racks.

MAKES 16 COOKIES.
CALORIES: 113   CHOLESTEROL: 15 mg   SODIUM: 49 mg   FIBER: 1 g

Health tip:
Use unsalted margarine instead of butter.
CALORIES: 113   CHOLESTEROL: 0 mg   SODIUM: 7 mg   FIBER: 1 g

TEFF
(Eragrostis tef)

Teff means lost, which may refer to the fact that each grain of teff is so tiny that it is easily misplaced, especially during harvesting.

One thing is for sure. Teff is an ancient grain that has been used for ages to make *injera,* a spongy sort of crêpe that is the national bread of Ethiopia. (Millet flour is also referred to as teff sometimes, and injera can be made with it, as well as teff flour.)

Types of Teff Available

Teff: It is the whole grain, and so tiny that it can't possibly be processed, so the germ and bran remain on the grain.

Teff flour: The whole grain ground into flour.

Texture and Flavor

Teff is a tiny reddish-brown seed that cooks up very much like a stiff cornmeal-mush. The grains retain some of their crunch, and the mouth feel can be likened to thick toasted-wheat cereal, better known as Wheatina.

Of all the more unusual grains, I find teff to be the most pleasing. The flavor is pleasant, something like wheat, with a natural sweetness and a hint of malt.

Cooked teff can be used the same way you would use ground nuts or small seeds: to add texture and subtle flavor to baked goods.

Compatible Foods, Herbs, and Spices

Because of its dense texture, teff is not suitable for stews or salads. Its best use is for baked goods, or as a binding agent or a thickener, and its definite texture can be used to advantage in smooth foods. Teff can also be used plain as a hot cereal.

Availability

Teff is available in most health-food stores and through mail-order grain catalogs (see page 21). I think it may be some time before teff makes its debut as a staple supermarket item.

Nutritional Content

Teff is high in calcium, iron, protein, and fiber.

Substitutions

Amaranth: It is the only grain that can be substituted for teff. However, since the flavor of amaranth is a good deal stronger, only use this substitution if the teff is a small part of the recipe.

Poppy seeds: Since teff is frequently called for to add texture to baked goods, whole or ground poppy seeds can just as easily be used in its place.

Ground nuts: They can be substituted the same way and for the same reasons as poppy seeds.

Basic Cooking Instructions

Please read *About Cooking Grains* beginning on page 7.

Stove-top method:

3 cups water
½ teaspoon salt
1 cup teff

In a 2-quart saucepan, bring the water and salt to a boil over high heat. Stir in teff and return to boiling. Reduce heat and simmer for 15 minutes, stirring every 3 to 4 minutes so that the grain does not form lumps.

MAKES 3 CUPS.

Microwave method:

2¾ cups water
½ teaspoon salt
1 cup teff

Place the water in a 3-quart, microwave-safe bowl. Cover with waxed paper. Microwave on high (100% power) for 5 minutes. Stir in salt and teff. Recover with waxed paper and microwave on high 4 minutes. Stir, then recover, and microwave on medium (50% power) for 3 minutes. Stir, then recover, and microwave on medium for 3 minutes. Stir, recover, and microwave on medium for 3 minutes more. Stir and let stand for 4 minutes.

MAKES SCANT 3 CUPS.

Reheating

If you are going to set the cooked teff aside, be sure to place a piece of plastic wrap directly on the surface of the grain. When the air dries it out, which happens quickly, the grains cling together and harden into a skin that is tough and like plastic. Teff binds and tightens considerably when it's chilled. In fact, it gets so stiff that it can be sliced. Steaming and microwaving will restore teff to its softer state.

TEFF RECIPES

*(*indicates easy recipes.)*

———————— ◇ ————————

Injera (Ethiopian bread)
Tibs Wot (Ethiopian stew)
Lentil Burgers
Potato-and-Teff Latkes
Teff Spoonbread *
Buttermilk Waffles, Teff-Style
Teff Scones
Molasses-Teff Bread
Teff-Nut-and-Date Bread *
Walnut-Teff Strudel

———————— ◇ ————————

Injera (Ethiopian bread)

This recipe was developed by Rebecca Wood, spokesperson for the health-food industry. Needless to say, she is an expert on all aspects of the "newer" grains, and she has written two books, "Quinoa the Supergrain" and "The Whole Foods Encyclopedia." Rebecca's injera is an Americanized version of the injera served in Ethiopia, where it is considered the national bread. Injera doesn't look like bread at all, or at least not what we think of as bread, but is more like a large and slightly spongy pancake or crêpe. Although there are only three ingredients in injera, and the actual procedure for making it is not difficult, it does take time, since the batter must ferment for up to a day to activate the natural wild yeast in the teff flour. In Ethiopia, the bread serves the purpose of both plate and eating utensils. Stews are served on top of the injera and then pieces of the bread are torn away and used to scoop up the stew.

2 cups teff flour
4 cups distilled water
⅛ teaspoon salt
Vegetable oil, for greasing skillet

In a large bowl, stir together the teff flour and water. Let stand at room temperature for 12 to 24 hours or until it gives off a slightly fermented aroma.

The following day, when ready to proceed, pour off any excess liquid on the surface of the mixture and stir in salt.

Heat a 9-inch slope-sided skillet over medium heat until a few drops of water sprinkled on the bottom of the pan bounce about before evaporating. Lightly grease skillet with oil. Pour about ½ cup of the batter into the skillet and swirl it around so that the bottom of the skillet is entirely covered with batter. Cover and leave undisturbed for about 3 minutes, or until surface of bread looks dry and bottom is browned. Remove from pan. Repeat this procedure with remaining batter. Serve warm or at room temperature.

═══

MAKES 4 BREADS.
CALORIES: 400   CHOLESTEROL: 0 mg   SODIUM: 33 mg   FIBER: 8 g

Health tip:
These are quite healthy just as they are.
═══

———————— ◇ ————————

Tibs Wot (Ethiopian stew)

A wot is usually eaten, quite literally, with injera (Ethiopian bread), which is broken into pieces and used to scoop up the stew. Wot, which is sometimes spelled *watt* or *wott*, can be made with beef (tibs), chicken, or vegetables. The common denominator is that it is *always* hot. This one is definitely hot, but not fiery. You can make it as hot as your mouth can stand by adding more red pepper.

2 tablespoons vegetable oil
1½ pounds beef cubes
2 cups chopped onion
3 cloves garlic, minced
1 teaspoon minced fresh ginger
2 tablespoons paprika
1 teaspoon salt
½ teaspoon ground red pepper
¼ teaspoon ground cardamom
¼ teaspoon ground coriander
Pinch ground nutmeg
Pinch ground cloves
1 cup water
2 tablespoons lime juice

In a heavy 4-quart saucepan or Dutch oven, heat the oil over medium-high heat. Add beef, onion, garlic, and ginger. Cook, stirring and tossing, until beef is no longer red and onion is softened. Add paprika, salt, red pepper, cardamom, coriander, nutmeg, and cloves, and stir until the spices are absorbed by the oil. Stir in water and bring to a boil. Cover and simmer for 1 hour. Uncover and simmer for 30 minutes longer, or until beef is tender and sauce is thickened. Stir in lime juice. Serve with injera.

SERVES 4.
CALORIES: 620   CHOLESTEROL: 153 mg   SODIUM: 647 mg   FIBER: 2 g

Health tip:
Omit salt. Use only 2 teaspoons of the oil and cook in a nonstick pan. Or, reduce oil to 2 teaspoons and cook beef, onion, garlic, and ginger in a large nonstick skillet, transferring to the larger pan to finish cooking.
CALORIES: 580   CHOLESTEROL: 153 mg   SODIUM: 114 mg   FIBER: 2 g

—————— ◇ ——————

Lentil Burgers

I make these burgers just firm enough so that they hold together as they cook. If you prefer a firmer burger, add extra bread crumbs to the lentil mixture. These are *very* filling.

2 cups cooked lentils, divided
½ cup cooked teff
⅓ cup chopped scallion, both white and green parts
1 clove garlic, minced
½ teaspoon salt
¼ teaspoon pepper
½ cup dry unflavored bread crumbs, divided
Oil, for frying

Place ½ cup of the lentils, teff, scallion, garlic, salt, and pepper in the container of a food processor. Cover and process until thoroughly blended. Stir in remaining lentils and ¼ cup of the bread crumbs. Shape mixture into 4 patties, then carefully roll in remaining ¼ cup crumbs.

Pour enough oil into a large skillet so that it measures ¼-inch deep. Heat until bubbles form when some bread crumbs are sprinkled on top of the hot oil. Cook burgers until browned on one side. Turn and cook until browned on second side.

SERVES 4.
CALORIES: 503   CHOLESTEROL: 1 mg   SODIUM: 412 mg   FIBER: 13 g

Health tip:
Omit salt.
CALORIES: 503   CHOLESTEROL: 1 mg   SODIUM: 103 mg   FIBER: 13 g

———— ◇ ————

Potato-and-Teff Latkes

These are simply potato pancakes with a plus: teff. I serve them with sour cream, but they're also good with applesauce or plain yogurt.

1 cup cooked and cooled teff
1 cup shredded raw potato
1 egg
2 tablespoons grated onion
½ teaspoon salt
¼ teaspoon pepper
Oil, for frying

If the teff is lumpy, mash with the back of a spoon to break up lumps. In a medium-size bowl, stir together teff, potato, egg, onion, salt, and pepper.

Pour enough oil into a large skillet so that it measures ¼-inch deep. Heat until oil bubbles when a small amount of batter is dropped into the skillet. Drop batter into skillet by rounded measuring tablespoonsful, then flatten slightly with a broad spatula. (The more you flatten them, the crispier the latkes will be.) Cook over medium-high heat until potato shreds are a deep golden, then turn and cook the second side the same way, adjusting heat, if necessary. (Make sure that the bottom of the pancake is cooked enough or you will have trouble turning it.)

MAKES 15 LATKES.
CALORIES: 70   CHOLESTEROL: 14 mg   SODIUM: 76 mg   FIBER: 1 g

Health tip:
Omit salt. Use scrambled egg substitute.
CALORIES: CHOLESTEROL: 0 mg   SODIUM: 8 mg   FIBER: 1 g

Teff Spoonbread

This is almost identical to traditional spoonbread made with cornmeal, but the teff gives it a slightly crunchier texture, which I find interesting. Serve it like the Southerners do, as a substitute for rice and potatoes, and with a big pat of butter melting on each serving.

2 cups cooked and cooled teff
1 cup milk
2 tablespoons sugar
2 tablespoons butter, melted
3 eggs, separated
2 teaspoons baking powder
1 teaspoon salt

Preheat oven to 350°F.

Grease a 1½-quart casserole or soufflé dish and set aside.

In a large bowl, stir together the teff, milk, sugar, butter, egg yolks, baking powder, and salt.

In a clean, grease-free, medium-size bowl, beat egg whites with clean beaters until stiff peaks form when beaters are lifted. Fold whites into teff mixture. Turn into prepared casserole.

Bake for 50 minutes, or until puffed and browned.

SERVES 6.

CALORIES: 214   CHOLESTEROL: 120 mg   SODIUM: 670 mg   FIBER: 3 g

Health tip:

Omit salt.

CALORIES: 214   CHOLESTEROL: 120 mg   SODIUM: 197 mg   FIBER: 3 g

——————— ◇ ———————

Buttermilk Waffles, Teff-Style

These are moist, chewy waffles, not at all crisp, but they do have a lovely flavor. They also freeze well and reheat nicely in a toaster.

1 cup teff flour
¾ cup all-purpose flour
⅓ cup sugar
1 tablespoon baking powder
1 teaspoon baking soda
1 teaspoon salt
⅔ cup buttermilk
3 eggs, separated
⅓ cup cooked teff
⅓ cup melted butter
1 teaspoon vanilla extract

Heat and grease a waffle iron as manufacturer directs.

In a large bowl, stir together both kinds of flour, sugar, baking powder, baking soda, and salt.

In a medium-size bowl, beat together the buttermilk, egg yolks, cooked teff, butter, and vanilla. Stir the buttermilk mixture into the flour mixture until well combined.

In a clean, grease-free, medium-size bowl, beat egg whites with clean beaters until they form stiff peaks when beaters are lifted. Fold beaten whites into the batter.

Spread about 1 cup of the batter onto the waffle iron. Cook until steaming has stopped and waffles are browned.

MAKES 8 WAFFLES

CALORIES: CHOLESTEROL: SODIUM: FIBER:

Health tip:
Omit salt; use unsalted margarine instead of butter.

CALORIES: CHOLESTEROL: SODIUM: FIBER:

Teff Scones

Teff adds just enough moisture to these scones to make them fairly moist. (Scones are usually a little dry for my taste.) Scones are one of the classic accompaniments to tea, but are also a wonderful breakfast treat. Spread generously with plenty of butter and strawberry jam.

1 cup teff flour
1 cup all-purpose flour
⅓ cup sugar
2 teaspoons baking powder
1 teaspoon baking soda
½ teaspoon salt
⅓ cup butter
½ cup raisins
2 eggs
⅓ cup buttermilk

Preheat oven to 400°F.
Grease a large baking sheet and set aside.
In a large bowl, stir together both kinds of flour, sugar, baking powder, baking soda, and salt. Using a pastry cutter or two knives, cut in butter until mixture resembles coarse cornmeal. Stir in raisins.
In a small bowl, beat together the eggs and buttermilk. Stir into the flour mixture just until the mixture forms a soft dough. Turn onto a floured surface and knead about 10 times. Pat into an 8-inch circle. Cut into 8 wedges and transfer to prepared baking sheet.
Bake for 15 minutes, or until lightly browned.

MAKES 8 SCONES.
CALORIES: 261   CHOLESTEROL: 73 mg   SODIUM: 412 mg   FIBER: 3 g

Health tip:
Omit salt; use unsalted margarine instead of butter.
CALORIES: 253   CHOLESTEROL: 60 mg   SODIUM: 232 mg   FIBER: 3 g

—————— ◇ ——————
Molasses-Teff Bread

This bread makes exceptional toast. The slight sweetness comes from the molasses, and the teff keeps the bread moist.

½ cup very warm water (105–115°F)
½ teaspoon sugar
1 package dry yeast
3 cups all-purpose flour, divided
1 cup teff flour
1½ teaspoons salt
½ cup milk
⅓ cup unsulphured molasses
1 egg
½ cup cooked teff

Grease a baking sheet and set aside.

In a glass measuring cup, stir together the warm water and sugar, then stir in yeast. Let stand until ¼ inch of white bubbly foam forms on top. (This foaming is called *proofing*, and if it doesn't happen it means that for some reason or other the yeast has not been activated. Discard this batch and try again, double checking the date on the yeast package and the temperature of the water.)

In a large bowl, stir together 1 cup of the all-purpose flour, teff flour, and salt. Stir in milk, molasses, egg, cooked teff, and proofed yeast mixture. Stir in 1 cup of the all-purpose flour. Turn onto a floured surface and knead in as much of the remaining 1 cup flour as necessary to make a smooth dough.

Form dough into a ball and place in a large greased bowl. Cover with greased plastic wrap and set in a warm spot, away from drafts, until doubled in bulk, about 1 hour.

Punch dough down and shape into a round loaf. Place on prepared baking sheet. Cover with greased plastic wrap and let rise until doubled in bulk, about 40 minutes.

Preheat oven to 350°F.

Bake for about 40 minutes, or until top and bottom are nicely browned.

MAKES 1 LOAF (18 slices).
CALORIES: 130   CHOLESTEROL: 12 mg   SODIUM: 196 mg   FIBER: 3 g

Health tip:
Omit salt.
CALORIES: 130   CHOLESTEROL: 12 mg   SODIUM: 9 mg   FIBER: 3 g

––––––––––– ◇ –––––––––––

Teff-Nut-and-Date Bread

My sister loves this bread and eats it like cake. (The teff in the batter will make you think you're eating poppy seeds.)

1 cup teff flour
1 cup all-purpose flour
2 teaspoons baking powder
½ teaspoon salt
¾ cup butter
½ cup sugar
1 egg
1 teaspoon vanilla extract
1 cup cooked and cooled teff
½ cup milk
1 cup chopped dates
½ cup chopped walnuts

Preheat oven to 325°F.

Grease a 9 × 5 × 3-inch loaf pan and set aside.

In a medium-size bowl, stir together both kinds of flour, baking powder, and salt.

In a large bowl, cream the butter and sugar until fluffy. Beat in egg and vanilla, then cooked teff. Add the dry ingredients alternately with the milk, stirring until well combined. Stir in dates and walnuts.

Spoon batter into prepared pan. Bake for 1½ hours, or until a wooden pick inserted in the center comes out clean. Turn loaf out onto a wire rack and cool.

MAKES 1 LOAF (14 slices).
CALORIES: 257   CHOLESTEROL: 43 mg   SODIUM: 243 mg   FIBER: 3 g

Health tip:
Omit salt; use unsalted margarine instead of butter.
CALORIES: 257   CHOLESTEROL: 16 mg   SODIUM: 69 mg   FIBER: 3 g

———————— ◇ ————————

Walnut-Teff Strudel

My Hungarian grandmother never used teff in her strudel, but I'm sure she would have approved of the addition in this case. This recipe makes two small strudels.

1 cup cooked teff
⅔ cup sugar
½ cup sour cream
1 cup ground walnuts
⅓ cup golden raisins
½ teaspoon grated lemon rind
8 sheets phyllo dough (9 × 13-inch), thawed according to package
   directions
¼ cup butter, melted
6 tablespoons corn-flake crumbs
Confectioners' sugar, for sprinkling on strudel

Preheat oven to 400°F.

In a medium-size bowl, stir together the cooked teff, sugar, and sour cream, removing any lumps of teff by pressing them against the side of the bowl with a wooden spoon. Stir in walnuts, raisins, and lemon rind.

Place 1 sheet of the phyllo dough on a work surface with a long edge toward you. (Cover remaining sheets of phyllo with a damp cloth to prevent them from drying out.) Brush sheet with melted butter, then sprinkle with about 1 tablespoon of the corn-flake crumbs. Lay a second sheet of phyllo on top of the first. Brush with butter, then sprinkle with another tablespoon of the corn-flake crumbs. Repeat this procedure with a third sheet. Place a fourth sheet on top and brush with butter.

Spoon half of the teff mixture along the long edge facing you, leaving a 1½-inch border from the edge nearest you and both ends. (You will have a "log" about 2 inches wide of the filling.) Fold the two ends of dough in over the filling, then, starting from the edge nearest, roll the phyllo into a "log," completely enclosing the filling.

Repeat this whole procedure with remaining ingredients. Place both strudels on an ungreased baking sheet and brush tops with any remaining butter.

Bake for 25 minutes, or until golden. Remove from baking sheets and cool on a wire rack for at least 30 minutes before serving. Sprinkle with confectioners' sugar when cool.

MAKES 2 SMALL STRUDELS (10 servings).

CALORIES: 256   CHOLESTEROL: 17 mg   SODIUM: 105 mg   FIBER: 3 g

Health tip:

Use unsalted margarine instead of butter. Omit salt when cooking teff.

CALORIES: 256   CHOLESTEROL: 5 mg   SODIUM: 35 mg   FIBER: 3 g

TRITICALE

Triticale (pronounced tri-ti-CAY-lee), a hybrid of wheat and rye, is the first completely man-made grain.

Research and development on triticale began in the last century, but agricultural scientists of the time were unable to produce consistent results, and the project was abandoned.

In the 1960s, when the hunt was on for high-yielding grain crops with good nutritional value that might help alleviate the third-world food crisis, the triticale project was revived and successfully completed. Triticale has some of the best qualities of each of its parent grains, and, in some cases, even better.

Unfortunately, there's a down side to this success story. Crop yields have never been as great as were hoped for, and there have been some other cultivation problems as well. To top it off, acceptance of the grain has been less than overwhelming.

However, triticale is a high-protein grain with a pleasant flavor and is certainly well worth incorporating into your diet.

Types of Triticale Available

Triticale groats or berries: The whole grain that has been hulled.

Flakes: The whole hulled grain that has been toasted and thinly rolled.

Flour: Triticale that has been finely ground.

Flavor and Texture

Triticale is a rice-shaped, beige-colored grain. It cooks into plump separate grains that have the texture of fresh corn kernels (a chewy skin and a starchy core), as well as a pleasant pop when the grains are chewed.

The flavor is mild and nutty with a very faint rye sourness and a slightly starchy aftertaste. The grain is very filling and has a quality of taste and texture that adds character to any dish.

Triticale flour has a flavor some place between whole-wheat flour and rye flour. Like rye, it is low in gluten, so it should always be used in combination with other flours that are high in gluten.

Compatible Foods, Herbs, and Spices

Because triticale has a mild pleasing flavor, it can be used with almost any food you like. It goes especially well with meats (particularly beef and pork), vegetables, cheeses, and virtually any member of the onion family.

Parsley and dill are the most compatible herbs to use with triticale, although other herbs and spices work well with it, too.

Triticale combines well with other starches, such as rice and potatoes, and is very complementary to dried beans.

Availability

Triticale can be found at health-food stores and can be purchased through mail-order grain catalogs (see page 21).

Nutritional Content

The protein content in triticale is slightly higher than either rye or wheat, its parent grains. Unfortunately, I was unable to find any other nutrition information regarding this grain, but I believe that when this information becomes available it will be similar to rye.

Substitutions

Wheat berries or flakes: The flavor and texture of these two grains are very similar, and can be directly substituted.

Rye berries or flakes: Since this is the other half of triticale, so to speak, the two can be used interchangeably. However, the rye is more sour.

Brown rice: It has a similar nuttiness and chewy texture that would be fine for any recipe calling for cooked triticale. But, since the cooking times differ greatly, that will have to be taken into account.

Whole-wheat flour: Can be substituted for triticale flour.

Rye flour: Can be substituted for triticale flour.

Other substitutes (in order of preference): White rice, barley, Job's tears.

Basic Cooking Instructions

Please read *About Cooking Grains* beginning on page 7.

Whole-grain Triticale (berries/groats)

Please note: When cooking the whole grain, salt must always be added after cooking, or the grain will not absorb the water. Do not cook triticale with broth.

Stove-top method:

> 2½ cups water
> 1 cup whole-grain triticale
> ½ teaspoon salt

In a 2-quart saucepan, bring the water to a boil over high heat. Stir in triticale and return to boiling. Reduce heat and simmer, covered, for 1 hour and 45 minutes, or until almost all of the liquid has been absorbed. Remove from heat and stir in salt. Let stand for 10 minutes.

MAKES 2½ CUPS.

Microwave method:

> 3 cups water
> 1 cup whole-grain triticale
> ½ teaspoon salt

Place the water in a 3-quart, microwave-safe bowl. Cover with waxed paper and microwave on high (100% power) for 5 minutes. Stir in triticale. Recover with waxed paper and microwave on high for 4 minutes. Microwave on medium (50% power), still covered with waxed paper, for 1 hour, rotating dish once, if necessary. Let stand for 5 minutes. Stir in salt and fluff with a fork.

MAKES 2¼ CUPS.

Triticale Flakes

Stove-top method:

1¾ cups water
½ teaspoon salt
1 cup triticale flakes

In a 2-quart saucepan, bring the water and salt to a boil over high heat. Stir in triticale flakes and return to boiling. Reduce heat, cover, and simmer for 40 minutes.

MAKES 1½ CUPS.

Microwave method:

1½ cups water
½ teaspoon salt
1 cup triticale flakes

Place the water and salt in a 3-quart, microwave-safe bowl. Cover with waxed paper and microwave on high (100% power) for 3 minutes. Stir in triticale flakes. Recover with waxed paper and microwave on high for 4 minutes. Microwave on medium (50% power), still covered with waxed paper, for 30 minutes. Let stand for 4 minutes.

MAKES 1¼ CUPS.

Reheating

Triticale gets a little chewier as it chills, but it can still be used without reheating. To restore its fresh-cooked texture, microwave or steam for a short time.

TRITICALE RECIPES

(*indicates easy recipes.)

———————— ◇ ————————

Triticale-Carrot Soup *
Parmesan Chicken with Triticale *
Fresh-Salmon-and-Triticale Salad *
Cornish Pasties
Greek Salad *
Succotash Salad *
Fruity Triticale Salad *
Spicy Tofu Salad *
Berries, Beans, and Black-eyed Peas *
Triticale and Cauliflower with Cheese Sauce *
Good-Morning Pancakes
Triticale Yeast Bread
Trail-Mix Bread

Triticale-Carrot Soup

The carrots and onions cook down to give this soup a wonderful natural sweetness. It's almost as good as chicken soup when you're feeling low.

8 cups water
2 pounds carrots, peeled and sliced ½-inch thick
1 pound beef short ribs or flanken
2 cups chopped onion
1 cup whole-grain triticale, rinsed
½ cup chopped parsley
¼ cup chopped fresh dill
1 teaspoon salt
⅛ teaspoon pepper

In a large soup pot, place the water, carrots, beef, onion, and triticale. Bring to a boil over high heat. Cover and simmer for 2 hours. Stir in parsley, dill, salt, and pepper. Continue to simmer, uncovered, for 30 minutes longer. Remove beef (make sure you get all the bones) from the soup. Shred meat and stir back into the soup, or serve the beef another time.

SERVES 8. (nutritional values for soup without beef)
CALORIES: 141   CHOLESTEROL: 10 mg   SODIUM: 347 mg   FIBER: 7 g

Health tip:
Omit salt. Skim off any fat from the top of the soup before serving.
CALORIES: 141   CHOLESTEROL: 10 mg   SODIUM: 81 mg   FIBER: 7 g

Parmesan Chicken with Triticale

Don't be deceived by the simplicity of this dish; you can serve it to company on any special occasion. Best of all, it can be made ahead of time, since it reheats beautifully. Needless to say, you can substitute other cooked grains for the triticale. For instance, wild rice would be *wonderful!*

3 tablespoons butter
1 pound skinless boneless chicken breasts, cut into strips
½ cup dry white wine
½ cup heavy cream
½ cup grated Parmesan cheese
¼ teaspoon pepper
2 cups cooked whole-grain triticale

In a large skillet, melt the butter over medium-high heat. Add chicken and cook until lightly browned and cooked through. Remove chicken from skillet and set aside.

Add wine to the skillet, stirring up any brown bits that cling to the bottom and side. Stir in cream, Parmesan cheese, and pepper. Cook over high heat until boiling rapidly. Add triticale and chicken. Cook, stirring, until heated through and sauce is thickened. (If making ahead, cool slightly, then cover and chill until ready to reheat and serve.)

SERVES 4.
CALORIES: 723   CHOLESTEROL: 137 mg   SODIUM: 350 mg   FIBER: 3 g

Health tip:
Eat this only occasionally, and enjoy every mouthful when you do.

Fresh-Salmon-and-Triticale Salad

I often order main-course salads when I go out to eat, and nowadays I often serve them to company. Everybody seems to enjoy these salads as much as I do, probably because they make a satisfying (and elegant) meal that's not too filling.

2 tablespoons butter
1 pound skinless salmon fillet, cut into ½-inch cubes
1 cup cooked and cooled whole-grain triticale
1 tomato, cut into wedges
½ small red onion, sliced
⅛ teaspoon salt
⅛ teaspoon pepper
⅓ cup mayonnaise
2 tablespoons sour cream
1 tablespoon chopped fresh dill or
  ½ teaspoon dried dill weed
2 tespoons lemon juice
1 teaspoon Dijon mustard
1 clove garlic, minced
4 cups mixed salad greens

In a large skillet, melt the butter over medium-high heat. Add salmon and cook, stirring and tossing, until just cooked through, about 3 minutes. Remove from heat and set aside to cool.

In a medium-size bowl, combine the triticale, tomato, red onion, salt, and pepper.

In a small bowl, stir together the mayonnaise, sour cream, dill, lemon juice, mustard, and garlic.

Divide salad greens among four dinner plates. Top with triticale mixture. Arrange salmon over greens. Spoon mayonnaise dressing over salmon.

SERVES 4.
CALORIES: 469   CHOLESTEROL: 103 mg   SODIUM: 495 mg   FIBER: 3 g
Health tip:
Substitute yogurt for mayonnaise; omit salt.
CALORIES: 389   CHOLESTEROL: 98 mg   SODIUM: 170 mg   FIBER: 3 g

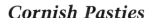

Cornish Pasties

This traditional Cornish recipe for a meat turnover can be served warm or at room temperature, and is typically packed for away-from-home meals for children to take to school or husbands to take to work. The basic ingredients of beef, onion, and potato in a flaky crust rarely vary, but the seasonings can be different from one town, or even one family, to the next.

Crust:

> 1⅓ cups triticale flour
> 1⅓ cups all-purpose flour
> 1½ teaspoons salt
> ⅔ cup solid white vegetable shortening
> ½ package (8 ounce) cream cheese or cream cheese with chives
> ⅓ cup ice water

Filling:

> 1 tablespoon vegetable oil
> ½ pound ground beef
> 1 cup ¼-inch-diced cooked potato
> ½ cup finely chopped onion
> ¼ cup sour cream
> ¾ teaspoon salt
> ¼ teaspoon pepper

To make dough, in a medium-size bowl, stir both of the flours and the salt together. Cut in shortening and cream cheese with a pastry blender or two knives, until the mixture resembles coarse cornmeal. Stir in the water and form the dough into a ball. Chill for 20 minutes.

While dough is chilling, make filling. In a skillet, heat the oil over medium-high heat. Add beef, potato, and onion and cook, stirring frequently, until beef is no longer pink and onion is softened. Remove from heat and stir in sour cream, salt, and pepper. Set aside to cool slightly.

Preheat oven to 400°F.

On a lightly floured surface, roll dough into an 18-inch circle. Cut out 7 6-inch circles, tracing around a plate, or anything that measures 6 inches in diameter, with the tip of a knife. Place equal amounts of the filling on each circle, leaving a ½-inch border. Brush borders with water and fold one side of the dough over the filling to form a half-moon. (You may find this a little tricky to do as there is quite a lot of filling for each pasty. The best way is to sort of hold the filling back with one finger as you fold the dough over it.) Seal each pasty by pressing the edge with your fingers or the tines of a dinner fork (you may need to dip the fork in flour from time to time to keep it from sticking to the dough). Place pasties on ungreased baking sheets. Cut vents in each pasty, or prick with a fork several times.

Bake for 25 minutes, or until golden. Serve immediately, or cool and serve at room temperature. Pasties may also be chilled and reheated, if that's more convenient.

MAKES 7 PASTIES.
CALORIES: 518   CHOLESTEROL: 52 mg   SODIUM: 833 mg   FIBER: 5 g

Health tip:
Omit salt.
CALORIES: 518   CHOLESTEROL: 52 mg   SODIUM: 72 mg   FIBER: 5 g

Greek Salad

This is a very full-flavored salad. The feta cheese, anchovies, and olives all have strong salty flavors. If you're not fond of or can't eat salty foods, you can omit the anchovies, if you like, and cut back on the feta cheese and olives. However, these ingredients are the heart of a Greek salad, and the anchovies and cheese do make it a complete high-protein dish.

1 cup cooked and cooled whole-grain triticale
1 cup coarsely chopped tomato
1 cup coarsely chopped peeled or unpeeled cucumber
¼ cup sliced scallion, both white and green parts
1 tablespoon olive oil
1 tablespoon vegetable oil
2 tablespoons red-wine vinegar
2 or 3 anchovies, cut into ½-inch pieces (about 1 tablespoon)
¼ teaspoon crumbled oregano
⅛ teaspoon pepper
½ cup crumbled feta cheese
12 pitted black olives, cut in half

In a large bowl, combine the triticale, tomato, cucumber, and scallion.

In a small bowl, stir together both oils, vinegar, anchovies, oregano, and pepper. Pour dressing over triticale mixture and toss gently to combine. Top with feta cheese and olives.

SERVES 8.
CALORIES: 146   CHOLESTEROL: 30 mg   SODIUM: 269 mg   FIBER: 1 g

Health tip:
Omit anchovies; reduce feta cheese to 2 tablespoons; omit olives.
CALORIES: 77   CHOLESTEROL: 1 mg   SODIUM: 126 mg   FIBER: 1 g

Succotash Salad

Chili powder and ground red pepper give this traditional New England dish a real Southwestern flavor. I would certainly think of serving this salad as a nice change from potato salad at a barbecue or a picnic.

1½ cups cooked and cooled whole-grain triticale
1 can (12 ounce) whole-kernel corn, drained
1 package (10 ounce) frozen lima beans, thawed and cooked as package directs, and cooled
1 cup sliced celery
½ cup chopped red bell pepper
¼ cup chopped red onion
3 tablespoons vegetable oil
1 tablespoon cider vinegar
½ teaspoon chili powder
¼ teaspoon salt
⅛ teaspoon ground red pepper (optional)

In a large bowl, combine the triticale, corn, lima beans, celery, red bell pepper, and onion.

In a small bowl, stir together the oil, vinegar, chili powder, salt, and ground red pepper. Pour dressing over salad mixture and toss gently to combine.

SERVES 10.
CALORIES: 136   CHOLESTEROL: 0 mg   SODIUM: 296 mg   FIBER: 4 g

Health tip:
Omit salt.
CALORIES: 136   CHOLESTEROL: 0 mg   SODIUM: 100 mg   FIBER: 4 g

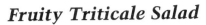

Fruity Triticale Salad

I think you'll like this sort of strange combination of fruit, cheese, nuts, and grain. I often eat this salad by itself for lunch, but it works just as well as a side salad, with broiled chicken, for instance.

1½ cups cooked and cooled whole-grain triticale
1 cup chopped tart apple (Granny Smith or McIntosh)
1 cup fresh peach slices
1 cup diced Monterey Jack cheese
½ cup chopped walnuts
¼ cup bottled Italian dressing
1 tablespoon fresh lemon juice
1 teaspoon Dijon mustard

In a large bowl, combine the triticale, apple, peach slices, cheese, and nuts.

In a small bowl, stir together dressing, lemon juice, and mustard. Pour over salad ingredients and toss gently to combine.

SERVES 4 (as a light main dish); OR 6 (as a side dish)
CALORIES: 537   CHOLESTEROL: 23 mg   SODIUM: 226 mg   FIBER: 11 g

Health tip:
Use a homemade dressing without salt, cook triticale without salt. Omit cheese.
CALORIES: 432   CHOLESTEROL: 0 mg   SODIUM: 20 mg   FIBER: 11 g

——————— ◇ ———————

Spicy Tofu Salad

I'm very fond of tofu, and the combination of tofu with whole-grain berries is a very healthy and nutritious combination. For my taste, the flavor of this salad is outstanding, but you may want to start with only ¼ to ½ teaspoon of the chili oil. As they say, you can always add more. If you think the chili oil will still be too hot, leave it out altogether and substitute Oriental sesame oil.

1½ cups cooked and cooled whole-grain triticale
1 cup diced tofu
1 can (8 ounce) water chestnuts, drained and chopped
½ cup julienned red bell pepper
¼ cup chopped scallion, both white and green parts
2 tablespoons vegetable oil
1½ tablespoons rice vinegar (available in Oriental grocery stores)
*1 tablespoon Japanese soy sauce (if you use a Chinese soy sauce, reduce
    to 2 teaspoons)*
*1 teaspoon chili oil or Oriental sesame oil (both available in Oriental
    grocery stores)*
1 clove garlic, minced

In a large bowl, combine the triticale, tofu, water chestnuts, red bell pepper, and scallion.

In a small bowl, stir together the vegetable oil, vinegar, soy sauce, chili oil, and garlic. Pour dressing over salad ingredients and toss gently to combine.

SERVES 4.
CALORIES: 165   CHOLESTEROL: 0 mg   SODIUM: 392 mg   FIBER: 3 g

Health tip:
Use low-sodium soy sauce. Omit salt when cooking triticale.
CALORIES: 165   CHOLESTEROL: 0 mg   SODIUM: 66 mg   FIBER: 3 g

———— ◇ ————

Berries, Beans, and Black-eyed Peas

I thought I didn't like either collard greens or kale or black-eyed peas until I cooked this. If you're of the same mind, this dish may make a convert of you, too.

3 slices bacon, cut into 1-inch pieces
2 cups firmly packed chopped collard greens or kale
½ cup chopped onion
2 cloves garlic, minced
1 can (10½ ounce) black-eyed peas, drained
1 cup cooked triticale berries
¼ teaspoon salt
¼ teaspoon pepper

In a large heavy saucepan or Dutch oven, cook the bacon until crisp. Remove bacon and drain on paper towels. Add greens, onion, and garlic to fat remaining in pan. Cook over medium heat, stirring, until vegetables are softened. Stir in black-eyed peas, triticale, salt, and pepper. Cook, stirring, until heated through, about 5 minutes. Stir in reserved bacon.

SERVES 6.
CALORIES: 115   CHOLESTEROL: 3 mg   SODIUM: 440 mg   FIBER: 6 g

Health tip:
Omit bacon. Cook in a nonstick saucepan with 1 tablespoon vegetable oil. Or, cook greens, onion, and garlic in oil in a nonstick skillet, transferring to the larger pan to finish cooking.
CALORIES: 115   CHOLESTEROL: 0 mg   SODIUM: 152 mg   FIBER: 6 g

Triticale and Cauliflower with Cheese Sauce

When you combine a creamy cheese sauce with cauliflower and triticale, what you get is an indecently rich and delicious side dish. You can also serve this as a meatless main dish, if you like, heeding the health tips below to cut back on the fat and sodium a bit.

4 cups cauliflower florets
3 tablespoons butter
¼ cup all-purpose flour
1½ cups milk
1 cup shredded Cheddar cheese
¼ teaspoon Worcestershire sauce
¼ teaspoon salt
⅛ teaspoon pepper
2 cups cooked triticale

In a 4-quart saucepan, steam the cauliflower in a small amount of water until tender. Drain thoroughly and set aside.

In the same saucepan, melt the butter over medium heat. Stir in flour until absorbed. Using a whisk, quickly stir in milk and cook, stirring, until mixture comes to a boil. Cook, stirring, for 1 minute. Stir in cheese, Worcestershire sauce, salt, and pepper, stirring until cheese is melted. Stir in cauliflower and triticale. Continue to cook, stirring, until heated through.

SERVES 8.
CALORIES: 208   CHOLESTEROL: 31 mg   SODIUM: 411 mg   FIBER: 3 g

Health tip:
Use skim milk instead of whole milk; substitute unsalted margarine for butter; omit salt.
CALORIES: 196   CHOLESTEROL: 14 mg   SODIUM: 114 mg   FIBER: 3 g

——————— ◇ ———————

Good-Morning Pancakes

Pancakes made with cottage cheese are not light and fluffy. In fact, these are moist and heavy with a slighty tangy taste from the cottage cheese and a grainy mouth feel from the triticale. So why eat them? Because they taste good and they aren't too fattening.

½ cup lowfat cottage cheese
2 egg whites
2 tablespoons 1-percent-fat milk
2 tablespoons sugar
¼ teaspoon vanilla extract
Pinch salt
¼ cup triticale flour
¼ cup all-purpose flour
1 teaspoon baking powder
Oil, for greasing griddle

Place the cottage cheese, egg whites, milk, sugar, vanilla, and salt in the container of an electric blender. Cover and blend until smooth. Add both kinds of flours and baking powder to mixture in blender. Cover and blend until combined.

Heat a griddle or a large skillet until a few drops of water sprinkled on the hot griddle bounce about before evaporating. Grease griddle lightly. Drop 2 tablespoonsful of the batter per pancake onto the griddle. Cook until bubbles on top burst. Turn and cook until the second side is browned.

MAKES 10 PANCAKES.
CALORIES: 37 CHOLESTEROL: 1 mg SODIUM: 130 mg FIBER: 1 g

Health tip:
Omit salt; reduce sugar to 1 tablespoon.
CALORIES: 32 CHOLESTEROL: 1 mg SODIUM: 91 mg FIBER: 1 g

——————— ◇ ———————

Triticale Yeast Bread

This bread is quite similar to a whole wheat bread, but it's a little heavier. It's this very quality that makes this an ideal toasting bread. You can use all-purpose flour if you have trouble finding bread flour, and rye or whole wheat flour if you can't find triticale flour.

½ cup very warm water (105–115°F)
½ teaspoon sugar
1 package dry yeast
1½ cups triticale flour
2½ to 3 cups bread flour
2 teaspoons salt
1 cup milk
2 eggs, beaten
¼ cup butter, melted

Grease a 9 × 5 × 3-inch loaf pan and set aside.

In a glass measuring cup, stir together the water and sugar. Stir in yeast and let stand until ¼ inch of white bubbly foam forms on top. (This foaming is called *proofing,* and if it doesn't happen it means that for some reason or other the yeast has not been activated. Discard this batch and try again, double checking the date on the yeast package and the temperature of the water.)

In a large bowl, stir together the triticale flour and 1½ cups of the bread flour, and salt. Stir in proofed-yeast mixture, milk, eggs, and butter. Stir in ¾ cup more of the bread flour.

Turn dough out onto a floured surface and knead in enough of the remaining ¾ cup bread flour to form a dough that is no longer sticky. (The dough will be soft and not as firm as most bread doughs, but it should not be sticky.) Place dough in a greased bowl and cover with greased plastic wrap. Set in a warm spot, out of drafts, and let rise until doubled in bulk, about 1½ hours.

Punch dough down and form into a 9-inch loaf. Place in prepared loaf pan. Cover with greased plastic wrap and let rise until doubled in bulk, about 45 minutes.

Preheat oven to 350°F.

Bake for 50 minutes, or until loaf is browned on top and bottom. Remove bread from pan and cool on a wire rack.

MAKES 1 LOAF (16 slices).
CALORIES: 148   CHOLESTEROL: 36 mg   SODIUM: 307 mg   FIBER: 2 g

Health tip:
Omit salt; use unsalted margarine instead of butter.
CALORIES: 148   CHOLESTEROL: 28 mg   SODIUM: 20 mg   FIBER: 2 g

———————◇———————

Trail-Mix Bread

I didn't start out to make a so-called trail-mix bread. I just thought that a slightly sweet bread with a mixture of nuts and seeds in it would be unusual. Then I got the idea to add the currants. As I struggled to name the bread, I thought about all the goodies I had measured out for it and realized that what I had made was a trail mix. This bread has a lovely kind of crumbly texture, but the slices hold together and are just waiting to be spread with butter, maybe even an exotic butter (like cashew or almond butter), and any kind of jam would be great!

½ cup butter
½ cup firmly packed light- or dark-brown sugar
2 eggs
½ cup currants
⅓ cup chopped cashew nuts
⅓ cup chopped pecans
¼ cup sunflower seeds
1 cup all-purpose flour
¾ cup triticale flour
2 teaspoons baking powder
1 teaspoon baking soda
1 teaspoon salt
½ cup buttermilk

Preheat oven to 350°F.
Grease a 9 × 5 × 3-inch loaf pan and set aside.
In a large bowl, cream the butter and sugar until fluffy. Beat in eggs. (The mixture will look curdled at this point.) Stir in currants, cashews, pecans, and sunflower seeds.
In a medium-size bowl, stir together both kinds of flour, baking powder, baking soda, and salt. Add the dry ingredients to the butter mixture alternately with the buttermilk. Spoon batter into prepared pan.
Bake for 50 minutes, or until nicely browned. Remove from pan and cool on a wire rack.

MAKES 1 LOAF (16 slices).
CALORIES: 171   CHOLESTEROL: 34 mg   SODIUM: 292 mg   FIBER: 3 g

Health tip:
Use unsalted margarine instead of butter; omit salt.
CALORIES: 171   CHOLESTEROL: 26 mg   SODIUM: 141 mg   FIBER: 3 g

BREAKFAST CEREAL

Say "cereal" to the average American and chances are, rather than thinking of any particular grain ("a grain suitable for food" is the first definition of cereal, by the way), row upon row and shelf upon shelf of brightly designed boxes come to mind. The boxes contain flakes, puffs, nuggets, and squares of breakfast cereal, ranging in color from shocking pink to dark brown, and, unfortunately, most of them are a far cry from what their original creators intended.

The story of breakfast cereal is an interesting one. It began in the middle of the nineteenth century, when preachers and doctors started advocating pure plain eating, and a campaign was launched against eating rich foods. Pork, salt, coffee, tea, sugar, and white flour, were only a few of the forbidden foods, and it was believed that consuming them would ultimately lead to physical and moral decay.

The first breakfast cereal was developed by Dr. James C. Jackson, a follower of Sylvester Graham, a Presbyterian minister, who urged his followers to embrace whole-grain flours. Jackson made loaves of bread from graham flour and water, which were baked slowly until they dried out. The loaves were then broken into pieces, baked again, and finally crumbled into even smaller pieces. Graham called his product Granula. It was to be served for breakfast after an overnight soak in milk

The cause of breakfast cereal was subsequently taken up by the Seventh Day Adventists, whose sanitarium in Battle Creek, Michigan was run by Dr. John Harvey Kellogg. Dr. Kellogg also advocated a diet of less meat and more roughage. (It's sort of amazing that Dr. Jackson's and Dr. Kellogg's diet guidelines are about the same as the ones we're hearing so much about today.) To help meet these requirements, Dr. Kellogg came up with a baked biscuit made of oats, cornmeal, and wheat that was ground into a breakfast cereal. He later went on to create the first flaked cereal by cooking wheat, rolling it thin, and baking it until dry. But it was not until he started to make the flakes out of corn and barley malt that his creation would gain widespread acceptance and popularity as—you guessed it—corn flakes.

Dr. Kellogg was not alone in the business of breakfast cereal. There was also Henry D. Persky, who created a wheat biscuit (which he baked, at the suggestion of Dr. Kellogg) that eventually became known as Shredded Wheat. And C.W. Post, who introduced a "scientific breakfast food" known as Grape Nuts, a cereal based on

469

Dr. Jackson's Granula. And so the breakfast-cereal industry, based on the latest principles of nutrition, began to grow.

Now, nearly 100 years later, it's ironic that the words "health food" would be about the last words any nutritionally knowledgeable person would use to describe most of today's array of cold cereals. Even those cereals that include "miracle" foods, such as fiber and oat bran, are also, in many cases, loaded with saturated fats in the form of coconut and palm oils, and sugar.

Hot cereals are more in keeping with the intentions of those pioneers of breakfast cereal. For the most part, cereals that are intended to be cooked and eaten are pure grain products, high in fiber and vitamin and mineral nutrients.

The best advice I can give you about buying cereal is to read, read, read those labels—especially the nutritional information—and make sure that what you take home is, in fact, a reasonably nutritious breakfast food that isn't loaded with saturated fats, sugar, artificial colors, and other additives. Keep in mind that brand names can be deceiving. For instance, a cereal that is named something like "total bran," I assure you, is not, since pure bran can only be compared to sawdust in both flavor and texture.

About Breakfast Cereals

The range of breakfast cereals available nowadays is so vast that it is impossible for me to discuss each product individually.

The recipes that follow, for the most part, use those cereals, which I consider to have at least some redeeming nutritional value, and will give you some ideas to help expand your repertoire beyond pour-into-a-bowl-add-milk-and-eat.

In some cases, you can make cereal substitutions: a corn flake for a wheat flake, for instance. In other cases you will have to use your own judgement, but the substitution should be more or less the same density and flavor. You can be a little more flexible when it comes to crushed cereals that are used for coatings and toppings, for example.

Cereals do have generic names, but they are so long and so ridiculously confusing that I have decided to just go ahead and call them by their familiar brand names.

I had a lot of fun creating these recipes, and I hope you enjoy them.

BREAKFAST-CEREAL RECIPES

*(*indicates easy recipes)*

———————— ◇ ————————

Spinach-Stuffed Flounder
Crispy Fried Sole
Spicy Chicken Strips
Crunchy Oven-Baked Chicken *
Stuffed Bell Peppers *
Thursday's Meatloaf *
Kasha Salad *
Mushroom Kasha *
Garlicky Stuffed Tomatoes
Squash-and-Carrot Casserole
Steamed Pudding with Brandied Topping
Honey-Bran Waffles *
Cream-of-Rice Pancakes
Banana-Bran Muffins *
Cereal Dumplings *
Raisin-Bran Oatmeal Cookies
Granola-Cheesecake Squares *
Frozen Maple-Pecan Pie
Viennese Farina
Cinnamon-Toast Bread Pudding *
Corny Apple Fritters
Baked Stuffed Pears à la Mode *
Fresh Peach Strada *
Ice Cream Layer Cake *
Granola Coffee Cake *
Krispie, Crunchy Chocolate Drops *
Maple-Wheat Candy *

471

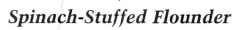

Spinach-Stuffed Flounder

You can substitute almost any fillet that is long and thin an‹ can be easily rolled for the flounder. There are also other col‹ cereals that are similar to Product 19 that can be used in th‹ stuffing.

4 medium flounder fillets (about 1¼ pounds)
3 tablespoons butter, divided
⅓ cup chopped celery
¼ cup chopped green bell pepper
¼ cup chopped onion
½ cup chopped tomato
1 tablespoon lemon juice
¼ teaspoon salt
¼ teaspoon crushed thyme
⅛ teaspoon pepper
⅔ cup Product 19, crushed
1 package (10 ounce) frozen chopped spinach, thawed and squeezed to
  remove as much of the liquid as possible

Preheat oven to 350°F.

Rinse the flounder fillets, pat dry on paper towels, and se‹ aside.

In a medium-size skillet, melt 1½ tablespoons of the butte‹ over medium-high heat. Add celery, green pepper, and onion an‹ cook, stirring frequently, until vegetables are softened. Stir i‹ tomato, lemon juice, salt, thyme, and pepper. Cook, stirring, unti‹ tomato is softened, about 5 minutes. Remove from heat and stir i‹ crushed cereal and spinach.

Place one-quarter of the spinach mixture on the broader end o‹ each fillet. Roll up and fasten with wooden picks. Place in a bakin‹ pan that is just large enough to hold the rolled fillets comfortably‹ Dot fillets with remaining 1½ tablespoons butter.

Bake for 25 minutes, or until fillets are just cooked through.

SERVES 4.
CALORIES: 258   CHOLESTEROL: 91 mg   SODIUM: 456 mg   FIBER: 3 g

Health tip:
Use 1½ tablespoons unsalted margarine in the stuffing only. Omit salt.
CALORIES: 220   CHOLESTEROL: 68 mg   SODIUM: 255 mg   FIBER: 3 g

———————— ◇ ————————

Crispy Fried Sole

Serve this fried sole (or flounder, or any white-fish fillet) with french fries and what you have is fish-and-chips. An accompaniment of tartar sauce and cole slaw tastes good, too.

4 medium fillets of sole (about 1¼ pounds)
2 eggs
1 tablespoon water
3 tablespoons flour
½ teaspoon salt
⅛ teaspoon pepper
¾ cup corn-flake crumbs (buy them ready-made or briefly process
plain corn flakes in a blender or food processor until flakes
form fine crumbs)
Oil, for frying

Rinse the fillets, pat dry on paper towels, and set aside.
In a wide shallow bowl or pie plate, beat eggs with water.
Place the flour on a piece of waxed paper and stir in salt and pepper. Place corn-flake crumbs on another piece of waxed paper.
Dredge fillets in flour mixture, then dip in beaten eggs. Pat corn-flake crumbs onto fillets.
Pour enough oil in a large skillet until it measures about ¼-inch deep. Heat until the oil bubbles when a few crumbs are sprinkled on it. Add fillets and cook over medium-high heat until browned, then turn with a wide spatula and cook until browned on the second side, adjusting heat as necessary. Drain on paper towels.

SERVES 4.
CALORIES: 302   CHOLESTEROL: 189 mg   SODIUM: 682 mg   FIBER: 0 g
Health tip:
Use a scrambled-egg substitute; omit salt.
CALORIES: 290   CHOLESTEROL: 85 mg   SODIUM: 378 mg   FIBER: 0 g

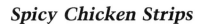

Spicy Chicken Strips

These delicate little strips also make an excellent appetizer, as well as a main dish. Offer honey mustard or honey-mustard mayonnaise for dipping.

1 pound skinless boneless chicken breasts
2 eggs
2 tablespoons water
¼ teaspoon liquid red pepper (Tabasco)
⅓ cup all-purpose flour
½ teaspoon salt
¼ teaspoon ground cumin
¼ teaspoon garlic powder
¼ teaspoon ground red pepper
1½ cups Special K
½ teaspoon spicy seasoned salt
¼ teaspoon pepper
Oil, for frying

Cut chicken breasts into 2 × ½-inch strips and set aside.

In a wide shallow bowl or pie plate, beat the eggs with water and liquid red pepper.

Place flour on a piece of waxed paper and stir in salt, cumin, garlic, and ground red pepper and set aside.

Place cereal, seasoned salt, and pepper in the container of an electric blender or food processor. Cover and blend until the cereal forms fine crumbs. Place crumb mixture on a piece of waxed paper.

Dredge the chicken strips in flour mixture, then dip into beaten eggs. Pat crumbs onto strips.

Pour enough oil in a large skillet until it measures about ¼-inch deep. Heat oil until it bubbles when a few crumbs are sprinkled on top. Add chicken strips and fry over medium-high heat until golden on both sides and cooked through.

SERVES 4.

CALORIES: 322   CHOLESTEROL: 169 mg   SODIUM: 714 mg   FIBER: 1 g

Health tip:
Use scrambled-egg substitute; omit salt.
CALORIES: 311   CHOLESTEROL: 66 mg   SODIUM: 198 mg   FIBER: 1 g

— ◇ —

Crunchy Oven-Baked Chicken

Coat the chicken early in the day, if that's more convenient, and then chill until ready to cook and serve.

3½ pound chicken, cut into pieces and skin removed
2 cups Grape Nuts, crushed
⅓ cup mayonnaise
¼ cup plain yogurt
1 tablespoon honey mustard
¼ teaspoon salt
⅛ teaspoon pepper

Preheat oven to 350°F.
Rinse the chicken and pat dry.
Sprinkle cereal crumbs on a piece of waxed paper.
In a medium-size bowl, stir together mayonnaise, yogurt, honey mustard, salt, and pepper. Brush chicken generously with this mixture. Roll in crushed cereal to coat. Place chicken on an ungreased baking sheet.
Bake for 50 minutes, or until cooked through.

SERVES 4.
CALORIES: 630   CHOLESTEROL: 180 mg   SODIUM: 878 mg   FIBER: 4 g

Health tip:
Use reduced-calorie mayonnaise; omit salt.
CALORIES: 546   CHOLESTEROL: 175 mg   SODIUM: 740 mg   FIBER: 4 g

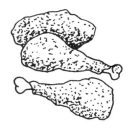

———————— ◇ ————————

Stuffed Bell Peppers

The microwave oven cooks these to perfection. Cover loosely with plastic wrap and microwave on high (100% power) for 10 minutes.

4 medium-size green or red bell peppers
¾ pound ground veal or beef
1 can (8 ounce) tomato sauce, divided
½ cup 40% Bran Flakes
¼ cup finely chopped onion
½ teaspoon salt
¼ teaspoon pepper
1 can (14½ ounce) Cajun-style stewed tomatoes or plain stewed
  tomatoes

Preheat oven to 375°F.

Cut off tops and remove seeds from bell peppers. Drop peppers into a large pot of boiling water for 5 minutes. Remove from pot. Drain and set aside.

In a medium-size bowl, combine meat, ½ cup of the tomato sauce, cereal, onion, salt, and pepper. Mix gently (I always use my hands to combine meat mixtures) until thoroughly combined. Spoon one-quarter of the meat mixture into each pepper. Stand peppers in a 9-inch-square baking pan. Mix stewed tomatoes and remaining tomato sauce together and pour over and around peppers.

Bake for 50 minutes, or until peppers are tender and meat is cooked through.

SERVES 4.
CALORIES: 268   CHOLESTEROL: 61 mg   SODIUM: 867 mg   FIBER: 4 g

Health tip:
Use ground veal; omit salt.
CALORIES: 268   CHOLESTEROL: 61 mg   SODIUM: 600 mg   FIBER: 4 g

Thursday's Meatloaf

Thursday was always my favorite lunch day in the high-school cafeteria. That's when they served the "type A" lunch consisting of meatloaf with mashed potatoes and canned green beans. I freely admit that I still eat this combination any time I'm in need of a little stroking. This is a very simple, down-home meatloaf. It's rather onion-y, but you can adjust that to suit your own taste.

1 egg
1½ pounds ground beef
1 cup spaghetti sauce, divided
½ cup finely chopped onion
½ cup slightly crushed corn flakes
½ teaspoon salt
⅛ teaspoon pepper

Preheat oven to 350°F.

Beat the egg lightly in a large bowl. Add ground beef, ½ cup of the spaghetti sauce, onion, cereal, salt, and pepper. Mix gently until well combined. Shape mixture into an 8 × 4-inch loaf in a baking pan. Pour remaining ½ cup spaghetti sauce over meatloaf.

Bake for 1 hour and 15 minutes, or until cooked through.

SERVES 5.
CALORIES: 422   CHOLESTEROL: 130 mg   SODIUM: 445 mg   FIBER: 1 g

Health tip:
Omit salt. Use extra lean beef.
CALORIES: 354   CHOLESTEROL: 112 mg   SODIUM: 268 mg   FIBER: 1 g

Kashi Salad

It was a simple Kashi salad, very much like this one, that was the inspiration for this book. I first tasted Kashi, a whole grain breakfast cereal, and whole-wheat berries) while I was on vacation at a health spa a few years ago and was absolutely bowled over by how delicious grains could be.

1¾ cups water
¾ teaspoon salt
1 envelope Kashi (1 cup less 2 tablespoons)
½ cup chopped red bell pepper
½ cup chopped green bell pepper
3 tablespoons chopped scallion, both white and green parts
2 tablespoons chopped parsley
2 tablespoons vegetable oil
1 tablespoon red-wine vinegar

In a 2-quart saucepan, bring the water and salt to a boil over high heat. Stir in kasha. Reduce heat, cover, and simmer for 1 hour. Remove from heat and set aside to cool.

In a medium-size bowl, combine the red and green bell peppers, scallion, and parsley. Add oil and vinegar and toss to combine. Add cooled kasha and toss again. Chill before serving.

SERVES 6.
CALORIES: 221   CHOLESTEROL: 0 mg   SODIUM: 267 mg   FIBER: 1 g

Health tip:
Omit salt.
CALORIES: 221   CHOLESTEROL: 0 mg   SODIUM: 7 mg   FIBER: 1 g

Mushroom Kashi

This is an excellent, easy-to-fix side dish for roast meat or poultry, steak, or chops.

2 tablespoons butter
½ cup chopped onion
2 cups sliced mushrooms
1 can (13¾ ounce) ready-to-serve beef broth or
*   1¾ cups vegetable broth (see page 19)*

1 envelope Kashi (1 cup less 2 tablespoons)
2 tablespoons chopped parsley

In a 2-quart saucepan, melt the butter over medium-high heat. Add onion and cook, stirring frequently, until softened. Add mushrooms and cook, stirring and tossing, until soft and lightly browned. Stir in broth and bring to a boil. Stir in kasha. Cover and simmer for 1 hour. Remove from heat and stir in parsley. Cover and let stand for 5 minutes.

SERVES 6.
CALORIES: 225   CHOLESTEROL: 10 mg   SODIUM: 244 mg   FIBER: 2 g

Health tip:
Use low-sodium broth. Use unsalted margarine instead of butter.
CALORIES: 225   CHOLESTEROL: 0 mg   SODIUM: 122 mg   FIBER: 2 g

———————— ◇ ————————

Garlicky Stuffed Tomatoes

Make these in advance, if you like, and bake them just before serving time.

2 large tomatoes
2 tablespoons butter
2 tablespoons minced onion
1 clove garlic, minced
1 cup crushed Wheaties
1/4 teaspoon crushed basil
1/8 teaspoon crushed thyme
1/8 teaspoon salt
1/8 teaspoon pepper

Preheat oven to 400° F.
Cut tomatoes in half, widthwise. Scoop out the centers and chop them. Set aside.
In a small skillet, melt butter over medium-high heat. Add onion and garlic and cook, stirring, until softened. Stir in chopped tomato and cook over high heat until the mixture is a thick sauce. Stir in cereal, basil, thyme, salt, and pepper. Spoon one-quarter of the tomato mixture into each of the tomato halves. Place stuffed tomatoes in a baking pan.

Bake for 15 to 20 minutes, or until tomatoes are heated through and the top of the stuffing is browned.

SERVES 4.

CALORIES: 91   CHOLESTEROL: 16 mg   SODIUM: 208 mg   FIBER: 2 g

Health tip:
Use unsalted margarine instead of butter; omit salt.
CALORIES 91:   CHOLESTEROL: 0 mg   SODIUM: 103 mg   FIBER: 2 g

———————— ◇ ————————

Squash-and-Carrot Casserole

This is an unbelievably delicious way to prepare vegetables, which I like to serve as a nice change from a sweet-potato casserole.

1 large butternut squash, peeled and cut into 1-inch cubes
    (you should have about 4 cups)
3 cups sliced carrot
⅓ cup firmly packed light- or dark-brown sugar
3 tablespoons heavy cream
2 tablespoons butter
2 tablespoons pure maple syrup
1 teaspoon grated orange rind
½ teaspoon salt
¼ teaspoon ground ginger
Pinch mace

Topping:

1 cup slightly crushed Special K
¼ cup butter, melted
2 tablespoons sugar

Preheat oven to 350°F.

In a large pot, boil water over high heat and cook the squash and carrots until tender, about 25 minutes. Drain thoroughly.

Place the drained squash and carrots, brown sugar, cream, butter, maple syrup, grated orange rind, salt, ginger, and mace in the container of a food processor. Process until mixture is smooth. (You can use a blender for this, but in that case you will probably have to puree the vegetables in two or three batches.) Spoon into a 1½-quart casserole.

To make the topping, in a medium-size bowl, stir together cereal, melted butter, and sugar. Sprinkle on top of vegetable puree.

Bake for about 25 minutes, or until casserole is heated through.

ERVES 6.
ALORIES: 294   CHOLESTEROL: 41 mg   SODIUM: 336 mg   FIBER: 5 g

ealth tip:
ubstitute half-and-half for cream; use 1 tablespoon unsalted margarine
nstead of butter in the topping, and omit butter in purée; substitute reduced-
alorie syrup for maple syrup; omit salt.
ALORIES: 257   CHOLESTEROL: 2 mg   SODIUM: 56 mg   FIBER: 5 g

— ◇ —

Steamed Pudding with Brandied Topping

This traditional pudding is just too good to make for holidays
nly, so serve it anytime you want to serve something a little
pecial—and impressive.

2 cups chopped mixed dried fruits
½ cup apple juice
1½ teaspoons ground ginger
1 teaspoon ground cinnamon
⅛ teaspoon ground allspice
3 eggs
½ cup firmly packed light- or dark-brown sugar
1 cup applesauce
¼ cup unsulphured molasses
2 cups fresh bread crumbs
1⅓ cups finely crushed Cheerios
1 teaspoon baking soda
¼ teaspoon salt
2 tablespoons melted butter

randied Topping:

2 tablespoons melted butter
2 teaspoons brandy or orange juice
½ cup confectioners' sugar

Generously grease a 6-cup ring mold and set aside.
In a medium-size bowl, combine the dried fruits, apple juice,
inger, cinnamon, and allspice. Set aside for 20 minutes, stirring
ccasionally.
In a large bowl, beat the eggs and brown sugar until thick. Beat
n applesauce and molasses. Stir in dried-fruit mixture, then bread
rumbs, cereal, baking soda, salt, and butter.
Spoon batter into prepared mold. Cover with greased waxed

paper, then two layers of foil. Wrap a piece of string around the mol(
to hold the foil down tightly and to make the covering waterproof

Place a wire rack in a large pot. (If you don't have a rack tha
will fit in the bottom of your pot, you can use three custard cup:
turned upside down and set the mold on them.) Pour enough boil
ing water into the pot so that it is just a bit lower than the rack
Place the mold on the rack, cover pot tightly, and steam for 2 hours
checking the pot occasionally to make sure that the water is no
boiling away.

Remove mold from pot and cool on a wire rack for 1 hour
Remove waxed-paper-and-foil covering. Run a knife blade aroun(
the mold's inner and outer edges. Turn pudding onto a servin;
platter.

Prepare the topping by stirring butter, brandy, and con
fectioners' sugar together in a medium-size bowl. Spoon toppin;
over pudding.

SERVES 12.
CALORIES: 285   CHOLESTEROL: 63 mg   SODIUM: 323 mg   FIBER: 2 g

Health tip:
Use scrambled-egg substitute for eggs; omit salt. Use unsalted margarine
instead of butter.
CALORIES: 278   CHOLESTEROL: 1 mg   SODIUM: 259 mg   FIBER: 2 g

Honey-Bran Waffles

These waffles are very moist, and the bran and wheat germ give them a nice texture.

1½ cups milk
⅓ cup butter
¼ cup honey
1 cup All-Bran
2 eggs
1⅓ cups all-purpose flour
¼ cup honey-flavored wheat germ
1 tablespoon baking powder
¼ teaspoon salt

Preheat and grease a waffle iron as manufacturer directs.

In a 2-quart saucepan, combine the milk, butter, and honey. Cook over low heat until milk is scalded (bubbles form around edge of pot, but milk should not actually boil). The butter may not be completely melted. Remove from heat and stir in cereal. Let stand for 15 minutes. Beat eggs into bran mixture, then stir in flour, wheat germ, baking powder, and salt.

Pour about 1¼ cup batter for each waffle into waffle iron. Bake until steaming stops and waffle is browned.

MAKES 12 WAFFLES.
CALORIES: 176   CHOLESTEROL: 52 mg   SODIUM: 277 mg   FIBER: 3 g

Health tip:
Use scrambled-egg substitute instead of eggs; substitute unsalted margarine for butter; use 2-percent-fat milk instead of whole milk; omit salt.
CALORIES: 168   CHOLESTEROL: 3 mg   SODIUM: 202 mg   FIBER: 3 g

─────── ◇ ───────

Cream-of-Rice Pancakes

The flavor of the cereal in these pancakes gives them a very special (and comforting) quality. They're light, yet definitely filling.

¾ cup water
¼ cup Cream of Rice
¼ cup butter
½ cup milk
2 eggs
¾ cup all-purpose flour
¼ cup sugar
1 tablespoon baking powder
¾ teaspoon salt
Oil, for greasing griddle

In a 2-quart saucepan, bring the water to a boil over high heat. Gradually stir in cereal. Cook, stirring, for 30 seconds. Remove from heat. Stir in butter until melted. Stir in milk, then eggs, until combined.

In a medium-size bowl, stir together the flour, sugar, baking powder, and salt. Stir into cereal mixture.

Heat a griddle or large skillet until a few drops of water sprinkled on the griddle bounce about before evaporating. Lightly grease griddle. Pour about ¼ cup of the batter for each pancake onto the griddle. Cook until bubbles on top of pancake burst. Turn with a wide spatula and cook until browned on the second side.

SERVES 4.
CALORIES: 302   CHOLESTEROL: 139 mg   SODIUM: 793 mg   FIBER: 1 g

Health tip:
Use unsalted margarine instead of butter, and scrambled-egg substitute for eggs; omit salt.
CALORIES: 290   CHOLESTEROL: 4 mg   SODIUM: 320 mg   FIBER: 1 g

Banana-Bran Muffins

Banana adds natural sweetness and moistness to these healthful muffins. Bake a batch when you have a few minutes, then freeze some for any time you'd like a wholesome pick-me-up. Reheat in the microwave oven to restore fresh-baked softness and aroma.

1¼ cups all-purpose flour
1 cup Bran Buds
2 teaspoons baking soda
1 teaspoon baking powder
¼ teaspoon salt
1 cup buttermilk
1 egg, beaten
¼ cup dark-brown sugar
¼ cup unsulphured molasses
1 ripe banana, mashed

Preheat oven to 350°F.
Grease 12 2½-inch muffin cups and set aside.
In a large bowl, stir together the flour, cereal, baking soda, baking powder, and salt.
In a medium-size bowl, stir together the buttermilk, egg, brown sugar, molasses, and banana until thoroughly combined.
Stir the liquid ingredients into the dry ingredients just until blended. Let stand for 5 minutes. Spoon equal amounts of the batter into each muffin cup.
Bake for 15 minutes, or until muffins spring back when lightly touched. Remove from pan and cool on wire racks.

MAKES 12 MUFFINS.
CALORIES: 120   CHOLESTEROL: 18 mg   SODIUM: 282 mg   FIBER: 3 g
Health tip:
Omit salt.
CALORIES: 120   CHOLESTEROL: 18 mg   SODIUM: 240 mg   FIBER: 3 g

—————— ◇ ——————

Cereal Dumplings

I like my dumplings a little on the heavy side, which these are. Drop the dumplings into soups, stews, or just a plain broth.

1½ cups milk, divided
⅔ cup Instant Cream of Wheat or Instant Cream of Rice
¼ cup butter
2 eggs
1 teaspoon salt
3 slices white bread, torn into bite-size pieces
½ cup all-purpose flour

In a 2-quart saucepan, bring 1 cup of the milk to a boil. Gradually stir in cereal. Lower heat and cook, stirring, until very thick. Remove from heat. Add butter and let it melt. Stir in the remaining ½ cup milk, then eggs and salt, then stir in bread and flour.

Bring a large pot of water to a boil. Drop the dumplings into the boiling water and simmer for 10 minutes. Drain thoroughly.

MAKES 24 DUMPLINGS.
CALORIES: 60   CHOLESTEROL: 25 mg   SODIUM: 136 mg   FIBER: .5 g

Health tip:
Use unsalted margarine instead of butter; omit salt.
CALORIES: 60   CHOLESTEROL: 17 mg   SODIUM: 24 mg   FIBER: .5 g

—————— ◇ ——————

Raisin-Bran Oatmeal Cookies

These just may be the best oatmeal cookies I ever ate. However, there aren't too many raisins per cookie, so if you really like them add a few extra.

1 cup butter, softened
½ cup firmly packed dark- or light-brown sugar
½ cup granulated sugar
1 egg
1 teaspoon vanilla extract
1 cup all-purpose flour
½ teaspoon salt
½ teaspoon baking powder
½ teaspoon ground cinnamon
2 cups Old-Fashioned Rolled Oats
1 cup Raisin Bran

Preheat oven to 375°F.

In a large bowl, cream the butter and both kinds of sugars until light and fluffy. Beat in egg and vanilla.

In a medium-size bowl, stir together the flour, salt, baking powder, and cinnamon. Beat flour mixture into butter mixture. Stir in both kinds of cereal until well blended.

Drop by measuring tablespoonsful onto ungreased cookie sheets.

Bake for about 10 minutes. Remove from cookie sheets and cool on wire racks.

MAKES ABOUT 36 COOKIES.
CALORIES: 95   CHOLESTEROL: 20 mg   SODIUM: 91 mg   FIBER: 1 g

Health tip:
Use unsalted margarine instead of butter; omit salt.
CALORIES: 95   CHOLESTEROL: 6 mg   SODIUM: 24 mg   FIBER: 1 g

---

◇

Granola-Cheesecake Squares

Everyone I've ever served these to raves about them and asks for the recipe. Needless to say, they're delighted to find out that the squares are so easy to make. Use any kind of ready-made granola that you like, or use the granola recipe given in this book on page 298.

½ cup butter, softened
¼ cup light- or dark-brown sugar
1 cup sifted all-purpose flour
1 cup granola, divided
1 package (8 ounce) cream cheese, softened
¼ cup sugar
½ teaspoon vanilla extract
1 egg

Preheat oven to 350°F.

Grease an 8-inch-square baking pan and set aside.

In a large bowl, cream the butter with brown sugar until light and fluffy. Beat in flour, then ½ cup of granola. Press into prepared pan and bake for 15 minutes.

While crust is baking, in a medium-size bowl, beat the cream cheese with sugar and vanilla until light and fluffy. Beat in egg. Pour over baked crust. Sprinkle with remaining ½ cup granola. Continue to bake for 25 minutes.

Cool cake on a wire rack, then refrigerate until chilled. Cut into squares to serve.

MAKES 16 SQUARES.
CALORIES: 195   CHOLESTEROL: 44 mg   SODIUM: 97 mg   FIBER: 1 g

Health tip:
Use unsalted margarine instead of butter.
CALORIES: 195   CHOLESTEROL: 28 mg   SODIUM: 66 mg   FIBER: 1 g

---

———————— ◇ ————————

Frozen Maple-Pecan Pie

The filling for this pie is a creamy, rich frozen mousse. Since the pie takes a little time to assemble and freeze, at some point you want a quick version of it. In that case, substitute butter-pecan ice cream (or any ice cream you like) for the mousse.

3 cups Cracklin' Oat Bran
⅓ cup butter
3 eggs, separated
1 extra egg yolk
¼ cup pure maple syrup
2 tablespoons dark corn syrup
2 tablespoons sugar
1 cup heavy cream
1½ cups chopped pecans

Preheat oven to 350°F.

Place cereal in the container of a food processor. Cover and process until cereal forms fine crumbs. (You can do this in a blender in two or three batches.)

Place the butter in a 10-inch pie plate. Place the pie plate in the oven for 4 minutes, or until butter is melted. Stir crumbs into melted butter until completely combined. Press crumb mixture onto the bottom and up the side of the pie plate to form a crust. Bake for 8 minutes, then set aside to cool.

Place the egg yolks, maple syrup, and corn syrup in the top of a double boiler. Beat with a whisk until completely combined. Place over simmering water and continue whisking until mixture is slightly thickened. Remove from heat and fill bottom of double boiler with ice water. Set the top part of the double boiler over ice water and whisk until the mixture has cooled.

In a clean, grease-free large bowl, beat egg whites with clean beaters until foamy. Gradually beat in sugar and continue beating until stiff peaks form when beaters are lifted.

In another large bowl, beat the cream until soft peaks form when beaters are lifted. (There's no need to wash beaters before beating cream.) Add egg-yolk mixture and egg whites to the whipped cream and fold in until completely combined. Fold in pecans. Turn into prepared crust and chill until firm, at least 8 hours.

Cut pie into wedges to serve. If you have a little difficulty getting the slices out of the pan, set the pie plate on a warm wet towel for about 5 minutes.

SERVES 10.
CALORIES: 398   CHOLESTEROL: 132 mg   SODIUM: 208 mg   FIBER: 4 g

Health tip:
Eat only half a serving—about once a year.

———————— ◇ ————————

Viennese Farina

When I was about 8-years-old, my aunt Annie and uncle Robert came to visit from Vienna. While she was with us, my aunt made a delicious dessert from farina that I have never forgotten, and this is my attempt to recreate it.

3 cups milk
¾ cup farina
⅓ cup sugar
⅓ cup butter
1 teaspoon salt
1 egg
½ cup golden raisins
1 teaspoon vanilla extract
1 can (16 ounce) pitted plums or 1 jar (16 ounce) pitted prunes, or any
    fruit packed in heavy syrup (optional)

Grease an 8-inch-square baking pan and set aside.

In a 2-quart saucepan, combine the milk, farina, sugar, butter, and salt. Cook over medium heat, stirring occasionally, until mixture comes to a boil and has thickened. Remove from heat.

In a medium-size bowl, beat egg. Stir ½ cup of the hot farina into the beaten egg, then stir the egg mixture back into the farina in the saucepan. Stir in raisins and vanilla. Pour into prepared pan and chill for 1½ hours.

Preheat oven to 400°F.

Bake the farina for 40 to 50 minutes, or until lightly browned. Remove from oven and let stand for 20 minutes. Cut into 9 squares. Serve topped with fruit, if desired.

SERVES 9.

CALORIES: 213   CHOLESTEROL: 52 mg   SODIUM: 343 mg   FIBER: 2 g

Health tip:
Use unsalted margarine instead of butter; omit salt.
CALORIES: 213   CHOLESTEROL: 34 mg   SODIUM: 57 mg   FIBER: 2 g

---

——————— ◇ ———————

Cinnamon-Toast Bread Pudding

I'm very partial to bread pudding, and when I feel truly decadent (or depressed) I serve it with a vanilla sauce or vanilla ice cream.

3 tablespoons butter, melted
5 slices soft white bread, cubed
1½ cups Cinnamon Toast Crunch, divided
3 eggs
⅓ cup sugar
1¾ cups scaled milk (bubbles form around the edge of the pan, but the milk should not actually boil)

Preheat oven to 350°F.
Butter a 1½-quart casserole and set aside.
Place the melted butter in a medium-size bowl. Add bread cubes and toss until coated. Place about half of the bread cubes in the prepared casserole. Sprinkle with 1 cup of the cereal and top with remaining bread cubes. Sprinkle with remaining ½ cup cereal.
In the same bowl you used for the melted butter, beat eggs with sugar until combined. Gradually beat in milk. Pour over bread and cereal in casserole. Let stand for 15 minutes.
Bake for 45 minutes, or until a knife inserted in the center comes out clean. Serve warm or chilled.

SERVES 8.

CALORIES: 207   CHOLESTEROL: 97 mg   SODIUM: 230 mg   FIBER: 1 g

Health tip:
Use unsalted margarine instead of butter; use scrambled-egg substitute for eggs; and use 2-percent-fat milk for whole milk.
CALORIES: 191   CHOLESTEROL: 5 mg   SODIUM: 211 mg   FIBER: 1g

Corny Apple Fritters

Deep-fried apple fritters are always a treat, and make a nice supper dish. The Corn Pops add a nice crunch.

1 cup all-purpose flour
3 tablespoons sugar
1 teaspoon baking powder
½ teaspoon salt
2 eggs
⅓ cup milk
1 tablespoon vegetable oil
½ teaspoon vanilla extract
1½ cups peeled chopped apple
½ cup lightly crushed Corn Pops (the Pops should be broken into pieces, but not actually crushed so finely as to be crumbs)
Oil, for deep-frying
Confectioners' sugar

In a large bowl, stir together the flour, sugar, baking powder, and salt.

In a medium-size bowl, beat together the eggs, milk, oil, and vanilla. Stir the egg mixture into the flour mixture until well blended. Stir in apple and cereal.

Pour enough oil into a 2-quart saucepan so that it measures about 2 inches deep. Heat oil until it bubbles when a little batter is dropped into it. Drop batter by rounded measuring teaspoonful into the hot oil. Fry until golden on all sides. Drain on paper toweling. Serve warm, sprinkled with confectioners' sugar.

MAKES 3 DOZEN FRITTERS.
CALORIES: 43   CHOLESTEROL: 12 mg   SODIUM: 45 mg   FIBER: 0 g

Health tip:
Eat just one.

———— ◇ ————

Baked Stuffed Pears à la Mode

Although these baked pears are just wonderful as is, when they are served with a scoop of ice cream on the side they are divine.

2 ripe pears
2 tablespoons butter, melted
1 tablespoon brown sugar
2 teaspoons lemon juice
¼ teaspoon grated lemon rind
¾ cup slightly broken up Cracklin' Bran
⅓ cup chopped walnuts
2 cups ice cream

Preheat oven to 350°F.

Cut pears in half and core them. Carefully scoop out about half the flesh in each pear half, leaving a ½-inch shell. Coarsely chop scooped-out flesh and set aside.

In a medium-size bowl, stir together the melted butter, brown sugar, lemon juice, and lemon rind. Stir in pear-cereal and walnuts. Set aside ½ cup of this mixture. Add chopped pear to remaining cereal mixture in bowl and toss until combined. Spoon one quarter of the pear-cereal mixture into each of the pear shells. Top each with 2 tablespoons of the reserved cereal mixture.

Bake 30 minutes, or until pears are fork tender. Serve warm or chilled with a scoop of vanilla ice cream.

SERVES 4.

CALORIES: 348   CHOLESTEROL: 45 mg   SODIUM: 184 mg   FIBER: 4 g

Health tip:

Use unsalted margarine instead of butter; skip the "à la mode."

CALORIES: 213   CHOLESTEROL: 0 mg   SODIUM: 85 mg   FIBER: 4 g

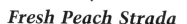

Fresh Peach Strada

Use peaches that are ripe, but still firm, or even slightly under-ripe, otherwise the dessert will be too mushy.

4 cups Sugar Frosted Flakes
¼ cup melted butter
1 teaspoon ground cinnamon
⅛ teaspoon ground nutmeg
2 pounds fresh peaches, peeled and sliced or
    4½ cups frozen peaches, thawed

Preheat oven to 350°F.

In a large bowl, combine the cereal, butter, cinnamon, and nutmeg. Place 1½ cups of the cereal mixture in the bottom of a 1½- to 2-quart casserole. Top with half the peach slices. Sprinkle 1½ cups more of the cereal mixture over the peach slices. Cover with remaining peach slices. Top with remaining cereal mixture.

Bake for 40 minutes, or until fruit is soft. (The time may vary depending on the ripeness of the peaches.)

SERVES 6.
CALORIES: 221   CHOLESTEROL: 21 mg   SODIUM: 254 mg   FIBER: 3 g

Health tip:
Use unsalted margarine instead of butter.
CALORIES: 221   CHOLESTEROL: 0 mg   SODIUM: 198 mg   FIBER: 3 g

---

———————— ◇ ————————

Ice Cream Layer Cake

You can use any flavor, or combination of flavors, of ice cream that appeal to you. But I found that all chocolate all the way was positively scrumptious.

1 cup (6-ounce bag) semisweet chocolate morsels
¼ cup butter
2 cups Nutrigrain Nuggets
½ cup flaked coconut
½ cup finely chopped almonds
2 pints ice cream, slightly softened

In the top of a double boiler over simmering (not boiling) water, melt chocolate morsels with butter. Stir in cereal, coconut, and almonds.

Pat 1½ cups of the chocolate mixture in the bottom of an 8½-inch springform pan and chill for 10 minutes in the freezer. Spread 1 pint of the ice cream over the cereal mixture. Sprinkle 1 cup of the remaining cereal mixture over ice cream. Return to freezer for 10 minutes. Spread remaining pint of ice cream over crumbs. Top with remaining crumbs.

Cover with foil and freeze until firm, at least 4 hours. Run a knife around the edge of the cake before unmolding.

SERVES 8.

CALORIES: 400   CHOLESTEROL: 45 mg   SODIUM: 180 mg   FIBER: 3 g

Health tip:
Eat only half a serving.

—————— ◇ ——————

Granola Coffee Cake

This is the kind of goodie I like to keep in the freezer for unexpected company.

1 cup granola
1 teaspoon cinnamon
2¼ cups all-purpose flour
½ teaspoon baking powder
½ teaspoon baking soda
¼ teaspoon salt
1¾ cups sugar
1 cup butter, softened
4 eggs
1 teaspoon vanilla extract
1 cup sour cream

Preheat oven to 350°F.

Grease and flour a 10-cup Bundt pan or 10-inch tube pan and set aside.

Stir together the granola and cinnamon on a piece of waxed paper and set aside.

In a medium-size bowl, stir together flour, baking powder, baking soda, and salt and set aside.

In a large bowl, cream the sugar and butter until light and fluffy. Beat in eggs, one at a time, until thoroughly combined. Beat in vanilla. Beat in the flour mixture alternately with the sour cream, starting and ending with the flour mixture.

Sprinkle ¼ cup of the granola mixture into the prepared pan. Spread half the batter over the granola, then sprinkle with remaining granola mixture. Top with remaining batter.

Bake for 1 hour and 10 minutes, or until a wooden pick inserted in the center comes out clean.

MAKES 20 SLICES.

CALORIES: 265   CHOLESTEROL: 72 mg   SODIUM: 165 mg   FIBER: 1 g

Health tip:
Omit salt; use unsalted margarine instead of butter.

CALORIES: 265   CHOLESTEROL: 40 mg   SODIUM: 78 mg   FIBER: 1 g

———— ◇ ————

Krispie, Crunchy Chocolate Drops

This is what I consider "junk" candy. If you are a chocolate afficionado, who loves the very expensive brands, this is not for you. But most kids, young and old, adore these make-in-minutes cereal candies.

1 cup (6-ounce bag) semisweet chocolate morsels
½ cup milk-chocolate morsels
1½ cups Rice Krispies
½ cup flaked coconut

Combine both kinds of chocolate in the top of a double boiler set over simmering (not boiling) water. Cook, stirring occasionally, until chocolate is melted. Stir in cereal and coconut. Drop by heaping teaspoonsful onto waxed paper. Let stand until hardened.

MAKES 40.
CALORIES: 42   CHOLESTEROL: 1 mg   SODIUM: 18 mg   FIBER: 0 g

Health tip:
Eat just one—if you can.

———— ◇ ————

Maple-Wheat Candy

These are something like little popcorn balls. They're not difficult to make, but it does take a little time for the sugar syrup to come up to temperature. And speaking of sugar syrup, remember while you are working with it that there is always the possibility of getting a severe burn if you're not careful. This is *not* a candy-making endeavor in which you will want little kids to help. Although I call for Puffed Wheat, you can use any puffed cereal in this recipe.

¾ cup sugar
⅓ cup water
¼ cup pure maple syrup
2 tablespoons butter
½ teaspoon white vinegar
3 cups Puffed Wheat

Place the sugar in a 2-quart saucepan, then pour water, maple syrup, butter, and vinegar over it. Bring to a boil, stirring occasionally. Insert a candy thermometer in the pan and cook over medium-high heat until the mixture reaches 290°F.

Place the cereal in a greased heat-resistant bowl. Pour syrup over cereal, stirring with a wooden spoon until the grains are well coated. As soon as the mixture is cool enough to handle (the syrup will harden as it cools), quickly form into 3-inch balls. (To protect your hands from the heat of the sugar syrup, keep them coated with butter while you make the balls. Better yet, use clean rubber gloves that are coated with butter.)

MAKES 8.
CALORIES: 120   CHOLESTEROL: 0 mg   SODIUM: 3 mg   FIBER: 1 g

Health tip:
Make balls half size.

Bibliography

Atlas, Nava. *The Wholefood Catalog*. New York: Fawcett Columbine, 1988.

Barrett, Judith, and Wasserman, Norma. *Risotto*. New York: Charles Scribner's Sons, 1987.

Brody, Jane. *Jane Brody's Good Food Book*. New York: W. W. Norton, 1985.

Brown, Elizabeth Burton. *Grains*. Englewood Cliffs, New Jersey, Prentice-Hall, Inc., 1977.

Carroll, David. *The Complete Book of Natural Foods*. New York: Summit Books, 1985.

Claiborne, Craig. *The (Original) New York Times Cook Book*. New York: Harper and Row, Publishers, 1961.

Cohen, Mark Nathan. *The Food Crisis in Prehistory*. New Haven: Yale University Press, 1977.

FitzGibbon, Theodora. *The Food of the Western World*. New York: Quadrangle/The New York Times Book Co., 1976.

Garrison, Holly. *Comfort Food*. New York: Donald I. Fine, Inc., 1988.

Greene, Bert. *The Grains Cookbook*. New York: Workman Publishing, 1988.

Hazan, Marcella. *The Classic Italian Cookbook*. New York: Alfred A. Knopf, 1982.

Hillman, Howard. *The Cook's Book*. New York: Avon Books, 1981.

London, Sheryl and Mel. *Creative Cooking with Grains and Pasta*. Emmaus, Pa.: Rodale Press, 1982.

McGee, Harold. *On Food and Cooking*. New York: Macmillan Publishing Company, 1984.

Robertson, Laurel; Flinders, Carol; and Godfrey, Bronwen. *Laurel's Kitchen*. Berkeley, California: Nilgiri Press, 1976.

Roehl, Evelyn. *Whole Food Facts*. Rochester, Vermont: Healing Arts Press, 1988.

Rombauer, Irma S., and Becker, Marion Rombauer. *The Joy of Cooking*. Indianapolis: The Bobbs-Merrill Company, Inc. 1931 (1981 edition).

Root, Waverley. *Food*. New York: Simon and Schuster, 1980.

Tannahill, Reay. *Food in History*. New York: Stein and Day, 1984.

Townsend, Doris McFerran. *The Cook's Companion*. New York: Crown Publishers, Inc., 1978.

Udesky, James. *The Book of Soba*. Tokoyo: Kodansha International, 1988.

Von Welanetz, Diana and Paul. *The Von Welanetz Guide to Ethnic Ingredients*. Los Angeles: J.P. Tarcher, Inc., 1982.

Wood, Rebecca. *The Whole Foods Encyclopedia*. New York: Prentice Hall Press, 1988.

Index

501

EASY SHOPPING GUIDE

	(trimmed weight)
1 cup shelled almonds	1 cup + 3 tablespoons chopped (5½ ounces)
1 medium apple	1 cup chopped or diced (peeled) (4 ounces)
1 large apple	1 cup shredded (peeled) (5 ounces)
5 medium asparagus	1 cup asparagus cut into 1-inch pieces (3½ ounces)
1 pound dried beans	2 cups beans (any kind), dried (16 ounces)
1 medium bunch broccoli	3½ cups flowerettes (9 ounces)
½ small head cabbage	4½ cups shredded (9 ounces)
½ small head cabbage	3 cups chopped (9 ounces)
1 large carrot	1 cup sliced (6 ounces)
1 large carrot	1 cup coarsely chopped (6 ounces)
1 large carrot	1 cup finely chopped (6 ounces)
1 large carrot	1 cup shredded (6 ounces)
1 medium head cauliflower	5 cups flowerettes (20 ounces)
2 medium ribs celery	1 cup sliced (4 ounces)
2 medium ribs celery	1 cup chopped or diced (4½ ounces)
2 medium ribs celery	1 cup finely chopped or diced (4¾ ounces)
1 large cucumber	2 cups chopped, sliced or diced (11 ounces)
1 medium eggplant	5 cups cubed (14 ounces)
⅓ pound green beans	1 cup green beans cut into 1-inch pieces (4 ounces)
1 medium green onion (scallion)	3 tablespoons sliced or chopped (white and green parts) (½ ounce)
1 medium green onion (scallion)	2 tablespoons finely chopped (white and green parts) (½ ounce)
1 medium leek	1 cup sliced (white and light green part only) (2½ ounces)
4 medium mushrooms	1 cup sliced or chopped (3 ounces)
1 cup shelled walnuts or pecans	1 cup + 1 tablespoon chopped (4 ounces)
1 medium onion	1 cup chopped or diced (4 ounces)
1 large onion	1 cup finely chopped (7 ounces)
1 small pepper (red, green or yellow)	1 cup sliced (4 ounces)
1 small pepper	1 cup chopped or diced (4½ ounces)
1 small pepper	1 cup finely chopped (5 ounces)
1 medium potato	1 cup cubed (5½ ounces)
1 medium potato	1 cup shredded (4¾ ounces)
1 medium tomato	1 cup diced or chopped (6 ounces)
1 small zucchini	1 cup sliced (3.5 ounces)
1 small zucchini	1 cup shredded (4.5 ounces)